ENVIRONMENTAL ARCHAEOLOGY

Principles and Practice

DENA FERRAN DINCAUZE

University of Massachusetts,
Amherst

CAMBRIDGE
UNIVERSITY PRESS

PUBLISHED BY THE PRESS SYNDICATE OF THE UNIVERSITY OF CAMBRIDGE
The Pitt Building, Trumpington Street, Cambridge, United Kingdom

CAMBRIDGE UNIVERSITY PRESS
The Edinburgh Building, Cambridge CB2 2RU, UK
40 West 20th Street, New York, NY 10011-4211, USA
477 Williamstown Road, Port Melbourne, VIC 3207, Australia
Ruiz de Alarcón 13, 28014 Madrid, Spain
Dock House, The Waterfont, Cape Town 8001, South Africa

http://www.cambridge.org

First published 2000
Reprinted 2002, 2003

Printed in the United Kingdom at the University Press, Cambridge

Typeface Minion 10.5/14.5 pt   *System* QuarkXPress™   [SE]

A catalogue record for this book is available from the British Library

Library of Congress Cataloguing in Publication data

Dincauze, Dena Ferran.
Environmental archaeology: principles and practice /
Dena Ferran Dincauze.
        p.   cm.
Includes bibliographical references and index.
ISBN 0 521 32568 4 (hbk.) – ISBN 0 521 31077 6 (pbk.)
1. Environmental archaeology.   I. Title.
CC81.D56   2000
930.1–dc21   99-39090   CIP

ISBN 0 521 32568 4 hardback
ISBN 0 521 31077 6 paperback

Environmental Archaeology
Principles and Practice

Archaeologists today need a wide range of scientific approaches in order to delineate and interpret the ecology of their sites. Dena Dincauze has written an authoritative and essential guide to a variety of archaeological methods, ranging from techniques for measuring time with isotopes and magnetism to the sciences of climate reconstruction, geomorphology, sedimentology, soil science, paleobotany, and faunal paleoecology. Professor Dincauze insists that borrowing concepts from other disciplines demands a critical understanding of their theoretical roots. Moreover, the methods that are chosen must be appropriate to particular sets of data. The applications of the methods needed for a holistic human-ecology approach in archaeology are illustrated by examples ranging from the Paleolithic through Classical civilizations, to recent urban archaeology.

DENA DINCAUZE is Professor of Anthropology at the University of Massachusetts at Amherst. Throughout her distinguished career she has written and thought about paleoenvironmental and epistemological issues. Her research area is northeastern North America, with a special interest in the Pleistocene–Holocene boundary.

This volume is dedicated to
Charles B. M. McBurney, Richard B.
Woodbury, and J. Grahame D. Clark,
extraordinary teachers and visionaries
whose enthusiasm for our complex
world inspired and sustained me.

Contents

Figures

TABLES

PREFACE

This volume is about synergy. It was born in my dissatisfaction with so much of environmental archaeology that focused on the application of single techniques to isolated data classes, and with the early prevailing notion of "environment" as background or stage set for human actions. As any thespian knows, the stage set is not passive; it constrains, and sometimes even inspires, particular actions and responses.

While teaching courses in environmental archaeology, I sensed the possibilities for integration based on the concept of environment as context for human actions – not an original insight. The essays that comprise the chapters of this volume explore the possibilities for interpretation of human contexts from non-artifactual, and some limited artifactual, finds. Only when I included the larger universe of off-site paleoenvironmental data at several scales did the integration begin to look feasible and powerful. In doing so I realized, as Aldo Leopold did long before, that humans are environments for other humans, for all living things, and for the physical world which they inhabit.

Detailed consideration of human environments is justified for what it tells about the conditions of life in which human choices and decisions are made. It does not entail deterministic interpretations, and no environmental determinism appears herein. Environmental effects upon human communities are mediated through technology and cognition, the specifically human means of adaptation. These impose upon the study of human adaptations certain constraints of scale which are foreign to many of the environmental sciences, so that archaeologists cannot simply shop passively for concepts, methods, and data appropriate to the study of the human past. Archaeologists must be selective in their use of methods and concepts from other disciplines; they must select data and methods at scales appropriate to archaeological problems.

Maintaining an explicitly "anthropocentric" point of view, the book examines aspects of global environments at micro- to macro-scales, attempting to give some notion of their diversity, while seeing human actions as contributing to the definition and dynamism of life, climates, and landforms as experienced by bipedal primates through a few million years. The five spheres of the climate system – atmosphere, geosphere, hydrosphere, biosphere, and cryosphere – form the skeleton of the volume, organizing the several scientific disciplines that contribute to knowledge and understanding of the context for life on planet Earth.

This book offers epistemological, philosophical, and methodological means toward integration across and within the disciplines that contribute to environmental archaeology. These approaches are suitable for use with any number of theoretical paradigms, as is appropriate for a genuinely useful methodology. Robust tests of theories, which are indispensable to the advance of understanding, require fully evaluated and integrated data, which in turn must be based on informed congruence between methods, data sets, and research goals.

Consequently, this book is about using pollen analysis, archaeozoology, soils science, and other techniques of paleoenvironmental studies in the pursuit of archaeological goals: thinking as archaeologists about the problems and potential of the sciences that study the planet and its biological and social systems. It was created to function as a guide into the literature of paleoenvironmental studies, an introduction to the concepts and language of a range of scientific and humanistic disciplines across which paleoenvironmental studies range. It is a study of methodology, not of methods or techniques, with some theoretical concepts that aid in the identification and application of methods appropriate to archaeological problems. My hope is that enough is expressed and explicated about the several disciplinary approaches to the past that the reader realizes effective means to integrate the results of many inquiries and apply them productively to the study of the human past.

Because the argument ranges across many disciplines, the text necessarily incorporates technical terms from ecology and from the geo- and life-sciences frequently encountered in archaeology. New terms are defined as introduced and utilized in the text, and are shown in **bold** face at first use. Words so highlighted may be found defined in the glossary, for ease of reference from any chapter.

This is not a didactic book; it does not advocate a single best way to do anything. The approach to methods and results advocated here is neither simplifying nor generalizing. Rather, it is an introduction that emphasizes critical thinking and non-linear models, reflexive processes and reflexive epistemology. I argue that the values of a successful environmental archaeology are firmly grounded in the idea that the universe is vast, multivariate, and constantly changing. Consequently, I present information, guidance, and opportunities for students and practitioners to explore thoughtfully on their own through the many growing disciplines that are building knowledge of paleoenvironments. The book remains one person's take on a complex enterprise: an introduction to newcomers, a moment's snapshot in a very fast-moving field. My purpose is to argue for integration, despite the difficulties, and for an educated awareness of the complexities of the world.

Ecology and paleoecology increasingly depend for growth on escaping from concepts of direct causation. Uniformitarianism plays only a minor role in the structure of the arguments presented here. Rather, I emphasize the importance of non-linear thinking for understanding living things and living systems. People and their behaviors are embedded in the dynamism of the planet, with everything changing at different rates. Ecologists and paleoecologists must learn to recognize eddies within turbulence, fractal motions, and sensitive responses to conditions encountered. To illustrate the reflexive qualities of paleoecological research, controversies are revisited. Discussions and case studies demonstrate that uncertainties can be productive when confronted rather than avoided.

Knowledge is contextual. We know more about any topic than the constraints of linear language permit us to say at any one time. A good question can elicit from a speaker or writer an answer richer than, and different in significant content from, a statement made to anonymous listeners or readers. This volume is presented with the hope that it will stimulate good questions and enrich answers from archaeologists confronting our multifarious, complex, interrelated, and fractal world. I complete this survey in an optimistic mood. Integration is possible; it is never easy, but it is essential for any success in the search for knowledge of our past.

ACKNOWLEDGMENTS

This volume took shape over surprisingly many years of research, learning, and teaching. Its completion has necessarily been a joint effort with many friends, students, and colleagues. Up front, I must thank Jessica Kuper and Margaret Deith for their faith in me over the years, which kept me buoyant, and my immediate colleagues at the University of Massachusetts, Amherst, for not teasing too much about progress. I thank the US Fulbright Commission for the introduction, early in my career, to inter-disciplinary scholarship at Cambridge University.

The deeply appreciated hospitality and fellowship extended by Clare Hall, and the facilitation provided by the Cambridge University libraries was essential to the development and completion of the work. I also owe gratitude to the University of Massachusetts libraries and librarians, and the Inter-Library Loan Department.

Collegiality is fundamental to efforts to reach across disciplines from archaeology. I owe generalized and deep gratitude to friends and acquaintances too numerous to name here. The extraordinary biannual meetings of the American Quaternary Association provide summaries of cutting-edge research and introductions to the foremost researchers. At Cambridge University I especially benefited from the conversations and guidance of Peter Rowley-Conwy, Margaret and Ivan Deith, Tjeerd H. van Andel, Paul Mellars, Geoff Bailey, and many others. David Harris and Gordon Hillman of the Institute of Archaeology at University College London have been graciously helpful. At the University of Massachusetts the generous mentoring of Raymond Bradley of the Department of Geosciences was crucially important. M. Pamela Bumsted, Elizabeth A. Little, and Robert J. Hasenstab have been long-term supporters and inspiring critics of this enterprise. From the world beyond Amherst and Cambridge, I have benefited especially from extraordinary help with reprints, concepts, and sources from Vaughn M. Bryant, Jr., Donald Grayson, Jeffrey S. Dean, George J. Gumerman, Walter Klippel, Karl W. Butzer, G. (Rip) Rapp, C. Vance Haynes, Vance Holliday, Charles Schweger, John C. Kraft, Gerald Kelso, James Schoenwetter,

Carole S. Mandryk, and Fred Wendorf. The manuscript-in-progress received alert attention from Margaret Deith, Raymond Bradley, Alan Goodman, Eric Johnson, Stanley Engelsberg, Susan Goode-Null, Tonya Largy, and Sharon Swihart, whose expertise and sympathetic support are gratefully acknowledged. Students in my Environmental Archaeology classes questioned enthusiastically, expanding my awareness. The supportive comments of two reviewers for the Press are gratefully acknowledged.

Of course, even the best of support systems cannot prevent errors by the author, and I take full responsibility for any that remain in this volume.

A generous grant-in-aid of research from Frederick H. West met some of the expenses of illustrations. The talented artists who provided them, and their work, are: Maureen Manning-Bernatsky (Figures 3.2, 3.5, 4.1, 4.2, 5.2, 6.5, 9.6, 10.1, 10.2, 10.3, 11.1, 12.1, 12.4, 15.3, and 15.4), Nancy Haver (Figures 13.3 and 13.8), and Linda Cahillane (Figures 3.3, 3.4, 3.6, 5.3, 6.1, 7.2, 7.3, 7.4, 8.1, 8.2, 9.2, 9.5, 9.7, 11.2, 11.4, 11.5, 12.3, 13.1, 13.2, 15.1, 15.2, 16.3, and 17.1). I thank them all for their skill and attentiveness to detail.

Quotations and illustrations used under copyright permission are generally cited in the text, with the following special exceptions. Material in Chapters 4 and 15 from the *Journal of Field Archaeology* is reproduced with the permission of that journal and the permission of the Trustees of Boston University. All rights reserved. The quotation from *Fossils in the making: vertebrate taphonomy and paleoecology* (p. 444) is reproduced with the permission of the University of Chicago Press, ©1980 by the University of Chicago. All rights reserved. The excerpt from *The living garden* in Chapter 15 (p. 433), © 1985, by George Ordish is reprinted by permission of Houghton-Mifflin Company. All rights reserved. The quotation by R. Lederman in Chapter 18 (p. 509) is reprinted by permission of the American Anthropological Association from *American Anthropologist* 98: 2, June 1996. Not for further reproduction. The quotation from E. Zahn in Chapter 7 (p. 148) is reprinted with permission from *Nature* 372: 621. Copyright 1994 Macmillan Magazines Limited. Quotations by D. Wolfman in Chapters 5 (p. 106) and 6 (p. 126), and the illustration in Chapter 6 from *Archaeomagnetic dating*, edited by J. L. Eighmy and R. S. Sternberg, © 1990, appear with the permission of the University of Arizona Press. The quotations by R. Netting in Chapter 4 (pp. 74 and 75) are reprinted by permission from *Cultural ecology*, 2nd edition, by R. Netting. Copyright ©1977 by W. A. Benjamin.

The cover illustration by Glynn Gorick, entitled *Garthinty*, evokes the five spheres of the climate system on which the text is based, and reveals, center front, a cultural landscape. This representation of a real place in Wales thus achieves iconic significance for the volume.

GLOSSARY

accuracy: the degree to which a measurement approximates an absolute standard – its
    "truth"

adaptation: biology: changes in gene frequency in a population conferring reproductive
    advantage in a particular environment; anthropology: innovations in technology and
    social structure (behavior) that reduce stress

aeolian: of materials carried and deposited by wind; typically well sorted in terms of particle
    size

albedo: a measure of surface reflectivity of solar radiation

allochthonous: deriving from a distance; not native to a place

allopatric: species occupying discrete habitats differing in some salient characteristics

alluvium: sediment deposited from flowing water

alpha particle (α):   a positively charged particle emitted in radioactive decay

altitude: height, or elevation, usually expressed as distance above projected sea level

amplitude: size or intensity of a wave, force, or environmental change

anaerobic: lacking access to free oxygen

analogy: a form of argument in which a known phenomenon is considered to represent
    crucial aspects of a less understood phenomenon; cf. no-analog problem

anthropogenic soils: site soils enriched by organic wastes due to human occupation

anthrosol: anthropogenic soils/anthropic epipedon

AP/arboreal pollen: pollen of tree species

aphelion: the point on the Earth's orbit at which it is farthest from the Sun

arctic front: the boundary where arctic air masses meet temperate ones

assemblage: materials recovered from a discrete sedimentary context

association: biotic species found together in a habitat of any scale

astronomical time: time calculated from the motion of astronomical bodies

atmosphere: gases surrounding the Earth; the medium for climate autecology: study of the habitat and niche adaptations and relationships of single species

autochthonous: originating in the place where found

autovariation: internally generated change within any one of the five spheres of the climate system, independent of external influences

axis: the imaginary line through the poles about which the Earth turns (cf. axle)

azonal: of soils whose characteristics are not predominantly determined by climate zones

basin: essentially concave landform; the catchment of a stream network bounded by the ridges of the watershed

benthic: fauna living at depth in the water column or on substrate beneath it

beta particle (β): subatomic particle emitted during radioactive decay, either positive or negative in charge

biocoenosis: an assemblage of living plants and animals; pl.: biocoenoses

biomass: all living organisms within an area of interest, the standing crop

biome: regional-scale unit of the biosphere

biosphere: the maximum spatial extent and systemic relationships of the living organisms of the planet Earth

biota: all living things in a defined place

biotope: small-scale unit of the biosphere

bioturbation: disturbance of sediments by living things

bolus: wad of chewed food or food residue

brackish: mixture of fresh and salt waters, as at river mouths and lagoons

calibrate; calibration: in chronometry, bringing one system of time intervals into close agreement with another; correlate

caliche/calcrete: more or less cohesive near-surface zone of carbonate deposition typical of arid-zone soils. May be hard as rock

carr: a boggy fen having woody swamp vegetation as well as peat

carrying capacity: the maximum number of organisms that can be supported in a given place; for the human species, it is always relative to technology

catena: sequence of soil profiles varying down slope on similar sediments

Cenozoic: the "recent life" age, encompassing the time since the extinction of the dinosaurs; Tertiary and Quaternary epochs

channel: a linear depression; bed of stream or river

chemical residues: organic molecules surviving during diagenesis; chemical indicators of substances remaining in sediments or tissues

chitin: a keratinous material in horn cores, hooves, arthropod exoskeletons, etc.

chron: a major, long-lasting episode of magnetic polarity

chronometer: anything used to measure time spans; instrumentation employed to do that

chronostratigraphic (adj.): a unit of stratigraphy defined by chronological boundaries

climate: statistical generalization of temperature and precipitation in a specified area

colluvium: sediment moved downslope by sheet wash or mass sliding; adjectival form: colluvial commensal: an organism living closely with another, without harm to either (sharing the table)

community: a concept of biotas as coexisting groups ("societies") of species changing along predictable trajectories toward mature "climax" formations controlled by climate

condition: the quantitative composition of a system

context: enclosing medium of archaeological remains that defines the stratigraphic and locational relationships with constituent data classes in a place (cf. matrix)

contingencies: unique, historical configurations of phenomena; particular environmental and social contexts in which events take place

crust: rocky tectonic plates at the Earth's surface, above the mantle

cryosphere: total mass of ice distributed around the planet

declination: of magnet: variance from true north

delta: triangular-shaped fluvial landform with an upper surface sloping gently into standing water and steeper margins on the sides

density: the number of individuals of a taxon in a given area

diagenesis: chemical and physical processes by which organic and inorganic sediments are transformed into rock; e.g., mineral replacement, compaction, chemical change

diamicton: redeposited regolith lacking sedimentary structure and sorting: e.g., tills, landslides, mud slides

diatoms: single-celled pelagic organisms enclosed in siliceous frustules

diversity: measure of the variety of taxa in a community, assemblage, region, etc.

domains: three basic divisions of life: Archaea, Bacteria, and Eukarya (Eucarya)

duration: span of time

ecology: study of relationships between organisms and their environments

ecosystem: a biocoenosis and its physical environment interacting as an ecological unit

ecotone: transitional zone between characteristic plant and animal associations at regional and local scales, usually expressed by enhanced diversity relative to the more homogeneous areas on either side

element (in archaeozoology): body part unit of skeleton; e.g., lower left front leg

eluvial: of the leached zone of epipedon, where water removes salts, oxides, and clays in solution or suspension; Table 11.2

endogenous: originating within the system primarily affected

environment: all physical and biological elements and relationships that impinge upon an organism

epipedon: the parts of a soil profile affected by surface conditions (O, A, E, or B horizons)

equifinality: principle that any particular state of a system can be achieved by many different historical combinations of variables or system trajectories; "many ways to skin a cat"

equinox: time when the Sun is directly above the equator; the time of equal length of night and day; the beginning of spring and autumn

Eukarya (Eucarya): organisms with cellular nuclei, including plants, animals, fungi, and protists eustasy: global changes in sea level

event: discrete occurrence to which some notice is given

exogenous: originating externally to the system affected

facies: lateral difference in sedimentary layers reflecting differences in environments of deposition

fan, alluvial: a triangular pile of complexly interbedded sediments built by a stream where channel gradient changes abruptly

feedback: process that amplifies (positive) or dampens (negative) deviations within a system

firn: coarsely recrystallized snow, a stage in the change to ice from snow

five spheres of the climate system: atmosphere, geosphere (sometimes lithosphere), hydrosphere, cryosphere, and biosphere

floodplains: areas of low relief adjacent to streams subject to periodic flooding and alluvial deposition

foraminifera: single-celled pelagic organisms with calcareous "tests"

formation: plant associations at the regional scale, limited by climate; the plant component of a biome

frequency: in a wave model, the distance or time between peaks of the wave or cyclical phenomenon

gelifluction: slippage of water-saturated surficial sediment over frozen subsoil

General Circulation Models (GCMs):   computer models simulating atmospheric circulation at various times in the past

genotypical: expression of the genes of a species

geomorphology: the study of landforms, especially the processes of formation and erosion

geosphere: rocks and minerals at and near the surface of the Earth that are components of the climate system

glacial: geological interval of cool climate during which glaciers form and expand

glaciation: glacial episode; the process by which ice accumulates on and moves over the land surface

glaciofluvial: originating in glacial meltwater

granulometry: quantitative description of sediments in terms of particle size

gyttja: muddy deposit consisting of plant detritus, often with algae as important components

habitat: environment utilized by a particular organism or species

half-life: time span in which half of an isotope's radioactivity is depleted

herpetofauna: reptiles and amphibians

HMA: Human Mode of Adaptation

Holocene: "most recent" geological time; epoch following the most recent ice age; the past 10,000 years

hominids: Hominidae; family-level taxon of primates including only people

horizon: contrastive zone in soil profile produced by pedogenesis

hydrography: the pattern of surface water drainage networks and drainage basins

hydrosphere: the water of the planet, on or below the surface

ichnofossils: traces of animal behavior preserved in sediments igneous: rocks formed by the cooling and solidification of molten magma

illuvial: zone of epipedon where groundwater deposits materials from suspension or solution

inclination: attribute of the magnetic field that pulls a magnet off the horizontal

insolation: amount of solar radiation reaching a surface

intensity (of magnetic field): strength

interface: conformable contact surface between two different beds in a stratified sequence

interglacial: relatively warm period between major glacial advances

isochron: line delineating the geographic limits of a taxon at a point in time

isopoll: contour-like line connecting mapped points having equal percentages of a pollen taxon

isostasy: buoyant uplift or subsidence of portions of the Earth's crust as overburdens are removed or emplaced

isotopes: atoms of a single element having different numbers of neutrons in the nucleus

karst: landscape in limestone eroded by streams flowing mainly beneath the surface; typically characterized by sinkholes and caves

keystone species: species that, by its position in the food web, influences the biotic composition of its habitat

lag deposits: coarse particles left behind on a surface scoured by wind that removed the fines; e.g., desert pavement

lapse rate: loss of atmospheric heat with altitude

latitude: distance measured in degrees and minutes from the equator toward each pole

levee: linear fluvial deposit paralleling a river channel, built as floodwater overflowing a bank deposited its coarsest load components

loess: medium- to fine-grained silt deposited by wind, typically massive

longitude: distance around the globe parallel to the equator, crossing meridians; measured in degrees east or west from the prime meridian at Greenwich, England

macrobotanical remains: visible and recognizable pieces and parts of plants such as pieces of wood, seeds and fruits, stems, leaves, buds, cuticle, and so on, preserved under special conditions

magnetic field: force field running through the center of the Earth, created by electrical currents originating in the fluid dynamics in the molten outer part of the core, roughly parallel to the surface at the equator, and approximately at right angles to the surface near the poles, varying with latitude between

mantle: stratified zone of heavy mineral matter in a viscous state, between the Earth's core and crust

marl: calcareous clays deposited from water

matrix: any enclosing medium that maintains the relative positions of archaeological remains and defines their immediate physical and chemical environment

meander: looping curve of a sinuous river channel; characteristic of streams carrying suspended load

meridian: imaginary line drawn from pole to pole on the cartographic surface of the Earth, to mark distances east and west of the prime meridian at Greenwich, England

mesic (adj.): of temperate climates

metamorphic: class of rocks recrystallized or indurated by high temperature and pressure

microbotanical remains: plant remains visible under magnification, principally pollen, spores, opal phytoliths, and microorganisms such as algae

midden: heap of refuse, piled by humans or other animals

minerals: inorganic chemical compounds in crystal form

MNI: minimum number of individual animals represented by bones from an analytical unit

moraines: landforms composed of till deposits, both sorted and unsorted glacial debris

morbidity: generalized illness in a population

mortality: death rate within a population

MSL: mean sea level

NAP/non-arboreal pollen: pollen of shrubs, flowers, and grasses

neoecology: study of living communities of plants and animals; special aspect of ecology devoted to the study of living species in their environments or in laboratory situations

niche: role of a species in a community, its manner of maintaining life and interacting with other species and elements of the environment

no-analog problem: difficulties following the recognition that states and conditions of organic and inorganic systems do not exactly repeat over time, limiting the validity of comparisons for interpretation

obsidian: volcanic glass formed by quickly chilled molten rock

ombrotrophic bog: rainwater-fed bogs developed above the water table

orbit: path of a planetary body circling another

order: stream orders are a hierarchical ranking of streams from smallest to largest in a basin; soil Orders are the highest rank in the USDA taxonomy

orogeny: episode of mountain building; the process of mountain building by crustal uplift or folding, or volcanism

outwash: debris deposited by glaciofluvial meltwater

paleoecology: application with disciplined inference of principles from neoecology to the study of organisms in environments no longer directly observable

paleosol: soil formed in past conditions unlike those of the present; sometimes, buried soils

palynology: study of pollen and spores (palynomorphs)

patch: local concentration of biotic resources that are discontinuous and clumped

patchy distribution: spatial heterogeneity of organisms, with contrasting clusters of species aggregates

pathogen: organism that causes disease in another

pedogenesis: process of soil formation at the surface of sedimentary bodies

pedology: science of soils

periglacial: pertaining to areas close to a glacier

perihelion: point on Earth's orbit at which it is closest to the Sun

phenotypical (adj.): of individualized expression of genes influenced by environmental factors physiographic province: geographic area characterized by distinct lithologic structure and relief

phytoliths: non-crystalline silica deposits in and between the cells of plants; some show diagnostic shapes

plaggen soils: cultivated soils enriched with manure and/or turves; a kind of anthropic epipedon associated with plows

plankton: organisms living at and near the surface of the sea

plate tectonics: theory that the Earth's crust is formed of a number of rigid plates in motion relative to one another; plates are formed at spreading ridges, and destroyed in trenches

plates (tectonic):   rigid segments of the Earth's crust

point bar: relatively coarse fluvial deposit along the convex curve of a meander, opposite the location of channel cutting

pollen diagram: graphic presentation of the frequency by depth of pollen taxa in a core or profile

potential niche: fundamental or potential niche is the essential ecological space of a species, in the sense of its ability to maintain life in the hypothetical absence of all imposed constraints (cf. realized niche)

precession: process by which the angle of the Earth's axis to its orbit changes through time, changing the relationship of seasons with the angle of the ecliptic

precipitation: water, snow, or ice condensed from vapor, falling from clouds

precision: fineness of resolution of a measurement; its replicability in repeated measurements

propagules: seeds, spores, tubers, etc.

protists: one of the five kingdoms of biology; single-celled organisms with cellular nuclei

proxy data: observational data used as surrogates for conditions not directly observable (e.g., pollen spectra interpreted in terms of climate)

quid: wad of plant fibers spit out after mastication

racemization: process by which amino-acid molecules reverse asymmetry after burial

realized niche: portion of its potential niche to which a species is confined by competition, geographical barriers, etc.; niche space defined by an organism's success in acquiring, in the presence of competitors, resources essential for its well-being and procreation

refugia: unglaciated areas where organisms survive during times of severe climate

regolith: unconsolidated mineral matter lying above bedrock, whether *in situ* or redeposited

regression: fall of sea level or rise of land, exposing landforms previously under water

relief: relative measure of surface ruggedness expressing vertical distance between highest and lowest spots in a given unit of land

resolution: degree of precision that can be attained in the measurement of a set of variables; potential for precision; property of being reducible to equivalent units

ridges: areas of uplift and spreading between tectonic plates; more commonly, the topographic divide between opposite slopes

rift zones: areas of uplift and progressive separation between tectonic plates on the surface of the Earth

RSL (relative sea level):   sea level relative to a land surface, acknowledging only relative movement, without claims for which component moved ruderals: plants that colonize disturbed ground; weeds

sapwood: young wood growth directly beneath the bark of a tree

scarp: steep slope or cliff

sea level: imaginary plane approximating the average elevation of the surface of the sea

sediment: unconsolidated mineral matter deposited on the surface of the Earth (see regolith)

sedimentary: rocks composed of matter transported by wind, water, or ice and consolidated after deposition

sequence: order of events in time

sidereal: pertaining to the stars, as "sidereal time" for astronomical time

slope: surface landform slanting between horizontal and vertical, usually $<45°$

soils: unconsolidated bodies of organic and physical particles that support plant life; chemically and mechanically altered terrestrial sediments

solifluction: process by which unconsolidated materials saturated with water slide downslope

spectrum (pl.: spectra): the total pollen count for each sample in a pollen diagram, read along the horizontal axis

speleothems: deposits of calcium minerals in caves, such as stalactites, stalagmites, and flowstone

state: qualitative character or structure of a system (cf. condition)

stenotopic: organism tolerant of a narrow range of habitats

strategies: consciously adopted means for adaptation

stratification: record of past events, processes, and states preserved in sequence within sediments

stratigraphy: interpretation of stratification by a stratigrapher, or the method of interpretation of strata

structure: of sediments, organizational attributes resulting from the manner of transport and deposition of particles constituting a sediment and its stratification; may also reflect subsequent transformation processes

succession: geological, ecological, or seasonal sequence of species within a habitat

symbionts: organisms living in close mutual dependence; e.g., lichens

sympatric: co-resident; living together in the same place; species sharing a habitat

synanthropic species: plants and animals that live in close association with *Homo sapiens* and are to an extent dependent upon anthropic habitats

synecology: interrelationships of several or many species within a defined habitat range

system: bounded set composed of entities and their relationships

taphonomy: study of the processes leading to burial and fossilization

taxon (pl.: taxa): basic unit in formal systematic classification of organisms (e.g., genus, species)

taxonomy: systematic classification

tectonics: movement and deformation of the Earth's crust: mountain building, plate movements, folding, etc.

tells: mounded or hill-like landforms comprised of the debris of ancient cities tephra: volcanic ash

terrace: segment of floodplain or erosional surface abandoned by river incision

texture: of sediments, the combined attributes of particle size, shape, and sorting

thanatocoenosis: death assemblage; a deposit of fossils

thermohaline circulation: global-girdling currents moving heat and salt in the oceans

till: diamicton deposited by a glacier, of two basic types: till deposited directly at the base of the glacier is called lodgement till, that deposited as the glacier melts away is called ablation till. Other common names for till, especially when the formation processes are less than certain, include "boulder clay" and "drift"

topography: elevational relief and form of the Earth's surface

transgression: advance of sea over land, caused by rise of sea level or subsidence of land

transhumance: herd management involving seasonal movements among pastures

transpiration: exhalation of water by elements of the biosphere, mainly vegetation

travertine: carbonate rock deposited in freshwater; tufa

trophic levels: feeding levels in an ecosystem, involving food producers, consumers, secondary consumers (carnivores), and decomposers

tuff: rock composed of indurated volcanic ash

unconformity: erosional surface between two beds in a stratified sequence

uniformitarianism: principle positing that geological and biological processes in the past were not different in kind from processes observed today

varves: paired lacustrine sediment layers showing seasonal variation in texture or color

vectors: organisms that carry pathogens from one host to another

ventifact: rock sculpted by wind-borne sand particles

vertebrates: animals with backbones

weathering: chemical and physical processes disaggregating or dissolving rock and sediments at the surface of the Earth

X-ray densitometry: X-ray images of tree-ring thin sections showing the relative density of cellulose in each ring as a measure of annual tree growth

zonal: of climate types, soils, and organic assemblages: distributed latitudinally on continents; of pollen diagrams: a characteristic suite of pollen representing a biostratigraphic unit within a sequence

zones, pollen: groups of stratigraphically adjacent samples in pollen diagrams showing similar combinations of selected taxa

zoonoses: disease organisms that infect animal hosts, especially those able to transfer to humans

PART I

Introduction

ENVIRONMENTAL ARCHAEOLOGY
AND HUMAN ECOLOGY

Ecology, a word so much in vogue in recent years that it has lost much of its original meaning, may be defined as "that branch of science concerned with [the study of] the relationships between organisms and their environment" (Hardesty 1977: 290). **Environment**, which is often confused with ecology, encompasses all the physical and biological elements and relationships that impinge upon a living being. Specification of an organism's environment emphasizes those variables relevant to the life of that organism – ideally, almost every aspect of its surroundings.

Advances in instrumentation for the observation and measurement of biological, planetary, and astronomical environmental phenomena have driven unprecedented recent growth in the historical geo- and biosciences. The maturing geosciences acknowledge unexpected complexity, diversity, and dynamism in the natural world, now slowly seeping into study of the social sciences as well. The biosciences have powerful new techniques for examining life at small scales, notably the molecular scale. The growth in these ancillary disciplines has opened opportunities for advances in archaeology on the basis of new data sources and richer understanding of processes and mechanisms in all historical sciences.

Archaeologists have embraced the novel results, and built on some of the new data, not always understanding the theoretical and methodological bases on which those results were founded; some of those foundations have since been shown to be unsteady. Premature adoption of poorly evaluated analytical techniques and their preliminary results has given archaeology a decade or more of spectacular claims and attendant rebuttals, creating an uneasy atmosphere.

In this atmosphere and by such means, environmental archaeology has gained a reputation as being driven by method at the expense of sound practice and genuinely

3

useful results. Some excellent, even extraordinary, work has been done in the environmental archaeology mode using the powerful new techniques and revised theories, most of it, however, applying one or at most two disciplinary data sets. Single data sets, utilized in isolation, have proven very vulnerable to rebuttal from other directions. Along with impressive improvements of field work and analysis, a chorus of dissatisfaction swelled as very few large, well-financed and staffed research projects achieved significant coordination and integration across the several disciplines which contribute to the practice of environmental archaeology.

This present exploration of human ecology emphasizes excellence in the methods and practice of environmental archaeology, worldwide. It begins with a brief review of the physical and cultural evolution of our species, identifying aspects of environment that have impinged most significantly upon human populations at various stages in prehistory. The argument emphasizes archaeologically recoverable information that enhances understanding of the human condition from an ecologically informed perspective.

ORGANIZATION OF THIS VOLUME

Archaeology has long been perceived as a borrower discipline, taking techniques and data from other sciences to help it meet its own goals, but giving back little. As I hope to show in the pages that follow, a mature archaeology can return to all the historical disciplines studying the last 3 million years a finer time scale, an enhanced database that integrates information from many disciplines, and a deeper understanding of the contributions, both positive and negative, of human lives in the evolution of the world we know today. As electronic communication expands and information flows more freely globally, it will be crucial for researchers to command the basic theory and assumptions of other special fields and disciplines, in order to evaluate claims for new methods, applications, and results.

The several parts of the volume group chapters related in terms of the data sets used in building interpretations of aspects of paleoenvironments. Thus, Part I presents the argument for multidisciplinary inclusiveness, which is developed further in each part that follows. Part II presents approaches to the construction of chronological frameworks, which are essential to the integration of data sets that cross disciplinary borders. It argues for active evaluation of methods used for chronology building, and for informed awareness of their limitations and best applications. Part III presents paleoclimatology in a framework of its relevance to archaeological data and problems. The concept of scales of data and interpretation is elaborated in Part III, and threads its way through all the later chapters.

Part IV presents structural geomorphology in paleoenvironments, again empha-sizing the importance of appropriate scales of analysis for different kinds of human experience. Part V introduces sedimentology as a fundamental aspect of archaeologi-cal context and of paleoenvironmental analysis. Soils science is given importance equal to sedimentology, while its special applications and rewards are argued, empha-sizing soils as archaeological matrices holding paleoenvironmental information and affecting relative preservation. Part VI presents paleobotany in its various manifesta-tions, introducing its several scales of inquiry with the data and methods appropriate for each. Part VII brings in animals, not only as objects of inquiry for zooarchaeology, but more centrally as aspects of human environments informative in themselves and biologically significant. Because the subjects of archaeology, people, are members of the world's Animal Kingdom, Part VII has three chapters instead of the two assigned to most of the other parts. Part VIII attempts to be both retrospective and forward-looking, discussing the enterprise of environmental archaeology in the context of the concepts presented throughout the volume, and attempting to evaluate its prospects for future success as a central element in the study of past human experience and human influences on many processes that define the home planet.

INTERDEPENDENCE

The Red Queen beyond Alice's Looking Glass huffed that the world and events were moving so fast that "it takes all the running you can do, to keep in the same place" (Gardner 1960: 210). Her plight has become the "Red Queen hypothesis" of ecology and evolution (Foley 1984; van Valen 1973): environments are constantly changing (at one scale or another) as climate varies, populations fluctuate, species' distribu-tions change, or behavior is modified. Each such change may entail behavioral, dis-tributional, or biological changes as species respond to the new conditions. The responses themselves in turn modify the environments of the target species and to some extent of all others sharing the same space. Thus, living things must continually monitor and respond to changing environments, even as their responses stimulate further change. Change presents problems and opportunities to all organisms; those that successfully solve the problems may be said to have adapted – ultimately, to survive. The emergence of the human species, within the last 2 million years or so, has complicated ecological relationships in ways that seem both to result from and to inspire the peculiarly human characteristic of high intelligence.

In traditional Western culture, human beings are conceived as separable from their environment, so that everything that is not human (and even some humans if sufficiently unfamiliar) is defined as "other" and considered to be subordinate and potentially exploitable. Ecology shows us that our very humanness is defined not by our separateness from the rest of the world, but by our unique but interdependent relationships to all those "others."

Homo sapiens is a creature of the Earth; humans would be different in fundamental ways if they had developed on any other planet, in any other solar system, at any other time. The elemental matter that comprises our planet condensed out of the primeval gases of the proto-Universe. Earth continuously receives bits of matter in the form of star dust that gravitates to it out of space: atoms of nitrogen, carbon, and other elements rain down on its surface, and are ultimately incorporated into organic and inorganic compounds (Morowitz 1983; Ponnamperuma and Friebele 1982). Humans ingest those compounds into our living substance from the foods we eat. Our genetic codes, partly inherited from ancestors millions of years remote from us, reflect the environments and selection pressures of marine and terrestrial habitats of a younger Earth. We move through, and breathe in, the Earth's unique gaseous atmosphere. Basic body rhythms, reset daily by sunlight, are in phase with the day lengths defined by planetary rotation; some appear to be responsive to the Moon's gravity. Our populations display biological characteristics that are responses to specific latitudinal and altitudinal stresses: biological adaptations to severe cold or heat, thin air, filtered sunlight, or high insolation. Our species is among many that emerged during the Quaternary ice ages, a prolonged period of unusually cool planetary climates. As we explore out into space, we cannot expect to find other creatures like ourselves.

We take our form of existence so thoroughly for granted that it appears inevitable. We cannot even imagine creatures fundamentally different from ourselves, and so we imagine them as distorted versions of ourselves – the anthropomorphized denizens of science fiction and fable. Perhaps if we can learn to know and understand the contexts that produced modern humans, we can better prepare ourselves for the future when our historically conditioned fitness will be put to harsh new tests (Potts 1996).

The human animal shares the basic needs common to all earthly life: food, shelter, and reproduction. We are born knowing something about supplying those needs, but from the first moment of life, we require other humans to help us satisfy them. We do not hatch out of an egg and begin to forage for ourselves. Society is a requirement of all contemporary human life. We can take that for granted throughout the human past, and perhaps should acknowledge it as a fourth basic need.

Becoming human

Human prehistory begins with relatively large-brained, bipedal, social omnivores in Africa. The original **habitats** (typical environments) seem to have been gallery forests and savanna edges, only a little cooler and drier than the Miocene home country of the immediately ancestral large primates. The climate was apparently equable, the terrain diverse and in many places actively volcanic. The vegetal environments were **patchy** (spatially heterogeneous) and linear, following river courses and lake shores. Early humans met some of the challenges of such environments by developing hand and eye coordination to new heights, building upon the alertness, curiosity, and manipulative skills characteristic of all primates. Enlargement of the brain went along with these adaptive developments. Throughout this volume there are passing references to biological/genetic change in humans; however, human evolutionary biology is not a central issue in this presentation of human ecology, which focuses on environments, not genotypes. Readers interested in current thinking and data on evolutionary physiology should seek primary sources on that topic.

Within this habitat, early humans made a **niche** (a species' role in a biological community) for themselves as social omnivores, foraging and scavenging a wide variety of foods on and under the surface of the land. The ability to acquire, consume, and digest almost anything not positively poisonous gave humans a special role and some advantages within their environment. Their broad niche made it possible for them to expand into habitats not closely similar to their original homes, and thus to proliferate. Human physiology is highly dependent on water; people cannot live long without replenishing body fluids. Where surface water was unavailable, they substituted liquids stored in the bodies of plants and other animals. The need for water imposed limitations on the locations of home bases and on effective travel distances.

The elaborated brain that distinguishes our species from all others extracted a price in extended gestation and lengthened periods of childhood dependency. Both constrained the mobility of women with young children and thus, probably, that of the residential group, placing a further premium upon generalizing behavior and diet breadth rather than specialization, which requires mobility. The development of the human brain apparently exceeded the requirements of natural selection in any conceivable environment. Evolutionary physiologists explain it by positing crucial feedback from social, cultural, and linguistic developments that synergistically improved the fitness of large-brained individuals (Tattersall 1998).

The emergence of language is not specifically revealed in archaeological data. Its origins and early development are matters of speculation (Mellars and Gibson 1996). However, even a rudimentary language that could allow foresight and planning (discussing what is not present or has not happened) would stimulate cultural elaboration and confer survival benefits upon its speakers. With elaboration came more effective communication, ritual and magic, and enhanced social cohesiveness. Language that allowed consideration of options and planning for contingencies would have been beneficial, if not essential, to the human groups that slowly moved out of familiar landscapes into new and challenging others.

Homo erectus, an intercontinental traveler, colonized well beyond the semitropical homelands (Fig. 1.1) into temperate zones of Europe and Asia (Tattersal 1998). Once fire could be controlled, expansion into higher altitudes and latitudes became possible and worthwhile. Using fire to drive game and clear underbrush could have been learned from observation of natural fires, but its use as a campfire opened unprecedented possibilities. Fires keep people warm, soften food, and push back the night. Fires kept prowling carnivores away from human groups, even those who took up residence in the carnivore lairs. In all these ways, fire enhanced the comfort and safety of the home base, contributing to the self-domestication of the human family.

Accumulations of trash in late Lower Paleolithic sites support the notion that home bases with fire were occupied for longer periods of time than earlier habitation and sleeping sites (Turner 1984). Home bases may also support larger interdependent groups, making accommodative social skills more important to survival. By keeping people together in one place home bases may have intensified the sharing and spread not only of food and cultural behavior but also of parasites and some communicable diseases. Thus, the institution of home bases had implications for both biological and social evolution.

ELABORATING CULTURE

Given that humans are primates, an order of mammals most of whose members are plant-eaters, major questions in human evolution involve when and how **hominids** (Hominidae: the human branch of the primates) began to eat significant amounts of meat, and when and how they began the purposeful killing of large mammals (Bunn 1981; Isaac and Crader 1981; Potts 1984). Chimpanzees and baboons kill and eat small creatures: predatory behavior is within the primate spectrum. In human prehistory, stone tools create an archaeological record more than 2 million years in duration, but we know very little about how those early tools were used in food-getting. In the archaeological record, scavenging as a means of meat acquisition is very difficult to distinguish from hunting, since both activities produce associations of broken bones and rough tools. Confidence in previous interpretations of purposeful hunting by early hominids has given way to cautious skepticism about the appropriateness of modern analogies (Binford 1981; Nitecki and Nitecki 1987; Potts 1984). Within the last million years or so, *Homo erectus* or early *H. sapiens* began to hunt large mammals, becoming the first hominids to share niche space with those powerful social hunters, the large cats and canids.

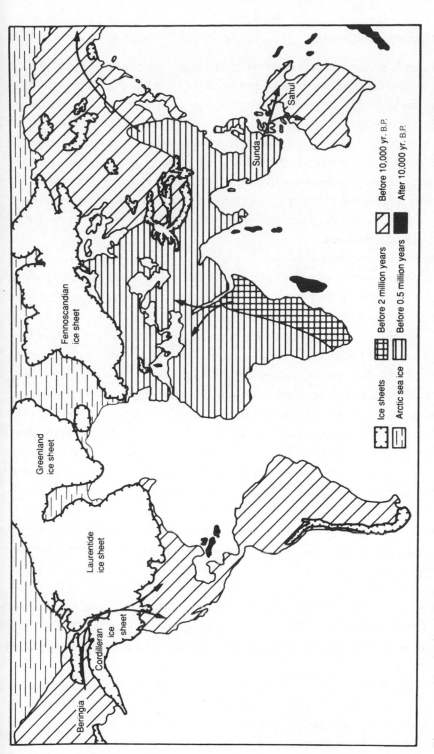

Figure 1.1 Hominid expansion across the continents, during the Pleistocene (hatchured and cross-hatched) and Holocene (solid) epochs. Entry routes into the Americas probably included water travel down the west coast. (Reproduced from Roberts 1989: Fig. 3.7, by permission of Blackwell Publishers.)

Labels on map:
- Greenland ice sheet
- Fennoscandian ice sheet
- Laurentide ice sheet
- Cordilleran ice sheet
- Beringia
- Sunda
- Sahul

Legend:
- Ice sheets
- Arctic sea ice
- Before 2 million years
- Before 0.5 million years
- Before 10,000 yr. B.P.
- After 10,000 yr. B.P.

Gatherers and hunters

Meat is a high-quality food, offering maximal energetic nutrition per unit of bulk or weight. Its consumption on a regular basis opened a new niche at the top of the food pyramid for hominids. However, hunting large game involves considerable risk of failure if pursued more than opportunistically; some alternative food-getting strategies are essential for buffering risk. Cooperative behaviors are institutionalized in the hunt: in the reliance on others to provide alternative foods, in the necessity for trust and sharing of whatever food is acquired. When hunters range widely, base camps must provide safety for infants and their caretakers, as well as secure places in which to consume large amounts of perishable food which is likely to attract the interest of other potential consumers.

There is a romantic fiction that people who live by gathering and hunting exist in a state of blessed nature, in benign harmony with the world around them. This idea has triumphed over earlier perspectives of gatherer-hunters living lives that were "nasty, brutish, and short." The purported harmony is evoked as the opposite of modern conditions where people clearly threaten the tenuous balances of the biological world. On the contrary, human beings have long been the world's great destabilizers, leaving almost nothing strictly as they find it (Goudie 1993). Long before bulldozers and dams, people were remaking the world to suit their visions, and before that, they were changing things by inadvertence if not always by volition. Gatherer-hunters, simply by being rather large and very clever animals, affect the world in which other species live. Where groups of them gather together and stay for any length of time, the local vegetation is trampled or removed. Their food and body wastes change the local soil chemistry. Their campfires ignite prairie and forest fires, establishing or maintaining fire-successional communities. In hard times they impose significant additional stress on prey species and on species with whom they compete for prey. Their game drives and fish weirs impose heavy predation burdens on local populations of game and fish. They move plants and plant parts around and may introduce species into new habitats. By changing the distribution and densities of flora and fauna, humans have always lived in a world partly of their own making (Dincauze 1993a). The physical remains of such behavior and its consequences make possible an archaeology of paleoenvironments and paleoecology.

By the Middle Pleistocene (Table 1.1), early humans expanded their ranges out of subtropical Africa into the Near East and Europe. In latitudes where they faced winter low temperatures, shelter became an imperative. Caves and small cave-like houses kept wind and rain outside; ultimately, clothing made the artificial "indoor"

Table 1.1 Geological epochs and Paleolithic stages, with ages

Time (millions of years)	Geological epochs	Paleolithic stages
0.01	HOLOCENE	
0.05	LATE PLEISTOCENE	UPPER PALEOLITHIC
0.1		
		MIDDLE PALEOLITHIC
0.5		
0.7	MIDDLE PLEISTOCENE	LOWER PALEOLITHIC
1.0		
	EARLY PLEISTOCENE	
1.5		
2.0	PLIOCENE	

climates portable for mobile hunters and foragers. The artificial microclimates of housing and clothing provide relatively benign conditions not only for people but for lice, fleas, and other insects. Small mammalian scavengers hiding in the dark corners of houses gain access to food. Houses create dead-air spaces, and smoky fires pollute that air. People relying upon houses and clothing are stressed by more and different diseases than are tropical people living mobile existences in the open air. Both genetic and behavioral selection is imposed by such novel stressors, including the social and psychological requirements for tolerating the close presence of others in winter quarters. Contemporary people, after thousands of generations of selection, still suffer from cabin fever or seasonal depression in long, dark winters. For all its benefits, environmental innovation entails major consequences.

Nevertheless, gatherer-hunters were phenomenally successful among the animals of the world. The environmental problems that constrained the ranges of the earliest hominids – inability to prepare portable high-energy foods, reliance on equable climates, and limited defense from predators – were solved well enough before 50,000 years ago to make life possible in all continents that were accessible by foot. Subsequently, by boat across the Pacific and Arctic Oceans and by foot into the last deglaciated terrains, they reached almost all habitable lands, mainly before cities rose anywhere. People learned to live successfully gathering and hunting the diverse plant and animal life of the planet from the high Arctic to the tropical forests, along the seacoasts, and in the mountains.

Domesticators

People first domesticated themselves, learning to live in social communities of their own invention. They then brought animals and plants into their communities and their houses, creating innovative social and economic relationships.

Dogs were apparently the first animals to be domesticated. The process of that achievement is unknown, but dogs genetically modified in the direction of modern domesticates appear in the archaeological record of Eurasia and North America by the end of the ice age (Davis and Valla 1978). Dogs accept food that they have not killed, and it may have been as scavengers that canids first came into close association with humans, joining human communities as secondary self-domesticators (Serpell 1995). Speculation has long centered on the usefulness of dogs to human hunters; their use prehistorically in hunting remains undemonstrated but possible. As pets, their intelligence and loyalty recommend them immediately; as alarm-givers, protectors, warmers, and comforters, and even as a convenient emergency meat supply, they offer appreciable benefits to humans who feed them. Dogs are good value: only in cities are their costs likely to exceed their contributions to group life.

There is no way of knowing how many other species humans might have tamed as pets; the keeping of individual animals rarely shows in the archaeological record. Nor do we expect to know how many species were experimented with as domesticates. We count the successes, and those were the small ungulates of the highlands fringing Mesopotamia. Sheep and goats were manageable; gazelles were not. On that difference hangs much of history and unmeasured ecological effects. The benefits of domesticating herbivores appear obvious in hindsight – a food supply conveniently close by, a ready source of milk, hair, fur, and other animal products, some control over the numbers of economically useful animals. In fact, some of the benefits could not have been immediately realized (sheep's woolly coats, for example, appeared later in domesticated flocks). We do not know what the impetus was for early efforts at domestication; more evidence of the context is required. In several parts of the world, people managed vegetation to increase the density of wild herbivores, achieving some of the benefits of domestication without the heavy costs.

Keeping domestic herds establishes unprecedented relationships between people and animals. While the seasonal **transhumance** of herders may seem not very different from the mobility of hunters, there are additional considerations. Herd animals, once captured, must be restrained, protected, fed, bred, and actively managed. The selection of the more docile for breeding, whether intentional or not, eventually produced animals ill adapted to fend for themselves. Successful maintenance or expansion of herds requires that the herders eliminate competitors and predators, and seek or supply essential food and water. All of these tasks entail human labor, requiring daily and seasonal scheduling. Later, when the original domesticates were augmented by cattle and when husbandry was expanded beyond the original homelands into the forests of Anatolia and Europe, labor requirements were increased by the construction and maintenance of facilities such as corrals and shelters. In Europe, early farmers kept their animals within their houses, presumably at night, thereby intensifying their own exposure to a range of contagious or vector-borne diseases. Close relationships with farm and herd animals directly affected human group size, territoriality, division of labor, niche breadth, diet breadth, mobility, and health, in both beneficial and deleterious ways. The changed conditions of life entailed genetic and social adaptations. With the invention of harness, humans were able to use large animals for traction, adding significantly to the benefits of animal domestication by increasing the energy and muscle power available to them.

Plant domestication emerged from foraging economies in many parts of the world during the early **Holocene** (between 12,000 and 10,000 years ago). In southwestern and southeastern Asia, Mesoamerica, and South America, seed-producing and starchy root plants were brought under human care and propagation by 10,000 to 8000 years ago. Because the archaeological record for leafy vegetables and fruits is impoverished by preservation problems, the chronology and location of domestication for some of our favorite modern foods is still unknown (Harris and Hillman 1989).

Competent gatherers of wild plant foods know well when the edible portions of various species are at their best, and they know where to find them in economic quantities. The easiest way to utilize plants in season is to go where they grow, gather and consume them until there are insufficient quantities left, then move on to other places. Population numbers, distance, or seasonality may encourage gathering more food than can be immediately consumed, with additional labor invested in preparing the surplus for later use. Such "harvesting" strategies bridge much of the conceptual distance between gathering wild plants and tending crops. The global warming that accompanied and followed the shrinkage of the ice sheets certainly brought climatic changes that in turn entailed changes in the compositions and distributions of plant and animal communities. Behavioral adaptations by human foragers followed; repeatedly, these involved deliberate manipulation of economically important plants. Plants colonizing new or disturbed surfaces, wild plants responding to drought, the sequential recovery of plant communities following fires, must all have been familiar to gatherers and understood well enough to permit human manipulation of the distribution or densities of favored species. Intentionally or inadvertently spreading seeds, as well as transplanting and weeding desirable plants and diverting or carrying small amounts of water for simple irrigation, are well within the technological competence of foragers. Small changes in human behavior, bringing minor, short-term benefits, do not show well in the archaeological record (chapters in Harris and Hillman [1989]; Watson and Kennedy 1991). Early experiments in plant management are even more elusive than the early successes at domesticating animals that seem to have been going on at about the same time in the Near East, at least.

The Farmer Trap was sprung later. The labor increase associated with early plant domestication must have been perceived as either a reasonable or necessary cost for a realized benefit. The varied diets of hunter-gatherers provide qualitatively better nutrition than do the simpler, more consistent, diets of subsistence farmers. Eventually, many foragers relinquished some freedom and mobility in exchange for a predictable sufficiency of a simpler and ultimately poorer diet. Crop-raising supports increased population and family size, typically at the cost of lowered nutritional status and diminished body size (Cohen and Armelagos 1984). Labor invested in the land requires a more sedentary life, which brings its own benefits and costs such as improved shelter, technology and its material products, labor requirements for the construction and maintenance of facilities and tools, and increases in density-dependent diseases. Lost mobility options make possible more intensive social control over individuals, beginning social stratification. The short-term predictability of domesticated crops is countered by the ecological fragility of specialization on only a few plants, which are subject to losses from diseases, unfavorable weather, insects, and animal predators.

The domestication of the landscape followed shortly on the establishment of subsistence agriculture. In Mesopotamia and the eastern Mediterranean lands its effects have been well documented archaeologically. "In their efforts to control the environment in the interest of reducing risk and increasing productivity, people unwittingly imposed a Near Eastern subsistence landscape on new and frequently unsuitable environments" (Butzer 1982: 310).

Landscape modifiers

The development of technology for landscape modification usually increases the **carrying capacity** of habitats for our unique species, making possible higher human population densities. With farming, land becomes valuable; land rights set up the conditions for social inequality and territorial conflicts at many scales. The discontents of civilization, as well as its material benefits, seem to be legacies from the same source.

Human effects on the biological landscape are inseparable from those on its physical aspects. Soils (Chapter 11) articulate the two very closely, so that what affects soils changes the **biota** (all living things in a defined place), and vice versa. Landform modification, of course, affects both. Even very simple plows, breaking the soil and exposing it to wind and water erosion, initiate significant changes in the distribution of soil types and superficial sediment bodies (e.g., Starkel 1987). Irrigation reorganizes surficial water flow and changes local water tables. New communities of plants and animals line up along irrigation canals. Pastured animals and manured cultivated fields further change soil characteristics. Soil depletion and erosion, progressive salinization of irrigated fields, deforestation to create fields and pastures and to obtain wood for buildings and fuel, siltation of lakes and rivers by agricultural runoff – these are ancient side effects of farming that change the natural landscape. As towns grew into cities, roads facilitated the movement of people carrying information, other organisms, and commodities. Urban populations, building anew on their own ruins, heaped cities into artificial hills.

Climate also is influenced by changes in biota and landforms. Deforestation and seasonally bare soils change the reflectivity of the Earth's surface, modifying air currents and thus weather patterns. When fragile plant communities are damaged, desertification can result – an expression of changed local climate, and in turn a cause of it.

City-dwellers

People hold strongly divergent opinions about cities as places to live; they feel ambivalent about these population concentrations that offer cultural richness and sybaritic comforts for some, with stressful social, economic, and biological challenges for the many. High population densities at a regional scale entail territorial and social circumscription. Sedentary communities are dependent upon outsiders to supply commodities not locally available, and importation of goods requires economic management. Managerial hierarchies everywhere bring taxes to pay for them, priests to justify the resultant inequality, chiefs to enforce it, and soldiers to protect it. High urban population densities amplify the benefits and costs of coresidence: houses and neighborhoods are more permanent, less clean. Urban conditions breed diseases; with cities came epidemics.

Cities not only concentrate population and energy, they consume them. Unlike rural hamlets and towns, cities rarely replenish themselves; they are instead replenished from their hinterlands, from which come commodities, energy, and population. The rate of population increase in cities tends to be orders of magnitude higher than biological potential; they are population sinks, and may always have been so (Barney 1980: 60–64; Watt 1973: 141).

Urban societies, concentrating power and wealth, support craftspeople and artisans whose products are not merely luxury goods but symbols of privilege and social power. Full-time craft specialists bring technology to new heights of achievement and complexity. The transformation of minerals by pyrotechnology that began in the work of potters and metallurgists is the foundation of all modern industry. Ore extraction and metallurgy began about the same time as cities in Asia Minor, although they involved also non-urbanized societies in the hinterlands.

The special needs of urban societies, and the wealth and power at their command, led to public works such as large temples, pyramids, palaces, and city walls. Beyond the walls were built canals, roads, and reservoirs to serve the inhabitants. Later swamp draining and land leveling expanded the food-producing potential. Irrigation, short-fallow regimes, and erosion eventually depleted the soils whose crops supplied the early cities. Native biota were displaced as the landscape was urbanized. Citizens kept pets, farm animals, and work animals. In shops, warehouses, and homes where food was stored, vermin such as rats and weevils proliferated.

Urban environments have their own distinct climates. Cities are notorious "heat islands," generating and retaining temperatures higher than the adjacent countryside. Rising air currents deflect local rainfall. Roofs and pavements shed water much as bedrock does, with the result that the local water table is lowered as water drains off outside the city center.

Urban environments have biological effects upon the residents. Privilege, poverty, stress, and density-dependent diseases all affect the quality and length of urban lives. We may expect, therefore, some selective effects on the gene pools in cities. However, these effects do not seem to have led to biological adaptation at the population scale. Cities, after all, are very recent phenomena in human environments, only about 5000 years old at the maximum. Because city populations rarely replace themselves, succeeding generations bring new genetic material from outside. Genetic adaptations to urban life remain for the future to observe and evaluate.

Cities raise to new heights human potential in the arts and in the art of living. At the same time, these special environments are transitory in the global scale of phenomena. The archaeological ruins of romance and fantasy are mainly those of dead cities. Where the early civilizations rose, the ancient centers stand abandoned in devastated landscapes. Over a hundred years ago, George Perkins Marsh urged his contemporaries to ponder the death of cities, that they might take some interest in the deaths of organisms around them in time to avoid a like fate (Marsh 1965 [1864]).

This rapid review of human environments in evolutionary perspective demonstrates that the human environment has become more complex through time – slowly at first, then at increasing rates, to arrive at today's startling pace of change and diversification. Today, worldwide, the sociocultural environment dominates individual lives, the fates of nations, and the destiny of other species coresident on the planet.

GOALS OF PALEOENVIRONMENTAL STUDIES

The global scale of human habitat is unique among creatures, most of which have environmental tolerances that limit their ranges. Humans invented personal and social environments that they carry about with them, permitting today almost any style of life to be lived anywhere on the globe. We bipedal omnivores with our powerful technologies modify the quality and distribution of climate, soils, water, vegetation, animals, and landforms. Paleoenvironmental studies, by no means esoteric historical exercises, are essential for elucidating the process by which this came about. Because of the interrelationships of organisms and their environments, past conditions continue to shape the present and future. Paleoenvironmental studies in archaeology have three kinds of goals: historical, philosophical, and policy-making goals.

Historical goals

The first task of paleoenvironmental study is the description and understanding of environments in the human past. As has been shown above, the traditional contrast between natural and social environments is no longer analytically acceptable; the two are mutually dependent and inseparable. The hypothetical question, "Are the modern densities of the human species attributes of its 'natural' or its 'social' environments?" defies analysis. Population density is central to the conditions of existence for any community, and begs to be understood on its own terms. Any adequate understanding must acknowledge the polydimensional character of environment, its physical, biological, and social aspects. Historical research can reveal how these characteristics developed and interacted to define our species as we find ourselves today.

Theoretical and philosophical goals

More abstractly, but not less significantly, we seek knowledge of the nature of *Homo sapiens* – the inherent potentials and limitations of the species. Significant issues include the uniqueness among mammals of our bipedal big-brained species, the interdependence of individuals and societies, the biological distinctions among populations, the social equivalence of our diverse societies, the problem of free will, the definition of "progress," and the ultimate questions of being and behaving. Paleoenvironmental data and insights will not resolve these issues, but it is unlikely that genuine understanding of them can be gained without a perspective on environmental contexts and the evolutionary processes that defined them.

The following chapters will amply demonstrate that an ecological perspective on human physical and social history and evolution is by no means determinative. People are the proximate causes of change in their societies; their environments reflect, amplify, or dampen change, and return changed conditions to the instigators of change, requiring new adaptations.

Policy goals

Insights and understanding gained during pursuit of the first two goals contribute to intelligent planning for the future. It is widely acknowledged that present generations must take action to assure a survivable world for ourselves, and we see that we cannot live in isolation from the worlds around us. The reciprocity between any creature and its environment is an inescapable fact of existence. Human ecology is not a simple phenomenon. Complex problems cannot be alleviated by simplification; what is needed is the understanding that permits creative insight and appropriate action. Ecology shows that static assumptions – the expectation that things will, or ought to, stay the same – are maladaptive. We need to build into the fabric of our daily lives an awareness of the global consequences of our activities. Human societies today, and for a long time, have found adaptation to each other both the immediate and the ultimate challenge. The threats we pose to each other, to all other living things, and to the physical world around us, are the adaptive challenges of today. Adaptation, fundamentally, is survival and reproduction. That always entails costs to individuals and communities.

Knowledge of past lifeways and foodways can illuminate dysfunctional aspects of contemporary lives, directly in the case of traditional people whose ancestry can be traced to archaeological sites, and indirectly in the case of urban and ghettoized populations. Significant policy implications can be developed from paleoenvironmental and paleonutritional research, to support improved living conditions for contemporary people (e.g., Brenton 1994).

Environmental studies in archaeology are not undertaken in expectation that descriptions of past environments will directly explain human actions, cultural developments, or change of any kind. The chapters that follow should make clear why such expectations are futile. The complexity of the natural world and, especially, of potential human responses within and to that world, defeats any hopes for easy, direct, causal connections between forms of human society or existence and the non-human world. However, no understanding of human conditions in the past can be achieved without some grasp of physical and biological contexts. The better we can know and evaluate the context of daily lives at any time in the past, the better to evaluate and understand the challenges faced, the choices made, and the changes engendered by human thought and actions. For archaeology, alone among the paleoenvironmental disciplines represented in this book, the human thinkers and actors retain primacy of place. Even though we can rarely identify individuals in the past, we cannot for a moment forget that it is the human beings whom we seek to understand, not simply the frequency of rains in past summers. As we learn more about both, the more likely it seems that the two phenomena are related.

CONCEPTS FOR PALEOENVIRONMENTAL RECONSTRUCTION

> If the theories behind borrowed concepts are not clearly understood and taken into account in the application of the concepts, not only will the results of the concept application be suspect, but misunderstandings may arise between practitioners of the science from which the concept was borrowed and the concept-borrowing archaeologists.
>
> CREMEENS AND HART 1995:16

The study of the human past requires knowledge of the solar system as well as of the home planet and its geophysical and biological systems, of which we are inextricably a part. The eternal fascination of archaeological research is that it challenges all our creativity, discipline, and enthusiasms; scarcely any knowledge is irrelevant to it. That is especially true of environmental archaeology – the study of paleoenvironments as human habitats. Habitats pose problems and opportunities for resident organisms of whatever size and complexity; humans are not excepted from this imposition. If we are to understand the behaviors of human beings in their unique cultural contexts, we must be able to define and examine crucial aspects of their habitats. Human environments, originally restricted to sub-Saharan Africa, now include the entire world and parts of space – so, the study of human ecology, which is at the core of environmental archaeology (Butzer 1982), is necessarily comprehensive and resolutely dynamic. Not surprisingly, it is still very immature and experimental.

The means for defining and interpreting elements of human environments, both past and present, are expanding. Archaeologists, especially environmental archaeologists, employ techniques and concepts developed in the disciplines of anthropology, biology, ecology, zoology, botany, geology, oceanography, climatology, and pedology (soils), among others. Of course, no one can be expert in all these subjects; both compromise and consultation are required. Under such conditions, it is fair to say, the borrowings have not always been efficient, or even effective.

Donald Hardesty (1980: 161) warned of "the hazards of crossing disciplinary boundaries on search and seizure missions." Borrowed techniques and methods should not be isolated from the concepts and theories with which they were developed. When people fail to respect that relationship, they create unnecessary difficulties. Too often, such failure has resulted in misapplication of methods, oversimplification of interpretation, and error. This work aims to minimize those hazards by introducing the fundamental concepts, theory, and vocabularies of the disciplines most often borrowed from, to help archaeology students cross the borders into the domains of other disciplines prior to specializing in any of them. Further specialization in one or more non-archaeological disciplines is strongly encouraged.

Research in the scientific mode is a search for insight and minimization of bias and error. There are many styles of scientific research. The physical sciences are experimental and quantitative. The natural and historical sciences are more descriptive and qualitative, less suited to controlled experiments. The former enjoy particular prestige for the **precision** of their methods and results. The latter stumble along dealing as well as possible with the complexities of the world and the intricacies of human perceptions, motives, and interpretations. The physical sciences are equally subject to the messy limitations of human cognition and conceptualization, but they deal with phenomena more radically distinct from common human experience. It can be argued that, in dealing forthrightly with complexity, the historical disciplines are more realistic than the conventional physical sciences.

Archaeology shares methodological constraints with all the historical sciences, from astronomy to paleontology. Among these are incomplete and discontinuous data sets that yield few representative samples and are inaccessible to experimentation, poor control of time for measuring rates, reliance on analog arguments, and no direct access to causation. Archaeology shares some of the strengths of historical studies as well, such as their long-term perspectives on change and historical processes and their respect for context and contingency.

Within the historical disciplines, the mode of discourse and the tone of reporting in the natural sciences may be less qualified, less hesitant, than that of the social sciences. That is tradition and style; it is not a reflection of a tighter grasp on "truth."

"[F]rustration with inherently imprecise data too often gives rise, in ecology as in the social sciences, to self-conscious 'schools' of thought, and to equally self-conscious obsessions with one or another 'scientific method' " (May and Seger 1986, *American Scientist* 74: 260).

Paleoenvironmental studies integrate the historical sciences in a manner similar to the way archaeology integrates the social sciences, by focusing on past worlds and ways to understand them. Science is no less scientific when it deals with variation rather than permanence, with change rather than continuity or stasis. The historical sciences, unlike chemistry and physics, deal with the dynamics of *particular* conditions in the past rather than with universal, static, laws. This emphasis on **contingencies** – unique, historical configurations of phenomena – is a powerful heuristic and seems to be the way the historical sciences do, in fact, proceed (Gould 1986). The acceptance of contingency is a far cry from the dogma of historical determinism. The importance of the historical sciences is that the past affects the present because past events and processes have constrained the range of options open to events and processes today.

There are further constraints in the historical disciplines. Scientific theory is often said to be quantitative and lawlike, and to aim for universal, rather than contingent, results. The study of quantitative relationships requires representative samples, which are rarely available and hard to recognize in historical data. Qualitative attributes, used in analogical and inferential reasoning, are more accessible in historical disciplines. Furthermore, several of the historical disciplines are based on concepts which have proven intransigent to quantitative definition or measurement. For example, anthropology has "culture," archaeology has "site," climatology has "climate," ecology has "system," and biology has "community." These concepts have been fundamental to the successes of their disciplines, yet are not amenable to the basic scientific activity of *measurement*, probably because they are artificially isolated from context. They appear to exist outside of time and space. If time and space are "added" in the sense that temporal and spatial limits are defined for each of the concepts, they become operational, but only within the constraints of the definitions. This state of affairs is a quality of these disciplines, not simply an attribute of their supposed immaturity. Efforts to impose quantification at the expense of qualification are futile diversions from the proper tasks of the historical disciplines.

Without apology, then, quantification will not be emphasized in this work, but will be discussed and applied when appropriate in various sections of the text. Scientific concepts that require quantification and assume representative samples are not a major feature of this work.

PALEOENVIRONMENTAL RECONSTRUCTION IN ARCHAEOLOGY

We seem perilously close to that characteristic failing of interdisciplinary study – an enterprise which often seems to merit definition as the process by which the unknowns of one's own subject matter are multiplied by the uncertainties of some other science.

SAHLINS 1972: 51

The discipline of archaeology has recently been through a period of methodological self-consciousness during which it tried to achieve scientific standards comparable to those of the quantitative physical sciences, while keeping its social science credentials. Historical context was devalued in the search for eternal verities ("laws" of human behavior).

Bailey (1983: 172) has noted that, in the same period, most of the natural sciences that archaeologists utilize became aware of the historical dimensions of their data; such awareness has been a powerful impetus to theoretical developments. Contextual richness and specificity have now been reinstated in archaeology, in both the natural-historical (Butzer 1982) and sociocultural (Hodder 1986, 1987) senses.

Multidisciplinary research has recently been afflicted by a mood of pessimism or skepticism concerning its potential for success (e.g., Thorson 1990b), especially in paleoenvironmental reconstruction. The problems are numerous and not trivial. They include intellectual as well as economic problems of cooperation, of coordination, of integration, and of differential reward. Investigators in the several disciplines involved in paleoenvironmental research are trained in distinct academic traditions and hired into separate departments and faculties. Consequently, they employ different vocabularies and perspectives on phenomena, perspectives that involve the scales at which they work as well as unexamined habits of mind. It is not unusual for members of an interdisciplinary team to be disconcerted by each others' mind-sets and work habits. The integration of results and the efficiency of cooperative work can be facilitated by a strong, appropriate research design, but the communication of research goals across disciplines can be remarkably difficult. Cooperative research in environmental archaeology appears to be especially difficult because of the incompatibility of scales of problems and data between archaeology, operating within the human dimension, and those of the natural-historical sciences, operating at the levels of species, region, and millennium.

All the disciplines involved in aspects of paleoenvironmental reconstruction have different goals, to which their characteristic scales of observation and data collection are appropriate. For archaeologists, the goal of paleoenvironmental reconstruction is the description of change in the physical and biological contexts of human existence.

The goal has often been only partially achieved because of temporal distance, the need to rely on indirect evidence, and the inherent difficulties of working in a multidisciplinary mode. A better understanding on the part of archaeologists of the basics of the cooperating disciplines can turn difficulties into strengths.

Integrating multidisciplinary research

Science is *learning*, not knowing. The writ of other disciplines is no more holy than that of one's own. All bodies of evidence and interpretation grow and change in time, because the scientific mode of learning involves recursive evaluation of hypotheses and insights, with adaptive change as indicated. Interpretations, especially, remain vulnerable to new data and new thought, and should not be accepted uncritically. There is a special intellectual excitement in working across disciplinary boundaries; all parties to the enterprise must be willing to stretch, grow, and reconsider what they believe they know. The personal rewards can be enormously gratifying.

The differences in scales and data sets in the several sciences can be a source of strength in multidisciplinary work. As definers and integrators of research projects, archaeologists can ease integration with the three *C* goals: *complementarity* of different data sources, *consistency* between data sets, and *congruency* of scale.

Complementarity enlists the strengths of diverse data sets to create interpretations more nearly complete than any single discipline can achieve. As the following chapters will show, the reconstruction of any aspect of ancient environments can utilize evidence from a number of other aspects from the same time and place. Since all data sources are subject to errors of association, representativeness, or interpretation, using diverse data sources reduces the likelihood of error caused by overreliance on any one source.

The goal of consistency requires that the reconstruction of any one aspect of paleoenvironments be compatible with the reconstructions of others. All the evidence, and the resultant interpretations, should agree – not necessarily in detail, but in presenting associations that are not inconsistent with plausibility. To take an extreme example: if pollen study implicates the presence of a lush deciduous forest in a given area and time, evidence from soils that permafrost existed at the same time is clearly inconsistent. As neither data set can be dismissed out of hand, additional research is needed to evaluate the alternatives.

The congruency goal recognizes the need to mediate among data sources at different scales. Paleoenvironmental data from different disciplines reach the archaeologist wrapped in concepts and scales that may not be equivalent. "To the archaeologist looking for an interpretation he can use, one form of biological evi-

Table 2.1[a] Exponential scales in space and time

Spatial scales	Area (km²)	Spatial units
Mega-	5.1×10^0 km²	Earth
	$<10^8$ km²	continents, hemispheres
Macro-	10^4–10^7 km²	physiographic province, region
Meso-	10^2–10^4 km²	site catchment, area
	1–10^2 km²	locality, city, large site
Micro-	<1 km²	locale, site, house, activity area

Temporal scales	Duration or frequency (yr)	Spans
Mega-	$>10^6$; >1 ma	more than 1 million years
Macro-	10^4–10^6; 10 ka–1 ma	10,000 to 1 million years
Meso-	10^2–10^4; 0.1 ka–10 ka	centuries to 10,000 years (millennial)
Micro-	$<10^2$; 0.001 ka–0.1 ka	less than one century (decadal)

Note: [a] Each higher unit incorporates and generalizes all those below. Scales in the two dimensions are not closely linked.

dence seems as good as another. But pollen grains are very different from snail shells; they get into the soil in different ways, they survive (in calcareous soils) for different lengths of time, and probably indicate ecological conditions over different spatial dimensions" (Dimbleby 1985: 64). Awareness of incongruence between the regional and local scales, and between short and long time spans, can help the archaeologist interpret each data set in terms of its own scales of time and space, to avoid comparing incomparable entities. Geologists face similar problems:

> At different scale resolution levels, which are mapped out according to our aims and abilities, different problems are identified; different types of explanation are relevant; different levels of generalization are appropriate; different variables are dominant; and different roles of cause and effect are assigned . . . It is also apparent that conclusions derived from studies made at one scale need not necessarily be expected to apply to another.
>
> CHORLEY ET AL. 1984: 12

Table 2.1 presents a scheme of exponential scales in time and space, with four divisions in each dimension. The units shown are heuristic only. They have logically no firm boundaries except when those are specified for particular cases. The four-part scheme simplifies reference to the several hierarchical levels of scale, but the exponents obviously can be subdivided more finely (e.g., Butzer 1982: 23–27). Relevant spatial concepts and methodological considerations vary with the scale under consideration.

In the temporal dimension, methods for measuring time vary with the scale, just as methods for inferring sociocultural phenomena also vary. Note that each higher unit incorporates and generalizes all those below; both detail and diversity are lost as research interest moves up the scale. For each level in each dimension, there are appropriate data categories that differ from those at other levels.

Reasoning and "recursive ignorance" in the paleoenvironmental sciences

Historical studies encounter the obstacle that the phenomena we want to study are rarely directly accessible to research in the present time. Consequently, indirect evidence is interpreted to increase knowledge. Astronomers study light spectra to learn about the chemical compositions of stars; paleontologists study bones to learn about the soft tissues and behavior of extinct animals; climatologists study pollen deposits to learn about atmospheric circulation patterns, and archaeologists study artifacts to learn about human behavior and societies. All of the historical disciplines rely on mathematical and statistical data and reasoning when those are appropriate, and rely on inference and comparisons with observable phenomena as necessary.

> Palaeoenvironmental analysis essentially proceeds by induction. Data from faunal, floral and sedimentological residues in bogs, lakes, river terraces and valley fills are used to infer past environmental conditions such as plant cover and hillslope and fluvial processes. These in turn are used to infer climatic parameters which may then form the basis of archaeological explanations. This may eventually produce a recursive ignorance as successive approximations move backwards and forwards, to and from the original inductive activity and may even prove circular as they are applied to explain the data from which they were derived. Despite the intrinsic shortcomings, which are widely understood, this approach continues to be widely practised in archaeology and geomorphology. Of the several reasons for this the two most important appear to be (i) a dismissal of essential limitations on the grounds that the ends justify the means, which is doubtful, or (ii) the reluctance to develop an alternative strategy or set of strategies to deal with the problem.
>
> THORNES 1983: 326

The following discussion responds preliminarily to Thornes' concerns; the bulk of this volume is devoted to them. If we are to escape from recursive ignorance, we need awareness of our habits of mind and level-headed clarity about our goals, so that we can select methods appropriate to our purposes.

Quantitative reasoning: sampling and probabilities

Archaeologists discovered sampling theory in the late 1960s; palynologists discovered it in the 1970s. Since then, its proper application has revolutionized the two disciplines, restricting or broadening acceptable inferences, depending on the case. In archaeology, inappropriate application of sampling theory and the sophisticated statistical analyses that accompany it has spawned a misleading and difficult literature, which has come under scrutiny and refutation (see, e.g., discussions in Cowgill [1986] and Shennan [1988]).

Formal sampling is a way of estimating what you can know about a population of data from examining a portion of it. The portion examined must be rigorously chosen to eliminate bias, and there must be enough of it to be representative, to a major degree, of the diversity within the population, which, of course, is what you want to know in the first place. Sampling is neither a magic solution to this dilemma nor hocus-pocus. Sampling works best with natural phenomena that are homogeneous at some scale. Unhappily, archaeological deposits are usually anything but homogeneous. George Cowgill has endeavored to elucidate the problems and potentials of sampling in archaeology; his work is the place to begin examining the issues (Cowgill 1970, 1986, 1989).

For paleoenvironmental studies, sampling problems are more prevalent than the literature indicates.

- In field work, the selection and size of samples are often defined casually, whether the subject is areas for investigation, sediments, or range of included materials.
- The descriptive literature is typically uninformative about the criteria for sampling in any given case, and
- the interpretive literature is frequently flawed by failures to consider responsibly the error probabilities inherent in the materials selected for study.

The aspiring student of archaeology or of the geosciences should be sensitized to this aspect of methodology, both in practice and in reviewing the literature. More sophisticated selection and evaluation of samples would go far toward correcting the kinds of error and circular reasoning that Thornes implicates in our "ignorance."

Samples for analysis must be representative of the phenomena under study, and appropriately sized for the analytical methods used. Representativeness of samples varies with the size of the sampling fraction and the distribution ("randomness") of samples collected. The more complex and structured the phenomena under study, the larger must a sample be before it can be considered reliably representative. For example, the diversity of sedimentary deposits within the walls of a single ruined room is likely to be orders of magnitude less than the diversity within the walls of a ruined town. However, if detailed behavioral and ecological interpretations are desired, a single sample from any room would not be sufficiently representative. These matters need to be addressed at the outset; good sampling plans can be modified to respond to circumstances, but selected collections of materials can never achieve the status of representative samples.

The decisions to be taken in designing a sampling program within a stratified deposit are different from those related to horizontal patterning. Good texts on excavation procedures (e.g., Barker 1993; Hester et al. 1997; Stein 1987) discuss the decisions involved in sampling – contiguous or non-contiguous units, small or bulk samples, at interfaces or central to stratigraphic units, and so forth. With any uncertainty, make the samples as discrete as possible, and the intervals small. While samples can always be consolidated later, they cannot be meaningfully subdivided after collection.

Since examination of all sedimentary contexts at any archaeological site is almost impossible, the student must be aware of the constraints on inference that are imposed by the sample available for study. The generality of an interpretive argument necessarily varies with the representativeness of the sample on which it is based. The strengths of sampling theory are that it can help estimate the degree to which the samples taken can be said to represent the diversity of the sampled phenomena. The relevance and appropriateness of samples to the problem(s) under investigation should be evaluated explicitly for each case, and carefully reported with the interpretation (Shennan 1988: Ch. 14).

Not even the best sampling plan can overcome the fact that all sediments and materials available from the remote past have been subject to non-random selection before they are scrutinized by researchers. **Taphonomy** is the study of the processes leading to fossilization of biological remains (Chapter 9 and Part V). While obviously an example of qualitative, not quantitative, evaluation, the recognition of taphonomic processes must be considered in any discussion of sampling, as they are major natural sources of non-randomness in deposits. Taphonomic processes include the original deposition of particles on the surface or in water, weathering, disturbance or consumption by living organisms, disaggregation and transportation of remains after death, burial at the site of death or redeposition, chemical and physical modification after burial, and whatever may befall the sedimentary context of burial. The complexities of individual histories of organic remains and their enclosing sediments are almost infinite. Rules of taphonomic inference are being developed by paleontologists and archaeologists to help regularize the observation and evaluation of relevant evidence (e.g., Behrensmayer and Hill 1980; Lyman 1994; Schiffer 1987). Palynologists are beginning to develop a literature on taphonomy, also, which will be noted in Part VI.

Qualitative reasoning: analogy, inference, and causation
Analogical reasoning is fundamental to paleoenvironmental and archaeological research. It is a form of inference by comparison. In historical studies, selected situa-

tions contemporary with the observer are assumed to share important characteristics with aspects of the past that are under investigation. Classic **analogy** is a form of logic by which one establishes the equivalence of two things that cannot be directly compared. The argument takes the form: A is like B; B is like C; therefore C is like A. Such logic is usually expanded to the more complex issue of comparing properties of entities. For example, if we observe that A and B have properties m, n, o, and p, and that C has properties m, n, and o, we may infer by analogy that C has p also. But, unless p is logically or essentially entailed by properties m, n, and o, our inference is only weakly grounded. In paleoenvironmental studies, effective comparisons can only be made if there is knowledge or the reasonable assumption that the entities being compared share the properties that we want to study, and that their similarities are crucial to the matter under investigation. When temporal distances between the two entities or situations are great, equivalence must be demonstrated, not assumed, lest we trap ourselves in circular reasoning. Analogies are invaluable for formulating research designs because they help specify what parameters are important for a particular question.

Analogical reasoning is a kind of pattern matching – the similarities of two entities or situations are explicated and evaluated. If the similarities are great, the usual assumption is that there are some causal connections among the shared characters so that they recur for similar reasons. This assumption is not, however, supported by the logic of analogy, which is a weak method for learning about causation.

Analogies (particularly in the form of metaphors) are basic to human speech and probably to human thought (Lakoff and Johnson 1980). However, analogical arguments rarely lead to new knowledge; typically, they show that some phenomena had or have wider distributions than was previously known. Lacking a stronger basis for inference, we must learn to use analogical reasoning responsibly and critically (Kelley and Hanen 1988; Wylie 1985). Analogies help us understand phenomena that are, for any reason, imperfectly observable. The analogical mode of reasoning permeates the historical sciences whenever practitioners not only seek to learn about past states and phenomena but also engage in rigorous observations of phenomena of the present in order to learn more about the past (a method called *actualism*).

In fact, analogical reasoning is so important to the historical sciences that it was elevated to the status of a principle during the nineteenth century. The geologist Charles Lyell is closely identified with the principle of **uniformitarianism**, the assertion that processes in the past were comparable to processes in the present. Taken at face value, this could mean that we are unlikely to learn anything surprising about the past, no matter how distant. Stephen J. Gould and others clarify this conundrum by recognizing that processes in the past were not necessarily equivalent in scale or duration to those of the present, only similar in kind and function. This distinction allows for the existence in the past of continental glaciers larger than any now observable, but requires that the processes that formed and controlled those glaciers were like those we can observe at smaller scales today. This kind of uniformitarianism is a *methodological principle*, not a statement of brute equivalence (Gould 1965; Rymer 1978).

A corollary of uniformitarianism is the use of **proxy** data in the paleoenvironmental sciences. Proxies are phenomena that indirectly relate to the phenomena we want to know about – especially, they are data that can be used to infer aspects of paleoclimates through analogies. For example, pollen evidence indicating the former existence of a spruce forest in an area now populated by temperate deciduous trees can be considered proxy evidence of a former climatic regime cooler than that of the present. The argument works through analogical reasoning because today spruce-dominated forests maintain themselves only in areas of severe winters and brief summers where temperate forest species cannot thrive. Similarly, the discovery of woolly mammoth bones in an area now temperate in climate is taken as evidence for ancient climates colder than those of today. Proxies are observable phenomena used to infer the presence or state of phenomena not directly observable – in these examples, forests and climates.

Some investigators have taken the argument further by recording and measuring attributes of biological systems associated with different climatic regimes today, and then mathematically "transferring" those climatic regimes into the past wherever they observe biological associations similar to those of the present. This extension of analogy has been cogently criticized for involving a great many unstated and untested assumptions about complex ecological relationships in both the past and present (Birks 1986; Hutson 1977; Lowe and Walker 1984: 155–156; Rymer 1978).

Chapter 7 demonstrates how widespread and essential is the use of proxy data in the study of paleoenvironments, and further discusses the methodology. Here it is sufficient to remind ourselves of the complexities of biological organisms and of their interspecific relationships within the various biota of the world. Even very simple organisms are capable of responding to environmental problems in more than one way, and when they occur together in associations of diverse species, the diversity of responses may defy codification. Proxy data for indirect inference about conditions in the past must be chosen carefully on the basis of knowledge as full as possible of their relevance for the issue of concern. Relevance involves such abstract qualities as scale as well as the clarity of the proxy's climatic signal. Both of these qualities are knowable only as they are expressed in contemporary, contingent situations. The application of analogical reasoning cannot eliminate the contingencies in the proxies, and thus the method is subject to the fallacy of transferring the present into the past. The best proxies for paleoclimates would be organisms so well known in all their diversity that the boundaries and mechanisms of their responses to particular aspects of environment could be directly specified and observed in fossil data. At present, we control (or believe we control) the boundaries for some organisms, but the mechanisms for almost none. For example, beetles are considered to be outstanding proxies for ambient temperatures, but only those qualities, as we shall see in later chapters.

As more is learned about the mechanisms of the various environmental systems (Chapter 3), investigators have confronted a new challenge to knowledge of the past: the **no-analog** problem. Environmental circumstances are highly complex and not fully determined by any finite set of known factors (Bradley 1999; Hutson 1977; Webb and Bartlein 1992). Because of the multiplicity of factors shaping any system of organisms, all prehistoric as well as modern systems are unique in some characteristics. No set of environmental circumstances is ever precisely replicated, and so no modern situation can serve as an accurate analog for any multivariate environment in the past. For example, the beetles that are used as indicators of temperatures cannot serve as proxies for rainfall, length of season, or vegetation. Contingency complicates inquiry in ecology and in all historical sciences; it limits the application of analogies of all kinds.

Another powerful limitation on the use of analogical reasoning is the principle of **equifinality**, which is that different sets of antecedent conditions may produce similar results. That is to say, no single set of causes can be readily assigned to each unique situation or circumstance. An example is that of a rising sea level, which may be the result of (1) an increase of water in the oceans, (2) sinking of the land, or (3) reduction in the size of ocean basins. Much more information than the simple observation of rising sea level is needed to distinguish among the possibilities. The principle of equifinality requires that multiple hypotheses be involved in any research (e.g., Haines-Young and Petch 1983).

CAUSATION AND SYSTEMIC RELATIONSHIPS

The gravest problem in actualistic research is assuming that a given agent is necessary and sufficient cause of an observable attribute when no such relationship has actually been established.

GIFFORD 1981: 394

The search for causes of observed phenomena and situations is deeply ingrained in the methodology of science and in the ways we all think about the world. Whenever some event arouses our interest, we seek its cause, in order to understand, commend, or blame. The historical disciplines have few methods for seeking causation. Conventionally, the observation of positively correlated variables (characters that always occur together or change at the same time) is taken to imply some causal link between them. However, the co-occurrence of two or more phenomena does not imply causation by any one of them, only the likelihood of interdependence and close relationship, possibly through a third variable. Also, pure coincidence may be confused with correlation. Pattern is not cause; arguments from correlation are research problems, not explanations. For the latter, we need to identify and understand the mechanisms in relationships – how things work together or affect each other.

In the middle years of this century, as computers aided the study of complex mathematical relationships, investigators applied ideas about systems and systemic relationships to data in many disciplines. **Systems** are bounded sets composed of entities and their relationships. It is characteristic of systems that a change in one entity will require compensating adjustments in others that are linked to it. We have already met an example of this in the discussion of the Red Queen hypothesis in Chapter 1.

Simple closed systems are assumed to be in a state of equilibrium unless disturbed, and to return after disturbance to conditions close to the original. In the mechanistic language of systems theory, the interactive responses of systems to disturbance, or to any change, are termed **feedback**, and may be either positive or negative. Positive feedback amplifies (increases) deviations from the original state of the system, leading to modified relationships among the parts. Negative feedback dampens (reduces) deviations or innovations to systemic relationships; its effects are to return the disturbed system to something like its original state or configuration. Open systems are those that receive matter, energy, or information from their environments. All complex systems involving living organisms are open and dynamic, with feedback responses initiated from inside as well as outside the system. Rather than tending toward static equilibrium states, feedback in complex systems approximates dynamic balance, with additional change the characteristic result of disturbance.

Systems models represent a major advance in realism from simpler models of linear causation. They emphasize multidimensional relationships among components of a system, and help focus attention on the feedback mechanisms that define the dynamic balances. Systems thinking was introduced into archaeology in the late sixties, most influentially by Lewis Binford (1965), David Clarke (1968), and Kent Flannery (1968, 1972). It rapidly transformed the terminology and metaphors of the discipline (Watson et al. 1984: Ch. 2). Formal systems theory is fundamentally mathematical. In the biological, environmental, and social sciences multivariate relationships are too complex for mathematical modeling even with the latest super-computers. Nevertheless, systems thinking as a way of dealing with complex rela-tionships that are multicausal has produced significant insights and improvements in understanding in all the sciences that deal in any way with living organisms.

THE EMERGING CHALLENGE TO CAUSAL THINKING

All the sciences of Western industrial society are based on a traditional mode of thought that can be traced back to Aristotle, at least, but was codified and established within the scientific enterprises in the seventeenth, eighteenth, and nineteenth cen-turies. It is exemplified in the work of René Descartes, Isaac Newton, and Charles Darwin. This mode of thinking, amounting to a world-view, an article of faith in the way the world works, assumes direct linearity in causation and a certain mathemati-cal determinism in systemic relationships. It has served brilliantly as the foundation of the mathematical and experimental sciences that have given humanity unprece-dented power over the natural world and the means to shape the destiny of life as we know it.

When linear causation and mathematical determinism are employed with suit-able analogies, it is possible to construct predictions for states of affairs in the future, or retrodictions for the past, that carry some scientific authority. A fashionable definition of "explanation" in archaeology equates it with the ability to make predic-tions that are borne out in the course of events. All of this has been intellectually grat-ifying; it is "normal" science. Recently, ideas emerging from studies of randomness in physics, ecology, meteorology, and epidemiology are beginning to cast doubt on the universal appropriateness of such deterministic assumptions. These investigations are converging in the "sciences of complexity," one aspect of which is "chaos" studies, a name chosen to attract attention but which unfortunately tends to mislead. In both standard and scientific English, "chaos" until now has meant true randomness, absence of patterning, signals that contain no information, existential "noise." Much of the strength and attractiveness of the new chaos theory, however, is that it asserts the information potential of phenomena that have been considered residual in tradi-tional science.

The new insights are extensions of systems theory that are rapidly superseding some basic concepts about systemic behavior. One of the major interdisciplinary findings of chaos investigations is that complex systems do not exhibit deterministic trajectories in either time or phase space; rather, systems of many different kinds tend to share a "sensitivity to initial conditions" (i.e., to their environments) that makes them liable to veer away from former "paths," to be unpredictable in all but the very smallest scales (Glass and Mackey 1988; Gleick 1987; Kauffman 1995; Schuster 1988; Waldrop 1992). This kind of randomizing system behavior can be replicated by fairly simple mathematical operations provided they are reiterated a great many times, with the results of one calculation feeding into the next. Rather than leading quickly to disorder, some randomness has been shown to be "creative" in ways that reduce disorder, and to be deterministic to the extent that it can be replicated at several different scales (fractals). Snowflakes, achieving an almost infinite diversity of forms based on six-part symmetry, are excellent examples of the creativity of sensitive dependence on initial conditions. The growth of snowflakes from water vapor exemplifies decreasing disorder, each flake developing a unique symmetry as it tumbles in turbulent air currents and encounters impurities in water vapor.

The two insights, that (1) there were states in the past that lacked any modern analogs, and (2) systems exhibit sensitivity to initial conditions, together undermine the authority of both proxies and the linear deterministic thinking that supports their use. One need not, however, abandon confidence in the principle of uniformitarianism. If even deterministic systems may exhibit unpredictable behavior, then contingency (context and history) is extremely important, equifinality cannot be ignored, and effects of scale may be paramount in understanding changes in system states in time and space (Gould 1986).

In this age of weather satellites, meteorology's failure to predict even threatening weather more than a few hours or days in advance is shown to reflect realities inherent in the atmosphere, not underfunding of technology. Retrodiction cannot be easier to achieve than prediction. There is no easy, scientific way to reverse time's arrow and observe conditions in the past. We can "know" the past only as the sum of the conditions that have determined the present, and some of those conditions will always be too small or too ephemeral to be observable.

The initial lessons from the new sciences of complexity confirm what philosophers have been saying all along about the limitations of analogical reasoning. The study of present-day phenomena and conditions can provide sound analogies for understanding the structure and mechanisms of systems of many kinds, including the planet's climate and biological cycles. However, analogies cannot be used directly to posit system states in the past or future. Theoretically informed close observation of existing systems exposes the relevant variables of each, and their interactions. This brings the observer to a better understanding of structures and mechanisms, which will lead in turn to enhanced abilities to learn about alternative states. The ability to posit numerous possible alternatives, and to reject those that are not possible permutations of things as we observe them, should bring us closer to the goal of learning about past and future that we thought to achieve by shorter, straighter paths.

Systems that are well understood in the detailed context observable today should permit some prediction, especially at small and medium scales of time and space. This is the case partly because some theoretical alternatives are precluded by immediately precedent situations, thereby reducing the number and complexity of possibilities in the short term.

Whether from the perspective of "normal" science or the new sciences of complexity, the advantages of multidisciplinary studies of complex systems are impressive. The compartmentalized disciplines of modern science have each special strengths for investigating a circumscribed range of phenomena. None can exhaust the complexities of any aspect of the world, but each can specify the likely states of some variables, and the relationships of variables within parts of a given system. Bringing many disciplines to bear on a problem, each contributing data from its special strengths, can significantly reduce the range of alternatives and uncertainties that must be considered in any given case. As complexity theory shows, what is "noise" from one perspective may be crucial information from another. In multidisciplinary investigations, it is very important that all investigators be explicit about the limitations and contradictions in their data, and about the kinds of data not gathered.

The paleoenvironmental sciences offer a vast array of methods of observation applicable to a significant portion of the variables recognized in contemporary environmental sciences. Experimental and descriptive investigations expand the available analogies that enhance understanding of crucial variables and relationships. The study of the past grows in power and insight with the study of the present, but it no longer merely holds a weak mirror up to the present. Informed by theory and experience, archaeologists in collaboration with other paleoenvironmental scientists can learn about a past that was unlike the present, illuminating both the present and the future.

3

MECHANISMS OF ENVIRONMENTAL CHANGE

Palaeoexperiments inevitably lack the rigour of true experimental science. Whilst a combination of replication, statistical validation, ingenuity and intellectual honesty can limit and constrain spurious reinforcement, the circumstantial nature of so much *post hoc* evidence, and the judgemental nature of critical aspects of sampling and interpretation will still influence the conclusions drawn.

OLDFIELD 1993: 18–19

Human beings perceive environmental change mainly as change in the **state** (qualitative character or structure) or **condition** (quantitative composition or amount) of nearby communities of living organisms, or of the weather. For example, a change of state for living communities might be gains or losses in the diversity of plants or animals represented; a change in condition might be an increase or decrease in the numbers of plants and animals. For the weather, a switch from winter rains to predominantly summer rains in mid-latitudes would constitute a change in state, whereas a marked decrease in precipitation over a month or more would be a change in condition. We notice such changes, because they violate our expectations that things vary little from year to year. Our experience and observations of the environment are at the local scale and are mediated by language and opportunity, so that each of us has a slightly different idea of things. Because of the ways we perceive environmental change, our "common sense" leads us to seek the causes of change where we perceive it – among living communities and in the weather systems. Recent research in geophysics and climatology has demonstrated that this approach is oversimplified and misleading.

Rockets, satellites, radar, and computers have revolutionized the study of the Earth's climate, and with it, knowledge of climatic and environmental change at scales ranging from that of the solar system to that of daily weather. This new under-standing has made research into environments of the past much more productive, permitting finer resolution in chronology and providing some understanding of mechanisms – the ways in which system components interact. With this greater control over a larger number of variables, scientists have relinquished hope for linear, unicausal, or independent explanations for environmental change. The compensation for this loss is a powerful awareness of the complexity and interconnectedness of environmental systems.

GEOGRAPHIC CONCEPTS

We must establish a working vocabulary for some basic ideas about our home planet. Images from space confirm that the planet is roughly spherical, mostly water-covered, icy at the poles, relatively dry part-way between the poles and the equator, and dominated by atmospheric circulation of gases and water vapor. In order to discuss distance and direction across the surface of the globe, geographers have defined certain conventions of measurement. The globe of the Earth is partitioned arbitrarily by lines of **latitude** running around it parallel to the equator; these help us define distance, in degrees latitude, between the equator and the poles. The equator is zero degrees latitude; the poles are each 90°, and any point in between, north or south, is expressed by degrees intermediate in value. Imaginary lines drawn from pole to pole on the cartographic surface of the Earth are called **meridians**; they mark distances east and west of the Prime Meridian at Greenwich, England, and converge at the poles. Distances measured at right angles to meridians are expressed in degrees of **longitude**.

Altitude is the measure of distance upward from sea level, which for this purpose is defined as an imaginary spherical surface projected across the continents, disregarding topographic relief and tidal variation. Height above sea level is also expressed as "elevation." At high altitudes (to about 8–10 km), and high latitudes, the air is cooler than it is lower down and closer to the equator. The loss of heat with altitude is the **lapse rate**.

CLIMATIC CONCEPTS

Climate cannot be directly observed; what we see and experience daily is weather. "Climate is the sum total of the weather experienced at a place in the course of the year and over the years" (Lamb 1972: 5). Climate is both the expected weather as well as extreme unexpected deviations from it, such as violent storms or protracted droughts. Weather and climate are both products of a number of factors comprising the "climate system," expressed as the range and seasonality of temperature and moisture. Moisture, in the climate system, is defined by the annual **precipitation** (water in any form condensed from vapor) minus evapotranspiration, water lost from the surface through direct evaporation and through the transpiration of plants.

At the global scale, climates vary over space and time. The distribution of solar energy varies systematically over the surface of the planet, resulting in a systematic variation in climates (Table 3.1). Glaciation, for instance, is a large-scale climatic state that is restricted to relatively high latitudes and high elevations, and is cyclical in time. Climatic variation over time is most systematic on the daily scale, with the predictable alternation of day and night and the temperature differences that follow. Temporal variation is more dramatic at the seasonal scale, especially in the temperate and polar latitudes, while seasonality is minimal in the tropics where it may be expressed most overtly as variation in rainfall. Thus, the expression of climate is always relative to the scale of space and time for which it is defined.

We have already established in Chapters 1 and 2 that we must abandon any idea that conditions of the present time can serve as a standard or major analog for any time in the past. "Other things," whatever they are, do not hold still and have not been "equal" to the present at other times. This restlessness is manifested by our home planet itself. Our search for understanding and integration of the environmental sciences begins, therefore, at the planetary scale, in order that we may use the best achievements of large-scale sciences to illuminate the environments of small-scale human societies at various distances in time.

Climatologists see the states and conditions of the climate system being affected by factors both "external" and "internal" to it. The external factors are mainly independent variables such as solar energy, orbital geometry, axial tilt, continental drift, and volcanism. The internal factors, on the other hand, are mainly dependent upon or closely influenced by each other. These are the **five spheres** of the climate system: the atmosphere, the geosphere, the hydrosphere, the cryosphere, and the biosphere. These "spheres" may be thought of diagrammatically as concentric, interpenetrating layers around the core of the planet. Although we perceive air, rocks, water, ice, and living things as separate, in fact they mutually interpenetrate even at the molecular level.

Atmosphere: the dynamic, life-sustaining layer of gases and suspended particulate matter that surrounds the planet and distributes the radiant energy of the Sun. Because gases are stratified within the atmosphere, its composition and character change at various heights. The Earth's weather is mainly determined by turbulence within the lower 10 km, the "troposphere."

Geosphere: the solid and viscous mineral matter of the planet, especially that manifested near the surface as rock and sediment.

Hydrosphere: the water on the planet in liquid form, whether salt or fresh, on or
within interstices of the geosphere.

Cryosphere: frozen water in the form of ice or snow, usually on and within a few feet
of the surface of the rocks, sediments, and water.

Biosphere: the living organisms of the planet, occurring on and in the rocks, sediments, water, ice, and lower few hundred meters of the air.

The five spheres are considered internal to the climate system because they are mutually interdependent: change in any one of them usually triggers responsive changes in
some of the others, which ultimately may stimulate feedback responses affecting the
initiating sphere. In practice, initiating events or changes can rarely be specified, but
for illustration let us imagine a change in the geosphere (which can be either an internal or external factor), perhaps earthquakes that raise a mountain range a few extra
feet. This could force changes in the tracks of winds striking the newly elevated
surface, causing rainfall to increase on the upwind side or decrease downwind.
Whether as differences in rainfall or in hydrography (distribution of surface water),
greater or lesser amounts of available moisture will change vegetation. Altered vegetation patterns change the reflectivity, and thereby the temperature, of the Earth's
surface to which winds are sensitive. All this could amplify changes in precipitation
patterns, leading to increased erosion, which would affect the local condition and
state of the geosphere. The internal factors are so interconnected that the ultimate
causes (or even the effective causes) of any observed change are rarely specifiable, but
they usually involve more than one sphere.

ENVIRONMENTAL CHANGE IN EXTERNAL FACTORS

Factors external to the climate system appear to change state spontaneously, without
being influenced from any other source. This perception, however, may be a product
of our ignorance of some critical relationships. As currently understood, the major
external factors in climatic change are variations in solar radiation and in the Earth's
orbit and axial tilt. Actually, some state changes in the geosphere appear to occur
independently of the other spheres, and therefore to act as external factors. Changes
in the geosphere, such as the positions of the continents, the height and location of
mountains, and the frequency of explosive volcanic eruptions, are considered for
now as if they were external to the climate system.

Table 3.1 Types of climate,[a] arranged zonally from the equator

EQUATORIAL ZONE

Warm and moist, with some seasonal differences in precipitation as the intertropical convergence follows the Sun north or south of the equator.

MONSOONAL ZONES

Marked seasonality of rainfall at the outer edges of the shifting equatorial rain belt. Temperature range is greater than in the equatorial zone, especially in the dry season.

TROPICAL AND EQUATORIAL HIGHLANDS

Rainfall amounts vary with aspect, elevation, and distance from the sea. Windward slopes may receive very high rainfall amounts, while rain-shadow effects may create locally dry areas. Seasonal differences are slight. Temperatures may reach temperate or more extreme ranges in higher elevations.

TRADE-WIND ZONES

Mainly oceanic and island climates, with steady breezes moderating tropical temperatures; they are subject to cyclonic storms. Mountainous islands may collect clouds and fog on windward slopes.

ARID ZONES

Trade winds over land and subtropical high-pressure zones reduce the precipitation reaching these regions, which is further reduced where high mountain ranges to the west collect rain. The spotty rainfall, sometimes locally torrential, is not reliable enough for forest growth.

SUBTROPICAL OCEANS AND ISLANDS

The mild temperatures and precipitation of these regions are defined by the high atmospheric pressure typical of these latitudes, and the moderating effect of the ocean. Tropical storms or cold air masses from the higher latitudes interrupt the regime occasionally.

SUBTROPICAL DESERT FRINGE ZONES ("Mediterranean" climates)

Warm, dry summers alternate with rainy, cooler winter weather brought by high-latitude air masses moving equatorward.

STEPPE AND PRAIRIE ZONES

Climatic zones of continental interiors in the mid-latitudes (35°–50°F), where mountains to the west wring out moisture from the eastward-flowing air masses. Hot summers, cold winters, and episodic precipitation, often in the form of storms, are characteristic.

TEMPERATE AND SUBPOLAR OCEANIC AND ISLAND ZONES

Mid- to high-latitude zones of prevailing westerlies have changeable, often stormy, weather. On the western fringes of northern continents, the sea moderates the temperatures, but leaves islands open to the force of winds, often bringing fronts.

TEMPERATE CONTINENTS AND ISLANDS IN THE NORTHERN HEMISPHERE

Away from the moderating effects of the seas, continental interiors and eastern islands in the temperate latitudes may have great seasonal extremes of temperature, with winters being much more severe than they are on the western fringes. High variability of weather from day to day and year to year is characteristic as weather systems move in from northern or southern zones.

Table 3.1 (*cont.*)

MOUNTAINOUS ZONES IN MIDDLE AND HIGH LATITUDES

The fall of temperature that occurs with elevation creates mountain climates that contrast with those of their neighboring lowlands. The windward sides concentrate precipitation, and may cause precipitation deficits leeward. Winter sunshine may be greater on the high slopes than below, producing higher temperatures when the lower slopes and lowlands are subject to cloudiness and temperature inversions.

NORTHERN LANDS ZONE

In the long days of the short northern summer, and in the long night of winter, the weather may be quiet. The spring and autumn are more turbulent, and the weather may be violent. Summer temperatures may be high if the 24-hour sunlight comes through clear skies, otherwise cloudy and cool, especially near the Arctic Ocean and over the swampy tundras. Winter temperatures reach low extremes.

ARCTIC OCEAN, HIGH ICE CAPS OF GREENLAND AND ANTARCTICA

Climate over the ice is quieter than over the high-latitude oceans, with clear skies typical in summer and winter on the ice caps. At the edges of the ice caps, strong winds blowing outward create harsh conditions for all forms of life. The amount of precipitation is not great, and it occurs on only a few days of the year.

> *Note:* The classification reflects the present-day atmospheric circulation modified by terrain and seasonality. No account is taken here of the effects of vegetation, which varies interzonally and affects the expression of climatic extremes. The classes are relatively permanent, although their spatial expressions, as well as climatic extremes, may have been somewhat different in the past. This adaptation emphasizes climates of major land masses at the expense of marine climate zones.
> *Source:* [a] After Lamb, 1972: 134–137.

Solar radiation

Variation in the amount of energy produced by our star, the Sun, may affect climate on the Earth on time scales that have relevance for archaeology. Research into correlations between the eleven-year sunspot cycles and aspects of the Earth's weather have produced to date only tantalizing hints (Chapters 7 and 8). Sunspots are localized cooler zones on the stellar surface; they appear when other solar activity seems to increase, and the combination probably marks some reorganization of the solar furnace. Although the effect of such changes on the Earth's climate is not well understood, historians of climate note that the "Maunder minimum," an observed period of very low sunspot activity spanning the latter half of the seventeenth century, coincided with the most severe years of the "Little Ice Age," some of the coldest weather of the Holocene.

Orbital parameters

The astronomical theory of ice ages relates changes in the Earth's orbital and axial geometry to variation in the amount and distribution of solar radiation reaching the globe over periods of different lengths (Berger et al. 1983; Imbrie and Imbrie 1979). Because the Earth's **orbit** (path around the Sun) is slightly elliptical, the distance from the Earth to the Sun varies through the course of a year (expressed as the "eccentricity" of the orbit); the distance is least at **perihelion**, greatest at **aphelion**, and the effect of the present configuration is a difference of ca. 7.0% in the amount of radiation received at the extremes (Bradley 1999: 35). The eccentricity of the orbit itself varies over periods of approximately 96,000 years, and can be greater than it is at present.

Days and nights on the Earth are defined by the rotation of the planet around an imaginary line through its poles – the **axis**. The angle that the axis forms with the plane of the orbit is now about 23.4° off the perpendicular. It varies from 21.8° to 24.4° over a period of about 41,000 years (Bradley 1999: 35). With the changing angle the amount of solar radiation reaching high latitudes changes seasonally (Fig. 3.1). Summer occurs in the hemisphere tilting toward the Sun, winter in the hemisphere tilting away, regardless of the relative distance to the Sun of the two hemispheres. The **equinox** is the time when the Sun is directly overhead at the equator, and day and night are of equal length.

Independent of eccentricity and obliquity, the axis defines a circular path over a period of 21,700 years. The effect of this cycle changes the timing of the seasons in respect to the Earth's position on the orbit, so that the seasons rotate through perihelion and aphelion (**precession** of the equinoxes). If perihelion occurs in the summer, summer temperatures will be accentuated; if in winter, winter temperatures will be moderated. The effects upon the two hemispheres are obviously opposite at any one time. Solar radiation (**insolation**) on the surface is greatest at perihelion, which currently occurs in the northern hemisphere in early January, with aphelion in early July; in about 10,000 years, these positions will be reversed, giving less solar radiation during the northern winter, more in summer, so that seasonal contrasts in that hemisphere will increase.

The different periods of these several mechanisms make their permutations complex; sometimes the changes cancel, sometimes accentuate, the effects. Moreover, the periods themselves vary over time, adding further complications. However, it is becoming clear that combinations of eccentricity, obliquity, and precession significantly change the strength of solar insolation and therefore seasonal climates in ways that, for example, support or weaken the growth of continental glaciers.

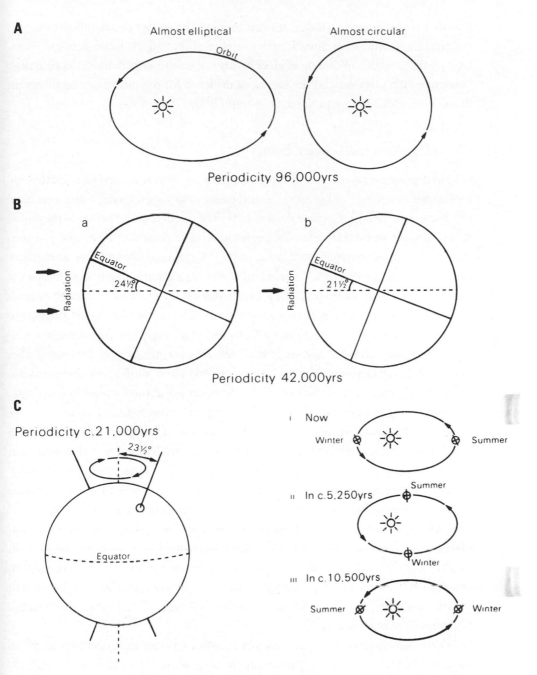

Figure 3.1 Orbital and axial variables, illustrating (A) orbital eccentricity, (B) axial tilt, and (C) precession of the equinoxes and orbital wobble. The orientation of the Earth's surface affects the amount of solar radiation received. (Reproduced from Lowe and Walker 1984: Fig. 1.5, by permission of Addison, Wesley, Longman.)

Exactly how these geometrical relationships affect the receipt of solar radiation and translate into contrastive climatic states, and just what effects those circumstances have on the growth and decline of glaciers, are not easily defined. More detailed discussions of the variables and the logic and evidence for the theory can be found in Bradley (1999), Crowley and North (1991), and Berger et al. (1983).

Geospheric independent factors

Within the last twenty-five years, the demonstration of continental drift (**plate tectonics**) has revolutionized geophysics and paleoclimatology, giving a dynamic new perspective on the past. The distribution of the continents across the face of the globe is now known to be transient, not permanent. The Antarctic continent has not always been at the extreme south pole, nor has Greenland always been far enough north to support an ice sheet. Very ancient continental glaciers flowed in what is now tropical Africa. The continents that we see today are arrangements of fragments of ancient continents and pieces of younger crust. The shape and size of the ocean basins also are recent configurations. The present arrangement of continents and oceans has been taking shape since the Mesozoic era, the age of dinosaurs. The modern Atlantic Ocean has formed within the last 150 million years, the northern part opening latest, toward the end of the dinosaur age about 60 million years ago. Recent measurements suggest it is still spreading at rates up to 2.0 cm a year.

The Earth is a layered sphere, with a dense hot core at its center. Surrounding the core is the **mantle**, a stratified zone of heavy mineral matter maintained in a viscous state by the heat of the core. On the mantle floats a lighter **crust**, which is the rocky surface of the Earth. As this less dense material includes the massive mountain chains of the continents, these comparative terms in this present context are far from their everyday meanings. The crust of the Earth consists of several rigid segments, called **plates**. Like plates of armor, for which they are named, the plates are capable of limited movement. Over time, they slide along the surface of the Earth, moving apart or sideways past each other, grinding into or overriding one another. The interested student can find many good books on the subject (e.g., Cloud 1988; Skinner and Porter 1995; Summerfield 1991).

Where hot material from the viscous mantle wells up to the surface at plate margins, the plates are driven apart, along the mid-ocean **ridges** and continental **rift zones**. The ridges circle the Earth through the ocean basins; one runs the length of the Atlantic, another loops from East Africa through the Indian Ocean, south of Australia and up the eastern Pacific (Fig. 3.2). On land they are observable as active zones of volcanism and rifting in Iceland and East Africa. Spreading in the rift zones

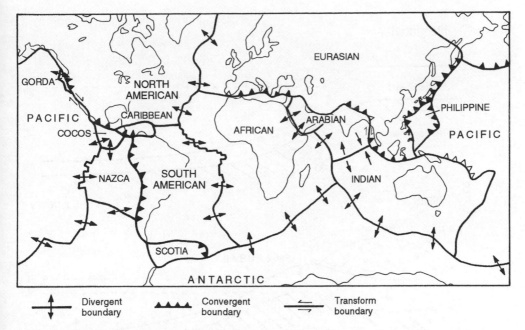

Figure 3.2 Major tectonic plates and types of plate boundaries. Mid-ocean ridges are one class of divergent boundaries; subduction zones are labeled convergent boundaries. A newly observed split in the Indian plate is added as of 1995. (After Summerfield 1991: Fig. 2.14.)

is compensated by folding or by "subduction" at the leading edges of plates, the latter being the process whereby an oceanic plate slips under a continental plate as they are forced together, and is melted into magma as it descends into the hot mantle. Chains of volcanoes occur along rifts and above subduction zones. Some volcanic areas isolated from rifts and subduction zones are formed where crustal plates are pierced by molten rock as they slide across hot spots below (e.g., the Hawaiian Islands). Where the continental plates collide, great folds form in the crust, eventually building mountain chains in a process called **orogeny**. Mountain-building does not reduce the bulk of the plates enough to counter the spreading that occurs in the rift zones. The difference is made up in subduction zones. All these processes are mechanisms of plate tectonics.

The crustal plates ride buoyantly on the heavier mantle, their height determined by their weight so that stability is maintained. When additional weight is added to the crust, as by crustal folding, massive sedimentary deposition, marine transgression, or the formation of continental glaciers, the crust subsides into the mantle. When weight is removed, as by erosion, the drying of large lakes, sea-level lowering, or

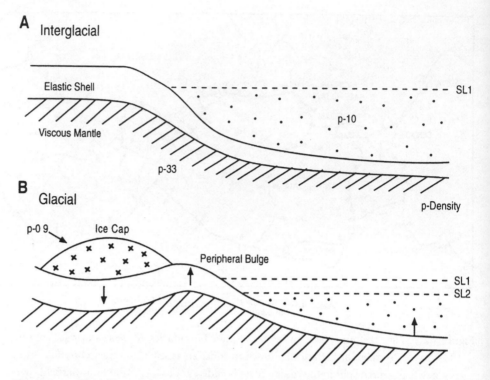

A Interglacial

Elastic Shell

Viscous Mantle

p-33

p-10

SL1

p-Density

B Glacial

p-0 9

Ice Cap

Peripheral Bulge

SL1
SL2

Figure 3.3   Glacial isostasy. The Earth's crust subsides into the mantle when it receives additional weight, and rises when the weight is removed. A shows interglacial or preglacial
conditions. B shows adjustments following ice loading on land, with sea level dropping from loss of water to ice sheets, and the mantle rising below it. The peripheral
bulge rises as mantle is displaced from under the weight of ice toward areas beyond the
load. (After Goudie 1983: Fig. 6.4.)

melting of glaciers, the crust rises. This adjustment of height according to weight is
called **isostasy,** or isostatic adjustment (Fig. 3.3; Summerfield 1991).

Isostatic adjustments of the continental masses change the relationship between
land and sea; rising continents result in locally lower sea levels and subsiding continents may be inundated by the sea. Sea level may change in other ways. When
changes in the relative levels of land and sea are the result of changes in ocean basins,
the process is called **eustasy.** Eustatic changes can occur if the shape or size of ocean
basins is altered, or if the amount of water in the basins changes. Isostasy and eustasy
are related but different processes; the distinction is important, although not always
easily determined. With plates moving, continents rising and subsiding, mountains
rising and eroding, and rivers transporting and depositing sediments, the solidity of
the Earth is obviously a relative concept. It will do to walk on, but we cannot assume

that it is unchanging. **Geomorphology** is the study of the diverse and changing shapes of the Earth's surface.

Mechanisms

With the recognition of so many interdependent variables, and of the large scale of the independent ones, research seeking explanations of climatic and environmental change is moving now from the search for correlations of variables to the search for *mechanisms*. This is an important shift in perspective, one which archaeology has yet to make, but in which environmental archaeology can begin to play a role. Correlations – the observation that two or more phenomena occur together in space or time, or even appear to vary together – stimulate hypotheses and help pose research problems; they cannot identify causal relationships or explain spatial or temporal coincidences. Only the demonstration of mechanisms linking variables can constitute explanations. A good example of this principle, and an instance of the historical shift of emphasis from correlation to mechanism, is the history of the "Milankovitch" or astronomical hypothesis (Berger et al. 1983; see "orbital parameters," p. 42 above).

Following suggestions from earlier researchers, in the 1920s and 1930s the Serbian geographer Milutin Milankovitch proposed that the known cyclic changes in the eccentricity of the Earth's orbit, the angle of the axis, and the precession of the equinoxes could together have caused the climatic changes that initiated **glacial** (an interval of cool climate during which glaciers form and expand) and **interglacial** (a relatively warm period between major glacial advances) periods. The periodicity of the orbital and axial changes could be calculated from mathematical principles, as could their effects on the amount of solar radiation reaching the two hemispheres. If they did indeed explain climate changes during the Pleistocene, then the timing of those changes could be known from astronomical calculations. Milankovitch worked out laboriously, before the days of electronic calculation, the geometry and timing of the permutations. At first, his work was seized upon as the chronological key to the glacial periodization (Zeuner 1946). Subsequently, as research expanded, it appeared that the timing and frequency of the astronomical events did not fit the phasing of glacial and interglacial events recorded on land. There seemed to be no good correlation, and therefore doubts about the existence of even a causal link began to dominate.

Later research on climatic cycles preserved in ocean sediments greatly expanded the observed number of glacial and interglacial cycles, demonstrating a better fit between the predicted and observed number and timing of cycles. Radiometric dating of the ocean sequences showed a good fit with the predictions of the astronomical theory. Mathematical modeling on computers corrected some of the original calculations and explored the scale of radiation changes induced by the changes of the Earth's position relative to the source of solar energy. The new work showed that the scale and timing of the radiation changes appropriately explained a large part of the cycling of glaciers. Consequently, the Milankovitch cycles are now considered to be external triggers of the Quaternary **glaciations** (glacial episodes), activating major climatic factors that were in a hypersensitized state because of mountain building and the positions of continents at and near the poles. These state changes constituted a necessary precondition to the ice-age effects of Milankovitch cycles, and explain why the cycling, which is older than the Pleistocene, has not caused perpetual ice ages. The observed correlation set off the search for mechanisms; once those could be specified, a limited explanation could be proposed and has been widely accepted. The correlation alone, isolated from mechanism, led to decades of debate and considerable confusion.

Of course, *environmental change* involves more than changes in climate, no matter how important that may be to all other elements of physical and biological environments. To understand human communities, past or present, we need a more comprehensive view of environments. The five spheres of the climate system can lead us toward such a view.

ENVIRONMENTAL CHANGE IN THE FIVE SPHERES

Each of the five spheres of the internal climate system includes "trigger mechanisms" that can initiate aspects of climatic and other kinds of environmental change. Each sphere responds to changes initiated within or outside itself, often setting up the conditions for further changes. Changes in state or condition often initiate long series of responsive perturbations, which are dampened as adjustments to the new states or conditions approach stability. Because adjustments to change may be widespread, requiring fairly long time spans to work through the series of perturbations, each sphere incorporates some evidence of earlier states and conditions that can serve investigators as proxies. A brief review of each of the spheres with these concepts in mind will lay a foundation for later consideration of research strategies and results.

Atmosphere

Atmosphere is the most sensitive of all to changes, whether those are internally generated or externally imposed, and it has the most pervasive feedback networks. All

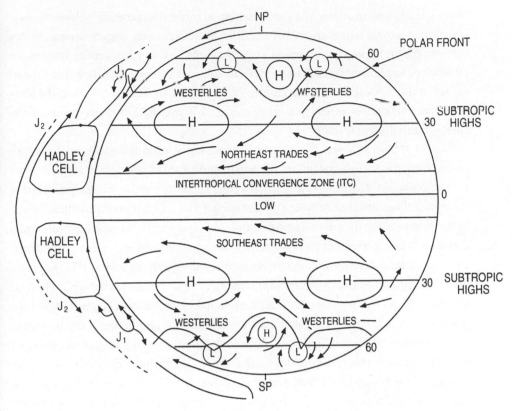

Figure 3.4 Planetary wind and pressure belts, and mixing cells in the lower atmosphere. (After Akin 1991: Fig. 1.5.)

the other spheres exchange particulate matter and gases with the atmosphere. The atmospheric composition changes with altitude; we are concerned here mainly with the lowest, most familiar part – the troposphere.

Large amounts of solar energy enter the atmosphere and reach the Earth in the equatorial zone; lesser amounts are received at the poles where the radiation strikes at a low angle and passes through more of the atmosphere before reaching the Earth. These relative differences in insolation create a strong heat gradient between the equator and the poles. The warm equatorial air expands and moves upward and outward, while the denser, cooler air at higher latitudes sinks and moves equatorward, causing winds (air in motion). The winds are deflected by the rotation of the Earth so that they flow more nearly parallel to the equator than perpendicular to it. In the mid-latitudes strong westerly flow prevails (Fig. 3.4). Prevailing directions of winds in adjacent zones tend to be opposite, thus the "trade winds" flowing from east to west in the subtropics of both hemispheres meet in the equatorial convergence zone. The counter motions of air masses help to move the warm air poleward; their contrastive temperatures create the pressure differences that trigger storms. Water vapor in the air masses is condensed as the air cools, whether from rising into cooler altitudes or losing heat by exchange or expansion, and the water is either precipitated as rain or snow or carried aloft as clouds. Precipitation, or its lack, as well as the temperature of air masses, is what is usually meant by "weather." The planetary wind circulation distributes weather.

The jet stream is a variable air current moving around the globe in the upper atmosphere in wave-like meanders, the length and height of which vary with the vigor of the circulation. The jet stream normally tracks equatorward in winter, poleward in summer (Oliver and Hidore 1984: 146), carrying major weather systems with it. Lower in the atmosphere are cells of low-pressure air (cyclones) and high-pressure anticyclones. When the temperature gradient from equator to poles is strong, the major air movement is westerly with relatively little south–north deflection (Fig. 3.5). The polar and equatorial air masses are kept separate, and storminess is reduced. This was the situation in large measure through the first half of the present century. When the gradient is weak and the jet stream flow is consequently sluggish, the jet stream meanders through a wide latitudinal band, creating high-pressure ridges (poleward loops) and low-pressure troughs (equatorward loops). The strongly developed meander pattern is called meridional flow, and it brings highly variable weather (Fig. 3.5). The steep ridges and troughs bring air from both higher and lower latitudes into the temperate zones, where contrasts in temperature, pressure, and moisture create stormy weather. Cells of high or low pressure may block meridional flow in places, creating "spells" of continuous weather that may last from several days to weeks.

Conditions in the troposphere, the lower atmosphere, affect the amount of solar energy actually received at the surface of the Earth. Particulate matter in the air, from volcanic explosions, dust storms, large fires, or pollution, plays an important role in mediating the receipt of radiation, as does the water vapor in clouds. Dust and water vapor reflect radiation back into space and water vapor absorbs heat, reducing the amount received at the planet's surface, and thus limiting the amount of heat available to land, water, and air. Volcanic ash, when injected in large amounts high into the air, predictably reduces temperature by reflecting heat. Gases may have different effects; carbon dioxide in the air allows the short-wave solar radiation to pass through to the Earth, but reflects back to the Earth long-wave heat radiation, preventing its escape into the stratosphere and beyond. This traps heat near the surface of the Earth; high concentrations of carbon dioxide in the atmosphere thus cause higher prevailing temperatures (the greenhouse effect) that may moderate factors favoring the growth of ice sheets.

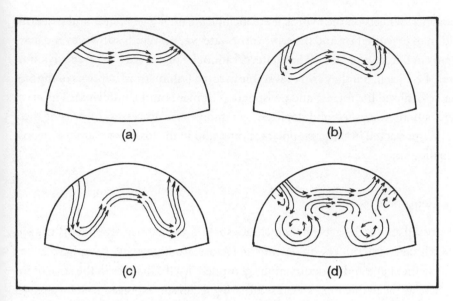

Figure 3.5 Westerly and meridional circulation patterns and blocking cells. Zonal circulation (a) limits mixing of tropical and polar air. When the waves become more meridional (flowing north and south, as in (b) and (c)), the exchange of cold and warm air is enhanced. Blocking cells are shown in (d). (After Oliver and Hidore 1984: Fig. 6.9.)

Some portion of the radiation that reaches the surface of the Earth and oceans is subject to loss by surface reflection. The ratio of energy reflected to energy received is called **albedo.** The effect is familiar in the difference, in sunny weather, between the solar warmth collected by a black coat (low albedo) in contrast to that reflected from a white one (high albedo). The ocean has, in general, low albedo; ice and desert sand have higher albedo.

The atmosphere, being composed of gases, does not preserve evidence of its past states and conditions; that must be sought in the other spheres, particularly the biosphere, cryosphere, and geosphere. Atmospheric states and conditions have direct and pervasive effects on the biosphere: heat and cold, and the amount and seasonal distribution of available moisture, directly determine the chances for life of species of plants and animals at any given place. Thus, the fossil record of life forms can be used as proxy for former states and conditions of the atmosphere. Atmospheric (climatic) effects on the geosphere are expressed in differential erosion and deposition by wind and water; landforms preserve in their structure and texture records of their experience of past climates and weather. Wind directions and intensities may be evidenced by the depositional patterns of dune sands and volcanic ash.

Atmospheric effects on the hydrosphere include the exchange of heat and gases, the addition of precipitation and the removal of water vapor. Winds stir waves and drive currents in the sea and lakes. These effects cannot be preserved within the dynamic hydrosphere itself, but they are recoverable in some fashion from deposits of the biosphere (fossilized life forms) and geosphere (sediments and landforms). The cryosphere is both nourished and depleted by atmospheric processes; records of these cycles are preserved in the great polar ice caps, and in the fossils of plankton deposited in the seas.

Geosphere

As discussed above, the geosphere includes some "external" (independent) triggers of the climate system. The independent factors are aspects of geosphere states, involving the shape and structure of the geosphere itself. Changes in the state of the geosphere affect all the other spheres, initiating feedback responses to such changes as continental drift, mountain building, and ejections of volcanic ash. Winds, water, ice, and living things must adjust to changes in these factors.

The Atlantic Ocean is spreading from the midline, driving Africa and the Americas ever farther apart. Antarctica separated from Australia 200 million years ago, moving to its present position at the south pole. Opening of the Atlantic ca. 150 million years ago, and the movement to high latitudes of the northern hemisphere continents and Greenland, created an almost enclosed sea in the Arctic. These arrangements, with a sea at the north pole surrounded by high-latitude continents, and a continent at the south pole surrounded by high-latitude seas, modified the mechanisms for global heat exchange between the atmosphere and hydrosphere, creating conditions propitious for an enlarged cryosphere. Without those changes, and others attendant upon them, the Pleistocene ice ages probably would not have occurred, regardless of the position of the Earth in respect to the Sun. The genetic isolation of biotic assemblages on the drifting continents allowed considerable evolutionary radiation, resulting in a non-climatic change in the biosphere initiated by geospheric changes.

As with the astronomical theory of ice ages, widespread acceptance of the hypothesis of continental drift, proposed originally on the basis of the complementary "fit" of shorelines across the Atlantic, had to wait upon some understanding of mechanisms. What was once only a curiously appealing idea became a powerful spur to research and understanding when the reality of continental drift was demonstrated by the recognition of evidence for the spreading Atlantic Ocean floor and the subduction troughs bordering the Pacific. While the full explanation of the mechanism lies in the future, it is known that volcanism and mountain building (orogeny) are related to continental drift, and that conditions in the core and viscous mantle of the Earth should hold the key to understanding them all.

Mountains and mountain ranges affect weather and climates through their influence upon the winds, varying with their orientation and height. The high Rocky Mountain range, running north to south through the middle latitudes of North America parallel to the eastern rim of the Pacific, interrupts the major air currents, deflecting them northeast, and creates a particularly stable atmospheric ridge which influences circulation far downstream (see Fig. 3.5). Mountain ranges oriented east and west, such as the Himalayas and the Pyrenees, also channel winds and define climatic zones, as can be seen in the behavior of storms that tend to follow seasonal tracks exclusively on one side or the other of the range.

Volcanic activity around the globe is related to continental drift and varies through time, perhaps with the configuration and dynamism of the moving plates. It is certain that the Pacific "Ring of Fire," the line of active volcanoes that border the ocean, is directly related to subduction zones at the margins of moving plates, and volcanoes elsewhere in the world have similar relationships. Icelandic volcanoes, on the other hand, are extensions above sea level of the volcanic mid-Atlantic ridge, a major axis of spreading. The environmental effects of volcanoes and volcanism are extensive; some are fairly transient, others large in scale and duration. We have already discussed how volcanic ash ejected high into the atmosphere interferes with heat exchange between the surface of the Earth and the upper air, reducing the heat received from the Sun. When eruptions release a large volume of carbon dioxide (CO_2) or sulfur dioxide (SO_2), the effects may be the reverse, with the gases in the atmosphere reflecting back to Earth the radiation leaving the surface.

Volcanic ash carries mineral nutrients that enrich soils; if it buries soil entirely, however, there will be some delay before the new deposit will support diverse life. Volcanic mudflows and lava flows and the accompanying fires cause environmental, but rarely climatic, change unless there are major effects on local albedo. Eruptions damage or eliminate life in their vicinities by venting hot poisonous gases, depositing ash or lava, initiating mudflows, and igniting fires. The surface of the Earth, and thus the basic conditions for subsequent life, is changed. Volcanoes influence the hydrosphere by changing the height and slope of land, by blocking and deflecting streams, and sometimes by interrupting the winds that bring rain. Crater lakes in calderas are created suddenly, and may be terminated equally suddenly. Volcanoes that build to great height support ice fields on their peaks and flanks, feeding rivers and nourishing glaciers.

In contrast to the apparently independent state changes, changes in the condition of the geosphere may be responses to changes in the other four spheres. Local and regional weather affects the rate and type of erosion experienced by rocks and land-forms, and the nature of the sediments that are transported and deposited by either wind or water. Moving water dissolves and separates rock constituents in the initial stages of erosion and moves sediments around, reducing them in one place, increasing in another. Ice affects rocks and minerals at several scales also, wedging apart crystals, grinding up rocks in glaciers, moving sediments at many scales, and shaping landforms. Living organisms such as plants and fungi also wedge rocks into smaller pieces, initiate acidic etching and rotting, and affect the locations and intensity of erosion and deposition.

Sediments, then, are produced by effects upon rocks of the atmosphere, biosphere, hydrosphere, and cryosphere. In their turn, sediments affect the other components of the climate system in ways that may induce additional feedback responses. The development or degradation of soils (Chapter 11) have great significance for the biosphere. Soils and sediments retain far greater amounts of water than do rocks, making water available to living organisms and at the same time holding it out of the surface waters and oceans of the planet. Sediments may clog or fill water channels and basins, thus changing the distribution and condition of the hydrosphere, at scales ranging from small spring ducts to channels and basins in the ocean. Dust plumes from exposed sediments carried by winds into the atmosphere reduce the solar radiation reaching the surface, just as volcanic ash does, affecting the motion and temperature of air masses at small and moderate scales. At larger scales the movement of dune fields, resulting from interactions between air and sediment, can increase surface albedo and change the distribution of both air masses and rainfall.

Hydrosphere

Water – around the land, under the land, and on the land – is the cradle of life on our planet and its fundamental essential, as well as the moderator of its climates. The Earth, despite its name, has more water than land on its surface. Of all the planet's water, 97% is in the oceans, most of it in the southern hemisphere.

The state and condition of the hydrosphere are interdependent with the other spheres, with which the hydrosphere exchanges heat (energy), moisture, and matter (Fig. 3.6). Since very little information about past states and conditions is retained in the hydrosphere itself, proxies for ancient hydrospheric conditions and states must be sought in the other spheres.

The hydrosphere, particularly its dominant oceanic portions, comprises the Earth's major reservoirs for heat and dissolved chemicals. Water's very high "specific heat capacity" means that a lot of caloric energy is required to warm it, and a lot of

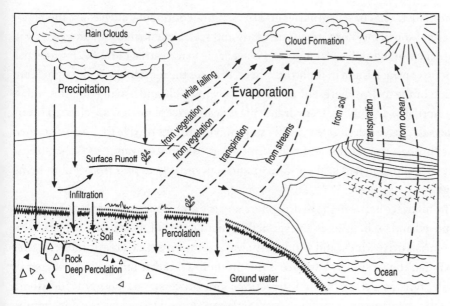

Figure 3.6 Simplified diagram of the hydrologic cycle showing water exchange among four spheres. Short- and long-term storage of water in the cryosphere is not modeled. (After Akin 1991: Fig. 3.1.)

heat is released when water changes state from vapor to liquid, or from liquid to solid ice. Oceanic currents move heat from the equator toward the poles, moderating the Earth's climate. Currents also move vertically, exchanging surface warmth for cold deep water. Many chemicals and elements are carried in the ocean currents. Some of these are exchangeable with the atmosphere, as carbon dioxide, for example, moves between the atmosphere and the oceans where it is readily soluble in cold salt water. It may remain in cold bottom waters until those reach an upwelling zone where they are recycled to the surface, bringing along old carbon and concentrated nutrients.

Moving water shapes the geosphere by erosion and deposition. Of all the fresh water on the continents, a bit less than 75% is frozen in ice, while close to 25% of it is groundwater beneath the surface. Lakes hold 0.3%, while about one-tenth as much as that flows in all the rivers. The remaining 0.06%, twice as much as in the rivers, is in soil moisture supporting plant life (Oliver and Hidore 1984: 71). The hydrosphere's normal erosional work is done by the 0.03% of continental water in the rivers, and by moving water along the shores of lakes and oceans. During the ice ages, more water was in solid form on land, and less in the ocean. The withdrawal of water from the oceans reduced the size and changed the shape of ocean basins, coincident with the isostatic adjustments of continental crusts and basin floors.

Water, of course, is a major component of the biosphere. Water habitats – marine, riverine, and lacustrine – are the oldest, and still the most important, support for life on the planet. The coastal estuaries and the shallow continental shelves are the major nurseries for marine life in its vast diversity and scale. Essential for life as we know it, less than 1% of the global water budget is available to terrestrial life as fresh water and vapor on continents and in the atmosphere. Perhaps the most biologically significant portion of the hydrosphere, although normally invisible and usually out of mind, is that internal to organisms. Dehydrated life is death, except to a few specialized invertebrates that have a desiccated resting stage. Living things recycle their incorporated water through respiration and transpiration, passing water vapor into the atmosphere to be precipitated again as rain or snow, eventually to pass from soil to living things.

The interface between the hydrosphere and the atmosphere, where heat and gases are moved and exchanged, is an especially dynamic part of the climate system. Heat differentials drive winds, and winds drive waves and currents. Climatic modeling has shown that the air–ocean interface is the mother of weather and a strong shaper of climate, but the details of the interactions and processes are poorly understood. Dramatic surprises are expected as research continues. Deepwater oceanic circulation affects the amount of CO_2 available to the atmosphere, influencing the "greenhouse effect" of the atmosphere on both short and long time scales (Boyle 1990) and thus dampening or amplifying other subsystems of the climate. The amount of greenhouse gases in the atmosphere correlated with major cool and warm cycles of climate for half a billion years or more (Berner 1990). The present interglacial, the Holocene, saw a dramatic rise in atmospheric CO_2 at its beginning (Kutzbach 1987). The Atlantic deepwater circulation influences the circulation of heat and salt (**thermohaline** circulation) in most of the other oceans, thereby mediating the major climatic states of the hemispheres (Broecker and Denton 1990).

The air–sea interface in the Pacific drives a major weather motor, the El Niño/Southern Oscillation (ENSO) system (Diaz and Markgraf 1993). High pressure and temperature shift periodically from west to east in the Pacific equatorial zone, affecting temperature and precipitation downwind in the eastern Pacific and from there over the globe and both hemispheres. On the seasonal scale, the dramatic monsoons of the middle latitudes are powered by temperature differentials between the cool wet air over the ocean and the warm, dry air over land. Freshwater bodies also moderate climates through interaction with the atmosphere at fairly local scales.

Cryosphere

In a special sense, the hydrosphere is interchangeable with, and complementary to, the cryosphere, since they are composed, respectively, of the liquid and solid states of

H_2O. Each expands at the expense of the other, but equally, each nourishes the other. The growth of glaciers on land is mediated by the atmosphere, which transports water vapor and precipitates it as snow through complex physical interactions with the hydrosphere. The melting of glaciers modifies the temperature, chemistry, and quantity of water in adjacent oceans.

The physical differences that accompany the change of state from liquid to solid H_2O are significant enough to justify considering the cryosphere distinct from the hydrosphere, even though the two exchange matter continuously. While only 2% of all the Earth's water is frozen, as much as 70%–80% of all water on land surfaces today may be in the form of ice (Lockwood 1985: 73). Ice caps at the poles account for most of it, but ice as permafrost, mountain glaciers, and seasonal snow and ice are important components with major environmental consequences.

The **Cenozoic** ("recent life" age; since the dinosaurs) drift of continental masses into high latitudes in the northern hemisphere and to the south pole seems to have set important preconditions for the most recent ice ages. The ice cap on Antarctica, the south polar continent, developed before any others. Ice-cap growth requires a large source of moisture for precipitation, cool temperatures to deposit snow, and a positive balance between deposition and melting so that snow accumulates from one year to the next. Once established and grown to some critical size, ice sheets tend to perpetuate themselves because of their effects upon adjacent atmospheric circulation. The high albedo of ice sheets keeps the surface cool and cools the air above, reducing snow melt and amplifying the heat gradients between the equator and the poles. Winds blow cool, dense air outward from the cold, elevated surfaces of ice caps, forcing the planetary circulation toward the equator and expanding the cryosphere with shelf and sea ice. These conditions can be triggered by a seasonal reduction in summer insolation at the pole, which is one effect of the orbital and axial variations. The northern hemisphere ice caps formed initially north and west of the Atlantic Ocean and along the eastern shores of the Pacific; in each case, the proximity of a major ocean assured a source of moisture to nourish the ice sheets. The orbital factors are the only external forcing mechanisms that can reduce solar insolation in high latitudes and increase it in the tropics. Increasing solar energy in the tropical regions ensures an initial supply of warm water, moving poleward, to provide abundant precipitation.

Eventually, however, the climatic effects of a growing ice sheet affect the oceans in ways that cut off the supply of moisture. Sea ice and cold winds bring cold Arctic water of reduced salinity farther south, changing the temperature and chemistry of the ocean basins. Fresh cold water at the surface of the ocean will freeze and, while increasing the albedo over the oceans to promote further cooling, seal the ocean surface against evaporation. Continental ice keeps water out of circulation in the oceans and atmosphere, lowering sea level and reducing the size and shape of the sea surface and ocean basins, with consequent changes in ocean currents. Under these conditions of a sea surface reduced in size and temperature, and seasonally at least partly sealed from the atmosphere, nourishment of high-latitude ice sheets is less effective. In combination with the extension of the ice fronts toward the equators, ice-sheet melting might increase faster than growth. Any shift toward higher summer insolation at high latitudes would, of course, accentuate the melting trends. These interactions among the ice, oceans, and geosphere, as water is shifted from ocean to ice and back, are involved in the growth and decay of ice sheets. Full explanations of the mechanisms and lag times in the interactions are not available now; it is possible that the ultimate understanding will involve additional variables, such as atmospheric dust and oceanic circulation (Broecker and Denton 1990; Imbrie and Imbrie 1979; Ruddiman and McIntyre 1981).

Continental glaciers modify terrestrial environments in more ways than by cooling climates. By removing water from the oceans, glaciers expose the continental shelves to colonization by terrestrial plants and animals, which in turn affect the local albedo, winds, and precipitation. The increased land area changes the local densities of species, permitting some relaxation of competitive pressures and perhaps leading to habitat expansions elsewhere. The equatorward shift of climatic zones during glacial expansion is paralleled by shifting distributions of plants and animals. Communities are disrupted and new associations develop in new habitats, changing the conditions of adaptation and competition for many species. As glaciers melt, deglaciated land is recolonized by successional sequences of plants and animals. New niches and habitats become available, competitive pressures are reorganized, and both speciations and extinctions may be expected within the terrestrial biosphere. Marine species are forced equatorward during periods of glacial expansion; they also shift toward higher latitudes with the return of more moderate climates. With the niche and habitat contractions, expansions, and redistributions, some organisms suffer extinctions and new species may form.

Glacial ice moving over land scours, transports, and deposits rocks and sediments, changing the conditions of the geosphere and hydrosphere at the regional scale. As ice piles up on the continents, the crust sinks to compensate for the weight; this isostatic adjustment changes the elevation and the pressure environments of the rocks. Displaced mass in the mantle may be shifted to the ocean floors, which rise in response to the removal of weight from them. Isostatic adjustments in the opposite direction occur with deglaciation, complicating our observation and measurement of eustatic adjustment of the sea level as the volume of water in the basins changes.

The sediments deposited by glaciers on deformed bedrock create postglacial land-scapes that may bear very little resemblance to those of preglacial times. Surface waters must excavate new channels to drain the deranged surfaces, and rivers may never return to preglacial routes. Immature drainage results in more water on and near the surface, with consequent effects on local climates and biota.

Non-glacial ice on land, whether seasonal as winter snow and ice, perennial but fluctuating as mountain glaciers, or long term as permafrost, limits habitable space for the plant and animal species in its vicinity. Ice stores, and usually releases, water in pulses over the course of the year; its expansion on freezing breaks rocks into their mineral components and initiates movement of the fragments. It heaves soil and sediments, aerating and displacing them (and with them any included archaeological materials). Shelf ice and sea ice, independent of glaciers, affect the climates and living conditions of high-latitude shores and near-shore seas. Ice conditions in pre-historic seas and landscapes can be studied through the proxy data of marine micro-organisms, shore landforms, and the periglacial effects of ice wedging, solifluction, and related periglacial landforms that may become "fossilized" through geological processes (Clark 1988; Lowe and Walker 1984). Knowledge of the cryosphere is still underdeveloped; paleoenvironmental studies will suffer until it is better understood.

Biosphere

The living things of the Earth, including people, are clearly dependent upon the inanimate spheres of the climate system to produce the conditions essential to life – conditions that may sometimes be narrowly defined. Modern ecology has shown that the inanimate spheres are in turn dependent upon the biosphere for the stability of their states and conditions. Earth and its climate is a unique system, in which living things are a fully participating component, inseparable from the others (Rambler et al. 1989).

The climatic zonation of the globe sets the conditions to which life adjusts, and life, in turn, modifies those conditions. Warm and wet conditions nurture diversity; there are more different forms of life per unit of space in the tropics than anywhere else on Earth. In the temperate zones, diversity is best expressed at the scale of associations of plants and animals that change gradually with latitude and altitude (Fig. 3.7). The lowest diversities are found in the deserts of the mid-latitudes and in the polar regions. With lowered diversity may come more numerous individuals per species, or individuals of greater body size. The strong seasonal contrasts of the higher latitudes are reflected in adaptive animal behaviors such as migration and hibernation, and in the rapid and brief growth spurts of plants interrupted by long periods of dormancy or annual cycling through seeds.

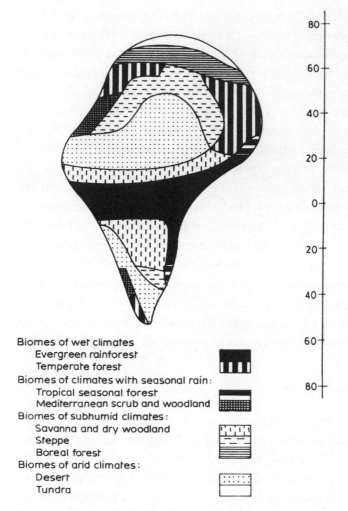

80—

60—

40—

20—

0—

20—

40—

Biomes of wet climates
    Evergreen rainforest
    Temperate forest
Biomes of climates with seasonal rain:
    Tropical seasonal forest
    Mediterranean scrub and woodland
Biomes of subhumid climates:
    Savanna and dry woodland
    Steppe
    Boreal forest
Biomes of arid climates:
    Desert
    Tundra

60—

80—

Figure 3.7 Latitudinal distribution of biotic zones in a generalized land mass. Compare to climatic zonation summarized in Table 3.1. (Reproduced from Tallis 1991: Fig. 2.2, by permission of Chapman & Hall.)

As we have seen above, the biosphere permeates all the other spheres. Living things are found on and in the surficial parts of the geosphere, in the hydrosphere and the lower atmosphere, and on and under ice. They do more than simply derive sustenance in all those places. Through complex feedback mechanisms, life influences all the other components of its environments. Nitrogen, carbon, sulfur and oxygen, carbon dioxide and water, are among the substances actively exchanged between the atmosphere and biosphere. The composition of the atmosphere, as we have seen, influences climate in direct but subtle ways, by affecting cloud cover, precipitation, and the degree of greenhouse warming. Plants and bacteria are the major players whose metabolism, respiration, and transpiration affect the composition of the air above the surface of the Earth, but all life is involved at some level.

Plant growth on the surface of the Earth, modifying the albedo, affects the amount of solar radiation that is retained as energy to warm the surface. The distribution of surface warmth in turn changes the patterns of winds, with consequent effects on both weather and climate. When forests are replaced by agricultural fields or grasslands, the local weather becomes drier and warmer; a change that is not necessarily beneficial to other life in the area.

Water is essential to life, and life forms permeate the hydrosphere, even to great depths in the oceans. Metabolic processes remove water and water vapor from active circulation and fix them temporarily inside living things. Metabolic processes such as waste excretion, respiration, and transpiration return chemically modified water to the hydrosphere and atmosphere, affecting the chemistry of oceans and other water reservoirs. The nutrients so cycled feed other life.

The biosphere modifies rocks of the Earth's crust, facilitating their decomposition or disaggregation by both chemical and mechanical means, producing acids that dissolve some minerals and mechanically wedging others apart by rootlet penetration and expansion. Plant cover reduces the rate of erosional displacement of sediments. Plants, animals, and single-celled organisms mix and enrich loose sediments, creating soil. Algae and bacteria fix metallic oxides in sediments, cementing loose aggregates into ores and rocks. Accumulations of organic sediments on ocean floors produce limestones and other sedimentary rocks.

The state and condition of the biosphere itself are defined significantly by internal factors, although triggers in the other spheres are more often considered the agents of change (Webb and Bartlein 1992). Photosynthesis, the chemical means by which plants create carbohydrates from sunlight and water, is at the base of all food webs. Photosynthetic exchanges of oxygen and carbon dioxide are essential to air-breathing animal life. Elsewhere in the web of life, decomposers release nutrients stored in the bodies of plants and animals, recycling them into the soil, water, and air. Population fluctuations in time and space, involving changes in distributions and diversity, boom and bust cycles, extinctions, replacements (niche changes), succession, and epidemics are other internally generated triggers affecting the biosphere itself. Some of those may be responses to external stimuli, but that is not always or necessarily the case.

The dominant element in the modern biosphere is, of course, our own species. Our vast numbers and our capacity for work have imposed an unprecedented burden on the biosphere as well as on the climate system. Fires, deforestation, monoculture, landform modification, soil depletion or exhaustion, irrigation with its attendant salinization, artificial drainage, fertilization, aerosols in the atmosphere, and the complex environments of cities all change the biosphere and aspects of the other four spheres as well. Although such changes are often presented as if they are recent insults to the Earth, many of them are old, even ancient, effects of human interventions that have defined the world as we know it (Dincauze 1993a; Roberts 1989). Even air pollution, whose beginnings are often assigned to nineteenth-century fossil-fuel burning, has ancient roots. Greenland ice cores indicate that lead and silver mining and smelting by Greek and Roman civilizations produced lead pollution of the troposphere at a hemispheric scale (Hong et al. 1994).

Human culture systems are not outside of planetary ecology; they are integral parts of it. Equally, the five spheres are inseparable from the contingent contexts of cultures. The challenge that such complexity poses for human understanding is profound.

> Ecology is not a second-class physics. It is infinitely more complex; so that, although physical science explains the driving mechanism for the biological system, it is not capable of explaining its behavior, nor do its simplistic attitudes apply . . . [W]ithout man there is no ecology and no physics; so that man's ecology is the ultimate science, and that is not subject to experiment.
>
> L. R. TAYLOR 1987: 21

HUMAN RESPONSES TO ENVIRONMENTAL CHANGE

> Prehistorians need to maintain a careful balance between explanations that are "elegant" and simple and those that are naïve and simplistic.
>
> DENNELL 1985: 1331

In an ideal homeostatic world, there would be little change. However, in a world such as Earth, dominated by living things, there can be no stasis, no equilibrium. For any organism, the successful continuation of life requires the ability to adjust to changed conditions. The paleoenvironments that were the contexts of past human actions must be known if we are to understand human history and evolution. Social environments, the crucial contexts of human planning and decision-making, are the subjects of anthropological and archaeological social theory, with their own vast literatures. In this chapter attention focuses on human strategic responses to changes in physical and biological environments, distinguished as much as possible from social environments.

Environmental change, loosely defined, is a departure from the "mean" or perceived normal state or condition of any aspect of the environment. Humans respond only to those changes that they perceive, and then only to those that affect conditions or resources that are important to them. To illustrate with a simplified example: a competitive replacement of one species of mouse by another on a mountainside should evoke no response whatever from a community of farmers in valleys nearby. The feeding habits of the new mice, however, could initiate changes in the ratios of grasses available to grazing animals, which might be crucial to pastoralists using the highlands. The pastoralists would observe the vegetative change, and might try to mitigate it by firing the grasses; they might not recognize the subtle role of the mice in the changed conditions.

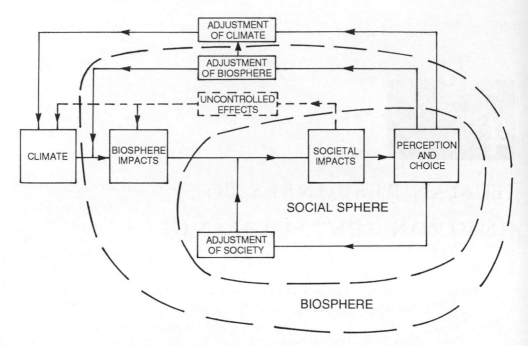

Figure 4.1   Climatic influences on human societies as mediated through the biosphere, with
feedbacks from human adjustments of technological strategies, including scheduling
(HMA). "Uncontrolled effects" are the inadvertent modifications of the biosphere or
climate resulting from anthropogenic changes responding to the initial stress. (After
Ingram et al. 1981: Fig. 1.3.)

In contrast to many other animals, humans can change their environments intentionally without moving away. This ability is a major complicating factor for investigators evaluating the impact of environmental change upon human groups (Fig.
4.1). Humans change their environments by manipulating aspects of their habitats,
typically using technology (tools and facilities of various kinds). People build
houses, irrigation canals, fish weirs, storage facilities, and other such amenities and
we clear land for farming and settlement. Except in basic housing, which has complements among some animal species (burrows, complex nests), human purposive
construction is unique in the biosphere; it imposes, sometimes heavily, upon other
species, as was shown in Chapter 1. This Human Mode of Adaptation (**HMA**) has
become in this century a major source of environmental perturbation, whose worldwide effects are now undeniable. Archaeology shows that, at lesser scales, the effects
of the HMA are very ancient – as old, at least, as the genus *Homo*.

Humans have dominated the biosphere for several thousands of years. We are not,
strictly speaking, an independent variable, but we are actual and potential triggers of

change. Our relative, conditional, independence of action does not absolve us from the effects of the changes we initiate; we are subject to feedback from the several spheres, usually with unanticipated consequences (Dincauze 1993b; Tenner 1996). The unanticipated consequences of human efforts to ameliorate their own environments include initiation of new systemic adjustments at local to regional scales in all spheres of the climate system, and ultimately in climate itself. For example, on the threshold of a new century we find our addiction to fossil fuels affecting climate on the planetary scale, even as we lack the technology, understanding, and discipline to respond effectively to the consequences.

Archaeologists grappling with issues in human ecology face fundamental theoretical and methodological problems; these problems pervade the literature, constraining interpretations, limiting understanding, and demonstrating the immaturity of the discipline. Without ranking, I present a list of some of the outstanding unsolved problems of human paleoecology, moving from theory to method:

- identification of the crucial *variables* in a situation (specification of the "initial conditions");
- identification of *mechanisms* that link variables (the keys to the articulation of systems or subsystems);
- identification and evaluation of *equifinalities* (the many potential processes giving similar results);
- elusiveness of *ideologies* in archaeological materials (the context of decision-making);
- *chronologies* precise enough to permit comparisons between systems and spheres (the key to situational context and systemic mechanisms);
- *preservation* biases in the classes of remains recoverable (loss of some critical categories);
- *recovery* biases in techniques and methodologies (especially sampling).

There is no shortage of ideas in the archaeological literature about how climate might have affected cultures. Especially outside of Eurasia, in areas where there is less literary ancient history dealing with human motives and social processes, archaeologists find the occasional coincidence of climate change and changes in culture a powerful incentive to postulate causal connections. Of course, with human cultures always changing in one aspect or another, and a growing body of theory and evidence for climatic changes, there is no end to such coincidences.

What is critically lacking in both archaeology and history is theory and method that will help focus such arguments from coincidence by implicating crucial evidence for linkage. Theory is required to specify mechanisms by which climatic change affects specific aspects of cultural systems. How can we distinguish between **endogenous** agents of change, developing within cultural systems, and **exogenous** agents, imposed from outside, when the linkages among them all are so intimate and, at the same time, complex? One source of the difficulties archaeologists and historians face is that the misguided search for causes displaces efforts to identify and understand processes and mechanisms.

Greatly refined chronologies are also essential to any progress, particularly in archaeology, where the best radiometric methods currently available work at the century scale, whereas change is fundamentally embedded in human behavior and decisions, maximally on the scale of years and decades. Consider the differences between challenges and responses to three different scales of change in the atmosphere and hydrosphere:

1 Any delay (lag time) between a flood and the responses of humans in its path could be fatal. The two events would be sudden and essentially synchronous in the archaeological record, as well as spatially circumscribed, so that the relationship could be readily noted.

2 Regional changes in the water table due to variation in rainfall over a few years occur at a scale compatible with regional studies of settlement patterns, where the responses are likely to be visible, so that environmental change and human response can be studied in tandem. Demonstration of coincidence may be difficult.

3 On the other hand, human responses to long-term climatic cooling initiating a glacial age will be strategically diverse as well as temporally and spatially diffuse; the relationships among them will be difficult to perceive or demonstrate in the archaeological record.

The complexities of paleoecological interpretations are well illustrated in a study reported by Seltzer and Hastorf (1990), which reveals unexpected complications in human responses to an apparently simple climatic reversal. Ecologists have long known that the effects of climatic stress are most clearly observed in **ecotonal** environments (where two or more modal landscapes meet), or those of simple structure ("marginal lands" – arid lands, high altitudes, high latitudes). For decades archaeologists have resorted to deterministic hypotheses in such environments, expecting to find close correlations between climatic and cultural change that will reveal causation. In an informed and sophisticated argument Seltzer and Hastorf use geomorphological observations and geoscience data (radiocarbon-dated mountain glacial readvances and ice-cap climatology) to postulate an episode of climatic cooling. They hypothesized that the cooling would have affected crop yields, and that information relevant to that effect might be observed in the archaeological record. Using modern crop and microclimate relationships as analogs, they postulated that the archaeological record would show a reduction in the ratio of maize to potatoes during the cooler climate, and supported this postulate with ethnographic data from the area of interest. Because maize is more sensitive than potatoes to climatic deterioration at the elevations involved, it was noted that moving maize fields and settlements down slope would be an effective response to the climatic change. The archaeological data showed the expected reduction in maize at the critical time. However, the settlement data showed that occupation moved up slope, against the direction expected as a strategic response to cooling.

Seltzer and Hastorf remark, "if it was only the climate that convinced people to give up their autonomy and resettle, they should have organized themselves to do so at lower elevations where they would have had more regular harvest" (1990: 411). Noting the archaeological evidence for political and economic troubles at the time, the authors conclude that sociopolitical conditions may have defined moves to more isolated and defensible locations. Climatic deterioration was not the unique stress to which people were responding, although "climate may have constrained some agricultural activities, possibly leading to increased social tensions" (1990: 411). The coincidence of the move upslope and the expected colder climate prevented unambiguous interpretation of either the stress or the response. This study demonstrates that paleoclimatic investigations are unlikely to explain cultural processes even in relatively simple biological systems (see also Fitzhugh and Lamb [1985] for a similar conclusion backed by data), but they can implicate some of the complexities, even contradictions, of cultural life. People typically had, and have, less than perfect freedom to act purely on economic grounds.

SCALES OF ENVIRONMENTAL CHANGE

Phenomena unfold on their own appropriate scales of space and time and may be invisible in our myopic world of dimensions assessed by comparison with human height and times metered by human lifespans.

GOULD 1993: 41

Environmental change is a relative concept – relative to cultural values, technologies, demographics, and scale. To illustrate the effects of **amplitude**, frequency, and duration, as well as the complexity of change, on the character of human responses, consider some hypothetical examples of changes originating outside of the cultural system that must respond to them. Such exogenous changes may originate in any of the five spheres as well as from other cultural systems. Exogenous changes may be

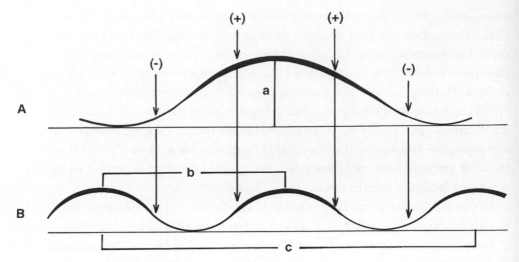

Figure 4.2 Wave model of change. Amplitude (a), wave length (b), and frequency (c) are illustrated as variables of form, time, or intensity. Synergistic relationships of processes interacting at different frequencies (curves A and B) are shown as positive (reinforcing) or negative (mutually canceling).

categorized in any number of ways; here we group them into two contrastive categories: *short-term changes* with durations or frequencies less than 10 years (high frequency), and *long-term changes* with longer durations or frequencies, generally greater than the span of a human generation.

Short-term changes

Evidence of this first class of environmental changes is only rarely observed in the archaeological record; however, it is the class of changes most salient to those people experiencing them, and most typically encountered in the historical and ethnographic literatures. These are the frequent, reversible changes of short duration with which we are all familiar. Examples include unusual weather such as droughts and warm winters, epidemic diseases, fires and floods, and various insect infestations.

For human beings, environmental changes that are fully realized within a span of less than a decade may be considered as "short-term" changes of brief duration. Such a brief span is not the usual definition of short term in the environmental sciences where, for example, the boundary of the short term for climatologists may be 100 years. For purposes of examining human responses, it is reasonable to focus on changes that may occur more than once in a human life span; those are generally incorporated into the normal range of behavioral and cultural variation. An example is the El Niño weather phenomenon along the Pacific Coast of Peru and Ecuador, which occurs when the normal coastal weather conditions are drastically reversed by changes in Pacific equatorial water bodies, and torrential rains drench the coastal deserts and foothills. Extreme as such changes are, they are expected and adjusted to as recurrent periods of economic stress and personal jeopardy.

Short-term environmental changes are of many kinds, and their many effects do not constitute a natural set. There are at least four attributes which can vary among them: duration, **frequency** (in a wave model, the distance or time between peaks of the wave or cyclical phenomenon), amplitude, and periodicity. While amplitude (size or intensity) and frequency tend to be inversely correlated, the set displays complex permutations. Events such as seasonal changes in the temperate latitudes may be characterized as events of short duration (a few weeks), high frequency (two or four times a year), moderate amplitude (mean temperature differences of 15 to 30 degrees Celsius), and regular periodicity (predictably annual). Major volcanic eruptions, on the other hand, are characterized by brief duration (a few days at most), low frequency (normally several generational spans), high amplitude, and no recognizable periodicity. Depending upon geography and history, human communities may consider both of these phenomena as normal variations in daily life, but the response patterns invoked by each clearly differ, mainly in respect to the differences in frequency, amplitude, and periodicity (Fig. 4.2).

Short-term changes that require immediate response are usually those that stress individuals or particular social subgroups by creating shortages or inadequacies of resources or leadership, or creating conditions exceeding the comfort or safety range of temperature or moisture. Such changes increase **morbidity** or **mortality**, or increase costs. Changes that do not impose stress may be simply accepted or, if especially beneficial, they may be celebrated as "blessings." Thus, the perception of a change as beneficial or deleterious will be a result of prior cultural norms and values, not merely of technological capacity for response. Changes characterized by regular periodicity and short duration, being more or less predictable, are usually managed within the normal repertory of cultural variability, using the tools and techniques ready at hand. They have, therefore, low archaeological visibility. Events of short duration, low frequency, and high amplitude, whether periodic or not, are likely to constitute crises and to stimulate innovative behavior. As the innovation may not become established in the cultural repertory, it also may have very low archaeological visibility even if the event itself is identifiable (earthquake, volcanic eruption, massive flood, landslide). Considering such singular, sudden catastrophes as examples of short-term environmental change appears to trivialize them; all the same, the analytical context can be productive.

Each of the five spheres of the climate system may produce short-term, reversible environmental changes of high amplitude, low frequency, and erratic periodicity that are likely to be perceived as "events," whether catastrophic or not. The hydrosphere and atmosphere, singly or in tandem, can initiate events such as floods, drought, winters without snow, and cold summers. The geosphere is the initiator of such events as earthquakes and tsunamis (tidal waves), landslides, and volcanism. The power of the cryosphere is seen in events such as ice dams on rivers with resultant floods, or sea ice driven ashore that endangers lives of coastal dwellers in the high Arctic (Newell 1984). Biospheric events include infestations of pests or diseases, dramatic changes in animal distributions and densities such as boom and bust population cycles and massive migrations, and major fires that set back plant successions.

Changes that occur as sudden events stress diverse aspects of cultural systems. Some systems, such as those of mobile foragers unrestrained by political borders, are elastic enough to absorb all or most of them without major adjustment. Complex systems may adjust to stressful events so subtly that the linkages are invisible in both the archaeological and historical records. Particular aspects of complex systems may bear the brunt of events so strongly that they never recover; their loss may affect other systemic parts in no archaeologically recognizable way. In any case, the adjustment is not made to the stressor, the event itself, but to its *effects*; adjustment is, therefore, culturally defined.

The massive volcanic explosion that buried the prosperous Bronze Age Minoan town of Akrotiri on the Aegean island of Thera must have been extremely disruptive to the social, economic, and political life of its time. However, decades after archaeologists recognized the event in the archaeological and geological record, there remains substantial uncertainty about its timing and about its relationships to other events of large amplitude and short duration in areas bordering the Aegean and eastern Mediterranean Sea (see case study in Part II, pp. 132–135). Not only does this stalemate keep archaeologists humble in the face of their own uncertainties, it shows clearly that societies can absorb destructive events by dispersing their effects throughout the cultural system, so that there are no clear correlations.

Long-term changes

Long-term, infrequent changes are those most familiar in the literature of the environmental sciences – the trend-like changes that reorganize regional and latitudinal environments over centuries. Examples include cooling or warming climates at the hemispherical scale. They are recognized as cumulative, directional, incremental changes. Because their onset and development typically occur over extended periods of time, long-term changes are difficult to date precisely and the human responses are diffused over long durations and probably usually through a number of different strategies. The archaeological literature on environments typically deals with trend-like changes of regional or larger scale (e.g., Gumerman 1988). Unless archaeological data are available at compatible scales, problems of causation and response modes, like those for short-term change, are highly intractable to solution by archaeological methods (Plog and Hantman 1990).

In the class of long-term changes there are few **events** (discrete occurrences to which some notice is given); we focus instead on low-frequency phenomena characterized by durations longer than 10 years and periodicities of recurrence considerably greater than a human generation. Amplitudes in this class tend to be low at the scale of human perception. The changes tend to be directional and cumulative; they may eventually result in conditions very different from the originals. Again, definition of such changes is relative to time span and geographical location; they are best measured over many years and at a regional scale. From the perspectives of human beings, such changes are perceived only in small increments, so that the responses are typically incremental also. The effects are expressed gradually, perhaps as increased or decreased energetic costs of normal activities, or as benefits accruing from the relaxation of environmental constraints on normal activities. At archaeological scales of analysis, the changes will be identified as cultural or biological changes, the products of series of biological, social, and technological innovations. Innovations that were adopted help to define the new condition of society and culture. They are visible in the archaeological record, although their relationship to the stimulus may be difficult to interpret. Innovations that were of immediate use only, were ineffective or abandoned, may be archaeologically invisible.

Long-term changes also originate in all of the five spheres. Glacial and interglacial climatic cycles and their attendant sea-level changes are of this class. Geospheric changes of long term include tectonic plate motions and local or regional isostatic uplift or subsidence, soil development and degradation, weathering, erosion and deposition, and changes of slope as hills are lowered and basins filled. In the hydrosphere, changes in ocean currents and water tables and in large-scale precipitation patterns will affect human societies either directly or indirectly through changes in local climates and the biosphere. In the biosphere, long-term habitat changes include the expansion or contraction of species' ranges and such processes as species competition and succession. These are perhaps the most significant environmental changes to which humans and human societies have adapted, because they define directly the conditions and raw materials for cultural life. For human beings, as living things, the biosphere mediates changes that occur in the other spheres. For the paleoenvironmentalist, the signals for most long-term changes in the five spheres are easily read. The signals for human responses, however, are elusive.

HUMAN STRATEGIC OPTIONS

"[C]ulture" is the result of situation-specific adjustments, reflecting the interaction of people adapting to particular environmental circumstances, by particular technological means, at a given point in their history.

MORAN 1982: 52

The social structure, technology, and ideology of a human group are critical determinants of its interaction with its environment. Human societies define their environments in relation to the technology available for exploitation of resources, which are themselves socially and culturally defined. Unrecognized resources, or those requiring technology outside the cultural repertory such as metal ores for people without pyrotechnology, are irrelevant. Significant change, from the perspective of a human community, is that which affects resources utilized by that community, regardless of where the change originates. The history of the environmentalist movements in contemporary society demonstrates this fully; different segments of society are aware of and threatened by quite disparate aspects of environmental degradation. For example, some factions in North America urge the return of wolves to western range lands to restore natural animal systems, against the fundamental opposition of ranchers. Water rights are contested between farmers, ranchers, and cities. Much of the contentiousness within and between environmental advocacy groups is attributable to these differential perceptions, even though the environment is not itself separable into discrete parts.

Change might not be perceived until it affects the amount, quality, or accessibility of important resources. Resource change, an aspect of environmental change, is also culturally relative. The spatial and seasonal distributions of resources are obvious and crucial variables in the definition of a group's environment, and responses to change in these circumstances will vary with that definition. For example, a midsummer flood inundating a river valley would create a temporary economic crisis for farmers whose crops were growing there; a typical response might be increased trade. A flood would pose a major economic threat to a factory on the floodplain, possibly entailing abandonment of the locale. However, such a flood would be a rich opportunity for hunter-gatherers who could harvest the fish stranded by receding waters. Neither farmers nor hunter-gatherers would be seriously affected by a flood in early spring, when plant growth was only incipient, but flood seasonality offers no relief to users of the built environment.

The catalog of potential human adaptive responses is extremely varied, ranging from biological evolution, through phenotypic plasticity, to adjustments in density and distribution of population, to behavioral changes at scales from the individual to the cultural, and to ritual and technological innovation. Emilio Moran (1982: 7) makes a distinction between **adaptation** and "adjustment," essentially contrasting genetic and behavioral responses to environmental constraints. Genetic evolutionary change is necessarily slow, involving changes in gene ratios and their expressions within populations. The concept of biological adaptation has only a limited usefulness in typical archaeological research, belonging to scales of time larger than those of archaeological units after the Lower Paleolithic. In biological evolution, adaptation is measured by population survival; maladapted populations go to extinction. There are no quantitative criteria for measuring the relative success of adaptations, or degrees of adaptedness, or for estimating potential survivorship in environments subject to change. Unfit individuals die; unfit societies change, move, or become extinct. Because the measure is survival, all populations that survive are by definition adapted to their environments – a tautological conclusion. Archaeological case studies of "adaptation" are, therefore, tautological in the long term, trivial in the short. It is more productive for archaeologists to devote attention to cultural concepts, leaving biological concepts to biological contexts.

"Adjustments" are responses that individuals make to negative feedback, which can be imagined as an on-going critique of their fitness in a particular environment. Behavioral changes are the most important forms of adjustment. Culturally defined, purposeful behavioral changes involve **strategies**. Strategies are "the modifications of behavior and material items that . . . peoples [make] in attempting to cope with one another and with the natural environment" (Cordell and Plog 1979: 409). The strategic options available within a particular cultural context vary with the scale of the change being responded to; short-term, reversible environmental changes permit a range of responses differing in kind and intensity from those appropriate to long-term changes. People, however, respond only to perceived change, and for most of human existence, perception has been effective only in the short term. Even today, scientists and policy-makers debate spiritedly whether a particular hot summer or mild winter is a harbinger of the greenhouse effect that will entail expensive long-term remedial efforts, or only an exogenous variation around the climatic mean. Long-term changes can only be recognized with hindsight supported by qualitative and quantitative records.

We have already seen that humans have uniquely complex behaviors available for adjusting to environmental changes and constraints. In response to changes in the qualities of both social and natural environments, people employ behavioral strategies that we may group into four sequential categories. This is the *strategy ladder*, whose steps are listed here in the order of increasing social and physical costs (i.e., upside down):

- individual behavioral flexibility,
- spatial mobility,
- innovative technology, and
- manipulation of social complexity.

The selection of any strategy from any of the steps will result in changed relationships between individuals and between persons and their non-human environments. Which strategic step is selected in any given situation is a matter of perception, values, constraints, opportunities, support, and the resources of the actors. The resulting cultural or social change may trigger either improved or deteriorated adaptedness. The outcome is rarely determinable in advance by the actors.

Culture, therefore, cannot be summarized or evaluated separately from the range of strategies practiced by its members, or from the environments they experienced throughout its duration. The ecological contexts of cultures, present or prehistoric, have contributed to the defining characteristics of those cultures. Paleoenvironmental study is essential to an adequate understanding of human cultures and to the knowledge we seek about the operation of cultures. In this context the concept of adaptation has some retrospective usefulness in that the social and natural conditions that human societies and populations have survived have shaped experience and to an undefinable extent imposed constraints on subsequent behavior. "The culture each of us inherits is a summation of coping devices that have proved their worth in the past, but they may not be equally effective in the present" (Netting 1977: 93). The conditions adapted to in the past set limits and define opportunities for the future.

Like cybernetic systems, cultures circulate energy, matter, and information (Flannery 1972). Energy and information are stored in artifactual "matter," the material culture with work potential that archaeologists recover. Material culture preserves clues to former information systems and, by its permanence, influences the forms of the future. Material culture, its spatial relationships, and its ecofactual associations are the observable phenomena available to archaeologists. Behavior, be it thought or action, must be inferred from those proxies.

The task of understanding ancient societies requires more than the descriptive reconstruction of their environments. Difficult as that is, it is inadequate because there is no simple, direct relationship between environment and culture. Archaeologists are groping for methods and theories that will help to specify those aspects of environments to which a particular society or subset is sensitive. Means for discerning the crucial from the coincident associations of environments and cultural systems are still elusive. Archaeologists face the added difficulty that both environment and resources are constructs of particular cultures and technologies, not independent of unique cultural contexts. Thus, again, one confronts the weakness of arguing from present-day analogics. Analytical methods and theories of greater precision and appropriateness are essential if archaeologists are to avoid the logical circularity inherent in this situation as it is now understood.

The ethnographic and ethnological literature offers minimal help in our quandary. "[E]cological analysis requires different kinds of evidence from those anthropologists have usually collected. To understand effective factors in the physical environment may require an accurate knowledge of rainfall, subsurface water, soil types, temperatures, plant varieties, and animal types" (Netting 1977: 83). These data, rarely of interest to ethnographers, are the sort accessible to the environmental archaeologist. Studies in ethnoarchaeology are tending to close this information gap, and bioanthropological studies of energy flow are even more promising for theoretical insights.

Short-term responses

Fundamentally, the human response to perceived changes is no different from that of other animals: all seek a minor adjustment in behavior or surroundings that will return them to the relative comfort of a former state. What is unique to humans is the range and complexity of the strategic choices available to them. Changes that stress a population through increased morbidity or mortality will be perceived as harmful; changes that provide additional resources or that decrease the energetic or other costs of traditional life will be perceived as beneficial. The strategies chosen for responses will vary with the nature of the perceived change (good or bad), the amplitude of the change, the flexibility of established lifestyles, the population structure and density, the amount of diversity in the environment, and the technology available to the group.

The first strategic options utilized in response to perceived change are likely to be conservative and reversible, moving up the ladder of response strategies from behavioral flexibility toward social complexity. They will draw upon the group's established behavioral repertoire, and will tend to minimize both energetic cost and demands for innovation. Such strategies include adjustments of task scheduling and personnel, of the intensity or scheduling of rituals, of the choices among resources sought, of key resource procurement behavior, of exchanged goods, of seasonal settlement patterns or sizes of social groups (by fission, fusion, or emigration), and of technologies by minor innovation or adoption. Short-term strategies, with the exception of emigration, may have very low archaeological visibility; they are local and may be only temporary. Moreover, because changes are likely to exploit the variability already inherent in the cultural system, new elements or new behaviors are rarely involved, only different emphases. Changes in social structure, the costliest strategies, are rarely necessary in the short term because individuals, rather than society, absorb the ill effects. Not until the number of stressed individuals is large enough to complicate normal function will the social structure be adjusted in compensation.

Long-term responses

Responses to long-term changes begin with the same conservative range of strategies that are applied to short-term changes. The difference is that as change endures or intensifies the new strategies become the modal strategies, entailing adjustments throughout the cultural system by positive feedback mechanisms. Once the system has adjusted to a number of changes, it achieves a new state; reversion to a former state is unlikely ever to occur. Also, in periods of continuing environmental change, strategies proliferate and accumulate. Extended response sequences move incrementally toward the expensive end of the strategy ladder. The result is cumulative innovation and technical and social restructuring that establishes, however inadvertently, a new cultural state – an irreversible change.

Over the long term, then, the results may be a gradual reorganization of major cultural subsystems, rather than just the tinkering with technology and scheduling that is immediately perceived by those involved. There may be reorganization of the socially defined habitat as groups expand or contract their territories. Redefinition of resources or reorganization of technology result in changes in the niche, and reorganization of settlement patterns at the regional scale amounts to changes in both niche and habitat. Changes in the habitat itself are likely to occur because of technological applications; an example is the changes in water distribution and life forms that follow from the construction of irrigation canals. Changes which affect the demographic structure of a population result in new ratios among age-grades. Severe morbidity or mortality may change the gene pool. Any of these major changes can impose a complementary reorganization of the social structure.

The chapters ahead offer examples of environmental attributes subject to long-term change requiring human response. Adequate discussion requires special concepts not yet introduced, involving the state and condition of aspects of the biosphere responding to state changes in the other spheres. As a generalization, we can note that any change that increases the spatial heterogeneity or spotty distribution of resources may create local shortages that could induce strategic cultural changes intended to average out the resource base for at least the dominant social groups in an area. Such "spatial averaging" strategies could be based on behavioral changes (e.g., modifications of exchange relations), mobility (movement to crucial resources or range expansion), technological innovations (storing food, adoption of agriculture), or changes in social structure (redefinition of access to resources, as in conquest and tribute).

Because response to any change typically begins conservatively, there is the danger that small-scale, incremental responses to long-term change or to a major infrequent event may be inappropriate in scale or kind. Inappropriate strategic choices, compounded and not offset, can lead to social and economic dysfunction and, ultimately, crisis. Social and economic change, however poorly defined, always precedes such crises. A crisis then may precipitate sudden and massive change, with rapid transformation of both society and culture (Flannery 1972; Renfrew 1979). Such rapid change is typically the result of stress internal to the society; its relationship to external stressors may be difficult to identify because of our inadequate understanding of mechanisms, lag effects, and intervening time or space.

> The fact that choices among a wide range of potential options are made with respect to available and acceptable information is critical, because decisions may be suboptimal, and in the medium- or long-range view they may even be maladaptive. Whether or not we can identify the cognitive dimension in an actual case study, explicit consideration of this variable serves to remind us that there can be no causality between environmental parameters and adaptive patterning and that adaptive response to an exogenic change cannot be uniquely predicted.
>
> BUTZER 1982: 293–294

The result of human adjustment to long-term environmental change, whatever its source, is cultural change, the form of which is not determined by either the initial state or the nature of the stressor. The change is visible in the archaeological record; the causes and processes must be inferred and interpreted.

IMPLICATIONS FOR ENVIRONMENTAL ARCHAEOLOGY

As Karl Butzer has effectively argued, environmental archaeology contributes *context* to the study of past human behavior. The reconstruction of past human environments enables us to recognize some initial conditions of human adaptations as well as changes in those conditions that have provoked adjustments. Knowledge of human environments will not explicate the ultimate causes of human evolution or history, but without detailed knowledge of past environments we cannot aspire to any deep understanding of human behavior. Ecologically grounded interpretations of human behavior are typically richer and more complex than those relying only upon analogical arguments or extrapolations of economic or political theories from observable contemporary circumstances.

The strategic choices that human individuals and communities make in response to changed environmental circumstances are the fundamental issues of anthropology and history. In order to understand them, we must be able to specify the sequence of challenges faced, the range of alternative resources and decisions available, the level of effort expended in implementing the choices made, and the location, within society, of the costs and benefits.

Successful environmental reconstruction enriches our understanding of the environmentally challenging HMA wherever it has occurred. Knowledge of paleoenvironments does not, however, *explain* any case or sequence of adaptive behavior. Archaeologists need to address the outstanding theoretical and methodological problems listed above and repeated here:

- identification of the crucial *variables* in a situation (specification of the "initial conditions");
- identification of *mechanisms* that link variables (the keys to the articulation of systems or subsystems);
- identification and evaluation of *equifinalities* (the many potential processes giving similar results);
- elusiveness of *ideologies* in archaeological materials (the context of decision-making);
- *chronologies* precise enough to permit comparisons between systems and spheres (the key to situational context and systemic mechanisms);
- *preservation* biases in the classes of remains recoverable (loss of some critical categories);
- *recovery* biases in techniques and methodologies (especially sampling).

In recent years, archaeologists have devoted impressive energy and innovation to the development of theories about knowledge of the past. Much less effort has been expended on refinement of the methods by which evidence is extracted from the sediments that enclose it. The last three problem classes are now constraining the realization of archaeology's sophisticated theoretical goals.

Archaeological research has established that hunting and gathering wild foods, the original subsistence mode, supported human life for about 99% of cultural time. Characterized by shared risks and shared bounty, it cannot be judged either ineffective or inefficient. Our species abandoned that mode and has exchanged it, over large areas of the world, for the discontents of urban life and industrialized subsistence. The benefits and risks of life are now unevenly distributed among vastly greater numbers of human beings. That evolution, neither obvious nor inevitable, is well established. How did it happen?

A salvage excavation in northern Syria revealed one part of the answer. At Tell Abu Hureyra excavations revealed a Mesolithic settlement on the banks of the Euphrates River. The gatherer-hunters lived there year-round, collecting plant foods and hunting a few animals in the river valley; once a year, in late April to early May, they staged a large gazelle slaughter as the migratory animals arrived to summer near the river. Eventually the location was abandoned and then resettled by farming people who kept a few sheep and goats but continued the annual gazelle hunt to supply the greater part of their dietary protein. The farmers' middens contain 80% gazelle bones, the same percentage as during the Mesolithic settlement. After about a thousand years, there was a rapid reversal of the percentages; gazelle was only 20% of the total meat bone, and the sheep and goat bones indicated that those animals were herded and managed. The zooarchaeologists found evidence to the south, in modern Jordan, of very large kills of gazelle in their winter range. These kills apparently devastated the herds, which then no longer arrived at Abu Hureyra in large numbers. The northern farmers had reluctantly adopted pastoralism as an essential alternative to the annual hunt. The impetus was human-induced resource shortage, and one response was intensification of a technology that had not been practiced intensively centuries earlier, when it was first available (Legge and Rowley-Conwy 1987).

This example reemphasizes that explanation of cultural behavior requires detailed information about conditions during and antecedent to the behavior of interest. Information is required about the diversity of extant conditions, the scale of changes involved, the mechanisms linking environmental and cultural variables, the timing and sequence of changes, and an awareness of equifinalities. The chapters that follow discuss research strategies and methods that archaeologists can use to collect data of the requisite quality and quantity for the study of past environmental contexts of human actions.

PART II

Chronology

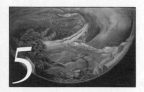

5

INTRODUCTION TO CHRONOMETRY AND CORRELATION

If there is one issue on which nearly all archaeologists can agree, it is the importance of chronology.

DEAN 1978: 223

Archaeology is necessarily about change, and all change is perceived by looking back from the perspective of one's own peculiar place in space and history. The differences perceived between now and then challenge us to explain them, and we try to do that by using assumptions about the world, time, and process.

For example, consider the story of Genesis as presented in the Judeo-Christian Bible. The Bible incorporates a serious effort to explain change from a legendary Golden Age (Eden) to the world of toil and sorrow most of us experience. In asking "How did the world begin?" we are expressing our assumption that there was a beginning, as we observe with every individual life. The Bible's answer is that God created the world in six days, and then rested. The world that God created was not significantly different from the world we see around us, except that it was Good, and the experienced world is not all Good. If the world in all its diversity and complexity did, indeed, come into being in six solar days, then its existence is proof of a Creation, and a Creator. Many people take comfort in that belief. However, geological and astronomical study has led scientists to posit a slow development of life on the planet, requiring over 2 billion years to shape the planet and its biosphere as we know it today. If this is a reasonably accurate statement of how the modern world was derived, it implicates almost continuous creation, which we call evolution, marked by many beginnings and endings (Gould 1989). This example demonstrates that the amount of time elapsed constrains the interpretation of process; the implied rates of change and duration of development in the two cases *require* very different inferences.

In order to organize and analyze events in time, we require concepts and methods for measuring time – chronometry. The concepts of event, duration, and sequence are essential to chronometry; they are at the heart of historical explanation and of prehistory. Events, or small clusters of events, are dated by various chronometric techniques available to the geosciences, according to the kinds of chronometric evidence available in each case. Two events of different ages define a duration, a span of time that has elapsed between them, and they also implicate a sequence because one is necessarily older than the other. **Durations** (spans between events of known age) are measurable only indirectly; their size depends on the accuracy of the event ages. The measurement of durations is crucial to the study of processes and of life.

Sequence (order of events) is the fundamental concept in chronometry. It can be established by a series of dated events or by various other kinds of sequential relationships among events (see below). Events lack historical significance until they can be ordered into a series by some means, and durations cannot even be defined until events are ordered. Sequence, then, is essential, permitting the ordering of events and estimation of durations. With this much information – events, duration, and sequence – we control relative time. With the addition of ages, however calculated, we achieve chronometry and can think about time in defined, comparable units (e.g., years, centuries).

But what, indeed, is "time" itself? Time is perceived only through the observation of processes that can serve as rough measures of elapsed time. Like language and music, perceived time is linear, experienced only moment by moment, not all of a piece. We speak of time in metaphors, rarely stopping to wonder about the concept itself. Metaphors such as distance ("far back in time") and movement ("time flies") define our sense of time; we are seldom aware that some of the metaphors are mutually contradictory. The concept of the linearity of time is supported by chaos theory and contingency, as well as by radioactive decay, in the sense that precedents cannot be reversed, or contexts of events changed without changing the event. However, because this support is partly tautological it cannot help us evaluate the appropriateness of our metaphors. The tautology is illustrated by the observation that although the concept of time travel is a theoretical possibility in a linear paradigm, it is impossible if time is irreversible (Bailey 1983).

Because we can only think about "time" as it is experienced through some external system of measurement, all expressions of time, past or future, are relative to the rates and ratios of the measurement systems we use. We utilize decay rates, pulse rates, revolution rates, and growth rates, as well as ratios such as the proportions of sand or water in an hourglass, of radioactive to stable isotopes, and of decay products to their parent material. Contrary to some regrettable terminology frequently encountered in introductory textbooks of archaeology (the purported contrast between relative and "absolute" time), *all* time is relative. We have no absolute measurements. Relativity theory has shown that even clocks and calendars are relative cultural concepts (see Bailey 1983). Time exists only as a duration which we can measure against some process or other.

In the historical sciences, the crucial chronological data are sequential relationships and durations. Dealing with events and processes, we ask such questions as:

- Did event A precede or follow event B; that is, is A older or younger than B, or are they synchronous? These are questions about sequence.
- Did process X (or event A) continue longer than process Y (event B)? These are questions about duration.

Given answers, we can then estimate durations and rates of processes and of historical sequences, essential first steps to explanations. Estimates of rates and durations require refined chronologies composed of ordered series (sequences) of small comparable increments of time; none of these relationships requires for its understanding direct measures of calendrical or sidereal time.

MEASURING TIME

The phenomena we use to measure time (**chronometers**) have different basic characteristics that make them useful in that role. Their chronometric characteristics may be *cyclical, serial,* or *progressive.*

- Cyclical chronometers are essentially planetary and celestial phenomena. For millennia, people have observed cycles of day and night and of the seasons, as well as the apparent movement of stars and planets, and have kept records of their changes and reappearances. Each cycle has a characteristic duration, and few of them are in phase with each other. Astronomers today track the movements of stars and galaxies and measure their cycles against atomic time. We also track and time subatomic cycles, and use those to create chronometers of unparalleled precision. Cyclical time is best for measuring durations.
- Serial chronometers depend upon the construction or knowledge of a series of unrelated or discrete events. Thus we relate some event to another, and thereby give it an approximate age and chronological equivalence or priority in relation to

others. References to events in such contexts as "in the Kennedy administration," "in gravel lens C," "in January," "before Joe was born," are references to unconnected serial events that nevertheless represent relative time. The series must be recorded or memorized to establish its sequence, and thereby its broader continuing usefulness.

- Progressive chronometers measure time as rates or ratios of phenomena subject to regular change. The changes may or may not have finite limits. Examples of finite progressions that are good chronometers include biological aging and radioactive decay. Radioactive accumulations, chemical changes, and stylistic changes are less finite but essentially linear phenomena that provide useful measures of time.

These many different systems of time measurement are not closely compatible. Think of the differences between the regular lengths of Moon months (counted as cycles of Moon phases as viewed from the Earth) in comparison to the calendar "months" which are unequal divisions of a solar year, compensating for the fact that 12 lunar cycles are completed in less than one solar year. Similar disharmonies between the rates or intervals of any two systems of time measurement are expectable. Even two systems based on annual increments, one biological (tree growth rings) and one geological (varve sequences), may fail to produce precisely comparable chronologies, because of inherent irregularities. Radiocarbon years are well known to be not always equal to solar years (see below); the rate of **obsidian** hydration changes with temperature and therefore the amount of hydration varies per solar year, and so on with many other methods. In order to compare any two or more of the large number of chronometers available, we must convert, correlate, or **calibrate** the incremental or ratio measures of age or duration to a standard; the standard of choice is calendar years, an approximation to sidereal time.

Sidereal time ("star" time) is a convenient and relatively precise convention with considerable heuristic value. As occupants of the third planet revolving around our star, the Sun, our bodies and minds have become accustomed to it. Star time provides a way of defining and measuring increments of time that are independent of almost every other phenomenon we measure chronologically, so that every rate or process that interests us can be expressed in units of star time (day, season, year), and thereby be compared directly with any other rate or process. Because of the centrality which such time expressions have gained in our thinking about time, measures of time that are precisely translatable into sidereal years are elevated in our esteem. Archaeologists' habitual preference for "dates" over "ages" seems to derive from our socialization to sidereal years as enshrined in calendars. This cultural preference is incompatible with the imprecision inherent in most archaeological chronometers.

It is crucial to bear in mind that there are constraints upon the **accuracy** and precision of all chronometric methods. Accuracy is a statement about the degree to which a measurement approximates an abstract, absolute standard – its "truth." Precision is a statement about the fineness of resolution of a measurement, or its replicability in repeated measurements (R. E. Taylor 1987: 106). A measure can be accurate and not precise, as in "Anne was born in 1940" (the correct year), as well as precise and not accurate, as in "Anne was born at 1:34 A.M. on July 1, 1943." While the ideal is an age statement that is both accurate and precise, in both archaeology and the geosciences one must balance the ideal against the possible. An awareness of the different potentials for accuracy and precision in various measurements of time is essential to good problem definition and clear thinking. In archaeological time-measurement we can settle for accuracy without precision when we are trying to arrange things in sequence. Precision is necessary when the degree of contemporaneity, or the fine-scale ordering of events, is at issue, as is the case in detailed studies of cultural processes. Precision without accuracy is always to be avoided.

Although archaeologists borrow most of their techniques of time measurement from the geosciences, the scale of time resolution desirable for most archaeological applications is much finer than what satisfies geologists and other Earth scientists. *Geological time* is typically measured in millennia or larger intervals, so that "± a million years" still makes sense to geologists, whereas in archaeology it is difficult to use such an interval even to think about the physical evolution of hominids. Archaeologists should try to achieve time intervals at scales that have some meaning in human societies; for *cultural time*, even a radiocarbon century is a bit coarse. Given the uncertainties and approximations of archaeological deposits and available chronometric methods, time intervals of less than a century can rarely be perceived. Therefore, problem formulations that require the *social time* of decades rarely fit archaeological data sets at all well. Archaeological time, in the context of the geosciences, requires high-frequency **resolution** (the potential for precision; the property of being reducible to equivalent units); that in turn entails pushing the available technologies to their limits in rigorous and imaginative ways (Table 5.1).

CALIBRATION

Calibration is the expression of one kind of measurement in terms of another, to establish equivalences. For example, measurements based on rates and ratios are expressed relative to various other processes independent of them; the preferred calibration standard is sidereal time. All chronometric methods have inherent uncertainties, and some inherit uncertainties from others with the calibrations. The uncertainties and ambiguities of chronometric methods are such that the best results

Table 5.1 Exponential scales in time with chronometric methods of appropriate precision

Temporal scales	Duration or frequency (a = yr)		Chronometric resolution
Mega-	$>10^6$	($>$1 ma)	K/Ar; paleomagnetism
Macro-	10^4–10^6	(10 ka–1 ma)	^{14}C; TL; ESR; K/Ar; fission tracks; U-series; paleomagnetism; obsidian hydration
Meso-	10^2–10^4	(0.1 ka–10 ka)	^{14}C; dendrochronology; TL; ESR; U-series; obsidian hydration; fission tracks; varves; archaeomagnetism
Micro-	$<10^2$	(0.001 ka–0.1 ka $<$ a century)	calendars; dendrochronology; ice layers; archaeomagnetism; (radiocarbon indeterminacy)

will be obtained when it is possible to use more than one technique to estimate the age of a particular event.

Each technique brings its own particular uncertainties and limitations, and its own calibration problems, but in combination there is strength. Even if chronometric results in a suite fail to correlate precisely, they make possible a rough estimate of the error factors involved in the comparisons (Aitken 1990; Betancourt 1987; Browman 1981; Tooley 1981). Archaeologists typically have preferred simple, single answers about age to multiple estimates that force evaluation of error sources, even when the first choice conceals large errors. We consider calibration further in the sections on particular methods.

The accuracy of clocks and calendars is achieved by definition; units are not precisely coterminous with any natural process, but are cultural conventions. We are reminded of the non-equivalence of the Hebrew, Chinese, and Roman-derived calendrical systems by colorful New Year's celebrations in different months. The elaborate and precise Mayan calendar, based on several astronomical cycles, "floated" unlinked to the conventions of Western calendars for many frustrating decades of research. Calendars themselves require calibration. The familiar annual calendar used in the Western world must be adjusted every four years by the addition of an extra day to keep it synchronous with the Earth's positions in its orbit around the Sun.

Cross-dating and correlation

The most desirable archaeological data are those that permit the recognition of discrete events, rather than palimpsets of the remains of many commingled events.

The goal in cross-dating and correlation is to relate an event in one context to an event in another. Jeffrey Dean defined a typology of events that is helpful in thinking about dating in archaeology (Dean 1978: 226–228). He calls those events of ultimate archaeological interest "target events"; these are the cultural or behavioral events whose age we wish to know. The event that provides the information about age is the "dated event," such as the death of a tree for tree-ring or radiocarbon dating. Fundamentally important to the dating enterprise is the conceptual distinction between the target and dated events; they are rarely identical. Only these two of Dean's four-class scheme will be used here.

Environmental reconstruction requires accurate correlations and cross-dating in order to compare events recorded in different universes of data. Again, relative age (sequence) is the critical information needed to establish chronological equivalence or priority. When events are separated in space, and therefore cannot be directly compared in terms of a single related event, cross-dating is required. Comparisons across space are facilitated by chronometers that are easily calibrated, such as radiometric techniques, tree rings, volcanic ash falls, or cultural associations (all of which represent relatively small spans of geological time). Calendars are important only as devices for comparison and calibration – for relating past events to our present sense of time.

The correlation of archaeological or geological deposits from one exposure to another can be accomplished by several different means. The best is continuous exposure, with sections and plans connecting two or more areas, but this is rare in archaeological excavation even at the site scale. Depositional units can be correlated by comparing the sedimentary structure, texture, chemistry, and the included fossils and cultural materials between the individual units (Part V). Because sediments have lateral extent, all of the above characteristics can change within a sedimentary unit that nevertheless retains integrity, thereby introducing a major complication. The geological concept of **facies** is helpful here – change of depositional environment within the same depositional episode. Note that adjacent archaeological profiles separated by baulks technically require correlation or cross-dating; they cannot automatically be considered equivalent while they are discontinuously exposed.

Artifactual cross-dating has a long and honorable history in archaeological chronologies, although its pitfalls are only now being fully realized (see the case study on pp. 132–135). Fundamental to the method is the demonstrable and repeated observation that styles of artifacts change through time. Objects of roughly the same age are most alike; the longer the time span between the production of two items, the less similar they are likely to be. On the assumption (rarely demonstrated and equally rarely tested) that items are reliably incorporated into archaeological deposits shortly after the time of their manufacture, archaeologists infer the synchroneity (coevality) of deposits that contain similar artifacts. The development of chronometric methods independent of artifacts has exposed the uncertainties, and sometimes the circular logic, on which long-distance correlations were assumed and cross-dates asserted (e.g., Hardy and Renfrew 1990; A. C. Renfrew 1973).

Similarly, the assumption that similar pollen assemblages can be used to establish the contemporaneity of stratigraphic units separated by space carries its own pitfalls, but has proven to be a valuable foundation for working hypotheses. The more complex and unique the pollen assemblages compared, the stronger the basis for the inference of equivalent age, with the additional caveat that the strength of the inference is negatively correlated with the spatial distances involved in the cross-dating.

Faunal materials offer special possibilities for cross-dating, and carry their own particular sources of error. The distance mobility of animals is related to their size, their environmental tolerances, and their means of locomotion; their usefulness for cross-dating cannot be separated from those characteristics. The presence or absence of faunal species in archaeological deposits rarely can provide chronological resolution within a millennium. Faunal cross-dating is most useful in the broad expanses of geological time, when millennia matter little, or in those instances of introduced species when the time of introduction can be reliably known. The case of the sixteenth-century Spanish introduction of horses to the Americas is an example of such an event; the introduction of the European rat to the New World, or to the British Isles by Romans, are other potentially datable events that can cross-date archaeological deposits.

Volcanic ash (**tephra**) may be carried by wind or water for great distances from its sources in volcanic vents; indeed, when ash is injected high into the atmosphere, it may travel around the globe several times before settling to Earth. Individual ash sources, and sometimes the products of individual explosions, are identifiable by their chemical or physical signatures. Their appearance in stratigraphic contexts permits cross-dating by "tephrochronology." Ash fall events are datable by means of radiocarbon, dendrochronology, thermoluminescence, potassium–argon, obsidian hydration, or fission-track dating (see below). When dated ash falls can be identified at distant points, they carry direct chronometric information and provide cross-dates at the event scale, sometimes less than a year.

Archaeologists and geoscientists have available a wide range of methods for determining age. Choice among them must depend upon the materials available and the problems addressed. The following brief summaries touch upon several kinds of chronometers that measure rates and durations in past time. All but the first group,

seasonal clocks and biological rhythms, give coarse resolutions for historical problems at the human scale.

SEASONAL CLOCKS AND BIOLOGICAL RHYTHMS

Time measurement methods derive ultimately from the natural cycles of the planet –
the alternation of day and night and of the seasons. Organisms of the biosphere are
sensitive to all these normal dynamic conditions of life. When biological responses to
these cycles accumulate without interruption, they can be interpreted to measure
duration and sequence at time scales familiar to us as fellow organisms of the planet.

Dendrochronology

Dendrochronology is the most precise chronometric method available to archaeology (Baillie 1995; Dean 1978), providing dates closely correlated to sidereal years,
sometimes even seasonal fractions of years. The method is based upon recording the
proportional widths of annual growth rings in climatically sensitive trees and then
matching pattern sequences from tree to tree back in time from a known year.
Chronosequences are created by matching "signature" sets of rings between trees of
different ages, to extend sequences back into the past (Fig. 5.1).

   Trees grow outward in annual increments, adding a sheath around the entire
tree just beneath the bark. In temperate zone trees, "early wood" composed of large
cells is emplaced by rapid spring growth. The "late wood" near the end of the
growing season has thicker and tougher cell walls. Trees are dormant during the
cold or dry season because growth is prevented by the fall of leaves or other mechanisms such as insufficient water or low temperatures. The following year's early
wood normally presents a visible contrast to the cells from the end of the previous
growth season.

Growth stressors

Ring widths vary according to (1) the growth conditions of the environment and (2)
the age and (3) size of the tree. In years with abundant water and sunlight rings are
relatively wide. Rings are narrow on young shoots, wider afterward, and narrower
again on large mature trees, because of the changing ratio of leaves to wood mass,
and therefore food available for growth. Ring widths also narrow with height, as distance from the roots increases. Trees growing in conditions where light and moisture
vary little from year to year develop rings closely similar in width, called "complacent" rings. In the American Southwest, where dendrochronology has long been an

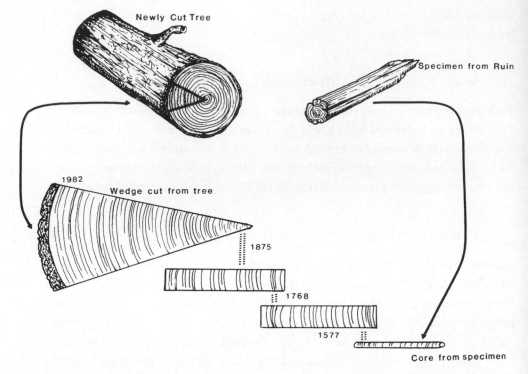

Figure 5.1   Schematic of chronosequence building in dendrochronology. See text for explanations. (Reproduced from Cordell 1984: Fig. 2.4 with permission of the illustrator, Dr. Charles M. Carrillo.)

important component of archaeological research, trees receive abundant sunlight; they are sensitive to (stressed by) varying rainfall. Elsewhere, inadequate sunlight can be a significant stressor, especially at high latitudes, where it is expressed as seasonal differences in insolation and temperature. The construction of dendrochronological sequences requires trees that respond to stressors at the regional scale, so that matches can be made over distance (Grissino-Mayer 1995). Very local stressors, such as earthquakes, slope changes related to landslip, and insect defoliation have subregional effects that must be interpreted to permit correct reading of ring sequences. Insect defoliation can halt growth in midseason, giving a narrow ring or a split ring if growth resumes later in the summer.

Tree death, the termination of growth of an individual tree, is the main dated event for dendrochronology. It is best marked by wood with bark adhering, secondarily by the **sapwood** directly beneath the bark. The relationship of tree death to any archaeological target event must be independently established (Baillie 1995; Dean 1978).

Methods

Tree-ring records are collected as wedges, slabs or cores, taken perpendicular to the bark. The surface to be read is planed or trimmed with a razor before counting. Ring-width plotting is the preferred method in arid zones (Fig. 5.1). Thin-sections are prepared for X-ray densitometry, a promising new technique in cool, wet environments where ring growth is typically complacent and the wood is waterlogged. Densitometry measures the varying density of cellulose in rings.

Counting is not a simple, straightforward matter. Rings may fail to form, or be doubled, under some conditions of stress. Wetland species are prone to ring complacency. We have noted that ring width varies over the life of the tree, independent of the regional variance, so that ring widths cannot be directly compared from tree to tree. Ring-matchers must disregard the actual widths of rings in favor of recording their relative widths and patterned clusters; a variety of techniques have been used, with electronic ones now dominating. The heart of the method is pattern-recognition; the actual physiological mechanisms creating the contrasting widths are complex and poorly understood. Short-term regional climatic variation is the basis for the patterned signatures that permit matching.

Ring matches are done not on the wood itself, but usually by scanning computer. Ring records are normalized to screen out life-cycle variation in order to create data of regional relevance (Baillie 1995; Parker et al. 1984: 216–217). Long-term regional trends are of interest mainly to climatologists (see Chapter 8); they may be statistically isolated in order to facilitate the construction of supraregional chronologies.

Regional chronologies

The time spans applicable for dendrochronology are controlled by regional preservation conditions, of which there are many kinds: roofed buildings; arid climates; saturated environments (bogs, lakes and rivers, ocean, anaerobic alluvium); charred wood; chilled wood (e.g., Arctic, high elevations). The ideal situation for establishing dendrochronologies is the recovery of multiple specimens of species sensitive to regional climatic variation, as exemplified in the arid Southwest and in the bogs of Western Europe and the British Isles.

Regional chronologies have been established in many parts of the temperate zones (Baillie and Brown 1988; Becker 1993). The first and for years the longest was the bristlecone pine sequence from the White Mountains of southern California, over 8000 years long. The oak chronologies of Ireland and Central Europe have now surpassed it, with over 11,000 years recognized in some areas (Becker 1993). The famous archaeological chronologies of the southwestern United States consist of many small regional sequences of varying lengths, few longer than a thousand years.

The southwestern American sequences are compiled from piñon pine and Douglas fir timbers from ruins, and bristlecone pine from mountain slopes. Red cedar is valued in the eastern United States because of its preservation and ubiquity, but it is relatively complacent (Stahle and Wolfman 1985). West European sequences use mainly oak, which is also preferred for sequences compiled from old furniture, building timbers, and painted wooden panels.

Applications

Dendrochronology is a useful tool for architectural history and art history, where its use is fairly straightforward since the specimens are usually closely related to the target event. Archaeological applications are often more complex and demanding. The target events are typically construction dates and use-spans of structures; for these applications, original timbers and repair timbers are sought, whose dated events are times of death (cutting). In dry and arctic climates, where dead trees may be useful construction timbers and fuel over many decades, problems proliferate. As for radiocarbon dates, the contextual integrity and cultural relevance of the sampled rings must be demonstrated on site (Baillie 1995; Dean 1978; Parker et al. 1984), and include sapwood to maximize precision and association.

Varves

The chronometric advantages of both stratigraphy (see below) and tree rings are combined in **varves**, annual increments of bottom sediments in certain lakes of the arctic and temperate zones. Annual laminations of lake-bed sediment, with typically a lighter-colored increment deposited in spring and summer and a darker layer in the winter, are usually thoroughly mixed by bottom-dwelling (benthic) invertebrate animals and by vertical circulation of water. However, lakes deep enough for the bottoms to be below the seasonal turnovers, and with oxygen deficits severe enough to inhibit benthic fauna, retain the laminations. Paired laminae may be formed in different ways, each of which produces a variant of the summer:winter contrast in sediments that receive a spring–summer influx of coarse material such as diatoms, calcareous or iron-rich sediment, and mineral sediments. The dark winter layers are formed by fine organic detritus deposited from suspension while the lake is sealed under ice. These seasonal rhythmites, or varves, retain the associations of all the material settling to the bottom of the lake, and offer annual resolution within the deposits, rather as tree rings do. Series as long as 13,000 years have been compiled (Stuiver et al. 1986).

Varves are utilized for fine-resolution chronology by palynologists and limnologists. Under ideal conditions, varve widths can vary as a climate signal with wet or warm summers giving thicker varves, permitting correlation of sequences from lake to lake. In this way, varve sequences have provided significant chronologies for Late Glacial events in Europe and North America.

Varved sediments, formed in the centers of deep lakes, rarely include archaeological materials, but nevertheless can be very informative about human activities in the watersheds. A notable example is Crawford Lake, Ontario, where maize pollen recognized in a core led to the discovery of significant late-prehistoric Iroquoian occupations on the windward side of the lake, and permitted the close dating of the maize, of woodland clearance episodes, and the integration of the pollen-core data with human activities (McAndrews and Boyko-Diskonow 1989). Studies of a varved lake in Finland have revealed a detailed picture and chronology of several episodes of land clearance and farming (cited in Saarnisto 1986). Varve studies produce high-resolution data on such environmental changes as fire frequency, disturbance by land-clearing, and eutrophication (oxygen depletion by phosphate enrichment) of lakes.

Ice accumulation banding

Analogous to varves in the manner of accumulation and study is the annual banding in glacier ice, observed at high latitudes and altitudes (Baumgartner et al. 1989). Deep cores drawn from the Greenland and Antarctic ice sheets, and from mountain glaciers in Peru and China, show annual banding defined by seasonal differences in accumulation on the snow fields. As the fallen snow turns to ice, the bands retain sufficient integrity to be traced to great depths in the glacier. Atmospheric dust and other contaminants permit some radiocarbon dates for calibration, with sufficient success that now, in heavily studied cores, reliance is placed not on radiocarbon but on counts of annual bands, which are defined by several different criteria (Hammer 1989). Such real-year counts make the ice-core chronologies potentially synchronous with **astronomical time**.

Volcanic dust layers and other unique event records support extension of ice dates to special cases far removed from the glaciers. The principal phenomena dated are changes in atmospheric circulation and temperatures, which reflect climate relevant to large areas (e.g., Mayewski et al. 1994; Thompson et al. 1990). Precision to single years is claimed in special circumstances, increasingly supported by multiple criteria isolating annual accumulations and by cross-checking adjacent cores (Thompson 1991).

STRATIFICATION AND STRATIGRAPHY

The only truth is stratification.

D. F. DINCAUZE

In archaeology, as in most of the field sciences, the basic method for establishing and measuring chronological relationships is **stratigraphy**. Stratigraphic relationships, properly handled, are the least ambiguous and arguably the most accurate of all time measurements available to archaeologists – they represent sequence, irreversible order. In addition, they are capable of relating to each other highly disparate kinds of data – in fact, the entire range of data that can occur within sedimentary matrices. Thus, mineral sediments, soils, pollen and plant macrofossils, micro- and macrofaunal remains, artifacts, features, and human remains can be related chronologically to each other to the extent that they co-occur and can be observed in the same stratified sediments. Co-occurrence of this sort is the firmest basis on which to establish sequence and synchroneity of data, and therefore of the events represented by those data. For this reason, "stratigraphic analysis . . . is the starting point for all palæoenvironmental reconstructions" (Tooley 1981: 47). It is crucial, therefore, that some fundamental concepts of stratigraphic analysis be established clearly right at the beginning.

Stratification is the record of past events, processes, and states preserved as phenomena and relationships in sediments. Stratigraphy is a record of the interpretation of stratification by a stratigrapher. These distinctions, although often ignored by archaeologists, are crucial, because no effort to understand can succeed if data are confused with interpretation. Stratigraphic plans and profiles, which are recording devices, encode the interpretations given to observations made in the field; they cannot be considered or interpreted as if they objectively represent field phenomena. As recording devices, they represent what observers were aware of seeing, and what they thought about their observations, including judgments about relevance, priority, scale, order, and diversity. Photographs record what the photographer aimed at, with technological limits on phenomena recorded; color and texture are not reliably recorded on film. Stratigraphic records reduce three-dimensional phenomena to two-dimensional pictures or to the linearity of language. By their nature such records must be selective, and therefore they represent an incomplete record of the complexity of field situations.

There is no reason to be apologetic or defensive about the fact of an interpretational screen intervening between phenomena and record; what is crucial to field science is an awareness of this screen, and a constant, conscious effort to make it as transparent as possible. To this end, archaeologists, like other field scientists, need to become self-conscious about their roles as stratigraphers – selectors and recorders of data. The simple acceptance of the principle that younger sediments overlie older ones does little justice to the complexities of either field situations or the translation of observation to interpretation within human minds (Ager 1993; Barker 1993; Stein 1987). Geologists have developed international standards for stratigraphic conventions and terminology (nomenclature), ratified by practicing scientists and observed by all who wish to communicate clearly. The terminology is changed and developed with need. Archaeologists should be aware of these standards, should use them when appropriate, and should refrain from arbitrary reinvention of stratigraphic terms and concepts (Farrand 1984; Gasche and Tunca 1983).

However, a basic distinction in stratigraphical practice must be made between geological and cultural stratification. The difference derives from the agents of transport and deposition, as well as from the environment of deposition. Discriminating between geological and cultural deposits is not always a simple matter, but it is crucial to archaeological interpretations (Stein 1987). In many sites, the two kinds of deposition and transformation processes may have alternated through time but, clearly, they must be distinguished if the sequence of events at a site is to be understood. Stratified archaeological sites normally involve both kinds of deposition, as, for instance, when human occupational debris is buried by river flood deposits, sand dunes, hillside slumping, or cave deposits. Outside of urban contexts, it is rare to find deposits that are entirely products of human transport and deposition. Cultural materials are more typically embedded intricately within natural deposits, and their interpretation entails understanding the relationship between the geological and cultural events that combined to create the stratification.

Stratigraphy

Stratigraphic units include *deposits* that are the result of discrete depositional events and processes, *erosional or constructional interruptions* (unconformities, pits, and walls) and the *interfaces* they define, and the lateral *gradations* that indicate a change in depositional environments over space ("facies" to geologists). Each of these units must be understood in three dimensions and recorded in such a way that the dimensional relationships can be understood by someone who did not see them *in situ* (Harris 1989). Because sedimentation is typically episodic, stratification is likely to be incomplete in the sense of not recording an unbroken sequence of events. Episodes of non-deposition and erosion separate episodes of deposition. Any assumption of steady rates of deposition must be tested, since rare and large-scale events are important in compiling the sedimentary record.

A deposit is an irreducible component of stratification, the result of a discrete event or episode of accumulation. The discreteness of a deposit must be observed, evaluated, and demonstrated *in the field*; it cannot be unambiguously reconsidered after excavation. Interfaces, including the interfaces that bound archaeological features whether destructional (pits) or constructional (walls), are equally important units of stratigraphy. The relationships of interfaces to all their contiguous deposits must also be clarified in the field, and recorded explicitly. The process of excavation, ideally, isolates every deposit and interface descriptively. There are many correct ways to do this, depending upon the nature of the deposits and the goal of the excavator, but there are an even greater number of incorrect ways to excavate and record archaeological phenomena. Progress has been made in rationalizing techniques of excavation and recording (Barker 1993; Harris 1989); everyone going into the field should be familiar with the most recent discussions of methods, in order not to repeat old errors. The conventional square, flat-floored archaeological excavation units usually include parts of more than one deposit. Unless the deposits are carefully discriminated in the field and recorded in standardized formats, there is the real danger of conflation of deposits and excavation units, resulting in confusion regarding the formation of deposits and their chronological relationships. Vigilance is required to clarify relationships in the field at every opportunity. Interpretation should be nearly continuous, in order that conflation be recognized and corrected as soon as possible.

Of course, neither depositional units nor excavation units can be assumed to be coterminous with units of cultural activity at archaeological sites, or to represent event-scale phenomena. Interfaces may sometimes have that quality, but deposits may occur over units of time varying from the instantaneous to the millennial. When a deposit or interface represents an episode of construction (walls, floors, etc.) or destruction (e.g., pit digging), the relationship between cultural event and depositional event may be very close. However, with natural deposits, or mixtures of cultural and natural deposits, the relationship must be teased out for each case.

The contents of individual deposits may vary greatly, even when the sedimentary materials themselves vary little. Deposits may include redeposited materials unrelated in origin to events or circumstances contemporary with the deposit itself. Cultural materials may be displaced across depositional boundaries by postdepositional processes, moving up or down across sedimentary units. Thus, the content and the matrix must be separately analyzed and their congruence evaluated (Barker 1993; Gasche and Tunca 1983; Harris 1989; Villa and Courtin 1983). Ideally, this is done without logical circularity so that the interpretations can be complementary rather than dependent.

Sampling in stratigraphy

If stratigraphic relationships are to yield their store of chronological information, they must be properly recorded; a crucial aspect of recording is sampling (Chapter 2). Samples are isolates taken from stratigraphic contexts in order that they may be minutely scrutinized and subjected to special analytical techniques. Sampling strategies must be integral parts of the research plan from the beginning. Everyone with responsibility for the field work and laboratory study (that includes everyone involved in the project) must understand what samples are needed, why they are needed, and how they are to be selected and handled. Materials removed from the field lose their representational value unless the purpose of sampling is reflected in the choice and handling (labeling, packaging, and storing) of samples.

Samples must be *adequate* for the intended analytical purposes (in size, target, and frequency), *discrete* (representing isolated sedimentary units), and carefully and fully *documented*. It follows that consultation between laboratory technicians and the field personnel is the best basis for field practice in sampling. The adequacy of a sample depends upon its being representative of the phenomena of interest, a relationship that can only be determined in the field (Fig. 5.2). It must be large enough to support the analytical techniques to which it will be subjected, and there must be a sufficient number of samples to assure comparability among the various site contexts.

Samples taken for any purpose are best when selected from within discrete stratigraphic units; the analytical resolution of a sample is compromised whenever stratigraphic boundaries are crossed. This concept will be encountered in various guises in the substantive chapters that follow (the exceptions for micromorphology are discussed in Part V). Discreteness has important implications for the kinds of interpretations that can be made from sample studies, and the problems may be very subtle. An example from pollen zone chronology exemplifies some of the complexities: "When comparing pollen zone boundaries that have been dated radiometrically, there is the problem that sample thicknesses [from cores] have varied, thereby increasing or decreasing the age range of material dated" (Tooley 1981: 17). Samplers selecting materials for dating must be alert to identify the range of contaminants that may affect the intended dating techniques, and for indications of stratigraphic disturbances that may have displaced materials. The discreteness and integrity of any sampling site is best considered a working hypothesis to be scrupulously tested both in the field and in the laboratory.

In interdisciplinary studies, field sampling requires close collaboration between specialists in the several disciplines, in order that samples be relatable across disciplines. Specialists in the different disciplines should be in the field together in order

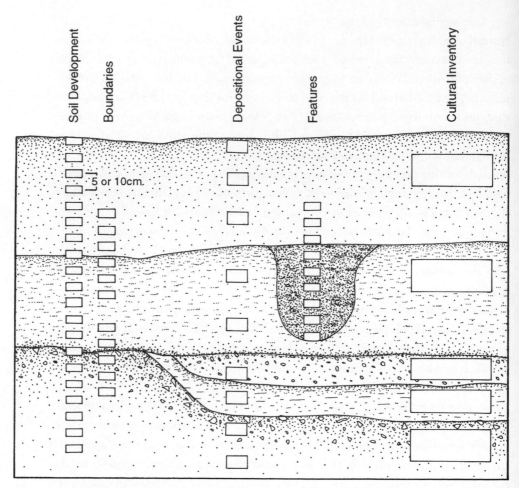

Figure 5.2   Sampling locations on an archaeological section. Five different sampling strategies are exemplified: collecting data for soil development, depositional boundaries,
depositional events, constructional features, and cultural inventories. Note that each
strategy requires special sample sizes and locations. The rectangles are proportional
to the sample sizes needed for different purposes; the smallest samples require
ca. 200 g. The soil development sample column on the left represents the case of a
single deep soil formation with multiple cultural surfaces. The buried soils shown on
the several surfaces each require its own sample series at smaller scale. (After Stein
1985: Fig. 1.)

to take samples closely and significantly related to each other (splits; adjacents), and to relate the different samples to the microstratigraphic controls (Fig. 5.2).

CHRONOMETRY BASED ON DIAGENETIC CHANGES

Diagenesis, the suite of chemical and physical processes by which organic and inorganic materials become rock, provides a number of ways by which relative and chronometric ages can be estimated. The rates of the several processes are closely dependent upon immediate environmental conditions and long-term climatic states, and so all must be calibrated if they are to yield information about time.

Organic and inorganic changes during diagenesis

The mineral and organic fractions of bones and shells (discussed further in Part VII) make possible a range of chemical dating techniques that can establish the relative ages of bone and shell within deposits, and sometimes between them. Such relative dating techniques are based on exchanges between buried organic tissues and minerals and various constituents of the sedimentary matrices surrounding them.

Bones buried in the earth are either leached and disintegrated into their constituent molecules and elements, or they become fossilized by mineral exchanges with groundwater. The rates by which these processes occur vary according to the density of bone, the duration of burial, the availability of groundwater, the temperature regime, and the chemistry of the soils and groundwater. Bones in the same place, buried for comparable lengths of time, should have roughly comparable rates of mineral exchange or disintegration. This principle is used to establish relative ages of bone materials in cases where other methods are not applicable, or where controversy surrounding finds has justified or required multiple avenues of research.

Fluorine and uranium, widespread in natural sediments and soils, are carried by groundwater and exchanged for some of the original constituents of the bone mineral hydroxyapatite. Their concentration can be measured by a variety of chemical and physical means and compared with that of other bones in the same deposits. Strong contrasts between bones in apparent association within a deposit imply that some of the material was added at different times, subsequent to deposition of the matrix. The infamous Piltdown Man hoax was exposed in this way (Weiner 1955).

The loss of organic components of bone, essentially the collagen, can be measured roughly by the remaining constituent nitrogen. Highly variable from one context to another, and from one tissue to another, such loss is a progressive and irreversible process, the development of which can be compared to other material to approximate relative ages.

These chemical methods are at their best in assessing relative contemporaneity, exposing mixtures of materials, and sorting out difficult stratigraphic situations. In such applications they are comparable to aminostratigraphy and obsidian hydration techniques (below). However, they are less suitable for calibration, since rates of change vary with the original material, age, temperature, groundwater, and other highly variable conditions of the soils. They cannot, therefore, provide independent rate-based estimates of calendar time.

Amino-acid racemization dating

The proteins that comprise living organisms are themselves made up of chains of amino acids, of which there are many kinds. Amino-acid molecules are built around a central carbon atom, with other atoms or atom groups attached to it at various angles in three dimensions. Most amino-acid molecules are capable of asymmetry: they can occur as mirror images ("stereoisomers"), with left ("L") and right ("D") versions that can be distinguished in polarized light. In living organisms the L form predominates; over time after burial the molecules change to the D form by a process called **racemization**. Thus the ratio of D to L forms ("isomers") increases with time, tending toward equality, and can be measured by gas or liquid chromatography. More complicated amino acids with larger molecules undergo a related change, producing converted forms that differ in some physical properties from the originals; these can also be measured as ratios that increase in time (Rutter et al. 1985; Wehmiller 1984). However, the changes are not simply dependent on time: temperature strongly affects racemization rates, and other complications are involved (Aitken 1990: 204–214; chapters in Hare et al. [1980]).

Because time and temperature are major factors in these chemical changes, isomeric ratios and racemization rates are utilized as measures either of time since death of an organism, or of the average temperature conditions affecting the buried remains. For these purposes, it is fortunate that different amino acids have different racemization rates. The amino acids most used are aspartic acid, leucine, and isoleucine; their different conversion rates result in different potential dating spans. Furthermore, the several rates may be used as internal checks against each other where rates overlap. The potential for amino-acid racemization dating is best in the meso- and macro-ranges, limited by contamination or the attainment of D:L equilibrium (Fig. 5.3). Recent work in shorter time spans shows significant promise at decadal scales in special conditions (Hare et al. 1997: 281–286). The analytical method requires only a very small (but

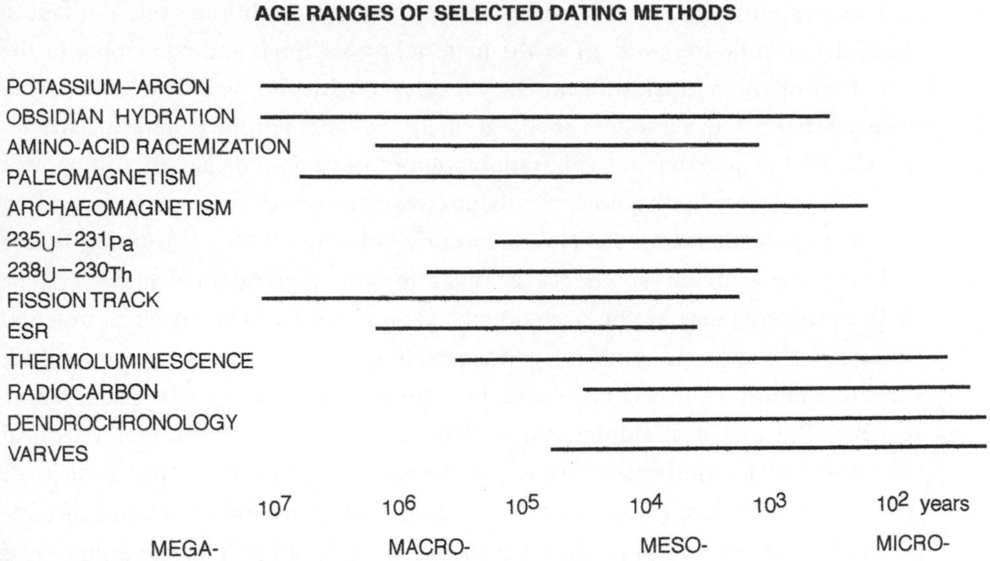

AGE RANGES OF SELECTED DATING METHODS

POTASSIUM–ARGON

OBSIDIAN HYDRATION

AMINO-ACID RACEMIZATION

PALEOMAGNETISM

ARCHAEOMAGNETISM

$235_U - 231_{Pa}$

$238_U - 230_{Th}$

FISSION TRACK

ESR

THERMOLUMINESCENCE

RADIOCARBON

DENDROCHRONOLOGY

VARVES

10^7 10^6 10^5 10^4 10^3 10^2 years

MEGA-   MACRO-   MESO-   MICRO-

Figure 5.3   Age ranges of selected dating methods. These ranges are subject to change with technical development. The spans shown are approximately those of Aitken (1990).

representative) sample of organic material, ca. 5 mg, depending upon the material employed. Laboratory comparisons have demonstrated a reasonably high level of replicability (precision) in the analyses involved to establish D:L ratios (McCoy 1987).

The application of amino-acid racemization to the dating of organic materials such as bone and shell is a secondary application of an analytical method that is mainly used to establish paleotemperatures. The method is quite successful in estimating the average temperature conditions for a buried sample of organic material, once the age of that material can be determined independently. For dating applications, however, departures from the simplifying assumptions of the method introduce serious difficulties.

The racemization rate is in fact a product not only of the average temperature but of temperature extremes; the process may be slowed almost to nothing by very low temperatures, and it is accelerated by high temperatures. A difference of only $\pm$ 2°C in the temperature estimate can reduce the accuracy of an age estimate by as much as 50%. Consequently, estimating a temperature average in order to solve for time does not give good results. It is now recognized that the depth of burial is also an important factor, since it involves heat sensitivity; burial depth, of course, can change over time due to disturbance, deposition, or erosion.

Experimental work has indicated additional factors affecting results. Micro-organisms introduce D-amino acids into buried material, and soil bacteria can influence racemization rates in collagen. Groundwater conditions (very difficult to establish for antiquity) will affect the material by leaching, and contribute to the definition of the temperature ranges. Rates vary with the type of organic tissue involved (bone, tooth, mollusk shell, eggshell) and differ among genera and species as well. That means that any calibration attempt must employ closely comparable material. Additionally, the molecules themselves convert at different rates depending upon their positions in the protein chains during diagenesis. Molecules bound on or within amino-acid chains convert at a faster rate than unbound molecules.

The problems may yet be overcome by careful comparative and experimental research. Geologists are achieving good results using racemization rates of mollusk shells to establish *relative* chronologies in order to check or cross-date stratigraphic sequences. Aminostratigraphy might supplant the more traditional chemical relative-dating methods using diagenetic changes in organic materials (see below). Aminostratigraphic applications could be useful in sorting and correlating discrete archaeological deposits, once the difficulties are overcome. For instance, amino-acid racemization analyses have reduced some of the uncertainties in correlating deposits within limited space, as among the several shell-rich archaeological middens at Klasies River Mouth in South Africa (refs. in Hare et al. 1997: 285). There, spatial separation of the middens precluded the establishment of relative ages by stratigraphic criteria.

Archaeological deposits and materials bring special problems as well as opportunities to racemization dating. The most favorable geological matrices are those that were rapidly buried and subsequently undisturbed. Archaeological matrices, in contrast, begin as superficial terrestrial deposits, subject to heating, mixing, complex chemical environments, and contamination. The method's promise for archaeological applications lies in the optimal time range, within 10^4–10^6 years, extending into the Middle Pleistocene beyond the limits of radiocarbon. If accuracy can be improved, racemization analyses might solve some problems of studying human development in the Middle Paleolithic. Regrettably, however, research applications on hominid specimens have been unsatisfactory. Bone has proven to be a poor material for racemization analysis because it is more subject to leaching and contamination than are more suitable carbonaceous materials such as various shells, both molluskan and avian. For instance, ostrich eggshell has unique chemical and physical properties that appear to make it an unusually appropriate material for amino-acid racemization dating (Brooks et al. 1990). Good results have been achieved with ostrich shells in Africa, leading to expectations for successful applications of the method to eggs of other bird species.

Obsidian hydration

Obsidian is a volcanic glass formed when molten silicate rock is chilled quickly upon exposure to air. Because it is not crystalline, obsidian is capable of taking water into its mass through a process of diffusion (adsorption), which is dependent on temperature. Water increases the bulk of the material, causing mechanical strains throughout the zone of diffusion, which progressively widens with time. A sharp diffusion boundary characteristically separates the saturated from the unsaturated zone. Rock surfaces of different ages thus have rinds of different thicknesses, varying with the age of the surface's exposure by fracture. The relative thicknesses of hydration rinds provide a measure of time elapsed since the exposure of the surface. At some point the saturated zone will spall off the mass of the rock, limiting the method's application in geological time.

In thin-sections cut perpendicular to the surface of the rock, the width of the diffusion zone can be clearly seen and measured under polarized light microscopy because the strains change the refractive index of the glass. Analysts measure the thickness in microns (μm: 1 millionth of a meter, 1 one-thousandth of a millimeter). The measurement technique itself is relatively quick, inexpensive, and precise, making this method useful for a number of purely archaeological applications, most especially for relative dating within sites with long occupation spans or complicated stratigraphy (Aitken 1990: 214–218). Where applicable, the method is superb for establishing sequences of artifacts or deposits.

The thickness of the hydration rinds can be used for chronometric dating of events (the exposure of a fresh surface) after calibration with stratigraphically associated objects of known age, so that a site-specific hydration rate can be calculated. Calibration has been variously based on the Egyptian calendar, radiocarbon, potassium–argon dating of the source lava flow, and dendrochronology. A successful calibration requires that (1) the association between the obsidian and the calibration standard is correctly known; (2) there is a suitably large range of rind widths within the collection, so that differences are significant; (3) the specimens are of known chemical composition; and (4) there is a suitably large number of samples (60–500) to avoid small-sample bias. Rates calculated from calibration necessarily incorporate whatever errors are characteristic of the calibration standard; the rates can be no more precise or accurate than the technique providing the calibration (Friedman et al. 1997).

As hinted above, the hydration rate is not simply a factor of time. It varies significantly with temperature, humidity, and the physical and chemical properties of different glasses (Ridings 1996). Therefore, no rate can be transferred from one glass to another, nor can a rate be extended over a very large area. Furthermore, the fact that the rate will vary with temperature, over the full range to which the glass has been exposed, introduces a strong unknown into the equations which solve for time, because paleotemperatures are notoriously difficult to determine and will vary additionally with depth of burial. This problem is comparable to the difficulties inherent in dating by amino-acid racemization. Research continues to refine a method for determining rates of diffusion directly, using samples in controlled laboratory experiments (Friedman et al. 1997; Mazer et al. 1991; Stevenson et al. 1996). The fundamental research on establishing diffusion rates has been overwhelmingly empirical; the rates are not yet understood as processes in contexts, so that research so far has not fully clarified the theoretical relationships between temperature, humidity, time, and composition of the natural glasses.

Where hydration rates have been established for glasses of known composition, the optical measurement technique provides inexpensive relative and calibrated ages for specimen series and deposits. Optimally appropriate for use within the range of Holocene temperatures, hydration measurement may be extended into Pleistocene ages in the subtropics. The method has proven itself in obsidian-rich areas such as Mesoamerica, and has important potential for East Africa, the Near East, and the Pacific rim.

SUMMARY

All dating methods are relative to some measure of time. As long as we choose to privilege astronomical time, dating based on rates or cycles must be calibrated to that master chronometer. Methods that yield what are sometimes called "absolute" time are those that can be closely calibrated to astronomical calendars. In the future, if atomic time supplants astronomical cycles, all methods will be recalibrated, their relative status thereby affirmed. The choice of a dating method will vary with opportunity and the scale and nature of the events to be dated. Whatever choices are made, they must be supported by appropriately precise sampling in the field. "I would strongly argue . . . that very precise relative dating with only a rough idea of absolute time is usually of much greater importance than absolute dating per se" (Wolfman 1990b: 344).

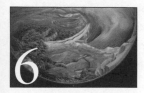

MEASURING TIME WITH
ISOTOPES AND MAGNETISM

Archaeological entities, processes and explanations are bound by metaphysical concepts of time and space.

CLARKE 1973: 13

Even metaphysical time is measured by means of geophysical processes. Ages calculated from measurements of processes such as radioactivity and magnetic-field variations have gained such prominence in archaeology that they threaten to eclipse the more fundamental stratigraphic method. Their claims to accuracy, however, have proven unreliable. It is essential that archaeologists understand the weaknesses as well as the strengths of these esoteric chronometric methods. The application of sound, careful stratigraphic methods of observation and recording in the field can help control for the grosser errors of radiometric and magnetic dating methods by calling attention to discrepancies that require special attention and interpretation.

CHRONOMETRY BASED ON RADIOACTIVE DECAY

Elemental atoms may have one or more unstable isotopic forms with different atomic weights, subject to loss of **alpha** (α) or **beta** (β) **particles** by spontaneous emission. A radioactive **isotope** has a characteristic **half-life**, the time during which half of all the radioactivity will be spent. The rate at which various materials emit particles, therefore, can be used to estimate the passage of time from a defined beginning point. Counting apparatus counts particle emissions; over a short span of time average emission rates can be recalculated as portions of half-lives. The emission of beta particles by radioactive carbon, and of alpha particles by uranium and its radioactive "daughter" products in decay series, are the basis of several chronometric methods that have redefined the reach and potential of the historical geosciences and archaeology. Particle counting methods are being replaced in many laboratories by mass spectrometry, to measure directly the mass of various isotopes in a sample. Direct measurements are considerably more precise than the particle counts for estimating the amount of radioactive isotopes, and thus are able to support more accurate age estimates.

Radiocarbon dating

We begin with radiocarbon, "this fortuitous isotope" (Butzer 1971: 30), because it is the premier archaeological method and because many other methods depend for their applicability upon calibration with radiocarbon time. The discovery by Willard F. Libby that the decay of the radioactive isotope of carbon can be used to measure the passage of time revolutionized the historical sciences and made possible paleoenvironmental studies as they are currently practiced. The importance stems not only from the relatively high accuracy and precision of ages calculated from radiocarbon decay, but principally from the fact that carbon is the element fundamental to all life forms on this planet, and is therefore practically ubiquitous. What is measured is the time since the cessation of metabolism in an organism incorporating radioactive carbon. The relevance of such a time measurement is left to the insight and ingenuity of the archaeologist to demonstrate.

Carbon occurs in the form of two stable isotopes (^{12}C and ^{13}C) and one radioactive isotope (^{14}C, radiocarbon), by far the rarest. Radiocarbon originates in the upper atmosphere when neutrons bombard nitrogen-14 and form carbon-14 + hydrogen ($^{14}N + n \Rightarrow {}^{14}C + 1H$). The radioactive atoms combine with oxygen to produce radioactive carbon dioxide, which is distributed by atmospheric turbulence and is then incorporated into the hydrosphere and biosphere (Fig. 6.1). While subaerial organisms live, the proportion of radiocarbon in their bodies remains close to that of the atmosphere. In the case of marine organisms the reference is to the upper levels of ocean waters. When organisms die and no longer metabolize new carbon, the finite amount of radioactive carbon in their tissues begins to diminish without replacement. Radiocarbon has a half-life close to 5730 years, which means that half the radioactive atoms disintegrate in that span, each producing a nitrogen atom and a beta particle ($^{14}C \Rightarrow {}^{14}N + \beta$). The time since the death of an organism can, therefore, be calculated from the concentration of the radioactive isotope in the material today. Because of the small amount of radiocarbon in the universe, and the length of its half-life, precise measurement of residual amounts is difficult in matter

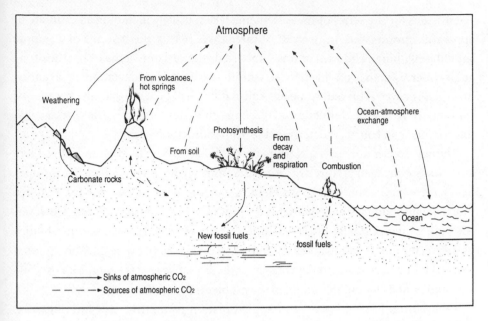

Figure 6.1 The carbon cycle, showing sources and sinks of CO_2. (After Oliver and Hidore 1984: Fig. 15.6.)

more than 30,000 to 40,000 years old; that is the effective range of the method in its conventional "beta-counting" mode. Accelerator mass spectrometry is expected ultimately to extend the range of measurement, but that improvement is elusive. Methodological refinements may permit extension to ca. 70,000 B.P. (Long and Kalin 1992).

Method

As indicated above, there are two ways to determine the amount of radioactive carbon in organic matter: count the emissions of the beta (β) particles, or measure the amount of the isotope directly. The β-counting methods were the first developed, and are conventional. The organic sample is cleaned and reduced to a purer form of carbon, in gaseous or liquid forms. Proportional gas counting and liquid scintillation are the main approaches for laboratories operating today. The purified carbon is placed in a counter and left for specified periods of time, during which the β emissions are counted by the apparatus. The counts are then averaged, and the average converted statistically into an estimate of age based on the half-life properties of the isotope (see R. E. Taylor [1987] or Aitken [1990] for technical details).

The age of the sample thus estimated is always accompanied by a figure expressed as a standard deviation ($\pm$ some quantity), which is the statistical deviation of the

β emissions for the series of measurements taken, usually including an estimate of apparatus error as well. In two out of three cases (68%), the true age of a sample should lie within the bounds of one standard deviation (one sigma or σ); the probability increases to 95% likelihood within two standard deviations. Certainty, however, is never achieved; some age calculations will be wrong simply because of the randomness of the β emissions. *Which* age estimates suffer from this inescapable uncertainty is, of course, indeterminable from the method itself.

The new accelerator mass spectrometry method (AMS or TAMS [tandem accelerator mass spectrometry]) directly counts the atoms of the several radioactive isotopes in a sample, thus avoiding the problem of random decays. This method requires much smaller samples and theoretically produces more precise results. However, AMS age estimates are also burdened by uncertainties related to machine instabilities that affect the precision and accuracy of the ages calculated (Gove 1992). The choice of method for the archaeologist depends upon the size and age of the samples, cost considerations, and laboratory interest in the problems being addressed.

Laboratories use a conventional approximation of the true half-life called the "Libby half-life" (5568 ± 30), which is shorter than the "Cambridge" half-life now universally acknowledged as more accurate (5730 ± 40). The Libby half-life is used so that all published ages since the beginning of the method are directly comparable. When accuracy is more important than comparability, the conventional figures can be converted to reflect the more accurate half-life by multiplying the age by 1.029. The *age estimates* calculated by the technicians, with their accompanying error ranges, are normalized by reference to the year A.D. 1950, a convention established by international agreement to calibrate all laboratory results to a single reference year ("before present"), and to express the utilization of a standard measure of ^{14}C concentration approximating the time before nuclear weapons testing changed the composition of the atmosphere ("before physics"). This resulting figure, compounded of a series of estimates, probabilities, and conventions, is the age "B.P." (or BP; "b.p." in English convention) of the sample, clearly a major departure from anything like an "absolute" age. A further simple calculation yields an approximation to calendar years: subtract 1950 to convert B.P. ages to B.C./A.D./B.C.E. dates. However, international radiocarbon reporting standards now discourage this latter shortcut to calendrical years.

Among investigators involved in paleoenvironmental studies, only the archaeologists tend to use ages converted to dates, and to talk in terms of calendar years B.C., A.D., B.C.E., and so forth. The reasons for this are perfectly sensible from the perspective of researchers who have access to calendrical precision for part of their time span of interest, and who wish to have their data in superficially comparable form. However, as we have seen, radiocarbon ages are properly expressed as a range of time

($\pm 1\sigma$) – a "span" not a "spot" (Orme 1982: 10). Even when expressed as calendar years, these spans do not command calendrical precision, and to pretend that they do is to confuse matters significantly. The special case of dendrochronologically "corrected" radiocarbon ages, and the calibration techniques related to them, are discussed below. In general, when working with interdisciplinary teams and combining archaeological and Earth-science data and results, one can avoid confusion and assure comparability by quoting radiocarbon assay results in terms of the direct expression of ages and durations, and remembering that these are counts of radiocarbon years, which are not always equivalent in length to calender years.

Complexities and uncertainties

The method is based on some key simplifying assumptions, three of which are classic.

1 The production rate of ^{14}C is constant,
2 All ^{14}C produced is rapidly and evenly distributed around the world, and
3 All organisms take up ^{14}C in the proportions in which it occurs in the atmosphere.

A fourth simplifying assumption has been recognized recently:

4 All laboratory results are comparable.

As it happens, none of these assumptions is actually true; reality, as with most of the world, is more complicated. The violation of the methodological assumptions (1–3) results in inherent, "systemic," uncertainties, uncertainties that are inseparable from the method. Fortunately, all four sources of imprecision are now fairly well understood. Even though their effects cannot be eliminated from the laboratory results, they can be allowed for and sometimes corrected by calibration.

The production rate of radiocarbon is not constant because fluctuations in the Earth's magnetic field permit different amounts of cosmic rays to enter the atmosphere at different times. Furthermore, the solar wind that carries the cosmic rays itself varies (secular variation). Variation in solar activity as measured by sunspots affects radiocarbon production such that quiet-Sun periods are periods of radiocarbon maxima, yielding spuriously young ages on the 210-year cycle of sunspot minima (Pecker and Runcorn 1990). The solar variation is not precisely predictable in its influence on radiocarbon ages. Its variability, in combination with the fluctuations in the Earth's magnetic field, limits the degree of resolution and accuracy that can be achieved within the method.

The secular variation resulting from fluctuations in the magnetic field and in solar activity is partly controlled for by enlisting dendrochronology in the service of

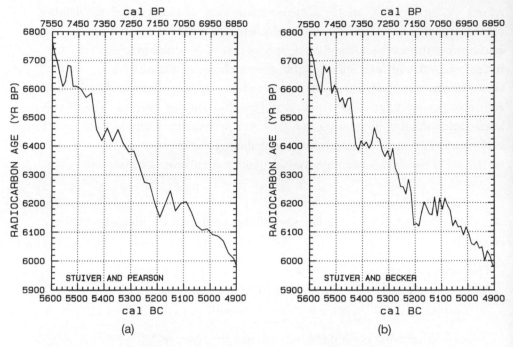

Figure 6.2   Two high-precision calibration curves for the period 5900–6800 B.P. in radiocarbon years. Curve (a) of Stuiver and Pearson (1993) was compiled by averaging 20-year (bidecadal) series of tree rings. Curve (b) of Stuiver and Becker (1993) was compiled from 10-year series. The calibration is read from the ^{14}C age at the left across to curve intersection, then up for cal B.P. or down for cal B.C. ages. Multiple intersections flag uncertainties. Note that curve (b) has more detail but less accuracy. "[B]idecadal curves should be used for most purposes" (Stuiver and Becker 1993: 35). (Reproduced from Stuiver and Pearson [1993: Fig. 1K] and Stuiver and Becker [1993: Fig. 20] with permission of *Radiocarbon*, © 1993 by the Arizona Board of Regents on behalf of the University of Arizona.)

radiocarbon dating. By testing tree rings of known age in high-precision laboratory apparatus, physicists calculate, decade by decade, the departure of radiocarbon ages from the "true" annual age of the sample. Calibration charts have thus been created, showing the spans of calendar date equivalents for radiocarbon ages (Fig. 6.2). Studies with old wood, particularly the tree-ring series that extend back more than 10,000 years, show that secular variation is of significant magnitude and is partly random: it cannot be predicted closely. Recent work in the northern hemisphere has produced calibration charts of refined precision for the last few thousand years as well as a computer program (CALIB 3.0.3) readily available to researchers (Stuiver 1993). Checking radiocarbon assays against dendrochronology revealed a disconcertingly large residue of error in ages previously published (Baillie 1990). Calibration of greater ages with other dating techniques and materials, including subtropical corals, glacial ice, and annually laminated sediments, discloses even wider separation in deep time (e.g., Bard et al. 1990; Kitagawa and van der Plicht 1998). Archaeologists should develop an attitude of informed skepticism about the precision of radiocarbon ages beyond dendrochronological calibration, and work to identify and avoid erroneous estimates (Taylor et al. 1996).

Properly calibrated dates typically have larger ranges of uncertainty than do uncalibrated dates or ages, as is also the case with properly calculated averaged ages. Furthermore, some precision is lost at the start to averaging multiple ages, because the age span represented in individual organic samples from archaeological contexts is typically considerably greater than the spans included in the tree-ring samples used to compile the calibration charts. Calibration corrections of radiocarbon ages should be used when it is necessary to compare events dated by ^{14}C to events dated by tree rings or calendar years, and whenever *rates* of change or processes are an issue. They can also be used to judge the integrity of "clusters" or "gaps" in radiocarbon series, by indicating major variational episodes in the secular trends (Fig. 6.2). Because of the fundamental differences between raw radiocarbon ages, calibrated ages, and calendrical dates, conventions for labeling them have been defined. The international standard for reporting ages is that conventional ages (as defined above) are reported as "years B.P. where 0 B.P. is the year 1950. Dendrochronologically calibrated ages are to be reported as cal A.D. or cal B.C., or, if required, cal BP" (Mook 1986). The international standard is a very useful reference tool for reporters and interpreters of radiocarbon ages; adherence to its several rules confers scientific credibility on the user.

The assumption of rapid and even distribution of CO_2 is violated because the Earth's deep oceans serve as reservoirs of dissolved carbon dioxide – 93% of all carbon in the exchange system (Aitken 1990: 61). The "reservoir effect" delays the redistribution of ^{14}C to the biosphere, and also regularly releases older stored ^{14}C into both the biosphere and atmosphere. Marine organisms, consequently, are impoverished in radiocarbon relative to most terrestrial plants, and tend to give radiocarbon ages greater than their actual age, reflecting not their contemporary atmospheres but the distortions of the marine reservoir amplified by the food chain, and with additional complications in special circumstances (e.g., Kennett et al. 1997; Little 1993). The tissues of modern North Atlantic seals have been radiocarbon-dated to as much as 400 years old. Pacific deep water is even older than that (Boyle 1990; Shackleton et al. 1988). Awareness of the exaggerated reservoir effect in the southern hemisphere, which has more marine than terrestrial surface, has inspired recent collaborative research into inter-hemispheric calibration.

The tissues of some organisms diverge from the atmospheric ratios of carbon isotopes because of metabolic fractionation: the organisms selectively metabolize carbon isotopes by their atomic weights, normally discriminating against the heavy ^{14}C. Plants that discriminate less than most against the heavy isotope ^{14}C (i.e., take in more) produce tissues with isotopic ages somewhat younger than those expected. Maize (Indian corn) is a notorious example of this, but it is only one of a number of plants, mostly tropical and semi-tropical grasses, which convert carbon dioxide to food through a special ("C_4") metabolic pathway that utilizes heavy carbon efficiently. Plants, the primary users of carbon dioxide, are the fractionating agents. Animals that consume fractionated plant foods accumulate the unrepresentative carbon signal, which can build up to significant levels over their lifetimes. The presence of fractionated isotopic ratios can be recognized by comparing the ratios of the stable isotopes, ^{12}C and ^{13}C; correction factors for the ^{14}C discrimination can then be calculated (Browman 1981; R. E. Taylor 1987). The ratio of the ^{13}C isotope in a radiocarbon sample, expressed as $\delta^{13}C$, is essential to evaluation of the age calculation. The standard is woody vegetation of the temperate zone, with a $\delta^{13}C$ value ca. -25%o ["per mil," parts per thousand]. Any departure of $\delta^{13}C$ values from the typical -25 %o is normalized as part of the calculation of conventional ages.

In order to evaluate the precision and accuracy of radiocarbon age measurements, one needs to know the sources of difficulties, and to be able to estimate their effects upon given sample ages. R. E. Taylor (1987) classifies the uncertainties and error sources in radiocarbon dating under four "factors" – sample provenience factors, sample composition factors, experimental factors, and systemic factors. Systemic factors and some sample composition factors (e.g., fractionation) are discussed above.

In archaeology, a significant source of dating error involves sample provenience factors: discrepancies between the real age of the organic material assayed and the age of the event of interest to the archaeologist. Dean's "event" concepts (introduced in Chapter 5) are useful for thinking about this. The target event is the event that the archaeologist wants to date; the reference event is the link between problem and method that permits dating of the target event. The dated event is the actual event whose age is measured. For example, in a case where the target event is the time during which a pithouse was occupied, the discovery of a hearth with charcoal in the middle of the floor may offer a reference event, to the degree that the use of the hearth is related to the occupancy of the house (i.e., the hearth was not intrusive). However, the dated event is the time of death of the tree; this may or may not closely approximate the time of the hearth fire. Clearly, rigorous stratigraphical observations in the field are essential for estimating the relationships between reference, dated, and target events; upon their integrity everything else depends.

Among the important sample composition factors are issues of sample contamination; these are likely to be especially prominent in archaeological sites because of the complex chemistry and depositional history of such areas. Fractionation problems aside, the introduction of organic matter of different age from that of the main body of the sample will complicate any assessment of the sample's age. Such contamination typically occurs after death and burial, and then normally involves the adulteration of the sample by humates or carbonates carried in groundwater, which may be deposited in the pores and interstices of the sample. These may be older or younger than the sample, while the intrusion of roots or the introduction of animal waste into buried samples can bring in younger materials. Contamination in the form of older or, more typically, younger material may also be introduced to a sample during collection, handling, and storage. Standard well-publicized handling procedures can minimize such error (Aitken 1990; R. E. Taylor 1987). Samples of organic material submitted for dating (Table 6.1) are cleaned to remove extraneous materials before the carbon is purified, as part of the laboratory processing.

The contribution of experimental factors to radiocarbon age uncertainties is under investigation. Experimental factors include those involved with counting random events, as expressed in the standard deviation that accompanies each age figure. Also included, but not often expressed, are the errors introduced by background or machine contamination in the laboratories, and machine error – those unpredictables that intrude into any elaborate and precise measurement technology. These errors are usually quite small, and therefore ignored, but can cause problems. They account for some of the differences, sometimes systematic, in the age calculations by different laboratories from "equivalent" samples. Among experimental factors, the statistical nature of radiocarbon measurements cannot be overemphasized, and must never be lost sight of. As discussed above, the probability of the true age of a sample lying within the interval expressed by one standard deviation is 68%; of two standard deviations, 95%. However, "the probability that the actual age of the sample is exactly equal to the value cited as the 'age' approaches zero" (R. E. Taylor 1987: 123). Radiocarbon measurements express *intervals*, not moments in time.

Laboratory pretreatment processes vary with the field and sample conditions, and can reduce the available size of the sample significantly. Chemical pretreatments vary with the sample material and suspected contaminants. The conventional treatments include washing in a strong base, NaOH (sodium hydroxide), for the removal of humic and tannic acids, and an acid bath in HCl (hydrochloric acid) for the removal of carbonates and certain unstable organic compounds (Aitken 1990; R. E. Taylor 1987). Since the pretreatment process chosen may affect the results, clients of radiocarbon laboratories should consult on any possible complications. It should be

Table 6.1 Typical sample sizes for radiocarbon dating

Counting mode	Sample preparation	Sample size in mg C[a]	Count time in hours
β decay	Standard gas/LS	250–5000	24–72
	High-precision gas/LS	10,000–20,000	72–168
AMS/TAMS	Solid	2–5	1–2

Notes:
[a] mg C = milligrams of carbon.
 LS = liquid scintillation.
Source: Adapted from R. E. Taylor 1987: 96, Table 4.1; see original for more details.

obvious that careful scrutiny of the sample in context at the time of collection, and full reporting of the context to the laboratory are both essential to decisions about appropriate pretreatment, and thus to the success of the assay.

In order to monitor and minimize such errors, radiocarbon laboratories check their results by separate runs and by inter-laboratory comparisons. Archaeologists should be aware that inter-laboratory differences are real. Even within a given laboratory, age estimates may vary with different pretreatment regimes and other factors still unknown. Tests have shown that laboratory variance may exceed the expressed error ranges, and that inter-laboratory differences may be greater still (Scott et al. 1998). The program of inter-laboratory testing is proving its advantages for defining, measuring, and controlling the discrepancies.

There is a large literature on problems of archaeological sampling for radiocarbon assays, amounting to a major body of cautionary tales and sound advice. Anyone anticipating the collection of samples for radiocarbon dating should become familiar with the literature, and should take special problems and questions to the radiocarbon laboratory prior to field sampling (see Aitken [1990: Ch. 4] and R. E. Taylor [1987: 107–112] for examples of sampling errors and things that go bump in the night). "[L]ittle reliance should be placed on an individual ^{14}C 'date' to provide an estimate of age for a given object, structure, feature or stratigraphic unit" (R. E. Taylor 1987: 105). Multiple dated samples from the same or closely related stratigraphic units, or dates on different fractions of the same sample, can help expose anomalies that indicate discrepancies. Anomalies are themselves information, implicating the need for further evaluation of the data in hand, or for more data. (See Kra [1986] for guidance in recording and submitting radiocarbon samples.)

Radiocarbon dating approximations create a number of subtle problems for the historical sciences, especially those, like archaeology, that depend on the ordering, correlation, comparison, and interpretation of cultural-scale events (Buck et al. 1994). The secular variation in radiocarbon production means that the lengths of radiocarbon years vary in time; especially in time ranges beyond the ninth millennium B.P., the length of radiocarbon centuries is significantly shorter than the length of sidereal centuries. An eloquent warning about the non-equivalence of uncalibrated ^{14}C years and the astronomical calendar (Braziunas 1994) might usefully be celebrated by archaeologists as the "Braziunas caveat," and heeded whenever comparisons are undertaken between the radiocarbon time scale and paleoclimatic chronologies. Periods of enriched cosmic ray bombardment result in radiocarbon "plateaus," spans of time within which fine chronological distinctions cannot be made. One such plateau complicates the isolation of chronology and event sequences during the Younger Dryas climatic reversal, coincident with the significant postglacial human population expansions into high middle latitudes in North America and Europe (Edwards et al. 1993; Hughen et al. 1998). Furthermore, because event sequences and chronologies are the foundations for inferences about processes, expect that further precision in dating methods will require reconsideration of some established models of historical and evolutionary processes.

With so many sources of possible error impinging upon radiocarbon measurements of elapsed time, it is strongly recommended that multiple interpretive hypotheses be entertained in efforts to understand any anomalies that are recognized. If the anomalies cannot be evaluated so that their sources can be identified, the responsible investigator will publish the results with a discussion of a range of possible explanations, to provide future investigators with clues for solving the problems.

Citation conventions

Archaeologists have habitually published their radiocarbon results in a variety of formats, some quite idiosyncratic. Furthermore, within the English-speaking world, archaeological conventions for distinguishing dendrochronologically calibrated ages from others, and calendar dates from ages, have diverged on both sides of the Atlantic. Here, assuming that the reader is familiar with at least the local practice, I call attention again to international conventions agreed by practitioners of the radiocarbon craft (Mook 1986). Archaeologists may benefit from the discussions addressed to them by Bowman (1990: 42) and R. E. Taylor (1987: 4–6). Most laboratories report in this "conventional" form whether the age is ultimately calibrated or not. Archaeologists should follow the format to enhance the clarity and usefulness of their published results. In brief, the published report of a "conventional" radiocarbon result should provide the following information:

- ages calculated with the Libby half-life of 5568 years
- the ages normalized to $\delta^{13}C = -25$ ‰
- the results in uncalibrated years B.P., with B.P. zero being A.D. 1950
- an error estimate of $\pm 1\sigma$
- the laboratory number.

Any calibration, correction of the half-life, or expansion of the error term to 2σ should be separated from the provision of this essential information. Also, interpretation will be facilitated if the $\delta^{13}C$ value of each sample is also provided. In other words, it should always be possible to distinguish the primary data on the radiocarbon age calculation of a given sample from later manipulations undertaken to compare ages to dates. A table with all the essential values is an ideal accompaniment to a discussion of ages. In every case, it is essential to realize that "The probability that a certain cal[ibrated] age is the actual sample age may be quite variable within the cal age range" (Stuiver and Becker 1993: 390). No matter how thoroughly manipulated, no radiocarbon age expression carries a guarantee of accuracy.

Prior to 1995, summaries of radiocarbon results regularly appeared in the journal *Radiocarbon*, which remains the best source for current and innovative research on methods and applications. Research results in the form of laboratory date lists are available in many different media now: on-line, on disk, in print. Consult radiocarbon laboratories in the area of interest; they are listed with addresses in *Radiocarbon*.

Uranium-series dating

The radioactive isotopes of uranium, ^{238}U and ^{235}U, decay through a series of "daughter" products to end after very long periods of time as stable isotopes of lead. The daughter products are many in each series, and all of them have their own particular half-lives. Some daughters may be separated from the "parent" materials by escaping the matrix as gases or precipitates, to continue on their own decay routes in other contexts. Because of the large number of different isotopes and elements produced during these decay series, there are various methods for measuring time elapsed since the series activity began in a particular material, and they cover different ranges of time, depending upon the critical half-lives. Some methods measure the decay of daughter products as ratios to the parent, others measure the accumulation of radioactive isotopes in materials since a given initiating event – the deposition, burial, or formation of the material.

U-series methods are applied to dating organic or inorganic carbonates, and have been successful in dating geological contexts and events. For archaeology, the most successful applications have been dating archaeological materials enclosed in **speleothems** (carbonaceous cave deposits). Methods frequently applied to date Quaternary geological phenomena and deep ocean cores vary in precision and accuracy among themselves (Aitken 1990: Ch. 5; Ivanovich and Harmon 1992).

The methods that have proven most useful in Quaternary paleoenvironmental studies measure the decay of ^{238}U through ^{234}U to ^{230}Th (a thorium isotope called ionium), and ^{235}U to ^{231}Pa (protactinium), or measure the ratios of ^{234}U to ^{238}U. In all cases, the crucial assumption is that the carbonate material whose age is being measured has constituted a closed system since the event of interest; that is, that no uranium or its major daughter products have entered or left the material in the time span being estimated. This assumption has been supported by research models and by results in coral reefs on raised beaches (taken out of the water) and in tufas and speleothems that crystallize after being deposited from groundwater. "Open system" involvement with groundwater contaminants typically complicates attempts to date carbonates such as caliche, bone, teeth, and mollusk shells.

Another problem with the methods is establishing the amounts of uranium or of the target daughter products that characterized the material at the time from which we wish to measure. In the case of uranium isotopes themselves, in sea water, the assumption of a constant ratio between them seems tenable, and their different rates of decay provide a measure of the time elapsed since they were taken up by marine organisms such as corals. In terrestrial systems, it is difficult to determine the amount of uranium available, for instance, in groundwater depositing calcites or aragonites in carbonates, bones, or shells.

The introduction of mass spectrometric methods for the measurement of isotope ratios established a new level of precision and usefulness for uranium series dating. A notable improvement in measurement of isotope ratios is TIMS (thermal ionization mass spectrometry), which permits greater precision and speed in U-series analyses (Wintle 1996: 134). Research published in 1990 measuring U/Th ratios in Barbados corals appears to have achieved precision and accuracy at least equal to that of radiocarbon, without the problems of radiocarbon's secular variation. The coral U-series ages match well their radiocarbon ages within the range of dendro-calibration. Beyond that, they diverge from the radiocarbon ages, but U-ages may be more accurate than ^{14}C for time before 9000 years ago (Bard et al. 1990). If the U/Th ages are as accurate as appears, the radiocarbon discrepancy may be as great as 3500 years by 20,000 years ago. If the accuracy of U/Th dating is indeed good enough to make it a calibration standard for ^{14}C, geochronology will be fundamentally improved worldwide and nearly all archaeological models of change rates in deep antiquity will require reconsideration.

Archaeologists must be aware of the highly experimental nature of these methods within the time spans and precisions that make them useful to archaeology. Referring to the most recent literature, mainly in geological publications, and consulting with investigators directly involved in development and application of the methods, are strongly advised.

Potassium–argon dating

A radiometric method based on the decay of radioactive potassium (^{40}K) has become indispensable to geologists. With a very long half-life, the decay of ^{40}K to its daughter product, ^{40}Ar, is capable of expressing the ages of certain rocks essentially from the first consolidation of the geosphere (Aitken 1990: Ch. 5; Faure 1986).

Potassium, which has one unstable and two stable isotopes, is a constituent of some of the most common minerals in igneous rocks. The decay of ^{40}K produces an isotope of the rare gas, argon, which is trapped in the crystal lattices. In rocks cooling from magma, gases are freed, and the newly solid rock is theoretically devoid of argon, thus setting a radiometric clock that will measure the time since cooling (compare the emptying of electron traps to set the thermoluminescence "clock," below). Measuring the amount of potassium in a rock sample, and then the amount of argon-40, permits calculating the age of the rock. The assumptions of the method, that (1) no residual argon remained after cooling, and (2) the system has been closed since, neither receiving nor giving up argon, are in fact violated often. Weathering or exposure of the rock may liberate argon or permit atmospheric argon to penetrate it. Various methodological refinements have reduced the errors introduced by the violation of the assumptions, but error ranges of a million years or so adhere to geological age determinations.

In the historical geosciences, K/Ar has helped build a basic chronology for the ice ages, and for the seafloor spreading that measures continental drift. Attempts to correlate geosphere events with climatic changes inferred from other kinds of evidence, including orbital parameters, are similarly beset with scale problems because of the large error ranges of this method.

The K/Ar dating of Cenozoic and Quaternary sites of hominoid and hominid finds has provided a rough chronology for the development of human beings and their earliest experiments in material culture, most notably in the Rift valleys of East Africa. It has made possible some comparability between sites widely separated in space, and some approximation to developmental rates. However, it is yet undetermined how much of the growing complexity seen in early human development may be attributed to the large imprecisions, and consequent inaccuracy, of this dating method.

Recent improvements in measurement technology have overcome some of the problems besetting classic K/Ar dating. Single crystal laser fusion (SCLF) has made feasible direct comparison of argon isotopes ^{40}Ar and ^{39}Ar, thereby increasing precision and circumventing some problems of sample contamination (Wintle 1996: 129). The precision so achieved has brought Ar/Ar ages into the time span of radiocarbon, offering the potential for lengthy calibration series.

CHRONOMETRY BASED ON RADIATION DAMAGE

Within the geosphere, natural radioactivity occurs in the form of alpha and beta particles and gamma rays, emitted by isotopic decay. This radiation, in combination with the weaker cosmic radiation, damages other elements, creating free electrons by ionizing radiation. The free electrons may recombine with nearby atoms or become trapped in gaps in crystal lattices. These trapped electrons may be freed by heating, in which case they emit measurable light (thermoluminescence). Alternatively, the density of trapped electrons can be measured by exciting them with microwaves and measuring the intensity of the resonance signal in a magnetic field (magnetic resonance). On the assumption that the intensity of the light or resonance signal of the electrons bears a linear relationship to the accumulated dose of ionizing radiation, these phenomena can be used to measure time elapsed since the electron trapping began. Further basic assumptions include (1) the expectation that the modern intensity of ionizing radiation at the collection site has been fairly stable over the time being measured, and (2) that the collecting material has neither lost nor gained electrons by any other means.

Groundwater is a major complication. Since water is more effective than other materials at absorbing radiation, its presence attenuates the radiation received by the sample, thereby reducing the dose, and consequently the apparent age. Water may also leach away or redeposit radioactive materials, thus changing the dose over time by violating the first assumption (stability). The difficulty in estimating the groundwater history of a site makes this complication particularly challenging for applications of radiation-accumulation dating methods.

Thermoluminescence dating

Electrons trapped in crystal defects are freed as light (thermoluminescence; TL) when minerals are heated above a critical point (ca. 300–450° C). If, at some archaeologically

significant time in the past, the material was heated enough to free all the trapped electrons and "reset" the TL clock, then the time elapsed since that heating event can be
estimated. The intensity of light measured correlates with the duration of electron
accumulation. Baked clay is an excellent material for this method; a range of other
archaeological and sedimentary materials can also be dated. The developmental
history of the TL method has been well summarized by M. J. Aitken (1985, 1990) and A.
Wintle (1996).

The method is self-calibrating: field and laboratory tests estimate the level of radiation dose a sample received at its burial point and the sensitivity of the particular
sample material to receiving, storing, and releasing the free electrons. With samples
up to 3000 years old, the method compares favorably in accuracy with radiocarbon
dating; it is less accurate with progressively older samples. However, as it is applicable
back to over half a million years, it is well worth development despite the complications and limitations. With improvements in U/Th dating, opportunities will
expand for calibrating ancient TL ages, to check on the accuracy and precision of the
latter method.

Several methods are used to prepare and read sample luminescence, depending
upon the characteristics of the sample and site (Aitken 1985, 1990; Wintle 1996).
Basically, a prepared sample is heated gradually, and the glow emitted by the sample
is graphed as a function of heat and intensity of light (sample glow curve). In combination with the information gained by the several self-calibration tests, the glow
curve can be interpreted as an expression of received dose ("equivalent dose"), which
permits calculation of time elapsed since the last heating of the sample.

The method incorporates two critical assumptions: (1) there is a linear relationship between the dose and the TL emissions, and (2) there has been no loss (fading)
of accumulated TL. Both of these assumptions are violated by reality, and special
tests for complications are required. Radiation sources may be both internal (in the
sample material) and external (in the matrix), along with a minor contribution from
cosmic radiation. The dose originating from the matrix can be measured on samples
in the laboratory or directly in the field with a dosimeter when conditions require,
providing there is close coordination between the excavators and the laboratory
technicians. Variations in the nature of samples and matrix necessitate choices
among several preparation and reading methods, and place special responsibilities
on the sample collector (Aitken 1985, 1990).

The method was first developed for archaeological use in dating ceramics, where
the mineral additives are the preferred target. In addition, TL ages since firing can be
calculated for burned flint, burned rock, and slags. For different reasons, the time
since deposition of crystalline calcite and aeolian sediments is also measurable by
TL. Calcites, essentially radiation-free at deposition, receive radiation from external

sources. Consequently, the age of speleothems can be calculated to help date archaeological materials in caves. Wind-blown mineral grains, on their way to becoming aeolian sediments, are bleached by exposure to sunlight, which removes most of the trapped electrons from the grains. Accumulation of electrons resumes after deposition and burial, incorporating a fresh TL signal representing the time since burial. TL dating of loesses, first developed in the USSR, has been widely applied in Quaternary studies, both terrestrial and marine (Wintle and Huntley 1982). The technicalities of all these age determinations are considerable; there is no substitute for consultation with a specialist while field investigations are in the planning stage. "TL dating is no routine work" (Wagner et al. 1983: 39).

The age of the sample or samples (they are best run in sets from a single context) is expressed as an average of the samples with two error figures. The first, usually the smaller of the two, expresses the statistical error in the calculation of the average age of the samples in the set. It is used to compare TL ages within a site or between similar contexts. The second, usually larger, uncertainty factor expresses the predicted systematic error, accounting for some of the field complications known to affect the sample. It is appropriately used when comparing TL ages with calibrated radiocarbon ages or between sites. Both error expressions are given as one standard deviation; both increase with the age of the samples, averaging 5–10% of the age (Aitken 1985: 31).

Used with sensitivity to its particular complications, TL can provide important information to several of the sciences involved in paleoenvironmental reconstruction. The range of TL, far beyond that of radiocarbon (to ca. 10^6 years), and its relative precision in comparison with other long-range dating techniques such as potassium–argon, promise an important future in geochronology.

Optical luminescence dating

A related approach to dating is showing promise for unburnt sediments, since it relies directly upon luminescence stimulated by light (Aitken 1990: 175–177; Wintle 1993, 1996: 132). This method, especially suitable for aeolian sediments because it quickly measures sunlight bleaching, is finding favor among Quaternary geologists for such applications, and for archaeological sites on or under aeolian sediments (Wintle et al. 1994).

Electron spin resonance dating

Electrons freed from paired bonds by particle bombardment may be trapped in crystal lattices of many materials, as summarized above for TL. Trapped electrons measured by electron spin resonance extend this accumulation clock to organic matter and calcite minerals. So far, it has worked better on teeth than on bone, and is applicable to mollusk shells, corals, foraminifera, speleothems, and **travertine** (massive carbonate rock deposited from freshwater). Contamination during diagenesis by radioactive minerals carried in groundwater is a serious complication, especially for bones and porous (poorly crystallized) carbonates.

The radioactivity of the sample material and of the sample matrix must be measured to determine the dose rate; the matrix can be measured in the field by a buried dosimeter. The efficiency of a sample for trapping electron charges (and positively charged "holes") in the lattice is measured, so that the environmental dose rate can be corrected to yield an accumulated dose rate specific for the sample. The accumulated dose is assumed to bear a direct relationship to time, although it has also proved to vary with ambient temperatures; the lower the temperatures, the slower the accumulation and thus the longer the time span that can be measured prior to saturation.

Measurement involves mounting a sample in a magnetic field of known force and subjecting it to microwaves to excite the trapped electrons. The intensity of the response by unpaired trapped electrons correlates directly with their number (a function of dose); consequently, it can be converted into a time measurement. The accumulated dose divided by the annual dose (established from rate and sensitivity) gives a measure of the time since crystal growth, or since subsequent significant heating that resets the chronometer.

The ESR method, still experimental and of unproven accuracy (Rink et al. 1996; Wintle 1996), has been used on archaeological teeth, shells, and calcite minerals with apparent success despite a wide range of uncertainties (Aitken 1990; Grün and Stringer 1991). Since it gives especially good results with hydroxyapatite in tooth enamel, it is being intensively developed for paleoanthropology because it is applicable to time beyond the reach of radiocarbon (Aitken et al. 1993: Jones et al. 1994). Nevertheless, experience is revealing an increasing number of complicating variables in the range of Middle and Lower Paleolithic sites (Grün 1997).

Fission-track dating

The massive nucleus of the heavy isotope of uranium, ^{238}U, is subject to spontaneous fission, releasing great amounts of energy and sending fragments outward at high velocity. These fragments damage other materials in their paths, leaving scar-like fission tracks in glassy mineral matter. On the assumption that the rate of decay is a constant, then the accumulation of tracks in a mineral is a function of time and the amount of uranium in the material. The applications of this dating method within archaeological time spans depend upon the presence of appropriate new material (uranium-rich minerals or glasses in a volcanic tuff) or some thermal episode related to the archaeological target event that would "set the clock" by raising the temperature of an appropriate material enough to eliminate older tracks by annealing (melting), so that damage since the annealing event could be counted (Aitken 1990: 132–136).

Materials suitable to this method include a number of glassy minerals (zircon, apatite, mica, etc.) and obsidian. Given such a material in primary association with an archaeological or natural event of interest, the analyst prepares the material by grinding a fresh surface and etching it, to emphasize the damaged zones surrounding the tracks. Sample preparation varies with the material, in recognition of different hardnesses and compositions. After preparation, the tracks are counted under a microscope. The uranium content of the material must be determined for each sample before time can be calculated (Wagner and van den Haute 1992).

The method is dependent upon some simplifying assumptions, which are not demonstrably accurate. The principal assumptions involve the uranium and the tracks themselves. It is necessary to assume (1) that the uranium decay rate is constant (although several different figures are in use for the constant), and (2) that the uranium is uniformly distributed within the material, which is sometimes demonstrably not the case. The analyst must also assume that all the tracks formed since the event of interest are still visible, that is, that none has healed naturally, and that the density can be adequately sampled by the polish-and-etch method. In fact, only some tracks intercepted by the polished surface can be seen on it; there are critical angles of interception that render some tracks unobservable. The damage is calibrated against damage inflicted on the sample in a nuclear reactor.

All of these uncertainties make the error in fission-track counting difficult to estimate; thus, both precision and accuracy can be in doubt. The method has wide application in geology, especially to volcanic rocks. Once enthusiastically embraced by archaeologists, the method is superseded in suitable materials by TL and ESR.

CHRONOMETRY BASED ON COSMOGENIC NUCLIDES

Cosmic rays, whose high-altitude bombardments make radiocarbon out of nitrogen atoms, also produce rare isotopes of many other elements. Some of these, especially ^{10}Be, ^{26}Al, and ^{36}Cl, with half-lives much longer than radiocarbon, have been used in experimental dating of geological and site surfaces. The concept is that the accumulation of these rare isotopes, or their ratios, can be used to estimate the time since a surface was first exposed (e.g., Bard 1997; Beck 1994; Plummer et al. 1997). The method shows promise, but the many complicating variables need more study (Tuniz et al. 1998). Watch for developments.

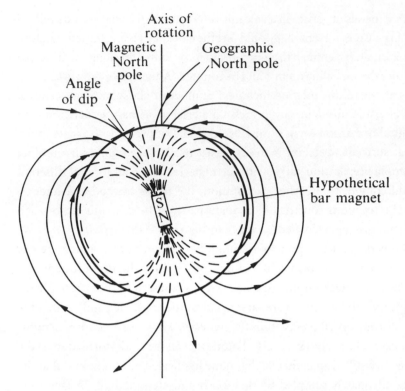

Figure 6.3   Earth's magnetic field, represented as a bar magnet. A small magnetized
needle would point along the lines of force. The close lines show relative field
strength or intensity. (Reproduced from Aitken 1990: Fig. 9.2, with permission
of Addison, Wesley, Longman.)

CHRONOMETRY BASED ON THE EARTH'S MAGNETIC FIELD

[A]rchaeologists are beginning to accept the fact that effective solutions of many of the
most crucial problems in the discipline will require their greater participation in a
wide range of natural-science applications.

WOLFMAN 1990B: 354

The Earth's **magnetic field** is created by electrical currents originating in the geodynamo, the fluid dynamics in the molten outer part of the core. Imagine the field as
the effect of a bar magnet running through the center of the Earth, at a slight angle to
its axis (Fig. 6.3). The force field produced is roughly parallel to the surface at the
equator, roughly at right angles to the surface near the poles, and at angles varying
with latitude between. The angle of force against the surface of the Earth is the **inclination**; it is that which makes compass needles dip toward the Earth's surface if free

to move in that direction. The poleward orientation of the imagined "magnet" defines the **declination** of the field, that is, its variance from true north. A third variable property of the magnetic field is its **intensity**, or strength.

The position of the magnetic pole, and therefore the declination, wanders almost constantly, although at varying rates. On short time scales it drifts around the direction of true (axial) north. Moreover, the period for changes in inclination is different from that of the declination, and these intervals are different from changes in the intensity. Therefore, all these phenomena can be used as dating methods if their changes through time are known (Aitken 1990: Ch. 9).

Additionally, over long but variable time intervals, polarity reverses direction, exchanging north for south. Polarity has reversed several times within the last few million years (Jacobs 1994). Wandering of the magnetic pole and reversals of the field are expressed in the "frozen" magnetism of rocks and sediments, especially volcanic rocks, which are dated by K/Ar and Ar/Ar ratios.

Paleomagnetic and archeomagnetic dating

The choice between these terms is often dictated by no more than the research specialty of the user: "paleomagnetism" is the term favored in the Earth sciences, "archaeomagnetism" in archaeology. However, there is a useful distinction to be made. Paleomagnetic dating as practiced in oceanography and geology is based on the sequence of polarity reversals in the Earth's magnetic field, which provide a reference chronology going back many millions of years. Archaeomagnetic dating is based on short-term changes in the orientation and intensity of the field in recent millennia, expressed at regional scales.

Archaeomagnetic dating is normally undertaken for archaeological materials within the Late Holocene, utilizing the secular variation of the Earth's magnetic declination, inclination, and intensity. Records of former positions of the declination and inclination, and of the intensity of the field, are held in minerals that are susceptible to magnetic force (the iron oxides magnetite and hematite dominate). Small magnetic "domains" within the mineral grains tend to align with the Earth's field when they are mobilized sufficiently to do so. This mobilization occurs when minerals cool out of molten rock, or cool after being heated up to ca. 700°C by fire or lightning, or when sediments settle freely through water and are then compressed, or are strongly weathered chemically.

Thermoremanent magnetism (TRM) is the signal of the Earth's field at the time the heated materials cooled; it remains fixed in its original orientation while the Earth's field changes around it, and is measured with appropriate instruments. The

TRM orientation in materials not directly dated is then compared to dated curves, and a date obtained by calibration. Similarly, detrital remanent magnetism (DRM) can be measured in fine sediments undisturbed since they settled out of water (Verosub 1988), and chemical remanent magnetism (CRM) from strongly weathered sediments. The latter (CRM), less stable than either TRM or DRM, is considered a contaminant.

Once research has established the meandering path of the magnetic pole (declination) and the vagaries of the inclination, as measured from points on the Earth's surface within an area of ca. 1000 km, and has dated reference points along the paths, then other measurements of these characteristics can be fitted to the data to provide approximate ages (Fig. 6.4). Dating accuracy varies in time and space; on dependably calibrated and well-dated curves, the accuracy can be within 25–50 years for declination and intensity.

The orientation of a sample in its original position is crucial information. Therefore, the best archaeological samples are baked earth under old fireplaces or ceramic kilns or the unmoved contents of kilns. Portable pieces of baked clay (ceramics) cannot give the positional data, but may sometimes be dated on the basis of intensity variation when curves for that have been established previously.

The critical assumptions for archaeomagnetic dating are: (1) the remanent magnetism reflects the field at cool-down or settling, and (2) in the case of TRM, there has been only one critical heating (that is, the sample must be relevant to the archaeological event of interest). As with other methods, exceptions to these assumptions complicate the applications. Remanent magnetism may decay in time, and it can be reoriented when sediments undergo chemical change (but that is usually obvious). Subsequent heating, e.g., by lightning or other fires, or resuspension in water, can reorient the particles. Errors may occur in sampling, by the selection of unevenly heated samples or of weathered samples, or by movement of the sample before or during recording or by simple recording errors. There are, as may be expected, additional complications in measuring the RM of samples and in creating the curves (Aitken 1990; Batt 1997; Eighmy and Mitchell 1994; Sternberg 1990; Wolfman 1984, 1990b), as well as a growing awareness of lability in the magnetic field.

Information on the varying locations of the virtual geomagnetic pole and other aspects of the secular variation of the field obtained from archaeologically dated samples are of interest for their own sakes to geophysicists (Verosub and Mehringer 1984). Variations of intensity inform about changes in the effective magnetic shielding from solar radiation, and thus, indirectly, about some aspects of climate and ^{14}C production that may enhance understanding of the linking of these systems (e.g., Stuiver et al. 1991).

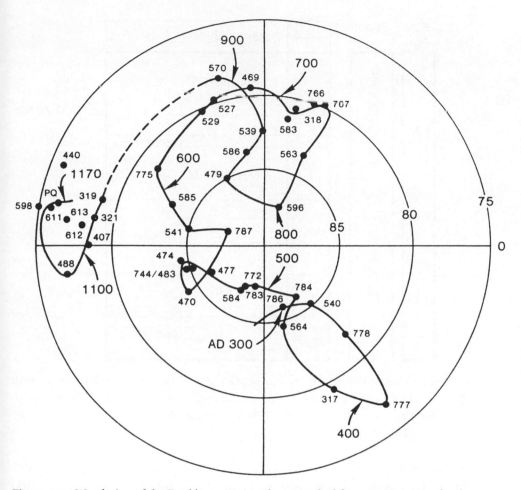

Figure 6.4 Wandering of the Earth's magnetic pole, as graphed from Mesoamerica for the period A.D. 300–1170. The curve is drawn on a polar projection above 75° latitude. Each point represents a "virtual geomagnetic pole" (VGP) calculated from declination and inclination in TRM at a particular sampling site. (Reproduced from Wolfman 1990a: Fig. 15.4B, with permission of the University of Arizona Press.)

Paleomagnetic dating based on polarity reversals provides a coarse chronology with a span in the millions of years. It is the basis for some of the dating of deep ocean cores, which are calibrated to potassium–argon-dated terrestrial volcanic materials that retain a TRM signal. Major, long-lasting polarity reversals are called **chrons**; briefer reversals are subchrons and excursions (Fig. 6.5). By matching the sequence and number of reversals recorded in the sediments of deep cores, investigators establish a chronology on materials otherwise difficult to date. Of course, with phenomena at such large scales, precision is impossible, and skepticism about accuracy may

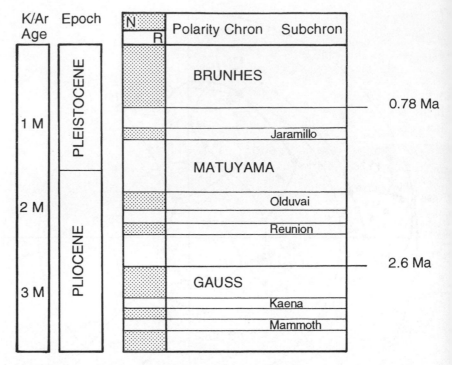

Figure 6.5   The most recent three paleomagnetic chrons (Brunhes, Matuyama, Gauss), with
subchrons and ages. Shaded areas are Normal polarity (N), others Reversed (R).
Polarity reversals are the basis for dating and correlating sedimentary and eruptive
events worldwide.

often be well founded (Bradley 1999: 95–96; Merrill and McFadden 1990). Nevertheless, for glacial and interglacial sequences far removed in time, and for early
hominid evolution, such dates may be the best currently available.

SUMMARY

Archaeologists and geoscientists can choose among an expanding array of methods
for measuring the passage of time (Fig. 5.3). These methods vary in their applicability
to various materials and situations, useful spans, precision and accuracy, and
expense. An informative example of synergistic ^{14}C applications in interdisciplinary
contexts is discussed by Bartlein et al. (1995).

   All methods have limitations and complexities, including some still undefined.
Archaeologists should be familiar with the basics of the methods currently most
useful, as summarized above, but need to understand that each method makes highly
technical demands upon its practitioners, so that no one can be expert in more than a

few. Once aware of the range of materials and situations that can be analyzed in terms of expired time, archaeologists must assume responsibility for consulting with expert practitioners prior to collecting critical samples.

All chronometric methods, even calendars and stratigraphy, are subject to improvement. Users should expect that refinements will render any textbook or handbook presentation obsolete at some point. New methods appear frequently as the Earth sciences receive better funding to study aspects of planetary ecology and climate change, among which knowledge of rates and processes of change are recognized as crucial for effective management. Archaeologists aware of the dynamism in geochronology can make informed use of it.

THE ELUSIVENESS OF TIME

Decades ago, B.P. (before 1950), dating Bronze Age sites in the eastern Aegean seemed direct and reliable, given artifactual cross-ties with the astronomically calibrated Egyptian king lists that served as calendars. For instance, the association of Late Minoan IA ceramics in a Greek tomb with Egyptian scarabs provided a *terminus ante quem* age estimate for the ceramic style at ca. 1500 B.C., a nice round, memorable date. Ceramics of LMIA style were buried when the Thera volcano erupted on Santorini island, north of Crete, and 1500 B.C. was proposed as the date of the event (Marinatos 1939). The scale of the eruption, devastating to the town of Akrotiri, led archaeologists to try to relate it to catastrophic fires and building destruction elsewhere in the Aegean. When radiocarbon dating became available, scholars wanted to use that method to refine the dating of the eruption and test its synchroneity with destructive events nearby. The result of those efforts, and applications of additional dating methods, has been a vast, expanding, contentious literature that remains inconclusive. Why?

In the decade of the 1970s, charred organic samples from the Akrotiri excavations were sent to the radiocarbon laboratory at the University of Pennsylvania, a respected research facility. The immediate results supported the traditional age, but tree-ring calibration produced dates implying an age greater than 1600 B.C. (Fishman et al. 1977). Efforts to explain the results focused at first on contamination by ancient carbon in volcanic gases venting nearby (Weinstein and Michael 1978).

As these issues were being pondered and contested (Cadogan 1978), other dating methods were applied. Archaeomagnetic studies on burned buildings in Crete and the tephra on Santorini showed diverse orientations: the destructive events on the two islands could not be coincidental in time (Downey and Tarling 1984; Liritzis 1985; Sparks 1985; Tarling 1978). Voices from western North America chimed in with a hypothesis for dating by teleconnection through climate proxy. Studies of tree rings in the California mountains disclosed notable frost rings at 1628/1627/1626 B.C., which were interpreted as evidence for a major volcanic eruption in the northern hemisphere. Those were correlated to Thera on the basis of some of the contested radiocarbon dates (LaMarche and Hirschboeck 1984). Although immediately assailed from the perspective of artifact cross-dating (Warren 1984), the claims soon attracted supporting evidence from tree-ring sequences in Ireland and Germany (Baillie and Munro 1988).

Geological stratigraphers joined the discussion, reporting on the distribution and relative dating of deposits of tephra from Thera as observed in marine cores and on land eastward into Anatolia (Turkey), which provided estimates of the size of the eruption and implied the possibility of more refined stratigraphic dating (Stanley and Sheng 1986; Sullivan 1988; Watkins et al. 1978). From the Dye research station on Greenland, ice-core studies produced another set of interpretations, building on the climate proxy argument begun by the tree-ring researchers (Hammer et al. 1987). These authors championed 1645 B.C. as the date for a major volcanic eruption with a strong sulfur signal observed in ice layers, retracting a later age they had proposed in 1980. By the late 1980s the radiocarbon debate had heated up again as more organic samples were distributed to several different laboratories. The conflicting results of the cross-laboratory tests pleased no one (Aitken et al. 1988; Betancourt 1987; Betancourt and Michael 1987; Manning 1988; Warren 1988).

There matters stood as the Third International Congress on Thera and the Aegean World convened in 1989 to consider the evidence. Conferees reported on radiocarbon analyses of sample sets carefully selected to avoid some of the problems raised earlier, which nevertheless produced similarly scattered results tending toward ages in the seventeenth century B.C. rather than the sixteenth (Friedrich et al. 1990; Housely et al. 1990; Hubberten et al. 1990; Nelson et al. 1990). Neither AMS dating of single seeds, the involvement of several laboratories, nor calibration of multiple dates clarified the situation. Champions rose to urge compromise on demands for precision, and to consider the ice-core and tree-ring ages to date the same volcanic event, which might be the Thera eruption. Their mediating efforts were properly rejected as compromising accuracy as well. Other voices argued against using the ice-core and tree-ring dates because the climate proxy argument could not be tested; volcanoes other than Thera might have produced sulfur veils and chilly climates in the centuries at issue (Pyle 1990).

The archaeologists considering the dating problems were incompletely familiar with geological advances in understanding the eruptions. At the conference stratigraphers called attention to evidence for several chemically and petrologically distinct tephra bodies on Santorini, and noted that tephra deposits elsewhere differentially matched more than one of them. Geologists demonstrated that the Thera volcano had erupted at least twice, with the possibility that the resultant ash deposits could be confused with one another (Hardy et al. 1990). The sequence of events as well as their synchroneity – eruptions, earthquakes, fires in buildings, destruction of buildings, sources of organic samples – was therefore exposed as an unresolved issue given the stratigraphic, archaeomagnetic, and radiocarbon complexities and contradictions (Housely et al. 1990). As the conference ended, consensus remained elusive despite significant gains in clarification of the arguments advanced (Manning 1990).

Since the Third Congress, new evidence and argument from high northern latitudes has called into question much of the debates that took place there. Investigators of paleoenvironments in Iceland published a strong caveat against confusing coincidences with correlations or correlations with causes, highlighting the unrealistic efforts of archaeologists to achieve calendrical precision through methods incapable of yielding it (Buckland et al. 1997). Tracing sulfur deposits in the GISP 2 core in Greenland, Zielinski and Germani (1998a) supplemented the seventeenth-century B.C. sulfur signal by extracting tephra sherds from the same ice layer and analyzing them chemically. They found no match for any Thera tephra, nor for those of four other eruptions close in time. Their responsible conclusion – the results neither support nor refute the relevance of the age of the sulfur signal for the Thera eruption – has survived one immediate challenge (1998b). Furthermore, research in Anatolia on tree rings and ash deposits has not yet clarified the situation, despite an attractive, but ultimately incomplete, argument supporting the early date from tree rings (Kuniholm et al. 1996). Inconclusiveness is properly a stimulus for research, not an embarrassment.

Why is this so important? Why have so many excellent investigations been directed to this enigma? The entire east-Mediterranean Bronze Age chronology rides on the results, since the validity of the traditional chronology based on links with Egypt is now strongly challenged. If LMIA is earlier than 1500 B.C., the entire archaeological scenario for the Bronze Age must be extensively revised and lengthened, with implications for connections in all directions.

Why has resolution been so elusive? When otherwise reliable methods fail to provide information, one must evaluate the assumptions that guided the choice and application of the methods. Even after the Third Congress eliminated some old assumptions, such as the reliability of the 1500 B.C. cross-dated age, other assumptions appear to be obstacles to resolution. The paleomagnetic and stratigraphic studies highlighted uncertainties in the sequence of events and assumptions of synchroneity; more rigorous stratigraphical analyses or new excavations on both

Santorini and Crete are needed. How many volcanic events, and of what kinds, affected the region? What was the magnitude of the eruptions, and can they be positively identified in Greenland ice cores? Do boundaries between archaeological periods relate in any way to external, natural events? Were the Cretan fires lit by human or natural agencies, and what was the sequence? How do stored seeds relate to the volcanic events at Akrotiri? Essential to any dating effort is a clear idea of what is to be dated, accompanied by rigorous selection of the appropriate methods and samples. An awareness of unforeseen complexities in human affairs is also necessary.

PART III

Climate

CLIMATE: THE DRIVING FORCES

For most of the food-producing regions of the world, the climate at present is better than it has been over 92 percent of the last million years.

ANTHES ET AL. 1981: 336

The last million years have seen the emergence of *Homo sapiens*, of the complex social fabrics that we call civilization, and of large-scale societies that expect and, to an extent, require some measure of climatic predictability or stability. Intensive food-production began within the most recent major warming cycle in the present ice age (the Holocene epoch); it has supported an unprecedented population expansion in our species. This population expansion has occurred mainly since the end of the "Little Ice Age" in the nineteenth century, in a time of warming and relatively stable climate (Grove 1988). The rate of population growth has steepened dramatically since industrialization, which occurred massively within the early to middle twentieth century, a period of unusually stable climate. Recent droughts and crop losses in Africa, and disastrous rains and flooding elsewhere, force us to realize how precariously balanced we are in depending upon intensive food-production in a world that may be fundamentally inimical to our present ways of doing things. Modern climates are neither typical nor normal in the perspective of world prehistory. Recent instabilities may presage major change.

Climate, as a statistical generalization about temperature and precipitation, varies from place to place, time to time and, especially, with the time duration and the size of spatial unit summed. Climatic statements should be understood as statements about the average and range of weather conditions at a place and time of specified scales. It is important that a student of past climates *not* slip into thinking of climates as normative conditions. Climates vary. They do so in ways that are at least partly systematic and determined, but as yet imperfectly understood. The climates of

our planet are the diverse expressions of a complex system involving many components which undergo continual dynamic adjustment to each other (Chapter 3). The
contributions of each component to a particular climatic configuration vary in
response to the states of all the other components. The climate system is composed of
the variations and mutual interactions of the internal factors – the five spheres:
atmosphere, geosphere, hydrosphere, cryosphere, and biosphere. As with all
systems, the components of the climate system affect each other through positive
and negative feedbacks between parts of the system in continuous mutual adjustment. Because many variables are involved, because the feedback loops are complex
and the relationships are poorly understood, systemic fluctuations are difficult to
quantify. Sometimes predictable in terms of their periodicity, fluctuations are very
elusive in terms of their effects – the direction and intensity of change. The external
climatic factors, independent of the five-spheres system, "force" states of that system.
As discussed in Chapter 3, the important external mechanisms include solar variability, changes in the Earth's orbital parameters, and geotectonics, including volcanism.

SCALES IN TIME AND SPACE

The components of the climatic system work at several different periodicities. It is
helpful to chart them exponentially, so that the components that affect climate most
strongly at different frequencies are displayed as nested scales, each successively
larger or smaller by a factor of 10 (Fig. 7.1). The exponential scale is a powerful heuristic device, displaying some of the variation in the time dimension without masking
its complexity. Each climatic mechanism may amplify or dampen the effects of
others, whether those others operate at the same or different scales.

An important additional complication in the expression of any climatic mechanism is the fact that historical considerations (contingencies) intrude. Processes
acting at large scales and low frequencies establish boundary conditions that constrain processes active at smaller scales. For example, the slow movement of continental masses into high latitudes in both hemispheres has apparently created
conditions in which rather small differences in seasonal distribution of solar radiation may trigger the large-scale cycles of an ice age (Crowley and North 1991).
Amplification and dampening effects work down the scales, defining the parameters
within which the variables at lower levels can be expressed. Forcing factors do not
repeat their combinations; the interactions of cycles at different frequencies do not
replicate patterns.

Because climate is so variable and dependent upon contingencies at many scales,
thinking in terms of climatic averages or norms is likely to be misleading, even when

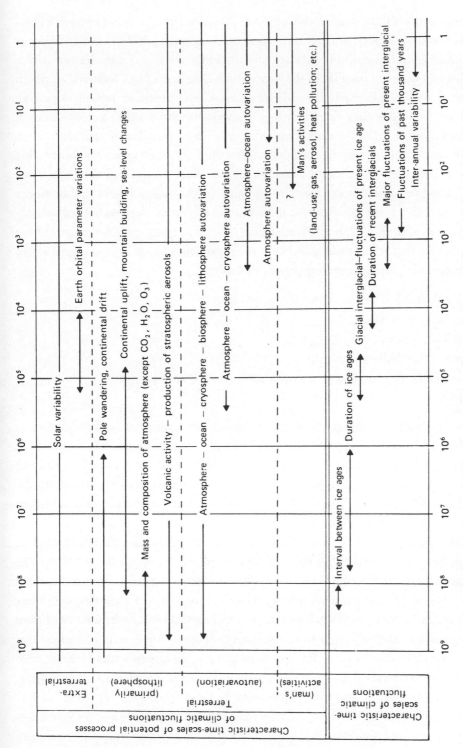

Figure 7.1 Examples of potential processes involved in climatic fluctuations and characteristic time scales of observed climatic fluctuations. (Reproduced from Kutzbach 1976: Fig. 2 with permission of *Quaternary Research*. Original caption.)

components of the system are the subject of discourse. It is better to emphasize dynamism and variability by describing climatic components in terms of their range (intensity) and duration (frequency of variation). These concepts are sometimes expressed in terms peculiar to the "wave model" described in Chapter 4, in which intensity is called amplitude and duration is wavelength or period (Fig. 4.2). Intensity and duration vary according to the particular climatic factors involved, which together define the scale at which any given factor is most influential.

Paleoclimatology entails consideration of all the known mechanisms affecting climate; a variety of techniques, therefore, is necessary for data collection, analysis, and interpretation (Bradley 1999; Crowley and North 1991). As Figure 7.1 shows, only certain of the climate mechanisms are relevant at any particular level in the exponential scales of time. To appreciate their expression and effects, it is necessary to have proxy data that reflect their influence at the appropriate temporal and spatial scales. For example, paleotemperature proxies include

- the altitudes of tree lines, snow lines, and cirques;
- pollen assemblages;
- stable isotope ratios;
- tree-ring widths and densities;
- marine, lacustrine, and terrestrial microfaunal associations; and
- paleosols.

Only some of these are available for any given time and place, and the luxury of choice and optimization is not always offered. On the other hand, the range of proxies is so wide that some useful data are normally available (Chapter 8). Much of the discussion in the rest of this book will be relevant to the reconstruction of past climatic conditions, even when techniques and data sets may be addressed to other, more proximal, research goals.

We have seen that both space and time can be organized according to a nested set of scales, in which each larger unit subsumes smaller ones subject to the influence of factors operating at the higher levels (Table 2.1). Chronological and spatial scales are loosely linked because of the hierarchy of climatic mechanisms and proxy data characteristics, from larger to smaller units. Scaling emphasizes the ever finer resolution of climatic detail that can be extracted from the paleoclimatic record as one moves from larger to smaller units. Processes operating at the largest scales of time ($\geq 10^6$ years) affect boundary conditions that are manifest at the global mega-scale of space, involving large-scale and low-frequency variables such as solar radiation receipts and the effects on atmospheric circulation of mountain building and the formation of polar ice caps. Mechanisms dominating at the temporal macro-scale of 10^5 years trigger processes that are expressed strongly at hemispherical and continental mega-scales of space. Subcontinental and regional macro-scale effects are characteristically visible as the results of factors operating at the macro-scale of 10^4 years, while subregional and local spatial meso-scales reflect processes operating at the higher frequencies: 10^3, 10^2, or 10-year scales. At the smallest micro-scales, the effects of stochastic, high-frequency changes are likely to be expressed with high spatial variability. Climatic data at the micro-scales are elusive because of their transience and because of problems in resolving physical data and chronology at those scales.

Each of the exponential levels of the climatic scale is characterized by processes which are expressed at frequencies on that scale (Fig. 7.1). Thus, the processes listed at the scale of 10^5 years are those that typically cycle at that frequency – roughly 10 times within a million years (e.g., glaciations). Because the levels are nested, lower-order scales are subject to the processes and forces affecting those at higher levels; so far as is now known, effects at lower scales are not significantly manifest at higher levels. There is the theoretical possibility that small-scale effects can flip large-scale systems when the latter are in sensitive states. An apparent example of such processes, the Younger Dryas climatic reversal, is discussed later in this chapter.

In the chapters that follow, scalar units will be referred to frequently. As proxy data sets are discussed, their relevance and utility at particular scales will be considered. A most gratifying aspect of looking at climatic processes in ranked scales will become apparent; proxy data sets are dependably useful across a limited range of adjacent scalar units, typically two or at the most three. This observation means that scalar concepts have direct applications in defining research goals and in identifying the data sets, and thus the methods, that are most appropriate for solving different kinds of archaeological problems. For example, climatic periodicities at the scale of 10^3 years or less are of interest to the student of culture history and specific cultural adaptive mechanisms, while larger-scale phenomena are the focus of investigation for climatologists and physicists. Small-scale phenomena ($<10^2$ years) attract ecologists and other field-oriented biological scientists, and are central to problems of human adaptive strategies – behavior at local and regional scales of space.

When attention turns to the relevance to humans of the nested scales of climatic processes, we move from cyclical to linear time, from thinking in terms of recurrent, scalar interactive processes to thinking about the historical trends and events that may be affected by those processes. This needs to be clear because nothing we know about historical trends suggests that they share any of the essential attributes of cycles. Historical trends are products of sequentially unique configurations of several cyclical processes interacting with one another in human and environmental history. It is possible and useful to isolate and consider evolutionary or historical developments at different scales. What is not useful is to assume that any two temporal spans of the same size would necessarily manifest comparable historical or evolutionary processes, as is indeed the case with cyclical phenomena. The evolutionary processes significant during the last 100,000 years of hominid evolution are not likely to be significantly similar to those of the next-to-last 100,000 years. This is so because of the interaction in history and evolution of many processes cycling at different wavelengths, and because unique historical events and non-cyclical processes – contingencies – create lags and deflections in the responses of systems. Therefore, in the sections to follow, each time the focus shifts from climatic to human systems, there is necessarily a redefinition of the terms in the time dimension, from cyclical to linear time.

FACTORS OPERATING AT LARGE (MEGA- AND MACRO-) SCALES

The highest-order scales (10^7–10^9 years) of climatic variation are of little direct concern for students of the human past, which is contained within the last 3–5 million years. These scales, summarized briefly in Figure 7.1, are mainly relevant to the very long-term perspectives required for study of the Earth's ancient history. Among the processes operating at such long wavelengths, those that continue to affect the climate to which humans have been exposed are fundamental structures of the climate system, expressed at such low frequencies as to be part of the invisible background, lost among those realities of life on Earth that all living creatures must take for granted. These background characteristics (Chapter 3) include (1) solar variables defining the long-term prevailing temperature ranges of the Earth, (2) the basic composition of the atmosphere, and (3) the distribution of land and water. Although such factors change very slowly, they affect all others, forcing the climatic system over very long terms. They set some crucial boundary conditions for atmospheric circulation and the receipt of solar radiation. Most of these factors are predictable on this scale; that is, their variation can be calculated and their theoretical contributions to climatic parameters calculated or modeled. Their effects in actually forcing the system or amplifying and/or dampening variation are poorly known and the expression of such effects will vary with feedback at shorter frequencies.

Million-year scale (10^6)

The boundary conditions within which Earth climate can vary at the million-year scale were established by processes working at the larger scales. The range within which such external factors as solar variability and polar wandering (Chapter 6) can have influenced the Earth's climates during the last million years was, therefore, partly predetermined by atmospheric composition and other variables defined at very low frequencies. The fact that both of these external factors are poorly understood in terms of their climatic expression, although fascinating in its own right, is of little concern to archaeologists.

External mechanisms of more direct relevance include the geosphere changes involved in continental drift, mountain building, and seafloor spreading. At the million-year scale, these changes can affect atmospheric circulation by raising mountain barriers to westerly wind flow and by redefining the shape, size, and latitudinal distribution of the oceans. All these characteristics affect ocean temperatures and circulation, and thus the exchanges of heat and matter (carbon dioxide and water vapor, principally) between the oceans and the atmosphere. In this way, climates at all spatial scales are affected.

Autovariation and feedback in all five spheres of the internal climate system are implicated in climatic variation at this scale (Bradley 1999; Kutzbach 1976). Geospheric processes of tectonism or erosion change the heights of continents, which in turn affect atmospheric circulation and temperatures. Structural changes in the ocean basins modify deep water circulation and thus heat transfer in the oceans. The coupling of ocean and atmosphere can change to some extent the distributions of heat and precipitation at the million-year scale, although this is more significantly expressed at shorter intervals. The state of the cryosphere is crucial to the development of major ice ages. Polar ice caps, high-latitude ice sheets, and sea ice are both preconditions of and effects of glacial ages. Variation within the biosphere seems mainly to be responsive to changes in the other spheres at this scale, but successful adaptation of plant and animal species to cooling climates, or to increased climatic variability, would themselves have climatic consequences defined by albedo and respiration effects.

The million-year scale can only be studied at a distance, at low resolutions, and within broad error ranges. Our ability to discriminate details and even magnitudes of variation on this scale is still very limited, as are the kinds of evidence available. Our precision in measuring is very coarse, as are the classes of proxy data. We rely heavily on large-scale theoretical and mathematical models to guide us in understanding the role of external forcing functions at large scales, with geophysical evidence that must be interpreted in terms of such forces. The "facts" of solar variation, polar wandering, continental drift, and mountain building are reasonably well established empirically. However, the relevance and force of their effects upon planetary climates and environments at large scales are only tentatively established. There remains also a great deal to learn about autovariation in all five spheres of the internal system, and in the coupling and feedback chains among them that amplify, dampen, and redirect trends of climatic change. At these scales, geophysicists resemble archaeologists in lacking crucial "middle-range theory."

In terms of archaeological relevance, the large-scale environmental and climatic factors that have been crucial for the evolution of the human species are even less well identified. What aspects of the environment helped select for bipedalism and large brains? Did the selection for large body size that we see in many Pleistocene mammals equally determine the increase of hominid stature since the Pliocene? How much of this selection pressure was climatic? Could a creature like modern humans have evolved in an Earth-time that was not an ice age? It is likely that the cultural environment was at least equally as significant as the natural environment for the evolution of the modern human species. However, until we know more about the conditions imposed by the climatic cycles within a major ice age, we will be unable to speak confidently about sources of critical environmental stresses and opportunities. One thing is certain: the last million years have been a period of relatively and absolutely high variability in Earth climates and topography, within the dominance of low temperatures. Some aspects of that variability must have contributed to the evolution of large-brained mammals, among which humans give themselves pride of place. Dinosaurs in equable climates managed to live very well with a fraction of the brain-power of mammals; perhaps none was as clever per ounce as a mouse.

Hundred-thousand-year scale (10^5)

The major ice advances of the Pleistocene pulsed at approximately 100,000-year intervals, roughly coincident with the cycling of the eccentricity of the Earth's orbit at 96,000 to 100,000 years. This cycle of major glacial–interglacial periods is superimposed on ice age background conditions defined by factors operating at larger scales. The 100,000-year cycles emerge from data on ice volume and ocean temperatures, as analyzed in deep-sea sediment cores and polar ice cores (Fig. 7.2; see Chapter 8 for a summary of methods).

The patterns displayed in Figure 7.2 have been duplicated in their essentials in marine cores around the world, indicating that the growth of ice sheets is a slow process and that climate fluctuates within major glacial phases. Ice-sheet retreat, on the other hand, is relatively rapid, resulting in the "sawtooth" shape of the graphs. The coincidence of this periodicity with the cycles of the eccentricity of the Earth's orbit strongly implicates that astronomical phenomenon as a leading cause of the alternation. Other factors, however, are major contributors.

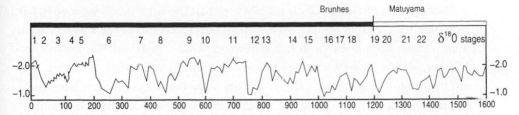

Figure 7.2 Oxygen isotope profile from core V28-238, with $\delta^{18}O$ stages of Emiliani, displaying sawtooth pattern of ice volume, the rapid onset of warm periods, and slow cooling. Isotopic "stages" are defined from these patterns: interglacial periods with low, or "negative," ratios of oxygen isotopes bear odd numbers, starting with the present interglacial; glacial periods with high, or "positive," ratios have even numbers. (After Shackleton and Opdyke 1973: Fig. 9.)

At our current state of knowledge, the dominant external climatic factors at the 100,000-year scale are orbital variations, and possibly solar variability. The cycle of the eccentricity of the Earth's orbit (Fig. 3.1) forces variation in the relative intensity of seasonal solar radiation. Glaciers grow best when summers are cool enough that the winter's accumulation of snow is not entirely removed before more is added. A highly elliptical orbit presents conditions for extreme glacier growth when precession brings the summer season into the part of the orbit farthest from the Sun. Although orbital rhythms at this scale have been traced in the record of sedimentary rocks for several millions of years, they were especially strong and effective in the last 2 million (Crowley and North 1991), when both the geosphere and cryosphere were in highly sensitive states. Orbital rhythms may account for about 50% of the variance in ice fluctuation during the Pleistocene, although they cannot be considered the cause of an ice age.

To the boundary conditions defined by the external forces, the components of the internal climate system add their own amplifications and negative feedbacks. Elevated mountain ranges, continents at high latitudes, polar ice caps, albedo effects of land and sea ice and of vegetation on newly exposed continental shelves were involved in various combinations. Interactions among the atmosphere, cryosphere, and ocean are particularly significant sources of additional variation, amplification, and even dampening. The role of volcanism at this scale is uncertain; there were certainly periods of active volcanism, but their effects at this scale are undemonstrated. The biosphere is responsive at this scale (10^5), through speciation and extinctions among fauna especially. Ice-core data show fluctuations in atmospheric concentrations of CO_2 and methane at these scales, indicating involvement of global vegetation. Vegetation both responds to climatic change and contributes to it.

Shifting from cyclical to linear time, we see that the last 100,000 years or so have been highly eventful in human development. Subspeciation of the sort that separated *H. s. neanderthalensis* from *H. s. sapiens* occurred in this span. Human speech, if not even older, certainly was fully established in this time period. And there were many possible topics for speech and curiosity in the last 100,000 years: active mountain building (earthquakes and volcanism), expansion and contraction of glaciers, lakes, and snowlines, transgressions and regressions of the oceans, as well as changes in regional and subregional distributions and densities of prey and vegetation. *Homo sapiens* expanded into higher northern latitudes than any earlier hominid had seen, elaborating technology for coping with a new range of climates in those challenging areas. Domestic fires created unique microclimates for small groups, while cave use and clothing opened new microhabitats. The era of human modification of the natural world was initiated with fire. Concurrent with the expansion into new habitats, our species experienced low rates of population growth.

FACTORS AT MACRO- TO MICRO-SCALES

Evidence for fast and abrupt climate variability . . . has shaken the paleoclimate community over the past two years.

ZAHN 1994: 621

Neither climatic forcing at very low frequencies nor its expression are issues of immediate concern to archaeologists. Correlations between such large-scale environmental phenomena and human behaviors can be no more than trivial. When the focus shifts to time spans of 10,000 years or less (the span of the Holocene), archaeologists become interested. At these scales, however, climatic conditions are influenced by many variables at many scales, likely including some factors still unrecognized. The predictability conferred by external astronomical forcing mechanisms at low frequencies yields to higher-frequency variability and increasing expression of contingency at smaller scales of time and space.

The low-frequency predictability and the high-frequency unpredictability of climate impose high variability on the biosphere, to which organisms respond – successfully or not. Human responses are the most complex of all. Human behavior in the face of environmental change always begins locally and is predicated on short time spans. Behavior need not, and may rarely, be predictable in advance, appropriate in hindsight, or efficient as measured economically or energetically. That our species has survived so far is due to our behavioral and biological flexibility, not the quality of our planning. Paleoecology sensitively done will increasingly provide examples of specific human responses to particular habitat changes; the best examples are likely to be complex and even counter-intuitive, as with the Andean case summarized from Seltzer and Hastorf (1990) in Chapter 4.

Ten-thousand-year scale (10^4)

The 10,000-year scale represents the frequency at which the alternation between glacial and interglacial periods is manifested. Whereas glacial periods tend to last several tens of thousands of years with minor interruptions, interglacials seem to average around 10,000 years each. Transitions from glacial to interglacial states are characteristically rapid; warming seems to progress faster than cooling (Fig. 7.2). Cycles at this scale are dominated by changes in the Earth's axis, obliquity, and the precession of the equinoxes, which affect receipt of solar radiation. Changes are expressed as greater or lesser contrasts of seasonality (Fig. 7.3) and as latitudinal shifts of radiation intensity. Volcanism also may be an effective external forcing mechanism at this scale, flipping sensitive relationships among subsystems into different states. When it blocks solar radiation from the lower atmosphere, volcanic dust can cause climatic cooling at very large spatial scales. However, the intensity and duration of episodes of explosive volcanism appear to be highly variable, not cyclic.

During the Pleistocene, in temperate and semi-tropical latitudes well beyond the extent of continental glaciers, lake basins were affected by dramatic cycles of high and low water. For a long time, lake levels at middle and low latitudes were believed to have pulsed in concert with the ice sheets. When ice sheets advanced, so the thinking went, the high atmospheric pressure over the ice shifted the prevailing westerlies south, carrying with them the precipitation belts. Thus, at latitudes equatorward from the great ice sheets, rainy periods known as pluvials filled lake basins that have, in many cases, been dry or markedly drier ever since. Better chronological resolution and computer models of glacial atmospheric circulation demonstrated that this correlation does not hold everywhere. Other mechanisms are involved. Obliquity cycles now appear to be the forces behind the low-latitude pluvial periods. When perihelion (Earth close to Sun) occurs during the northern hemisphere's summer, the opposite of current conditions (Fig. 3.1), the increase in solar radiation on land masses at low latitudes causes summer low-pressure systems that draw intensive monsoon rains over the continental interiors. The extra precipitation fills the lake basins. In an elegant study, J. Kutzbach and F. A. Street-Perrott (1985) demonstrated a close and predictable relationship between axial factors and

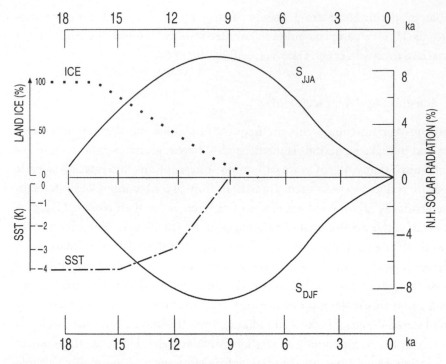

Figure 7.3 Variation in seasonal solar radiation in the northern hemisphere as percent difference from that at present, calculated on the basis of obliquity of axis and precession of the equinoxes. The diagram shows summer (JJA) and winter (DJF) radiation for the last 18,000 years, since the height of the last glaciation. Percent difference in solar radiation is not expressed directly as temperature, which is defined by complex interactions of many additional variables. SST = sea surface temperature. (After Kutzbach 1987: Fig. 1.)

pluvial periods; the behavior of monsoons predicted by the mathematical model correlates with data on lake location, size, and timing. This model even accounts well for the incongruent timing of pluvial periods between the American West and sub-Saharan Africa.

The atmosphere, oceans, and cryosphere respond in complicated ways to external forcing at the scale of 10^4 years, both in autovariation and in their interactions. Because these cycles are relatively brief and we have access to data on many more variables and relationships, some of the complexities are yielding to research. Crucial variables within the hydrosphere include the amount of water in the oceans, the state of the deep-ocean currents that circulate water masses of different temperatures and salinities, and the latitudinal and longitudinal location of the boundary of Arctic water (the polar front) in the North Atlantic (Fig. 7.4).

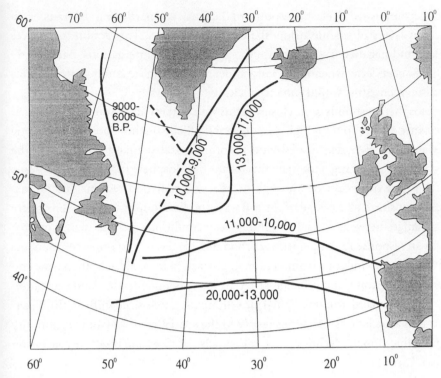

Figure 7.4 Deglacial shifts of the polar front; the position during the Younger Dryas reversal is averaged at 11,000 to 10,000 radiocarbon years ago. (After Ruddiman 1987: Fig. 8.)

Atmospheric responses to axial forcing and to states of the ocean involve shifts in the latitude of the **arctic front** (where arctic air masses meet temperate ones), the concentration of CO_2, and the latitude and longitude of persistent atmospheric blocking highs (important boundary conditions forcing either **zonal** [latitudinal] or meridional circulation; Fig. 3.5). The cryosphere is especially sensitive at this scale, with continental ice sheets waxing or waning, and the location, amount, and duration of sea ice varying dramatically as expressions of both autovariation and responses to atmospheric and oceanic conditions. The state and condition of ice on land and ocean influence the global heat gradient and thereby affect the location and intensity of atmospheric convection cells, atmospheric highs, and the jet stream (Akin 1991), as diagramed in Figure 3.5.

Sea-level changes responding to the formation or decay of continental ice sheets entail isostatic adjustments in the geosphere, in directions opposite to the accumulation of water (Fig. 3.3). The geosphere is depressed into the mantle by added weight of ice or water; it rises in compensation with release of the load. The vertical motion is partly accomplished by elastic response of the crust, and partly by mass transfers in the viscous layers of mantle below the continental rocks. This action introduces some lags and negative feedbacks into the ocean–air–ice interactions, particularly during ice-sheet decay when rising land under the melting ice could protect the ice from submergence that would enhance melting.

The biosphere responds quite closely at this scale to these land–water–ice changes; lag effects are obvious only at higher frequencies. Albedo on the exposed continental shelves and on newly deglaciated land is controlled at the landward side by the quality and density of vegetation; by this means the biosphere may contribute some feedback to the other spheres through its effect on radiation receipts and atmospheric composition at the edge of ice and water bodies. Responses in the biosphere during changes between glacial and interglacial conditions include swings of productivity in response to temperature, carbon dioxide levels, and other components of climate such as wind speeds and seasonal contrasts in insolation. Both marine and terrestrial biota exhibit such changes; they are best documented for land vegetation and for planktonic microfauna in marine sediments. Large-scale shifts in the distributions and associations of species testify to the spatial resorting and community disruption that climatic cycling at this scale entails (Huntley and Birks 1983; Jacobson et al. 1987; Part VI).

A problem in chronological precision haunts attempts to model environmental conditions affected by external forces by means of proxy data derived from the biosphere. Radiocarbon years are not equivalent to solar years and depart increasingly from them back in time (Chapter 6). Therefore, the ages of events or system states that are to be correlated to Milankovitch cycles must be translated from radiocarbon B.P. years into calibrated years, to reduce the errors of time measurement inherent in the former (e.g., Braziunas 1994).

Homo sapiens sapiens, the only hominid species to survive the last major glaciation, successfully spread a unique gene configuration over all the major continents of the world between 50,000 and 10,000 years ago. Human communities achieved significant degrees of technological dominance within local environments everywhere, establishing home bases and territories and competing successfully with other large predators by means of weapons, traps, drives, and fire. The distribution of the species was partly constrained by the climatic cycling that fed and consumed continental glaciers, exposed and submerged coastal lowlands, and permitted or discouraged the establishment of edible plants and animals. Choice within those imposed limits was also constrained by cultural factors, among which the state of technology was preeminent.

Millennial scale (10^3)

At the millennial scale (1000 years), climatic variation is poorly understood; no single astronomical cycling is known to drive it. Large-scale patterning is obscured by small-scale variation, some of which may result in mutual amplification of cycles. The boundary conditions within which variation takes place are set by mechanisms operating at all the higher scales. External forcing at this scale involves solar variability, again poorly specified, and geophysical effects including volcanism, the effectiveness of which varies with clustering and intensity. The geographical scale over which generalizations can be made begins to contract.

As the precessional cycle plays through its variations, receipts of solar radiation progressively change their seasonal effects. O. Davis (1984) argues that during the Holocene in the northern hemisphere the shift of perihelion successively through the summer months affected various ecotonal communities at different times. As perihelion occurred progressively later through the summer months, species and communities sensitive to early summer sunshine responded differently from those controlled by early frost. Changes in biotic communities stressed by rapid climate fluctuation may have contributed significantly to the megafaunal extinctions at the end of the last glacial stage (Chapter 16; Graham 1986; Haynes 1991).

The internal climatic system dominates the millennial scale, especially the coupling between atmosphere and ocean that is expressed at relatively high frequency as changes in atmospheric temperature and trace gases (Bond et al. 1997; Mayewski et al. 1993). Rapid reversals of climatic trends, such as those between stadials and interstadials within glacial periods, can be forced by sensitive short-term feedback loops between the atmosphere and hydrosphere. The cryosphere can be involved in amplifying the trends, in accounting for some lag effects, or even in triggering rapid changes. The Younger Dryas cold period of glacial readvances in the eleventh millennium B.P. (see below), as well as Neoglacial episodes within the Holocene, are climatic phenomena of this type; their immediate causes are not yet fully understood, although their effects can be observed at even local scales.

Variation at the millennial scale is best visible to archaeologists within the last 10,000 years, the Holocene. Cultural and perhaps social pressures influenced the course of human **genotypical** and **phenotypical** change within the span of the Holocene, taking precedence over selection pressures from the physical and biological environments. It is still not clear whether climatic variation at this scale has any profound importance for human cultural or biological evolution at the global scale, except that the options represented by techniques of food production, and therefore population increase, would have been greatly constrained in the absence of the Holocene warming (DeVries 1981; Wigley et al. 1981).

Beginning many millennia ago, in many societies, cultural buffering reduced direct selection pressure originating in the inanimate environment, even while introducing a novel range of cultural pressures induced by the demands of complex technologies and of sedentism and urbanization with their attendant disease and stress loads. There are evolutionary consequences for the species in genetic and phenotypical adaptation to suboptimal nutrition, to epidemic diseases and high loads of endemic disease, and to the stresses of urban crowding. The role of paleoclimates as direct influences on the cultural and behavioral records becomes less accessible to archaeologists at the millennial scale, since the immediate effects of climate are mediated through the biosphere. The biosphere itself is sensitive to feedbacks from the behavior of our most meddlesome species. The human population explosion within the last thousand years had profound effects on the biosphere and, through it, is now encroaching upon conditions in the atmosphere and hydrosphere. Within the last millennium, human activities have certainly affected local climates, even if the precise sequences and effects of the mechanisms involved remain unclear.

Massive deforestation has occurred in some parts of the world for several millennia; its effects on the atmosphere, and thus climate, occur through changes in local albedo and evapotranspiration, affecting atmospheric temperature and moisture and the routes and speeds of air currents. Urban heat islands deflect rain-bearing winds. For all these reasons, climatic parameters associated with human settlements in the last several millennia (temperature and moisture ranges and variability) cannot be considered completely independent from the human world itself. At the millennial scale, we make our own local climates and have done so for some time (Roberts 1989).

Century scale (10^2)

The effective forcing factors at the century scale (100 years) are, like those at the next highest level, poorly understood. The expression of forcing factors at such high frequencies is strongly influenced by spatial attributes such as latitude and altitude, topography, vegetation, distance from large water bodies, albedo, and so forth (Table 3.1). Consequently, at smaller temporal and spatial scales high variability is characteristic of the record, masking the identity of effective forcing factors. Climate at local and regional scales is affected by oceanic and atmospheric heat distributions, volcanism, autovariation within mountain glaciers and sea ice, as well as albedo effects, including anthropogenic albedo changes. There are hints of cycles of 125 years that may be caused by variable solar activity (Scuderi 1993). Expression of larger-scale phenomena such as eustatic changes in sea level may be suppressed or even reversed by local isostatic or tectonic responses of the geosphere. Thus, the rate of eustatic marine transgression during the early Holocene (1 meter per century [van Andel 1985]) tells the archaeologist very little about conditions at the site scale, and nothing about effects at any given place, which must be established individually.

Autovariation within the biosphere, consequent upon human activities, emerges at this scale as an important forcing function for climatic variation. We saw the beginning of this emergence at the millennial scale. In the smaller spatial units that are significant at the century scale, deforestation, urban heat islands, and agriculture affect local wind speed, evapotranspiration, albedo, soil conditions (warmth, dryness, deflation) and distributions, and therefore temperature and precipitation.

Ironically, the temptation to interpret events in human history in terms of climatic causation becomes almost irresistible at this scale, because of the existence of written records, and because the archaeological record itself is often resolvable to centuries and cultural change is perceptible. In temporal units of 10^2 years we are observing change at the generational and family scale. Folklore and historical records alike reference weather and climatic phenomena as causal agents in human history. Interpretation, however, rarely has moved beyond the logic of correlation to examine mechanisms. Recently, with climatic shifts better dated and cultural theory better established, this has begun to change. Human choices, along with constraints imposed by human institutions and technologies, are increasingly acknowledged as significant factors in historical responses to climatic change.

Certainly, weather extremes affect individuals and small family groups, particularly if they are isolates. Short-term climatic variation can be extreme; its effects on human communities need not be so. Strategic responses and cultural buffers intervene between communities and catastrophes much of the time. Societies are likely to survive, even when the loss of individual lives is high. The exceptions, we are learning, may be socially determined. Certainly, social and cultural adjustments to significant climatic change are necessary; these may be resolved by emigration or by technological or social innovation. Close observation of the conditions in which societies failed to survive climatic change is a responsible alternative to the facile invocation of climatic causation. McGovern's (1981) analysis of the failure of the Greenland Viking colony is a convincing example of a case in which severe climatic and environmental change certainly occurred, but only one of two neighboring societies collapsed under the challenge; ideology is strongly implicated in the failure of the European settlements, while the Inuit survived.

Anthropogenic effects on climate can be monitored and demonstrated at the century scale for several millennia. Land clearance, soil impoverishment and salinization, erosion and redeposition, urban heat islands and urban changes in microrelief and elevation – all these affect air circulation and hence climate at the local scale and over short time periods. Increasing amounts of CO_2 released by human combustion of fuels, and methane from biological wastes, add to the greenhouse gases warming the planet. The reality of these effects can be recorded today; they are emerging in trapped gas data in ice cores. Obviously, their influence on ancient regional climates should be considered, to reduce circularity in interpretations.

Decadal scale (10^1)

Until recently, climatic change at the scale of decades was beyond the reach of paleoclimatic research; it is beginning to dominate the literature as concern rises about anthropogenic effects on climate at the end of the twentieth century. Long-term, high-resolution climate records in ice cores, corals, speleothems, and tree rings are demonstrating that boundaries between major phases of warm and cold climate can be as short as a decade (Gu and Philander 1997; Mayewski et al. 1993). This scale of change is much finer than can be observed in marine cores and pollen records, and is apparently much more important in large-scale climate change than anyone had previously imagined.

Atmospheric autovariation dominates the climate system at the decadal scale, bringing high-frequency variation (weather) of low predictability. The solar variation expressed as sunspot cycles, in periods of eleven years more or less, has long been suspected of affecting climate. No demonstrable mechanism has emerged, but the possibility continues to beguile researchers (Kerr 1996). Volcanism or other sources of aerosols may force short-term perturbations at the scale of a few years (Porter 1986), but without a cyclic component.

Extended cycles of wet and dry years are emerging from studies of annually laminated ice caps on several continents (e.g., Thompson data in Ortloff and Kolata 1993), and in extended tree-ring sequences in the American Southwest (Swetnam and Betancourt 1990). Severe droughts lasting more than a decade correlate with major cultural and population disruptions in the archaeological record of societies dependent on farming (Gumerman 1988; Ortloff and Kolata 1993; Shimada et al. 1991; Weiss et al. 1993). The responses of the societies involved in each case initiated unique, complex sequences of cultural change.

Anthropogenic changes in temperature and precipitation frequently force modifications in farming practices, and may even lead to drought. Deforestation results in increased evaporation and run-off of water from the exposed land, as well as increased insolation of the surface, so that the range of daily and seasonal temperatures on the deforested plot is increased. The results are analogous to the infamous diurnal swings of temperatures in deserts – hotter days, colder nights, even without major climatic changes.

Annual scale (1 yr)

Everyone is familiar with the high variability of weather over periods of less than 10 years. At inter-annual scales, it is weather rather than climate that is most strongly felt by people. People live by the weather, and they influence local weather by changing vegetation. The long-term effects of short-term weather extremes, if any, are likely to be invisible in the archaeological record, except when they are manifested in changed frequency and scale of floods and landslides. Cultural buffering, however, is usually effective except when catastrophe may affect individuals or small groups.

At annual frequencies, so many variables interact in sensitive states that the resulting processes appear random, even chaotic, but are yielding to analysis (Shukla 1998). Paleoclimatic reconstruction may be achieved at yearly scales under ideal conditions, when dendroclimatology or ice-core layers can be interpreted. These ideal circumstances are quite rare in the archaeological universe, but their number might increase as archaeologists refine their chronologies.

One short-term climate system that has yielded its structure to analysis is the El Niño/Southern Oscillation (ENSO; Chapter 3), which occurs in the equatorial zone of the Pacific Ocean but has effects at the planetary scale (Diaz and Markgraf 1993; Gu and Philander 1997). "Except for the annual cycle, the El Niño/Southern Oscillation (ENSO) is the dominant signal in the global climate system on time scales of months to several years" (Thompson et al. 1992: 303). Zones of warm, moist air and high sea-surface temperature swing from the western to the eastern Pacific and back again at periods of two to five years. When the high-temperature zones are in the east, the coastal deserts of Peru in South America receive heavy rains, and the cold upwelling oceanic currents that feed marine life swing west away from shore; life zones and economies are disrupted as croplands erode and marine biotic resources fail. Atmospheric changes driven by the Southern Oscillation are reflected widely over the globe; summer droughts and severe winters in parts of the northern hemisphere seem to cycle with the warm El Niño phase in the east (Swetnam and Betancourt 1990).

Intra-annual scale (<1 yr)

Weather cycling at periods of less than a year is of course the most familiar, and the astronomical causes for those are unequivocal. Seasonal contrasts are defined by the tilt of the Earth's axis. The hemisphere facing toward the Sun experiences summer; that facing away, winter. The season and amount of rainfall constrains agriculture. The contrast between day and night is created by the axial spin, constantly changing the area of the planet's surface exposed to the sun's rays. Biological and behavioral adaptation to seasonal and diurnal contrasts is essential to all forms of life except those species living permanently in caves and other sunless places; it is typically managed physiologically by metabolic (circadian) rhythms.

Weather patterns at the scale of weeks may be partly predictable, but anyone planning a picnic knows how undependable is the forecast for tomorrow's weather. Short-term storms, floods, and droughts can have perceptible, even severe, effects on the geosphere and biosphere, changing the density or distribution of prey species, killing off livestock, increasing turbidity of water, changing the courses of rivers, redefining the boundary conditions for vegetation and thereby changing the species mix, the albedo, and even local temperatures.

At daily to decadal scales, very local and short-term weather can impinge on individual health and effectiveness. The unpleasant psychological and physiological effects of dry, warm, positively charged mountain winds such as the European Fohn and Californian Santa Ana are examples. The lethargy we feel in extreme heat or cold is another, while the energizing influence of ideal conditions of temperature, pressure, and humidity keeps travel agents in business. Even in technologically simple societies, cultural buffering against threatening weather is usually effective, although energetically expensive. Failure of cultural buffering, as in the Bangladesh and Central American floods of the 1980s and 1990s, is even more costly. Catastrophes of such scales should have been rare to absent prehistorically, among smaller societies and before anthropogenic environmental damage was as dramatic as it is today.

MECHANISMS INVOLVED IN A MESO-SCALE CLIMATIC REVERSAL

Milankovitch cycles may lull us into thinking of climate changes at regular intervals separated by periods of stability. Analyses of ice cores in Greenland and elsewhere show that climatic states flip more frequently than can be explained by orbital/axial factors. Internal autovariation and feedbacks among the five spheres are strongly implicated. These occur at intervals approximating archaeological relevance: 1000 years or less. Rapid reversals between cold and warm climate states are now recognized during glacial periods as well as during interglacials. Mechanisms have not been identified securely, partly because chronological precision is inadequate to specify initiating changes or distinguish those from responses. Solar variation is gaining respect as an initiating mechanism for high-frequency changes at the century and smaller scales.

The search for explanations of climatic fluctuations has focused interest on a period of about 1000 years near the end of the last glaciation, when the strong warming trend that was melting the glaciers was interrupted by a period of renewed severe cold. The cold period that spanned most of the eleventh radiocarbon millennium B.P. is called the Younger Dryas period, from an arctic flower (*Dryas octopetala*) that is the signature of renewed arctic climates in northwest European pollen cores and peats. The climate reversal, recognized about a century ago, is receiving renewed attention now as a model of short-term, abrupt climatic change.

In northwestern Europe the Younger Dryas period (YD) is recognized in such cold-climate indicators as readvancing mountain moraines, new cirque glaciers, reversals of vegetation sequences recorded in bogs and lakes, cycles in loess stratigraphy, signals in marine and ice cores, and in beetle sequences. Other evidence varies in specifics, proxies, and intensity with distance from the North Atlantic. Single-celled organisms in marine cores signal a readvance of the polar water into the middle latitudes of the North Atlantic, after a period of dramatic withdrawal to the north and east (Fig. 7.4). Ice cores in Greenland show increased dust in the air and decreased snow accumulation, both signals of cold, dry glacial-type climates (Alley et al. 1993). Evidence for cooling was first recognized in northwest Europe; other indicators of climate change tied to the period have been reported eastward into central Europe, in northeastern North America, in Alaska, the Levant, East Africa, eastern Asia, and the southern hemisphere (e.g., Broecker 1994; Peteet 1995; Thompson et al. 1995). Mechanisms that initiated cooling interrupting a strong warming trend, as well as the involvement of other aspects of the climate system, are matters of active controversy. Recognition of global-scale cooling recasts the search for mechanisms.

Information about the timing of the onset and end of the YD interval is sought in peat beds and other organic sediments, glacial lake varves, pollen cores, ice cores, marine sediments, loess sequences, mountain moraines, and corals. Correlations of several data sources are attempted by radiocarbon dating, tracing of volcanic ash deposits, ice-layer counts, oxygen-18 sequencing, and thorium dating (e.g., Edwards et al. 1993; Mangerud et al. 1984; Rundgren 1995). As is usually the case, with more data come more details and enhanced controversy. The ages indicated for the initiation and end of the YD cold spell vary with place and medium, but for the most part cluster into the eleventh radiocarbon millennium B.P. Efforts to develop a replicable YD chronology are hampered by radiocarbon uncertainties, secular changes in radiocarbon production related to solar activity, which we saw in Chapter 3 also affect climate. The radiocarbon calibration record for the eleventh millennium B.P. includes a major plateau of uncertainty occupying much of the eleventh millennium (Edwards et al. 1993; Hedges 1993). What seems clear is that the cold spell ended abruptly, perhaps within 40 years (Taylor et al. 1997), and was probably completely over around 10,000 radiocarbon years ago. Ages from ice-core counting and Th dating are older by about 2000 years, emphasizing the need for calibrated ^{14}C ages.

Age differences from place to place require reconciliation by improved understanding of the mechanisms driving the climatic reversals, their expressions at different places, and by the relationships of the several chronometers to those processes. Numerous mechanisms for the YD reversal have been proposed, invoking the atmosphere, the cryosphere, the ocean, the geosphere, and external forcing; the strongest combine two or three factors into ingenious synergisms. Doubtless by the time this volume appears, there will be more. Changes in ice-sheet forcing of atmospheric and oceanic temperatures with downwasting of the Laurentide ice sheet have been suggested (Ruddiman 1987). Meltwater from the massive Laurentide ice sheet of North America is of the right magnitude to cool the ocean directly (Broecker et al. 1989), but is far from the whole story. An attractive scenario involves sudden diversion of Laurentide meltwater from the Gulf of Mexico to the North Atlantic, capping the high-latitude ocean with a layer of cold, fresh water (Broecker and Denton 1990), modifying the global thermohaline marine circulation, and interrupting the northward flow of warm water that heats the atmosphere over Western Europe. However, as evidence accumulates from areas of the globe distant from northwest Europe, the relevance of a local cause is less likely.

Changes in atmospheric gases have been noted during the YD interval; their role, whether as forcing factors or response factors, is unclear. Volcanism, known to cool climates by reflecting solar radiation, is demonstrably involved, according to evidence from Greenland ice cores, but is not seen as a sufficient trigger for change on this scale. Recently, ice- and marine-core data amplify these suggestions. The latter show that near the end of the YD cold episode, terrestrial sediments pulsed into the North Atlantic in icebergs, leaving a signature in marine cores characteristic of the glacial "Heinrich events" (Bond et al. 1997), although less intense. The ca. 7000-year cyclicity of the Heinrich events implies a mechanism so far undiscovered. The direct calendar time of the ice-sheet layers provides a tighter, crisper chronology for the YD that facilitates correlation by paleoclimatologists of spatially separated data (Taylor et al. 1997). Archaeologists may soon be able to correlate cultural events with dated climatic episodes and begin to understand human adaptations to climatic stresses.

At present, none of the competing scenarios is completely convincing. Some of the mechanisms proposed as causes are likely to be shown eventually to be responses to change initiated or intensified by more independent mechanisms. A complex set of synergisms seems to be involved, requiring more precise and more dynamic notions of interaction than are now available. General Circulation Models of the YD atmosphere and conditions of global surfaces have been called into the game (Overpeck 1991). Powerful computer models seem the best means for understanding the interactions of so many factors cycling at different frequencies and involving different scales of space and different parts of the climate system: orbital and axial positions, thermohaline circulation, global atmospheric states including El Niño conditions, the behavior of the jet stream (Fig. 3.5), and monsoon strengths. The widespread evidence for the YD episode and its new dating together create an unparalleled opportunity for research into the complexity of climate mechanisms on the 1000-year frequency band.

Archaeologists have big stakes in attempts to understand the YD period. It directly affected regions in northern Europe and North America where humans were, at the time, colonizing recently deglaciated landscapes. In northeastern North America, Paleoindians were moving into the country around the Great Lakes and the St. Lawrence lowland; the landforms open to them, and the habitat conditions developing there, were partly defined by the expression of YD variables including temperature, precipitation, vegetation, and the volume of summer meltwater flow in the St. Lawrence River. The extreme conditions make the Paleoindian colonization of New England and the Maritime Provinces problematic rather than inevitable. Similarly, peoples with Hamburgian and Ahrensburgian cultures on the North European Plain must have confronted YD cooling that cannot have been very welcoming. If the evidence of abrupt termination is realistic, the final flip to climatic warming must have seemed magical to observers on the spot, who would have been challenged to change most of their coping strategies, as did their prey.

In the land that is now the Levant, populations of hunter-gatherers appear to have adopted strategies of plant cultivation in response to the environmental stresses of YD time. In the immediate Late Glacial warming period, people in Western Asia enjoyed relative plenty in a moist climate: they harvested fruit and nut trees and wild grains and hunted gazelles and goats. The YD cooling brought a sudden reversion to cool and dry climate; vegetation changes included a sharp decline in the temperate-zone food products favored during the warming, which were replaced on the landscape by species better adapted to cool steppe climates (other subtle aspects of the change are discussed in Part VI). Relatively sedentary "Natufian" communities in the area around the Dead Sea and northward began to tend and encourage edible seed plants, altering their previously opportunistic plant-collecting habits. The result of their efforts to stay in place and prosper in the new conditions was the beginning of a radically new style of human life – farming. Centuries passed before the implications of the change were revealed and the self-domestication of humans was irrevocably in a new phase (chapters in Harris 1996).

CODA

This brief review of the forces that define world climates establishes that climatic fluctuation is differently expressed at different scales, and that the sources of variation change with scale. Also, the significance of climate in human affairs varies with the scale at which it is observed. Archaeologists need to take this lesson to heart. As a factor in paleoenvironmental reconstruction, climate is the crucial fundamental. However, its definition is neither the beginning nor the end of paleoenvironmental analysis. Climate must be understood, and its details defined, at the scale at which it was significant for the archaeological studies at hand. The choice of scale will vary with the field situation, the age and size of the site or regional group being studied, and the human social, behavioral, and cultural problems posed. In studies of culture history, the role of climate cannot be assumed, but must be demonstrated for each case; surprises lurk.

CLIMATE RECONSTRUCTION

[I]nvestigators must know exactly what questions they are asking so that they can determine the kinds of data needed to answer those questions and, in turn, the procedures needed to obtain these data.

WATSON ET AL. 1984: 137

Climate – the mean and range of temperature and precipitation prevailing over a defined area of the globe – is complex in its causation and expression. Reconstructing climate, the effort to describe and measure climates of the past, must necessarily be a complex and technical undertaking. Climates leave only indirect, proxy evidence of their past states and conditions. The reconstruction of past climates, therefore, requires accumulation of indirect and partial evidence from many diverse sources, which must be carefully evaluated and compared. Archaeology and archaeologists contribute important sets and classes of data to the undertaking, but the task of reconstructing climate is not archaeological. It requires the integration of data from many sources by means of concepts and techniques that are themselves interdisciplinary.

The reconstruction of ancient climates involves specification of the distributions and amplitudes of temperature and precipitation in space and time. Once an exercise in inspired analogy, paleoclimatic study entered a dynamic phase in the 1970s, when the Earth's orbital and axial variations were demonstrated to be fundamental forcing factors for large-scale climatic states (Chapter 3). With basic mechanisms identified, paleoclimatology has been a lively research frontier since the 1980s. No survey such as this can be either complete or current. This chapter is an introduction for archaeologists, who may then explore further in the specialist literature. More detailed and technical treatments of the methods of paleoclimatology can be found in texts and handbooks such as those by Berglund (1986), Bradley (1999),

Crowley and North (1991), and Lowe and Walker (1984). Doubtless, references cited here will be superseded by new work in this fast-moving subject before this volume is in print.

Archaeologists rarely contribute data to climatic reconstructions above the site scale; that research is the domain of climatologists, geologists, geographers, ocean-ographers, and astronomers. Because archaeologists apply the results of such research to their own problem domains, they should be familiar with the assumptions that guide and the error factors that constrain the research, and they should develop sensitivity to appropriate archaeological applications of the results.

The discussion below follows the structure of Chapter 7 in separating the largest scales of paleoclimate reconstruction from those more familiar to archaeologists.

DEFINING CLIMATE AT LARGE SCALES

Atmospheric circulation distributes heat and moisture over the globe along paths that change as the intensity of solar radiation at different places on the Earth is modified by Earth's axial spin and tilt and seasonally variable distance from the Sun. The received radiation (insolation) is further modified by the extent of ice and snow on land and water. The winds that distribute weather are affected additionally by **topography** – the elevational relief of the surface. Once the major atmospheric circu-lation patterns are defined and modified for relief, the parameters of large-scale cli-matic conditions can be specified for a given time and space.

With external factors defined, paleoclimatologists can consider the contributions of the internal system's five spheres. As we have seen, the states and conditions of the five spheres (Chapter 3) are studied through proxy data – observable phenomena specific to each sphere that reflect changes in temperature and/or precipitation responding to climatic forcing. Paleoclimatologists have developed powerful com-puter models to simulate atmospheric circulation at various times in the past. These **General Circulation Models (GCMs)** are helping to refine knowledge of past major climatic states, especially within the last 18,000 years.

Modeling the external factors

At mega-scales of 10^6 years or more, astronomical and global factors define major low-frequency climatic trends. Therefore, the data utilized in studying the boundary conditions at very large scales derive from astrophysics and geophysics. In large measure, the orbital and axial variations that drive the glacial–interglacial alterna-tion can be calculated from knowledge of planetary motion. Because of this, orbital and axial variations are the foundations for the master chronologies of the glacial climate cycles, and of the General Circulation Models.

As discussed briefly in Chapter 3, the eccentricity of the Earth's orbit varies on a frequency of approximately 10^5 years (Fig. 3.1). The alternation between glacial and interglacial periods cycles at that frequency. The precession of the equinoxes and the cycle of axial tilt (obliquity) vary at frequencies approximating 23,000 or 41,000 years, respectively, defining the alternations of stadial and interstadial periods within glacial periods. Precession and tilt most directly affect the latitudinal distribution of solar radiation, and therefore the major patterns of atmospheric circulation that are accessible from mathematical models.

Computations of the variation of received solar radiation under orbital forcing provide information on temperature variations at scales ranging upward from monthly. Energy receipts under orbital forcing vary with latitude as well as on all the different frequencies of the several orbital parameters. For example, maximal summer solar radiation during the Holocene in Arctic latitudes is calculated to have occurred around 10,000 years ago, at a time when traditional climate modeling indicated the Arctic to have been still in the grip of the ice age. Pollen from organic sediments in the unglaciated Mackenzie Delta region of northwestern Canada reveals tree growth that meets that prediction of optimal growing conditions (Ritchie et al. 1983). This, with other research at high latitudes, indicates that responses to maximum radiation receipt occur at different rates in the several spheres, varying with latitude and medium. A great deal of the Earth's climatic complexity may someday be explained as variable-rate responses to radiational forcing. Radiational estimates from astronomical theory seem capable of supporting reasonably accurate models of temperatures and atmospheric responses at scales in the 10^5 to 10^3 range, within reach of archaeological research.

The most influential research demonstrating and validating the astronomical model of large-scale climate change has been study of sediments, comprising biological ooze, on the ocean floors where the alternation of warm and cold periods of sea-surface temperature through long sedimentary records shows a close fit with astronomical predictions for climate change (Imbrie and Imbrie 1979). Because the chronology of the astronomical variables is given by planetary cycling rates in sidereal (solar/calendrical) time, there are problems matching data to the several chronometric methods used by the Earth sciences. This should be kept in mind by archaeologists who work with terrestrial data and all the chronometric uncertainties that those entail, especially for times prior to the Holocene.

Research into relationships between solar variability and Earth climate has had a checkered career, and has only become productive in the late 1990s. If the complex chains of mechanisms suggested for relationships between sunspot cycles and climatic changes can be tested outside of computer models the 11-year cycle may be shown to be significant (Haigh 1996). This prospect fits well with the evidence for short-term rapid changes in climate within both glacial and interglacial stages.

Large-scale processes in the geosphere, such as plate tectonics and mountain building, define the latitude and elevation of continental masses and the distribution of oceans. The relative positions of continents and oceans in turn affect the amount of solar radiation that is absorbed or reflected by the Earth's surface, providing some of the parameters for atmospheric circulation of received heat. Continents constrain the oceanic and atmospheric currents that redistribute heat. Movements of the continental plates (Fig. 3.2) over the surface of the globe, at scales of 10^7 years and greater, are tracked by the orientation of remanent magnetism locked into rocks (Chapter 6) as well as by matching lithologies, rock series, and structures. Studies involve paleomagnetic reversals, archaeomagnetic orientations, structural geology, and biogeography.

Continental rocks are deformed into mountain ranges or pierced by volcanoes as tectonic plates push against one another. The height, latitude, growth rate, and chronology of mountain chains are important data for understanding ancient patterns of atmospheric circulation affected by elevational change. The growth and destruction of mountains, occurring at scales of 10^7 to 10^6 years, is studied by geophysical and geomorphological methods (Chapter 9).

Modeling the internal system

Within the parameters set by the external climate factors, autovariation and interactions within the five internal spheres produce the climatic states and changes at the higher frequencies and smaller spatial scales that are most useful to archaeologists. Understanding the states and conditions of each of the five spheres at any particular time theoretically would provide a helpful limitation on the degree of variation that could have been present. At mega- and macro-scales, the most determinative constituents of the internal climate system are the atmosphere, geosphere, hydrosphere, and cryosphere. Reconstructions of states of the biosphere are discussed below only in the second section (scales of 10^4 and smaller). The separation of the five spheres in the discussions that follow is purely for analytical clarity. The integration of disparate data sets, and the task of deriving from them a coherent picture of global, hemispheric, or regional climates, is the domain of mathematical models that are briefly considered below.

General Circulation Models (GCMs), abstract numerical simulations of climatic systems, incorporate proxy data from many sources. Many different GCMs have been developed, utilizing different ranges of data and processes and achieving different degrees of precision. Two of the most ambitious and detailed research projects using GCMs are those called CLIMAP (Climate: Long-range Investigation Mapping and Prediction) and COHMAP (Cooperative Holocene Mapping Project). Both projects involved international teams of scientists gathering and collating information about climate proxies worldwide, in order to provide data for computer simulations of climate at specific target years. The simulations aim to model atmospheric circulation patterns in the past – in the case of CLIMAP, at 18,000 radiocarbon years ago, the height of the last ice age.

The CLIMAP team established a limited set of boundary conditions for their simulation: surface albedo, sea-surface temperature, ice-free water area, sea-ice area, ice-sheet area, and "bare land" area (CLIMAP 1976). The effects of these conditions on present climatic variables were modeled by computer, on a simplified world map. Once the model was judged to simulate the current averages reasonably well, the modern values for the boundary conditions were replaced by values determined from a number of proxy calibrations for 18,000 years ago. To the extent possible, the values were derived directly from data, although extrapolations and estimates were used when necessary. With the ancient data set, the computer mapped conditions at the extreme of the last ice advance (e.g., Fig. 8.1).

Twelve years later, with experience and new information, another team published maps of successive climatic states at 3000-year intervals from 18,000 to 3000 B.P. Data on ice-sheet area, extent of sea ice year-round and in winter, land and ocean areas, effective moisture relative to the present, distributions of oak and spruce pollen where relevant, and key species of **foraminifera** in the Atlantic and Indian Oceans were put into the simulation. From these data and astronomical modeling, the COHMAP simulation reconstructed the major wind patterns and high-pressure blocking zones in the northern hemisphere. Tests of the climate models against selected data sets indicated that realism had been impressively approximated, but not achieved (COHMAP 1988). For example, the model predicted temperate forest vegetation in eastern North America earlier than palynological data indicate it. Problems with uncalibrated radiocarbon ages in the ranges of 15,000–25,000 years may explain some of the difficulties. The astronomical (true year) chronology for the forcing functions is seriously incongruent with radiocarbon ages prior to 10,000 years, where the model's divergence from data is greatest (Chapter 6). Other problems are likely to be found in assumptions about realistic climatic environments for pollen distributions, and for the speed with which plants can expand their ranges with climate change. Research continues, with GCMs providing powerful tools for approaching understanding of the effective mechanisms of the climate system at

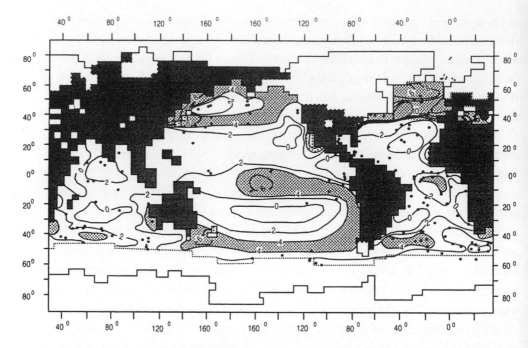

Figure 8.1 An example of an early GCM, plotting differences between August sea-surface temperatures 18,000 years ago (last glacial maximum) and modern averages. The contour interval is 2°C. The map is shown on a coarse grid of units 4° of latitude and 5° of longitude. (After CLIMAP Project Members 1976: Fig. 2.)

10^3–10^4 years and hemispherical spatial scales. Sellers et al. (1997) offer a useful review of the development of GCM technology to 1996.

Data sources for the atmosphere

Because the atmosphere distributes heat and moisture over the globe, its past states are of greatest interest to the paleoclimatologist. These states are studied by calculating and modeling the external and internal mechanisms that alter them, through analyzing ancient air samples in ice (Chapters 3 and 7), and through the effects of the altered states recorded in proxy data. A major complication in using proxy data for reconstructing atmospheric states is that the available proxies often discriminate very poorly between changes in temperature and changes in moisture, distinctions which are crucial for climatic reconstructions.

The reconstruction of atmospheric states at large temporal scales (10^5 years and above) is facilitated by computer processing of quantified, multivariate data in GCMs. The "scientific" cast of such research tends to blur for archaeologists the fact that resolution of detail at the low frequencies and large spatial scales that GCMs entail cannot be any better than the data on which it is based: the traditional proxy data from geology and paleobiology. Whatever the methods and data sources employed, climatic research at large scales is dominated by chronological considerations. Chronometers provide ages that permit data to be compared from one domain to another; the available refinement of the chronology employed defines the resolution of the data.

The oxygen isotope composition of ancient water can be deduced from calcareous molluskan shells and tests of single-celled organisms, which provide a deep-sea record of chemical composition for that crucial distant sphere. While there are serious uncertainties about the mechanisms involved and the amount of variance related to temperature, $^{18}O/^{16}O$ ratios in ice cores are considered responsive to air temperatures at the time of water vapor condensation and deposition (Bradley 1999: 132). Sea-surface temperatures, reflecting the interaction of air and ocean, affect some part of the isotopic signal in **planktonic** organisms recovered from marine sediments. Other chemical constituents and ratios in ancient atmospheres are being measured in air samples trapped in glacial ice (Alley et al. 1993; Mayewski et al. 1993).

The geosphere provides proxies for atmospheric conditions in both landforms and sediment sequences. Indeed, it was through observations in terrestrial sediments and landforms that the climatic changes of the ice ages were initially recognized, and it is in landform and sediment analysis that the bulk of traditional paleoclimatic work was done before the middle of the twentieth century. Geological evidence for climatic change is applicable at time scales in the middle to upper ranges, from 10^3 years to Earth age, with some younger exceptions, so that coordination with events at archaeological scales is typically poor. Major exceptions to this situation are varved lake sediments and loess deposits that provide stratified records of climatic changes at high chronological resolutions. Alluvial and aeolian sediments record in their textures and structures information about the moisture and energy in their environments of deposition (Birkeland 1984; Retallack 1990). Landforms and sediments of glacial origin inform about both temperature and moisture in past climates because they retain evidence of their environments of transport and deposition. The history of atmospheric moisture is read from proxies in the other four spheres as well, most of which contribute data that help define the crucial variables in GCMs.

Data sources for the hydrosphere: marine

For the reconstruction of climate at spatial scales of regions and above, data on the state and condition of the oceans are crucial. The distribution of water temperatures, salinity, currents, and major water masses over the globe sets the conditions of water–air interaction and of global heat circulation. The transfer of water between the oceans and ice sheets affects many elements of the climatic system.

Sediments accumulating on continental shelves and in deep ocean basins are mixtures of biogenic and mineral matter. The biogenic material is mainly the fossilized and subfossil remains of marine biota – the plants, animals, and single-celled organisms that live in the water column and on and in the floor of the ocean, although some comes ultimately from land (e.g., pollen). Mineral matter of terrestrial origin contributes climate data. Terrestrial sediments are flushed into the oceans by rivers, eroded by wave action from the shores and moved out to sea by currents, or transported as wind-borne particles and deposited from the atmosphere. The accumulation in one place of material from so many sources makes possible a wide variety of investigations into synchronous states of the land, air, freshwater bodies, and of the oceans themselves. Study of deep-sea cores has (1) increased the number of recognized cycles of glaciation during the last ice age from the four that were counted in continental deposits to over twenty, (2) revised estimates of the size of continental ice masses and the corresponding sea-level responses, (3) revealed periodicities in the deposits that have implicated the orbital forcing of Pleistocene climatic cycles, and (4) provided a rough chronology of climatic states for the last several hundred thousand years. These impressive accomplishments were achieved by analytical and interpretive methods still under development, and on the basis of rather small data sets. Further surprises and revisions of these results are expected.

The most informative proxy data on marine conditions are unicellular organisms with calcareous or siliceous "tests" (shell-like cell structures) that live in the water column both near the surface (planktonic) and on or within the sediments at the bottom (**benthic**). Foraminifera and coccoliths are the principal calcareous forms. Radiolaria and **diatoms** secrete siliceous structures and tend to accumulate under chemical conditions different from those that produce the calcareous forms. There are contrasts also between the biota of shallow continental shelves and those of the deep sea. The use of biological proxies in marine studies shares with terrestrial studies certain problems, such as inadequate knowledge of habitats and the biased representativeness of death assemblages, which do not mirror living populations closely. Death assemblages in the deep seas are subject to mixing by currents and by organisms living in the ooze, and the organic matter that reaches the sea floor has been subjected to selective dissolution of silicates and carbonates, so that the most fragile structures are unlikely to survive at all. These problems create difficulties in using living populations as analogs for interpreting the habitats of species assemblages recovered from cores (Hutson 1977). There is much to be learned about the life cycles and habitat tolerance ranges of these tiny organisms, in order that investigators may be able to specify the boundary conditions each represents. In addition, as with all living creatures, there are vital factors that complicate relationships between organisms and their habitats. Some species are known to change habitats seasonally or during their life cycles; some have wide tolerances for certain conditions and perhaps narrow tolerances for others. The critical habitat parameters of extinct species cannot be known with any certainty. All these complications make the choice of species for any given study a crucial decision in the research design, and limit the interpretations that can legitimately be made from different kinds of analyses.

The earliest major studies of deep-sea cores were achieved by examining species ratios and distributions. By recording the presences and frequencies of species whose temperature and salinity sensitivities are known or inferred from their modern distributions, investigators map sea-surface temperatures and salinities at different depths in cores, equating them with progressively older time periods. Plotting species distributions along transects, they track the changing distributions of major water bodies in the Pleistocene oceans. Variations and refinements on this approach include mapping species associations, mapping species which changed aspects of their morphology in different habitats, and translating species assemblages into quantitative expressions of temperature or salinities. For example, the foraminifer *Globorotalia truncatulinoides* coils its test to the right in warm water, to the left in cooler water: this single species thus gives some relative indication of temperature changes. By selecting critical species for counting in numerous cores, oceanographers have mapped the changing position of the polar front in the North Atlantic through the Late Pleistocene (Fig. 7.4).

Studies of oxygen-isotope ratios in calcareous microorganisms have been in the forefront of paleoclimatic research since the 1960s (Faure 1986). The two stable isotopes of oxygen, ^{16}O and ^{18}O, occur in fixed ratios in the Earth's water cycle as a whole (Shackleton 1977: 2: $^{16}O = 99.725\%$; $^{17}O = 0.0374\%$; $^{18}O = 0.2039\%$), but are differentially distributed within it. Oxygen isotope ratios in sea water and ice are expressed in terms of a fixed standard: Standard Mean Ocean Water (SMOW; corrected to VSMOW [Kra 1995]); those in calcareous materials are expressed in terms of a standard measured in an ancient belemnite from the PeeDee formation of South Carolina (PDB; VPDB [Kra 1995]). The ratios are, therefore, expressed as departures, in a positive or negative sense, from those standards, and are written as deviations, $\delta^{18}O$, in parts per thousand (per mil: ‰; Table 8.1). The lightest isotope evaporates most readily, and is more stable in water vapor than are the heavier ones. Therefore, at times when large amounts of water are transferred from the oceans to ice caps by evaporation and precipitation, the lightest isotope is differentially removed from the oceans, and the ocean is thereby enriched in the heavier isotopes. Larger amounts of

Table 8.1 Conventions in isotope analyses

Isotope conventions and symbols

^{12}C; ^{15}N: the superscript on the left identifies the isotope number of the element indicated.

δ: lower-case delta stands for "difference" from some agreed standard.

‰:   parts "per mil": as 1% is 1 part in a hundred, so 1‰ is 1 part in a thousand.

Carbon isotopes

δ^{13}C: the difference (δ) between the carbon isotope ratio of a sample and the ratio of a standard, in parts per mil, e.g. $\delta^{13}C_{sample} = [(R_{sample}/R_{standard}) - 1] \times 1000$, when R is the ratio of ^{13}C/^{12}C.

negative numbers: see PDB.

PDB: the Pee Dee Belemnite standard for carbon isotope ratios. The ^{13}C/^{12}C isotope ratios in CO_2 derived from the carbonate shell of a mollusk from the Cretaceous Pee Dee Formation of South Carolina, chosen to be free of ^{14}C. Organic materials have a smaller (lighter, or depleted) ^{13}C ratio, thus a negative δ^{13}C value in respect to the standard.

Typical values of δ^{13}C

  atmosphere: -7 ‰

  C_3 plants: -26.5 ‰

  C_4 plants: -12.5 ‰

  marine mollusk shells: $+4.2$ to -1.7‰

  freshwater molluskan shells: -0.6 to -15.2‰ (riverine species are more negative than lacustrine spp.)

Nitrogen isotopes

AIR: the standard for nitrogen ^{15}N/^{14}N ratios. The unmistakable acronym technically stands for "ambient inhalable reservoir."

Typical values of δ^{15}N, based on AIR standard $= 0$

  Terrestrial food chains

    legumes $= 0$

    terrestrial plants: ca. $+3$‰

    herbivores: $+4$ to $+7$‰

    carnivores: $+7$ to $+9$‰

  marine food chains

    algae $= 0$

    swordfish and seals: $+15$ to $+20$‰

    polar bear: >20‰.

  terrestrial values are higher in dry regions, complicating the interpretation of differences between marine and terrestrial foods in dry coastal regions.

Sources: Ambrose 1993; Bumsted 1985; E. A. Little (pers. comm.); Keith et al. 1964; van der Merwe 1992.

the heavy isotope then are incorporated into the hard tests and shells of organisms that live in the sea, creating a proxy signal for glacially lowered sea levels. In organisms secreting calcium carbonate, the concentration of ^{18}O is also to some degree dependent on seawater temperature, a relationship complicated by the changing isotope ratios in the sea water itself. Differential temperature effects are best expressed among organisms living on or near the surface, so that the calcareous structures of planktonic species, separated out from sediment cores, are used to make rough estimates of sea-surface temperatures (SST) (Bradley 1999). The deep-dwelling benthic species living in the cold bottom waters incorporate the isotopic ratios of the deep waters. Deep-sea isotope ratios are reasonably comparable worldwide because of the relatively rapid mixing of the world's deep-water masses. The data can generally be resolved to within a thousand years (10^3), and occasionally to a century, depending on the mixing rate, resolution preserved in the mixed sediments, rates of sedimentation, and sizes of samples processed.

Oxygen-isotope ratios have varied markedly and rhythmically through the last several hundred thousand years, showing characteristic "sawtooth" patterns when graphed (Fig. 7.2). The alternation of glacial and interglacial climatic conditions is clearly exemplified. For sea-surface paleotemperature studies the derived temperature values are usually expressed as difference from modern averages rather than in absolute terms.

The worldwide expression of the oxygen-isotope stages make these patterns excellent stratigraphic markers for the correlation of cores from different parts of the world as well as cores analyzed on different data sets. They provide a reasonably reliable relative chronology of glacial and interglacial periods in the world's oceans. Cores can be dated by radiocarbon for the period of that technique's usefulness, by uranium-series measurements and by paleomagnetic reversals. Between points on a core that can be dated by one or another of these means, dead reckoning and matching of dated biostratigraphic markers are used, with fitting to the calculated periods of the astronomical chronology. Some stratigraphic correlations between terrestrial and marine data sets have been achieved using identifiable volcanic ash falls and well-dated sea-level changes. The farther back in time, the less firm is any chronological control on the core data and, by extension, on the climatic and marine episodes that are interpreted from them, but within the time span of significance to archaeologists, the controls seem adequate.

Data sources for the hydrosphere: terrestrial

Proxy data on ancient or low-frequency states of moisture on land masses are more elusive than those for the oceans. Precipitation regimes, especially major alternations between wet and dry states, can be studied in lake-bed sediments, vegetation proxies, ice cores, and faunal associations. The terrestrial biosphere, vitally sensitive to the availability of essential water, is a source of eloquent proxies for it (tree rings and pollen spectra) in both the atmosphere and hydrosphere.

Oxygen-isotope studies of **marls**, mollusks, and single-celled organisms in the beds of freshwater lakes and ponds reveal climatic signals related to water temperatures and biological productivity. The climatic relevance of these signals is attenuated by a number of non-climatic factors, including differences in the sources of the precipitated moisture, influx of older carbonates from the watershed, stirring and redeposition of sediments, and organic fractionation by the carbonate-fixing organisms themselves. Such complications mean that the oxygen-isotope method can provide only qualitative estimates of temperatures (Berglund 1986). The $\delta^{18}O$ ratios in fresh water are essentially mirror images of those in the sea: cold-climate periods show a relative enrichment in the light isotopes precipitated from the atmosphere. Studies of $\delta^{18}O$ in lake-bed cores can be calibrated with pollen and other data sources reflecting different aspects of climate, and can be resolved to time periods and geographical spaces significantly smaller than those of marine cores, especially in varved sediments (e.g., McAndrews and Boyko-Diskonow 1989). Fluctuating water levels in closed freshwater basins have been shown to reflect orbital forcing of the low-latitude monsoonal system (Kutzbach and Street-Perrott 1985). Other methods for interpreting environmental signals in freshwater sediments are discussed in Part V.

Data sources for the cryosphere

Information on the past distributions and conditions of ice on land and sea comes from a variety of sources, principally ice cores, marine cores, landforms, and sediments. High-latitude and high-elevation ice coring has revolutionized the study of the cryosphere as much as marine coring has that of the hydrosphere. Snow accumulating on continental glaciers gradually packs under the weight of further accumulation, recrystallizes into the coarser state called **firn**, and eventually compacts and partly melts into ice, which may then flow. Seasonal variation in snowfall amounts and accompanying particulates makes annual layers visible in snowfields and ice, sometimes to great depths. Cores drilled into deep ice sheets reveal a record of accumulation and the transformation of snow into ice that can be used to recreate aspects of the ice sheet's history and of the conditions in which it grew. Ice cores reveal the accumulation rate of ice, and the qualities of air and precipitation under which it formed. Such studies have been most successful for Holocene time ranges, and have been used in archaeological applications in both the northern and southern hemispheres.

The same reasoning that related $\delta^{18}O$ ratios in water to major temperature cycles of the planet can be applied to ice sheets, which are accumulations of precipitated condensed water vapor, which came ultimately from the oceans. Therefore, we could expect that ice sheets would reflect, through very low heavy-isotope ratios, the cold conditions under which they formed; to a point, those expectations are met. Large, old continental ice sheets have some of the lowest $\delta^{18}O$ values recorded on the Earth. However, the filters that have selectively screened out the heavy isotope of oxygen from precipitation at high latitudes and high altitudes reflect many variables of water-vapor source and distance, season, transport, and condensation. These variables are difficult to quantify and their results cannot be separated in the final product. In addition, subsequent movement of the ice at depth through the glacier, distortion of the annual layers by compression at depth and with ice movement, and diffusion of isotopes under pressure in ice further complicates the isotopic history (Bradley 1999: 126–135). Although empirical evidence has shown a relationship between $\delta^{18}O$ values in high-latitude precipitation and hemispheric mean annual temperatures, the reasons for such correlation have not been fully demonstrated. The relationships may be scale-dependent, so that at high frequencies (small temporal scales) such as archaeologists prefer, the spatial representativeness might be significantly smaller.

Dating ice cores is another challenge. Initially, investigators used a mathematical model of ice flow through and out of ice sheets to estimate the age of ice samples at depth. The model, based on several simplifying assumptions, provided only approximate ages. Over the years, the chronologies proposed for long ice cores have been recalculated on the basis of different sets of boundary assumptions (Dansgaard et al. 1969, 1971, 1982). Any use of ice-core data in correlation with climatic events distant in space will be affected by the chronology adopted. Recent advances in discrimination of annual layers in ice have pushed a high-resolution chronology back toward 80,000 years in Greenlandic cores, and demonstrated broad departures from uncalibrated radiocarbon years at the end of the last glaciation (Mayewski et al. 1993), as discussed in Part II.

Marine cores close to shores can reveal, through the presence of diatom species that live under ice or the absence of microorganisms that live at the air–sea interface, the former extent of ice frozen to the shore. The distribution on the ocean floor of iceberg-rafted sediments is an indicator of iceberg pulses and their equatorward extension at various times.

Ice-core research is contributing revolutionary insights to paleoclimatology at global and smaller scales. Advances in counting annual layers will likely provide a radiocarbon calibration standard complementary to tree rings. Nevertheless, extrapolation of ice-core climatic models to distant places, particularly at cultural scales of time and space, must be undertaken with great care.

DEFINING CLIMATE AT MESO- AND MICRO-SCALES

Archaeologists must rely on climatologists for information and interpretations of paleoclimates at all but the micro-scale. As the scales of phenomena studied become finer, as must those relevant to cultural interpretations, archaeologists are more directly involved in recovering evidence that can implicate climatic states and conditions. They must, therefore, be able to recognize evidence in the ground, and know enough to recover it in usable condition from well-recorded contexts. Archaeologists have the responsibility to know (1) how to use the climatological literature responsibly, (2) how to collect climatological data at the micro-scale, and (3) how to consult with specialists for interpretation and integration of the data at all scales.

Archaeological data may be extremely valuable for paleoclimatologists when they come in fine chronological packages, giving more dating control than is usually available. Archaeologists sensitive to proxy data on climatic and weather conditions therefore may contribute evidence that can advance interdisciplinary research. For the archaeologist, such involvement requires familiarity with climate proxies, a sharp eye and active curiosity, and effective collaboration. Successes in these endeavors are discussed in several chapters below. Primarily, making the best use of proxy data in field situations demands of the archaeologist forethought in problem formulation and team composition, and flexibility in the face of new opportunities.

In short time spans and at small scales, weather is the expression of climatic bounding conditions. Weather is what humans experience on a day-to-day basis; weather is the context for their behavior and sometimes for their options in decision-making. Evidence for weather, however, is not easily recovered from proxy data that are by their nature cumulative and integrative. Most such data sets are relatively insensitive to variability at the micro-scale, unless the data are recovered from unusual, micro-stratified matrices such as varves. Tree rings are the best sources for climatic data at fine resolutions; under ideal conditions, seasonal weather patterns can be interpreted from them. Ice cores from high-accumulation areas such as Quelccaya in the Peruvian Andes can match the resolution of tree rings.

With refinement of spatial and temporal resolutions, evidence is emerging for significant regional diversity in the expression of climate. Diversity appears in chronological differences in the onset and end of climatic and vegetational phases, in contrastive trends of temperature and precipitation inferred from a variety of proxy sources, and in the differential dominance of internal and external climatic mechanisms. Thus, species dispersal rates, differential competition, soils development, distance from glacial **refugia**, and human manipulation are all recognized as significant non-climatic determinants of vegetation patterns in the Holocene at higher frequencies (Davis 1986; Ritchie 1986; Roberts 1989). As postglacial vegetation is mapped with increasing sensitivity to fine details the broad-scale coherence that has been so highly valued as a climatic indicator disappears (see Lowe 1993). There can be no question but that climate is one of the determinants of vegetation associations, especially at range limits. Its role at other times and places is now less than entirely obvious and deterministic, especially during the dynamism of Late Glacial warming trends. It is no longer so easy as it once was to confuse pattern with process, or to leap from the inference of process to the assumption of mechanism. Some of the complexities of adapting paleovegetation data to archaeological contexts are exemplified in the Elm Decline case associated with this Part (pp. 188–191).

As Table 8.2 shows, proxy sources for climatic data are much the same at the macro- and meso-scales, except that the resolution of marine cores is unsatisfactory for archaeological applications more recent than the middle of the Holocene. After about 5000 years ago, with written language, historical archives become important data sources. By the Middle Holocene, anthropogenic impacts on environments, and even climate, increase (Chambers 1993a; Roberts 1989). Hence, the skills and data sets applied to reconstructing late Holocene climates differ qualitatively from those utilized for earlier times.

For consistency's sake, this second half of the chapter is organized according to the five spheres to emphasize individually the climate proxies in each; at the smaller scales of space and time, data from separate spheres begin to cross-reference each other. This overlapping complementarity is an important characteristic of proxy data at these scales that becomes an organizing principle for archaeological use of climatic data.

Data sources for the atmosphere

Direct evidence of atmospheric composition in recent millennia is available in the form of particulates and gases trapped in glacial ice. Identification and quantification of airborne particulates such as volcanic ash and desert sands reveal source areas, wind strengths, and dust concentrations. Air enclosed within fallen snow is sealed into bubbles as the snow compacts to the coarser crystalline firn and from firn to ice. By crushing the ice under vacuum, investigators recover samples preserved in air-filled cavities, revealing the concentrations of gases within ancient

Table 8.2 Exponential scales in time with appropriate sources of proxy data on climates

Temporal scales	Temporal range	Proxies	Information classes
Mega-	$>10^6$	marine cores	T, Cw, B, A
		GEOMORPHIC FEATURES	T, H, V, L
		sedimentary rocks	H, Cs, V, L, A
Macro-	10^4–10^6	marine cores	T, Cw, B, P
		ice cores	T, H, Ca, B, A, V, S
		sedimentary rocks	H, Cs, V, L, A
		lake sediments	T, H, Cw, B, V, A
		TERRESTRIAL SEDIMENTS	H, B, A
		FAUNA	T, H, Cs, B
		POLLEN	T, H, B
		PALEOSOLS	T, H, Cs, V
		corals	Cw, L
Meso-	10^2–10^4	TERRESTRIAL SEDIMENTS	H, B, A, V
		PALEOSOLS	T, H, Cs, V
		POLLEN	T, H, B
		TREE RINGS	T, H, Ca, B, V, S
		FAUNA	T, H, Cs, B
		lake sediments	T, H, Cw, B, V, A
		ice cores	T, H, Ca, B, V, S, A
		corals	Cw, L
		historical records	T, H, B, V, L, S
Micro-	$<10^2$	historical records	T, H, B, V, L, S
		TREE RINGS	T, H, Ca, B, V, S
		varves	T, H, Cw, B, V, A

Notes:
KEY:
A = atmospheric particulates
B = biomass
C = chemical composition of air (Ca), water (Cw), or soil (Cs)
H = humidity or precipitation
L = sea levels
S = solar activity
T = temperature
V = volcanism

Some major proxy data sets used to reconstruct climatic parameters at the scales which archaeologists can utilize. SMALL CAPS TYPE distinguishes data sets that may be recovered during archaeological field investigations. Most of the data are studied by a number of different analytical and interpretive techniques, which will be considered in the chapters to follow. This table may be compared with the dating techniques of Table 5.1, which are crucial to the application of proxy data.

Source: Modified from Bradley 1991: 7.

air, including sulfur gases, methane, and carbon dioxide that directly influence the receipt of solar radiation (Bradley 1999: 167–169; Crowley and North 1991: 58). Attempts to sample ancient air in archaeological environments such as tombs and sealed containers have been less successful, because of diffusion and gas exchange in near-surface environments.

Additional records for atmospheric particulates include wind-borne dust recovered from datable loess sheets, lake beds, and marine cores. The source area of the dust implicates wind direction and the size of the particles indicates wind speed. Less dust is in the global atmosphere during warm and moist climates than during cold, dry times, because vegetation holds mineral sediments in soils when growing conditions are optimal and wind speeds less.

Changing $\delta^{18}O$ values are tracked at close intervals for the timing of oscillations between warm and cold air regimes and relative precipitation (Meese et al. 1994). Investigations of ancient air confirm what marine cores imply – atmospheric CO_2 concentrations were lower during glacial periods, and enriched during interglacials such as the present. Cores from deep-water basins in the oceans reveal that the oceans conserve CO_2 during cold periods and release it as solar radiation increases at the beginning of warm periods. Trapping heat in the lower atmosphere, CO_2 amplifies radiational warming, contributing to the rapid disintegration of large ice sheets.

Proxies for atmospheric temperatures include oxygen-isotope ratios from marine cores, ice cores, corals, and terrestrial speleothems. Apparently good cross-correlations among these several sources are building confidence in such methods and the resultant chronologies.

Data sources for climate change from the geosphere

The geosphere participates in feedback adjustments of the internal climate system at smaller scales. Isostatic adjustments of the crust and mantle under shifting loads of ice and water appear to have been important in deglaciation; in some circumstances they increased contact between glacial ice and water, and thus melting rates. Elevational differences created by postglacial uplift, especially at high latitudes, influence wind patterns and intensities, at least at local scales, and thus affect climate. The relatively high terrestrial albedos of deserts and land newly emerged from a regressing sea all reflect solar radiation back to the atmosphere, with climatic effects. Geomorphology and sedimentology provide the data to reveal changes of these sorts, although estimating their contributions to climatic change remains a great challenge.

Landforms indicative of major changes in the cryosphere and hydrosphere, such as till deposits, dune fields, **glaciofluvial** (glacial outwash) features, and raised beaches, reveal the spatial scales at which interactions among atmosphere, ice, and ocean took place. Similarly, evidence for small ice bodies, such as snow lines at high elevations that were lowered during periods of colder climates, gives roughly quantifiable estimates of the atmospheric lapse rate, the lowering of temperature with elevation. Old shorelines of major lakes indicate, by successive elevations, how lake levels fluctuated at times in the past. While the explanation of those fluctuations may require data from other sources, and may implicate climatic components other than the atmosphere, changing lake levels indicate that either temperature or precipitation changes were likely involved, especially if geotectonic or isostatic movements were not contributing. Ancient dune fields and loess sheets are landform elements that implicate climatic limitations on vegetation, providing evidence about ancient temperature and precipitation regimes. Wind-polished rock surfaces and stones (**ventifacts**) record periods of strong wind scour and the removal of fine sediments; when they can be dated, even stratigraphically, their evidence for atmospheric conditions can contribute to climatic reconstructions.

Sediments – terrestrial, lacustrine, marine, speleological – are the media of archaeological investigations. They contain considerable information about past states of climate, even episodes of unusual weather. Archaeologists alert to such possibilities can enrich the environmental contexts of the human behavior they are digging to investigate. As noted above, wind strengths and directions can be inferred from dune fields, loess sheets, ventifacted bedrock, and even dust plumes in marine cores and ice cores, as the strength of the transporting wind is reflected directly in the size of the sediments moved. The amount of sediment moved varies with the moisture available at its source, providing information about dry and moist periods at the sources of the sediments (Krinsley and Doornkamp 1973). The character of soils developed on and within sediments varies with a number of environmental factors (Part V) including temperature and moisture; analysis of paleosols, therefore, can contribute information on ancient atmospheric conditions.

Alluvial sediments, deposited from moving water, hold information about past precipitation conditions. Only abundant water can move large masses of sediments and sizable pieces of rock. The shapes and compositions of alluvial sediments reveal details of the environments in which they were transported and deposited. Information about long-term precipitation regimes, as well as instability in prevailing climates, can be gained directly from alluvial sediments and their associated landforms (Chorley et al. 1984; Summerfield 1991).

Volcanism affects climate at shorter frequencies by contributing to the atmosphere particulate matter that deflects away from the Earth solar radiation reaching the upper atmosphere. In this way, major episodes of volcanism can produce markedly cooler climates at hemispheric scales, the time span of which varies with the intensity and frequency of volcanic eruptions (Scuderi 1990). Volcanic ash falls (tephra) can be traced in terrestrial and marine sediments and in ice cores, potentially establishing contemporaneity in all three depositional environments; the age of a tephra layer can be measured by potassium–argon dating, ice-flow modeling, paleomagnetism, or association in datable contexts. Sulfuric acid in high-latitude precipitation can be traced in ice cores, where it records major explosive volcanism. Volcanism appears to be an effective trigger mechanism for initiating cooler climatic episodes at scales of 10^2 years and below. When other systems are in particularly sensitive states, volcanism may be enough to flip the climate from a warm to cool trend. Thus, defining and dating episodes of volcanism contributes importantly to understanding climatic changes (Bryson 1989).

Data sources for climate change from the hydrosphere

The oceans of the world are major factors in climate definition, through their exchanges of heat, moisture, and gases with the atmosphere. Terrestrial fresh water, crucial to life on Earth, is a product of precipitation, which has been variable in the past and seems to have become especially variable in the latter years of the twentieth century. Information about the state of the hydrosphere at any point in time is crucial for understanding human habitats.

Marine cores yield information about temperatures at the interface of air and water, and about the circulation of heat and cold around the globe. We have seen in Chapter 7 the importance for paleoclimate reconstruction of the oxygen-isotope records in marine cores. Recent expansion of marine core information through correlation of Heinrich events and rapid climate oscillations (Bond et al. 1997) has improved chronometric resolution and has brought those data sources into fruitful cooperation with ice-core studies of atmospheric changes. The resultant linkage of sea and air changes is revolutionizing GCMs.

Some of the most promising work on marine conditions and states at small scales derives from research on the ENSO system of the central Pacific, a major definer of short-term climate and weather variation over large areas of the globe (Diaz and Markgraf 1993). Short-term atmospheric fluctuations related to the ENSO system have been traced in historical records, in temperate zone tree rings, in South American alluvium, in ice cores, in coral reefs, and in shellfish growth, to provide both fine-resolution chronologies and crucial climatic data for archaeologists (papers in Diaz and Markgraf 1993; Moseley 1987; Rollins et al. 1986; Sandweiss et al. 1996).

Limnological study of terrestrial freshwater states and conditions relies on interpretation of lake-bed sediments to measure fluctuations in water depth and quality at very high resolutions. Oxygen isotopes in marls and travertines, ostracods and diatoms, pollen and grain-size studies all contribute information (e.g., Binford et al. 1983; chapters in Berglund 1986).

Landsat imagery has revealed the courses of rivers now buried in sand (Ghose et al. 1979), leading to crucial insights into past climates and habitats. Water running under the surface of the Earth deposits calcitic speleothems in caverns, where the isotopic signals of surface conditions are crystallized for later study (e.g., Dorale et al. 1992). Experimental work recovering paleotemperatures from analysis of gases in deep groundwater looks promising (Stute et al. 1992).

Data sources for climate change from the cryosphere

The very existence of continental and mountain glaciers, as well as their size variation in the past, are direct indicators of the relative coolness of climates of the last several hundred thousand years (Hambrey and Alean 1992). Geomorphological techniques applied to glacial landforms give evidence about the minimum volume, shape, and ages of glaciers, and about the scale and timing of episodes of advances and retreats (Denton and Hughes 1980; Sibrava et al. 1986). These classic glaciological methods have provided most of what is known about individual ice sheets, their action on the continents, and their climatic effects. Ice in formerly frozen ground is revealed by the characteristic **periglacial** features that form in perennially frozen sediments – patterned ground, pingos, and solifluction. Periglacial features are discussed in Part V.

Ice cores are taking their place among the best recorders of moisture and temperature regimes at high latitudes and altitudes. The research on trapped gases and particulates (volcanic dust, terrestrial dust, salts), along with accumulation measurements, provides a rich choice of proxies for several different climatic variables: atmospheric composition (trace elements and isotopes); relative precipitation at a seasonal scale; temperatures of deposition (Dawson 1992; Oeschger and Langway 1989; Thompson et al. 1998).

When organic particles in ice permit radiocarbon dating, the ages can be approximated within the precision of that method. In cases where the annual layering of glaciers can be sensed chemically or optically, counting yearly accumulations gives a chronology as precise as tree rings. Ice-core research on several continents is expanding and clarifying understanding of the crucial ENSO system on a global scale (chapters in Diaz and Markgraf 1993). Interpretations change rapidly; archaeologists should seek guidance and collaboration from active practitioners of the art when they wish to utilize current understandings for their own purposes.

A recent application of annual measurements of ice accumulations to cultural problems in Peru provides a glimpse of high-frequency paleoclimatology in the new mode. Ice accumulation records from the Quelccaya ice cap in the southeastern Peruvian highlands were used to develop an ecological explanation for the collapse of the prehistoric empire of Tiwanaku, centered near Lake Titicaca about 200 km south of the ice cap (Ortloff and Kolata 1993). Ortloff and Kolata describe several different kinds of intensive agricultural technologies within the empire at different altitudes, proposing a scenario for their differential vulnerability to droughts, and hence the sequence in which they would fail. The authors compare ice-core data indicating an especially long-lived dry period to the archaeological records of the disintegration of various parts of the Tiwanaku empire. They consider a wide range of cultural processes – technological, economic, political, and social. Within the limits of archaeological chronology, less exact than that of the climate changes, their explanation holds extremely well. This study is especially notable for the fine resolution of the paleoclimate reconstruction based on research at Quelccaya, for the support given this reconstruction by limnological study of lake sediments, and for the detailed specification of a range of cultural effects of the climate change. It sets new standards for effective interdisciplinary collaboration in cultural history.

Data sources for climate change from the biosphere

As part of the internal climate system, the biosphere contributes significantly to the definition of climates at all scales. It is also, as we saw above for pollen associations, a source of crucial proxy data. To avoid tautologies climatologists must scrupulously distinguish these two roles for biological data. Both roles are briefly discussed here.

The biosphere contributes to the stability or variability of the climate system principally through regional-scale adjustments of vegetation that are changes of state rather than of condition (Ganopolski et al. 1998). Changes such as those from forest to grassland, or from grassland to desert scrub, have implications for moisture, gas, and particulate interchanges with the atmosphere, as well as albedo effects. Changes at such scales affect local climates, and may in turn force further changes downstream in atmospheric circulation patterns. Reconstructions of regional-scale vegetation, therefore, can help elucidate the biosphere's contribution to climates of the past, including their role in testing GCMs with the observed distributions of climate-sensitive species. Palynology and macrobotany provide direct data about the states and conditions of terrestrial plant communities at local scales. Data sets on terrestrial biota are characteristically available in relatively brief or discontinuous sequences. Cases in which biological data are continuous through time ranges greater than 50,000 years are precious indeed. Examples include pollen sequences extending back through the last glacial stage into the last interglacial, documented in France (Woillard 1978), Australia (Kershaw 1978), and Florida (Grimm et al. 1993).

Biological proxies introduce into climatic reconstruction sampling issues such as representativeness and integrity of context. These issues are evaluated by the methods of taphonomy, the study of the processes leading to burial and fossilization. Awareness of taphonomy is an important aspect of the field collection of biological proxy data (Gifford 1981; Parts VI and VII).

Plants

Reconstruction of regional climatic regimes, and by implication air masses, from evidence of former plant associations and distributions was a pioneering method in paleoclimatology. For most of the twentieth century the Blytt–Sernander peat stratigraphic zones established for the Holocene in northwest Europe, amplified by pollen analysis and dated by reference to varve counts and later by radiocarbon, stood as the standard proxy for climatic evolution in the northern hemisphere since the last glacial maximum (Fig. 8.2). The sequences of plant species associations were assumed to be determined by and in equilibrium with climate, so that climatic states were inferred and characterized for each phase. The appearance in a peat sequence or pollen diagram of a selected temperate forest species, for example, was interpreted as a record of the establishment of a temperate, moist climate in the area. Although these simplified assumptions no longer command respect (Blackford 1993), plant remains both microscopic and large continue to inform paleoclimatic studies.

Similar assumptions about correlations between vegetation and climates lie behind statistical expressions of relationships between modern pollen associations and modern climatic parameters (Bryson 1985; Webb and Clark 1977). Statistical relationships (transfer functions) are used to calculate climatic parameters for pollen associations observed in ancient sediments. While these relationships hold reasonably well at scales of 10^3 years and above (Webb and Bartlein 1992), they are subject to all the caveats and pitfalls of analogical arguments. This has become increasingly clear with the recognition that many of the pollen associations observed in Quaternary deposits have no close correspondence with any modern pollen rains,

Years B.P.	Blytt–Sernander period	Climate	Peat evidence	Pollen zone
—1000 —2000	Sub-Atlantic	Deterioration cold and wet	poorly humified Sphagnum peat	VIII
—3000 —4000 —5000	Sub-Boreal	warm and dry Climatic Optimum	pine stumps in humified peat	VIIb
—6000 —7000	Atlantic	warm and wet	poorly humified Sphagnum peat	VIIa
—8000 —9000	Boreal	warm and dry Rapid Amelioration	pine stumps in humified peat	VI V
—10000	Pre-Boreal	subarctic	subarctic plants in peat	IV
	Younger Dryas	Cold		III
—11000	Alleröd	Cool		II

Figure 8.2 Blytt–Sernander vegetation periods and the climatic states attributed to them. (After Lowe and Walker 1984: Tables 3.4 and 3.5.)

and the demonstration that the relationships among axial and orbital boundary conditions do not repeat in time. Furthermore, the basic assumption of direct climatic control of plant associations has come increasingly under attack as (1) the claims for synchrony of vegetation changes in different areas have suffered under the contrary evidence of radiocarbon-dated pollen diagrams from many areas of Europe and North America, (2) higher resolution in pollen studies has shown that species' appearances over space are time-transgressive, and (3) alternative methods for inferring climatic regimes have shown a lack of congruence among the several data sets (e.g., temperature indications from pollen and beetles) (Birks 1986; Lowe 1993; Magny 1982). Additional complications for the analog argument come from high-resolution data on atmospheric CO_2; carbon dioxide concentrations different from those of today affect the growth efficiency of plant species in different ways, so that associations in the past could reflect growing conditions unlike any observable today (e.g., Street-Perrott et al. 1997). Archaeologists should beware of misapplying climate reconstructions built at regional and millennial scales. For cultural interpretations, use data at the finest resolutions available.

Thomas Hardy's fictional nineteenth-century Wessex countrymen knew that "a warm summer permanently marks the ring in the tree-trunk corresponding to its date" (*The Mayor of Casterbridge*). Dendroclimatologists take good advantage of this, using both ring width and wood density to study small-scale atmospheric patterns and past climates at micro-scales (Baillie 1995; Hughes et al. 1982). Compilations of such observations, statistically compared at meso- and macro-scales, are informative about latitudinal and longitudinal shifts of major air masses (Fritts 1991) and of trends in climate change at short and long intervals (Dean et al. 1996; Jacoby et al. 1996).

Animals

Animal proxies for climate change come into prominence at small scales, where they can provide appropriate resolution. Small animals, particularly, offer special opportunities for information about past climates at the local and micro-scales because they may have fairly narrow tolerances for temperature and moisture conditions, especially in comparison with large mammals. Vertebrates with strongly migratory habits, such as some birds and fish, reliably represent seasonal temperature ranges by their presence or absence in stratified deposits, as can animals such as reptiles and amphibians that avoid seasonally stressful conditions by means of dormancy. Small mammals may have very close tolerances for selective conditions; their mobility keeps them within their tolerance ranges, and their presence in sediments attests to those conditions within time spans consistent with genetic stability.

Invertebrates are especially beloved of paleoclimatologists. The ubiquitous insects can be preserved indefinitely in wet sediments, where they may be very numerous and diverse. Small size and short life spans make them very sensitive to certain aspects of their habitats. Taxa which select for particular foods or substrates are not useful for paleoclimatology, but those requiring specific temperature or moisture ranges are ideal. Certain beetles, especially, are more sensitive to climatic conditions than to specific food sources or habitats; they are extremely mobile in their quest for comfort and by their presence they provide direct analogical evidence for ambient temperatures (Coope 1977). Late Glacial beetle faunas on both sides of the Atlantic have been shown to indicate temperatures significantly higher than are inferred from the immediately surrounding vegetation (Coope et al. 1971; Morgan 1987). In dry or alkaline soils small gastropods are good proxies for microclimates as well as for habitat conditions such as soil and vegetation (Bobrowsky 1984; Evans 1976). Sessile aquatic invertebrates such as bivalves are closely adapted to particular water depths, temperatures, and chemistry. Their presence in archaeological deposits informs about nearby water conditions, and even ENSO episodes (Sandweiss et al. 1996).

Biological carbonates deposited by animals as external shells or tests, coral reefs, or specialized internal structures provide climatological data in the form of oxygen-isotope ratios, trace-mineral ratios, amino-acid racemization rates, and growth rings. Racemization rates are sensitive to ambient temperature since burial (Chapter 5; McCoy 1987). Seasonal increments on the growing edge of shells and the ear-bones of fish (otoliths) record periods of temperature-mediated rapid and slow growth that can be read as indicators of seasonal conditions.

CODA

Climatic reconstruction in archaeology may be based on a great variety of data sources, some generated from archaeological research, most derived from paleoclimatology itself. Climatic information in biological proxies is further explored in later chapters, where it complements information about other aspects of paleoenvironments. Some of the peculiar difficulties of deriving paleoenvironmental and paleoclimatic signals from biota influenced by human actions are exposed in the case study on the elm decline, which begins in this Part.

WHEN IS AN ENVIRONMENTAL CHANGE A CLIMATIC CHANGE?

How do we recognize climate change in the cacophony of proxy signals in the paleoenvironmental record? A prime criterion has long been recognition of the same or similar change over regional or larger spatial scales. The idea is that only climatic forcing can elicit parallel and nearly synchronous response over significant distances. Is this criterion sound, and is it adequate? The history of the concept of the European "elm decline" is the story of efforts to explain a phenomenon that has exercised the ingenuity of scientists for over fifty years, yet its environmental significance remains unclear at best.

Early in the development of the northwestern European pollen studies, investigators noticed a sharp mid-Holocene decline in the abundance of elm pollen, a loss of 50% or so in a century. Peat-bog stratigraphy indicated that the decline occurred very close to the transition between the Atlantic and Sub-Boreal phases of the Blytt–Sernander scheme (Fig. 8.2). That transition had been earlier interpreted as the result of climatic change from a wetter "Atlantic" to a drier "Sub-Boreal" phase, both falling within the postglacial peak of warmth. Efforts to interpret the elm decline in causal terms emphasized (1) the wide geographic extent of the decline throughout northwestern Europe, (2) its apparent synchrony, and (3) its coincidence with the Atlantic/Sub-Boreal transition. In the years before abundant radiocarbon dates, the latter two criteria were themselves interdependent, as well as both being dependent upon the *definition* of the A/S-B (Atlantic/Sub-Boreal) boundary as a regional **chronostratigraphic** marker and upon the adoption, by the 1940s, of the elm decline as the marker for the A/S-B boundary (Garbett 1981: 573). The argument, therefore, was circular in respect to criteria 2 and 3. Nevertheless, these observations convinced many that a climatic change was behind the decline.

As pollen diagrams accumulated and resolution improved, investigators noted episodes of apparent forest disturbance and regrowth early in the Sub-Boreal period, with cereal and weed pollen present. They interpreted these as evidence for Neolithic forest clearance and burning as early farmers claimed land by the slash-and-burn method familiar among tropical horticulturalists. Because these "landnam" (land-claiming) episodes typically followed closely upon the elm decline, the idea became established that the elm decline was roughly synchronous with the first appearance of farming economies in northwestern Europe. Selective clearance by farmers of elm stands, which grow on some of the most fertile and best-drained soils, was therefore suspected as the cause of these coincidences – intentional competitive clearance.

An even more attractive explanation was advanced by Troels-Smith (1954), who was convinced by Iverson's (1941) idea that the European forests of the Atlantic period were dense, dark, and lacking in understory plants to nourish herbivores. Troels-Smith therefore argued persuasively that early husbandmen could not pasture their cattle until they had opened pastureland, and he suggested that the live-stock would have been initially penned and provided with fodder by the farmers' own efforts. The selective lopping of elm branches for such fodder was suggested, elm leaves being known as nutritious and palatable for herbivores. Massive cutting of elm branches would have stressed but not killed the elms; it would, however, have prevented the trees from flowering and thus producing pollen. This hypothesis was especially attractive to ecologists, who, during the environmental consciousness of the 1960s and later, embraced it as an object lesson in anthropogenic environmental destruction. The idea was particularly powerful in this role because it suggested that ancient human populations, although small and possessing an experimental economy, had been able to inflict recognizable damage at a very large scale. On the basis of a very fine-grained study of a pollen sequence in the west of England, Garbett (1981) published a strong defense of the foddering explanation.

A hypothesis of soils depletion consequent on deforestation for agriculture had also been proposed. Depletion of Holocene soils by the progressive leaching of bases and the formation of podzols and hardpans is a well-recognized phenomenon in the moist climates of northwestern Europe. Deforestation and farming practices includ-ing pasturage are known to have contributed to the impoverishment of soils in post-Neolithic Europe. However, the argument that soil depletion caused the elm decline confronted the facts that other species of trees were not similarly affected, that the decline was widespread and simultaneous very early in the establishment of agricul-ture, and that both soils and topography throughout the elm range are highly diverse. That diversity alone would ensure that soils depletion was incapable of resulting in simultaneity of effects over the entire range. However, once the elms had been severely reduced in number, by whatever mechanisms, it is likely that competition for their preferred soils and habitats by established or invasive farmers could have contributed significantly to the slowness of regeneration of the woodlands.

Another contending hypothesis – elm disease – had been proposed in the late 1950s. The idea had few adherents initially for lack of any relevant data on prehistoric epidemics, as well as the strength of the prevailing notion that Dutch elm disease was a phenomenon peculiar to the twentieth century. The ravages of the disease in Europe and America in the third quarter of the century brought the large scale of its expression forcibly to public notice after 1970, providing opportunities for research on its mechanisms and manifestations. Margaret Davis' work on the mid-Holocene hemlock decline in North America clarified palynological criteria for recognizing disease (Allison et al. 1986; Davis 1981). In England, Oliver Rackham developed historical and dendrochronological data disproving the notion of the disease's recency; that refutation reopened the discussion (Rackham 1980). Radiocarbon dates demonstrated that the decline occurred throughout Western Europe within a couple of centuries of 5000 B.P. The rapid spread, in combination with the geographic extent, reaching to the environmental limits of elm trees in Europe, supported the disease hypothesis.

There are, therefore, five contending hypotheses for explaining the prehistoric elm decline: climatic deterioration, human exploitation of the species, human competition for the tree's habitat, soils depletion, and disease. A number of lines of evidence converged to weaken the classic landnam argument; these are discussed further in Part VI.

How did the original hypothesis of climate change fare? Current data on postglacial maximum temperatures show that highs occurred prior to the Sub-Boreal period, and there is now evidence indicating that some cooling affected the northern hemisphere beginning around 5000 B.P., which is expressed by the retreat of treelines in northern Canada and Scandinavia and by some advances of mountain glaciers at that time. However, as climatic change and its manifestations are better understood, investigators have begun to challenge simple univariate models. Both Rackham (1980) and Magny (1982) took issue with the idea that climate change at the Atlantic/Sub-Boreal transition was unidirectional and equally severe over a wide geographic range. They cited diversity in the expressions and effects of climatic change, varying with latitude, soils, elevation, and other factors (e.g., insolation, vegetation). These arguments, and the fact that no other species was similarly affected, weaken the case that climatic deterioration was the effective cause for the loss of elms throughout their range in northwestern Europe.

The disease hypothesis reemerged strongly in the 1980s with the discovery of wing cases of the *Scolytus scolytus* beetle at Hampstead Heath (Girling and Greig 1985), stratified just below the evidence of the elm decline. This is the beetle that spreads the fungus of Dutch elm disease. The beetle itself does no great harm to the trees; only when its breeding tunnels in elms are infected by the *Ceratocystis ulmi* fungus does it spread the fatal spores. The presence of the beetles alone, therefore, does not prove the presence of disease, only the presence of the requisite vector. The specificity of the decline, affecting elms far more than any other species at the time, implicates disease. In 5000 years, however, there is plenty of scope for changes in both pathogen and hosts. Rackham observes that a "virulent mutation" of the pathogen could cause a major outbreak of the disease as a unique, or almost unique, event. The intensity of the Neolithic decline could also have been exacerbated by human actions that weakened the standing trees by pollarding (cutting branches to stimulate growth of leaves on new stock for fodder) and exposing elms at the edges of forest clearings where they would have been more accessible to the beetle than in closed woodlands (Rackham 1980).

The hypothesis of a climatic cause for the elm decline was considerably weakened by new information, but climatic deterioration as a contributing factor, particularly at the northern edge of the range, cannot be dismissed. The argument for soils depletion as a cause seems fairly well refuted, but the contribution to the decline and slow regeneration of elm woodlands of human competition for arable and pasture land remains a factor (see review by Edwards [1993]). Human cropping of elm leaves for fodder may have occurred, but cannot be the effective cause of the decline. The scale, synchrony, and specificity of the decline point strongly to a virulent pathogen whose effects may have been amplified by human activities (Part VI).

What is clear is that the elm decline, and probably the entire phenomenon of the Atlantic/Sub-Boreal transition, provides very poor evidence in itself for any climatic change, in Europe or elsewhere. It remains as a useful chronostratigraphic marker in northwest European pollen diagrams; its significance to regional climates, human history, and forest history remains to be defined. Rapid and widespread expression of the elm decline, once an argument for climatic change, is now seen as too rapid and too widespread over diverse habitats and latitudes to support the argument. The reinterpretation suggests that the A/S-B transition is best relegated to a stratigraphic convention.

At mid-century Faegri (1950: 194) knew: "Palæoclimatology suffers from the disadvantage that those who can judge the evidence [biologists, geologists, etc.] cannot judge the conclusions, and those who can judge the conclusions [paleoclimatologists] cannot judge the evidence." The growth of interdisciplinary cooperation in the second half of the twentieth century has improved the situation; recognition of the inconclusiveness of extant explanations for the elm decline is in fact a significant achievement.

PART IV

Geomorphology

9

LANDFORMS

Geology . . . is a historical science concerned with past configuration of the Earth, dealing with successions of unique strictly unrepeatable events through time.

HALLAM 1981: 11

For as long as the Earth has had an atmosphere, its surface has been continually shaped by air, water, and ice disaggregating, transporting, and depositing mineral matter. Human lives are lived on surfaces, but archaeological surfaces are not necessarily those on which the archaeologist walks. Depending on their age and situation, ancient surfaces have been buried or lost to erosion.

Conceptual reconstruction of past landforms and surfaces is an essential aspect of modern archaeology because the spatial context of a site is crucial to its interpretation, and to understanding its relationships to other sites. Space and landscapes define the resources available to any human group, and landform changes through time are related variously to changes in other elements of the environment – climate, hydrography, and biota (mainly vegetative). The mechanisms by which landforms, as elements of the geosphere, are shaped by processes originating in the hydrosphere, cryosphere, atmosphere, and biosphere are imperfectly known although believed to be determinable. Because of these interdependencies, landform reconstruction informs about the past states of variables in all five spheres. However, as with all complex dynamical systems, our ability to predict future states or understand past states and conditions is limited by the element of chance influencing combinations of mechanisms in several scales of space and time.

The "reconstruction" of ancient landforms is not done with earth-moving equipment; it is, rather, a conceptual exercise based on the study of remnants available for observation in the present. The results are perspective drawings, maps, or descriptions of landforms whose past shapes, sizes, and positions in space are approximated.

Unlike past climates, the reconstruction of which is dependent on proxy evidence, landforms can leave within the geosphere some accessible evidence of their former states, evidence that can be found by applying the methods and insights of geomorphology. For example, field prospection and recording of tangible remains provide evidence of past states of the surface of the Earth. **Sediments** preserve some records of past landforms, accompanied by evidence about former states of the atmosphere, hydrosphere, cryosphere, and biosphere. All these kinds of data are, in turn, used to reconstruct former landscapes with their climates, hydrography, and biota.

As geological data have earned a more central place in archaeological interpretation, a new specialty has emerged within archaeology, that of the geoarchaeologist. Self-identified geoarchaeologists have tended to be much more interested in sediments than in landforms (e.g., Waters 1992). When geoarchaeological study is taken beyond the immediate site locale and into the realm of past landforms, the assistance of an archaeological geologist is typically required – a geologist with a predilection or tolerance for problems at archaeological scales. The two combined terms indicate that in each case field workers are crossing disciplinary boundaries and dealing in part with concepts, terminology, problems, and scales that are exotic to their primary training (Butzer 1982; Rapp 1975; Stein 1993; Thorson 1990b). Archaeologists typically gain more from the expertise of a geomorphologist working with them than the geomorphologist expects to gain from the archaeologist, because the small-scale resolution and historical particularity which the archaeologist seeks may be less familiar or even useless for the research geomorphologist. Archaeologists should cultivate assiduously those geomorphologists whose interest in rates and processes incline them to work on Holocene phenomena, and who therefore can potentially benefit from the fine spatial and chronological resolution intrinsic to much archaeological field research.

Collaboration can be successful only with a great deal of discussion, cooperation, mutual goodwill, and intense communication between the investigators. "[A]rchaeologists and geologists, to work effectively together, must be aware of each other's values and paradigms, and of the strengths and limits of their respective data sets" (Thorson 1990b: 33). As part of their own preparation for field research, archaeologists should know at least something about how geologists and geomorphologists think about the Earth and approach its study. Control of basic geomorphological concepts and vocabulary by archaeologists will facilitate communication and enhance cooperative research.

INTRODUCTION TO GEOMORPHOLOGY

Geomorphology, the study of landforms, has developed from being mainly a qual-itative and descriptive discipline to being a science based on a systems paradigm and quantitative methods. Like other sciences, it is moving beyond mechanistic systems models toward the complexities of process–response models for morphogenesis. Concepts of scale and process currently dominate in explanations and research designs, succeeding emphases on form and age. Advances in instrumentation have made possible the study of a larger number of variables in both the field and labora-tory. Landscape evolution involves complex combinations of processes working at different scales of space and time; the major landforms take shape over time dura-tions in the 10^6–10^7-year scales. Observation, on the other hand, rarely can be under-taken over more than 10 years and in limited areas; such prolonged or repeated studies are still exceptional. Theory in geomorphology, therefore, currently lags observation and mathematical modeling; complex four-dimensional problems (the fourth dimension being time) are not yielding readily to explanatory models built in two and three dimensions. The assumptions and premises underlying geomorpho-logical studies, once implicit, are being explicated, challenged, modified, and replaced (Schumm 1991; Thorn 1988).

Much research in geomorphology has been undertaken in order to describe and understand paleoclimates by using landforms as proxies – the literature of glaciology and Quaternary geomorphology especially is dominated by such concerns. The link to climate history, particularly strong in Europe (e.g., Summerfield 1991: Table 1.4; Tricart and Cailleux 1972), originated with the discovery of terrestrial ice ages through interpretation of landforms on the basis of alpine glacial analogies. More recently, appreciation of the number and complexity of variables involved in land-form processes, and the realization that cycling between stable and unstable states can occur at different scales and involve time lags, has tempered expectations of reading the details of climatic changes from landforms. To the extent that landforms can serve as climate proxies, they must be used as such in combination and comple-mentation with proxies from different data domains, and with comparative data sets at a range of scales (Bull 1991). Research directed toward the measurement, explica-tion, and interpretation of land modification processes has exposed the scope of our ignorance about the critical variables and the measurement of rates. Investigators have turned to laboratory and computer models in hopes of identifying the critical variables and vectors in systems at different scales. These developments make modern geomorphology more valuable to archaeologists because of its enhanced explanatory powers and finer chronological resolutions, at the same time that it becomes less accessible because of its increased technicality (Chorley et al. 1984; Goudie 1981; Thorn 1988; Summerfield 1991).

For archaeologists, ancient landforms are of interest as the locales and geographical contexts of sites – the home spaces and habitats of human communities. At large scales, landforms define the physiography and other elements of the environment in which human communities exist, and in many respects the climates and resources available to them. At intermediate scales, landforms constrain communication and travel, and to various degrees determine both the state and condition of the biotic resources that are available to humans. At small scales, sedimentary landforms may comprise the matrix or physical context of sites, and thus must be understood for chronological control. Human modification or construction of landforms is often evident at small and medium scales, and may require interpretation. Description and interpretation of small-scale landforms in terms of formation and deformation processes become crucial for understanding the location, integrity, and natural history of a site. Understanding landforms at all scales aids in correlating a site location with other coeval surfaces across space, and thereby interpreting the spatial component of human behavior.

SCALES OF LANDFORM ANALYSES

In conformity with the discussion of scales presented in previous chapters, we can consider landforms within a nested series of four scales (Table 9.1). At the mega-scale, global or hemispherical landforms lack immediate relevance for archaeologists, although they are important, even prominent, in paleoclimatology. Mega-scale landforms of continental size, involving areas of 10^7–10^8 km^2, are relevant as background to human evolution and behavior, and to large-scale climatic phenomena. Macro-scale phenomena include physiographical provinces involving areas ranging between 10^4 and 10^7 km^2; they have direct relevance to human territoriality, resource exploitation, and communication and are perceptible components of habitat. The typical archaeological scales of region and locale, with areas as large as 10^2–10^4 km^2, belong in the meso-scale division, leaving the micro-scale for very local and site-scale phenomena.

Landform analysis and reconstruction can be undertaken at any of these scales, each having its particular degree of archaeological relevance. The processes and variables that define landforms vary with the scale under consideration (Table 9.2). Continental-scale landforms reflect mainly crustal structure; province-scale landforms reflect mainly the intensity and duration of erosional planation and tectonism. At smaller meso-scales, the diversity and number of relevant processes and

Table 9.1 Landform scales

Spatial scales	Area (km²)	Illustrative landforms
Mega-	global: 5.1×10^8	(geoid)
	continental: $<10^8$	continents; ocean basins
Macro-	physiographic province: 10^4–10^7	mountain ranges; continental glaciers; major drainage basins
Meso-	regional: 10^2–10^4	sand seas and loess sheets; river basins; volcanoes; karst terrains; fault zones
	locality: 1–10^2	small volcanoes and lava flows; river floodplains and terraces; minor drainage basins; dune fields; glacial valleys; mesas; arroyos
Micro-	local: <1	river channel features; glacial kames and minor moraines; periglacial features; beach ridges; buttes

variables become very large, while at the scale of microrelief, definable short-term processes dominate.

The analyst's ability to isolate the relevant variables, and consequently the completeness and accuracy of the resulting analysis or reconstruction of landforms, is likely to be best at the largest and smallest scales. This rule holds for two basic reasons: (1) at the extremes of scale, fewer variables control the processes, and (2) the variables are likely to be comparable in scale themselves (clearly either large or small) and therefore to present similar measurement or sampling problems. We can illustrate this best by looking at the extremes. Phenomena at the continental scale reflect mainly atmospheric and structural states of long duration and low frequencies. The controlling variables are, therefore, few in number and among the most stable and regular processes involved in landform development. At micro-scales, on the other hand, landforms are very closely responsive to the small-scale and high-frequency processes that shape them in the short term; the identification of relevant variables is least complicated because they can generally be observed directly. Small-scale landforms deserve close attention by archaeologists because they are likely to be unstable and therefore to reflect conditions of the present rather than of the past.

For archaeologists, these observations bring both cheer and disappointment. Geomorphological analyses can be very helpful for the particularistic kinds of problems posed at micro-scales, to define and interpret landforms supporting and

Table 9.2 Landform processes at four scales

Spatial scales	Area (km^2)	Selective morphogenetic processes
Mega-	global: 5.1×10^8	plate tectonics
	continental: $<10^8$	crustal structure; tectonism
Macro-	physiographic province: 10^4–10^7	orogeny; tectonism and faulting; continental glaciation; hydrography; erosion; climate
Meso-	regional: 10^2–10^4	erosion; tectonism and isostasy; hydrography; volcanism; aeolian deposition; river-basin development; chemical solution; glaciation and deglaciation; regional climates
	locality: 1–10^2	volcanism; fluvial processes (floodplains and channels); gullying; fans and deltas; aeolian deposition (dunes); valley glaciation; glaciofluvial processes; slope processes; mass wasting; seismicity; isostasy; local climates
Micro-	local: <1	small-scale fluvial processes; glaciofluvial processes; periglacial processes; volcanism; beach processes; solifluction and gelifluction; seismicity; microclimates

Note: The duration and age factors vary by scale; the processes expressed in large-scale landforms influence form over longer time spans than do those affecting the smaller scales. The processes effective at each descending scale are to a greater or lesser degree dependent upon those at larger scales, which set parameters. No priorities are implied by the order within lists.

enclosing archaeological sites. When attention moves to the meso-scale, the habitats of human communities, description will be more easily and less equivocally attained than will interpretation. It is specifically at the meso-scales, where human activities are diverse and adaptationally crucial, that the number and complexity of environmental variables affecting landforms is also greatest, reducing seriously the analytical resolution obtainable with the methods and concepts currently available to geomorphologists (Stein 1993). This is not a brief for avoiding the issues; the need for landform analysis to support archaeological investigations at meso-scales is very great, and neither technical nor theoretical difficulties pose insurmountable obstacles. At these scales, human influences on landforms are often recognizable, while some landforms, particularly glacial and glaciofluvial features, may be mistaken for human artifacts. It is especially at the challenging meso-scales where the relatively fine-grained resolution of archaeological chronologies can be of most help to the field geomorphologist, and where archaeologists, therefore, can help to repay their debt to their colleagues, potentially advancing both disciplines in the process.

Archaeologists excavate sediments and erosional disconformities that must be interpreted in terms of the processes that formed them. Were the critical changes at regional or local scales? Were they triggered by climate, land use, or other factors? What spans of time and what ages were involved in the cycles? How did the changes affect human societies? How did human responses in turn affect erosive cycles? How have archaeological sites been preserved under sediment or destroyed by erosion, and where? All these issues and more come into play in archaeological investigations; the range is brilliantly exemplified in Karl Butzer's study of the ancient site of Axum in Ethiopia (Butzer 1981a). Chapters in Bell and Boardman (1992) and Wagstaff (1987), displaying archaeology's capability to contribute to the history of landforms, should inspire archaeologists to master the concepts and language of geomorphology. The need is being met by new publications addressed to archaeologists (Herz and Garrison 1998; Rapp and Hill 1998).

PROCESSES AND CONCEPTS IN LANDFORM ANALYSES

Among the five spheres of the climate system, those most important in geomorphology are the physical, abiotic ones. Landforms result from the action of air, water, and ice on the geosphere. The biosphere responds to and modifies the products of the other spheres.

Geosphere

Chapter 3 introduced plate tectonics, orogeny, isostasy, and eustasy to explain the distribution of continental crust on the face of the planet, its elevation above sea level, and the location and form of mountain ranges. The crustal plates are subject to additional constructional processes at smaller scales, principally in the form of volcanism. Volcanoes, individually or clustered, form mountains very dissimilar to folded and faulted ranges. Smaller landforms related to eruptions of ash or lava may be prominent at meso- and micro-scales. Lava flows can extend over hundreds of square kilometers, inundating older landforms under a hardening sea of molten rock.

Starting with these constructional geological features in place, geomorphologists are fundamentally concerned with the resulting surface **relief** – a relative measure of surface ruggedness that expresses the height difference between the highest and lowest spots in a given unit of land: the vertical distance between hilltop and valley bottom. This fundamental expression of landform is analyzed in terms of smaller segments of form such as **slopes** (surfaces slanting at angles typically less than 45°), **scarps** (steep slopes or cliffs), **basins** (essentially concave landforms usually encompassing the catchment of a stream network), and **channels** (linear depressions; beds of streams or rivers). It should be clear from the definitions that basins incorporate most of the other forms; in fact, basins are considered the "basic geomorphological unit in many terrains" (Chorley et al. 1984: 316). It is at the scale of basins that the fundamental destructive processes of erosion, discussed below, are observed.

Atmosphere

The solidity attributed to rock is a prevailing simplification, even misrepresentation, of the fundamental material of the continental surfaces. Much rock is actually aggregates of crystalline matter or of small sedimentary elements such as microfossils or grains of sand or silt. Such aggregates are penetrated by joints and cracks that permit water vapor to infiltrate the mass and begin the process of disaggregation. Obsidian is supercooled liquid (glass), which tends to crystallize and weaken as it ages. The transition from rock to sediment begins when rock is exposed, at or near the surface, to the influence of the climate system. Cycles of warm and cold temperatures, high and low precipitation, and atmospheric pressures lower than those characteristic of environments where rock formed, result in physical and chemical changes in the minerals constituting the rock. All rock is susceptible to disaggregation by either mechanical or chemical **weathering**, most by both.

Mechanical weathering includes those processes that physically break up rock, by wedging it apart or reducing it by abrasion or glacial plucking. Mechanical weathering includes such processes as frost wedging, caused by the expansion of freezing interstitial water; differential thermal expansion and contraction of minerals subjected to extremes of temperature; salt wedging caused by the crystallization of saline interstitial water or chemically transformed minerals; and root wedging, caused by the growth expansion of rootlets, which prise apart minute cracks in rock. Chemical weathering is effected by water, in liquid or vapor form, which dissolves and ultimately carries away soluble minerals or mineral compounds. Rock disaggregates into its constituent minerals or insoluble residues, which may remain in place or be carried away by gravity or moving water, ice, or wind. Sediments created by redepo-

sition of weathering products are discussed in Part V. The technical term for unconsolidated mineral matter lying above bedrock, whether remaining *in situ* or redeposited, is **regolith**. The erosion of regolith by wind, water, ice, or gravity results in
destructional landforms; redeposition creates constructional landforms.

Still air, by itself, can do little work other than serving as a medium from which
water vapor can be deposited onto surfaces. However, air in motion – wind – can carry
mineral particles and be an effective erosional agent, shaping and even creating landforms. Wind is capable of transporting particles ranging in size from the finest silts and
clays to small buildings (as in tornadoes). The stronger the wind speed, the larger the
particles moved. The smaller the particles, the more likely they are to be transported
long distances in suspension. Reduced wind speed deposits particles in order of their
size: largest first. **Aeolian** deposits are therefore composed of materials well sorted in
terms of particle size, although they may derive from different places and distances.

The largest aeolian landforms are **loess** plains: deposits of well-sorted medium- to
fine-grained silt (2–64 μm) that may blanket prior landforms to great depths. They
typically form in mid-continental areas downwind of sediment sources exposed by
extreme aridity or cold. The largest formations are products of the cold, dry climates
of glacial periods. The high winds characteristic of glacial margins mobilize the silts
and fine sands and transport them varying distances until the wind velocity is slowed
by distance from the glacier, by encountering vegetation, or by rising elevation.
Being derived from freshly weathered bedrock, aeolian silts are typically calcareous
and highly fertile if watered; in temperate climatic regimes, the silts readily support
vegetation, stabilize, and develop soil profiles.

Dunes are smaller constructional forms, although dune fields may be of immense
size. Dunes form where there is a source of medium to fine sand (64 μm–2 mm),
wind velocities sufficient to move it, and some factor suppressing vegetation. When
sand-laden winds are slowed by surface roughness, they deposit sand. These conditions typically occur in zones of arid climate, whether warm or cold, or along sea-
shores where sand is plentiful and strong winds and salt air suppress vegetation. In
temperate climatic zones, old relict dunefields may be remobilized and reshaped if
the vegetation cover is destroyed by catastrophe or human abuse. Flat sand sheets
form when winds carrying medium sands are slowed with less turbulence than that
resulting in dunes.

The sediment sources from which winds remove materials are generally less dramatic than the depositional landforms. Winds move finer sediment grades from
exposed deposits, leaving behind coarse **lag deposits**. Winds mobilizing previously
sorted deposits, such as dry river channels, dunes, or sand sheets, create hollows
called blowouts. Both lag deposits and blowouts are problematic for archaeologists

since archaeological materials exposed in them lie on surfaces below those on which they were originally deposited and may be associated with materials deriving from more than one episode of deposition.

The intimate relationships between climate and landforms are the subjects of climatic geomorphology, a subdiscipline which, while losing favor as an approach to paleoclimatology, has much to offer for the understanding of geomorphological processes. While climate is undeniably a strong influence on landforms, it cannot be shown to be predominant. Landforms are polygenetic, the result of many different factors interacting over time spans of varying lengths with changing climatic regimes (Bull 1991). The number of relevant variables grows as measuring techniques and models are refined. Some correlations of landforms with climate are strong, as with the destructional landforms created by glaciation, the buttes and mesas of dry semitropical mid-continental areas, and the slopes and valleys of wet tropical areas thickly mantled with unconsolidated weathered sediments. However, no correlations between climate and landforms can be assumed strong enough to permit confident retrodiction of one from the other.

Hydrosphere

Water exists in the hydrosphere in liquid and gaseous states, with the liquid form episodically moving or depositing sedimentary matter. Increases or decreases in the annual amount or seasonal distribution of precipitation can initiate or reverse cycles of erosion and deposition, modifying landforms.

The potential of moving water to do work varies with the steepness of the land (slope or "gradient"), the compactness and roughness of the surface, and the volume of water; together these factors define the speed ("velocity") and thus the force of the water – its ability to erode materials and to carry them away. Moving water carries material in three forms: dissolved load, suspended load, and bed load. Dissolved load is derived mainly from products of chemical weathering of rocks and sediments, and secondarily from ions brought down by rainwater. Suspended load is the fine particles of clay and silt that remain in suspension in moving water, while bed load is the heavier particles that are slid, rolled, and bounced along the bottom of a stream. Bed load moves best when water is flowing at high volume and speed, and thus is transported episodically, while suspended and dissolved load may be carried almost continuously downstream. Both the amount and maximum size of material moved vary geometrically with velocity; small increases in velocity greatly increase a stream's ability to move material. That is why even very small and gentle summertime brooks may have bouldery beds that testify to powerful spring freshets.

Slope processes

Unconsolidated material on slopes moves under the influence of gravity, but most such moving material has been dislodged or lubricated by water. Mass wasting occurs in many forms and scales, from rapid massive landslide to slow soil creep; the latter is implicated as the dominant process in surficial geomorphology. In all cases, material is dislodged and moved down slope where it is more accessible to erosion by surficial water. Archaeological materials move in the same ways, being sorted by size as they are moved, separated and recombined in new associations, and suffering the destruction or even reversal of their stratigraphic relationships (Rick 1976). While the loss of archaeological integrity in landslides is rarely an issue, mudslides and **solifluction** (saturated sediments moving downhill), as well as surface displacement by creep, have presented daunting problems of archaeological interpretation and many opportunities for misinterpretation. The sediments resulting from slope processes are typically mixed, poorly sorted, and difficult to interpret when old. To express uncertainty responsibly, geomorphologists use the term **diamicton** for redeposited regolith which lacks sedimentary structure and sorting and for which, therefore, the generative processes cannot be demonstrated. The term carries no connotation of origin; it applies equally to landslides, some glacial deposits, volcanic mudflows, **gelifluction** (sediments moving over frozen substrates), and so on. Diamicton is an excellent example of an ambiguous word that increases precision of expression at the expense of accuracy; it perfectly expresses "I don't yet know what caused this mess."

Fluvial (river) processes

Water, being both heavy and shapeless, responds strongly to gravity, coalescing into streams that follow the lowest surface irregularities. Over the years and over most of the planet's surface, water has been the force shaping landforms. The water available for erosion and transportation of weathering products varies in space and time according to its receipt of precipitation and loss of water vapor into the air through evaporation and **transpiration** (exhalation of water by elements of the biosphere, mainly vegetation). As precipitation increases, or evapotranspiration diminishes, more water is free to run across and through sediments, redistributing and reshaping them (Fig. 3.6).

The structure, climate, and geological history of a physiographic area together define its unique properties. All of these factors influence the **hydrography** (the pattern of drainage and drainage basins). Streams flowing on the surface of the ground do not create an infinite variety of possible patterns; rather, a few generalized classes of patterns subsume the observed variation (Fig. 9.1). Stream patterns, observable on large-scale maps and aerial photos, are strong clues to fundamental

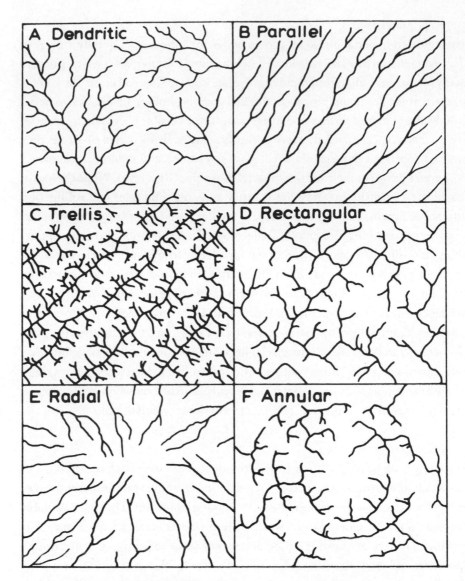

Figure 9.1   Selected stream pattern diagrams: dendritic, parallel, trellis, rectangular, radial, and annular. Dendritic patterns form on mildly sloping terrain; parallel on steeper slopes without strong bedrock controls. Trellis and rectangular patterns typify uplifted eroded folds (see Fig. 9.5, "fold mountains"). Radial patterns form on domes and volcanic cones, annular patterns on eroded domes of stratified bedrock (see Fig. 9.5). (Reproduced from Chorley et al. 1984: Fig. 13.3, with permission of Methuen & Co., publishers.)

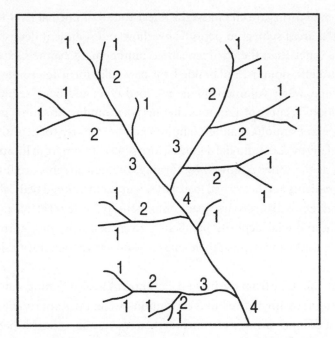

Figure 9.2 Strahler stream ordering begins with the streams initiating surface flow, which are "first order." Higher order streams are formed only by the confluence of equal orders. Where two first-order streams meet, they form a second-order stream. Two second-order streams form a third, and so on. (After Catt 1988: Fig. 2.33.)

underlying lithological structures at province and regional scales. Drainage that has been disrupted by glacial deposition comprises the major exception to the patterning rules, and may itself thus be readily interpreted.

The smallest, most numerous streams in a drainage basin, or catchment, tend to occur on the higher ground, while fewer large streams dominate the lowlands. This tendency can be quantified, and turns out to display mathematical regularities that are used to describe and compare different stream basins. The number of streams of each relative size class, or **order**, and the proportion of basin area that they drain, have regular relationships to the other orders, varying mainly with the surface relief. In this way, qualities of drainage basins which are significant to human settlement choices (slope, elevation, water availability) can be expressed as indices that are directly comparable from basin to basin. Among several available descriptive systems, the Strahler system is widely used and the most suitable for archaeology (Fig. 9.2).

Fluvial landforms are produced by dynamical responses of flowing water to changes in volume or to changed conditions of slope or sediment load (Leopold

1994). The fundamental forms are channels, the linear routes of normal river flow, and **floodplains** – the areas subject to periodic overflow and sediment deposition when there is more water than the channel can accommodate. Channels exist in three basic forms: straight, sinuous, and braided, the particular form determined by variables such as slope, water volume (discharge), load type, and bank sediment composition. Each looping curve of a sinuous channel is a **meander**. Erosion typifies the convex outer curves of sinuous channels. The inner curves are areas of deposition where **point bars**, relatively coarse fluvial deposits, form downstream from locations of channel cutting, as the water is slowed by turning. Braided streams are fluvial responses to steep gradients and heavy bed loads; they wind across broad beds, alternately depositing and remobilizing coarse load components (Chorley et al. 1984: 309, 349). **Levees** are linear fluvial deposits paralleling river channels; they form as floodwaters overflow banks and deposit their coarsest load where the velocity slows rapidly.

Channel gradient, the slope from the highest elevation of freely running water to base level, varies along a stream course but is continuous; water does not run uphill. Base level, the lowest point to which a channel segment can erode, is established by effective obstructions to erosion such as rock outcrops, standing water in ponds and lakes, or sea level. Obstructions in a channel cause a change in slope; the stream will pond and deposit sediment (aggrade) until it can flow over the obstruction. The new deposit decreases the gradient immediately upstream of the obstruction. Lowering of a base-level control can occur by tectonic adjustment, erosion of obstructions, or lowering of sea level. Rivers respond to base-level lowering by eroding (incising), which steepens the channel gradient upstream from the changed condition. Incision continues upstream until blocked by another base-level control. Aggrading or incising streams change the form and gradient of their channels as part of their response to new conditions of flow – faster and steeper or slower and flatter. The new conditions may destabilize river banks and adjacent slopes, bringing more sediment into the stream, thereby increasing the stream load or clogging the channel. The response of a stream to a change in base level at one place is expressed both upstream and downstream from the change; matters are further complicated by compensations triggered in tributary streams that join a stream under adjustment.

"Natural systems are inherently complex" (Schumm 1991: 85). River responses to base-level change can be extremely complex, with aggradation and incision cycling until a new state of stability is achieved. The concept of "complex response" in hydrography as developed by Schumm (1977) is crucial to understanding the dynamics of fluvial systems (Fig. 9.3). It is also a fundamental concept for natural systems of

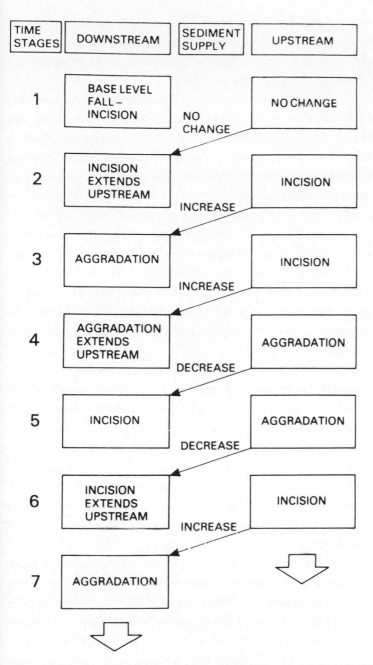

Figure 9.3 Complex response in a drainage system with fall of base level. Adjustments in regime work both upstream and downstream from the point of change, as the gradient steepens or flattens and the velocity of the flow is affected. (Reproduced from Summerfield 1991: Fig. 9.27, with permission of Addison, Wesley, Longman.)

all kinds. The complexity of response to perturbations is due to the combination of external and internal triggers of instability in a system. Systemic compensation for external triggers is likely to trip internal triggers, which in turn entail further changes within the system, and so on (Leopold 1994).

Stream responses to changes in gradient or water volume affect the width and the relief of valleys and the elevation of valley floors. Stream incision leaves floodplain fragments on valley walls above a new floodplain. For instance, a glacio-eustatic lowering of sea level will increase the gradients of all rivers running into the sea, causing them to incise their channels beginning at the mouths, leaving former floodplain segments elevated as **terraces**. Cycles of adjustment result in the creation of step-like terraces along valley walls – abandoned fragments of former floodplains adjusted to different conditions. Terraces may contain bedrock components, but most are composed of alluvial sequences, sometimes including older buried surfaces. Terraces are numbered up from the active floodplain, 1–n, from youngest to oldest. The sequences on facing sides of a valley may not be equivalent. Paired terraces form when incision dominates the valley-formation processes. Rivers meandering widely are likely to cut unpaired terraces at staggered levels on valley sides (Chorley et al. 1984; Summerfield 1991).

A stream adapting to an abrupt change in channel gradient will deposit some of its load at the point of change. The typical landform where gradient flattens abruptly is an alluvial **fan**, a triangular-shaped pile of complexly interbedded sediments over which the stream flows in braided channels. Alluvial fans are prominent features of semi-arid climates at the foot of mountain ranges, but they can form wherever gradient change is too abrupt for smooth transitions (Summerfield 1991: 224–225). In arid landscapes, fans may be important aquifers, with springs emerging at the margins or foot of the fan. Humans attracted to the springs are likely to leave archaeological deposits on the surfaces or edges of fans where they may be rapidly buried by sediments to form stratified sites.

In arid climates where precipitation is seasonal and episodic, river beds may be dry for large parts of the year. During the monsoon season, or following storms, these channels may carry impressive and destructive flows of water. Seasonally dry stream beds, often littered with boulders that look strangely out of place, can fill very suddenly with water, as many an unwary camper has learned the hard way. When active, these streams can incise or aggrade their beds very quickly, changing shape and sometimes course. In the Near East these features are called "wadis," in the Americas and Spain, "arroyos."

In contrast to superficial fluvial channels, water may flow underground through channels in bedrock. In areas of adequate rainfall and limestone bedrock, extensive river systems may be created by chemical dissolution of carbonates, running for miles through tunnels and caverns. When solution of the bedrock is far advanced, cavern and tunnel ceilings may collapse, opening the subterranean landscape to the surface and creating a karst topography, with or without underground caves. Maturely eroded karst landscapes are characterized by finely scaled and abrupt changes in relief, expressed either as depressions below the surface or as rock pinnacles rising above the levels of streams and floodplains. Caves, rockshelters, underground rivers, and dolines (closed depressions in a limestone surface, not components of fluvial networks) are typical features of karst terrains (White 1988). Limestone caves, which provide spectacular non-architectural archaeological sites, focus occupation and debris deposition spatially, and provide excellent preservation conditions for bone and antler artifacts and other remains. Repeated use of the same limited space forms stratified sites of great structural complexity.

Cryosphere

We are still in an ice age; at no time during the existence of the human species has the globe been free of ice. At the last glacial maximum, three times as much land was covered by ice as is now the case. Over a typical year today, snow and ice cover varies seasonally from ca. 8% to 16% of the planetary surface (Bradley 1985: 19).

The properties of glacial ice that make it an effective agent of erosion are its mass and its motion. The mass is the result of many years' accumulation of snow, compressed under its own weight and become ice. With continuing accumulation, the mass deforms by plastic flow, expanding outward toward areas of less pressure. The outward motion is channeled by any unevenness in the ground beneath the glacier. If snow continues to accumulate on it, the mass may grow upwards to the point where it constitutes an area of high elevation regardless of the relief or elevation of the land below; the ice may then flow "uphill" over opposing slopes. Water may exist under the ice, contained at high pressure. High pressure raises the freezing point and increases the erosional capabilities such that subglacial water is a significant agent of erosion. Mineral matter in glacial water and in moving ice increases the erosive capabilities of both. Gritty ice, moving over bedrock, grinds away rock surface, especially any that is weathered. Basal water infiltrates cracks in rock or unconsolidated sediment below the ice; if it freezes, mineral matter is incorporated into the moving ice, "plucked" up, and carried away. The leading edge of an ice sheet shoves unconsolidated sediments like a bulldozer, scouring the landscape down to solid rock. In ice, on the ice surface, in water, or in front of the moving edge, debris of all sizes is transported from its original location.

Rock debris and sediments incorporated into glaciers are eventually deposited as a glacier overrides its own excessive bed load or melts away. Material deposited from ice is called **till**, poorly sorted sediment of two basic types: till deposited directly at the base of a glacier is called lodgement till, while that deposited as a glacier melts away is ablation till. The latter may be subdivided on the basis of evidence for meltwater involvement. Other common names for till, especially when the transport and deposition processes are less than certain, include "boulder clay" and "drift," both now being replaced by diamicton. Lodgement till occurs in sheets or pockets, often beneath a deposit of ablation till, and more typically in ovate hills called "drumlins." Drumlins, which form in clusters ("swarms") when conditions are propitious, may be small enough to be mistaken for artificial mounds, but can be readily distinguished by their sedimentary fabric. **Moraines** of many depositional varieties are landforms of low to moderate relief composed of till deposits that may be highly controversial with respect to their origins, being typically composed of both sorted and unsorted debris.

Periglacial landforms

Ice distorts sedimentary bodies, creating characteristic small-scale landforms that can be powerful indicators of past climates. The proximity of glaciers establishes extreme climates where frost remains perennially in the ground to great depths. Seasonal thawing at the surface mobilizes water into sediments; it expands as it freezes in cracks and pockets, forcing sedimentary material sideways and upwards. Such periglacial processes create networks of interconnected ice wedges that may be outlined by rocks forced to the surface by cycles of freezing and thawing. Water-saturated sediments on frozen ground may slide on even slight slopes (gelifluction), folding and overturning as they settle. The stratigraphic and associational relationships of any archaeological materials in geliflucted sediments are likely to retain no integrity, although the deposits may mimic stratification by duplication of layers in folds. Archaeologists working in formerly glaciated terrain should be aware of the full range of periglacial landforms, and ready to deal with their interpretive problems (Clark 1988).

Biosphere

Living organisms influence landforms by controlling cycles of erosion and deposition both directly and indirectly. The type, density, and distribution of vegetation influence the exposure of sediments to erosive forces such as wind and water. Plants trap and hold sediments above and below the surface; their presence stabilizes slopes. The absence of vegetation, whether resulting from fire, herbivory, human land-use practices, or climate change, exposes sediments to erosion. In special cases such as the mounds and pits left by uprooted trees, plants create microrelief that itself mobilizes sediment. Small to medium-sized animals that live parts of their lives under the surface of the ground also disturb sediments and create microrelief features at the surface. Artificial landforms built by humans have increased the complexity of the surface for thousands of years. Depositional features such as middens, mounds, agricultural terraces, roads, and more recently cities, testify to the effectiveness of human construction of landforms. Erosional features such as canals, plowed fields, and artificial leveling have achieved scales matching those of natural forces.

BASIC GEOMORPHOLOGICAL METHODS

The fundamental descriptive field techniques in geomorphology are cartographic skills; it is on those, especially, that geomorphology and archaeology converge most closely. The basic mapping skills essential to good archaeological reconnaissance at local and regional scales are classics of geomorphology – both plane-table and transit surveys, photogrammetric mapping, air-photo interpretation, and the use and refinement of standard topographic and surficial maps of the sort that government agencies produce in many countries for many strategic purposes. The availability of maps of different kinds varies greatly from place to place. Most widely available are standard topographic contour maps at scales between 1:25,000 and 1:250,000; these are a great boon to archaeologists although they lack accuracy at site scales. Maps showing surficial geology or soils types also have immediate applications in archaeology. Archaeologists engaged in field work should be thoroughly familiar with the full range of map types and mapping conventions used in their area, and with the literature that supports their productive exploitation (e.g., mapping manuals supplied by the governmental agencies that publish the maps; Monmonier 1993). Although these maps are the first gift of geomorphologists to archaeologists, many of the specialized maps are still underutilized by the latter. The new technology of Global Positioning Systems (GPS), whereby suitably equipped persons on the ground can find their geographic position electronically from satellite coordinates, promises unprecedented precision for map-makers everywhere (Hofmann-Wellenhof et al. 1993; Leick 1995). Areas of the world not well served by conventional cartographic methods are now accessible by means of aerial photography and GPS (Maschner 1996).

Archaeologists have benefited from remote sensing of terrain as long as any such techniques have been in use. Aerial photography, beginning with primitive cameras held by balloonists, is now a highly technical specialty developed for military purposes but with immediate applicability for archaeological survey. While low-altitude photographs – oblique, mosaics, or orthogonally corrected – continue to be the most useful, photography from satellites and manned spacecraft has revealed classes of data previously undreamed of by archaeologists. The paleoenvironmental applications of aerial photography and other remote-sensing techniques extend far beyond the identification of landforms and vegetation suites. Infrared films record the growth rates of different types of vegetation that are sensitive, among other things, to the water content and mineral enrichment characteristic of the soils on archaeological sites. Normally invisible subsurface features are visible from the air under special conditions of ground cover or seasonal humidity. Satellite-borne cameras have transcended the traditional earthbound limits of spatial scales to give highly accurate records of current landforms and vegetation. Some archaeological applications are cited in chapters that follow. The technology is currently outpacing the literature (Foody and Curran 1994; Leick 1995; Scollar 1990).

Geophysical remote-sensing techniques such as radar, geomagnetic mapping, and electromagnetic and multispectral scanning are revealing new kinds of geomorphological data on the Earth's land surfaces, some of which have immediate archaeological relevance. Imaging radar that scans surface relief through dense vegetation and surficial sand sheets has revealed previously unsuspected agricultural systems in tropical jungles as well as ancient river networks buried under desert sands. Computer enhancement of remote-sensing data and photographs increases the resolution of data displays by orders of magnitude (Scollar 1990). Small-scale buried land surfaces and constructional features are mapped using subsurface radar scanners, sonic reflection techniques, proton magnetometers, and resistivity surveys – all techniques developed for geomorphological and engineering applications before being adapted for archaeological work (Clark 1990; Conyers and Goodman 1997). Data from many sources can now be formatted to a common scale by computer processing and combined into information-rich Geographic Information Systems (GIS) data displays (Fig. 9.4; Allen et al. 1990; Maschner 1996).

Large-scale buried landforms are sought and mapped by various satellite imaging techniques, ground-penetrating radar, and seismic refraction in addition to the older methods of drilling or trenching through layers of sediment. Buried soils revealed by digging, coring, or remote sensing trace former surfaces that may bear little resemblance to contemporary landforms in the same place. Former landforms may also be estimated by extrapolation from surface remnants across locations now eroded away or moved by faulting or isostatic adjustment (e.g., Bailey et al. 1993; Roberts 1987; Rolph et al. 1994).

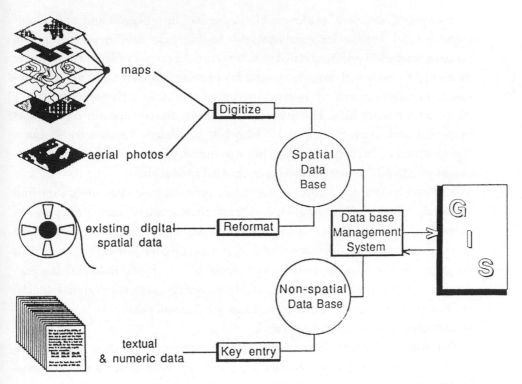

maps

Digitize

aerial photos

existing digital spatial data

Reformat

Spatial Data Base

Data base Management System

G I S

Non-spatial Data Base

textual & numeric data

Key entry

Figure 9.4 Geographic Information Systems equipment and process. (Reproduced from Madry 1990: Fig. 15.3, with permission of Taylor & Francis.)

Analytical techniques

Regardless of their sophistication, imaging techniques are inadequate for interpretation. Analytical description of bedrock and unconsolidated sediments (lithology) is the essential complement to the description of form. Aspects of sedimentology and **pedology** (soil science), particularly at archaeological scales, are the topics of Chapters 11 and 12. The order of presentation here, which places form before content, must not be interpreted as diminishing the importance of lithologic study in the field and laboratory. In most cases it is the sediments, rather than the landforms, which should engage the archaeologist's primary attention. The dominant analytical techniques in geomorphology are based on small-scale observations of contemporary conditions (Goudie 1981; Chorley et al. 1984; Thorn 1988: 110). Their relevance for the interpretation of larger, older, actual landforms may be problematic.

In contrast to the readiness with which archaeologists borrow techniques for discovery and description of landforms, geomorphological developments in analytical and interpretational techniques seem to be adopted slowly and reluctantly by archaeologists. Renewed awareness of site-formation processes and taphonomy (Schiffer 1987) is stimulating archaeologists to undertake field investigations into processes that affect unconsolidated sediments and the rates at which these act under different environmental conditions to modify or create landforms. The pace of innovation and development of analytical techniques in geomorphology defeats any effort to summarize here. The newest, fastest, most precise methods are best met in professional journals such as *Geomorphology, Geology, Quaternary Research, Holocene, Geoarchaeology,* and others more technical, where advances in mathematical, physical, and chemical methods are reported and evaluated.

Measurements of soil creep, sedimentation processes and rates, infiltration and chemical change, and bioturbation and cryoturbation are beginning to appear in archaeological publications (Chapters 11 and 12) although they are typically retarded in comparison to the capabilities displayed in the geomorphological literature. To a far greater degree than the tectonic and glacial processes that dominate the geomorphological literature, these small-scale processes are relevant at archaeological scales of space and time. It is at the small scale that human impacts on landforms are best revealed (Boardman and Bell 1992).

Constructional landforms are usually directly interpretable because of their characteristic forms and internal sedimentary structures. Destructional and erosional landforms are more problematic because the generating processes are subtractive, sometimes leaving no direct evidence of their presence, and because the original forms are modified or even lost during erosion. Lost landforms may be partly retrievable with expertise and appropriate techniques. Archaeologists who collaborate with geomorphologists find their interests very well served (e.g., Bettis 1995; Wagstaff 1987).

Geochronology: time concepts in geomorphology

Among the basic issues of world-view that complicate collaboration between archaeologists and geomorphologists, concepts of time and scale vie for first place. Archaeologists deal typically with radiocarbon time and local scales; geomorphologists with stratigraphical relative time and regional-scale process models. Professionals working on phenomena at one set of scales develop mind-sets that hinder their recognition of phenomena at other scales of space and/or time. These issues have been clearly addressed in the volume edited by Stein and Linse (1993), which defines the essential first steps toward awareness that will lead to resolution of some of the difficulties.

Earth-time and human-time are not easily correlated. Not only are the scales of temporal units different, but also the resolutions and comparability of the many chronometric methods available (Chapters 5 and 6). In addition to all the chrono-metric methods used by archaeologists, geomorphologists studying processes also utilize methods appropriate for very short time spans at the scales of decades (e.g., a lead isotope, ^{210}Pb, with a half-life of 22 years). As discussed in Chapters 5 and 6, different chronometric techniques employ distinct units, relevant time spans, and error ranges, all of which must be calibrated to some common scale before compari-son. A continuing source of complications in interdisciplinary research is the uncrit-ical correlation of incomparable time scales, such those of radiocarbon and orbital cycles (e.g., Braziunas 1994).

While archaeologists are comfortable assuming rough synchrony between events and even deposits separated in space when they contain similar artifact forms, geo-morphologists are sensitive to equifinalities, complex responses, and process lags that produce superficially similar landforms independently in time and space. Productive collaboration across disciplines requires explicit evaluation of contras-tive assumptions about phenomena and processes in culture and nature. "Because geologic processes and human behavioral processes commonly operate at different rates, the chronological information inherent in these processes is incapable of resolving the different scales" (Dean 1993: 59). Dealing with phenomena of mutual geological and archaeological interest within the classes of nested scales alleviates immediately some of the incongruity between them.

LANDFORMS AT MEGA- AND MACRO-SCALES ($>10^4$ KM^2; 10^{6-9} YEARS)

Anyone curious about the observable diversity of landforms has wondered about the large-scale processes that have shaped the surface of the Earth. Mountain ranges were thrust up and worn down by processes which we can observe in operation now, although we see and measure only brief segments of those long waves of change. Because of the large scales of these processes, we can measure them only at low resolu-tion; error factors may exceed a million years. Furthermore, large landforms change relatively little in the time spans that are significant for archaeological studies; change at the scale of continents and provinces is rarely important even for Paleolithic archaeology. Therefore, interpretation at large scales rarely concerns archaeologists, who can adopt interpretive conclusions from responsible scientists without evaluat-ing the details of methods and logic. Archaeologists do, however, need to understand the terms and concepts of structural geology sufficiently to interpret and adapt the descriptive literature of their research areas, because however it is explained, the gross shape of the landscape matters to people living on it (Skinner and Porter 1995).

Continents

We have seen above, in Chapters 3 and 7, that the latitudes and elevations of continental masses over the Earth are major determinants of climate. The geosphere thus sets the parameters defining the dynamics of the hydrosphere and atmosphere at large scales. Although the motions of the plates are very slow, and change is manifested only gradually in geological scales of time, at any one point in time the arrangement of oceans and continents, mountains and plains, is unique and determinative. The arrangement and timing of unique configurations cannot be ignored by the paleoenvironmentalist. For archaeology, however, continental-scale phenomena remain background.

Physiographic provinces

The continental masses are traditionally subdivided into more or less discrete **physiographic provinces** on the basis of distinct rock structures and relief. The boundaries of such units are generally quite obvious on the ground. Despite the expansion during the twentieth century of information about deep structures, age, and formation processes, early descriptive works on physiography retain a basic validity regardless of fundamental changes in interpretation required by the concepts of plate tectonics.

Provincial boundaries are typically defined by geologic **unconformities** created by plate movements and tectonic deformation, usually but not necessarily involving orogenies (mountain-building episodes). Figure 9.5 illustrates four types of orogenic structure, greatly simplified diagrammatically. Structures are best displayed in the youngest mountain ranges, among which are the Cascades and Andes ranges in North and South America and the Himalayas in Central Asia. All of those are situated on the margins of actively moving plates and are still being pushed up, even as they erode at the surface. Mountain ranges of very great age, such as the Appalachians of eastern North America and the Urals of European Russia, nevertheless form distinctive physiographic zones contrasting strongly with adjacent areas manifesting different origins and histories. The rugged relief of mountain ranges is a product of interactions among structure, lithology, and processes of erosion and transportation.

The interiors of continental plates are usually tectonically stable areas, typically characterized by essentially horizontal bedrock and by low relief. Physiographic provinces in such areas may be very large. Depending upon the dominant climatic regime, the interior provinces may be plains, steppes, deserts, or tropical lowlands.

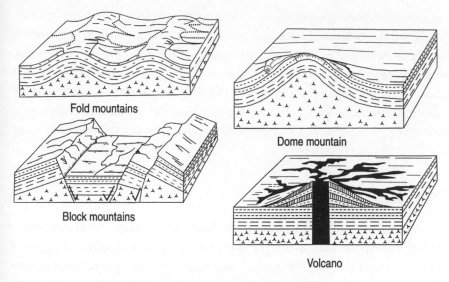

Figure 9.5 Four kinds of orogenic structures. The arrows showing relative movement in the block mountains are oversimplified. (After Hunt 1974: Fig. 3.5.)

Some are interrupted by upland areas contrasting in lithology and relief, such as the Ouachita Mountains in North America and the Urals of Eurasia. These represent very ancient plate boundaries, no longer active.

At the scale of physiographic provinces, climates are largely determined by the latitude, elevation, and orientation of landforms, but smaller-scale effects begin to be expressed. The location and size of mountain ranges, and their orientation in respect to prevailing atmospheric circulation, will affect precipitation patterns and the strength of seasonal differences, and thus define the dominant processes of erosion and deposition. Distance to oceans is also crucial. Landforms typical of physiographic provinces are well described in the literature of geology and geography and are readily available to archaeologists. When interpretation involves large time scales, the skills of a historical geologist or geomorphologist are essential to success.

LANDFORMS AT MESO-SCALES ($< 10^4$ KM^2)

Intermediate-scale landforms are affected by a wide range of processes, and by rates at many frequencies. The processes operative at the macro- and mega-scales set the parameters within which those of shorter wavelength can be expressed, while high-frequency processes may complicate analysis by imposing over the basic structures surficial landforms of short duration. Thus, there is practically no scale of landform, process, or rate that can be totally ignored during interpretation of features at meso-scales. The most immediately relevant processes, however, are those controlling weathering of rock and erosion and deposition of the resulting mineral grains. Translocation of mineral matter from higher to lower elevations, with consequent reduction of regional relief, is the business of these middle-scale processes, working through wind, water, and ice. Countering the prevailing elevational reduction are the geospheric processes expressed at meso-scales, principally volcanism and isostatic uplift.

Volcanism

Volcanic eruptions occur at or near boundaries of tectonic plates, or at intra-plate geothermal "hot-spots" such as the Hawaiian Islands. Zones of active rifting or of subduction display the conditions for volcanic eruptions, where liquid rock at very high temperatures rises from the mantle to emerge onto the surface of the Earth. The molten rock moves along pipes or fissures in the crust, and may emerge at the surface as flows of lava or as explosions of gas or steam with or without broken rock. The form of release varies with the chemical composition of the liquid rock, the form of the opening and other factors, not all of which are understood. The typical volcano is a conical pile of shattered rock and dust, often interlayered with solidified lava flows. The volcano grows by the ejection of new material onto its slopes, and can rise dramatically in short bursts of activity (Fig. 9.5). Volcanoes can also, as in the case of the Santorini volcano in the Aegean or the recent eruption of Mount St. Helens in Washington State, USA, destroy themselves in violent explosions and subsidence.

Volcanic eruptions can also create depositional landforms less dramatic than cones. Lava flows may fill preexisting valleys and blanket other topography, flowing for many kilometers from the fissure or pipe that released them. The rough, knotted surface of flows is inimical to most forms of life for a long time. Caves may be formed during lava flows when bubbles of gas create voids in cooling lava, or when the hot interior liquid flows away from the chilled, hardened surface. Clouds of fine volcanic ash (tephra) accompanying some explosions can smother both plants and animals. After settling and weathering, tephra forms a fertile substrate for new plant growth. Ash falls can be massive and destructive; very hot ash deposits may harden into rock (**tuff**) that defines a new surface and new landforms where it lies. If an explosion melts snowbanks or glaciers on the slopes of the volcano, or if it is accompanied by heavy rain, massive mudslides (lahars) may roll down the mountain and spread along the valleys, killing all life on their routes and changing the landform. Needless

to say, lava flows, ash falls, and lahars are capable of creating or destroying archaeological sites almost instantaneously (Sheets 1992; Sheets and McKee 1994).

Isostasy

The relatively thin crust of rock that forms the continents and underlies the ocean
basins rests on more viscous material of the mantle. When additional weight is
imposed upon the crustal rocks, they deform elastically, sinking as pond ice may
subside under the weight of a skater. The mantle material below slowly flows away
from the depression, forcing crustal rock elsewhere to rise (Chapter 3). When weight
is removed, as by the melting of a glacier, the draining or drying of a lake, the erosional removal of surficial sediments or rock, or the regression of the sea, isostatic
crustal uplift occurs. The uplift is a subtle effect; however, fluvial responses to
changed base levels and raised beaches of pluvial and glacial lakes indicate that the
scale of landform change can be considerable. The seacoasts of Scandinavia and
Labrador with their step-like raised beaches are dramatic demonstrations of the
potential scale of isostatic landform change: 8000 years after the ice sheets melted,
those northern coasts are still rising. Effective reconstruction of landforms deformed
by isostasy requires modeling changes in elevation and slope over time.

Aeolian landforms

In arid lands, where vegetational cover is thin and surface sediments easily mobilized, wind erosion may be the dominant agent of surface modification. Air whirl-
ing at tornado speeds (hundreds of km/hr) picks up and transports objects as large
as trees and houses, leaving behind both denuded spaces and new debris piles.
Where large amounts of unconsolidated sediments are available to be transported
by wind, aeolian landforms such as sand sheets, dune fields, and loess deposits may
dominate the landscape, blanketing earlier landforms. Loess deposits of well-
sorted silts sometimes cover thousands of square kilometers to depths of many
meters, as in the American Midwest ($\geq$30 m in Kansas), the South American
pampas, Eastern Europe, and in Central and Eastern Asia ($>$100 m deep) (Lowe
and Walker 1984: 112).

Dunes take many shapes, their forms responding to aerodynamic principles and
reflecting prevailing or dominant wind directions and speeds as well as the supply of
sand. They may be linear, crescentic or parabolic, star-shaped, or domed, and their
orientation may vary from transverse to longitudinal in respect to the winds (Fig.
9.6). Every geomorphology text provides details about dunes.

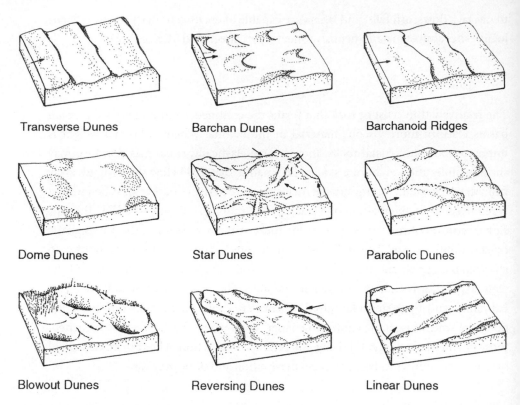

Figure 9.6 Typical dune forms; arrows indicate wind directions that influence the dune formations. (After Waters 1992: Fig. 4.4.)

Fluvial landforms

The most archaeologically relevant landforms created by moving water have been discussed above. Floodplains and terraces, river channels and channel forms are important elements of archaeological landscapes (Chapter 10). Terraces, levees, and the higher segments of floodplains have been for millennia favored places for human activities. As these landforms are all accretional, stratified sites may be found in them.

Glacial and glaciofluvial landforms

Landforms created by glacial erosion and deposition are easily identified, if not interpreted, but often difficult to date. Although archaeologists must be concerned far more with the dating of glacial features than with the details of their form and formation, it is helpful to understand some of the basic concepts and language of glacial geomorphology.

Landforms shaped by glaciers, and the low-temperature periglacial landforms that accompany them, are obvious at local and regional scales in the affected latitudes. For the most part, the features are local elements of limited size and extent, but they are typically distributed regionally. Features resulting from continental-scale ice sheets are rarely themselves continuous in space at comparable scales; they form, and are preserved, discontinuously, and must be interrelated by interpretation based on theories about glacial growth, flow, and disintegration. Most of what is known about glaciers has been learned from observation of currently active mountain glaciers and snow fields, features of much smaller size than the great ice sheets of the past. Research now under way in the high Arctic, in Greenland, and in Antarctica is producing the first significant sets of direct observations on large-scale ice bodies, and is making very clear how much is still to be to understood. The landforms remaining after the melting of ice sheets and valley glaciers, however, are available for direct observation; their forms and composition, therefore, are better understood than are the processes that shaped them (Bowen 1991).

Terminal moraines are ridges of unstratified material left at the outer edges of ice that has ceased to move. They may be traceable for long distances across terrain, but upon close examination are frequently found to be composed of deposits laid down by separate episodes of glacial-edge halts. Stratified debris, deposited from water, forms in cracks and at the edges of glaciers as well as in front of the ice margin. Within the ice zone the most common kinds of stratified deposits formed are small hills and mounds called "kames"; they may be of any shape, but are typically elongated because they formed as water-laid deposits in cracks or along the margins of ice and hillsides. Meltwater carrying debris away from glaciers as **outwash** may form extensive, level, sloping plains as it dumps its burden, the coarsest component near the ice, the finer farther away, in the manner of alluvial fans. Outwash plains and **deltas** are prominent features of postglacial landscapes at the edges of melting; their level surfaces and good drainage make them favorite places for human settlements and airfields. Outwash sediments are favored for sand and gravel quarries.

Like drumlins, small-scale glaciofluvial landforms such as kame deposits may be small enough to be mistaken for artificial landforms created by people. As discussed above, the distinction is easily made from observation of sedimentary structures in sections or cores. For further details about glacial landforms, consult any recent text on geomorphology or glaciology. As the field is developing quickly, texts more than 15 years old are no longer reliable, and the specialist literature is highly technical.

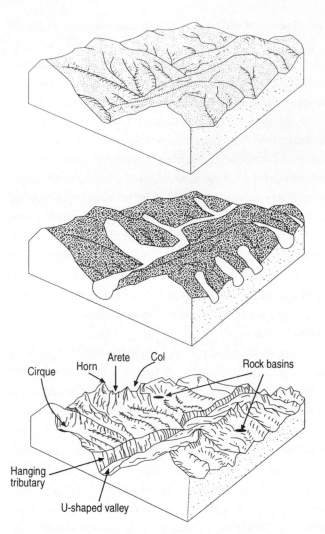

Figure 9.7 Stream-eroded uplands (top), subjected to alpine glacial erosion (middle). The bottom block diagram shows a U-shaped valley, cirques, hanging tributaries, and other classic valley glacial landforms. (After Flint and Skinner 1974: Fig. 11.12.)

Landforms shaped by glacial erosion are best developed in areas of high relief, where the flow of ice was strongly channeled and where bedrock was extensively exposed (Fig. 9.7). In areas of low relief and limited bedrock exposures, glacial erosional features are less available to observation, being typically covered by glacial or postglacial sediments. Striated and streamlined bedrock features are the most widely distributed erosional landforms, marking the passage of ice but usually affording no clues as to the time of the event.

Anthropogenic landforms

At the distance of orbiting spaceships, the view of Earth has been reassuring in that human impacts upon the continental surfaces are not immediately obvious, except as light patterns at night. However, aerial and satellite photographs demonstrate that at meso-scales roads, canals, cities, and the Great Wall of China are perceptible modifications of the planet's surface. Constructional and destructional forms such as irrigation systems, agricultural terraces, road and rail networks, dikes, landfills, airports, and urban sprawls are important geomorphological features. Humans have imposed on the Earth artificial landforms to which natural systems must adjust. Landforms influence the flows of air and water and, through them, local climate. The most pervasive effect of humans on landforms, however, is probably their "alteration in the rate at which geomorphic processes operate" (Summerfield 1991: 25). Anthropogenic vegetation clearance and regolith disturbance have effects far beyond the immediate places and times of the activities. The complexities of "down-stream" effects of human meddling with geomorphological surfaces remain to be understood (Boardman and Bell 1992).

LANDFORMS AT MICRO-SCALE (< 1 KM^2)

At the micro-scale, in spaces less than 1 km^2, geomorphological analysis emphasizes not only processes, but actual agents and small-scale variables such as soil temperature and moisture. Prominent among the effective agents are humans. Having reached the scale at which human activity is readily influential, we must contend again with the occasional difficulties of distinguishing purely natural (non-artifactual) phenomena from the products of human artifice.

Modern urban-dwellers may live their lives in casual disregard for the shape and composition of the landscape beneath their feet. This obliviousness is a fairly recent luxury for the species; the locational attributes of ancient dwelling and activity sites display the sensitivity of former societies to the topography and lithology of their habitats. Living sites and cemeteries are so consistently sited on topographic rises, even in areas of very subtle relief, as to leave no reasonable doubt that the founders selected for drainage and for visibility. Any settlement with pretensions for perma-nence needed a ready supply of potable water, as well as abundant water for industrial uses and, ideally, transportation. Every rocky outcrop on the surface of the globe has surely been scrutinized at some times in the past to ascertain its potential for raw materials; the known distribution of ancient quarries seems to be limited only by the abilities of field archaeologists to recognize them for what they are. Every cave and rockshelter on the face of the Earth has surely been evaluated as living space many times. In addition to analyzing the natural history of inhabited landscapes, archaeologists need to understand the advantages that landscape features offered to people in the past.

Among the many small-scale glacial landforms easily confused with results of human labor are perched rocks – boulders balanced precariously on smaller rocks or outcrops, which appear to some people as so completely unlikely natural phenomena that they "must" be artifacts. Large erratic boulders and boulder fields emplaced by glaciers have been similarly overinterpreted by people insistent on their mythic qualities. An informed appreciation of landscape, and the ability to test hypotheses about agents, are effective antidotes to such error.

On the other hand, human actions such as digging and piling and bringing and taking can reshape natural landforms until their original morphology is irrecoverable. Furthermore, the scale of some artificial platforms, created to elevate and support religious and secular structures of consequence, can easily compete with natural formations, and may be misunderstood in turn. The Eurasian **tells** composed of the debris of ancient cities rival hills in size, and the amount of earth movement involved in constructing some European Iron Age hillforts compares favorably with some terminal moraines. Indeed, many ancient urban areas, wholly artificial landforms, exceed the micro-scale here under consideration.

The variety of landforms at the micro-scale worldwide is very great, but within given regions is usually finite and even predictable. Archaeologists should familiarize themselves with the natural forms common in their areas, including the full range of variation involving frozen-ground phenomena, water-laid sediments, aeolian action, forest-floor morphology, animal burrows (from ants to rodents), and the products of mass movement on slopes. Observe small-scale processes such as rainwater splashes moving sand grains, water transporting material down slope in rills and gullies, and clay deposits forming in puddles. Many of these phenomena are ephemeral within archaeological time scales, even within seasonal durations, but familiarity with them in their many guises will sharpen awareness not only of the climatic and biotic agents involved in their formation and disappearance, but of the cultural agents from which they should be distinguished. Moreover, the scope and scale of the damage micro-scale processes can do to archaeological sites will become obvious.

10

LANDFORMS OF SHORES AND SHALLOW WATER

> The coast of a continent is a great boundary between two realms, land and water. Along this, as along other boundaries, two very different realms must adjust to each other, and conflict occurs.
>
> FLINT AND SKINNER 1974: 245

The conflict of land and water creates the dynamism characteristic of shorelines, whether of rivers, oceans, or lakes. Humans are drawn to water because it is essential to the maintenance of organic life, and is therefore the location of basic resources. Archaeological sites on the shores of lakes and oceans present special opportunities and challenges for paleoenvironmental studies. Sites near water typically exhibit preservation conditions conducive to the survival of a range of organic materials. The sediments in and near them are likely to be organically enriched as well and hence excellent sources of climatic proxies and remains of plants and animals. Landforms shaped by waves and currents are typically informative about past climatic and geotectonic states and conditions. The dynamism of sedimentary regimes typically creates stratified sites, which are nevertheless subject to frequent erosion.

COASTAL GEOMORPHIC CONCEPTS AND PROCESSES

Landforms at the edge of water, like those on land, are shaped primarily by processes in the atmosphere, geosphere, hydrosphere, and cryosphere. The biosphere's influence is expressed mainly at small, local scales. The large-scale processes most responsible for changing the elevational relationships between land and water, and thus initiating erosion and landform evolution, are tectonism and climate change, and their combined product – eustasy.

Because the boundary between land and sea fluctuates constantly, the notion of **sea level** is merely a convention – a plane extended across and through the continents at the average elevation of the surface of the sea (mean sea level [**MSL**] or sea level elevation relative to land: relative sea level [**RSL**]). Although casually considered a fixed datum from which elevations on continents and on the sea floors are measured, sea level varies ceaselessly. During the Cretaceous epoch at the end of the Mesozoic (dinosaur) era, sea level everywhere was relatively higher than today, overflowing the continents as warm shallow seas. The global trend has been downward since, with many significant fluctuations. Today, most shores are sinking relative to MSL, although some are rising (Pirazzoli 1991). Tides, of course, ebb and flow twice daily along most coasts and the tidal ranges vary semi-monthly and with weather; tidal ranges are averaged in the expression of sea level.

Processes in the geosphere

The Pleistocene epoch was characterized by the unusual frequency and intensity of both isostatic and eustatic variation in the relative levels of shore and sea. Continental platforms and ocean floors moved up and down relative to each other as ice and water were exchanged, creating dynamic coastlines worldwide. Isostatic depression of the continents under the weight of ice is partially compensated by viscous flow in the mantle, causing uplift of the nearby ocean floors and thereby minor reductions in the capacity of ocean basins. Rebound of land after glacial melt, and subsidence of the ocean floor under the renewed load of water, are slow processes that continue today in the higher latitudes. Dropping sea levels (**regression**) expanded terrestrial habitats, subjecting large areas previously underwater to subaerial erosion and deposition (Chapter 9). With rising sea level or sinking land the sea encroached (**transgression**); surf and currents rearranged unconsolidated surface sediments to create coastal landforms as the shore shifted inland and the edges of continents became submerged continental shelves. Ancient shores, therefore, may lie below or above present sea levels. Any combination of processes that elevates the land relative to sea level will raise coastal and shallow-water landforms out of the realm of waves into that of weather. When land–water relationships move in the opposite direction, low coasts and terrestrial landforms created by subaerial processes are inundated. In either case, appropriate description and interpretation of landforms is the first step in understanding landscape history along shores.

Sea-level change is understood theoretically, but the details involve so many variables and so many scales that much remains to be learned. The trend of lowering seas ver the past 80 million years still remains to be fully explained, as do details in the Pleistocene history of sea-level fluctuations (Pirazzoli 1991). Explanations for these fluctuations involve minimally three types of change: changes in the volume of water in the oceans, changes in the capacity of the ocean basins, and changes in the "geoid," the shape of the sea surface over the planet calculated as if MSL were influenced by gravity alone and the ocean could flow into continental areas. The geoid is mentioned here only for completeness; we can ignore it for present purposes, but it does matter in certain reconstructions (see Kellogg [1988: 84] and chapters in Tooley and Shennan [1987] for further particulars). Isostatic and eustatic adjustments following the last glaciation are expressed as relative sea-level change along various segments of the continental shores. The explanation of the changes, whether movement of land or sea, should be explored for each case, and may be indeterminate.

Since the last glaciation, changes in the volume of water in the oceans are mainly glacio-eustatic – defined by the growth and decline of ice masses on the continents, with a minor component defined by water temperature – and thus dependent upon climate. Long-term changes in the capacity of the ocean basins are functions of geotectonic processes, as well as isostatic adjustments to the loading and unloading of water, ice, and sediments. The geotectonic processes involved are ocean floor rifting and subduction, introduced in Chapter 3, and continental warping, with some lesser changes caused by volcanism (Summerfield 1991: Ch. 17).

Lake shores are similarly affected by changes in water volume, basin shape, and capacity. Water volume in a lake is sensitive to the elevation of the lake outlet, to climatic availability of precipitation and groundwater, and to tectonism and isostasy. As with the oceans, if the water level in a lake drops, beaches are abandoned above the new level; if it rises, beaches are submerged. The drainage or evaporation of very large lakes, such as Late Glacial Lake Bonneville in western North America, results in isostatic uplift of the locale, raising the abandoned beaches to higher elevations than they occupied when active.

Processes in the atmosphere

Climate is a major player in sea-level changes, as we have seen. Cold climates foster the accumulation of ice as glaciers on the continents, diminishing the amount of water available to flow back into the oceans. In addition, the volume of sea water changes on both long and short time scales according to prevailing temperatures, expanding with warmth, contracting in cold.

Climatic control of large lakes is rather more complicated and to an extent more direct, depending as it does on precipitation to fill lakes and maintain groundwater. The Milankovitch astronomical factors come into play at seasonal and larger scales, as do glaciation, sea level, ocean and atmospheric temperature distributions, an planetary wind patterns. During glacial phases, large lakes in northern temperate latitudes were greatly expanded by increased precipitation pushed south by high pressure over the ice sheets, and maintained by reduced evaporation due to cool climates and cloud cover. These temperate lakes were drier and lower during interglacials, including this present one. In contrast, levels of subtropical lakes are controlled by monsoonal rains that shift latitudinally with the winds of the intertropical convergence zone (ITCZ), itself sensitive to the seasonality of perihelion and other cyclical factors (Chapter 3; Bradley 1999: 317–324). Subtropical lakes, therefore, were low during the last glacial maximum, high in the early Holocene and, with perihelion in the northern winter, they are again low today (Kutzbach and Street-Perrott 1985).

Winds drive waves on the surfaces of large water bodies. Coastal erosion is accomplished by the energy of waves and wind, typically working together. Waves and currents erode coastal landforms and move sediments in water; winds mobilize loose sediments above water level and redeposit them. Storm waves do more work than do normal tides and breakers, because wave size is partly a function of wind speed. Coastal dunes are built by aeolian reworking of beach sands; archaeological sites are frequently buried in them. Dunes, typically stabilized by vegetation close to humid shores, may be driven inland considerable distances in arid climates and bury landforms and archaeological sites (Moseley et al. 1992).

Processes in the hydrosphere

Coastal landforms, like those inland, are shaped by the action of moving water on regolith. Coastal landforms are overwhelmingly the products of the hydrosphere; tides, waves, and currents mobilize, transport, and deposit sediments. Water in ocean basins, lakes, and rivers initiates shoreline evolution that tends toward subduing the topography and regularizing the shoreline. Regardless of the initial landform, and of variation at local and regional scales, nearshore topography worldwide displays a limited range of characteristic forms.

The marine shoreline is defined by sea level; the major perceptible variation in sea level is, of course, the twice-daily fluctuation of tide. Tides are water's response to the gravitational attraction of the Moon and Sun. The pull is strongest (spring tides) when the Sun, Earth, and Moon are directly in line, twice a month; it relaxes as the configuration changes. Tidal range is measured conventionally as elevation symmetrical around mean sea level, which varies from a few centimeters in the Mediterranean Sea to over 15 m in the Bay of Fundy, Nova Scotia (Fig. 10.1; Chorley et al. 1984: 373).

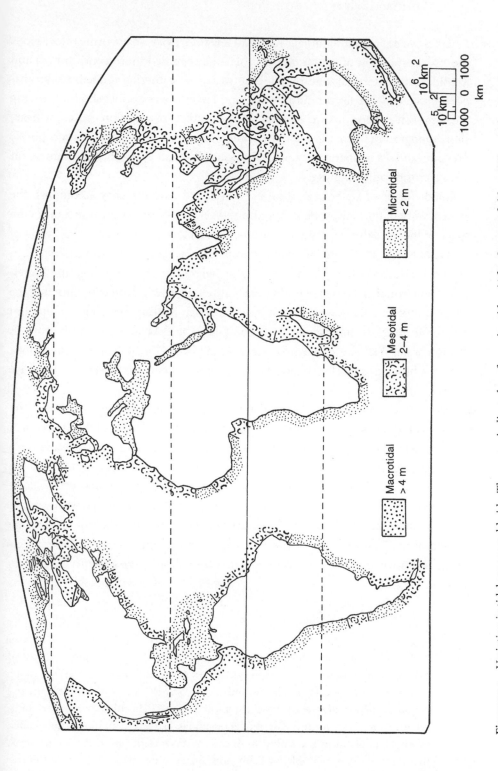

Figure 10.1   Variation in tidal range worldwide. The ranges indicated are for spring tides. (After Summerfield 1991: Fig. 13.9.)

Macrotidal
>4 m

Mesotidal
2–4 m

Microtidal
<2 m

Tides cycle at regular intervals: high and low tides twice a day, spring tides twice a month. Storm tides, of course, are irregular. The exposed shore between high and low tides is the intertidal zone, the site of most active weathering and sediment transport. Large tidal ranges run more water and larger waves against shores, bringing greater erosive energy. However, tidal range is subject to variation caused by nearshore topography, storms, gravitational pull, wind direction and speed, atmospheric pressure, and sea temperature, so that the potential exists everywhere for significant coastal erosion and sculpting.

Major forms of water in motion are waves and currents; they accomplish the erosive work of the hydrosphere. The size and velocity of a wave are functions of the speed of the wind driving it and the distance it travels over open water (the "fetch" of a wave or wind). The length of a wind-driven wave in open water is the distance from crest to crest, across the trough between; the height (amplitude) is measured vertically from trough to crest (review Fig. 4.2). Although waves travel with the wind, the water comprising the wave does not itself move far, instead revolving in loops and returning nearly to its original position (Fig. 10.2a). As waves touch bottom in shallow water near shore they slow, steepen, fall over ("break"), and rush upslope onto the beach as surf (Fig. 10.2b). Powerful erosive energy is directed at the wave base.

Water driven onshore by tides and waves returns to its source in the form of currents that follow the major slope of the shore under the influence of the direction of the waves. Longshore currents run parallel to the beach until turning seaward as rip currents (Fig. 10.3a). The speed of the water and the turbulence induced by the change of wave form provide the erosive energy of the surf that attacks the shore. Sediments are driven upslope in the swash zone, and may be returned basinward in currents draining the slope. Currents carry very significant sediment loads along the beach and seaward until their energy dissipates in deeper water. All these principles pertain whether the basin is the sea or a lake, despite the obvious differences in scale.

Figure 10.2   Wave zones and shore landforms in the littoral zone of sloping and cliffed shores, section views. (a) Wave height, wave base, and wave change on shore. (Modified from Waters 1992: Figs. 6.1 and 6.6.) (b) Littoral zone with breaker zone and bar, surf zone, swash zone and beach, berm, and dune. High and low water levels indicated against shore forms. (After Waters 1992: Fig. 6.6.) (c) Landforms on a cliffed shore: shore platform and cliff with sea cave. With isostatic uplift or lower sea level, such caves become available for habitation. (After Waters 1992: Fig. 6.5 and Butzer 1982: Fig. 4.4.)

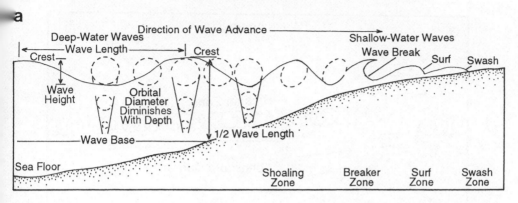

a

Direction of Wave Advance

Deep-Water Waves

Shallow-Water Waves

Wave Length

Wave Break

Crest

Crest

Surf

Swash

Crest

Wave
Height

Orbital
Diameter
Diminishes
With Depth

Wave Base

1/2 Wave Length

Sea Floor

Shoaling
Zone

Breaker
Zone

Surf
Zone

Swash
Zone

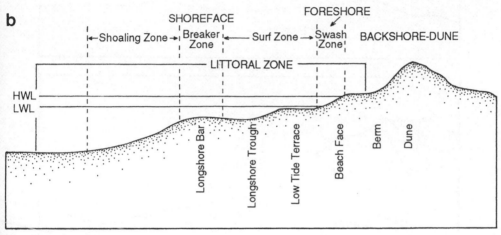

b

SHOREFACE

FORESHORE

Shoaling Zone

Breaker
Zone

Surf Zone

Swash
Zone

BACKSHORE-DUNE

LITTORAL ZONE

HWL
LWL

Longshore Bar

Longshore Trough

Low Tide Terrace

Beach Face

Berm

Dune

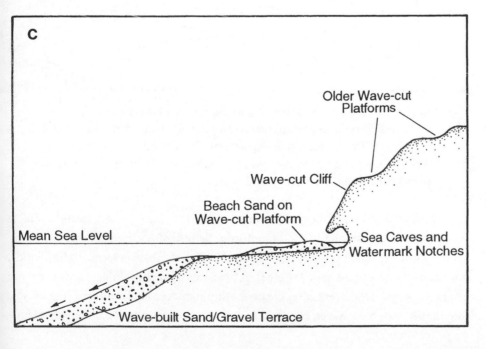

c

Older Wave-cut
Platforms

Wave-cut Cliff

Beach Sand on
Wave-cut Platform

Mean Sea Level

Sea Caves and
Watermark Notches

Wave-built Sand/Gravel Terrace

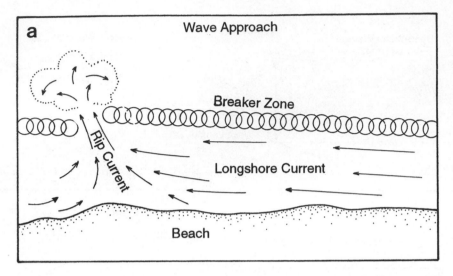

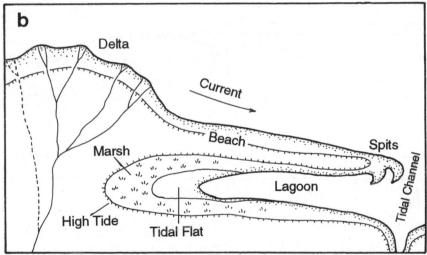

Figure 10.3   Selected coastal and near-shore landforms and currents in plan view.
(a) Longshore currents and rip currents on a sloping shore. (After Waters 1992:
Fig. 6.3.) (b) Delta, beach, spits, lagoon, marsh, tidal flats, and tidal channel
typical of shallow shores in unconsolidated sediments. Delta shows active and
abandoned distributary channels and lobes.

The surge of waves and the sweep of currents move sediments underwater to create
erosional and depositional coastal landforms. Sediments carried by longshore currents may be deposited as sand spits and bars that parallel beaches, extend headlands,
and block the mouths of bays. Where large amounts of unconsolidated sediments are
available, longshore currents may create the dominant coastal landforms (Fig. 10.3b).
Regularly reshaped by waves, currents, and wind, near-shore and shallow-water land-

forms are ephemeral structures. They are stabilized only when they are exposed above water as elements of terrestrial geomorphology, or are inundated to water depths below wave base where erosion is greatly reduced.

Beach-front properties were attractive locales long before the popularity of suntans, being close to the sea's biological riches and offering easy mobility for people equipped with boats. Beaches are normally composed of sediments of medium grades – pebbly gravels and sand-sized particles – but on high-energy shores they may include remarkably large boulders. Beach landforms such as ridges built by storm waves and aeolian dunes are built above the level of normal high tides where they are only episodically affected by wave energy. Cheniers are special kinds of beach ridges built of coarse materials, including shell debris, winnowed from mudflats. Barrier islands, storm ridges, and dunes are the predominant coastal landforms on which archaeological sites are situated and preserved, although preservation may be very conditional (Figs. 10.2b and 10.3b).

Shores where wave and current energy is low typically display no sharp demarcation in relief between land and water. Low-energy shores include those in the lee of dominant wind direction, and those on very gradual slopes. Typical low-energy shore landforms include lagoons, estuaries, marshes, and mangrove swamps, among others (Fig. 10.3b). In such areas fine sediments, both mineral and organic, are deposited in basins of quiet water, which itself is typically **brackish** rather than fully marine. Sediments deposited under shallow waters dominate preserved low-energy shores where inundated archaeological sites may be found (e.g., Eddison and Gardiner 1995).

Sea level is the ultimate limit for fluvial processes on the continents; it is the ultimate "base level" below which rivers cannot erode (Chapter 9). Rivers entering the ocean or a lake basin deposit their coarsest load near the point of entry, progressively dropping finer sediments as the current speed slows in deeper water. The result, as in lakes, is a delta (Fig. 10.3b). Fine materials in suspension and dissolved load are carried beyond the delta and deposited on the sea floor or lake bed in deep or quiet water, such as under ice during the winter. The large active deltas at the mouths of major rivers around the globe are recent constructions, having formed only since slowing of the postglacial rise of sea level, after 8000 years ago (Stanley and Warne 1994). With sea-level rise, deltas tend to build upstream concordantly with the marine incursion; they also sink isostatically under the weight of accumulating sediments. The history of each delta is unique, varying with climate, elevation, sediment load, and local sea level.

The shores of inland lakes and ponds are shaped by processes essentially equivalent to those of the seacoasts but usually at much smaller scales. Very large mid-continental lakes have tides, breakers, and currents and may display shore forms closely comparable to those of the seacoast. Smaller bodies of water experience lower wave energy and fewer of the erosive processes, but can develop typical elements of beaches and deltas resulting from storms and water-level fluctuations.

Processes in the cryosphere

Glaciated shores record the processes of glacial erosion and deposition both above and below sea level. Until they reach water deep enough to lift them off the bottom, glaciers continue to erode rock and sediments, cutting far below sea level. Once afloat, glacial ice deposits sediment on the floors of lakes and seas. Sedimentary particles carried by meltwater drop to the bottom of water bodies, or spew out from under the ice to form fans and deltas. Heavy materials melting out of ice drop at the edge of the glacier or, frozen into calving icebergs, are carried out into deeper water. Continuous deposits of boulders on shallow continental shelves may indicate the former presence of glaciers floating above; trails of scattered boulders extending out to sea track icebergs. Finer materials carried in meltwater into lakes and the ocean may be deposited in the still water under ice as massive or varved clay beds. These shallow-water phenomena are relevant to archaeologists when isostatic rebound or other processes raise the glaciomarine landforms above sea level, where they may become terrestrial landscape elements whose origins need to be recognized.

More immediately relevant to archaeology is the non-glacial winter freezing of the sea surface in high latitudes, where shelf ice forms on surface waters of low salinity. Ice shelves extending seaward from the shores of eastern and northern Canada were seasonal hunting grounds for people taking seals and fish, utilization areas lost every spring. The Inuit and earlier Thule peoples of northern Canada built their snow houses (igloos) on shelf ice that was seasonally frozen fast to the shore (Savelle 1984). Marine shore ice or ice cover on lakes may be driven ashore by storms with considerable violence, pushing up beach deposits, creating new small landforms, and damaging or destroying archaeological sites (e.g., Newell 1984).

Processes in the biosphere

Coastal vegetation is a counter-force dampening the dynamics of wind and waves. At the strictly local scale, vegetation stabilizes sediments and the landforms they comprise. Grasses hold dune sands in place and also roughen the surface, slowing winds and facilitating dune growth by the deposition of additional sand. In shallow water, salt-marsh plants collect, contribute to, and hold fine sediments near high-tide level. Mangrove swamps in the tropics play similar roles. Swamps, marshes, and lagoons are nurseries for aquatic animals of all kinds, and consequently rich data sources for paleoenvironmental studies (Part VII).

METHODS OF LANDFORM RECONSTRUCTION

The applicability of conventional topographic survey techniques ends just off the beach, in water too deep for surveyors to stand in. Commercially available maps of coastal landforms include the familiar topographic maps produced by government surveys almost everywhere (Chapter 9), complemented by nautical charts that show soundings into coastal waters. The datum for soundings is low water, to provide minimal depths for navigation, rather than the mean sea level typically used for topographic maps. Consequently, there is a gap between whatever low-water datum is used for the subaqueous readings and the datum for the terrestrial elevations, roughly equivalent to half the tidal range. It is also likely that the contour intervals underwater will differ from those on land, expanding with depth. Nautical charts may show more detail underwater than topographic maps do, but they are produced at different scales and sometimes measured by different systems. A transect or profile running from inland to offshore, therefore, will require recalibration at the shore. As discussed above, the bottom surface near shore is formed mainly by unconsolidated sediments responding to tides and currents; it rarely preserves significant elements of drowned subaerial paleotopography. Instead, the underwater surface reflects different depths of tidal scour, dredged channels, bedrock outcrops, and areas where a variety of undesirable debris is dumped. Genuine paleotopographic data must be acquired by coring or by remote sensing.

Direct observation

Closer observation of sediments and structures underwater involves coring, diving, or both. Diving, of course, is the glamorous choice, although it is best done in shallow, quiet warm waters. Turbulent water compromises visibility and increases risk. Diving to survey inundated landforms and archaeological sites has in fact been most successful in the Mediterranean Sea and on the shallow continental shelves of the Gulf of Mexico off the west coast of Florida (Dunbar et al. 1992; Muckelroy 1980), and in sinkholes and lakes.

Coring is the traditional means for close examination of sediment sequences at depth, whether underwater or underground. Small hand-held soil samplers provide useful information about the sediment sorting and structure of surficial landforms such as dunes, **middens** (accretions of refuse), and some beach ridges. For dealing with coarser sediments or greater depths, mechanized coring devices are essential. Sequences of deep cores are the best methods now available for reconstructing inundated landforms. Examples of coring methods and their results are discussed below (Fig. 10.5) and in Part V.

Remote sensing

Aerial photographs and satellite scans are as suitable for imaging coastal landforms as they are for those inland; as a bonus, coastal photos are typically dramatic and revealing because so few alternatives exist for gaining a distant perspective on coastlines. Photographs, it must be remembered, show moments in time, not the generalized landforms of maps. A series of photographs taken over months or years will display aspects of coastal dynamism otherwise unobservable and unmapped. An impressive example is the 40-year sequence of beach ridges on the Peruvian coast displayed by Moseley et al. (1992: 220).

Underwater remote sensing has had a major role in coastal archaeology for some time, where side-scan sonar and seismic profiling have been used to locate shipwrecks and to map Quaternary landscapes submerged on continental shelves (e.g., Stright 1986a; van Andel and Lianos 1984). Side-scan sonar produces relatively fine-scale relief maps of the bed of the ocean, large rivers, or lakes. It is useful for examining the sea-bottom surface for small relief features, particularly shipwrecks. Sound waves are produced by an apparatus towed from a boat and the resulting sound, reflected off the seabed or lake bottom, is recorded electronically. The apparatus for seismic sub-bottom profiling is packed in a pod which is either towed or mounted in the hull of a research vessel. Depending upon the nature of the bottom sediments and the resolution desired, the apparatus emits sound waves of different frequencies that penetrate sediments vertically. Waves are reflected from surfaces of different densities representing stratigraphic interfaces between sediment layers. The computer printout resembles a fuzzy stratigraphic profile (Fig. 10.4). Neither technique has the resolution to map in detail archaeological sites lacking major structural elements such as walls, stone quays, or ships. Both techniques reliably provide information about sediment interfaces underwater, although precision and resolution are typically compromised by navigational uncertainties in terms of absolute position and the depth from apparatus to the bottom, which varies with each wave.

Analysis

Chapter 9 explicitly noted that shape description alone is insufficient for full interpretation of terrestrial landforms. That is somewhat less the case with coastal land-

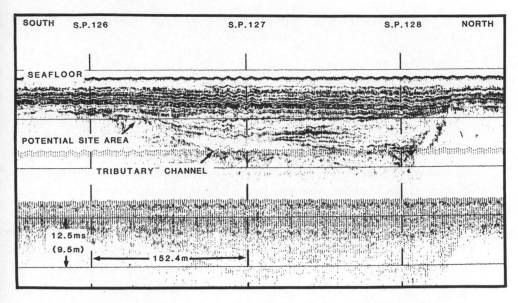

Figure 10.4 Sub-bottom profile under the Gulf of Mexico off the northeastern Texas coast, showing a tributary channel in the submerged portion of the Sabine River Valley. The area indicated as "potential site" was chosen because of its gentle slope and possible preservation opposite the channel-cut bank. (Reproduced from Stright 1986a: Fig. 8, with permission of the Society of Exploration Geophysicists.)

forms because these are less diverse, highly determined, and tend to occur as suites of historically related and spatially associated structures. The associations support interpretations for the landforms. However, as for terrestrial landforms, so for coastal geomorphology: sedimentological analysis (Chapter 11) is essential for detailed understanding. Sedimentological analyses are indispensable whenever it is important to know (1) whether a given set of, say, raised beach features represents one or more instances of sea-level stand at that elevation, (2) when the sea lapped there, (3) what were the respective contributions of wind, waves, and currents – the depositional environments. When inundated landforms of lagoons, estuarine shores, ponds, and so forth are at issue, sedimentology may be the only recourse. Samples for analyses are obtained by excavation or by coring.

Sediment samples from coastal landforms are likely to include biological as well as mineral matter. Fragments of carbonaceous or chitinous shells, bones, and single-celled organisms may be present, as well as pollen. Organic remains always help to answer the dominant analytical questions of when, how, by what means, and in what conditions deposits formed. Macrofossils in organic sediments are likely to include roots, stem fragments, and leaves of plants that grew in and near the water, as well as bones and shells of marine animals. Macrofossils are informative about water depth, chemistry, and temperature as well as about the local biota (Parts VI and VII).

Geochronology

Landform studies in archaeology always involve issues of time – it is essential to know when landforms were created and their age in relation to other landforms and to archaeological sites in the area. Stratigraphy is always the best method for determining relative age. When stratigraphic superpositions are not observed, then age information must be sought in chronometric methods that can deal with non-contiguous data.

Because the study of coastal landforms is predominantly about former sea levels, expertise and ingenuity have been devoted to refining chronometric methods for determining ages and durations. The literature of old sea levels, within and beyond archaeology, is replete with interpretive errors arising from erroneous age assignments. This is not surprising given the number and magnitude of the assumptions that underlie most of the chronometric methods currently in use (Part II) and the recent recognition of the complexities of eustatic, isostatic, and tectonic adjustments of coasts. As each dating method is refined and its applicability better delimited, earlier applications have to be reconsidered. It is easy to forget that published interpretations and conclusions, by the fact of publication alone, lag behind the current state of disciplinary knowledge.

Once it was relatively easy to play "date the beaches"; there was widespread acceptance of the assumption that eustatic sea levels were expressed globally and could be correlated from one region to another, even intercontinentally, by the elevation of surfaces. One counted back from the present interglacial to obtain a relative age for a raised beach in a coastal sequence, assigning each beach in a sequence to an interglacial in the four-glaciations model. Now we understand that, because of isostatic and tectonic movements affecting many coasts, and because of differential postglacial histories for coasts, none of the conclusions so achieved can be relied upon in the absence of detailed and explicit evidence of age.

With multiple geochronological methods available today, the principal difficulties are calibrating the several methods to achieve agreement that will support scrutiny. Uranium-series ages on corals and speleothems, radiocarbon ages on recent organic materials, and amino-acid racemization sequences on shells may fail to agree because of either methodological considerations or sampling error (Bard et al. 1990; Pirazzoli 1991; Törnqvist et al.1996). For coarse-grained estimates, Milankovitch cycles or oxygen-isotope stages defined in deep-sea cores provide some chronology for major relative sea-level movements, but the tightness of those correlations is in doubt (Gallup et al. 1994). Ice cores are weighing in now with potentially correlatable isotope and element profiles. The challenge is to choose the strongest method in a given instance, and to reconcile differences by discriminating tests.

At the smallest scales of geochronology, sampling problems dominate over analytical ones. In order to realize the relatively fine resolution possible with radiocarbon analyses, it is essential that the relevance of a sample be beyond question. In organic sediments, that relevance is not always achievable. Organic materials deposited in mucks, for example, may derive from numerous source areas and ages, coming to rest together on a surface either older or younger than their time of death. Organic materials in growth positions, such as shellfish in beds or roots of marsh plants, are coeval with the surfaces on or from which they grew; the integrity of the surface must then be demonstrated, as well as its age in respect to the older sediments that surround roots beneath that surface (Kellogg 1988). The stratigraphic relationships and relative ages of materials buried in or grown into near-shore silts and mucks may be very difficult to establish.

Interpretation

Reading the landscape is the first step in interpreting ecosystems. Reconstruction of coastal landscapes supplies data relevant for past climates, geotectonics, habitats past and present, and human adaptations and behavior. Because coastal landscapes represent tightly integrated subsystems involving all five spheres, many sources of data can, and should, be utilized. Here we limit consideration to geomorphology because other data sources are discussed later. Sedimentological data are crucial for interpreting coastal landforms, but their power is discussed in Part V, making them available here only in anticipation.

Interpretation of relict shores standing above or below modern water planes begins with efforts to define the sea level that formed them. Past tidal ranges cannot be estimated by analogy from modern conditions, since they vary with RSL and with landform shapes near shore. Key landforms represent former tidal ranges – mud flats mark the intertidal zone; marsh deposits or cliff notches mark high tide; wave-cut or sedimentary platforms below low tide mark the wave base (Fig. 10.2a and c). When possible, successful measurement of tidal range on relict coastal landforms is the ideal beginning for interpretation of former shore environments. From that datum one can address relative sea-level elevation and proceed to a reconstruction of landform associations and to selection of samples for chronometry.

Beaches and coastal features raised above water are the most readily interpretable, although exposure to subaerial erosion and deposition will in time obscure their original forms. Erosion of sediments obscures the relationships between extant land surfaces and former sea levels. Because such complications are rarely definable, projections of former sea levels onto modern landforms will not provide reconstructions accurate in their details. However, when key elements of earlier coastal landforms (e.g., beaches) are observable, they can be correlated across space to provide the best possible estimates of surface loss and of the extent and position of former topography. Landward extrapolations of elevations referenced only to sea-level curves are likely to be unreliable for ages of more than a few millennia.

Landform reconstructions undertaken from underwater survey are necessarily even less accurate. Submerged landforms are truncated by wavebase erosion or buried under additional sediment; key details of original morphology may be hidden or lost. Underwater contours on bathymetric maps, like those on land, average elevations between plotted points (soundings), smoothing away the edges and slope changes crucial for paleotopographic interpretation. In addition, they show modern subaqueous forms such as tidally scoured channels that should not be extrapolated into the past. Methodological uncertainties intrude into more technical work as well. For example, measuring depth from water surface to a feature observed in a seismic profile (Fig. 10.4) is beset with small errors inherent in the equipment, which are in turn surpassed by the errors involved in trying to be precise about the elevation of the sea surface at any particular moment in time when measuring from a boat bobbing amid waves. Exacerbating these inaccuracies are the problems of precision in dating underwater landforms. A concise exposition of the uncertainties is given by J. Shackleton (1988: 12) and elaborated in references she cites. Regardless of these uncertainties, which surely rival Heisenberg's, reconstruction of ancient coastal landforms is among the most fascinating of paleoenvironmental exercises (e.g., Bailey and Parkington 1988; Bloom 1983; Gifford et al. 1992; Stright 1986a; van Andel and Lianos 1984; van der Leeuw and Brandt 1988; Wilkinson and Murphy 1986).

Once a portion of an old coast is mapped, the temptation to relate it to a sea-level curve is apparently irresistible. The essential controls are (1) a sound age for the coastal features expressed as a span of time, not a unique moment or single radiometric age, and (2) a coeval tidal range or ranges measured from landmarks. Given these and (3) a dated *local* sea-level curve, good agreement may be achieved. Failing any one of the three essentials, estimates necessarily proliferate, not least because sea levels may repeat in time (the curves have "wiggles"). Lacking suitable data, investigators too often resort to curve-matching at any scale available. For these and other reasons, controversy is a nearly constant companion of sea-level reconstructions in archaeology (Kellogg 1988).

COASTAL LANDFORMS WITH ARCHAEOLOGICAL SITES

[T]he events described in the *Iliad* and *Odyssey* occurred in a dramatically different geographic and geomorphologic setting from that described heretofore by archaeologists.

KRAFT ET AL. 1980: 782

The world's seacoasts include some of the most attractive habitats for people. Continental shelves exposed during times of full-glacial low sea levels were occupied by plants and animals, including people, prior to being inundated as melting glaciers released water into the seas. Consequently, coastlines were rolled onto land, plants and animals backed up and shallow-water environments expanded. Waves, currents, and surf truncated and filled landforms they overran, reducing archaeologists' access to ancient coastal sites and habitats. Rivers aggraded to keep their mouths level with rising seas, burying terrestrial sites.

The archaeology of coastal habitats may be pursued in diverse situations. Wherever coastal zones have risen isostatically since deglaciation, old coasts are accessible upslope. Stable coasts offer remains of various ages, sometimes stratified under storm beaches or dunes. Where coasts have sunk or been overrun by rising seas, excavation opportunities are limited. Shelf landforms inundated by low-energy underwater environments may be preserved for archaeological excavations (Fig. 10.1), but are challenging to find. Extensive wetlands created as rising sea levels raised water tables on the land have proven to be especially rich in preserved organic remains. Investigations of wetland sites, most of them on coastal lowlands, have yielded exciting results in recent decades (Coles 1992).

Landforms of regional scale were classic objects of geomorphological study prior to the current interest in processes, although few of them are appropriate for archaeological interpretation. Exceptions include extensive raised wave-cut platforms that can be dated (usually to interglacials), the undersea karstlands of the last glacial period west of the Florida peninsula (Dunbar et al. 1992), the isostatically raised beaches of Labrador and Norway, and very large estuarine or lagoonal systems. Interpretations of features at these scales tend to focus on sea-level data, with some attention to chronology and the distribution of sites on coeval surfaces. For the most part, however, regional-scale reconstructions must allow for local-scale exceptions to generalizations about river basin evolution, isostatic adjustments, and microclimatic effects, all of which are particularly sensitive near shores.

Geomorphology best serves archaeology at local scales, explaining and interpreting small landforms and their relationships to human behavior. Notable work has been done on coastal sites both above and below water, but much is clearly experimental and often inconclusive (Johnson and Stright 1992).

Subaerial landforms

Archaeological sites on and near the shores of present-day lakes and seas have been among those most intensively investigated since the nineteenth century. Shell middens, particularly, are often large, highly visible landforms typically rich in artifacts of bone and shell in addition to the usual stone and ceramic classes. Shell middens (*sambaquis*) are heaps of refuse, predominantly food remains, left by humans or other animals. Because shelly middens resemble beach ridges and cheniers created by high-energy waves, and because bird feeding and nesting activities create shell piles, the human origin of middens was an early question in archaeology. It still surfaces occasionally today (Bailey et al. 1994; Sullivan and O'Connor 1993). Beach ridges and dunefields were everywhere favored locations for dwellings or food-collecting sites because they are above wave action and local water tables, but still close to the shore and its resources. Sea caves raised above the active shore have all the usual cave amenities amplified by proximity to coasts. Especially numerous around the shores of the Mediterranean and southern Africa, they were heavily utilized from Paleolithic time.

Volcanic islands and coral reefs

Volcanic islands formed above rift zones and mantle plumes cutting the sea floor are widespread in the world's oceans, clustering in the western and northern Pacific, the Caribbean, and mid-Atlantic Ridge. Raised by magma and ash deposited on oceanic crust, they later sink as the crust adjusts to the added weight. Coral reefs form near the edges of tropical volcanic islands, typically enclosing lagoons as the islands sink progressively below the sea surface.

The islands of American Samoa are volcanic vents that have recently emerged above sea level in the southwest Pacific Ocean. Archaeological investigations on a small island at the eastern edge of the archipelago included in their problem orientation interpretation of the local geomorphology. Ofu Island is a small, steep-sided volcanic cone rising from the ocean floor, fringed by coral reefs but lacking both lagoon and encircling reef. On the south shore of Ofu today, a narrow beach terrace extends seaward a short distance from the slope of the volcanic cone, providing the major horizontal surface on the island. Homes and gardens occupy the shelf.

Research had established that sea level in that area of the Pacific had been higher during the mid-Holocene and had dropped during the last 2000 years (Dickinson et al. 1994). On the shelf at the base of the volcanic cone lies a deep pile of rock and sediment fallen and washed from the upland. Those terrestrial sediments interfinger seaward with sandy sediments eroded from the reef and deposited on shore by winds. Archaeological investigation in the 1980s was attracted to one area of the terrace by prehistoric artifacts revealed by earthmoving (Kirch and Hunt 1993).

The archaeologists approached their excavations with questions about the formation of the terrace and its relationship to changing sea levels. When sea level was higher, waves lapped close to the cone, cutting a rock platform near shore. A coral reef formed off shore. Lowered sea exposed the reef and rocky edge of the platform to wave erosion that ground them into sand-sized particles. Exposed sand blew shoreward, mixing volcanic rock and reef debris together into the terrace sands. Volcanic rock and clays slid down the steep slopes of the cone onto the near edge of the terrace. As the terrace accreted outward toward the reef, less and less of the volcanic rock was exposed for inclusion in the sediments. Reef-derived calcareous sands came to dominate the terrace deposits. The archaeologists realized from the relationships of landforms and sediments that the terrace surface has been available for homes and gardens only in the last 2000 years. The earliest human occupations were likely buried under the debris pile near the cone; test excavations confirmed their model predictions. Furthermore, isostatic sinking of the island has brought the beach into the active wave zone again, and erosion is cutting away the shore edge of the terrace.

Beaches

Archaeological sites situated on beaches are preserved only when separated from the active zone of beach erosion. Beaches on stable shores may build seaward (prograde) when excess sediments moved by longshore currents are deposited as ridges of sand or gravel. Such ridge sequences are progressively younger toward the sea. At Cape Krusenstern and other locales on the Chukchi Sea coast of Alaska, ridge sequences provide crucial relative chronologies for sites (Giddings and Anderson 1986; Mason 1992). Beaches are raised above sea level by isostatic rebound of a deglaciated shore or isostatic compensation for dynamic loading nearby, or by tectonic uplift. Raised beach series are readily visible as step-like series of terraces on the tardily deglaciated Atlantic coasts of eastern Canada and western Norway. As with beach ridges, the isostatically raised beaches provide relative ages of sites situated on them so long as the assumption holds that the sites were located close to the shore of their time. For Arctic and subarctic sites that assumption seems valid and is supported by ethnology.

Geomorphologists and archaeologists both use such sequences to advance their investigations (Clark and Fitzhugh 1992; Helskog 1974).

Ancient raised shorelines on the coastal zones of the Mediterranean, and north-western and southern Africa early attracted attention as possible vehicles for relative chronologies for Lower and Middle Paleolithic sites. The idea was that the old beaches faithfully represented the elevations of high interglacial seas, and could therefore provide relative dating for sites on them since the number of interglacials was taken as known from terrestrial glaciation data. The guiding assumptions are no longer defensible in detail. Many of these classic old surfaces have been redated by more precise geochronological methods.

Sea caves

Among the most dramatic sites on raised beaches are elevated sea caves that occasion-ally shelter archaeological deposits. Sea caves form at high-tide level (Fig. 10.2c); they are, consequently, not habitable when on the active shore. Dating the shore provides only a maximal age for associated sites. Ancient sea caves in a sandstone quarry at Sidi Abderrahman on the northwest coast of Morocco contained Lower Paleolithic arti-facts and human remains. Heroic efforts were made to use the elevations of the caves and beach deposits to fix the age of the archaeological materials, but consensus was elusive (McBurney 1960: 114–118). Restudy might permit assignment of organics in the beaches to dated oxygen-isotope stages of the marine core chronology.

Inundated and subaqueous landforms

As soon as we step off the beach into water, we confront the limitations of our under-standing as well as of our physical and technical equipment. Dating landforms on the continental shelf has proven more difficult than expected, and continues to elude enthusiastic investigation off the coasts of the Americas, for example. Intensive search for sites potentially buried under sediments of a transgressing sea produced promising results off the northeastern shore of Texas in the Gulf of Mexico near Galveston. Predictive modeling from dated sea-level curves, followed by sub-bottom profiling and coring, led investigators to areas on the margins of a Pleistocene channel system southwest of the present mouth of the Sabine River, draining to a low sea-level (Fig. 10.4). The areas were 9 m or less below the present seafloor, appropri-ate to ages of 12,000–6000 years ago (Stright 1986a). Limited coring following the geophysical investigations brought up sediments that, on analysis, appeared to indi-cate midden-like deposits containing shell, bone, and charred materials (Stright 1986b), but no conclusive results were achieved.

Estuaries where fresh water meets the sea, and other shallow-water coastal areas such as mangrove swamps, lagoons, and extensive marshes are biologically diverse and attractive resource areas for people. Archaeological sites often cluster close to such low-energy shores, where they are subject to inundation (microtidal zones in Fig. 10.1). Preservation of archaeological sites during inundation requires protection from wave-base erosion and scouring by surf under sedimentary blankets. Peat mats and lagoonal muds extending over sites in advance of marine erosional forces provide the best protection. Such sites can be accessible in shallow water or under sediments near shores where excavation is feasible, although challenging and often expensive. Investigations of estuarine and coastal marsh sites on the shores of England are setting new standards for recovery of environmental contexts and of archaeological materials, especially organic artifacts and waste materials (e.g., Eddison and Gardiner 1995; Wilkinson and Murphy 1995).

Estuaries in other natural and cultural environments also have dynamic histories. A notable case is ancient Troy, where Homer's war may or may not have taken place. Schliemann's claim to have found Troy at Hissarlik south of the Dardanelles strait in Turkey was disputed partly on the basis of geography that corresponded poorly to the descriptions in the Homeric epics. A Turkish/American interdisciplinary investigation of the region explained much about the changes, restoring credibility to both Homer and Roman writers (Kraft et al. 1980). Figure 10.5 illustrates the modern and ancient situations, displaying dramatic infilling of 10 km of the bay since Troy was settled, and enough since the estimated time of the Homeric battles (Troy VI/VII) to have left the site far inland today. Note that the seacoast to the west changed significantly in the same time span. Alluviation of the bay occurred during and after a time of rising sea levels. Tectonics may have complicated estimations of RSL: ancient Troy also suffered earthquake damage. Sediments flushed into the bay by the Scamander River had been mobilized by upstream deforestation for agriculture and for fuel. The reconstruction was achieved by a combination of coring and other paleogeographic studies; the report is good reading.

Wetlands

Rising sea levels do not merely back up the rivers that run into the sea. Fresh water floats on heavier salt water, so that a marine incursion raises groundwater to and above the height of MSL. Coastal lowlands are transformed into freshwater swamps fringing brackish estuaries; the water table overwhelms archaeological sites formerly on dry ground. Wetland archaeology near the North and Baltic Seas has been notably enriched by the preservation afforded organic materials by rising groundwater.

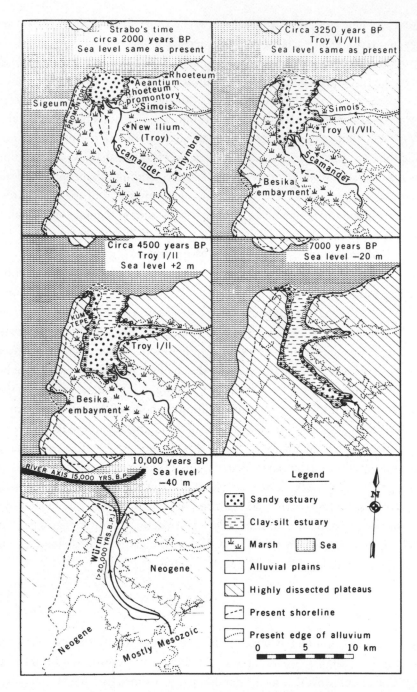

Figure 10.5   Reconstructions of Holocene paleogeography in the vicinity of ancient Troy, showing wave-cut cliff retreat to the west and deltaic progradation and alluvial aggradation in the embayment. The embayment is depicted in terms of the quality of bottom sediments. (Excerpted with permission from Kraft et al. 1980: Fig. 6, © 1980 American Association for the Advancement of Science.)

The island today called Britain was a peninsula of Europe during glacial low-sea conditions. Paleolithic and Mesolithic people walked across land now under the Channel. When the sea broke through between the cliffs at Dover and Calais, cutting off the island, tidal scour deepened the strait. As sea level continued to rise, the weight of rising water induced compensating isostatic depression, supporting increased tidal amplitude (Fig. 10.1). The North Sea widened into the lowlands of East Anglia and the Netherlands, creating huge estuaries that **alluvium** has since nearly filled. In East Anglia, alluvial aggradation and the rising water table pushed fen conditions inland, turning low hills into islands. Neolithic burial mounds (barrows) built on gravel were overwhelmed by fen peats (Evans and Hodder 1987). Following a mid-Holocene marine incursion that deposited widespread clay, fresh-water peats again dominated, providing resources and wet footing for Bronze Age and later human occupants of the area.

Pumping behind dikes for land reclamation in the Netherlands exposes archaeo-logical sites as deep as 10 m below MSL today (van der Leeuw and Brandt 1988: 153). The Assendelver Polder Project investigated for several years a large prograding delta north of Amsterdam. Paleogeographical and geological investigation aimed to describe and understand changes in landforms and land use at the supraregional and regional scales, while smaller natural and cultural phenomena were investigated at settlement and intra-settlement scales. An intensive coring project was the basis for landform investigation. The area once was a coastal estuary zone fed by large rivers and bordered by dunes and barrier beaches. Over the last 3000 years, the estuary mouths were driven north by longshore current deposition of abundant sediment and the growth of dunes. Between the dunes and eastern uplands was an expanding area of peats, mudflats, and drainage channels with levees. From the Neolithic period into the Iron Age, opportunistic use of the natural resources of the area was carried on from shifting bases on the higher surfaces of sand and peat. Early in the second millennium B.P., farmers and herders began to settle on the levees and dunes, digging drainage ditches around their holdings. The population increase that fol-lowed led eventually to more ambitious manipulation of the land, with diking begun about 900 years ago. Dike construction, of course, intensified with the development of pumping technology, which transformed the marshy area into an agricultural landscape. The area is now greatly reduced in both landscape and biological diversity from its condition of 3000 years ago, even as it supports a higher human population and greater cultural diversity (Brandt et al. 1987). Pumping has lowered the surface of the land by extracting water, and is likely to continue to do so. The present extreme elevational contrast between farmland and the excluded sea is a cultural product just as much as is the landscape; a relative sea level that to a major degree obfuscates the acceleration of expense and effort required to maintain the modified, simplified landscape of coastal Holland.

Wetland archaeological sites are among the world's most diverse and interesting, with their special preservation conditions and obvious close relationships between the natural conditions offered for human exploitation and the ingenuity, skill, and effort expended to overcome the most relentlessly constraining of them. Large timber villages, pile dwellings and ritual sites, human burials with flesh and clothing, lengthy walkways, and ingenious fish weirs all attract interest and public support. All are excellent vehicles to teach and demonstrate the achievements of our species as well as our ultimate, reflexive dependence upon the natural world as we have reshaped it.

CODA

Holocene sea-level rise has affected human cultural adaptations and cultural beliefs at every meeting of land and sea, worldwide. Clearly, at the local scale all such factors must be studied together. Like many other phenomena once considered natural, relative sea level (RSL) includes significant anthropogenic factors. The Red Queen (Chapter 1) moves just as fast with her feet wet.

LANDFORM RECONSTRUCTION AT LAETOLI, TANZANIA

Landform reconstruction in archaeology is most challenging with truly ancient sites, as in the study of human origins. The site of Laetoli in the southern part of the Serengeti Plain in East Africa is rich in hominid and other fossils and, uniquely, in footprints on a buried land surface about 3.6 million years old. Among the prints are those of upright, bipedal primates walking with a "shambling" gait (Leakey and Hay 1979) on thin layers of volcanic ash. What we can know of the context of those prints and of the landscape in which those strolls were taken – the habitat of a remote ancestor – we must learn from landform analysis, sedimentology, and paleontology. Diligently applying skill and imagination to these complementary sets of data, Richard L. Hay (1981) achieved a remarkable reconstruction of a Pliocene landscape at the beginning of human time.

The current landscape at Laetoli is a product of plate tectonics; continental plates are pulling apart and new crust is forming by volcanic action in the East African Rift Valley. Large-scale faulting has shaped a landscape of abrupt changes in relief and elevation, where dry uplands loom over lakes in the basins. South of Olduvai Gorge in northern Tanzania, the Eyasi Plateau lies on the uplifted northwest side of a major fault. Near the fault on the south edge of the plateau, the Laetoli area rises to an elevation of 1800 meters; at the foot of the fault lies Lake Eyasi. Occupying the divide between the Olduvai and Eyasi drainages, the Laetoli area has a seasonally dry climate with savanna vegetation. During the wet season grasses provide forage for large herbivores – the famous Serengeti fauna with elephants, giraffes, many antelopes and gazelles, along with the carnivores that prey upon them. The reduced forage of the dry season supports fewer and smaller animals that remain in the area year-round.

The volcanic Laetolil Beds are the oldest exposed members of a deep series of ash falls deposited on an erosional surface formed on ancient rocks. The Laetolil ash (tuff) was deposited from eruptions of the extinct volcano Sadiman onto a dome-shaped uplift of Pliocene age. The beds are now exposed discontinuously by faults on the plateau and in valleys. Stratigraphic relationships show that ash deposition preceded by over a million years the faulting that formed the Rift Valley and raised the Eyasi Plateau. Potassium–argon dates on the upper beds with fossils and animal footprints indicate an age of about 3.6 million years, placing the formation of the beds well into the Pliocene epoch. Faunal remains, related but not identical to modern fauna, confirm this.

Hay's study indicated that the ash, from a series of separate eruptions, fell in beds generally less than 15 cm thick that were superficially cemented, apparently soon after deposition, by calcareous and clay minerals derived by atmospheric moisture from the ash itself. The ash, partly reworked by wind after it had fallen, had been subjected to only minimal stream action. A few thin layers within the fossiliferous beds preserve footprints. One of these, the main Footprint Tuff, also preserves rain prints – splash-marks made by scattered raindrops hitting unconsolidated material. Because the thin beds show no sign of erosion the Footprint Tuff is considered to have accumulated over a relatively short period of time, "certainly less than a year" (R. L. Hay 1981: 19). The preservation of both bones and footprints was due largely to the rapid burial of surfaces by new ash falls and the quick cementation of the superficial sediments. The rain prints are interpreted as having been made during the latter part of a dry season; the beds above, some redeposited from water, are assigned to the rainy season of the same year.

Reconstruction of the Pliocene landscape was based on field and laboratory observations and analyses including intensive sedimentological, lithological, and stratigraphic work. Exposures of the Laetolil Beds were scrutinized for evidence that would indicate the landforms on which the ash fell, the vegetative cover and climate that constituted the environments of deposition, and any indication of the animal life of the time. Between outcrops the discontinuous beds were correlated by comparing their composition and structure. Old surfaces of low relief were traced along interfaces, while surfaces of larger scale, such as the doming of the underlying basement rock, were delineated by mapping the slopes of drainage channels.

The Footprint Tuff was traced along exposures and sometimes excavated. The rain-print ash followed the low relief of the landscape closely, like a blanket on a sleeper. Except for the footfalls and raindrops, it had been little disturbed between settling onto the surface and cementation, while the layers of ash above, partly reworked and displaced by moving water, were thinner on the mounds and thicker in the swales. Both sets had been cemented quickly after deposition, setting the prints that were soon covered by further ash falls. The carbonaceous composition of the Sadiman ash was easily leached by water that then precipitated calcium carbonate cement.

Fossil bones indicated a faunal suite differing little from that of the Serengeti today. The animals included both extinct and modern forms, the extinct taxa being in most cases related to modern genera. The paleontologists identified cattle-like forms including buffalo, extinct relatives of rabbits, giraffes, rhinoceros, zebras, warthogs, and elephants, as well as various rodents, carnivores, and primates in that order of frequency (Leakey et al. 1976). Snakes, tortoises, and birds, as well as land snails and slugs were present. The rodents, being non-migratory and having reason-ably well-defined ecological tolerances, are particularly important for understand-ing the climate and vegetation. The footprints correspond quite closely to the animals represented by bones, but identification is difficult, particularly for the extinct animals whose footprints are otherwise unknown. Elephant, rhinoceros, ancestral rabbit, guinea fowl, baboon, and hominid prints are confidently identified.

With these sets of data, Hay was able to describe significant aspects of the ancient landscape on which the hominids walked. Uniformitarian assumptions and analog arguments based on modern phenomena guided his interpretations. Analog argu-ments were particularly important for using faunal evidence to infer climate and vegetation. The reconstruction appears successful at the local scale, including some seasonal indicators. At a distance in time removed by more than 3 million years, such precision is an unexpected gift. The accuracy of the reconstruction, on the other hand, is difficult to judge; at mega-scales of time, one lives with large uncertainties.

The potassium–argon age of the Footprint Tuff, confirmed by stratigraphic rela-tionships within the series of dated tuffs and lava flows, places the ancient surface well prior to the development of the Rift Valley that defines the present landscape. The domed shape of the old surface, rising to the northeast toward Sadiman volcano, was inferred from the radial pattern of drainage cut by seasonal streams. The tuff beds, traced for various distances in the outcrops, indicate a surface of low relief on which ash falls from Sadiman accumulated to unmeasured depths. Successive sur-faces were interpreted as arid, with little vegetation, because the ash falls were moved around by wind and, less often, by apparently seasonal water. Hay considers the ancient situation comparable to the modern environment of the eastern Serengeti, a "grassland savanna with scattered brush and *Acacia* trees, where highly seasonal rainfall averages 50 cm per year" (R. L. Hay 1981: 16).

The faunal assemblage was also comparable to the modern Serengeti, with differences that could be expected given its age. It was an upland savanna community lacking any elements indicative of aquatic habitats. In the succession of the Footprint Tuff, seasonal differences could be discerned; the footprints in the lower part were "chiefly rabbit, rhinoceros, guinea fowl, bovids, and other forms which remain in grassland savanna during the dry season. Footprints in the upper part include a wide variety of forms not found in the lower part" (R. L. Hay 1981: 19). The wet-season beds showed redeposition by water and included footprints of elephant-like animals, equids, baboon, and the hominids; the former three, especially, are characteristic of the rainy-season migrants on the upland savannas of the present day. A rodent in the fossil fauna, the "tree-rat," has today a very narrow niche occurring only in open grassland with thorn trees; thus, one specific element of the flora is strongly indicated. The presence of the "naked mole rat" especially interested Hay because the modern representative of the genus does not live on the Eyasi Plateau, where the night-time temperatures are too low for it. The temperature on the ancient upland may have been warmer, implying a lower elevation than that of the modern Eyasi Plateau. Such an inference is strongly supported by the evidence that the faulting that raised the plateau occurred long after the burial of the Footprint surfaces.

The evident complementarity of these several data sets provides a detailed picture of the immediate area. We see here early hominids active, at least occasionally or seasonally, outside of the lowland gallery forest and waterside environments that have been characteristic of all other finds of this age. The uniqueness of this upland site may, however, be an artifact of preservation. Deposits of this age on uplands are vulnerable to erosion and loss; deposits in lowland basins have a better chance for long-term survival.

PART V

Sediments and soils

BASIC PRINCIPLES OF SEDIMENTOLOGY AND SOILS SCIENCE

To the field archaeologist the most obvious – and often the most abundant – constituent of a site is dirt . . . Dirt, properly called soil or sediment, is the subject matter of sedimentology.

SCHIFFER 1987: 200

Sediments are composed variously of particles of disaggregated rock, dust from whatever source, bits of dead animals and plants, and chemical precipitates. Their deposition on the surface of the Earth or the bottom of lakes and seas creates three-dimensional sedimentary bodies (deposits) which are subsequently modified in characteristic ways by the five spheres of the climate system. In company with bedrock, sediments underlie the landforms on which life processes occur. For archaeologists, sediments are the enclosing medium and the environment for the physical and chemical remains that comprise archaeological sites.

INTRODUCTORY CONCEPTS

In contrast to the readiness with which archaeologists borrow geomorphological techniques for identification and description of landforms, developments in petrographic techniques seem to be adopted slowly and reluctantly by them. Methods for the technical description and interpretation of sediments and **soils**, particularly, need further development and more intensive application in archaeology. As with fish that cannot be expected to be aware of water, archaeologists often take for granted the materials within which their sites occur, rather than seeing them as problems and interpretive opportunities. Skilled geoarchaeological work remains, regrettably, a specialist domain instead of being incorporated as a matter of course in all field work.

Minerals are inorganic chemical compounds in crystalline form; rocks are composed primarily of minerals, sometimes accompanied by organic detritus and chemical precipitates. Mineral matter of the regolith recirculates through cycles of exposure, erosion, deposition, and burial at the surface of the Earth. Rocks and sediments are disaggregated by weathering; the resulting particles are eroded and transported by components of the atmosphere, hydrosphere, cryosphere, and biosphere that rearrange the surface of the Earth and remodel landforms. Sediments form when particles in transit are deposited, as transport media lose energy. The conditions of transport and deposition can often be inferred from attributes of the sediments, which are important sources of proxy data on former environmental states. These potentials are discussed below under the headings of "Lithology," the study of rocks and minerals, "Sediments as archaeological contexts," the study of sediments in sites, and "Pedology," the study of soils.

Lithology

The primeval rock of the planet cooled and crystallized from a molten state to form the continental and oceanic crusts of early geological time. Igneous rocks, cooled from the molten state called "magma," include such materials as granite, diorite, basalt, and obsidian. **Igneous** rock that flowed on the surface of the Earth as lava is "extrusive"; that which infiltrated under pressure into or between bodies of rock is called "intrusive." Igneous rock bodies may be very extensive; the massive "shield rocks" that form the stable ancient cores of the continents belong to this class. In our own time volcanic eruptions are common enough to remind us that molten material continues to emplace new rock on the crustal plates. The extrusion of lava along rift zones beneath the oceans is probably nearly constant if the rifts are considered as a whole.

Sedimentary rocks are composed of mineral matter transported by wind, water, or ice and consolidated after deposition. The consolidated material may be minerals weathered from older rocks, chemical precipitates from water, or detrital organic materials. Sediments are consolidated and lithified (transformed into rock) by cementation or compaction or both, resulting in such rocks as sandstones, limestones, and siltstones, all reflecting in their names their sedimentary origins.

Metamorphic rocks are modifications of lithic material from the other two groups that has been subjected to great heat, as from contact with magma, or both heat and pressure, as occurs during mountain building when rocks are folded and faulted. In such extreme conditions, both igneous and sedimentary rocks are modified by formation of new crystal states that are stable at high temperatures and pressures. For example, granite can be changed to gneiss, limestone to marble, silt-stone to slate.

Before there can be sedimentary rocks there must be sediments, masses of uncon-solidated particles of mineral or biogenic materials. Sediments are always deposited on geosphere surfaces, which may lie beneath air, water, or ice, with obviously different consequences for their archaeological relevance. Sediments are fundamen-tally important to archaeologists because they constitute the **matrix** for archaeologi-cal remains, the enclosing medium which keeps the remains in place and defines their immediate physical and chemical environment. Sediments constitute also the **context** of archaeological remains and sites, locking them into stratigraphic and locational relationships with other classes of data. The attention paid by environ-mental archaeologists to this second characteristic of sediments is what primarily distinguishes them from their non-environmental archaeologist colleagues, who may consider sediments no more than expendable "dirt." The amount of archaeolog-ically relevant information that can be wrung from the analysis of sediments is limited only by our skill, imagination, and funding (Fritz and Moore 1988).

Sediments as archaeological contexts

In the absence of sediments there can be no typical archaeological sites. Piles of worked stones on bare bedrock can qualify by definition as archaeological sites but, by providing the investigator with the utter minimum of information about the piling event or accompanying conditions, they limit investigation to elements of form; they are artifact aggregations, rather than sites. Sediments provide context and structure. Sediments enclose artifacts and features, maintain relationships among objects, and protect buried materials from a range of disturbances. In their role as burial environments, sediments may also disturb and damage archaeological ma-terials. Additionally, it is always worth asking whether or not the original deposi-tional surface is preserved in the sediments.

Archaeological sites occur in most kinds of sediments. Sites in primary context may be buried by aeolian, alluvial, **colluvial**, volcanic, marine, or lacustrine sedi-ments. Redeposited artifacts, provided they survive transportation, also occur in a great variety of sediments, although once moved from their primary locations they lose much of their strictly archaeological information and become a special class of geological phenomena. Each class presents its particular physical and chemical characteristics and interpretational problems, each in turn requiring a special set of analytical methods.

In order to understand the crucial relationships between a site or deposit of artifacts and its enclosing medium, archaeologists need to know as much as possible about five characteristics of sediments:

1 the source of the material, whether it is residual or derived, the nature of the parent rock, and, if derived, from which direction and what distance;
2 the transport medium which moved and deposited it;
3 the depositional environment in which it came to rest;
4 any subsequent natural transformations of the deposit, including mechanical or biological disturbances and chemical or physical changes such as soil formation, cementation, or compaction; and
5 any subsequent cultural transformations.

Hay's study of the Footprint Tuff in the East African Laetolil Beds (R. L. Hay 1981; Part IV Case Study) exemplifies the kinds of data and logic involved in determining these five characteristics. The fact that he was working in lithified sediments changes some of the techniques, but not the basic research strategy. The source (1) of the volcanic ash that comprised the tuff was traced to the extinct volcano Sadiman by observing the slope of the beds and by matching the chemical composition of the ash in the two locations. The transport medium (2) was the force of the volcanic explosion, with subsequent fall through air; after the initial deposition, the ash was determined to have been disturbed only by rainwater. These conclusions were reached by observing that the bedding of the dry-season tuffs was about the same thickness across the minor relief of the surface, indicating that, unlike other ash-falls in the series, it had been only lightly disturbed by wind. The upper tuff showed some redistribution from topographic highs to low points, and water transport was suggested for that. The depositional environment (3) for most of the Laetolil Beds was inferred to be a dry savanna, on the basis of the included fossils and some wind movement of the ash which indicated little vegetation to offer obstruction; the rainfall that disturbed the upper layers of the Footprint Tuff was interpreted as seasonal. Natural transformations (4) subsequent to deposition included the footprints, subsurface disturbances by termite colonies and rodents, the formation of a carbonate crust, the cracking of the crust by the movement of burrowing animals, and, ultimately, lithification. None of the investigators who have crawled over the Footprint Tuff in the years since its recognition have found any evidence of cultural transformations (5). While disappointing, this is not surprising given the great age of the tuff, which antedates by over a million years any cultural remains or behavior known anywhere.

Pedology

Pedology is the science of soils – chemically and mechanically altered terrestrial sediments. Soils form on and beneath the subaerial surfaces of sediments that are stable or only slowly aggrading. The formation of a soil requires above all else time; therefore, a soil represents a period in which deposition occurred only slowly if at all – a depositional hiatus and a time of relative stability. A surface that is rapidly building or rapidly eroding will not support the formation of a soil. While the deposition of a mass of sediment may be thought of as an event, with a beginning and an end, the formation of a soil is always a process, and soils must be understood in processual terms. The process has a beginning, which is usually coincident with the formation of a stable sedimentary surface. However, it is not known that soil formation as a process has an inherent endpoint; the process typically ceases with an environmental change that leads to burial or removal of the sediment supporting the soil. Archaeological materials, even entire sites, occur within soils, but the relationship of soil processes to a site or an artifact must be independently determined in each case. The soil may have been formed before archaeological materials were deposited on or in it; it may have formed after the creation of the site, or it may have been disturbed by human activity and then continued to develop with appropriate adjustment to the environmental change.

The primary literature on soils was developed within agronomy and is directed toward improving growing conditions for economically important plants. Geologists and geomorphologists, who also work in and around soils, have developed a literature that meets their special needs. The soils literature directed to the needs of archaeologists is limited (Cornwall 1958; Holliday 1990, 1992; Limbrey 1975; Waters 1992) and is not sufficiently detailed to be of substantive help in local situations. Archaeologists, therefore, need to use the soils literature as it exists, and build on it in consultation with local experts (Chapter 12).

There are at least three working definitions of the term "soil," which can complicate communication. To agronomists, soils are surficial materials that support plant growth. Agronomists ignore buried soils, even to the point of not recognizing them, and tend to evaluate archaeological deposits (**anthropogenic soils**) in terms of their horticultural potential. Nevertheless, agronomists can be helpful, provided full communication about analytical goals is established before analyses are undertaken. To construction engineers, "soil" is all unconsolidated materials that can be "dug" rather than "blasted." Their soils are our sediments and regolith; it is helpful for an archaeologist to know this before trying to interpret engineering drilling logs that may constitute the only preliminary glimpse of subsurface sediments in urban areas.

To geologists, "soil" is surficial sediment altered by weathering, whether buried or not. This definition is closest to the archaeological usage, and Quaternary geologists share with archaeologists an enthusiasm for buried soils and their information content (Holliday et al. 1993). However, geologists may include archaeological deposits in their concept of "soil," failing to distinguish them because geologists are trained to notice and interpret phenomena at scales larger than those typical of archaeology (Stein and Linse 1993). Archaeologists, who must communicate with all three groups of specialists, should be alert to the need for clear understanding of the language in use in particular situations.

Although sediments occur across the extent of the globe itself, and soils cover the continents, both sediments and soils are highly variable at the micro- and meso-scales. Generalization is difficult, since archaeologists need to apply soils analyses principally at the local and micro-scale. The text that follows here and in Chapter 12 constitutes the barest introduction to the complex world of surficial sediments and soils. Further reading could well begin with *Soils in archaeology* (Holliday 1992) and *Reconstructing Quaternary environments* (Lowe and Walker 1984: Ch. 3), progressing to chapters in specialized texts such as *Soils and geomorphology* (Birkeland 1984). The archaeological literature on soils analysis can be quite unforgiving to neophytes, pre-suming as it does a technical basic vocabulary. Ultimately, the descriptive soil surveys published by most national governments provide the most detailed information that is available outside of the analytical laboratory for the site and local scales.

STUDY TECHNIQUES IN SEDIMENTOLOGY

Sediments constitute the context in which archaeological materials are deposited and retained; their identification and analysis can inform about the history of the materials and the site itself, about agents of site burial, about the environment in which human behaviors that defined the site took place, and about chemical and physical conditions that determined the preservation of remains. Understanding of these processes properly begins with an understanding of sediment source and history.

Interpretation of sediments and soils requires an informed combination of field and laboratory techniques. Field observations are crucial; sedimentological consul-tants who are simply given bags of materials for laboratory analysis cannot be as fully supportive of archaeological investigations as their methods and expertise ideally allow. Sediments and soils are three-dimensional bodies, whose horizontal extents usually far exceed their vertical extent; they typically display variation in all direc-tions. Variation necessarily raises issues of sampling adequacy that can only be resolved by field investigations. The discussion in this section is directed principally toward the investigation of sediments exclusive of soils.

Sources of sediments

With respect to origins, regolith (mineral aggregates) is either "residual" or "derived." Residual regolith (technically "saprolite") formed in place by disintegration of underlying bedrock, while derived regolith (sediment) has been deposited after transport. Weathering products may be fragments of rock, grains of mineral matter, chemical solutions, or all three. They are strongly determined by the mineral composition of the parent material and by the climatic conditions and weathering mechanisms that obtained during disintegration. For instance, granites subjected to extremes of heat and cold in very dry environments break up into their constituent mineral grains – quartz, feldspars, and micas – and undergo no further disruption. In moist climates, however, granites are reduced to grains of quartz and mica, while the feldspars weather into clays. If these residues are subjected to water transport, the grains of mica and to a lesser extent those of quartz will be further reduced by attrition; the clay will be carried off in suspension. The original three minerals, after transport, may be deposited in very different locations under distinct hydrodynamic regimes, because of their distinct specific gravities. While the minerals are all together, identifying them as the weathering products of a particular granite is fairly straightforward; once transported and separated, they cannot be traced to their origins. Rocks of more elaborate mineral composition, particularly those containing minerals less common than quartz and clay, may be recognized as the sources of mineral associations even after displacement over long distances.

Residual deposits form in place as bedrock is disaggregated by weathering agents (sun, water, ice, wind, salts, acids) attacking the inter-crystal bonds. If the loose material is not moved by wind, water, or ice, plants will colonize it and soils will begin to form. Without disturbance this process can continue, perhaps at slowing rates, to great depths. Organic detritus forms sediments in place, normally settling from water.

Derived sediments constitute the largest class of regolith, since the most likely fate of unconsolidated material is movement by wind, water, ice, and the force of gravity. Gravity, whether or not aided by ice and water, draws loose matter from cliff faces to form talus slopes; from cave roofs to floors; downhill to form colluvium; and through water to form subaqueous sediments in lakes and oceans. Moving ice carries materials on, in, and beneath it and deposits them as till. Moving water carries sediments away from ice sheets and other sources; as water slows or becomes otherwise overloaded, it drops its load to form any of a series of diverse fluvial deposits. Water currents moving along the shores of lakes and oceans sort and deposit coarse materials along beaches. Carbonate-rich water bubbling up in springs or flowing through limestone caves deposits calcareous "tufa" or travertine that hardens into rock. Fast-moving wind lifts and carries sand and silt-sized particles, sometimes to great distances, depositing them in dunes and sand sheets or in beds of loess. Wind also disperses volcanic ash after it has been exploded into the air.

Archaeological sites occur in all these kinds of deposit. Incorporation of archaeological materials into residual deposits occurs in the course of soil formation and the churning of sediments by organisms and ice. The mechanisms of incorporation into various derived sediments are research problems in each case; the challenge is to learn which of a large but not infinite set of agents and processes was involved.

Knowing the source of a sediment is a long step toward knowing its history. As the granite example above shows, tracing sediments to their sources is not a simple task with a guarantee of success. In cases where highly characteristic or unique suites of minerals survive transportation and deposition, their identification in a sediment can indicate the probable source or source area. It is self-evident that the source area for any sediments will be found in the direction from which the transporting agent came: upstream for wind, water, and ice. This rule of thumb can greatly simplify the task as long as non-human agents are at issue. Identifying the source of rock fragments, which by definition constitute a suite of minerals, is much more straightforward than is sourcing disaggregated minerals. Petrographic methods such as thin-section microscopy, X-ray diffraction of clay minerals, neutron activation for trace elements, and the set of spectroscopic methods all give good results when properly chosen. Many of these techniques are used by archaeometricians tracing the raw materials of lithic artifacts and clays; the principles and methods are the same for rocks in natural deposits.

Organic sediments composed of macrofossils, such as peats, generally accumulate where the plants grew, or in depositional basins very close by; vegetative detritus does not travel well. However, with the intervention of human agents, such materials (e.g., peat, lignite, and coal) may be transported for use over great distances. In such cases, sourcing is possible only when the material is clearly exotic and the original plant association is obvious, as might be the case for montane forest plants carried into a desert. Subaqueous sediments composed of microfossils such as diatomites and foraminiferal oozes can be traced only by identifying the characteristics of water bodies in which they formed, and in the case of ancient rocks, the known ages of the fossils. While such information may on occasion contribute to archaeological investigations, especially in submerged sites, it is mainly limnologists and paleoclimatologists who need to know about the temperature and salinity of water bodies. Such

Table 11.1 Velocity of transporting agents and sizes of particles moved (selected)

Water transport	
Stream velocity (miles per hour)	Sedimentary particles moved
⅙	clay
⅓	fine sand
1	gravel up to pea size
2	gravel up to thumb size
3	gravel up to size of hen's egg
Wind transport	
Wind velocity (meters per second)	Diameter of grains suspended (mm)
0.5	0.04
1.0	0.08
5.0	0.41
10.0	0.81

Source: Hunt 1974: 141.

determinations are made on the basis of assumed analogies with the modern habitats of organisms closely related to the fossil forms.

Transport media

Water, wind, and ice transport sedimentary materials more or less parallel to the surface within characteristic ranges of distance. These several media sort materials by size and shape, according to the energy in the system (Table 11.1). The coarsest materials are moved by high-energy systems such as glacial ice, fast-moving water as in rivers in flood and storm waves along a beach, wind in tornados and other cyclonic storms. The finest grades of materials, silt and clay-sized particles, may be carried by wind and water for great distances, from the centers of continents to the deep oceans. Gravity can be the agent of vertical transportation through characteristically short distances involving the settling of particles in place, or falling from a cliff or cave roof. Gravity acting alone does not sort particles, affecting all indiscriminately as Galileo demonstrated at the Leaning Tower.

Transport media are reflected primarily in the **texture** (particle size and sorting) and secondarily in the **structure** (bedding) of sediments, because of the close relationship between the energy in the system and its capacity for sorting the particles carried. In high-energy systems, in addition to sorting there may also be significant attrition of particles during transport, further reducing their size. The mill-like action of glaciers, which can reduce rock to fine "flour," is the extreme example, but given enough time media such as particle-loaded water and wind can work similar transformations. Unsorted and unstratified mixtures of coarse and fine particles may be difficult to interpret in terms of transport media. They are classed as diamicton unless there is some additional evidence indicating their origin as glacial till, land-slides, or mudflows – all involving a significant component of gravity. Although no members of this confusing class of sediments are good preservers of archaeological sites, enough claims have been made for sites in and under such deposits that archae-ologists need to be alerted to their characteristics and the potential confusions they bring (e.g., Shlemon and Budinger [1990]; see selected references in Dincauze [1984]). Alluvium, sediment moved by and deposited from rivers, is characteristically "graded," which means that the sediments deposited are sorted according to the speed of the water. Slowing water drops coarse materials first. Coarse materials typically ini-tiate a graded depositional sequence, the characteristic "fining upward" signature of overbank floodwaters with finer materials toward the top. Such graded sequences may be repeatedly deposited as stratified sediments. Aeolian deposits (sand particles in dunes and silts in loesses) are usually well sorted by wind speed (Pye 1987; Pye and Tsoar 1990). Dune sands may show the characteristic cross-bedded structure.

Both the topography and internal structure of sedimentary bodies provide evi-dence of the transport media that deposited them. Terminal moraines, river terraces, and dunes normally testify by their scale and form to deposition from ice, water, and wind, respectively. The sorting and grading that are typical of variable speeds of transport by wind and water result in bedded (stratified) sediments, the individual beds of which may be internally complex, thus providing a number of analytical cri-teria for discrimination of the transport medium (Fig. 11.1). Alignment of particles within a sediment body is also indicative, being best developed in water-laid materi-als where elongated particles tend to align with the axis of movement. Magnetic alignments are best developed in particles settling from still water, as in deep lakes. Unconsolidated sediments moved downslope under the force of gravity (colluvia-tion, solifluction, gelifluction) are poorly stratified, if at all, but may be roughly aligned.

Depositional environments

When sedimentary bodies enclose or bracket archaeological materials, inferences made about the paleoenvironmental conditions at their deposition can be used to

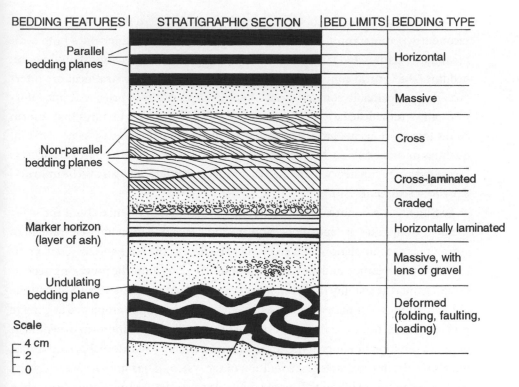

| BEDDING FEATURES | STRATIGRAPHIC SECTION | BED LIMITS | BEDDING TYPE |

Parallel bedding planes — Horizontal

Massive

Cross

Non-parallel bedding planes — Cross-laminated

Graded

Marker horizon (layer of ash) — Horizontally laminated

Massive, with lens of gravel

Undulating bedding plane —

Deformed (folding, faulting, loading)

Scale

4 cm
2
0

Figure 11.1 Terminology for stratification and bedding structures. The cross-bedding structure forms as wind or water deposits sediments over ripples and down the farther slopes, with the ripples moving downstream. (After Waters 1992: Fig. 2.12.)

understand the environments of the materials or sites. In this section, we address the *environments of deposition*, related essentially to sediments themselves. For archaeological interpretations, depositional environments are only part of the story, since we also need to understand the *environments of incorporation* – how the archaeological materials came to be associated with the sediments and the environments of burial. Those issues are developed in Chapter 12.

Materials mobilized by ice, water, or wind are carried as long as the transporting agent maintains sufficient energy to move them. Deposition, therefore, represents a change of environment for both the materials and the transporting medium. This change is recorded, more or less clearly, in the structure of the deposit itself, whether stratified, graded, sorted, or not. Variation in physical characteristics within sediment bodies, in either the vertical or horizontal dimension, indicates variation in the immediate environments of deposition. Vertical differences reveal the stratification of a sediment mass, expressing change in time. Horizontal differences in sediment bodies (facies) reveal environmental differences in space.

Depositional environments are interpreted primarily from structural evidence, secondarily from textural characteristics. Structural evidence includes both sedimentary structures and landforms. Sedimentological concepts important here are: bedding, the vertical contrasts in sediment bodies that define stratification; **interface**, the conformable contact surface between two different beds; and unconformity, an erosional surface between two beds. Particle surface textures that inform about transport agents are also relevant for depositional contexts, as are textural qualities of sediments such as sorting and grading. The degree of particle packing, measured as the frequency of interstitial air spaces in a deposit, can also be informative about sediment history.

Sedimentary structures (bedding, lenses) incorporate evidence about the scale, frequency, and rates of depositional and erosional events. The major determinant of sedimentary accumulation rates everywhere is climate: the scale and seasonal distribution of precipitation and the frequency of storms determine the prevailing depositional agents, the stability of sedimentary systems, and the frequency and amplitude of interruptions. For these reasons, sedimentary landforms are employed as climate proxies. It is crucial to realize, however, that the stability of a landform or sediment body is a function not only of the strengths and frequency of external perturbations but also of the internal state and condition of the system. The internal characteristics control response rates and the energy available for response to stimuli. Even when perturbing factors are similar, responses in one system (e.g., a fluvial basin) may be different from those in other systems.

Subaerial deposits

Sediments deposited in glacial and periglacial environments dominate major portions of the northern hemisphere, but their direct relevance to archaeological sites is limited. Obviously, no archaeological sites are contemporary with the deposition of till or glaciofluvial (outwash) deposits. Sites associated with such deposits are centuries or more older or younger than the formations themselves, and by their very existence reflect less extreme environments.

Periglacial deposits, on the other hand, may be intimately involved with human settlement and activities, now as in the past, but they have never been environments conducive to large concentrations of human beings. Modern periglacial areas, where large-scale freeze–thaw processes are studied, are mainly far removed in time and space from the ice age periglacial environments occupied by Paleolithic communities in the Old and New Worlds and are likely to be significantly different in the details of their seasonality and temperature ranges. Therefore, paleoclimatic and paleoenvironmental studies based on periglacial characteristics in sediments must be undertaken with informed caution (Clark 1988; Washburn 1980). Active peri-glacial environments are characterized by gelifluction and subsurface disturbances related to permafrost, by wind erosion and deposition, and by seasonal fluvial action of typically overloaded, braided streams; all of these have characteristic sedimento-logical structures (Chorley et al. 1984; Summerfield 1991; Washburn 1980). Dramatic secondary sedimentary structures such as ice and sand wedges, soil involutions, and gelifluction lobes (Fig. 11.2) may be encountered by archaeologists working far from the Arctic. Interpretation of such features requires the involvement of experts who can scrupulously evaluate their relevance for any associated archaeological remains which, outside of the Arctic, may postdate them by large spans of time.

Strong periglacial winds that lift the finer grades of sediment from exposed outwash and till deposits carry silt-sized materials far downwind from the periglacial environments themselves, to deposit them as loess in the cool, usually dry, steppe and grassland environments of continental interiors. Loesses are typically massive deposits with strongly vertical structure and with bedding rare or only subtly devel-oped. Because pollen is unreliably preserved in calcareous loesses, terrestrial gastro-pods constitute the major source of incorporated evidence about climate and vegetation. Buried soils mark depositional interruptions and provide evidence for temperature and precipitation cycles. Sequences of buried soils in mid-continental loesses have been shown to correlate well with the glacial–interglacial cycles identified in deep-sea sediment cores (Kukla and An 1989).

Temperate sedimentary environments, on the other hand, are dominated by fluvial erosion and deposition by perennial streams (Table 11.2). Terrestrial fluvial deposits are typically local in scale and therefore both highly sensitive to local condi-tions and variable in time and space. Unless disturbed, abundant vegetation in tem-perate environments reduces the effectiveness of erosional forces, maintaining relatively stable sediment bodies. When surfaces or slopes are destabilized, either by denudation of vegetation or by water saturation, sediments may move quickly, forming colluvial deposits or alluvial fans, making their particles available for further fluvial transport. Otherwise, periodic deposition on floodplains is the sedi-mentary environment most typical of temperate zones. Archaeological sites oriented toward rivers and streams may be preserved within or under floodplain deposits.

The complexity characteristic of fluvial deposits challenges generalization. Responses to changed conditions vary according to the state of the system involved; they may be complex or simple, massive or very limited in area. A change in either climate or base level can evoke cyclical erosional and depositional responses in a stream network, varying in space and time (Chapter 9). Since archaeological scales of observation are essentially finer than geological scales, the complexity of fluvial

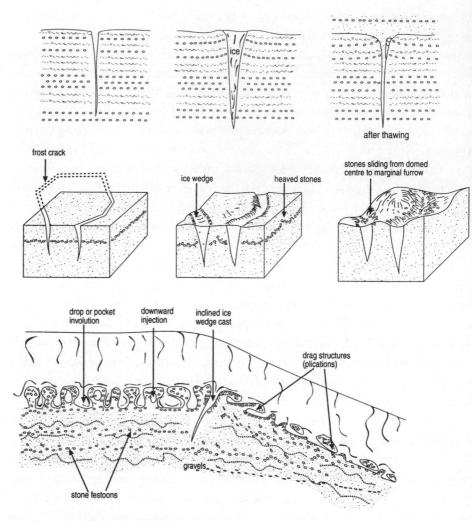

Figure 11.2   Schematic of the formation and form of selected periglacial sedimentological features: ice wedges, sorted polygons, and involutions. The ice wedges contribute to the polygonal cracking patterns that may result in polygons. Involutions sliding downslope complicate solifluction structures. Note that, to the unwary, each structure can resemble archaeological features such as postholes, hearth circles, and stratigraphy. (After Catt 1988: Figs. 2.49, 2.51, and 2.52.)

systems can seriously mislead archaeological efforts at understanding environments of deposition and the triggers of change. Extrapolation from archaeological-scale observations of fluvial deposits to regional processes is not recommended.

Sediments in subtropical arid environments reflect the special processes and landforms of those areas. Precipitation is strongly seasonal and episodic; vegetation cover is consequently sparse. These circumstances are conducive to episodic floods

Table 11.2 Flow words

The following related words are based on -*luv*-, a root meaning "flowing," derived from Latin *fluere*, to flow. The prefixes change the meaning in obvious ways. The adjectival form is given for regularity.

f-	luvial	*fluvial:* flowing in rivers, or pertaining to a river
al-	luvial	*alluvial:* of sediments deposited by rivers (flowed to)
col-	luvial	*colluvial:* of sediments sliding down hill, usually lubricated by water (hill flow)
e-	luvial	*eluvial:* of solutes and fines removed by water in suspension or solution. The A or E zone of a soil (flowed out)
il-	luvial	*illuvial:* of solutes and fines precipitated or deposited by groundwater in the B zone of a soil (flowed in)
p-	luvial	*pluvial:* of abundant rain; a rainy season or period

with large erosional and depositional events, as well as to large-scale aeolian activity moving and depositing sediments. Arid subtropical fluvial sediments are typically poorly sorted, as in alluvial fans and gravel spreads on pediments and in arroyos (Chapter 9). Fine-grained sediments at the downstream limits of fans and arroyos provide material to winds that carry away sands, silts, and dust. Winds removing sands and silts leave behind lag deposits forming gravelly desert pavements. Ephemeral shallow bodies of water dissolve salts and carbonates from the dust deposited in them and, on drying, leave mineral-rich crusts on the surface of playas (dry lake beds).

In rainy tropical environments, dense vegetation stabilizes slopes and retards erosion of sediments. In such climates, chemical weathering dominates and chemical erosion and eluviation of the finest sedimentary particles are characteristic. Consequently, slopes and elevated surfaces are deeply mantled with residual regolith. Episodically, the loose material becomes unstable, usually when saturated, and slumps or slides downslope where it becomes accessible to mobilization by rivers. Tropical rivers carry mainly clay-sized particles in suspension and colloids and ions in solution. Broad floodplains are seasonally inundated and typically swampy between floods. Archaeological sites in the tropics tend to be situated on the more stable, raised landforms, but they are subject to burial under colluvium and dense, clay-rich alluvium.

Deposits in caves and rockshelters vary with the specific conditions and climates of their host landforms. Stringently localized, speleological deposits are nevertheless an especially diverse group. The open fronts of caves and cliff shelters receive particulates from running water that ponds inside and from winds that are stilled there. Alluvial and aeolian sediments create a mixed record of very local sequences of changing depositional environments related to external conditions. Caves and shelters form by the loss of rock mass from cliffs and roofs; their floors accumulate rock shatter (clasts) and finer particles from those sources. Deposition of shattered rock is episodic, partly reflecting cyclic extremes of atmospheric temperature or moisture, partly responding to conditions on the surface of the rock mass itself. For a long time the degrees of sorting and of angularity of rock waste in limestone caves was interpreted as direct proxies of climates, especially of glacial–interglacial cycles. The history of such deposits is now recognized as being far more complex (Butzer 1981b; Straus 1990). Limestone caves, the surficial areas of underground drainage systems, are characterized by carbonate deposits called speleothems (stalactites, stalagmites, and travertine), which contribute essentially to the special strangeness of these interior spaces as well as to the preservation of diverse materials deposited on the floors and subsequently sealed under crystallized crusts. Because they lie underneath a stretch of surface, caves and shelters may also receive groundwater from cracks or openings in their roofs and back walls. Water coming thus from outside may either erode or deposit sediment on the floors of enclosures.

Subaqueous deposits

Lake and pond deposits constitute special classes of organic sediments. Their importance in paleoenvironmental reconstruction (see Berglund 1986) gives them a role far in excess of their frequency on the face of the Earth. Being subaqueous, lake and pond sediments do not form soils and do not support archaeological sites, although they may incorporate archaeological materials. Their importance to archaeologists lies in their centrality for paleoenvironmental and paleoclimatic reconstructions utilizing the organic particles such as pollen, diatoms, and macrofossils included in them. Ponds and lakes of temperate zones collect heavily biogenic sediments in typical postglacial sequences running upward from abiotic clay to **gyttja** (algal-rich organic detrital mud) and/or mud, and finally peat, as the water body is filled by sediments and plants. In basins so deep that they lack oxygen at the base of the water column, and thus do not support life in their depths, sediments may show strongly seasonal variation in texture or color, forming sequences of annual deposits (**varves** or rhythmites) that may be counted like tree rings (Chapter 5). Large deep lakes in tectonically active areas are prized for their thick, stratified, climatically informative sediment bodies. Shallow saline lakes in arid lands form less diverse paleoclimatic records, and have less archaeological relevance.

Near-shore marine sediments are of interest to archaeologists as the locations of inundated terrestrial landscapes or as platforms for shipwrecks. They merit special expertise, but the principles for their study are novel only in scale. The floors of lagoons, estuaries, and coastal ponds are mixtures of alluvial, organic, and marine current deposits, reflecting the energy levels of the local aquatic systems. Offshore, inundated terrestrial and coastal landforms may complicate matters at the landward edge of continental shelves. Postglacial marine transgression over the shelves typically planed off preexisting sedimentary landforms and deposited a broad sand sheet as the surf zone moved landward (Belknap and Kraft 1981).

Organic inclusions

Plant and animal remains included in sediments are among the richest evidence for depositional environments provided they are interpreted with care and informed imagination. Inclusions can range in size from the bones of whales or mammoths to grains of pollen. Not all organic materials relate to depositional environments. The bulk of the inclusions may derive from animals and plants living in or on the sediments subsequent to deposition (remnant), while others may be elements of communities that were carried along with the sediments, finally coming to rest far from their native habitats (redeposited). The distinction is, of course, crucial to the interpretation of environments relevant to any archaeological materials involved, which must themselves be evaluated for their status as remnant or redeposited materials. Remnant (**autochthonous**) fossils are problematic as to their time of introduction into a body of sediment, belonging normally to times following the subaerial depositional event itself. Their environmental signals must be evaluated for their chronological relationships to the depositional event and to the archaeological events under investigation. Naturally redeposited (**allochthonous**) materials belong to earlier times and distant space in relation to any deposit that contains them. As elements of sedimentary history, they represent environmental conditions at their source. They may, consequently, either complement or contradict the autochthonous evidence. How much time and space separates them from the deposit itself is to be determined in each case; it is never irrelevant to interpretation of the deposit. Organic materials introduced to a deposit by people may be exceptions to both these relational rules.

Bogs, fens, marshes, and swamps, as depositional environments, are intermediate between subaerial and subaqueous environments – more ambiguous even than fluvial deposits. A globally useful typology of wetlands is provided by Retallack (1990: 213–214). Wetlands attract people, not as comfortable places to be, but because of their rich biotic resources. Archaeological sites were rarely formed on such surfaces; more often they are underneath them, having been incorporated by wetlands expanding beyond their margins. Occasionally sites were built above them, as in the cases of trackways, refuge villages, and ritual sites, famous for their degree of organic preservation. Because the sediments enclosing such materials are composed predominantly of vegetation, they are discussed in Part VI.

Field methods

Observation of sediments in the field depends upon visual access, which is achieved by seeking out natural exposures of subsurface materials (scarps, eroded surfaces), by creating exposures (usually vertical) excavated for the purpose, or by using special equipment to pull cores from beneath a surface that is not more directly accessible. For geological and archaeological investigations, the vertical exposure, a "section" or "profile," is preferred since it minimizes distortion and provides good two-dimensional access. The larger the exposure, the better the investigator may observe spatial variation in the sediment body.

Particles that comprise a sediment may vary in composition, size, shape, orientation, sorting, grading, packing, and cementation. In combination, these characteristics create the texture and structure of the sediment. Texture is defined by the combined attributes of particle size, shape, and sorting, which together determine whether a sediment is fine or coarse grained, homogeneous or heterogeneous. Structure, on the other hand, is the result of the manner of transport and deposition of the particles constituting a sediment and its stratification, and may also reflect subsequent transformation processes. Materials deposited from wind, moving water, still water, ice, or other agents vary in characteristic arrangements of particles within the sediment in their orientation, packing, and size grading. Postdepositional disturbance of sediments by ice, plants, or animals will be recorded in structural attributes. Structural and stratigraphic observations in the field are essential preconditions to adequate sampling, since samples must be obtained from each discrete stratigraphic unit.

Description of sediments in the field must be undertaken with awareness that sediments are *both* matrix and context. Therefore, description of observed materials and structures should be accompanied by active questioning and hypothesis formulation, to collect data for alternative interpretations. Once the number and boundaries of lithostratigraphic units in a study section have been defined, each unit may be sampled. Sampling locations should be selected to represent the full diversity of the sediments, and each sample should normally include material from only one unit. If the full diversity cannot be sampled along a single transect, additional sampling locations should be selected as complements (Fig. 5.2). Sedimentary samples from exposures may be taken in bags, tubes, or sampling boxes; the choice of container and sample sizes depends on the research questions to be addressed and therefore the kinds of analyses that are anticipated (Catt and Weir 1976; Courty et al. 1989; Stein 1987). Sampling of inaccessible sediments by coring presents a special range of technical problems and challenges. Sediment sampling and analysis is distinct from sampling for particular kinds of archaeological data; it should be pursued by lithological methods (e.g., Aaby and Digerfeldt 1986; Gale and Hoare 1991; Reineck and Singh 1980; Stein 1987).

Lithostratigraphy

In a stratigraphic section, interruptions in texture, structure, or mineralogy of the sediment column are the criteria for defining sedimentary bedding units. Comparisons with sedimentary sequences beyond the immediate locality are aided by reference to a formally defined hierarchy of lithostratigraphic units. Lithostratigraphic units ("formations," "members," and "beds" in declining order of scale) are defined and described at type localities that are standards for comparison and formal naming. The local scale of archaeological sites places them most directly in a member or bed of a regional lithostratigraphical sequence. Deposits at archaeological sites of Holocene age are rarely classified into formal lithostratigraphic units, those being merely implied by the surficial deposits involved (e.g., alluvium, loess). The assignment of older sites to their correct lithostratigraphic member or formation can be a difficult endeavor but rewarding for chronological clarity (e.g., the Laetolil case study). Hence, archaeologists should be aware of the formalities of lithostratigraphic classification. Although not needed every day, the rules of stratigraphic nomenclature and classification are important for comparison and correlation of deposits at regional and larger scales. The intricacies of the formal system are well defined and accessible to non-experts in sources such as Ager (1993), Catt (1986: Ch. 4), Farrand (1984), Stein (1987), and Waters (1992: 60–88). The official international standards and nomenclature are set out in the periodically revised reports of the North American Commission on Stratigraphic Nomenclature (NACSN 1983).

Lithostratigraphic analysis and interpretation require *scrupulous distinction between description and interpretation* of observed phenomena (Stein 1990; see also Barker 1993). In the field, description should be as precise and interpretation-neutral as possible. Such care will keep the description useful as interpretive hypotheses are subsequently tested against analytical data. When interpretation is kept separate from description, multiple analytical techniques and their different kinds of data can more effectively be brought to bear on problems. Only the simplest of historical questions is likely to be answered definitively by a single analytical technique. The distinction between field description and interpretation is clearly demonstrated in Figure 11.3, a diagram from a complex English site of Middle Pleistocene age.

Laboratory methods for determining composition and structure

There is no ideal or required list of laboratory analyses that can be mechanically invoked to satisfy the demands of a scientific approach. The methods selected and the results obtained should have direct relevance for research questions, especially those that arise during field examination of sediments. No analysis can be any better than the quality and appropriateness of the samples available and the research questions asked. Archaeologists must, therefore, ensure that there is effective communication and coordination between personnel in the field and in the laboratory; the best situation is for sedimentological consultants to be involved in both places (Rapp 1975).

The physical and chemical properties of sediments and particles are informative about the sources and transport media of particles and the depositional environments and subsequent histories of the sediments. The methods cited here are for illustrative purposes only; they are definitely not exhaustive. Anyone planning to undertake or to utilize such analyses should obtain the necessary information and instruction from qualified practitioners. There is a wide range of choice among methods, even for a particular class of information; the choice will vary with the information required, the nature of the sample, the resolution desired, and the equipment available (Holliday and Stein 1989). Applications of these methods will be referenced in discussions that follow in this and later chapters. Fuller discussion of these methods and their limitations, and references to the primary literature, may be found in Gale and Hoare (1991).

Sedimentary particles and cementing minerals can be identified by a variety of chemical and mineralogical techniques, starting with simple chemical tests for a key element. The choice among mineralogical techniques, such as examination of thin sections under polarized light, atomic absorption spectrometry, electron microprobe, X-ray fluorescence, and X-ray diffraction, will depend on whether heavy minerals or clay minerals are involved, and whether information on mineral concentrations is needed. Analysis of the organic content of sediments is traditionally done by combustion and reweighing, but wet methods may be better choices in some instances (e.g., Lowe and Walker 1984: 93; Waters 1992: Ch. 2). Quantitative description of sediments in terms of particle size (**granulometry**), important for a variety of interpretive issues, is done by dry or wet sieving, hydrometer, pipette, sedimentation column (Gale and Hoare 1991; Goudie 1981: Pt. 3), or one of the newer electronic

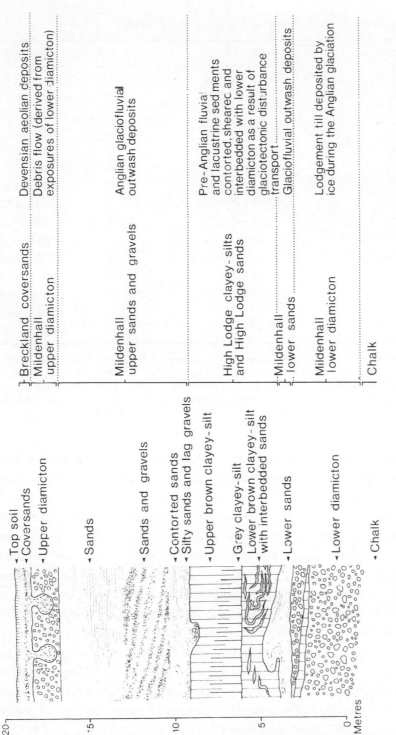

Figure 11.3 Schematic section through deposits at High Lodge, with the field description, lithostratigraphic classification, and interpretation of the units. (Reproduced from Ashton et al. 1992: Fig. 3.1, with permission; original caption, © the Trustees of the British Museum, British Museum Press.)

Table 11.3 Particle size classes: the Wentworth scale and phi (ϕ) units

Wentworth scale	phi (ϕ) units	mm equivalents
Boulder	− 8.0 and larger	>256.0
Cobble	− 6.0 to − 8.0	64.0 to 256.0
Pebble	− 2.0 to − 6.0	4.0 to 64.0
Granule	− 1.0 to − 2.0	2.0 to 4.0
Very coarse sand	0.0 to − 1.0	1.0 to 2.0
Coarse sand	1.0 to 0.0	0.5 to 1.0
Medium sand	2.0 to 1.0	0.25 to 0.5
Fine sand	3.0 to 2.0	0.125 to 0.25
Very fine sand	4.0 to 3.0	0.0625 to 0.125
Coarse silt	5.0 to 4.0	0.0312 to 0.0625
Medium silt	6.0 to 5.0	0.0156 to 0.0312
Fine silt	7.0 to 6.0	0.0078 to 0.0156
Very fine silt	8.0 to 7.0	0.0039 to 0.0078
Clay	8.0 to 12.0	0.00024 to 0.0039
Colloid	<12	<0.00024

Note: The Wentworth scale is quantified in mm units (3rd column); the categories granule to cobble are subdivisions of gravel. The phi scale is logarithmic, based on $0 = 1$mm. The conversion is $-\log_2$ of the diameter in mm; the advantage is that the scale is then based on whole numbers. Negative numbers represent particle classes larger than coarse sand; positive numbers represent the progressively finer categories. *Sources:* Adapted from Lincoln et al. 1982, Lowe and Walker 1984, and Waters 1992.

sensing devices employing laser beams. Particle size definition can be accomplished by direct measurement or by reticules used with microscopes, except for the small size ranges (Table 11.3).

The analysis of particle shape is more problematic than that of size, since methods for rapid and objective determination of shape classes are still being developed. In cases where particle shape is a critical element for interpretation of sediments (uncommon in archaeology), it is best to consult someone working actively on this subject. The surface textures of sedimentary particles themselves contain useful information about the transport and depositional environments of particles. Viewed under high magnification in a scanning electron microscope (SEM), quartz grains, especially, display a wide range of surface textures and microtopography developed in different environments (Krinsley and Doornkamp 1973). While the interpretation of these forms is less than direct and obvious (Brown 1973), there are occasions when this method in the hands of an experienced researcher can distinguish between otherwise ambiguous possibilities: e.g., the distinction between beach and dune sands.

Box samples of sediments retain the fragile three-dimensional relationships among the mineral, air, and water contents of a sediment. Measurements of mass, density, porosity, and moisture content, quickly and reliably achieved, may refine description and interpretation of the sediment. Analyses of the "fabric" of a sediment involve measurements of the preferred orientation and dip of major particle classes, and of the proportion and distribution of air spaces ("packing") among the particles. Orientation studies, traditionally important in the analysis of glacial deposits, are also relevant to the study of alluvial material, in which context these studies may have archaeological applications. Widely applicable in sedimentology but still underutilized in archaeology, is X-radiography (Butler 1992). Radiographs illustrate even small structures in aqueous and aeolian deposits, such as ripples that indicate the direction and velocity of the transporting water or wind, as well as a range of inclusions. Thin sections of impregnated sediments studied under magnification reveal fine details of structure and content not otherwise visible (Bullock et al. 1985; Catt 1986: 180–181; Courty et al. 1989).

PEDOGENESIS AND DIAGENESIS

> Soil is never truly in equilibrium with its environment although we often assume an equilibrium state in order to develop an understanding of processes.
>
> WILD 1993: 90

We have seen that rocks at the junction of geosphere and atmosphere are modified by weathering. Similar chemical and physical changes modify sediments after deposition, during periods of relative stability. Groundwater acidified by carbon dioxide dissolves and redeposits salts and oxides to begin the long process of diagenesis – turning sediments into rock. Physical churning and chemical changes induced by plant and animal life on and in deposits, aided by moisture and temperature changes, begin almost immediately to form soils, a process called **pedogenesis**. Humans, also, have been active agents in soil formation and degradation for a very long time. The overriding difference between diagenesis and pedogenesis is that the latter process is dependent upon living organisms; organic matter and biological activity are essential to the transformation of mineral deposits into soil.

Natural transformation near the surface

Pedogenesis is a continuous, reversible, and interactive process. It works progressively from the surface down into underlying sediments. Organic matter collecting on the surface releases acid compounds that, carried down in water, begin the chemical transformation of mineral matter through differential leaching and deposition. Classic definitions of pedogenesis recognize five "soil-forming factors" (Jenny 1941):

- climate
- biota
- topography
- parent material
- time.

Within each factor many different processes react with sediments to produce soils that vary strongly but systematically in space and time (Brady 1990; Catt 1986; Johnson et al. 1990). Because the five factors cannot be quantified, are not independent, may vary through time, and operate at different scales, soils scientists seem rather embarrassed by them (Birkeland 1984: 162–168). However, they comprise a useful mnemonic for the major contributors to pedogenesis and the environmental constituents that may be studied through soils.

The climate of any particular place is a product initially of the moisture and temperature ranges defined by atmospheric circulation interacting with the elevation, slope, and aspect of landforms (Fig. 11.4). Extreme climatic components interrupt or delay pedogenesis. For example, wet sediments slide downslope, interrupting pedogenesis. Sediments below the water table resist the normal oxidizing reactions that typify active soils. Permanently frozen sediments do not form soils, although they develop characteristic structural features that record environmental conditions (Washburn 1980). Very arid climates delay soil development and produce typical desert soil characteristics, such as subsurface carbonate concentrations. In temperate climates, on level to moderately sloping ground, vegetation strongly influences both temperature and moisture at the ground surface. High temperatures in the tropics accelerate oxidation and leaching, causing soils to mature rapidly.

Biota in life and death contribute the essential organic matter from which pedogenic chemicals are derived. The physical churning of sediments and soils caused by animals and plants is collectively termed **bioturbation** (disturbance by living things). "The soil is clicking, turning, and changing with the energies of a fantastic variety of occupants" (J. Hay 1981: 38). Bacteria, and animals on a scale from minute mollusks through ants, earthworms, and larvae to insectivores, rodents, and lagomorphs (rabbits, hares), live within or actually derive their food from the soil. Some prey upon each other, entirely underground. In the course of their daily routines, some of these animals displace or digest significant masses of sediment, some of which is then redeposited on the surface. Plants, which we tend to think of as static creatures, disrupt the soil that supports and nourishes them as they expand in

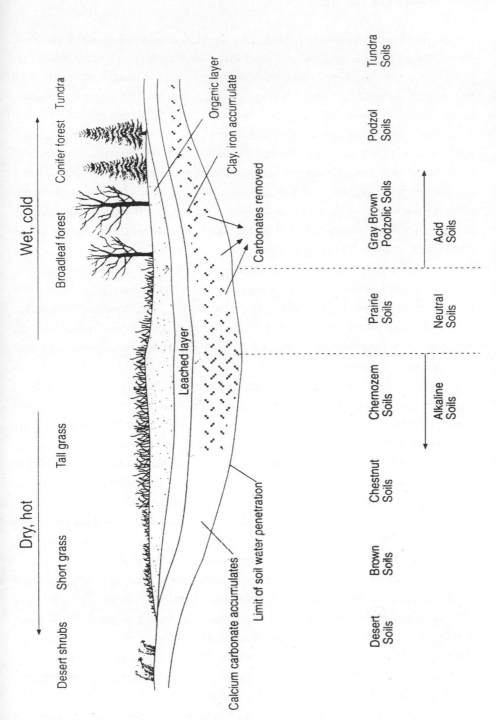

Figure 11.4 Diagrammatic transect through North America from southwest to northeast, showing pedogenesis varying with vegetation and climate. (After Hunt 1974: Fig. 6.6.)

size and increase in numbers, prying apart the sediments to make space for their roots. When roots die and rot, sediment drops into the hollow spaces left. Trees, when mature or aged, may be toppled by storms or their own failing strength; root masses tear out sediment which then gradually falls back, destroying the original structure.

Topography's influence on soil formation derives from the effects of slope, relief, elevation, and aspect. Any slope at all permits movement of unconsolidated materials to lower elevations. The steeper the slope, the thinner is soil likely to be because of the shorter residence time of particles in any one place. Elevation and aspect influence microclimate, and thus the biological activity in sediments. Even adjacent slopes on the same parent material will support soil differences according to the direction faced and solar energy received.

"Parent material" is simply the original deposit of sediment, which determines some of the soil's potential for development in terms of chemistry, grain sizes, compaction or permeability, and other characteristics that set parameters for interactions with groundwater and air. Over time, soil-forming processes will modify all such characteristics by the cumulative effects of chemical action and physical churning (Wilding et al. 1983).

Despite the diversity of factors and components, some basic processes characterize all soil development. Rainwater is acidified by carbonic acid and humic acid, the latter from the decomposition of organic matter. Acidic water leaches salts, oxides, and clays from the upper range of sediment, the **eluvial** zone, and carries the solutes and fine particles deeper into the sediment column where they may be deposited in the **illuvial** zone (Table 11.2). The subtraction of fine materials from the top and their deposition below create soil **horizons** within the sediment body: contrastive zones parallel to the surface. In vertical section, such bands constitute a soil profile (Table 11.4; Fig. 11.5). The color, texture, and properties of successive zones are changed by the pedogenic processes acting in place, progressively deeper with time.

Soil horizons are formed by change *in situ*, subsequent to the deposition of sediment. They are not lithostratigraphic units, not layers, beds, or strata. In fact, the color and textural changes of horizonation eventually destroy original stratification by homogenization and chemical modification. Therefore, *soil horizons are not stratigraphic markers*. Although they are occasionally so used in archaeological field work, such usage seriously distorts the concept of stratification and may preclude any clear understanding of depositional events at a site.

All the soil factors play out their roles, harmoniously or competitively, as long as a sediment body remains in place. The relative influence of any factor varies with conditions, and the others adjust in turn. Soils are ecosystems; pedogenesis is nothing if

Table 11.4 Soil horizon nomenclature[a]

Master horizons recorded in field studies

O horizon	Organic material accumulated on the surface.
A horizon	Humified organic matter mixed with mineral substrate near surface; typically dark-colored.
E horizon	Light-colored mineral horizon from which oxides, clays, and organic matter have been chemically leached (eluviation zone).
B horizon	Mineral horizon underlying O, A, or E horizon with little evidence of original sediment structure. May be zone of accumulation (illuviation) of sesquioxides, carbonates, and/or clays. Typically red in color.
K horizon	Subsurface horizon impregnated with carbonate so that carbonate dominates the structure. Typical of soils in arid climates.
C horizon	Parent material of the soil, only minimally transformed by pedogenesis, underlying A and B horizons. May show some evidence of weathering.
R horizon	Hard bedrock.

Note: [a] Soils nomenclature, even for horizons, is more detailed than this, and varies geographically.
Source: Adapted and simplified from Birkeland (1984: 7), which see for details.

not dynamic. Over time, barring interference, a soil develops from rawness to a maturity that supports a richly diverse biota within and above the soil.

Soils are considered immature or mature, according to the extent to which they inhibit or permit the full climatic potential of vegetation. However, maturity is not stasis; soils continue to change until they are destroyed. Pedogenesis is reversible, usually by burial or climate change, but soils can also be exhausted by vegetation demands. Eventually, the natural permeability of any soil is compromised by increasing clay concentration, compaction at depth, or development of carbonaceous or mineral hardpans, depending on the type of soil. The amount of time required for such degradation varies with everything that influences pedogenesis, and so cannot be predicted closely (Johnson et al. 1990). Birkeland (1984: 204–220) suggests that an organic A horizon develops to a steady state within a century or so, whereas a B horizon takes thousands of years. Local factors will override these generalities, and it is worth noting that soils utilized for farming or grazing do not have natural histories. Old unburied soils, called relict soils, continue to evolve and change as long as they remain at the surface; their histories are partly recorded in their chemical and physical compositions.

The B horizons of soils are the most dynamic areas in profiles. Soils taxonomies offer a large set of labels for different kinds of B horizons (e.g., Holliday 1990), the

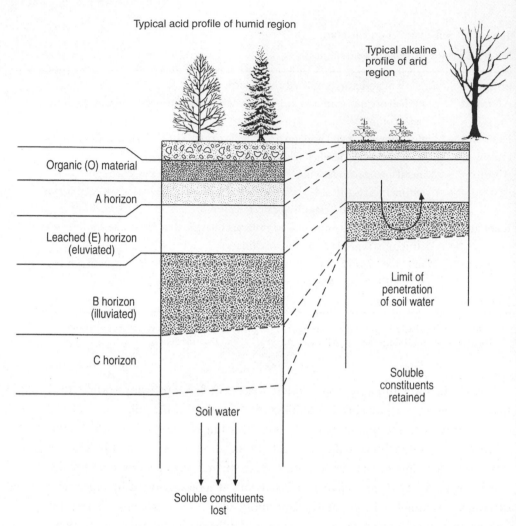

Figure 11.5   Soil horizons under two different climatic regimes. (After Hunt 1974: Fig. 6.4.)

most used of which are Bt for clay accumulations and Bk for calcareous concentrations. The former are typical of soils in moist environments; the latter, in arid climates. Both clays and carbonates accumulate in soils from two sources: chemical changes within sediments due to weathering, or the addition of fine particles from airborne dust. In both cases, the fine particles accumulate in the B zone where they may ultimately dominate completely over original constituents. Soils with very high clay contents, from either original deposition or illuviation, shrink when drying and swell on wetting (Vertisols). The deep cracks that can form when such materials dry out cause slumping and the introduction of surficial materials at depths. The intricate cracking of sun-dried mudflats is a familiar small-scale example of such activity. Carbonate concentrations in soils range from fine thread-like features to massive, cement-like secondary deposits called **caliche**. Discussions of B horizons particularly useful for archaeologists are found in the volume by Retallack (1990: 264–276).

Cultural transformations of soils

Human activities strongly influence soil development by disturbing superficial sediments and by changing their chemical composition. Humans are major bioturbators of soils and agents of deposition. Their dominance today relates to sheer numbers as well as to the efficacy of their tools for digging, transporting, and depositing (Schiffer 1987). Plow zones are such ubiquitous phenomena that they have a soil horizon designation of their own (Ap). In the US soil taxonomy, surficial horizons chemically enriched by human wastes and food debris have been given a special taxon: anthropic epipedon. **Epipedon** is the technical name for horizons near the surface (O, A, E, B); the meaning of "anthropic" should be self-evident. Archaeologists speak of "**anthrosols**," but this term has not established itself in soil science. It is only a matter of time before it must be recognized as another class of **azonal** soils (Chapter 12). Anthrosols are characterized by physical disturbance, high organic content, and phosphate enrichment typically due to high concentrations of animal wastes (Eidt 1985). Exotic sedimentary particles (e.g., artifacts) are diagnostic of anthrosols only in company with chemical and structural changes.

Analysis of ancient agricultural soils is a developing methodology. Chemical analyses and micromorphological (thin-section) methods have been most successful in identifying the changes in soil chemistry and structure attendant upon long-term plowing, fertilization, and irrigation (Artzy and Hillel 1988; Groenman-van Waateringe and Robinson 1988; Sandor 1992). Less attention has been paid to hoe horticulture and agriculture without animal wastes as those affect soils, but interest and a literature are growing (e.g., Denevan et al. 1987). Paleolimnology also has provided insights into the scale of soils transformation and disruption due to hand cultivation (Binford et al. 1987; Deevey et al. 1979; O'Hara et al. 1993).

Transformations at depth

In the C horizon, below the surface levels at which soils are forming, sediments may be compacted, cemented, churned, and chemically changed by processes involving acids and ions carried in groundwater. Such subsurface processes collectively are termed diagenesis, and although they resemble some of the processes that form soils, their distinctiveness is important to archaeologists because they indicate different aspects of subsurface environments in which archaeological remains may lie. Because many diagenetic processes take place at the water table or below it, they can be useful indicators of the water table's dynamics. Oxides and salts carried in groundwater tend to be deposited at the water table. Iron oxides may accumulate, singly or in sets, as wavy red lines that superficially resemble either bedding planes or genuine soil horizons, but are very different from both. This red color may also be confused with burning. Hydrated manganese and iron compounds may impart distinctive gray colors to sediments at depth, creating mottling or the more pervasive *gleying* that can puzzle the uninformed by suggestive resemblance to buried soils. Oxides deposited from groundwater have been involved in many disputed archaeological interpretations. Massive accumulations of oxides and carbonates create "hardpans," cemented rock-like layers that have no history related to surface exposure.

Clays leached from surficial zones of soils and redeposited at depth resemble units of stratification. Nodules of clay or oxides resembling small stones may form within sediments at depths determined by groundwater; their presence must not be interpreted as a "stony layer" indicative of stratification. The gradual settling and compaction under pressure of overburden experienced by water-saturated sediments such as pond muds and peat deposits is an aspect of diagenesis with special implications for any included archaeological materials.

Soils formed originally at the surface may be later buried. After burial these **paleosols** cease to develop as soils and become subject to subsurface modifications by any of the processes active at their location. They may undergo eluviation, illuviation, cementation, compaction, or other processes that change their characteristics (Retallack 1990). Buried soils retain for some time the attributes and inclusions they acquired while at the surface and, as a class, are among the most valued repositories of paleoenvironmental data. At the time of burial they cease to be organically active and thus, unless truncated, may be more readily dated by radiocarbon than their equivalents at the surface, which actively incorporate new organic matter throughout the zone of bioturbation. In time, organic materials and the A zone are lost to diagenetic changes that transform soils properties (Brady 1990).

Soils chemistry

The destructiveness of soils acids has long been recognized as limiting preservation within the archaeological record. Such recognition has established the notation of soil pH (hydrogen ion concentration) as a standard item in archaeological field reports, typically with no further discussion. As with the phi scale of particle size (Table 11.3), pH is a negative logarithm such that the higher the hydrogen concentration, the lower the index number. On a scale from 0 to 14, 7 is neutral, lower numbers are increasingly acidic, and higher numbers are increasingly alkaline. In highly acid soils, organic macrofossils are rapidly destroyed; however, the inhibition of oxygenating bacteria in such soils results in good preservation conditions for pollen grains. Soils with high pH are poor environments for the preservation of pollen, but are excellent for preserving bone and shell. Consequently, carbonate crusts in archaeological sediments are worth a close look; they may contain important organic materials.

Water-saturated soils effectively exclude oxygen and thus preserve from decomposers otherwise fragile organic matter, including artifact classes rare in other environments (Coles 1984). Damp or wet soils have another property significant for archaeological materials: they support the transfer of ions between buried organic materials and their soils matrices. The resultant chemical changes, tending toward homogenization, complicate chemical analyses of archaeological materials (Lambert et al. 1984; White and Hannus 1983). Chemical analyses can be useful complements to other environmental study of soils formation and history, helping to test alternative interpretations (McBride 1994).

Pedogenesis and the archaeological record

The dynamism of pedogenesis has implications for archaeology and for the condition of archaeological sites that are only recently being appropriately exploited. Pedogenesis as a process affecting the environment of burial is progressive, continuous, variable, and reversible. Because soil, as matrix and environment of burial, affects what is available for archaeological study and the integrity of observed associations, as well as the condition in which materials are recovered, a basic awareness of pedogenesis is essential to successful field work.

Postdepositional disturbance of sediments and soils by the churning actions of organisms and/or ice has dismayed many observant archaeologists. Artifact associations and features underground can be disaggregated or rearranged by such mechanisms, eliminating parts of the record and creating false associations (Johnson and Watson-Stegner 1990; Wood and Johnson 1978). Such destructiveness is inherent in pedogenesis; it is nearly ubiquitous and must be anticipated by responsible archaeologists (Barker 1993).

Regrettably for archaeologists, archaeological sites are not exempt from the natural processes of erosion and deposition that ceaselessly reshape the surface of the

Earth. Erosional processes destroy landforms and displace everything on them. With each loss, the fabric of ancient landscapes is torn. Depositional processes bury surfaces, subjecting them to compression, deformation, and diagenesis underground. Overburden not only changes the environment of sediments, it also introduces mechanical stresses that result in compaction, displacement, and particulate sorting within them. Pedogenesis and diagenesis, erosion and deposition, all restructure the archaeological and paleoenvironmental records, requiring of interpreters precise, thoughtful observation and application of informed imagination (Schiffer 1987).

SOIL SCIENCE

There are many reasons why archaeologists must know something about soil science; in fact, the more the better. However, it is a discipline of its own, not something one can pick up as a sideline. Here, with the emphasis on paleoenvironmental reconstruction, a few matters are presented with the hope that they can ease readers into the sometimes arcane literature of an important discipline (Fanning and Fanning 1989).

The analytical language of soil science is probably the major obstacle to its use in archaeology. Contemplating the formal soil taxonomy used in the United States and increasingly elsewhere, Birkeland notes (1984: 42) that it "carries such exotic combinations of Latin and Greek as Cryaqueptic Haplaquoll, Aquic Ustochrept, and Natraqualfic Mazaquerts." No matter; for the archaeologist the real problem with the US soil taxonomy is that the criteria for classifying soils do not include historical (genetic) concepts (Guthrie and Witty 1982; Hallberg 1985; Soil Survey Staff 1975). Furthermore, and perhaps for this reason, in practice the soil units shown on local-scale soils maps bear only a tenuous relationship with the geological sediments of the parent materials. The Canadian system includes more genetic information and is therefore more immediately applicable to archaeological and paleoenvironmental uses (Canada Soil Survey Committee 1978). Most industrialized countries have a system of their own (e.g., Avery [1980] for Britain, Stace et al. [1968] for Australia). UNESCO is developing international conventions for soils maps (Fitzpatrick 1980), but in the short run, archaeologists must familiarize themselves with the system in use locally, and learn the limits of its reliability and applicability (e.g., Catt 1986; further discussion in Chapter 12). Beyond that, active collaboration with a soil scientist is the best approach.

Because of the way that they form, soils on contiguous landform surfaces vary with the topography, vegetation, parent material, and microclimates. Soils, therefore, provide information on the development and environmental history of landforms and surfaces. **Catenas** are sequences of soils profiles varying downslope. At the top of a slope soils are typically well drained, but subject to erosion and therefore relatively thin. At intermediate elevations slopes may be more gentle and soils development deeper. At the foot of a slope, sediments accumulate; soils may be deep, but any drainage limitations will directly affect the soils on such landforms. Geomorphologists exploit catenas to study the subtle diversity of landform histories and the complex play of the soils-forming factors (Birkeland 1984: 238–254; Daniels and Hammer 1992; Gerrard 1992; Knuepfer and McFadden 1990).

Standard analytical methods that provide clues to soils' histories include the conventional chemical spectra, grain-size analysis (granulometry), and percentage of organics (e.g., Holliday 1990; Macphail 1987: 361–363), which provide information about the parent material and the transformations it has experienced. The transformations are sometimes interpretable in terms of the soil-forming factors that dominated in the past. Analysis of the relative degree of eluviation and illuviation amongst horizons provides information about relative ages of soils and the contributions of the five factors of soil formation. Soil thin-sections reveal evidence for disturbances and microstructures in the soil that are directly relevant to environmental history (Bullock et al. 1985; Goldberg 1992; Limbrey 1992).

Paleoenvironmental information is derivable from soils once one learns to elicit it analytically. In a volume addressed to paleopedology at geological scales, Retallack (1990) presents particularly clear discussions of the potentials and limits of soils for paleoenvironmental inferences. Fine resolution is rarely possible, but if, say, the climate during soil formation differed significantly from that at the time of observation, some evidence of that difference may survive. Changes in the height of the water table can be read in some subsoils. Resolving the differences in terms of time, however, is difficult. Soils contain biological residues such as pollen, charcoal, and microorganisms that serve as climate proxies when they can be dated. Buried soils are the best sources of paleoenvironmental data; when the time of burial can be specified, they can be eloquent. A promising technique for reading past environmental states directly from stable carbon isotopes in soils is based on the differences in carbon metabolism between tropical grasses and other vegetation (C_4/C_3 ratios). In suitable areas, vegetation community successions, interpreted as changes in microclimates, have been tracked by carbon-isotope ratios in organic residues in soils (Ambrose and Sikes 1991). Biological data derived from soils are considered further in Parts VI and VII.

There is a growing, tantalizing literature on direct dating of soils (Andersen 1986; Matthews 1993; Scharpenseel and Becker-Heidmann 1992). Archaeologists cannot help but be attracted, even tempted, by the preliminary results and claims.

Nevertheless, this subject must be approached with critical awareness. Organic matter is certainly available in soils and can be extracted for dating. The difficulty is in knowing which organic matter is equivalent in age to the archaeological event to be dated. Soils development is a time-transgressive process. Organic matter cycles in and out of soil throughout the active life of the soil; roots and burrowing animals penetrate deeply into the B zone. Bulk sampling of soil carbon in the A zone will give ages averaged over the duration of the soil with bias toward the youthful side; technically, what is dated is the "average residence time" of the organic matter sampled. Now that AMS dating permits the selection of definable components of soil (charcoal fragments, humates), sample selection will define the age determined. Soluble humates tend to be younger than bulk charcoal, but they may sometimes be older. Dating of close-interval samples through a sequence of soil horizons often demonstrates that soils are frequently churned, although the progressive translocation of older carbon compounds into the B zone may impart some semblance of stratigraphic order to the sample ages. Soils with archaeological materials include organic matter both younger and older than the anthropogenic materials. Soils processes are continuous; archaeological deposition is episodic.

CODA

Sediments and soils are the essential contexts of field archaeology; on their appropriate interpretation rests all understanding of the relationships among artifacts and aspects of environments, past and present, as well as understanding of relative ages. The results of pedogenesis must be correctly distinguished from variation in sediments. The structural priority of sediments over soils developed in them is a fundamental tenet of analysis. The field relationships of sediments and soils must be demonstrated convincingly before interpretation of included archaeological remains can begin.

ARCHAEOLOGICAL MATRICES

> The excavator's aim should be to explain the origin of every layer and feature he encounters whether it be structural or natural; made by man, animal or insect, accidental or purposeful.
>
> BARKER 1982: 68

Every surface on which humans lay foot or artifact is a potential archaeological site, requiring only that subsequent processes not dislodge and transport the surficial deposits. Of course, disturbance of surficial sediments of every kind is the normal case. This vulnerability ensures that archaeological sites are neither ubiquitous nor permanent.

The focus of this chapter is on sediments and soils as matrices of archaeological sites, at local and micro-scales. We occasionally lift our eyes to regional-scale phenomena, as in considering the information potentials of widespread deposits of loess or volcanic ash, but we pay no attention here to the mega- and macro-scales of phenomena or to regional-scale interpretations.

MESSAGES IN THE MATRIX

Sedimentological analyses are undertaken to learn about the sources, transportation agents, depositional and transformational history of the materials comprising deposits (Chapter 11). Although archaeologists typically treat that information as background, environmental archaeology must begin with the environments in which materials, whether cultural or natural sedimentary particles, were brought to a site, deposited, and affected by postdepositional processes including pedogenesis and diagenesis. The enclosing matrix is the fundamental source of information about all the processes essential to understanding the context of human behavior at a site. Not all evidence is visible, and not all is extractable by techniques currently known. However, for sites lacking written evidence the matrix is the only source of non-artifactual information; for sites with written histories, the matrix will variously confirm, expand, or contradict elements of that record.

Archaeological matrices are very complex deposits. Altogether they represent a significant subset of the geological diversity on the surface of the Earth, compounding that diversity with incorporated cultural debris. The complex chemical and compositional attributes of archaeological matrices are worthy of more intense analytical scrutiny by geologists and archaeologists than they have typically received (Stein 1987).

Burial and incorporation

Archaeological materials and structures go underground within a wide range of environments of burial or incorporation, but in any single instance the range is finite and potentially determinable. Archaeological materials deposited on surfaces may be (1) buried by sediments added on top or (2) incorporated into existing sediments by pedoturbation or other disturbances. Many different materials and processes are capable of burying surfaces and whatever is at rest on them. Overbank floodwaters, rising lakes and seas, wind-borne particulates, expanding peat bogs, volcanic ash, colluvium, and carbonates precipitating from solution may all bury sites, gently or violently. On the other hand, everything that disturbs the soil, from ice crystals through burrowing animals to mechanized excavating tools, may contribute to the incorporation of archaeological materials into regolith. The burial and incorporation processes, whether episodic or continuous, are always potentially reversible: deeper is not always older.

Environments of incorporation determine the diversity of environmental data that is included and preserved in matrices. The full range of matrix constituents is almost never buried or incorporated at the same time; that is, incorporation is nonsynchronous for the artifacts, ecofacts, and other materials included. Whatever archaeologists retrieve must be evaluated for its relevance and synchroneity to the cultural constituents.

Transformations

As the discussion in Chapter 11 showed, materials under the surface are not at rest. Rather, they are subject to all the equifinalities of pedogenesis and diagenesis that keep the regolith in a dynamic state. Materials close to the surface are affected by pedogenesis at rates varying with climate and other soil-forming factors. The chemical changes of soil formation and diagenesis influence the relative preservation of ma-

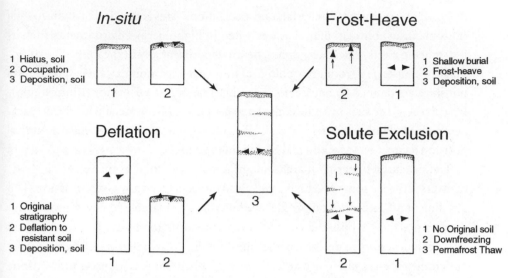

Figure 12.1 Four hypothetical original stratigraphic states resulting in the situation shown in the central column. The numbers indicate the sequence of states and transformations in the four cases. Black triangles represent artifacts. "Solute exclusion" is cases where permafrost or hardpans stop groundwater above the base of sediments, concentrating leachate after deposition. (After Thorson 1990a: Fig. 3.)

terials. Bioturbation by resident organisms modifies original spatial relationships. Objects below the surface – pebbles, cobbles, and boulders no less than archaeological artifacts and ecofacts – will be moved up, down, and sideways by living creatures and by ice wedging when the climate supports that (Fig. 12.1; Thorson 1990a; Wood and Johnson 1978).

No degree of exquisite excavation technique in archaeological matrices is likely to reveal absolutely pristine spatial associations; careless excavators unconcerned about the messages in the matrix recover only inadequate approximations to the relationships there (Barker 1993). Everything about the matrix – color, texture, structure, microstructure, water content, pH, biota, particles, and so forth – has a message to tell about the history of the materials it encloses. The history is analyzed first at the site and more intensively in the laboratory; the two opportunities are complements, never substitutes. Post-excavation analyses cannot overcome deficiencies in excavation observations, recording, or sampling.

Integrity

Archaeological accumulations buried gently under fine-grained materials, ideally either totally dry or anaerobic and permanently wet or frozen, may retain much of their original integrity of materials and associations. This is the ideal of archaeological context. In contrast, materials deposited in high-energy environments such as fast-moving rivers, glacial ice, dunes, beach deposits, or any of the range of diamictons are transferred from archaeological into geological context; their spatial relationships are defined by natural forces rather than human behavior (Binford 1981). In such cases, the sites must be considered geological phenomena with the artifacts being simply "rather specialized particles" among many others subjected to transport and deposition (Macklin and Needham 1992: 10).

The structural integrity of archaeological matrices can be evaluated on the basis of diverse criteria, some of which are likely to be available in any given situation. The first line of attack is the soil profile: are horizons comparable in development and condition to those within the same substrate away from the archaeological deposits? If not, it is necessary to decide whether the differences can be explained by anthropic enrichment of site soils, by age differences, or by disturbances (Johnson and Watson-Stegner 1990). Are features such as hearths and pits visibly intact in the substrate? Are artifacts in resting positions, not turned on their edges by cryoturbation (Wood and Johnson 1978)? Do the artifacts appear to be sorted by size or weight, as would happen to those affected by clay turbulence in Vertisols, by cryoturbation, or by slippage of water-saturated sediments on even moderate slopes? Are animal burrows evident or likely given the nature of the deposit (Erlandson 1984)? Are earthworms numerous (Armour-Chelu and Andrews 1994; Stein 1983)? Are artifacts of recent age present at depth in the sediments? Small objects such as the once ubiquitous pop-tops for aluminum cans, coins, nails, broken glass, and such can be informative about soils disturbances. Alertness to all these matters as the trowel moves is crucial to an ultimately successful interpretation of samples of any kind from the matrix. Without field records explicitly addressing such issues in terms of presence, absence, and patterning, *post hoc* claims for integrity of association or its antithesis can never be more than hypotheses beyond the reach of testing (Barker 1993; Schiffer 1987; Waters 1992: Ch. 7).

The chemical integrity of soils and sediments, especially, cannot be assumed. Recent and ancient anthropogenic contaminants need bear no relationship to any archaeological materials included in a matrix. Acid rain and other modern pollutants similarly need have no great age to be significantly misleading to analysis. Even beyond the site area itself, modern or ancient contaminants may thwart the search for analogs and comparative samples needed for interpretation of soils histories. Soils with a history of deforestation and agriculture are distinct from forest soils, in ways that change their chemistry to the detriment of archaeological analyses (Kaiser 1996; Trumbore et al. 1996).

Paleoenvironmental data

The enormous range and diversity of paleoenvironmental data in archaeological sites exceeds the capacity of this volume to inventory. Evolving knowledge of sediments, soil processes, and living things, complemented by improvements and innovations in methods of examination, outpaces the ability of archaeologists to encompass them in investigations. A brief review here may help establish the value of expanding awareness. Additional information about these techniques is in Chapter 11, Parts VI and VII, and sources noted.

In sediments

Laboratory analyses for interpreting environments of deposition or incorporation of archaeological remains will normally begin with the sediments. As techniques are being developed all the time, there is no need here to recommend specifics, only to review some of the currently most informative approaches.

In most situations granulometric methods based on the Wentworth or phi scales (Table 11.3) suffice for interpretation of depositional agents; at the least, they can indicate situations in which further analysis is necessary for resolution. The major caveat for direct interpretation of depositional agents on the basis of granulometry is the fact that archaeological sediments typically include materials added by human activity – sediments tracked or carried onto living floors, debitage and trash accumulated during processing, damage to exposed bedrock on site, erosional byproducts of mudbrick or fired clay, plant and animal refuse. All such additives must be eliminated from samples processed for interpretation of natural agents but, of course, they are informative about the full suite of formation processes at a site. Organic detritus observable in screening, flotation samples, or thin-sections will be informative about biogenic disturbances as well as environments during and following deposition.

Identification of the mineral suite in a deposit may help to define the source of the sediments; at the least, it can be the basis for distinguishing successive depositional events should those require clarification. Clay mineralogy reflects processes of pedogenesis and diagenesis. Micromorphological analysis of thin-sections can be very informative about the history of deposits, especially the illuvial (B) zones of soil horizons where disturbances of many sorts leave characteristic signatures (Courty et al. 1989; Fitzpatrick 1993). Organic remains and signals of bioturbation present problems for synchroneity, but offer information worth reaching for.

In soils

Information is sought in soils about former environmental conditions near the surfaces on which they formed. The proxies required are those properties or inclusions of soils that reflect conditions of precipitation and temperature prevalent at times of interest in the past. The purely pedological proxies relate to transformations of sediments in the epipedon – chemical and mineralogical changes brought about by weathering, eluviation, and illuviation. The distributions and states of minerals and simple compounds, as well as small structural changes within the epipedon, can provide information about climates: warm or cold, wet or dry episodes at scales above the seasonal (e.g., McBride 1994).

Paleoenvironmental inferences based on soils data are less reliable for archaeology than is often assumed, because of the coarse chronology and multiple sources and ages of soils constituents. Nonetheless, coarse as the resolution of soils data may be, they have important roles in environmental archaeology (Holliday 1992; Matthews 1993; Waters 1992). The Comprehensive Soil Classification System of the United States Department of Agriculture (Soil Survey Staff 1975) offers an internationally applicable, high-level classification of soils. The great soil Orders, at the top of the hierarchical taxonomy, are defined in terms of selected attributes of environments in which they formed: precipitation, temperature ranges, seasonality, and some chemical attributes. Six of the ten Orders are zonal soils classes, whose distributions reflect the influence of zonal climates. In Figure 12.2 these are shown as they would be distributed on a hypothetical continent in the northern hemisphere lacking major contrasts in relief. The remaining four azonal soil Orders are less constrained by climate, but emphasize attributes of soils relevant for archaeology. Table 12.1 lists the ten Orders, their major characteristics, and the suffixes that identify them in creating names for "Suborders" in the taxonomy.

The limitations of soils data for reconstructing environments at archaeological scales are less constraining in the geosciences, where most paleoenvironmental research has been done (Lowe and Walker 1984; Retallack 1990). The older the archaeological site and the more geological the context, the more useful will be geological data. For archaeology, the optimal contexts for recovering environmental data are those rapidly deposited and sealed by human agency, not soils of any kind. Deposits at intimate scales of time and space, effectively protected from pedogenesis, retain integrity. Surfaces buried immediately under structures, microstratified deposits such as middens, and the contents of deep pits are the treasuries of paleoenvironmental data. Their abundance in urban contexts justifies recent excitement about paleoenvironmental research in urban and town sites (Deagan 1996).

TERRESTRIAL MATRICES

The range of sediments in which archaeological materials occur is essentially bounded only by the range of unconsolidated materials on the planet (Chapter 11).

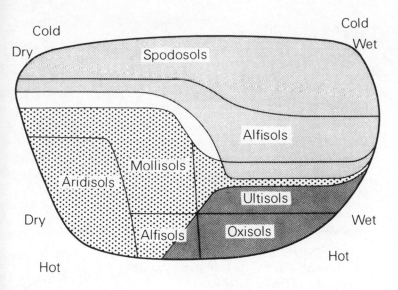

Cold
Dry

Spodosols

Cold
Wet

Alfisols

Mollisols

Aridisols

Ultisols

Dry

Wet

Alfisols

Oxisols

Hot

Wet

Hot

 Podsolization

 Calcification

 Laterization

Figure 12.2   Schematic representation of the great soil Orders on a hypothetical continent in the northern hemisphere. (Reproduced with permission of Blackwell
Publishers from Goudie 1993: Fig. 2.11. Original caption.)

Here we consider some typical sediments, classed by depositional environments, to
emphasize characteristics of subaerial matrices, including soils, that set boundaries
for paleoenvironmental investigations in archaeology.

Alluvial sedimentary matrices

Recent geoarchaeological literature presents us with contrastive statements such as
this pair. "Holocene alluvial sequences are arguably unique in the way that they integrate and record environmental change (natural and anthropogenic) over a wide
range of spatial and temporal scales" (Macklin and Needham 1992: 20, working with
alluvium in the British Isles). On the other hand, Ferring (1992: 15), working in the
arid American Southwest, claims: "In too many cases . . . direct evidence for paleoenvironments, such as pollen, snails or plant macrofossils, is poorly preserved in alluvial sediments." Both statements have merit; they highlight the importance of
context, contingency, and multidisciplinary research designs suited to specific cases.

Table 12.1 Ten soil Orders of the USDA soils taxonomy[a]

Order	Suffix	Characteristics
Alfisols	-alfs	soils with argillic horizon and moderate base content; woodland and forest soils of temperate regions
Aridisols	-ids	soils of deserts and semi-arid areas; likely to have calcified B horizons
Entisols	-ents	new soils, slight development; strongly expressing sedimentary features
Histosols	-ists	soils composed of plant tissue accumulated in waterlogged areas; peats
Inceptisols	-epts	young soils, esp. on alluvium; precursors of other Orders
Mollisols	-olls	soils with dark, loose A horizon and high base content; usually grassland soils
Oxisols	-ox	soils with strongly oxidized B horizon; typically formed in hot, moist climates; laterites
Spodosols	-ods	podzols; soils rich with iron and aluminum compounds in the B horizon; cool moist climates
Ultisols	-ults	forest soils with argillic horizon but low base content; pronounced seasonal rainfall
Vertisols	-erts	soils with high clay content subject to cracking and shrink–swell turbulence

Note: [a] The ten soil Orders are the highest classificatory categories in the USDA taxonomy. The suffixes combine with additional syllables to form the Suborders, which are more specific, and more numerous, categories. Six of the Orders are zonal categories, identified with zonal climates. The other four (Entisols, Inceptisols, Histosols, and Vertisols) are azonal soils that form under special conditions in any zone. Sources: Definitions after Birkeland 1984, Goudie 1984, Holliday 1992, Retallack 1990: 107–111, and Waters 1992.

Alluvial sediments and soils are polygenic, complex, and potentially very informative matrices for paleoenvironmental study that must be addressed appropriately, in recognition of their sensitivity to climate.

The biological necessity for water explains the frequent association of archaeological sites with alluvial deposits on floodplains and terrace surfaces. The dynamism of riverside environments brings a range of special problems and opportunities for the archaeologist. Old floodplain landforms are typically discontinuous, difficult to find or trace over distance even when not buried, and sensitive to disturbances from tectonics, climate change, human activities, or fluvial dynamics. Alluvial deposits originally laid down on floodplains are eventually buried by aggrading rivers or isolated as components of terraces after river incision. Archaeological sites encountered on fluvial terraces, therefore, may have been established originally on a floodplain, a very different environment. Artifacts in alluvial sediments unaffected by pedogenesis are most likely to have been deposited from water, whether or not they display transport damage, because they are not associated with surfaces. In such cases the only environmental issues that can be investigated are those of deposition of the displaced artifacts. Artifact clusters in soils, particularly if heterogeneous in the sizes and shapes represented, are likely to have been introduced by people occupying a stable land surface. If the depositional agents were people, and the matrix retains integrity, the way is open for investigation of environments prior to, during, and after human use of the location (Rapp and Hill 1998).

The mechanisms that bury archaeological sites in or on alluvium vary with the original topographical location of the site. Active floodplains can be used by humans only seasonally; even so, people are likely to favor elevated landforms. On meander stretches or large deltas, sites tend to be located preferentially on levees near channels or oxbow lakes. High-energy floods that overtop or break through levees may destroy such sites. Quieter floodwaters (slackwater) simply inundate a location and deposit a fresh layer of silt. Slackwater flooding occurs typically upstream of bedrock constrictions in valley walls, and inland from active channels. Quiet flooding, whether away from the channel or simply due to a minor overbank episode, may create stratified sites or merely "overthickened" A horizons in soils. Sites on terraces above active floodplains may be buried by hillslope processes such as mass-wasting or colluviation, or by windblown sands and silts. Burial processes differentially influence the integrity and preservation of sites.

For most of the twentieth century, paleoenvironmental studies in alluvium emphasized interpreting alluvial deposits directly in terms of climate change. The idea, unadorned, was that extensive gravel deposits represented cool wet periods, and soil development represented warm periods. The case study of alternative interpretations of Greek valley fills (pp. 320–325) introduces the importance of chronology in such studies, to test synchroneity of fluvial sequences from valley to valley (review Fig. 9.3). Clarity about the causes and timing of valley alluviation is important well beyond archaeology, because paleoenvironmental inferences find applications in modern land-use policies. In a thoughtful review of recent studies of human influences on alluvial processes, Bell (1992b) concludes that both climate and culture contribute to cycles of valley erosion and deposition in temperate latitudes. He notes differences in fluvial responses according to latitude and climatic regime, especially related to continentality, a geographical complication not yet well developed in the wider debate. Human behavior is a significant component of geomorphological systems worldwide but neither its influence nor the reflexive effects on human culture are well understood.

Aeolian sedimentary matrices

Archaeological sites are deposited on the surfaces of aeolian sediments, but they are often recovered within them. Sites may be incorporated within aeolian sediments during accumulation episodes, may be buried by them, and may be exposed, disturbed, sorted, and reburied by wind action. Beaches and dunefields occupy the high end of the energy continuum, with loess deposits at the other; archaeological sites in loess are less likely to be damaged than are those in beach or dune sands. As dunes often form by aeolian reworking of beach deposits (see below), determination of the environment of deposition can also help clarify the relative ages of sediment bodies.

At local scales, aeolian deposits can be subtly misleading. For example, in 1968 excavation began in Manchester, New Hampshire, USA on a river terrace high above a major waterfall. The soils survey had mapped fine-grained deposits there as "alluvium," implying overbank flooding at a considerable elevation above the modern river. Archaeological testing revealed nearly 2 meters of black anthrosol, rich with artifacts. Excavation exposed a late Holocene sequence of artifacts, hearths, and pits, underlain by artifacts not recognized in the taxonomies of the time. Senior archaeologists dismissed the deposit as colluvium displaced from a famous site on the bluff above. Geologists recognized that hearths in place belied that interpretation, but thought the dark soil represented an old bog. Granulometry indicated that the sediments were sandy aeolian deposits on a truncated alluvial terrace, supporting interpretation that human use of the surfaces was synchronous with their accretion since the early Holocene (Dincauze 1976).

Dunes and sand sheets

Dunes, forming downwind of extensive sources of lightly vegetated sand, represent and perpetuate microclimates. Dunes do not themselves constitute full climate proxies since they can form in temperate climates where vegetation is stripped, as well as in regimes unsupportive of vegetation. Absence of vegetation reduces the surface friction that would interfere with wind velocity, and increases albedo-caused temperature differentials at the land surface. Dune sands are not homogeneous; they may display strong cross-bedding produced by variable winds during deposition. The challenge of dunefields to archaeologists is to determine whether archaeological sites found in and among dunes were deposited before, during, or after dune formation. Each situation has a different implication for environmental contexts of the sites.

Archaeological deposits overtaken by developing or moving dunefields will likely be disturbed. Unless protected by a vegetated soil and rapidly buried, archaeological deposits will be exposed by wind deflation of finer sediments enclosing them. Wind erosion leaves particles heavier than sand grains in more or less their original locale as lag deposits, perhaps with surfaces polished, pitted or striated, and effectively isolated from their original matrices. Such lag deposits can comprise artificial associations of materials of different ages sorted only by their relative weights, lying on surfaces created by processes younger than themselves. The underlying surfaces, whether sand, bedrock, or even paleosols, cannot be assumed to bear any original relationship with the artifacts resting on them.

Dune sands do not hold water; rapid percolation and oxidation of the sediments militates against the preservation of organic matter. Stabilized dunefields colonized by vegetation support slow pedogenesis and may be chemically altered by both pedogenesis and diagenesis. Soils typical of stabilized dunefields include Entisols and Aridisols. Stabilized dunefields may support inter-dunal pools if the concave surfaces intersect the local water table or if water is held on pedogenic hardpans. Such pools may become foci for human activity or residence, and ultimately the locations for archaeological sites younger than the period of dune stabilization. In such cases, only the environmental evidence associated with the ponds, and possibly the period of soil formation, is relevant to the human activities. Humans, fires, and climate change all destroy dune-stabilizing vegetation, initiating periods of remobilization that in turn can destroy human settlements and agricultural fields as well as any archaeological sites in the vicinity. The dynamism of active dunefields equals that of floodplains.

Notable paleoenvironmental work in desert sandsheets and dunefields has been accomplished in northwestern India and in northeastern Africa (Allchin et al. 1978; Misra and Rajaguru 1989; Wendorf et al. 1993). Research in arid zones elsewhere, particularly in the American Southwest and Australia, is elucidating the diversity and challenges presented by such archaeological locations.

Loess deposits

Loess covers thousands of square miles in the centers of continents. The largest deposits formed during periods of glacial retreat, when meltwater deposits of rock flour were exposed prior to colonization by vegetation and carried away by strong winds blowing from the glaciers. Silt-grade particles are transported to great distances because they are deposited only from winds slowed to near-exhaustion.

No matrix is more conducive to a pleasant excavational experience than loess, which is easily disaggregated and maintains vertical faces because of its homogeneity and compactness. Because of their high pH, loesses retain for millennia carbonaceous organic matter such as bones and mollusk shells. In addition, sites on loess were buried gently and therefore usually retain significant spatial integrity. Loess sheets typically accumulate episodically, with increments separated by paleosols. Mollusks in loesses add their oxygen isotopes and racemized amino-acids to the available climate proxies (McCoy 1987), offering alternatives to the missing, mixed, and damaged pollen. Because loess deposition is a Late Glacial process, cryoturbation of loesses can be extreme, roiling and even overturning original stratification.

Littoral sedimentary matrices

Studies of archaeological sites on beaches typically emphasize landforms and RSL. Archaeologists have only recently confronted the challenges of understanding processes of incorporation of archaeological sites into active beach sediments, and explicating methods that will advance such understanding (e.g., Bailey et al. 1994; Thorson 1990a; Johnson and Stright 1992). They have been rather complacent about these issues, overlooking what sedimentologists could tell them and being content with very little ("beach" does not even appear in the index to Schiffer's survey of formation processes [1987]). Research such as that of Kirch and Hunt on To'aga (1993), summarized in Chapter 10, shows the advantages of paying attention to beach formation processes. The deceptive dynamism of beach sands was dramatically revealed at the Lower Paleolithic site of Terra Amata in southern France, where artifact refitting exercises showed that what appeared to be a series of stratigraphically separated living surfaces was belied by extreme vertical distributions of matching fragments (Villa 1982). Such special archaeological analyses of sediment integrity are invaluable in deposits formed by waves or wind, subject to *in situ* reworking.

Beaches are narrow, linear, geographically constrained landforms marked by dynamic sedimentary histories and locational shifts over time. Only the backshore zone and inter-ridge swales (troughs between ridges), where deposition by storm waves or aeolian sand is episodic and erosion minimal, are amenable to the creation and preservation of archaeological sites (Chapter 10). Occupation on beaches, spits and barrier beaches, or islands is usually seasonal, represented by middens and lenses of anthropic soil within sorted aeolian or poorly sorted storm deposits. Careful discrimination during excavation may reveal microstratigraphic sequences, which, nevertheless, must be evaluated for their agents, periodicity, and integrity before being overinterpreted as "annual" or other regular deposits. Thorson offers a sobering discussion of formative and destructive processes on Arctic beaches, where tsunamis and ice dynamics further complicate matters (1990a: 413).

Beach sites are best preserved where they are raised above sea level; there, their special littoral characteristics may be overlooked. On sinking coasts, old beaches are subject to shore erosion, a typical mechanism exposing ancient shell middens. The erosion and reworking of coastal sites present important problems for regional-scale settlement patterns and seasonality studies, and for estimates of paleodemography. Improved understanding of coastal use throughout prehistory requires that more attention be paid to the dynamics of coastal site formation and deformation. Evaluation of beach environments should include consideration of offshore conditions in both water and foreshore, which may be represented in shore deposits of driftwood, molluskan and vertebrate remains, and seaweeds, occurring in cultural deposits and as wrack in storm beaches.

Shell middens, special kinds of beach deposits, deserve mention here; they are further discussed among anthrosols below. As with other shore landforms, middens may be destroyed and redeposited by storms and transgressing seas, appearing then as artifact-rich versions of cheniers (Fig. 12.3).

Volcanic sedimentary matrices

Explosive volcanic eruptions throw fine rock "ash" (tephra) into the wind and the stratosphere. The fine particles return at varying rates and distances according to their size, wind speed, and altitude. Many tephra deposits are identifiable chemically to their sources and may be dated by organic materials on the surfaces on which they fell. Tephra falls provide the best indicators of synchronic, long-distance land surfaces available to the geosciences. Tephra chronostratigraphic markers have been recovered from cave deposits, alluvium and lakes, buried land surfaces (soils and peats), and marine cores (e.g., Dugmore and Newton 1992; Sheets and McKee 1994).

Volcanic ash deposits are extraordinary matrices for paleoenvironmental study, as excavations at Pompeii demonstrated in the eighteenth century. Thick layers of volcanic ash seal living surfaces quickly, holding intact much of their microrelief and associated objects. Analysis of ancient gardens in Pompeii revealed patterns of planting and, in some cases, the species involved, by analysis of root casts (Jashemski 1979). Research at Ceren in Central America set new standards for archaeological data recovery and paleoenvironmental interpretation under tephra (Sheets 1992).

Rockshelters and caves

Rockshelters and caves, special sheltered environments, are only partially open to the weather. They have their own microclimates and localized sediment sources, and may offer unusually favorable preservation conditions. They concentrate and circumscribe activities within them, and the deposits that result. They are occupied,

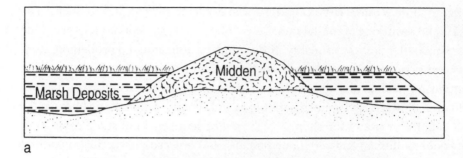

a

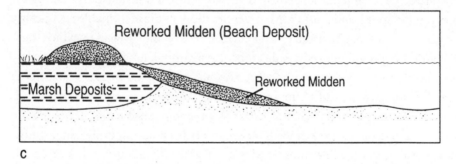

b

c

Figure 12.3 Redeposition of a coastal midden. Preserved by marsh overgrowth as
water rose, the midden is destroyed and redeposited when attacked by waves. It
is transformed by wave action from an archaeological to a geological deposit.
(After Waters 1992: Fig. 6.15.)

synchronously or serially, by many different species including microorganisms. Cave
and shelter deposits, once heavily relied upon for cultural sequence data, are now
recognized as dense taphonomic challenges that yield data on sequence and environments only to critical, disciplined analysis.

Beyond their natural fascination and rich archaeological remains, caves and rockshelters with deep stratigraphic sequences have been especially attractive to archaeologists seeking definitive paleoclimatic data from sediments and inclusions (e.g.,

Laville 1976). However, tracing deposits from outside into shelters, to support chronological comparisons, is difficult. Many deposits are endogenous (originating inside), or polygenetic. Sediments in caves and rockshelters do not support soils development comparable to that on sediments outside. Organic remains and some sediments are brought into caves by creatures other than humans (e.g., Andrews 1990).

Whether synchronous with human occupations or not, environmental change within caves and shelters can rework deposits, erode sediments, and move, damage, or destroy artifacts (e.g., Bar-Yosef 1993: 19–22). The sequence of sediment types, as well as their integrity, must be evaluated as part of the environmental investigation: do stratigraphic interfaces represent old surfaces or erosional truncation? Spatially concentrated and repetitious occupation by humans and animals results in physical disturbance and chemical changes in the sediments. The environmental information potential varies with the area's access to external sediment carriers – wind, water, people, animals. Over time, the entrance may be blocked and reopened, according to very local circumstances.

Rockshelters

Shelters are typically formed by erosional undercuts in cliff faces, usually alluvial or marine erosion into the face of a sandstone or limestone cliff. They may also be formed by the collapse of lava tubes or karstic structures, and by rock layers of differing integrity and resistance to erosion. In glaciated regions, on the slopes of volcanoes, and at high-energy shores, sheltered spaces may be created by rough piles of boulders. The semi-enclosed environments of rockshelters form a continuum between open sites and cave mouths.

Rockshelter floors have a characteristic microrelief, dominated by a linear pile of sediments at the dripline directly below the overhanging cliff edge (Fig. 12.4). Water and sediments sliding down the cliff hit ground at the dripline, which forms a watershed directing falling sediments and water both outside and inside the sheltered space. Large rock fragments dropping from the cliff face usually form a talus pile outside the dripline. Rock fragments falling from the roof or back wall land inside the shelter, where they create topographic relief. Humans using rockshelters typically concentrate domestic activities in the sheltered space between the dripline and back wall, where they receive protection from precipitation and strong sunlight. If there is a ledge or level ground beyond the dripline, which is not always the case, people may situate hearths and activity areas there in fair weather.

Sediments within shelters include both exogenous (from outside) and endogenous elements. Typical of exogenous materials are fluvial, lacustrine, or marine

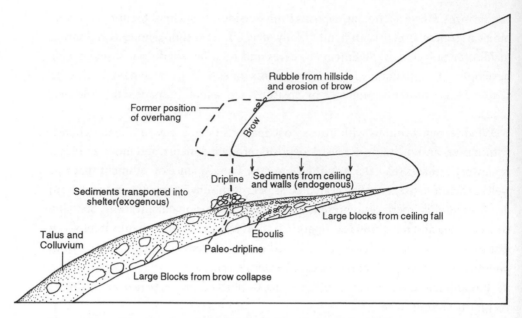

Figure 12.4　Cross-section of a rockshelter, showing retreating cliff face, overhang, dripline, roof-fall, talus. (After Waters 1992: Fig. 5.13.)

deposits related to the original formation of the undercut, colluvium washing or sliding in from the sides or over the top, materials falling from above the cliff onto the dripline, aeolian sediments deposited by winds slowed by the cliff, and materials of all kinds brought in by users of a shelter – humans, denning carnivores, small mammals, and birds. Endogenous materials include rock fragments and minerals dislodged from the shelter walls and roof by weathering, precipitates from springs and groundwater, and organic debris created by resident fauna and plants. The sedimentary sources and environments vary with distance from the entrance, and through time.

The dripline, therefore, separates contrastive sedimentary environments as well as microclimates; humans may enhance its effectiveness in the task with structural elements such as walls. The interior space may be damp or dry; the outside is usually more variable in temperature, precipitation, and windiness. Bedrock bases of shelters formed by erosion are often close to the local water table. Because of this, springs and seeps commonly form within shelters. Sheet wash on surfaces above the cliff may flow along the wall to drain into the back, marking its passage with flowing stains or deposits on the wall. On the other hand, deep shelters and those in arid environments with appropriate protection may be dry year-round; such places offer comfortable living space with good preservation for organic debris. As with all landforms based on relief, the orientation of a shelter is crucial to its efficacy as living space.

Shelters opening to the Sun were utilized much more often than those that face away. Shelters open to seasonal storms have seasonally constrained habitation potential.

Caves

Caves proper differ from shelters in being enclosed at the sides as well as back and ceiling. They are most typically formed in karstified limestone or dolomitic bedrock, where they are the surficial openings of large solution cavities. Special cases of cave-like enclosures include large lava tubes and bubbles in extensive basaltic flows (e.g., Barba et al. 1990). Because caves are more fully shielded from exterior climatic conditions than are rockshelters, their sediments contain larger proportions of endogenous materials. Sediment sources such as roof-fall (rock fragments and fine particles), reprecipitated limestones (speleothems: crusts, flowstone, stalagmites, stalactites, tufas/travertine), residual minerals left after solution of carbonates (silicas, metal compounds, and clays), and fluvial deposits originating within the karst drainage system reflect in their content and structure the disparate environmental conditions within the cave space. Behind the entrance, aeolian and cultural sources of sediment diminish rapidly, temperature stabilizes, and light dims. Beyond the reach of daylight interior cave environments are used by humans only for special ritual purposes or exploratory visits. Preservation of organic materials such as bone, coprolites, and plant materials is enhanced in stable interior environments, both damp and dry. Dryness and high pH are especially favorable factors in preservation, as are layers sealed under flowstone (Straus 1990; Waters 1992: 240–247).

External environments are represented in caves by aeolian materials, drainage into fissures, slope wash and colluvium, and particles deposited by high water reaching the cave mouth. In brighter and drier parts of a cave are concentrated hearths and other cultural deposits created by human activities. Along with those, and sometimes extending deeper into the enclosed space, are materials brought in and deposited or tossed by humans and animals, including bones and other food wastes, dung, seed caches, and bedding. Packrat middens are paleoenvironmental features of caves and fissures in the American West.

Postdepositional changes in cave deposits were ignored for a long time while cave strata were confidently interpreted as climate proxies. *In situ* weathering and carbonate impregnation of sediments transform chemical and physical attributes of the deposit, reduce mass, and translocate elements after deposition. Deposits may be eroded away at the surface and undermined at depth (e.g., Tankard and Schweitzer 1976). Trampling by occupants in the confined spaces of caves, and subfloor digging, add cultural disturbances to the list. When these possibilities are considered with awareness that microclimates inside caves are distinct from those of the exterior, it is clear that the paleoenvironmental interpretation of cave sediments is no straightforward task. Careful discrimination of sediment sources and depositional agents is essential to identify the several source environments. Even so, the potential for equifinality is high; many variables at play in complicated interactions make the interpretation of cave deposits tenuous at best (Barton and Clark 1993; Butzer 1982: 77–87; Straus 1990).

With regional-scale climates so imperfectly represented in caves, the potential of cave sediments to serve as proxies at that scale is drastically reduced. Any respectable effort will require minute attention to the structure and stratification of deposits in place, followed by laboratory analyses selected to reveal attributes relevant to the interpretation. Increasingly, analysts are devoting attention to the smaller classes of sediments – moving down the phi scale (Table 11.3). Sediment components attributable to human activity must be removed prior to textural analyses intended to illuminate climatic factors (Butzer 1981b). Micromorphological study of thin-sections has proven its worth in cave studies, where events as intimate as a gust of wind stirring the ashes of a Paleolithic hearth buried thousands of years ago may be interpreted (Courty et al. 1989: 214).

There is now less reason to stretch the study of cave deposits so far beyond their best use in search of paleoclimatic data. Regional-scale climatic proxies are multiplying all the time, as Chapters 7 and 8 show. Cave sediments are most appropriate for interpreting cave environments, which can change without external influences as floors build up, roofs fall, and entrances are sealed or opened. Caves inhabited by people qualify as domestic space, subject to modification by humans, whose hearth fires, large bodies, and interior constructions change interior climates. The study of cave microclimates can reveal much about living conditions at intimate scales if we relax our grander expectations of them.

Soils as matrices

Soils form from the stable surfaces of sediments, where human lives are lived and biological wastes are deposited. Soils are the typical matrices into which archaeological data are incorporated, and in which such data are preserved or transformed. The archaeological literature shows very plainly how variable is the preservation potential of diverse soils, subject to both pedogenesis and diagenesis. The soils Orders (Table 12.1) provide a basis for discussing some regularities. For further specifics on soil Orders see Brady (1990) and Fanning and Fanning (1989).

The Spodosols, formerly "podzols" as their name suggests, develop on sandy parent material in cool, moist climates in the middle and high latitudes. They are

Table 12.2 Abbreviations for some common chemical elements

Al	aluminum	N	nitrogen
C	carbon	Na	sodium
Ca	calcium	O	oxygen
Cu	copper	P	phosphorus
Fe	iron	Pb	lead
H	hydrogen	S	sulphur
I	iodine	Si	silicon
K	potassium	Sr	strontium
Mg	magnesium	U	uranium
Mn	manganese	Zn	zinc

characterized by low pH, concentrations of Al and Fe oxides in the B horizon (Table 12.2), and bio- and cryoturbation. They cycle organic matter rapidly into humus and leachates, and yield to archaeologists only calcined bone, stone, ceramics, and some oxidized metals. The acidity may be tempered locally by concentrated organic wastes or wood ash, permitting preservation of some bone or shell materials. Ants, rather than earthworms, are the typical bioturbators, cycling particles from within the B and C horizons and redepositing them on the surface. The churning moves artifact-sized particles ever deeper into the soil profiles. Cryoturbation may bring them up again. Very small-scale, intensely colored Spodosols can form under anthropogenically or biologically enriched deposits, such as pits and ditches, in areas of abundant rainfall. Hardpan development in Spodosols can raise water tables and support bog formation.

Alfisols form mainly under woodlands on base-rich parent materials, and develop a B horizon rich in clay. Their carbonate content makes them less corrosive for organic matter than the Spodosols, so that they are likely to yield more paleoenvironmental proxy data. Mid-continental grasslands are the typical location of Mollisols – base-rich, organic, dark-colored fertile soils. They form in a wide range of climates, and in drier areas can preserve bone and shell constituents very well. Aridisols, the soils of dry climates, typically have calcic cemented B horizons because rainfall is inadequate to leach away soluble salts and oxides. They are not strongly weathered, but loose in texture and light in color. Their preservative qualities vary widely with rainfall and seasonality.

Ultisols are typically ancient forest soils of humid warm climates. They also form a clay-rich B horizon, but are low in bases and therefore more deeply weathered than Alfisols. Tropical rainforests are the usual vegetation on Oxisols – deeply leached, typically red clayey lateritic soils. Oxisols preserve for archaeologists neither organic materials nor spatial relationships.

Azonal soils (Table 12.1) include the Histosols, composed of plant remains with minimal mineral matter (e.g., peats). Whether acidic, as is typical, or carbonaceous, their preservative properties are legendary (see below). Vertisols are clay-rich soils that shrink and swell, crack and churn, preserving no spatial relationships for any inclusions. They form in seasonally dry climates on flat terrain in clay-rich parent materials. The microtopography characteristic of Vertisols complicated the interpretation of Maya agricultural techniques in wet lowlands of Central America, creating decades of controversy that has been productive of alternative hypotheses and ultimately enhanced understanding (Jacobs 1995).

Entisols are too immature to be classified as any of the zonal soils. They are found on recently deposited materials, excessively drained substrates such as dune sands, and newly exposed eroded surfaces. The parent material is modified very little. Archaeological sites are rarely found in Entisols because of their recency and instability. Inceptisols show the beginnings of soil horizonation on parent material of no great age, typically alluvium or colluvium. They form under almost any climatic regime on parent materials of diverse sorts.

A model of conditions conducive to the preservation of various kinds of organic matter was developed for paleosols on the basis of "Eh," a measure of "the extent of oxidation and reduction reactions in . . . soils" that varies with water content and the soil pH (Retallack 1990: 218). The model elegantly predicts the kinds of organic remains that will be preserved under diverse conditions of pH and drainage (Figure 12.5), and appears to be appropriate for archaeological matrices.

Soils on alluvium

Alluvial contexts and matrices for archaeological sites, especially where sequences of buried soils are involved, offer opportunities for the study of environments at microscales. Changes in microclimates at the immediate site location may be directly recorded in the relative intensity of processes such as leaching, gleying, illuviation, or subsurface deposition of carbonates – all of which reflect temperature and precipitation regimes that may differ from those at the time of observation. When additional climate proxy evidence is preserved in alluvial sediments, especially near or below water tables, the circumstances may be excellent for paleoenvironmental work. Of course, recognition of changed water tables offers no direct evidence for the causes or times of such change. Refined stratigraphical and chronometric data are required to show (1) whether materials associated in alluvial deposits are truly synchronous and not simply mixed together during fluvial deposition or pedogenesis, and (2) how

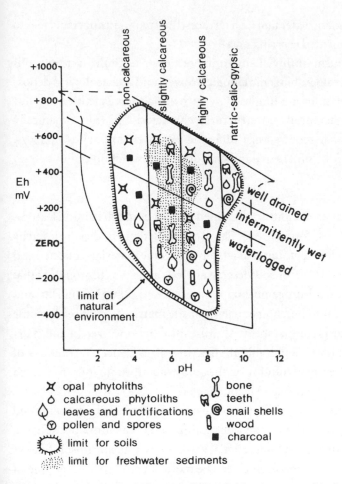

Figure 12.5 Theoretical Eh–pH stability fields of common kinds of terrestrial fossils preserved in paleosols. (Reproduced from Retallack 1984: Fig. 11, with permission of *Paleobiology*; original caption.)

changes in one place relate to similar or even opposite changes spatially distant. Successful paleoenvironmental reconstruction at scales above that of the site depends entirely upon control of time at fine resolution, coupled with evidence permitting extension of the local paleotopography to the regional scale.

The surfaces of active floodplains are neither very stable nor likely to be old. Consequently, they are characterized by Inceptisols and Entisols that carry little paleoenvironmental information, and may be kept immature by periodic additions of sediment (Table 12.1). Terrace soils are likely to be more useful, supporting Zonal soils which, although offering no more than confirmation of regional soils types, may include proxy data of some antiquity. Sealed paleosols in floodplain deposits are likely to be below the modern water table; on terraces, they may be important clues to old landforms now fragmented (Ferring 1992).

The notorious dynamism of fluvial environments alerts us to the fact that soils may vary locally in mineralogy, biogenic climate proxies, and archaeological deposits. Long-distance correlations are hindered by such variability. Paleosols on alluvium also share many textural and structural characteristics with organically rich flood deposits, which require very different interpretations (Brown 1997). Micromorphology will be helpful in making such difficult distinctions.

Anthrosols

Anthrosols (anthropogenic soils; anthropic epipedons) are as much cultural features as are pits, hearths, and house foundations. They are sedimentary bodies enriched by chemicals, mineral particles including artifacts, and biogenic materials collected and discarded by human beings. Anthrosols deserve analysis at least as thorough as that devoted to other complex culturogenic compounds such as ceramics, mortar, and metal slags. The disdain for sedimentary analysis of site matrices expressed by some archaeologists even today is comparable to the dismissal of bones, seeds, and charcoal earlier in this century – deplorable destruction of evidence. Techniques of micromorphology promise to revolutionize the study of anthropic soils, for which they seem unusually appropriate (e.g., Macphail 1994).

The dark color and greasy feel of developed anthrosols derive from concentrated organic wastes, especially carbon, nitrogen compounds, calcium, phosphates, amino acids, lipids, and diverse colloids. Spatial variation within anthrosols follows from different activity distributions, which can be plotted from on-site mapping of phosphates (Eidt 1985) and other constituents (Dillehay 1997: Ch. 10). Research refining the extraction and interpretation of organic compounds from soils, wet sites, and cave earth is regularly reported in such journals as *Journal of Archaeological Science*, *Archaeometry*, *Nature*, and *Science*. Organic particles typical of anthrosols and middens, such as pollen, insect parts, mollusk shells, and animal bones contribute to the definition of micro-scale site environments.

Most middens qualify as landforms composed of anthrosols and rubbish (Kolb et al. 1990; Lawrence 1988). Urban landforms, including tells, enclose anthrosol lenses. Ancient and modern urban backyards and privies share many characteristics and information content with more conventional anthrosols (Macphail 1981; Reinhard et al. 1986). The living surfaces of non-urban sites are likely to display some chemical traits typical of anthrosols. Another signal of concentrated human activity in such soils is enhanced magnetic susceptibility induced by iron oxides modified by burning (Catt 1986: 177; see also Bellomo 1993).

Anthropogenic deposits in dry climates, such as the Near East and southwestern North America, may be treasure troves of paleoenvironmental data, with no pedogenic modifications at all. Such sediments have traditionally been separated by sieving or flotation, and the constituent elements inventoried in sets by size or kind. Micromorphological techniques permit analyses of actual associational sets, with behavioral interpretations supported as well as paleoenvironmental ones. Box samples from a Mesopotamian city, transformed into large thin-sections and examined microscopically, revealed details about living conditions within dwellings, brick-making, and insect infestations in food and other trash (Matthews and Postgate 1994).

Shell middens may be distinguished from natural shore features such as shelly cheniers, all else failing, on the basis of their anthrosol component, which may be discontinuously distributed. Normally, the artifact and feature contents of shell middens are adequate to distinguish them from other kinds of shell concentrations (e.g., Bailey et al. 1994; Sullivan and O'Connor 1993), but in cases where structure has been damaged, soils chemistry may be definitive. Molluskan shells, large calcareous particles, give midden soils typically high pH which preserves bones and bone artifacts. Shell middens are not choice sediments for pollen preservation; pollen analyses should be undertaken only when local questions can be answered by special situations.

Culturally modified soils include "agric" and **plaggen soils**; the first are plowzones, the second heavily manured soils such as those of gardens, fields, and pastures (Behre and Jacomet 1991; Simpson 1997). These are best developed in areas of population concentration and intensive cultivation, such as urban gardens and terraced fields. Both are identifiable by their chemistry and structure (e.g., Groenman-van Waateringe and Robinson 1988; Macphail 1994; Macphail et al. 1990; Sandor 1992). Sandor reports that the obvious changes in Peruvian terraced soils are thickened A horizons enriched with organic matter, nitrogen, and phosphorus; they develop distinctive soil structures and pores and become more acidic (Sandor 1992: 237). Limbrey (1992) reports successful discrimination in thin-sections between tilled and untilled sediment bodies. Agricultural soils lose humus and carbon to a degree detectable by radiocarbon analysis (Harrison et al. 1993; Trumbore et al. 1996). Enhanced erosion of tilled fields, now an international concern, began in antiquity (Bell and Boardman 1992).

Soils culturally modified for other purposes are receiving attention. Depletion of soil carbon, nitrogen, and fungal biomass following clear-cutting of timber retards growth of new seedlings (Moffat 1993). Such depletion reverses pedogenesis in formerly forested tracts, and might be detectable in isotopic ratios. Pastured tracts can be identified by suites of phytoliths characteristic of animal foods, by changes in soil mollusks, and by symbionts such as dung beetles (e.g., Powers-Jones 1994; Robinson 1988).

WET AND FROZEN SITE ENVIRONMENTS

Excavating frozen ground is a tediously slow process that can make young knees into old knees in a single field season.

SCHWEGER 1985: 128

The special preservation conditions of archaeological sites at the interface of land and water have long been appreciated. **Anaerobic** burial conditions impede bacterial decomposition and preserve archaeological deposits rich in organic materials. Anaerobic sediments, saturated or frozen as well as special cases such as tar pits, are important sources of paleoenvironmental data well represented in the archaeological literature (Coles 1984; Purdy 1988). Exploitation of such situations is increasing as constraints on excavation are overcome by technology (e.g., Dillehay 1997).

Sites and objects preserved in wet or frozen contexts were either originally subaerial or were deposited intentionally into water or wet media. For a proper understanding of environments of incorporation, it is obviously essential to determine which situation obtained in each case. The long, contentious history of reinterpretation of the Swiss Neolithic "Lake Villages" and their associated middens indicates that the issue is not always as unambiguous as a shipwreck. For excellent preservation, either rapid inundation or original submergence are the best circumstances. Since organic materials are subject to rapid decomposition by bacteria and fungi in air, their condition on recovery can indicate the relative duration of exposure prior to submergence, and thus the rapidity of incorporation and the integrity of associations in the matrix.

Histosols as matrices

The natural continuum of wet sites begins on land, with waterlogged depositional environments such as bogs, fens and **carrs,** swamps and marshes. Definitions are helpful, because the environments differ, as does the likelihood of archaeological deposits in each. **Ombrotrophic** (rainwater-fed) bogs covering uplands are the classic archaeological "blanket bog" sites, best developed in northwest Europe and the British Isles, and less extensive elsewhere. Other terrestrial wetlands form where the water table intersects the surface of the ground. Sphagnum peats growing in acidic groundwater pools or shallow ponds create the classic bogs. Quaking bogs are peat mats floating on water but attached to shore; cherished by frogs, they are not suitable archaeological environments. Fens are boggy landscapes formed in alkaline or neutral groundwater; carrs are variants supporting woody swamp vegetation in addition to peat. Swamps are terrestrial habitats formed where woody vegetation alternates with stretches of open water. Marshes typically have grassy herbaceous vegetation that may be partly submerged in water. Coastal marshes in brackish water are further characterized as low-energy depositional environments; with rising sea levels archaeological sites may be protected under the vegetation mats of coastal marshes transgressing inland. Fens, ombrotrophic bogs, and coastal marshes are of greatest interest here, as most likely to cover terrestrial archaeological sites. In each case, the matrix will be a Histosol, with the characteristic good preservation of organic remains.

Acid Histosols preserve plant materials including pollen, and animal soft tissues, very well; they are less kind to bone (Clymo 1984). In contrast, alkaline groundwater is credited with remarkable soft-tissue preservation at the Windover site in Florida, where early Holocene burials recovered from peat retained brain tissue in a shallow pond with neutral pH (Doran and Dickel 1988: 285). The preservation of bog bodies in sphagnum bogs depends on more than acidic suppression of bacterial action; complex chemical reactions in humates derived from sphagnum explain the loss of bone mineral components and the preservation of soft tissues (Painter 1994). Acidic Histosols of fens, carrs, and ombrotrophic bogs have preserved the renowned peat sites of Great Britain and northwestern Europe, where environmental archaeology began. The preservation of plant macrofossils and pollen along with insect remains, occasionally bones, and abundant wooden structures and artifacts supported multi-disciplinary studies beginning in the 1930s (Coles 1992). Excavation in wet peats is an exacting and expensive undertaking, which yields its extraordinary surprises slowly (e.g., Pryor 1991, 1995).

Nearshore matrices

Sites below the strandline in lacustrine and marine sediments, exclusive of shipwrecks and such material deposited from the surface of the water, represent times of lower water levels. By their very existence, they implicate different environmental conditions. Typically they exist in a matrix of peat or silt, permanently or mainly waterlogged. Saturation and the lack of pedogenesis usually permit better preservation of organic materials than in terrestrial sites. Nearshore sites occur at the edges of lakes with climatically fluctuating water levels, in estuaries and shallow sea coasts with barrier beaches, and wherever rising sea levels lift water tables on land. The postglacial rise in oceans inundated numberless sites, a few of which have been investigated, most of them only a few thousand years old, visible under water or exposed by tides or during periodic low-water stages in lakes. Tectonic elevational changes, particularly in the eastern Mediterranean and western North America, have added others. Areas inundated early in the Holocene are, for the most part, lost at depth and probably essentially destroyed.

The shallow foreshore or intertidal sites that are available to archaeologists lie on terrestrial sediments but are enclosed in subaqueous sediments. Each of these deposit classes offers a different suite of potential paleoenvironmental data. Investigation of such contrastive and complementary deposits demands special expertise for interpretation of the transport and deposition agents, the range of biological inclusions, the chronology of inundation, and the best techniques for disaggregation. Excavating by pumped air or water, common enough in underwater archaeology, puts special responsibility on managers for the collection of crucial environmental data, which may take second place to the spectacular and valuable artifacts typical of such sites.

Sites under fresh water

Freshwater deposits enclosing archaeological sites and data are very diverse. The simple cases are those (e.g., fishweirs, quays) under rivers, which are covered by sands and silts if protected at all, and those under lake waters in sand, silt, clay or marls, or peats. Sites of the early Holocene or older also occur in deposits of various salt playas, and in tufas and travertines near springs.

These several matrices preserve organic materials suitable for paleoenvironmental studies; some offer unique opportunities. For example, investigation of travertine deposits in western North America yielded diatom evidence, for the period of human use (1500–1000 B.P.), of organic enrichment of water sources that disappeared when the area was subsequently depopulated (Blinn et al. 1994). Excavation at a wet site in Japan revealed "a series of rice fields of the Yayoi, sealed and preserved by flooding silts, with, in places, the individual rice plants still visible in the fields, planted 2000 years ago" (Coles and Coles 1994: 5). Large lakes with fluctuating water levels have revealed sites under water throughout Europe, but few have been investigated elsewhere. The Swiss lakes are among the most famous, with houses, furnishings, and food remains receiving most of the publicity. An Upper Paleolithic campsite, left on a Late Glacial shore of Lake Neuchatel, was inundated gently enough to preserve hearths and activity areas. A rescue dig, mounted in 1985, explored the site after pumping out the shallow water within a cofferdam (Stickel and Garrison 1988). The paleoenvironmental potential of lake sites remains to be exploited appropriately.

Shallow marine sites

Seacoasts worldwide offer opportunities for wet-site archaeology, especially within the tidal zone. Beyond that, maritime archaeological methods and problem foci dominate. Where shores offer a wide expanse between high and low tide there are opportunities to excavate or at least sample archaeological sites. Estuaries and lagoons, semi-enclosed near-shore fringes of the sea, are among the most attractive locales for human exploitation and habitation (Chapter 10); their brackish mixture of fresh and salt waters has a high biotic potential, with characteristic fauna including shellfish. Archaeological sites are often found near or under intertidal swamps on such shores.

The potential for site integrity in such locations can be estimated in preparation for searches (Belknap and Kraft 1981). Site preservation potential will vary with the slope of the inundated surface, the depth of water and tidal range, wave energy, abandonment time in relation to rising sea level, and other local factors. Preservation of paleoenvironmental data will, of course, depend on the integrity of the site itself. Environments during active use of sites may have differed significantly from those at the time of abandonment, as well as from the environment at inundation. Reasonably intact sites near shore should include preserved wood and other organics. Protection under mucks in zones of low wave energy, especially lagoons, may be optimal. In silts, environments of deposition, incorporation, and inundation may be studied in sedimentary textures and structures, and in included fauna, microfauna, and pollen. Sites are destroyed if the surf zone reaches them. Sites in deeper water offshore will have been subjected to compaction of the enclosing sediments, with resulting distortion of organic materials and disruption of associations.

Permafrost and periglacial matrices

No soils form on frozen ground, but ice is a more powerful disrupter of sediments than is pedogenesis. Periglacial and Arctic cycles of freezing and thawing may preserve incorporated organic materials, but disrupt associations and structures (Washburn 1980). Permafrost holds water tables near the surface during periods of thaw. Archaeological materials deposited on surfaces may sink into muck during thaws, to be mixed with whatever other discrete particles they join there. Excavation in permafrost requires removal of small thawed increments, to facilitate further thawing. Thawed ground is little different from waterlogged muck.

The superb preservation of organic materials and artifacts made from them recompenses excavators for the discomforts and challenges of digging in permanently frozen ground, but in sediments with histories of alternate freezing and thawing, observation and interpretation of archaeological associations and structures is at or beyond the limits of feasibility. Thus, the recovery of a broad suite of paleoenvironmental data from Arctic sites is dependable, but the interpretation of associations and synchronies is not (Waters 1992: 292–299, 302–304). Cryoturbation in sediments subject to deep freezing results in churning of sediments and sorting and displacing of particles that are comparable to those of Vertisols, or worse (Schweger 1985; Thorson 1990a). Included objects are displaced both upward and downward; sediment layers slide and fold. Prior to widespread awareness of these processes, false "stratigraphic" relationships were reported from Arctic sites on the basis of superposed folds of geliflucted sediments. The chronological problems created by churning cannot be solved, but they are now widely recognized.

Paleolithic sites in areas not now subject to frost disruption may be misunderstood if cryoturbation is not recognized. The dramatic disruptions at the High Lodge site in England were not disentangled for years (Ashton et al. 1992). Figure 11.3 indicates some of the difficulties ultimately overcome through a harrowing investigative process.

Seasonally frozen ground in middle and high latitudes and high altitudes suffers a related set of disruptions and displacements, varying with the depth and duration of freezing and the frequency of thaw cycles. Archaeological sites in ground subject to freeze–thaw cycles will have heavy particles shoved toward the surface, flat objects rotated vertically, and everything subjected to lifting by ice expansion from beneath and to dropping into frost cracks. In northern North America, sites of Paleoindian age (twelfth to eleventh millennium B.P.) rarely offer any evidence of intact fireplaces or postmolds, and rarely preserve even charcoal for radiocarbon dating. The implication, which must be tested, is that the sites were subject to severe freeze–thaw cycles in the distant past, if not currently.

Permanently frozen archaeological sites, on the other hand, are among the most complete, as is evident in the case of the Eneolithic fugitive in the Tyrol (Spindler 1993), the Pazyryk graves from Central Asia, and Arctic sites with intact house interiors. Environmental archaeology is never easier than with such complete site preservation.

CODA

The matrix of an archaeological site is the environment of burial, the source of diverse information, and a labile, corrosive storage medium. Archaeological matrices vary with climate, sediment class, history, disturbance processes, and original contents. Retrieval of paleoenvironmental information requires that the excavator be informed, alert, and innovative in observing and recovering data classes. Sampling schemes should be defined to catch the entire range of variation within a site and to permit comparisons to off-site contexts that are similar except for the cultural materials.

DID THE CLASSICAL CIVILIZATIONS DESTROY
THEIR OWN AGRICULTURAL LANDS?

The Classical lands of the Mediterranean present the thoughtful observer with the paradox of the homelands of great early civilizations in landscapes now characterized by limited and discontinuous arable soils, bare rocky hillsides, and silted harbors. Already in late Classical times writers speculated about the destruction of formerly richer landscapes by abusive land-use practices. Early environmentalists used the Mediterranean case as a moral lesson, threatening similar impoverishment to heedless peoples elsewhere (e.g., Marsh 1965). This view of things is necessarily based on the assumption that the damage had been done during classical times and that later populations simply endured the burden of their poor inheritance, which doomed them to economic marginality in the modern world.

By the decade of the 1960s, informed observers had noticed that the massive alluvial deposits in circum-Mediterranean valleys contained Roman and younger sherds, and that in some instances they buried Classical and Byzantine sites (e.g., Judson 1963). These observations particularly impressed Claudio Vita-Finzi, who inspected valley fills around the Mediterranean and published in 1969 a monograph on his investigations.

Vita-Finzi observed two major episodes of Mediterranean valley fills, which he called the "Older" and "Younger" Fills. The older and more massive was very rocky in places, was typically a deep red color, and had been deeply incised by stream-cutting before the deposition of the Younger Fill that was "nested" within it. Along the coasts, the Older Fill extended seaward, as if emplaced during times of lower sea level, and was overlain by more recent beach deposits of the postglacial transgression. Interpreting the stony component in the fill as evidence for frost weathering, Vita-Finzi concluded that the Older Fill was a product of the last glacial age. He saw that, in the twentieth century, streams in the valleys in which the Younger Fill lay were not depositing sediments but were instead incising and carrying seaward some of the Younger Fill. The Younger Fill itself, gray or brown in color, usually finer in texture and far less massive than the Older Fill, and apparently graded to modern beaches, he interpreted as a Holocene deposit created under environmental conditions different from those of the present.

His archaeological observations led him to conclude that the younger fills were of medieval age everywhere he looked. At the same time, climatologists were demonstrating that a Little Ice Age had begun in northern Europe and North America in late medieval times, and Vita-Finzi tentatively suggested that such a climatic change might have brought heavier or less episodic rainfall to the Mediterranean lands, thus reversing regional stream regimes and reinstating the erosion-and-deposition cycle that he claimed had emplaced the Older Fill during the last glaciation. He was convinced that only climatic change could have caused such a reversal over the entire region within the limited time span of the last two millennia. Moreover, he assumed that the fill sequences were synchronous over the entire Mediterranean basin and therefore represented only two discrete cycles of events. He rejected agriculture and husbandry as explanations of the change because they had characterized the region for a far longer time span.

Vita-Finzi's claim for large-scale Late Holocene landscape remodeling, developed and expounded strictly at a geological rather than archaeological scale of resolution, influenced thinking about classical and modern economies alike. Vita-Finzi concluded that Classical land-use practices had not been ruinous, that climate change was responsible for the redistribution of unconsolidated sediments from hill slopes to valley bottoms, and that this redistribution, painful in its immediate consequences, ultimately provided modern farmers with excellent and accessible arable soils.

The hypothesis was embraced and expanded by John Bintliff (1977) who claimed that field situations in many areas of Greece supported Vita-Finzi's conclusions, although he did change the dating of the Older Fill, assigning it to the early part of the last glaciation rather than the height of the ice age.

Attractive as the Vita-Finzi hypothesis was in some quarters, it was immediately challenged. Karl Butzer (1969), reviewing Vita-Finzi's book, noted that the mechanisms by which climatic change could trigger reversals in stream regimes were not demonstrated and that the data presented were inadequate to eliminate the alternative hypothesis of abusive human land-use practices as local causes. Moreover, he stated that the argument failed to account for complexities recognized even in the Older Fill components. Butzer later demonstrated that several different modes of land use influence stream regimes and hill-slope erosion, and that interactions of climate change and human land use may be so complex that interpreters cannot emphasize either as the critical factor (Butzer 1969, 1981a, 1982).

The assumptions on which the climatic conclusions were based came under closer scrutiny, as Davidson (1980) challenged both the generality and the synchroneity of the Younger Fill. He thereby weakened the necessity for invoking a universal large-scale mechanism such as climate change. Wagstaff (1981), citing geomorphological and sedimentological research on the behavior of intermittent streams in dry climates, argued that the Mediterranean field data of Vita-Finzi and Bintliff were not only inadequate to refute the hypothesis of human agency, but also were themselves not strongly supportive of the climate-change conclusions (see also Bell 1982). Basing his argument partly on complex-response theory in hydrology (see Chapter 9 and Figure 9.3), Wagstaff claimed that the alternation of cut and fill regimes, as well as local differences in mode of sediment transport and deposition, implied far more complex processes operating at local, not regional, scales. "Variation [in stream activity] could result from differences in the location of the site studied, local topography, soil quality, vegetation and climate, as well as from diachronic alternations in human activity" (Wagstaff 1981: 253). The modern range of variation in rainfall, in both time and space and on seasonal, annual, and larger scales, could easily account for the variability cited in the stream regimes. Furthermore, there was then little independent evidence supporting the inference of climatic change of the scale and age necessary for the hypothesis. Wagstaff's forceful argument for the testing of alternative hypotheses closed with a call for a technical interdisciplinary study involving geomorphologists, climatologists, and archaeologists, with detailed attention to variation and correlation through a range of temporal and spatial scales.

An interdisciplinary study meeting some of the stated requirements began about the same time in the Southern Argolid area of Greece, a small, seagirt peninsula which incorporates within its limited area much of the native landform diversity of modern Greece. Geological field work was carried out in conjunction with an intensive archaeological survey, and data on regional population densities, land-use practices, and economic conditions were gathered from administrative and literary sources (Pope and van Andel 1984; van Andel et al. 1986). The results gave strong new credibility to the anthropogenic erosional hypothesis, but still fell short of settling the matter, even locally. A closer look at the methods and conclusions will help explain the complexities involved.

Examination of multiple exposures in most of the valleys of the Southern Argolid revealed that both the Older and Younger Fill bodies were the products of multiple episodes of valley deposition, and thus of hill-slope erosion. The major episodes of valley fill were themselves internally diverse, some beginning with debris flows followed by stream channel deposits and ending with overbank deposits of fine silty alluvium, others lacking the channel deposits, still others involving only the channel and overbank deposits. For all but the most recent sequences of deposition, active sedimentation was followed by episodes of local stability within which soils formed on the exposed silts. The soils, being progressively younger through the sequence, provided a reasonably reliable means of correlating distinct episodes of deposition between adjacent valleys, a correlation that could not be made on the basis of the deposits alone except when appropriate archaeological inclusions helped to refine the chronology.

As many as four distinct episodes of deposition followed by soil development were discerned within some of the Holocene fills in the Argolid, each dated by archaeological criteria or radiometric dating. The oldest Holocene unit recognized was assignable to the Early Bronze Age (Early Helladic), about 4000 years ago. It characteristically began with debris flows indicative of catastrophic hill-slope erosion. Debris flows occurred again in deposits assignable to medieval times (Middle Byzantine/Frankish period). Both of these events occurred during periods of major population expansion, and in each case are thought to have been triggered by extensive land clearance lacking effective conservation measures. The earlier Neolithic land clearance is interpreted, on the basis of the small numbers of sites involved and the absence of evidence of erosion, as localized and probably based on long fallow rotation, so that no great amounts of sediment were at risk at any one time.

Following the Bronze Age soil losses, a long period of stability ensued in which streams neither aggraded nor gullied and little soil was lost from the hills. The stability lasted through the time of high population associated with the Mycenaean civilization; the investigators propose that the landforms and agricultural surfaces were stabilized by effective conservation tactics that, given the high population, are more likely to have been terraces and check dams than long fallow intervals. The depopulation that followed the collapse of Mycenaean civilization was not accompanied by massive soil mobilization. The investigators, noting that today the natural scrub vegetation quickly stabilizes the soil of abandoned agricultural terraces, posit a similar natural healing to explain the continued stability of the valley floors. The population expansion that preceded the prosperity of Classical Greece did not trigger soil losses either, presumably because terracing technology was understood and properly employed.

The political and economic upheavals following the Alexandrian empire and Roman conquests led again to reduced population in the Argolid, and for a second time slopewash from abandoned fields carried sediments into the valleys, where they were deposited as channel gravels. In this case, it is thought that the hillside terraced fields were used as pasture for sheep and goats, preventing the natural vegetation from asserting itself, while the terrace walls were allowed to disintegrate. While the same effects could have been achieved by increased rainfall, there is no other evidence for such a change, and the brief duration of the event, dated by archaeological means to the Hellenistic period, makes the case for neglect much the stronger. With economic recovery the soils were stabilized again; the stability continued through another depopulation, when evidence from pollen analysis indicates the regeneration of the native scrub vegetation. The last sporadic episode of valley deposition, dating to the most recent couple of centuries, correlates with observable neglect of terrace walls and upland fields as economic attention shifted from agriculture to herding or tourism.

The Southern Argolid investigators concluded, therefore, that cycles of economic and population expansion and contraction, in conjunction with changing land-use practices, account effectively for most observed Late Holocene cycles of slope erosion and valley deposition (van Andel et al. 1986). Pointing out that either increased rainfall or terrace neglect can trigger slope erosion, and that either terracing or natural vegetation cover can stabilize the slopes, they rely on historical evidence and archaeological and radiometric dating to discriminate among the possibilities. However, the absence of field evidence for significant climatic change within the last 5000 years raises unanswered questions, given evidence accumulated recently for climatic reversals at the end of the fifth millennium and during the Little Ice Age of late medieval time.

The reinstated anthropogenic hypothesis is convincing because it is based on more observations, finer chronological control, greater analytical detail, more fully developed theories of stream processes, fuller historical and prehistorical evidence for the human factor, and sounder arguments than were lavished on the climatic hypothesis (Zangger 1992). It is incomplete because the complexities of the natural and cultural records could not be revealed or dated to the degree required for assessment of the relative contributions of the several possible agents involved in the scenarios (Bintliff 1992).

Whenever there are equifinalities involved in explanations, as with the choice above between terrace neglect and greater rainfall, it behooves the investigator to identify the crucial variables in the instances under investigation. In the Southern Argolid, it was not possible (1) to measure past rainfall amounts, (2) to find evidence of the seasonality of precipitation, (3) to establish the nature or abundance of the local vegetation in anything but gross approximations, (4) to date closely either episodes of soil displacement or agricultural terracing, or (5) to reconstruct in detail the ancient stream gradients and their sediment sources. Neither are the antique agricultural systems well understood. Without such detail, neither the sensitivity of the stream basins to local changes nor the contributions of the several relevant trigger factors can be realistically assessed. Note, for instance, that a change to greater precipitation accompanied by less marked seasonality of rainfall might allow more robust vegetation cover in the region, making soil erosion far less likely rather than the reverse. We see in later chapters that study of molluskan microfaunas in the soils could provide relevant information on past vegetation covers, even where pollen is poorly preserved. On the other hand, stream basin regimes can change longitudinally because of basin morphology and sediment yield without any necessity for external triggers (e.g., Patton and Schumm 1981).

A revised climatic argument draws strength from the neo-catastrophism of recent climatology, which recognizes the episodic and rapid nature of short-term climate change, exemplified by the extraordinary storms of the past three decades (Bintliff 1992). The argument is tempered by new data that suggest that the dramatic depopulation cycles following economic expansions in ancient Greece may have been triggered by the literal collapse of the agricultural base. The weakness of linear causation models based on too few key variables once again is exposed. As the debate continues in the Mediterranean, a growing literature on Holocene valley fills in temperate Europe and the British Isles is revising the historical geomorphology and land-use history of those regions. The potentials and problems of such research agendas are well discussed by John Boardman and Martin Bell (1992). Bell summarizes cogently: "environment is the product, not only of natural factors, but the history of their interrelationship with human activity" (Bell 1992a: 21).

PART VI

Vegetation

CONCEPTS AND METHODS IN
PALEOBOTANY

At times, evidence from different sources may on the face of it appear to be
contradictory. Ultimately, of course, there can be no contradiction.

DIMBLEBY 1985: XI

Not long ago the biosphere encompassed by definition two taxonomic kingdoms:
Animals and Plants. Fungi and algae were included in the plant kingdom, and bacteria
were somewhere between. The currently dominant **taxonomy** (systematic classification), based in large measure on organic form, recognizes five kingdoms, with bacteria and some algae included in Monera, other algae and simple "eukaryotic" organisms
(having discrete nuclei in their cells) in Protista, and Fungi in a kingdom of their own
(Margulis and Schwartz 1982). The kingdom of Plantae includes most of what we recognize as plants (vegetation) – trees, shrubs, flowers, mosses, ferns, and so forth.
Recent research in microbiology has forced reconsideration of the organization and
history of life, and initiated a period of classificatory revisions. An emerging taxonomy
based on molecular criteria proposes three "**domains**" at the foundation of life:
Archaea (microbes unlike bacteria), Bacteria (with blue-green algae), and **Eukarya** (all
organisms with distinct cell nuclei). Members of the newly recognized group, Archaea,
are separate from but differentially related to the two other groups, and with bacteria
comprise the prokaryotes (organisms lacking cell nuclei). The domain of Eukarya
includes plants, animals, fungi, and **protists** (single-celled organisms with cellular
nuclei). As the new criteria are tested against extant classifications, the results are
likely to rearrange classes even further and modify phylogenetic trees (Pace 1997).
Archaeologists can wait for these developments but should be aware of the new uncertainties and alert to the need for clear analytical language.

In Part VI we ignore prokaryotic microbes except for awareness of their positive and negative consequences for the health of more complex organisms. The organisms most central to environmental archaeology are eukaryotic. Plants, some protists, and occasionally some fungi are here discussed under the vernacular term "plants," and their study is called variously botany, plant science, or phytology. When more specificity is needed, technical terms are introduced.

Plants in the widest sense are the foundation for all other forms of complex organisms. Using carbon dioxide and sunlight energy, plants and bacteria synthesize the carbohydrates, amino acids, and fatty acids essential to the proliferation of living things. From soils and water they derive additional chemicals for organic compounds. Plants grow nearly everywhere; with microbes, algae and more complex organisms live in and on the geosphere, within the hydrosphere to great depths, and on ice surfaces. Abundant and widespread plant remains are the basis of our knowledge of paleoenvironments.

Three classes of primary data support studies of past states of the biosphere and of human relationships with plants: **macrobotanical remains** (visible and recognizable pieces and parts of plants); **microbotanical remains** (plant parts and products requiring magnification for study); and molecular and **chemical residues** and traces coaxed out of sediments, charred crusts, or animal tissues. Macrobotanical remains are pieces of wood, seeds and fruits, stems and roots, leaves, buds, cuticle, and so on that are preserved under diverse special conditions. Microbotanical remains include principally pollen and spores, microorganisms such as algae and diatoms, and inorganic intracellular deposits such as opal phytoliths and calcitic crystals. Indirect evidence for past plant **associations** (habitat groups) and species distributions comes from such proxy sources as sediments and soils, animal remains and, for recent millennia, artifacts such as graphic representations and historic texts. This chapter introduces these classes of evidence.

Theory for bioarchaeology

The basic bodies of theory for the life sciences are those of genetics and evolution in the widest sense. Those concepts, which underlie much of what is discussed here, are not considered in detail. Taxonomy (the theory of formal classification and systematics), fundamental to description and identification, is more important in the applied biosciences, including bioarchaeology, than in the academic life sciences today. Ecological theory developed in the study of modern organic systems and **biomes** (regional-scale units of the biosphere) must be modified for application to paleoenvironments that cannot be observed in action; in this chapter and that which follows, applications and modifications of ecological theory are indicated. The emphasis here is on **synecology** (the study of interrelationships of species within a defined space), rather than on concepts of community ecology. Paleoethnobotany is too young a discipline to have a developed body of theory. It borrows some theory from the biosciences and the rest, properly, from anthropology and archaeology. The emphasis of bioarchaeology today (paleoethnobotany and zooarchaeology/ archaeozoology) is on special skills and clear reasoning rather than on advanced theory. As the studies mature and criteria for good work are clarified, theoretical issues will come to the fore.

Taphonomy and sampling

The process by which a living organism is translated from the biosphere to the geosphere is the subject of taphonomy. It begins with the death of an organism and continues through deposition of the remains, possible transportation of all or some of them, to decay and burial, and ends with the remains being either fossilized or disintegrated and recycled (Chapter 2). Because taphonomic processes follow many possible routes and reach many possible outcomes, consideration of taphonomy is essential to interpretation of any organic samples recovered from deposits.

Sequences and agents of transportation, deposition, burial, and preservation are directly relevant to the evaluation of organic remains as representatives of the living populations from which they were derived. Organic remains in archaeological sites present additional taphonomic routes related to human actions and intentions: for example, importation, cultural selection, modification, and discard. Ethnobotanical and ethnoarchaeological studies are important sources of insight regarding the histories of plant materials on archaeological sites.

The archaeologist's choice of recovery and sampling methods further complicates issues of representativeness. Samples recovered during field studies must be defined for congruence with research goals. Sample attributes such as size, distribution, diversity, and frequency are differentially relevant to studies of human behavior and paleoecology, varying with the transport and depositional processes represented.

The archaeological literature on paleobotany leans toward exposition of cultural and behavioral interpretations – paleoethnobotany. In this volume, since paleoenvironmental and ecological interpretations are of paramount interest, cultural information is invoked as a control for understanding taphonomic processes. Clearly, neither cultural nor environmental information can be ignored in the geosciences, and no value judgment is implied by the emphasis presented.

MACROBOTANICAL REMAINS (PLANTAE AND FUNGI)

The gulf between the biophysical environment as perceived by archaeologists through the extant material evidence, and that perceived by a contemporaneous person within that environment is significant and probably unresolvable.

O'CONNOR 1991: 4

Macrobotanical remains are the most identifiable and least ambiguous class of plant remains, being parts and pieces of vegetation, more or less familiar as tissues and structures of plants and fungi. While they are usually recognizable as vegetative remains, their identification and interpretation require training and a special analytical vocabulary (e.g., Körber-Grohne 1991).

A paleobotanist must be familiar with plants in fragments, as those are retrieved waterlogged, desiccated, charred, or fossilized from several preservation contexts. Access to systematic collections such as those in herbaria is essential to identification and interpretation of fragmented remains of plant tissues, organs, and **phytoliths** (Pearsall 1989). Publications that aid the identification of cuticle fragments, fibers, bark, leaves and leaf skeletons, wood, stems, seeds, flowers, fruits and nuts, and underground organs and tissues (roots, bulbs, corms, rhizomes) are scattered and specialized. Most specialists build their own reference collections for the areas in which they work.

Taphonomy and preservation

Plant remains in organic deposits, including Histosols, are likely to have grown locally. Peat deposits are most representative of the plant associations from which the remains are derived, subject mainly to preservation biases. Exceptions proliferate when fluvial transport is involved or charcoal fragments are carried by wind. Macrobotanical remains in geological contexts are subject to post-mortem transportation and secondary deposition; information about their taphonomic histories should be sought before they are removed from context. Far more complex histories may be involved in archaeological sites because plant materials may be derived from great distances, selected according to strong cultural values, nurtured nearby despite being unsuited to the local natural conditions, or deposited where found after site abandonment (Fig. 13.1). All that one can conclude unequivocally about plant remains found in a given place is that they were available by some means to be deposited there. The range of means is then open for investigation (Miksicek 1987; Smart and Hoffman 1988: 176–180).

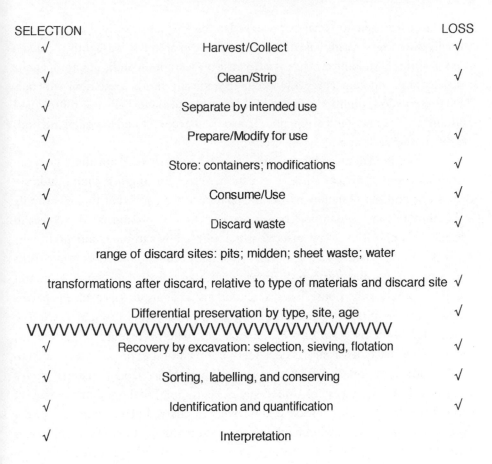

SELECTION		LOSS
√	Harvest/Collect	√
√	Clean/Strip	√
√	Separate by intended use	
√	Prepare/Modify for use	√
√	Store: containers; modifications	√
√	Consume/Use	√
√	Discard waste	√
	range of discard sites: pits; midden; sheet waste; water	
	transformations after discard, relative to type of materials and discard site √	
	Differential preservation by type, site, age	√
	VVVVVVVVVVVVVVVVVVVVVVVVVVVVVVVVVVV	
√	Recovery by excavation: selection, sieving, flotation	√
√	Sorting, labelling, and conserving	√
√	Identification and quantification	√
√	Interpretation	

Figure 13.1   Taphonomic processes and human behaviors and choices involved in the deposition, reduction, and recovery of plant materials in archaeological contexts. The column on the left highlights human choices; that on the right, the points of loss of material or information. Few materials pass through all stages diagrammed; some may loop through several, repeatedly.

Macrobotanical tissues are preserved through archaeological and geological time spans when they fall into depositional conditions that impede decay and disintegration – when they have been carbonized, deposited and held below the water table in anaerobic conditions, mineralized, frozen, or kept very dry. These special conditions retard decay by limiting either the moisture or the oxygen required by decomposing microorganisms. Plant materials deposited on subaerial surfaces are rarely preserved. Additionally, molds of plant parts, showing very good morphological details but lacking tissue remains, may be preserved in volcanic ash or as impressions in clay (usually but not essentially baked); these should be expected to be slightly shrunken from heating (J. M. Renfrew 1973: 15). Because preservation conditions are spatially restricted, macrobotanical remains occur sporadically and become rarer with age. Each preservation condition poses special opportunities and challenges for retrieval and study of macrobotanical remains. Appropriate recovery and handling methods are different in each case.

Carbonization (reduction) of organic materials occurs with burning in oxygen insufficient to support complete combustion. Water and fugitive compounds are driven out and the remaining structural materials are converted to a chemically stable mineral state which preserves most aspects of form and is not subject to organic decomposition. Plant macrofossils preserved by carbonization are usually the more massive tissues such as wood, seeds, stems, tubers, and roots, some fruits and nuts, and occasionally fibers. In archaeological sites they occur typically and frequently in pits, hearths, house floors, and middens. They are also recovered in palynological cores as minor components of bog and pond deposits, brought by wind or water after forest or grass fires (Tolonen 1986). The occurrence of carbonized remains in archaeological sites is dependent upon a number of variables related to site function, duration, and mode of burial. Studying charred plant material from a village site in the southeastern United States, Hally (1981) identified five sources of variability related to the presence and recovery of charred plant materials: (1) the duration of occupancy, including the season or seasons; (2) the site's function and the range of activities carried on there; (3) the nature of the abandonment of the site or structures, especially whether houses were burned; (4) the timing of the abandonment (whether precipitous or gradual); and (5) the methods of excavation and sampling. The likelihood of plant materials being burned by intent or accident in the course of normal site activities and materials processing is a primary consideration affecting various classes of materials differently (Hally 1981; Smart and Hoffman 1988).

Natural or archaeological features that intercept the water table, such as bogs, ditches, pits, wells, and cisterns, create anaerobic conditions likely to preserve plant macrofossils. In perennially wet conditions, even large wooden structures and artifacts such as boats and fish weirs, trackways over bogs, even houses, may be preserved essentially intact for millennia. On archaeological sites, wet plant remains are usually accompanied by other organic materials including animal tissues – leather, skins, bone, and insect carapaces.

Macrobotanic remains comprise the Histosols of bogs, swamps, and similar wetlands at the intersection of the geosphere and hydrosphere. Wetlands transgressing land surfaces in response to rising groundwater are most typically involved with archaeological sites, since only very special and limited classes of sites are formed directly on wet vegetation. Therefore, coastal marshes and terrestrial bogs and fens are most commonly met in the archaeological literature, while swamps, ponds, and such water-based systems are domains of paleobotanists. Particularly in northwestern Europe, there is a large literature on bog investigations involving significant archaeological finds as well as paleoenvironmental research. More typical in the Americas are archaeological sites buried in transgressing coastal marshes and swamps.

Peat deposits, whether coastal or terrestrial, are dynamic environments that may cycle repeatedly between saturated and unsaturated states. It is not uncommon to find horizons in deep peats which represent former forest floors, containing the remains of sizable trees. Frozen environments are a special class of wet; not only are the materials protected from air, but the low temperatures further constrain bacterial decomposition. Frozen sediments in the high Arctic yield plant remains from Late Glacial times, sometimes even mammoths with hair and remains of their last meals.

Permanent dryness is an even better preserver of plant materials than permanent wetness. Deposits of plant materials in dry areas are usually cultural, because natural collecting agents are rare. An exception is the woodrat (packrat; *Neotoma*), which accumulates middens in dry dens and crevices in the American desert West; the plant and other debris collected from the rodents' immediate neighborhoods is cemented by a varnish-like urine and kept dry in sheltered spots. Paleoecologists use the clumps as datable samples of the immediately local flora (Betancourt et al. 1990). Desiccated macrofossils in archaeological contexts are recovered from caves and rockshelters, burials, tombs, and other structures in arid environments. Despite the brittleness that is a characteristic of dried plant materials, the remains are frequently astonishingly complete and easily identified. Woodworking and constructional techniques are well represented in dry archaeological sites, where domestic architecture and household interiors may be studied. Dietary evidence is also dependably preserved; in dry sites food remains reveal all stages of on-site food preparation and consumption in the contents of storage caches, the remains of meals and food preparation, and the composition of coprolites.

Preservation of plant materials in volcanic ash (tephra), while rare, can be spectacular, as sites such as Pompeii, Herculaneum, and Akrotiri attest. In catastrophically buried cities, houses and furnishings may survive in remarkable condition, with meals on tables, and garden plots (Meyer 1980). In tephra, plant materials are preserved by desiccation or molding, or some combination of the two. The phenomenon of molding, in which organic material is leached away but the impression is preserved in a fine matrix, occurs under special conditions of matrix composition and groundwater. While organic materials themselves disappear, their original form may be faithfully modeled, permitting confident identification.

On geological sites

Non-cultural agents accumulate macrofossils in bogs, pond and lake deposits, animal nests, and perennially frozen ground. Unless rivers were involved in the transportation and deposition of the materials, off-site deposits normally are relevant sources of data for immediately local environments. They preserve parts of plants that grew nearby, although such remains cannot be considered statistically representative of the full diversity or proportions of the living plant communities. When the stratigraphical or chronological resolution of deposits permits close dating, such **assemblages** (suites of remains in a deposit) may be related to human activities nearby. Natural deposits can reveal evidence for human impacts on plant associations; archaeologists should be alert to opportunities to test them for evidence of human effects (e.g., fires, deforestation, removal or introduction of species).

On archaeological sites

The full range of preservation conditions for plant materials is found on archaeological sites; not, of course, all together. Dry caves or tombs, and true desert conditions preserve plant materials superbly, as do deposits in permafrost. Wet macrobotanical remains are restricted to small-scale features that provide good preservation, such as pits, wells, and privies. Archaeological sites within wet natural features such as bogs and transgressing marshy shores, or shipwrecks under water, offer exceptions. Typical of terrestrial sites are carbonized plant remains distributed discontinuously because of their primary association with different kinds of activities. The rare impressions in clay, including plant parts and artifacts such as matting and cordage impressed in pottery or in baked clay floors and hearths, are limited to the appropriate materials. In the southeastern United States, where plant materials are unusual in early sites, mat flooring 8000 years old was revealed in a site buried in alluvium, preserved in burnt clay near a hearth (Chapman and Adovasio 1977). Houses, furnishings, and garden plots may survive under tephra deposits, as noted above.

Recovery

On-site vegetation data are typically retrieved by archaeologists themselves, less often by specialists collaborating with archaeologists. In contrast, off-site data are generally retrieved by specialists other than archaeologists, with archaeologists sometimes involved. The choice of recovery methods directly affects the quality of data recovered and the range of applicable analytical methods. Advance planning and consultation for recovery and sampling is, therefore, essential to success, as is forethought in providing for appropriate handling and conservation.

Sampling

The quality of the sampling design is crucial for any field investigation. Successful sampling entails an informed awareness of taphonomic biases and of the range and representativeness of the materials preserved (M. K. Jones 1991). The full range of proveniences available in any research locale or site should be evaluated for potential contributions to problem-oriented sampling. Each sample context must be interpreted in the field to identify its cultural or non-cultural origin, depositional agent, and full suite of stratigraphic relationships. The ideal situation for sampling is a specialist taking the samples directly, for specific analyses; failing that, there must be consultation beforehand on the full range of information to be collected. Identification of the depositional agent is essential information regardless of whether the material is cultural or non-cultural. Cultural contexts are appropriate for investigating aspects of human behavior relating to plants, particularly selection for use (Hastorf and Popper 1988; Pearsall 1989). Cultural contexts also provide information about the size, diversity, and quality of the environments utilized for resources (the site catchment; e.g., Jones 1984). Natural contexts, where animal or physical agents have deposited or concentrated plant materials, reveal aspects of environments less directly under human control. In archaeological research, neither of these complementary contexts is complete without the other; confusion between them leads to error.

Retrieval and treatment

Recovery of organic materials from either archaeological or geological field situations is a major subject best dealt with in the specialist literature rather than thinly summarized in a volume such as this. Here, we touch on only the range of problems and situations relevant to macrobotanic specimens. Plant macrofossils are usually recovered from clumps of matrix, ranging from peaty deposits and mucks, coprolites, carbonate crusts, and packrat middens, to food stores and artifacts. Paleobotanical samples are acquired by coring or bulk sampling, from pond and bog sediments (Aaby and Digerfeldt 1986). The enclosing clumps of matrix are then disaggregated to separate the seeds, stems, leaves, and fruits for study.

Except for structural timbers and water craft, which should be uncovered and recorded *in situ*, waterlogged plant materials are best recovered in lumps of wet matrix, to be washed free in the laboratory where conditions can be controlled and treatment started expeditiously (Körber-Grohne 1991; Schoch 1986; Tolonen 1986). Wet materials may be separated by hand and by washing, with sieving for small items. Wet specimens must be kept wet until treated; they shrink and crack upon exposure to air. Proper treatment can prevent the distortion that reduces interpretive and display values. The special needs of wet materials should be anticipated as part of the planning for any field work that might encounter them. Equipment requirements normally include hoses or sprays to keep things wet during exposure, wet tanks to receive large specimens, and those modern marvels, plastic sheets and bags, to protect them from excessive exposure to air. Special materials and facilities for transport and storage should be provided when required (Cronyn 1992; Sease 1987). Prior to treatment, wet materials may be stored in distilled water or under refrigeration to keep them moist and to reduce bacterial action. Treatment may include the leaching of contaminants such as salts and humic acids.

Carbonized and desiccated materials, because of their fragility, require special care in cleaning and handling prior to identification. Archaeologists typically recover carbonized plant materials by flotation or dry sieving (Pearsall 1989: Ch. 2; Toll 1988; Wagner 1988), more rarely, when pieces are large, by isolation in place. Charred plant materials in pollen cores are usually only counted, or quantified as a ratio of the pollen and spores in the core; charcoal is not usually identified, given the variety and small sizes of fragments involved (Schoch 1986; Smart and Hoffman 1988; Tolonen 1986). Carbonized plant materials are stable if allowed to dry out very slowly and protected from compression or shocks that might further fragment them. Desiccated plant remains must be recovered with great care, taken up in lumps as they occur or cleaned carefully by dry brushing in place or sieving. Being fragile, they require careful packing and support during transport and storage, to prevent sagging, cracking, or compression. They may need no other preparation for museum storage, but it is imperative that they be protected from dampness (Cronyn 1992; Sease 1987). Desiccated coprolites are rehydrated in a chemical solution and then separated as for wet materials (Fry 1985; Reinhard and Bryant 1992).

Recovery of impressions and molds requires mainly alertness on the part of excavators, and appropriate response to the opportunity. In Pompeiian gardens, under ash, molds of tree roots were recovered and identified after being filled with plaster (Jashemski 1979). Recognizing impressions of matting on a clay floor requires another level of responsiveness on the part of excavators; the possibility should be part of every field archaeologist's kit of expectations. Impressions of sticks, seeds, leaves, mats, basketry, and cordage in potsherds, bricks, and mud daub can be examined and recorded in the laboratory if collected in the field.

Study techniques

The first step in analysis and interpretation is identification, in terms of plant taxa and tissue parts, of fragments recovered in altered chemical and physical states. Plant tissues, "complexes of cells of common origin . . . may consist of cells of different form and even different function" (Fahn 1990: 79). Knowledge of cell types and tissue structures is basic to identification of plant remains (Esau 1977). There are no dependable shortcuts to training in systematic botany for that initial task.

Botanical keys and systematic collections are essential for the identification of plant materials. Systematic herbarium collections prepared for the region involved are the only reliable bases for identifications, although special challenges are posed by recovered species that no longer live in an area. The shrinking and distortion characteristic of charred materials require that reference collections include carbonized specimens, prepared for the purpose if not otherwise available (Schoch 1986). Specimens preserved in wet conditions should also be included, to display the chemical and physical changes they undergo. Fragments, so long as their identification is in no way problematical, are valuable components of a study collection, as even breakage patterns may be diagnostic (Bohrer 1986). Intact specimens may be identified from comparative material by the naked eye, provided eye and mind have been trained to observe the crucial determinants of tissues, genera, and species. Because carbonized materials are typically fragmented or distorted, while wet materials may be corroded, distorted or both, microscopic examination may be essential to identification. In some cases thin-sections (along more than one plane) are the best preparation for identification of characteristic structures, as they are of wood. Electron microscopy has proven its value with small macrofossils (Pearcy et al. 1989). The degree of taxonomic specificity attainable varies with the size, condition, and parts preserved, and with the diversity and distinctiveness represented in the native vegetation (Hather 1994; Körber-Grohne 1991; Smart and Hoffman 1988; Sobolik 1994; Wasylikowa 1986). Plant materials modified in the course of early experiments in domestication may be impossible to identify to the species level.

A list of recovered species and plant parts is the beginning of interpretation of a collection. From that beginning, studies proceed toward understanding aspects of ancient environments and human behavior related to management and exploitation of plants.

Interpretation

Once plant materials are identified and interpretation has begun, the value of a disciplined sampling design is demonstrated. When every sample can be unambiguously related to its spatial coordinates and context of origin, its depositional environment interpreted, and its taphonomic history related, interpretation problems are minimized and competing hypotheses are testable.

While study of plant macrofossils was important in the early development of Quaternary paleoenvironmental research, it was superseded before mid-century by pollen analysis. Recently it has again attracted attention from phytogeographers and paleobotanists. Macrofossil interpretation is based on analogies with modern flora and vegetation associations, expanded and circumscribed by paleoenvironmental inferences from as many other sources as can be brought to the task (Fig. 13.2; Wasilykowa 1986). Saturated plant remains and associated materials recovered from pond margins and bogs complement rather than duplicate the palynological data associated with them. Representing species growing on the recovery site or nearby, they typically include some of the insect-pollinated, vegetatively reproducing, or rare species that are poorly represented in pollen deposits. Moreover, macrofossils can be identified to the species level, which is rare with pollen. Large wood specimens offer, in addition to forest composition, data for dendrochronological and dendroclimatological interpretations.

Macrofossils in geological context are direct relicts of natural vegetation, offering insights into past environments different from those achieved through the study of similar materials on archaeological sites. They are sounder evidence for the local presence and associations of ancient plants than pollen alone can provide, since pollen can be carried over considerable distances by wind or water. However, macrofossils are not statistically representative of their source populations. Taphonomic processes intervene significantly between the production of plant components and their deposition in preservative environments. Edible plant parts are subject to predation by herbivores of all sizes; the most nourishing may be rarely preserved. Diverse reproductive strategies influence the likelihood of preservable parts being deposited in anaerobic conditions; for example, plants that produce small, lightweight, and numerous seeds are far more likely to be represented in pond sediments than are those producing a smaller number of heavy, hard nuts and seeds that fall close to the parent plant. Similarly, some mechanisms for fruit and seed dispersal may make preservation opportunities exceptional. Transportation of plant parts by animals, wind, or water retains no semblance of original ratios within the source populations. For all these reasons, preserved terrestrial vegetal remains provide only qualitative information about past vegetation at very local scales.

Interpretation of even the same items of vegetation in cultural contexts requires sensitivity not only to issues of representativeness and selective deposition, but also to cultural biases (Fig. 13.1). Charred materials in archaeological sites, for instance,

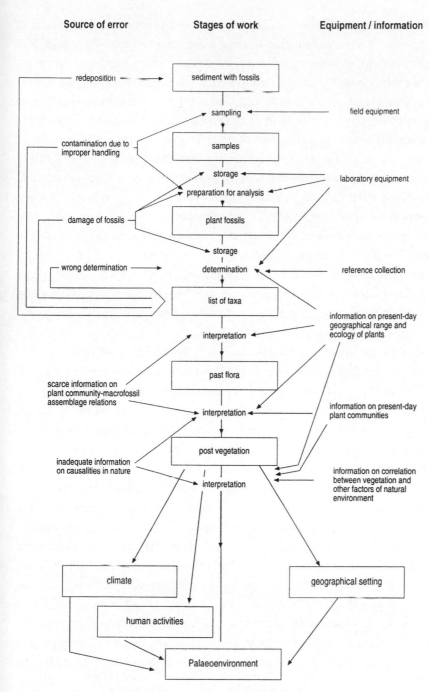

Source of error

Stages of work

Equipment / information

redeposition → sediment with fossils

sampling ← field equipment

contamination due to improper handling

samples

storage ← laboratory equipment

preparation for analysis ←

damage of fossils

plant fossils

storage

wrong determination → determination ← reference collection

list of taxa

interpretation ← information on present-day geographical range and ecology of plants

past flora

scarce information on plant community-macrofossil assemblage relations

interpretation ← information on present-day plant communities

post vegetation

inadequate information on causalities in nature

interpretation ← information on correlation between vegetation and other factors of natural environment

climate

geographical setting

human activities

Palaeoenvironment

Figure 13.2 Schematic sequence of steps for retrieval and study of plant macrofossils, from sediment to interpretive reconstruction of paleoenvironments. The top half of the diagram is data collection; the lower half is interpretation. (After Wasilykowa 1986: Fig. 27.1.)

result from a far more complex mixture of events and processes than do those in natural deposits. While identification of large pieces may be relatively straightforward, interpretation of their significance is subject to considerable uncertainty (Smart and Hoffman 1988). Carbonized material may be derived from, and represent, plants growing on or near the site, plants or plant parts brought in by people or other animals from any distance as food and economic resources for occupants of the site, waste and debris of food preparation or other activities, or combinations of the preceding. Desiccated plant remains typically owe their preservation to cultural selection and manipulation; their presence in a deposit is subject to seasonal differences of use and preservation, and to differential selection for special purposes. Without strong contrary evidence, the safest assumption is that on-site plant remains of all classes only distantly reflect the environment of the site and its surroundings. They directly reflect (1) cultural selection for a variety of purposes, (2) special environments in and near human habitations, and (3) special preservation conditions. The biases, always significant, pose problems for the paleoecologist who wants to understand natural associations, and offer opportunities for the archaeologist who is interested in human behavior.

Because of the numerous variables determining plant preservation in archaeological sites, the equifinality issue is pervasive. The number of means and agencies by which a given set of plant remains might have been assembled on a particular spot is very large, and each has implications for interpretation. Rigorous sampling, imaginative testing, and collection of complementary data can help to narrow the scope of responsible interpretations, but in archaeology the temptation to push beyond the data limits is rarely overcome. Thus, statistical treatments of recovered macrofossils appear in the literature, especially when site data are being applied to environmental reconstructions. Investigators presenting such arguments do not always justify the assumptions behind the statistical techniques employed, or establish a priori the representativeness of the remains for either the total site content or the question being investigated. Even frequency counts, dependent as they are upon the degree of fragmentation of the materials, the size and location of samples collected, and the fineness of subdivisions defined within the site (pits, strata, activity loci, etc.), may mislead by implying standards of objectivity and representativeness that cannot be met by the data (G. E. M. Jones 1991). Unless conditions are demonstrably appropriate to numerical treatments, macrofossil data should be interpreted as the qualitative data they typically are.

For all these reasons, therefore, macrobotanical remains are more significant in their presence than in their absence; the interpretation of absence, particularly, must not be pressed. Statistical treatment of the data is only appropriate when sample sizes are large; this condition is rarely met. With sources of variability deriving not only from the parent plant populations but also from processes of selection, transportation, processing and consumption, deposition, preservation, and recovery, no direct or statistical relationship between any environmental factor and plant macrofossil assemblages can be assumed.

MICROBOTANICAL REMAINS: POLLEN AND SPORES

Tiny and abundant, pollen grains and spores pervade the near-surface zones of the five spheres of the climate system. This ubiquity, in combination with their remarkable resistance to decay and destruction and the relative specificity of their morphologies, is at the foundation of **palynology**, the scientific study of pollen and spores. Pollen grains are produced by the male reproductive organs of flowering plants and conifers; they are dispersed by a variety of mechanisms to fertilize the female organs, which then produce seeds. Spores are the asexual reproductive cells of non-flowering plants (cryptogams) such as mosses and ferns, and of fungi. The size, ruggedness, and morphological specificity of spores are comparable to those of pollen grains but their function is more nearly akin to that of seeds; each can initiate the growth of a new plant, although in an alternative generational form. The genetic matter in pollen grains and spores is protected by a durable outer coat, or exine, made of sporopollenin, a plant polymer highly resistant to enzymes and acids and resilient under stress or abrasion. Exines, therefore, may survive in environmentally favorable deposits for very long periods of time, retaining the identifiable form of the pollen grain or spore (Faegri and Iverson 1989; Moore et al. 1991; Fig. 13.3).

Palynology has dominated paleoenvironmental studies since the second decade of the twentieth century, following its development by the Swedish botanist, Lennart von Post, as a stratigraphic tool to correlate varved lacustrine deposits and layered terrestrial peats. Like other historical sciences including archaeology, palynology has been changed recently by the adoption of quantitative concepts and ecological principles, which initiated creative reconsideration of some of its fundamental assumptions and basic methods (Birks and Gordon 1985; Faegri and Iversen 1989; Moore et al. 1991). Deeper awareness of the complexity of the natural world and of the interdependence of all the environmental sciences entails new standards for data evaluation and demonstration of conclusions. For example, palynologists are increasingly sensitive to evidence implicating human interference in natural systems, even in the distant past, and are increasingly able, in collaboration with archaeologists, to evaluate it. As a consequence of this innovation and growth, papers on theory and method

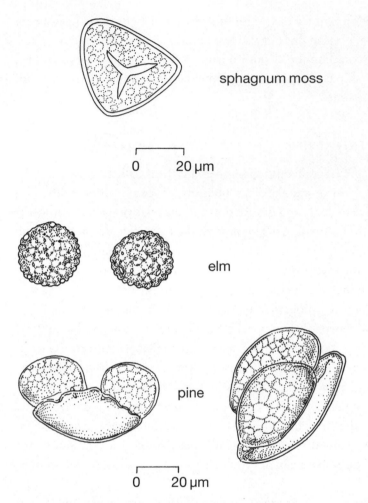

sphagnum moss

0   20 μm

elm

pine

0   20 μm

Figure 13.3   Pollen grain morphologies: pine and elm grains, moss spore, with scale. The bladder-like wings on pine pollen facilitate wind dispersal. (After Bradley 1985: Fig. 9.1, and Lowe and Walker 1984: Fig. 4.1.)

dominate the literature, and much of the classic interpretive work of the first half of the twentieth century is under revision.

Pollen grains and spores are adapted for passive dispersal by a variety of means. Some, buoyant in the wind, soar over great distances. Some are adapted for dispersal by animals, having sticky surfaces or small hooks that cling to insects, fur, and feathers. Tough exines permit grains to survive water transport as well, although they may suffer abrasion and some loss of surficial features in the process. The pollen of some aquatic plants is spread exclusively under water. Wind-pollinated species, particularly trees, tend to produce more pollen and disperse it more widely than do the species relying upon other mechanisms; consequently, tree pollens dominate the deposits typically sampled by palynologists. Because of diverse species-specific specializations for dispersal, pollen grains are produced, and deposited in sediments, in proportions different from the representation of the parent plants in the standing vegetation (see discussions of dispersal in Faegri and Iversen [1989] and Moore et al. [1991]).

Deposits receiving pollen and spores vary in the sizes of their catchments (the areas from which they receive pollen), preservation characteristics, and postdepositional stability. For example, a large lake receives pollen from the air and from its influent streams; it collects grains from considerable distances. Lake-bottom sediments may be seasonally churned by burrowing organisms, and be subject to settling and sliding to the detriment of stratification. In contrast, a small bog will receive most of its pollen from plants that grow on its surface and margins, with less contributed by running water and moving air. Although bog sediments suffer only compaction in place, pollen may trickle down with rainwater through air spaces, blurring the stratigraphic integrity. A lake will yield a generalized picture of pollen rain at the regional scale, while a bog will collect data mainly representing changes in its native and immediately neighboring vegetation (Jacobson 1988; Larsen and MacDonald 1993). Neither lake nor bog presents a truly representative picture of vegetation associations at scales important to people living nearby.

Palynologists collect pollen from lake and pond sediments, peat deposits, and soil for several different research purposes. Collection sites and techniques vary with research goals, and the results will be partly constrained by those choices. Interpretation of the data must be done in full awareness of the biases. At least five different research emphases are represented in contemporary palynological literature: (1) vegetational history, (2) phytogeography, (3) climatic history, (4) plant ecology, and (5) human intervention in and use of natural systems. A sixth emphasis, formerly more important, was using stratified pollen sequences to provide chronological control and stratigraphic correlation for other paleoenvironmental studies. Expansion and improvement in physicochemical dating techniques have superseded this application of biostratigraphy. The optimal sampling locations and techniques for each research emphasis are not mutually exclusive, but nevertheless vary considerably, as does resolution of resulting laboratory analyses. Archaeologists, who frequently select palynological data from the literature on the single criterion of geographical proximity to archaeological phenomena of interest, need to be aware of the original research purposes that shaped the data collection, analysis, and interpretation of published data.

The fundamental limitations of pollen accumulations as environmental data derive from the facts that palynological accumulations record mainly plants that are wind pollinated, and that pollen is identifiable primarily at the genus level (e.g., Solomon and Webb 1985). Such limitations have many, variously serious, implications for paleoenvironmental studies. Many plants important as human food, both wild and domesticated, are poorly represented in the pollen record. The morphological specificity of pollen grains, which makes it possible to identify many taxa unequivocally, is relevant mainly at the generic level. When a particular genus comprises more than one species, each of which may have very different environmental requirements, such low resolution in the database introduces serious indeterminacies. Moreover, pollen deposits do not faithfully represent the local diversity of plant associations; they are biased by the areal extent (size) and spatial distribution (direction and altitude) of vegetation associations in the catchment. Even extensive vegetation stands contribute differentially to a pollen deposit, according to their composition and location in respect to prevailing winds and to watersheds.

Efforts to refine interpretation of pollen deposits by discriminating among the many factors that contributed to their composition led palynologists to examine plant **community** ecology and to study processes and rates of community development. On Quaternary time scales, rates of species colonization and dispersal, the dynamics of species competition, differential degrees of climatic control of distributions, rates of soils development, occurrence of plant pathogens, and human interference with landscapes must be considered equally with climatic changes in the interpretation of pollen diagrams and **spectra** (the pollen grains associated with a stratigraphic sample). With experience in the description of actual pollen rains came the recognition that many pollen spectra of the past are not matched in modern pollen rain. This is the basis of the no-analog problem: in the absence of good modern matches for fossil pollen spectra, analogous reasoning for interpretation is severely constrained. Analog arguments are weak tools for dealing with differences, but we still lack theoretical principles that can reach beyond analogs. For all these reasons pollen diagrams cannot be directly interpreted in terms of vegetation, and never directly in terms of climate at any scale (Faegri and Iversen 1989; Ritchie 1986). Paleoclimatologists have made their peace with the uncertainties, and continue to work toward refinements that will provide better resolution (Bradley 1999: 363–364).

Preservation conditions

Pollen preservation requires anaerobic (oxygen-free) or acidic environments that hinder decomposing bacteria. In sediments that are aerated, even seasonally, pollen is destroyed by bacteria and oxidation; in neutral or alkaline sediments (pH over 6.0), pollen gradually decays unless the sediments are perennially and thoroughly desiccated. The best sedimentary environments, therefore, are both anaerobic and acidic, or totally arid. Bogs, the basal sediments of oligotrophic ponds and lakes, archaeological features and deposits below the local water table, acidic soils such as podzols, and dry cave Earths all offer environments variously conducive to the preservation of pollen. Certain metallic salts, such as oxides of copper, inhibit bacterial action and preserve pollen in contact with them. Sediments sheltered immediately under objects such as large stones or bivalve shells may also yield pollen. Thus, the archaeologist has a variety of favorable situations in which to find pollen, and should be alert to recover samples that can illuminate aspects of past plant associations or human exploitation of plants (Bryant et al. 1994; Davis and Overs 1995; Dimbleby 1985; Faegri and Iversen 1989; Gremillion 1997).

Recovery

Palynological investigations have many goals and for each purpose there are optimal and less ideal sites from which to extract pollen samples, because each kind of deposit collects pollen and spores from a different range of sources more or less appropriate to the research aims. Basically, it is essential that the pollen in a given deposit be derived from sources at spatial and temporal scales congruent with the research questions: large catchments (e.g., lakes $>1 \, km^2$) for regional paleoenvironmental or paleoclimatic studies, smaller catchments (e.g., bogs and ponds) with fine stratigraphic resolution for studies of plant ecology or human exploitation. When small catchments are used, they are sampled optimally in sets, to intersect a range of microenvironments (Jacobson 1988). In archaeological deposits, each discrete class of contexts which preserves pollen should be sampled, and on habitation sites each member of each class might be examined in order to investigate the full range of variation represented.

The study of pollen in soils, rarely undertaken by palynologists unless they are working with archaeologists, presents special problems because scale factors are not well controlled and stratigraphic integrity is difficult to evaluate. Soils represent an indeterminable span of time for accumulation and chemical and biological modification; soils processes may mask depositional events, and there may be a large range of pollen sources and vectors represented (Dimbleby 1985). Pedoturbation (soil mixing) and pollen percolation further complicate pollen stratigraphy, but their effects may sometimes be discriminated (Kelso 1994).

Pollen samples are typically collected either by coring or by taking a series of discrete samples from an exposed stratigraphic section. Lakes and ponds, for obvious reasons, are sampled by coring, either from boats or from the more stable platform of ice cover. Bogs may be cored, usually requiring a series of segments through the deposits; they present challenging technical problems because of compaction of sediments during coring. The best results are obtained when sections are exposed so that they can be cleaned and sampled sequentially (bottom-up) through the depth of the deposits. In stratified archaeological deposits, collecting a sequence of small contiguous samples through the section is the recommended procedure; the smaller the sampling interval, and therefore the larger the number of discrete samples, the better the resolution of the stratification during analysis (see Fig. 5.2). In purely archaeological contexts, where individual features and small depositional contexts are sampled, it is best to collect samples as large as possible, being scrupulous in bounding and subdividing them to represent as fully as possible the range of *discrete* depositional incidents. The methods and equipment are discussed in any good palynological handbook (Dimbleby 1985; Faegri and Iversen 1989; Moore et al. 1991).

Palynologists study actual pollen rain in relationship to standing vegetation in order to define biases inherent in sampled deposits of older pollen, as a test of representativeness. Good summaries of these studies are readily available in palynological handbooks. The major biases are only briefly referenced here to indicate the scope of the problems. Pollen and spores are sampled from deposits with good preservation characteristics, but there are always likely to be preservation differentials among taxa and between depositional layers of different ages and chemical and physical composition. In addition, any change in depositional rates will bias the pollen representation, and any physical disturbance of the matrix during consolidation will mix pollen of different ages. We have already seen that plant species produce pollen in widely differing amounts and that different agencies disperse it over diverse spatial scales. Any geomorphological or hydrological changes in the catchment area, such as stream capture, or human action in clearing land and modifying drainage, will change the size and character of the area sampled. Such changes in the pollen source area may be difficult to distinguish from vegetational changes of other kinds if the pollen sample itself provides the only data considered.

A sobering example of the subtleties of pollen contexts has been revealed by research in southern New England, USA. A research program seeking macrofossil remains in Late Glacial and Early Holocene sediments revealed abundant macrofossil specimens in the basal parts of cores, with minimal representation of pollen. The ratios were reversed in the core sections dated later than 9000 B.P. Interpretation of the macrofossil matrix indicated that the earliest deposits were considerably more alkaline than later ones. Alkaline conditions preserve macrofossils but destroy pollen; acidic conditions later had the opposite effect (McWeeney 1994: 186–188). Low pollen concentrations observed in Late Glacial sediments in this region may be artifacts of sediment chemistry rather than reflections of impoverished vegetation.

Transportation of pollen in moving air introduces further complexities; understory plants release pollen into winds slowed by standing vegetation, while pollen released near the top of the canopy layer may travel far in faster winds, reaching into the upper atmosphere (Moore et al. 1991: 10–21; Tauber 1967). Pine and oak pollen grains, adapted to airborne transport, are notorious travelers; they soar beyond the range of the parent trees to be deposited, for example, beyond the tree line in tundra and sites at high elevations. Heavier pollen such as that produced by beech and larch will settle close to the originating vegetation. One study indicated that 99% of wind-dispersed pollen grains settle within one kilometer of their source (Brasier 1980: 67), well within our local scale, implicating serious underrepresentation of diversity at the regional scale. Pollen carried in water can settle at considerable distances from its source, even onto the continental shelves. Running water can liberate old pollen from sediments and redeposit it with younger material. Spring snow melt and floodwaters flush sediment and pollen into depositional basins, complicating studies of depositional rates. Grains of different sizes and weights entering standing water settle out differentially, the more buoyant being carried by wind and wave action to the shore zones. Sediments under shallow water are subject to resuspension during the seasonal turnover of the waters and to bioturbation in place, mixing the upper layers. Pollen samples taken from lakes deep enough to preserve annual varves, and those from annually laminated snow and firn deposits, are less affected by such disturbances.

Sample preparation and identification

In the laboratory, standard-sized subsamples are taken from cores or box samplers so that each stratum in a sequence is represented by at least one subsample and thick strata are subsampled sequentially at regular intervals. The frequency of subsampling will depend upon the size of the core, the concentration of pollen in respect to other sedimentary materials, and the degree of resolution desirable for the investigation, just as similar decisions are made in the field when an exposed section is being sampled.

The pollen in each subsample is separated from matrix materials and concentrated by a series of chemical treatments and washes and by centrifuging. Humates, carbonates, silica, and cellulose are removed chemically from the matrix. Strong acids are used, including hydrofluoric acid to dissolve silica, testifying to the toughness of pollen exines that survive the treatment intact. The procedures require special equipment to ensure the safety of the handlers; beginners must be fully and carefully supervised (Moore et al. 1991: 41–44). The concentrated pollen grains from each subsample are fixed to a microscope slide and examined grain by grain under magnification. The grains are identified by comparison with pollen keys and reference collections (e.g., NOAA 1994); like any skill it becomes easier with practice, but always requires painstaking accuracy and patience. The identification of pollen grains that have been damaged or partially decayed is especially challenging, but is now recognized as an important source of information about the integrity of the sample (Kelso 1993). Taxa less susceptible to destruction than others over comparable time spans may dominate deeper parts of a deposit (Hall 1981; Havinga 1984). Typically, specimens more degraded than the rest in a sample are likely to have been secondarily deposited from older or exotic contexts. By identifying and accounting for them, analysts can distinguish between pollen natural to the deposit (autochthonous) and that foreign to the context (allochthonous).

The analyst counts each sample until a predetermined number of grains has been identified. The number is defined in terms of the diversity of pollen in the samples and the completeness of representation required by the research goals. For some purposes, identification of absolutely rare pollen taxa is not important and so counting may be limited at around 200–250 grains per sample. If rare species are sought, as in investigations of sub-regional assemblages or of anthropogenic effects in the vegetation (including domesticates, which rarely disperse pollen very far), then counts as high as 1000 grains or even more may be undertaken (Fig. 13.4). Expanded counts are expensive and must be justified by the research goals (Berglund and Ralska-Jasiewiczowa 1986; Dimbleby 1985). For some purposes, only the pollen of tree species (**AP: arboreal pollen**) is counted; this was the standard procedure during the early years of palynology. Studies of vegetation environments, ecology, or human effects require attention also to the pollen of shrubs, flowers, and grasses (**NAP: non-arboreal pollen**); these are now typically included in pollen diagrams (Table 13.1 displays Latin and common names for some common northern-hemisphere taxa). For archaeological research, rare pollen grains may be extremely informative; even when their presence cannot be easily or immediately interpreted, recognition is important. Again, weighing research goals against costs, counts for pollen samples from archaeological contexts should ideally be on the high end of the range; sometimes this means counting the total sample, especially when, as is frequently the case, the concentration of pollen is low.

Depositional biases, bioturbation, settling, compaction, and sliding of sediments clearly affect the associations of pollen grains, and thus the counts. These random errors are typically ignored once counting begins, with the justification that they affect all samples equally. Of course, random errors are not evenly distributed; their

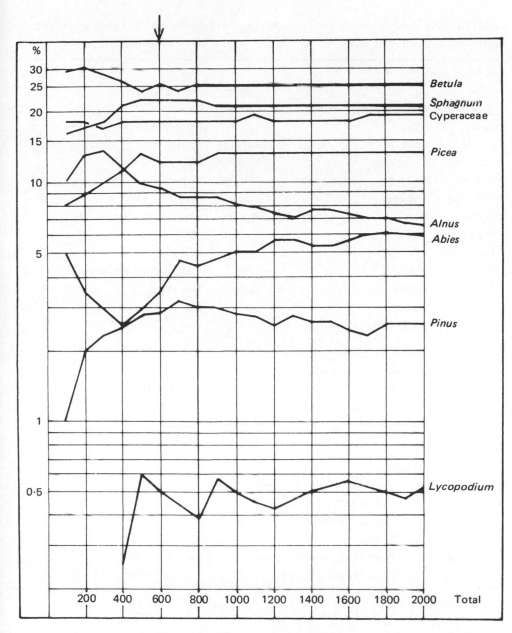

Figure 13.4 Change in pollen percentages and diversity of taxa with larger counts. The numbers on the x axis are total grains counted. (Reproduced from Birks and Birks 1980: Fig. 8.9, with permission of Cambridge University Press.)

Table 13.1 Latin and common names of some major plant taxa in northwest European and eastern North American pollen diagrams

---

A. Arboreal genera

Abies	Fir		*Myrica*	Myrtle/Bayberry
Acer	Maple/European Sycamore		*Nyssa*	Tupelo
Alnus	Alder		*Ostrya*	Ironwood/Hop-hornbeam
Betula	Birch		*Picea*	Spruce
Carpinus	Hornbeam		*Pinus*	Pine
Carya	Hickory		*Platanus*	Plane/American Sycamore
Castanea	Chestnut		*Populus*	Poplar/Aspen
Corylus	Hazel		*Prunus*	Cherry/Plum/Almond, etc.
Fagus	Beech		*Quercus*	Oak
Fraxinus	Ash		*Salix*	Willow
Ilex	Holly		*Tilia*	Lime/Basswood/Linden
Juglans	Walnut		*Tsuga*	Hemlock
Juniperus	Juniper		*Ulmus*	Elm
Larix	Larch/Tamarack			

B. Non-arboreal genera

Ambrosia	Ragweed		*Phragmites*	Reed
Artemesia	Sagebrush/Wormwood		*Plantago*	Plantain
Calluna	Heather		*Pteridium*	Bracken fern
Dryas	Mountain avens		*Rumex*	Dock, Sorrel
Hedera	Ivy		*Typha*	Cattail

C. Non-arboreal families

Amaranthaceae	Herbs and herbaceous shrubs
Chenopodiaceae	Goosefoot/Lambsquarter, etc.
Compositae	Daisies, Sunflowers, Asters, etc.
Cyperaceae	Sedges
Ericaceae	Heaths (e.g., blueberry, rhododendron)
Gramineae	Grasses, including cereals

Source: various sources.

methodological dismissal affects results. Pollen counts, representative of no vegetational reality, must be interpreted.

Data presentation

The grains identified are summed by **taxon** (discrete class) and each taxon is expressed as a percentage of the total count for each sample. Sometimes the total is the sum of arboreal pollen only (ΣAP); more usually now the total pollen count (ΣTP) is the sum used. Obviously, any interpretation depending upon relative representation must take account of the reference sum actually used in the calculation; this should always be given with the results. Percentages are presented in **pollen diagrams**, for which several graphic styles are in use (Fig. 13.5; Grimm 1988). Time (or stratigraphy) is represented on the vertical axis; taxa as percentages of the total count are shown separately on the horizontal axis. The total of each sample can be read along the horizontal axis of the diagram, as a pollen spectrum. In this way the relative representation of each taxon is immediately comprehensible, and can be easily compared with any other. However, the use of the percentage statistic means that a real change in the frequency of any one taxon entails a statistical adjustment in the percentage of all others, so that the diagrams conflate actual and statistical representation, introducing serious methodological bias. Moreover, the percentage statistic is a relic of an earlier disciplinary paradigm, in which issues of proportional representation of pollen in the pollen rain and of depositional, preservational, and retrieval biases were ignored (Birks and Gordon 1985; Faegri and Iversen 1989: 149–155). Percentage representation is a convention; its conventional status must be fully understood by anyone intending to interpret or use pollen diagrams. Because percentages of species adjust with every change, interpretation of actual increase or decrease in a *particular* species of interest requires additional data, independent of a single diagram.

An alternative or complement to the percentage calculation is the calculation of "absolute counts," either "absolute pollen concentration or frequency" (APC; AP_{conc}; APF) or "influx" (API; AP_{influx}) statistics. The concentration of pollen grains in samples is measured by counting grains derived from standardized subsamples to which exact numbers of exotic marker grains or spores have been added. Counts of the marker grains yield a percentage of the total added, which is used as a basis to estimate the actual frequency of other counted taxa in the subsample, giving a pollen concentration figure, usually expressed as grains per cubic centimeter of sediment. The deposition rate of the sediment is calculated from a series of direct radiocarbon dates through the sediment column, or by counting annual deposits. Pollen influx is calculated as the number of grains falling on one square centimeter of surface per year. Although the absolute status of such figures is a polite fiction (Colinvaux 1978), concentration and influx calculations are advantageous for some kinds of research. The concentration figures can be weighted in terms of known pollen production rates for different taxa. Such manipulations provide closer approximations to the ratios of various plant taxa in ancient landscapes, and permit displays of the relative frequencies of individual taxa through time with less statistical distortion than percentage diagrams offer. The archaeological applications are especially appealing, as the figures are the best available approximation to biomass estimates.

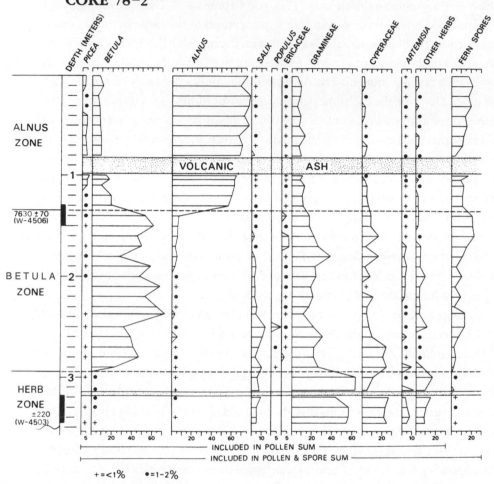

Figure 13.5   Examples of pollen diagrams; both at 10 cm intervals. A. Percentage diagram with tephra, Puyuk Lake, Alaska. (Reproduced with permission from Ager 1982: Fig. 6.) B. Pollen percentages (a) and influx values (b), at Lateral Pond, Yukon Territory, Canada. Notice how different are the emphases by species between (a) and (b), and the marked change in biodiversity at 12,000 B.P. (Reproduced with permission from Ritchie and Cwynar 1982: Fig. 3. Both © 1982 by Academic Press.)

B

(a)

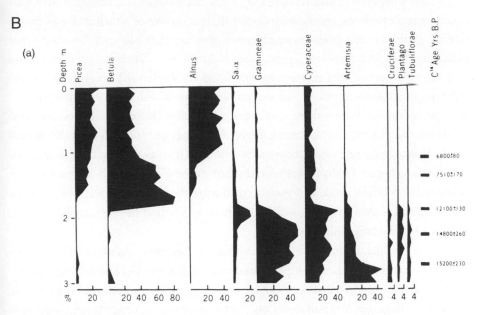

Lateral Pond, Yukon Territory

(b)

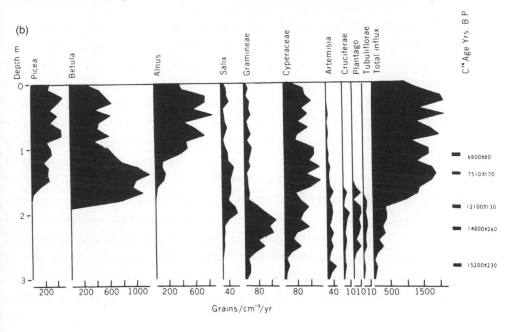

Grains/cm⁻³/yr

The advantages of concentration and influx calculations are, unfortunately, balanced by real problems, the most obvious and least serious of which is that preparation of an influx calculation is much more time-consuming, and therefore more expensive, than preparation of a percentage diagram. The significant problems come with the assumptions that are basic to the method. Calculation of pollen concentrations requires the assumption of a constant rate of deposition between dated points – an expectation that is unrealistic and usually untestable. Influx calculations depend fundamentally on the concentration figure. A number of problems both theoretical and technical make rate calculations conventions of greater or lesser, but in any case untestable, accuracy (Aaby 1988; Prentice 1988). Some of the complications in calculating sedimentation rates, and ways to minimize them, are cogently discussed by Berglund and Ralska-Jasiewiczowa (1986) in an article that has direct relevance for archaeological stratigraphies as well.

Some investigators present both percentage and influx/concentration counts, in order to benefit from their complementary strengths and weaknesses (Fig. 13.5B); there is no question but that such compound diagrams are an advance over simple percentage diagrams. For pollen in soils, influx counts are strongly recommended as alternatives to percentages, since soils mixing and degradation of pollen in such matrices make percentages fundamentally misleading (Dimbleby 1985). In such contexts, however, influx counts may really be equivalent to preservation counts.

To facilitate comparison among pollen diagrams reflecting both very local as well as regional factors affecting pollen frequencies, diagrams are subdivided into **zones** that group sequential spectra into sets. The zones are defined so that each has a characteristic suite of pollen and they are labeled with numbers, letters, or combinations of both. In this way, a sequence of biostratigraphic units is defined, which can be compared from diagram to diagram across space and time. The drawing of **zonal** boundaries has been until recently a subjective, even intuitive, activity, lacking rules to guarantee comparability of either criteria or subdivisions. Quantitative computer algorithms are standardizing the definition of zones so that intra- and inter-regional comparisons will not be unduly influenced by arbitrary personal criteria (Berglund and Ralska-Jasiewiczowa 1986; Birks and Gordon 1985; Moore et al. 1991: 178–180). In regions where many pollen studies have been carried out, zonation schemes tend to be self-perpetuating, gradually taking on auras of accuracy and generality that they have not earned on their merits. The schemes become reified, as was the case with the northwest European schemes which initially were equated uncritically with the Blytt–Sernander climatic phases based on bog stratigraphy. Biostratigraphic units should not be assumed uncritically to be determined by climate, or to reflect everywhere the same directionality and timing of change. Relationships among vegetation change, soils development, climate change, geomorphological and anthropogenic changes must be investigated for each instance, not assumed. They will vary in time and at different spatial scales (see the excellent discussions of various factors affecting pollen production and deposition in *Vegetatio* [vol. 67, no. 2, 1986]). For pollen diagrams representing NAP influx as well as tree pollen, zones may be defined in such a way as to reflect human interference with natural systems – a desirable product for archaeology.

When many dated pollen diagrams are available in a region it is possible to map distributions of pollen in time and space. Taxa may be mapped singly to show their representation at different points in space at one time, using the graphic convention of **isopolls**, contour-like lines connecting points with equal percentages of a pollen taxon (Fig. 13.6A; Huntley and Birks 1983; Jacobson et al. 1987). Pollen concentration or influx data can be mapped the same way, giving patterns that may depart significantly from those of percentages. **Isochrons**, lines delimiting the geographic limits of a taxon at a single point in time, display other kinds of information (Fig. 13.6B; Gaudreau and Webb 1985). Pollen associations defined by the zonation of diagrams can also be mapped spatially, to show large-scale synchronic distributions of gross vegetation types (e.g., Delcourt and Delcourt 1981). These cartographic conventions, based as they are on interpretations of quantitative data, require evaluative interpretation in turn; they are not representations of demonstrable facts. They present *data patterns* relevant to reconstruction of paleoenvironments and phytogeography. Clearly, they are all great favorites with archaeologists, who are eager consumers of patterned data – most particularly dated patterns. Archaeologists must be informed consumers of such patterns, (1) recognizing the methodological, logical, and interpretational complexities that underlie them, and (2) applying them to archaeological problems at congruent scales. Because of the need to extrapolate and generalize in any mapping exercise, but particularly with still scanty pollen data, the best uses of these maps are in environmental studies at regional and larger scales.

Interpretation

Application of data from pollen diagrams and maps to significant research problems in paleoenvironmental studies entails evaluative interpretation for which both theoretical concepts and a responsible sensitivity to logic and limitations are essential. With the growth of palynological research and plant biology in the last few decades much has been learned, and much necessarily unlearned, about the interpretation of pollen data.

The hard-won realization that many Late Glacial and Early Holocene pollen spectra

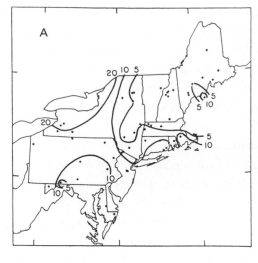

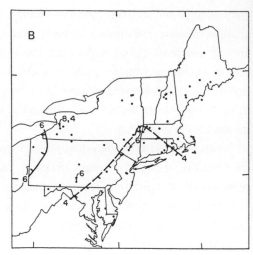

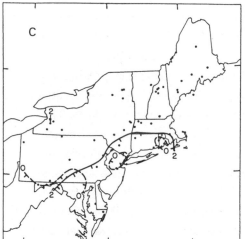

Figure 13.6 A. Isopoll map showing % of ragweed (*Ambrosia*) pollen in northeastern United States today. Note that percentages decline outward from a center. B and C. Isochron maps showing changing distributions of hickory pollen (*Carya*) at 3% frequency from ca. 8 ka to today. On all maps, the sprinkle of dots indicates data sites. (After Gaudreau and Webb 1985: Fig. 14 and Fig. 13a, b, by permission of the American Association of Stratigraphic Palynologists.)

have no modern analogs shook much of palynological reasoning to its foundation. The first victim of obsolescence was the idea that plant communities and regional associations maintained their compositional integrity as they "shifted" toward or away from the poles when Quaternary climates warmed or chilled. As data accumulated at the regional scale, as sampling intervals were reduced and dating achieved finer resolutions, it became clear that the spatial changes in vegetation had been accomplished at the taxon level, each taxon changing its distribution and density in response to many interacting environmental parameters, at rates defined by both biology and ecology. The idea of stable associations was invalidated; equilibrium became a relative concept, and research attention turned to the elucidation of processes.

Once the multiplicity of processes defining pollen representation came under scrutiny, researchers realized that many of the classic questions of palynology, particularly those related to climate, could not be answered with the available methods. With the new emphasis on quantification, issues in sampling theory emerged and it became clear that more questions could be put to the data if scalar distinctions in time and space were carefully respected. Thus, recent palynological studies examine the effects on pollen production and representation of such local factors as topography (relief and elevation), catchment size, depositional environments, soils maturity, disturbance and successions within plant associations, competition, pathogens, consumer effects (herbivory), and human interference with the physical and biological environments. These concepts are not elaborated here, but their promise for expanding paleoenvironmental studies should be clear.

The powerful concepts and methods adopted for studying rates and processes revealed the need for better control of the time dimension in pollen deposits. Beyond the problems of the radiocarbon method itself (Chapter 6) are the complications related to internal dynamics of the deposits sampled, and complications introduced by sampling methods. Collecting organic material for dating from small-diameter cores of sediments with varying proportions of organic material meant that different dated samples represented different *spans* of time; the several radiocarbon dates could be no more than averages of individual, undefined spans. Such data compromise precision, and therefore comparability. In the lake sediments that have been favored for regional pollen studies, mixing of sediments by moving water and bioturbation blends annual pollen deposits into zones representing a decade or more. In combination with the imprecision of dating technologies, the uncertainty complicates and limits correlation among cores and sites (Solomon and Webb 1985). The validity of pollen isochron and isopoll maps, even assemblage maps, depends among other factors upon a reasonable accuracy, if not precision, in correlation among diagrams; that is not easily achieved (Pilcher 1993).

Specification of the spatial dimension represented in pollen deposits is also challenging. In deposits outside of archaeological contexts, the size of the catchment can usually be estimated, according to the characteristics of the depositional basin. One estimate suggests that typical catchment sizes range from 50 to 3000 km^2 (Solomon and Webb 1985: 63), a range that measures vegetation from the scale of watersheds to landscapes. The selection of sampling sites appropriate to the scale of a problem under investigation is crucial, as is awareness of the relevant scales in any interpretation of the data. Pollen rain on archaeological sites includes elements of local and regional floras, but the special conditions of deposition and preservation on sites are unlikely to preserve representative samples of pollen rain. Interpretation entails critical consideration of possible or likely sources for all taxa. In particular, pollen that finds its way into features that were once inside an enclosed space may represent very special or temporary conditions within the space itself (room, cave, etc.). Plants and plant materials may be collected and brought to a site by people, animals, or insects, introducing pollen that could not have reached the place naturally. Pollen deposited in fecal matter, especially in cesspits and latrines, may represent a highly diverse, selective, and widespread range of source locations (Greig 1982; Reinhard et al. 1986). In archaeological investigations, where the research problems are fitted to the data as often as the data are selected for the problem, an educated awareness of the spatial scales represented in diverse pollen samples is essential to interpretive success.

The realization that modern plant associations are products of numerous specific and interactive processes shifted attention from pollen zones and assemblages to indicator species as the bases for the study of plant associations (Birks and Birks 1980; Bryson 1985). Field studies reveal the modern parameters of climate, soils, or other factors that seem most determinative for the presence or absence of sensitive species, and the relationships so revealed are used to infer environments of the past on the basis of pollen spectra. This form of analog argument entails assumptions that we have seen are undemonstrated and vulnerable to challenge. First, there is the assumption that the relative importance of constraints on species in modern associations is unchanged through the duration under investigation. The assumption that plants are in equilibrium with climates (now and in the past) is a variant of this. Second is the assumption that consistent and close relationships hold between the observable ecological relationships of a particular species and that species' manifestation in the pollen record. Extrapolation from observations of plant associations to the interpretation of pollen spectra is made more difficult by the fact that field observations are made at the taxonomic level of species, whereas pollen is mainly identifiable at the genus or even family level, where ecological tolerances may be quite broad.

Pollen analysis supports strong inferences about paleoenvironments when they address the state and condition of vegetation mainly at regional (formation) scales (Berglund 1986; Birks and Birks 1980). Such interpretation stays closest to the data, requires the fewest undemonstrated assumptions, and benefits greatly from research on pollen–plant relationships. Excellent work has been done in both North America and Europe mapping the major plant associations of the Holocene (Huntley 1990; Huntley and Birks 1983; Jacobson et al. 1987).

Close-interval sampling and growing interest in sampling and comparing small basins to study local effects is producing excellent results at small scales, where bio-

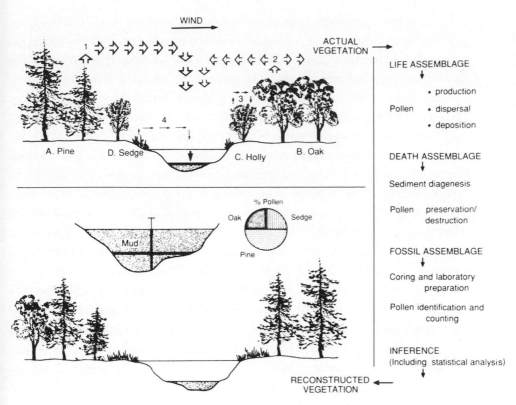

Figure 13.7   Reconstruction of vegetation from pollen analysis, showing biases skewing representation and distribution of species. Factors such as prevailing wind direction (1 & 2), differential pollen production (3), and relative proximity to collecting basin (4) are shown to overrepresent pine and sedge in the pollen spectrum, while underrepresenting oak and eliminating from consideration the insect-pollinated holly. (After Roberts [1989: 24], where more detailed discussion is available; with permission of Blackwell Publishers.)

logical factors dominate over those of the physical world (Peglar 1993; Smith and Cloutman 1988). Despite the possibility of greater precision when sampling intervals and sampled universe are both small, small-scale paleoenvironmental reconstructions may well be necessarily less accurate than the large-scale work. Inaccuracies in the data and assumptions will be more prominent in results at small scales (Fig. 13.7). Archaeologists can benefit from paleoenvironmental reconstructions based on pollen analysis, even when the reconstructions are not done with or for archaeologists, as long as they bear in mind (1) the requirements of scale congruency, (2) the need to be critically aware of the assumptions behind the work, and (3) the inherent limits of resolution or accuracy (King 1985).

Research into human effects on plant associations is intensifying in palynology as phytohistorians become aware of the range and scales of human influences and the antiquity of the phenomenon (Behre 1986; Starkel 1987). Palynologists are providing data on fire regimes, forest clearance, resource management, and introductions of exotic species. Human disturbance of natural systems is now recognized as a major environmental determinant, not confined to the period of industrialization or even of urbanization. The discrimination of anthropogenic effects from other habitat disruptions requires sophisticated analysis not only of pollen data but of other environmental proxies as well. Wherever human activities were concentrated enough to produce a recognizable archaeological context, the crucial distinction between background and cultural sources of pollen is at best difficult. An example of the difficulties is provided by the case study of the elm decline in this section. It is not idle speculation to wonder if Holocene vegetation anywhere in the world developed without some human influence (Roberts 1989). The idea of a "natural" environment or even "wilderness" free from human influence is problematical. Recognition of the antiquity and ubiquity of anthropogenic effects has important implications for the use of proxy data in any paleoenvironmental reconstructions. The biological success of *Homo sapiens* is more than a side issue in the study of Late Quaternary environments at any scale (Dincauze 1993a).

MICROBOTANICAL REMAINS IN MINERAL FORM

Growing plants and algae deposit in their tissues oxides and crystals that may outlast the organic remains and be diagnostic of former vegetation. Non-crystalline silica bodies that form in and between the cells of plants and encase some algae are significant categories of microbotanical remains. Delicately elaborate diatom frustules (box-like cases enclosing cytoplasm) recovered from subaqueous deposits inform about the chemistry and temperature of water bodies. As they rarely occur in archaeological contexts or yield information about terrestrial habitats, they are noted here but not further discussed (see Chapter 8, and discussions in Bradley [1999], Lowe and Walker [1984], and Williams et al. [1993]). Micromorphological studies of archaeological sediments have revealed potentially identifiable plant remains in the form of crystals of calcium oxalate and calcitic ash. These have been observed at high magnifications in floor accumulations and middens in dry climates, and in ash deposits from hearths (Matthews and Postgate 1994; Wattez and Courty 1987).

Phytoliths

Phytoliths ("plant stones") are opaline silica bodies formed in and around plant cells from silica (SiO_2) taken up with water. Constrained by the walls of cells, they harden into shapes that are characteristic of some plant taxa. When plant tissues decompose, the inorganic silica bodies typically remain where they fall, to be incorporated into soils and sediments. Their durability is less than that of crystalline silica (quartz) but is not well quantified; they have been shown to degrade with depth in soil (Fisher and Kelso 1987). Radiocarbon dating of organic inclusions in phytoliths showed considerable, but not infinite, age averaged for a set (Wilding 1967). Phytoliths form in many kinds of plant tissues; their sizes and frequencies vary with available moisture and other factors poorly understood (Pearsall 1989: Ch. 5; Piperno 1987; Rapp and Mulholland 1992; Rovner 1983, 1988).

Phytolith shapes, which may be amorphous, generalized, or distinctive, are consistent within taxa and are used for paleobotanical reconstructions within the limits of their specificity (Fig. 13.8; Piperno 1987). While there are several manuals for pollen identification, phytolith systematics is only just developing (Rapp and Mulholland 1992). Phytoliths are best known and therefore most useful among the grasses, and have been successfully applied to studies of domestic landscapes (lawns and meadows), pasturage and grain crops, particularly maize, and successional sequences in grasslands. Because phytoliths are preserved in climates and soils inimical to pollen, they offer advantages worth the development costs in pollen-poor areas such as tropical climates (Piperno 1989), grasslands, and urban deposits. Phytolith research, approached with discipline and imagination, promises a conditionally useful complement to pollen analysis.

Pioneering phytolith studies held out the promise of species-specific shapes; recent work has demonstrated that using suites of phytolith shapes to identify plant associations has a firmer foundation in the reality of phytolith variation and recoveries (Powers-Jones 1994; Rovner and Russ 1992). Research in archaeological middens in the Outer Hebrides shows that degraded cattle and sheep dung, as well as peat, can be identified by discrete phytolith suites (Powers-Jones 1994).

The small size of phytoliths creates difficulties in separating them from sedimentary matrices, where they tend to concentrate in the chemically similar silt fraction. They are separated from other sedimentary components by heavy-liquid flotation and centrifuging with deflocculation to separate them from clays. Pearsall (1989: 356–404) summarized a number of experimental laboratory methods for preparations of phytoliths, leading toward standardization. Counts of identifiable classes and degraded specimens are displayed in formats like those of pollen analysis. In the

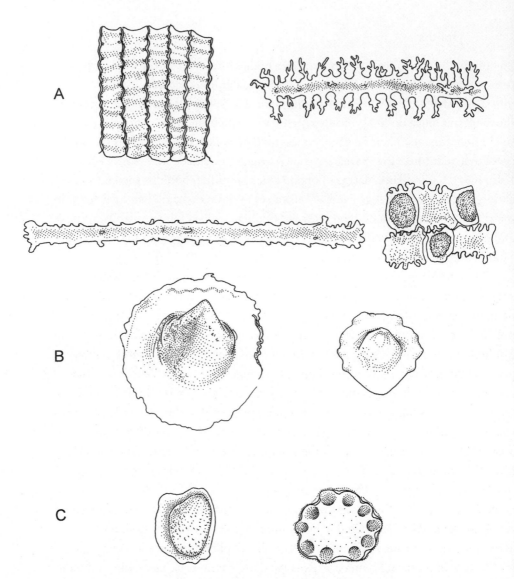

Figure 13.8 Selected phytolith shapes from Old World cereals, few of which are strongly diagnostic. A. Sheet elements from epidermal surfaces of oats (2), wheat, and rye-grass; B. Long cell appendages from oats and wheat; C. Epidermal cell elements from rye-grass and wheat. (After Kaplan et al. 1992: Figs. 8.2–9, 19–22, scales diverse. Identification and explanations are in the original source.)

current developing state of phytolith analysis, interpretation is best supported by comparison with patterns of pollen and other paleoenvironmental indicators.

Phytoliths have been recovered from contexts other than sediments, including tooth calculus (Middleton and Rovner 1994), cooking residues (Pearsall 1989: 312), and the working edges of flint tools. In those contexts they have explicitly archaeological implications for human activities and environments.

CHEMICAL TRACES AND PROXY DATA

Subcellular plant remains in the form of ratios of stable isotopes and **chemical residues** also provide data on former vegetation. Chemical analyses of tissue constituents and residues retrieved from sediments, soils, and cooking and storage vessels can indicate the past presence of plant taxa that have left no visible remains.

Stable isotopes

Plants use solar energy to synthesize organic compounds by photosynthesis. There is more than one way to do it. Three photosynthetic pathways are recognized: C_3 (Calvin, with 3 carbon atoms in a primary compound), C_4 (Hatch-Slack, with 4 carbon atoms), and CAM (crassulacean acid metabolism), which involves aspects of the other two, according to available light and moisture. Since the photosynthetic paths involve different degrees of discrimination against heavy carbon isotopes, they are distinguished analytically by their ratios of stable carbon isotopes ($^{13}C/^{12}C$) (O'Leary 1988). C_4 plants discriminate less against ^{13}C (that is, utilize more) than do C_3 plants, and therefore their photosynthetic compounds have higher values of ^{13}C (expressed as less negative $\delta^{13}C$) in comparison to an established standard (Table 8.1). Photosynthetic pathways differ among taxa, reflecting adaptations to diverse regimes of temperature, moisture, and possibly light. "At different temperatures it pays to gather gas in different ways" (Colinvaux 1981: 5). CAM plants are typically desert succulents; C_3 plants characterize temperate regions; subtropical grasses constitute a major C_4 group. Because the pathways differ among environments, isotope ratios in plant tissues are proxies for regimes of temperature and effective moisture.

The ratios of heavy to light isotopes continue through the food chain, from plants to herbivores, to carnivores and omnivores, and can be measured in the tissues of consumers. Fortuitously, the C_4 group includes major subtropical human food plants such as maize, sorghum, millet, rice, and sugar cane. When such plants are introduced and cultivated in temperate environments naturally dominated by C_3 plants, their isotopic signature values can be read in the tissues of consumers.

Significant research in prehistoric human and animal diets is founded on this observation (van der Merwe 1992). Such research, based on animal tissues, is discussed further in Part VII.

Analysis of plant tissue fragments from soils and sediments shows isotope values varying regularly by altitude on the slopes of an African mountain as a result of adaptations to conditions of light and moisture (Tieszen et al. 1979). The phenomenon offers an approach to tracking climate change and vegetation responses (Ambrose and Sikes 1991). Especially where moisture regimes are close to critical values, habitat change would stimulate adaptive response from plants, normally by changes in distribution or proportional representation of species within the vegetation. It is not necessary that the tissues be closely identified to taxa in order to serve as isotope proxies of vegetation changes but, of course, identification improves sampling control.

Chemical residues

Examination of food residues adhering to cooking vessels is a promising line of inquiry into chemical analyses of plant constituents in human foods. After a slow start, the literature is growing in specificity and breadth (Biers and McGovern 1990; Charters et al. 1993; Fankhauser 1994; White and Page 1992). Both wet and dry analytical methods are showing success. Various lipids (fat molecules) have been extracted from ceramics and chemically identified to plant sources (Evershed 1993; Heron and Evershed 1993). For example, analysis of pots from an early medieval site in central England has indicated the cooking of cabbage or turnip leaves and also leeks (Evershed et al. 1992: 203), an indication of recipes to come. Cacao residues have been identified in Maya food vessels (Hall et al. 1990), in an area where plant remains are rare. A glimpse of the future is provided by Hillman and his colleagues (1993), who find that "long-chain lipid systems offer greater potential than proteins and carbohydrates as they are less vulnerable to fungal and bacterial attack." Work continues to refine methods, identify complications, improve experimental controls, and reduce costs and processing time.

Research on trace elements and crucial molecules that can identify vegetatively reproductive plants has achieved preliminary results in Peru (Ugent 1994). The classic trace element suites of nitrogen and strontium ratios in animal bones, long used to distinguish plant from animal dietary emphases, must be refined to escape from some long-standing abuses of interpretation (Radosevich 1993).

Methods under development for utilization of chemical residues in paleoenvironmental research include extraction of DNA from plant residues, and trace chemical analyses. The literature is currently experimental and partly unevaluated, but improving (Andrews 1994). At present, plant DNA seems better preserved and easier to clone (Weising et al. 1995), under many conditions, than animal DNA, which is particularly susceptible to fungal contaminants.

Proxy data for paleobotany

Indirect evidence for past vegetation and human use of plants comes from both natural and purely cultural (artifactual) sources. Gross aspects of plant associations can be inferred from paleosols, since vegetation is a prime soil-forming factor (Chapter 11). Forest soils contrast significantly with soils formed under grasslands; in the absence of identifiable plant remains in soils, such basic differences can usually be distinguished, although chronology is likely to be problematic. The addition of paleoclimatic information can strengthen the inference or at least restrict alternatives. Reconstructed ancient landforms and hydrography help narrow the range of possible vegetation types by implicating constraints such as elevation, slope, and drainage.

When something is known of past faunal associations, analog arguments can suggest likely foods for herbivores and habitats for animals whose ecological requirements are well known. Age is a limiting condition for such inferences, because the further the analogy must be stretched from present conditions, the less likely is a good match to past conditions and therefore the weaker the analogy. For example, insects often have narrow ecological niches, being adapted to particular plant species, but because many are genetically very plastic they are not dependable indicators of past vegetation. Beetles, which apparently rely more on migration to suitable environments than on genetic adaptation, have been a useful exception to the rule on insects. Small herbivorous mammals are comparable to mobile beetles in this respect; they contribute to vegetation reconstructions in many investigations. Herbivores such as terrestrial mollusks may be useful indicators of past vegetation associations. Snail sequences recovered from pits and ditches at the Danebury hillfort, in England, implicated a period of reforestation after site abandonment (Evans 1984). Stable carbon isotope ratios in animal tissues can help refine gross estimates of past vegetation by implicating proportionate consumption of C_3, C_4, or CAM groups.

Artifacts representing identifiable plants are excellent evidence of what the artificer has perceived. Drawings and sculptures of plants from archaeological periods as ancient as the Upper Paleolithic provide such information. As with artifactual data of all kinds, however, the source is not specifiable from the findspot or associations. Portable plants smaller than shrubs and plant organs such as fruits and seeds may have been accessible to an artist who was never within many miles or hundreds of kilometers of the home soil of a given plant. Depictions of plant associations, such as the marsh panoramas in Egyptian tombs, are excellent evidence of habitats closely observed, whose locations might be inferred from their characteristics.

CODA

Plants and bacteria that make food (autotrophs) are fundamental to life and nearly ubiquitous. Plant remains in great variety are preserved differentially in dry, wet, or charred condition, and as pollen, spores, phytoliths, crystals, molecules, DNA, isotope ratios, and suites of trace elements. Artifacts provide indirect evidence. Archaeologists who maximize the amount and diversity of recovered plant remains, and diversify laboratory analyses, enhance studies of prehistoric human paleoecology and behavior in many disciplines.

VEGETATION IN PALEOECOLOGY

[I]nterpreting palaeoecological data is rarely a matter of unambiguous, objective certainty.

OLDFIELD 1993: 16

Vegetation, with bacteria, is the foundation of the biosphere, the base of the food chain, the mediator of atmospheric composition, the organizer of the water cycle, and the pulverizer of the geosphere. Human biological and cultural adaptations today and in the past grow out of relationships with plant communities at all scales, and must be understood in those contexts. This chapter presents some basic concepts of ecology and **paleoecology** (the application of principles from the ecology of living systems to the study of organisms in environments no longer directly observable), and indicates some methods for achieving knowledge of aspects of past vegetation states and conditions and the mutual relationships between those and human societies.

ASSEMBLING THE DATABASE

Paleoenvironmental reconstruction begins with defining, assembling, and describing the data available, and moves on to interpretation. Again, description and interpretation must be separate and sequential, although ideally there are reflexive loops in each process.

The diversity of data sources for paleovegetation is advantageous since the entire set is rarely if ever available at once. As discussed in Chapter 13, plant and animal remains, soils classes and distributions, paleotopography and paleohydrology, paleoclimate data, and ecological theory all potentially contribute to reconstructions. Data can be assembled from archaeological sites (on-site data) or from the locale and region (off-site data). The more diverse the data and the sources, the more reliable the results. The best information comes from research projects clearly defined and structured so that sampling has been broad, careful, and suitable to the goals. Samples from a range of contexts, comparable in size and consistent in collection methods, are the only sound basis for evaluating taphonomy, and thus the biological entities sampled (M. K. Jones 1991; Prentice 1988). In addition, the chronological resolution of samples must be adequate for the scale of reconstruction attempted.

Vegetative data

Plant parts and fragments – macrofossils – are direct evidence for past vegetation. As discussed in Chapter 13, their interpretation in terms of standing vegetation and associations requires knowledgeable awareness of sources and of agents of transport and deposition, as well as preservation and recovery biases. When these taphonomic and sampling factors are well controlled, macrofossils provide direct evidence for vegetative habitats.

Plant microfossils (pollen, spores, and phytoliths) are far more numerous and widespread than macrofossils. Chapter 13 explains how the assumptions and methods for constructing pollen diagrams smooth and generalize the diversity and dynamism of biotic systems. Phytoliths, which like pollen are also limited in taxonomic specificity, are more reliably local in origin than is pollen. Palynologists compensate for lost detail by utilizing statistical and graphic techniques for displaying dynamics at appropriately large scales, such as regional- and continental-scale maps of plant ranges (Grimm 1988). Analytical techniques such as large sample counts, close-interval sampling, expanded recording of NAP, and pollen concentration and influx calculations benefit archaeologists by conserving details in historical reconstructions based on pollen.

Pollen derived from anthropogenic deposits presents a special set of problems and opportunities (Davis and Overs 1995; Dimbleby 1985). Taphonomic problems dominate. Pollen in sites may be derived and redeposited by natural and cultural means; it is brought into settlement areas on clothes and animals, in food and fodder and excrement, in bedding and floor covering and roofing material, in peat fuel, bulk commodities, cultivated plants, ritual behavior, and many other ways. In addition, the mode and seasonality of site use is likely to influence the kinds of pollen that predominate in the deposits. Other forms of persistent remains, principally phytoliths and residues, are indicative of ancient plants (Chapter 13).

Climatic data

Typically, paleoclimatic reconstructions are heavily reliant upon vegetation proxy data. As GCM approximations increase in complexity, they become both more accurate and less directly reliant upon pollen distributions. Meanwhile, a lively debate continues about the degree to which climate controls plant distributions and the speed by which vegetation associations respond to climate change (see discussion of this issue below).

Certainly, alternating glacial and interglacial climatic regimes strongly influenced the distributions and durations of plant **formations** (the plant component of a biome) at large scales (Fig. 14.1). Just as certainly, modern correlations between plant associations and local climates have been poor guides to past conditions in the fossil records. The no-analog problems in pollen spectra and other ancient data sets must cool enthusiasm for vegetation reconstructions based on modern analogs.

What is clear is that most plant species, especially the long-lived trees, withstand short periods of unfavorable climate by slowing metabolism and survive to thrive in improving conditions. Climatic forcing is most effective at the edges of species distributions where favorable climates support range extensions or unfavorable climates suppress growth and ultimately cause local extinctions. The resolutions of paleoclimate reconstructions available now are not fine enough to be helpful in modeling plant associations or distributions in the past at local scales. When locally relevant data from non-vegetative sources strongly implicate climatic conditions known to be favorable or unfavorable to specific species, those interpretations should be considered useful controls for vegetative reconstructions based on other data sets. At the very least, there is no point in modeling a **mesic** (temperate) forest on paleosols that reflect development under arid conditions. A basic congruence among the full suite of data sets is the minimal requirement for a realistic reconstruction of vegetation.

Topographical data (geomorphology and hydrography)

Similarly, while topographical data may at first glance offer little to vegetative reconstructions, the congruence rule (Chapter 2) assures the relevance of topography. Critical variables such as elevation, relief, aspect, slope, water table, and hydrography constrain potential vegetation at any location. These variables may or may not be straightforward. In tectonically active terrain none of them can be taken on faith without investigation of the prehistoric stability of the locales.

Even outside dramatically unstable terrain, surfaces on unconsolidated materials

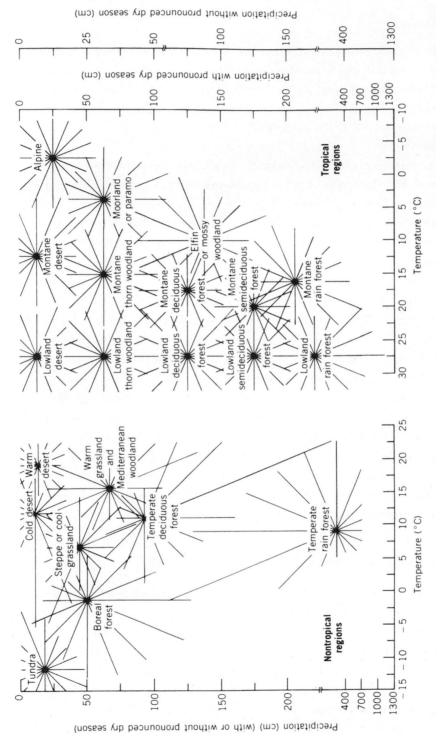

Figure 14.1 Major vegetation formations related to present climates. Horizontal axes are average annual temperature clines; vertical axes are average annual precipitation. (Reproduced with per- mission from Forman and Godron 1986: Fig. 2.4. © 1986 by John Wiley & Sons, Inc.)

may be significantly recent. Large-scale erosion can change slope, elevation, and drainage fairly rapidly, as we saw in the case studies on valley fills in Part V. Anthropogenic changes of this kind have modified landscapes and entailed vegetative adaptations in both tropical and temperate zones at least since the beginnings of farming (Bell and Boardman 1992). More recently, extensive deforestation related to industrial development has been a major contributor to erosion, landslides, and valley-fill episodes worldwide. Such landform perturbation both follows and forces changes in vegetation.

Paleotopography can be especially important near the seacoast, notoriously variable in the last million years. Sea-level changes affect the elevation, slope, and shape of landforms, the height of water table, and the chemistry of air and water – all directly influencing plant habitats. Although the scale of the changes may be small, their ecological effects are large.

Soils data

Soils are crucial repositories for the diverse plant remains discussed above. They also contain evidence of past states of geomorphology and hydrography. Because of their wealth of direct and indirect evidence for vegetation, soils have come to play central roles in paleoecological studies in archaeology (Chapters 11 and 12).

Paleosols can be useful proxies for vegetation at local to regional scales, when used with awareness of process. Since living organisms are important soil-forming factors, past vegetation leaves some relatively persistent signatures in soils. Vegetation formations such as forests, grasslands, heaths, and bogs shape their characteristic soils' chemistries, textures, and profiles. Because other soil-forming factors are also active, paleovegetation signatures fade in time to reflect later conditions. The strongest paleovegetation evidence is preserved in buried soils as chemical and material signatures. Relict soils at or near the surface do not retain reliable evidence for old vegetation assemblages. When observed soil characteristics are employed in paleoenvironmental reconstruction, it is important to be aware of the central role of time in the process of soils formation. Soils development is not only progressive but also mutable and even reversible. Soil pH drops through time with base leaching. Acidic conditions may support the development of hardpans that impede drainage and degrade soils. Changes in water tables revise the conditions for plant life.

Soils maps, created for economic development, have been utilized for decades for information about vegetation patch structure and major associations and distributions in and near archaeological sites. Their utility varies with the taxonomic system they are based on (Chapter 11) and the amount of climate and vegetation change intervening between them and the target age. Soils maps offer the best foundation currently available for giving pollen data spatial distributions at the local scale. They can reward the effort required to overcome their idiosyncrasies and limitations for paleoecology (Retallack 1990). Regional-scale pollen diagrams are poorly suited to such applications, which require data at the scale of the soils maps if the results are to transcend triviality and circular reasoning.

Faunal data

The fate of animals as individuals and populations is dependent on plants at the base of the food chain (trophic ladder). Information about the presence and distribution of herbivores is useful proxy data in paleovegetation modeling when employed with awareness of the problems of scale, source, contemporaneity, and congruence. Because such interpretations normally are analog arguments, it is well to keep in mind that species niches are mutable, and avoid extending analogies to extinct taxa. Chapters 15 and 16 address paleofaunal reconstructions in more detail.

Large animals are useful vegetation proxies only at large scales; they may indicate changes in plant formations that take place slowly over large areas, such as succession between forests and grasslands. For archaeologists, smaller animals are more informative. Rodents and lagomorphs especially, with their small home ranges, are excellent indicator species for biomes. An unusual instance of plant formation data derived from faunal remains is reported from Alabama, in the southeastern United States, where a cultural cave deposit yielded over 3000 identifiable bird bones in an extensive faunal assemblage including 21 taxonomic families and 70 species. The majority of the birds were aquatic and semi-aquatic, while prairie chickens indicated nearby grassland or savanna habitats throughout the 9000-year duration of the deposits. Other birds implicated forests on the bluffs and riverbanks (Parmalee 1993).

In herbivore remains, plant information is where you find it. Tooth form alone implicates the general niches of extinct proboscidians: mastodonts as browsers, mammoths as grazers. Masticated plant tissues have been recovered as **boluses** from bison teeth (Akersten et al. 1988), and phytoliths identified in tooth calculus (Middleton and Rovner 1994). Stable isotope ratios of carbon and nitrogen extracted from collagen in animal tissues enable insights into the vegetation of their habitats (e.g., Ambrose and DeNiro 1989). Microfauna such as insects and soil mollusks are data sources for local habitat conditions and their own preferred foods (e.g., Elias 1994; Thomas 1985). Microfauna richly complement pollen analyses and can substitute for the latter in alkaline soils inimical to pollen. Evans (1991) presents an approach for inferring vegetation from terrestrial molluskan assemblages that mini-

Table 14.1 Exponential scales in space and time[a]

Spatial scales	Area (km^2)	Ecological units (paleo- and neo-)
Mega-	global: 5.1×10^8 continental: $<10^8$	biosphere
Macro-	physiographic province: $10^{4-}10^7$	formation
Meso-	regional: $10^2–10^4$ locality: $1–10^2$	biome mosaic? association
Micro-	local: <1 km^2	fossil assemblage biotope; patch

Temporal scales	Duration or frequency (yrs)	Units
Mega-	$>10^6$	eons; eras
Macro-	$10^4–10^6$	epoch
Meso-	$10^2–10^4$	century; millennium
Micro-	<10	years

Note: [a] Each higher unit incorporates and generalizes all those below. Scales in the two dimensions are not closely linked.

mizes reliance on analogs; he warns that archaeological contexts as well as modern ones are likely to be influenced by human activities. Insect remains complement other data about plant assemblages and formations. Their adaptability in respect to habitat requirements eliminates most herbivorous insects as sources of novel or fine-scale information about plants; even symbiotic links to specific plants can evolve rapidly.

SCALES OF RECONSTRUCTION

Reconstructing past vegetation associations at scales from the continental to the backyard is a major goal of paleoenvironmental archaeology (Table 14.1). Just as archaeological science at its best has not succeeded in bringing past human communities to full life, paleoecological science cannot do that for other aspects of paleo-biotas. The full vitality of past life cannot be regained. Important aspects of its composition and complexity can be described, and the direction and magnitude of its differences from today may be realized. What can be achieved is more impressive every year, despite maturing awareness of the equifinalities and uncertainties of the task.

Mega-scale (global: 5.1×10^8 and continental: $<10^8$)

Reconstruction of vegetation at the scale of the biosphere is the domain of paleo-climatologists, who began the compilation of worldwide data for GCMs (CLIMAP 1976; COHMAP 1988). The broadest patterns of climate rule at this scale, defining the sequential changes and spatial patterns of vegetation. There is no better source of vegetation information at this scale than compilations of pollen diagrams. Paleontological distributions of herbivores are useful indicators. The global scale is appropriate for archaeologists working in long time spans and evolutionary perspectives over the last 2 to 3 million years, the period during which humans expanded into habitats beyond their subtropical environments of origin.

Continental-scale mapping of paleovegetation involves phytogeographers as well as paleoclimatologists. The first large-scale isopoll maps, spun off the projects that produced CLIMAP and COHMAP, changed conceptions of vegetation history with their clear demonstration of the no-analog problem (Bernabo and Webb 1977; Delcourt and Delcourt 1981; Huntley and Birks 1983). Those in turn revolutionized archaeological approaches to paleoecological modeling. At the continental scale, vegetation influences the quality of human and all other lives, and establishes the parameters of biomes. Recent interest in life at this scale ("macroecology": Brown and Maurer 1989) acknowledges the importance of large-scale patterning for the diversity and complexity of life. For cultural history and human behavior, however, continental-scale patterning is background.

Macro-scale (subcontinental: 10^4–10^7 km^2)

Paleoclimatologists and phytogeographers modeling vegetation at the macro-scale realized that the resolution of maps was constrained by spatial differences in the quality and density of pollen studies. In addition, the imposed generalization of spatial distributions in isopoll maps and of temporal change in isochrone maps suppress the representation of diversity and dynamism in plant formations. Archaeological use of such maps has not always reflected awareness of these limitations. Large-scale cultural patterning is appropriately modeled at this scale; behavior is not. There is no site-scale relevance in subcontinental-scale maps of vegetation formations. Such maps do provide excellent heuristics for considering large-scale historical processes in the revegetation of deglaciated landscapes, as the best of them clearly demonstrate (e.g., Delcourt et al. 1983; Gaudreau and Webb 1985; Huntley and Birks 1983; Jacobson et al. 1987).

At the macro-scale, both climate and topography control the composition and structure of plant formations. Soils, at the scale of soil Orders, are influential. Herbivores, including insects and some pathogens, can change the structure and diversity at this scale for relatively short periods of time; more typically their effects are expressed at smaller scales. Humans are an important exception; prehistorically, human influences were not salient at the macro-scale, but they have become increasingly significant definers of the composition and structure of plant formations. Today humans are the **keystone species** worldwide, influencing the composition of biota.

Pollen analysis remains the principal source of information about plant history at subcontinental scale. The best data for large-scale vegetation histories come in pollen cores from lakes with large catchments. Data from many such sources are evaluated and compiled by comparing chronologies and pollen zonations. Vegetation formations so defined are high-level generalizations, losing significant resolution of diversity (Prentice 1985).

Meso-scales (locality and regional: $>1–10^4$ km^2)

Vegetation reconstruction at the regional scale remains the domain of phytogeographers, who typically work at larger scales. Nevertheless, their work has been seized upon by archaeologists eager to utilize the most recent or detailed isopoll and pollen isochrone maps and GIS plots. Archaeologists rarely have been informed consumers of such data, failing to notice that the detail and resolution lost in compiling data at the subcontinental scale cannot be reconstructed by simply enlarging map segments. The lost detail hinders archaeological interpretation of behavior and resource patterning. Improvement of this situation requires innovative cooperation of archaeologists with phytogeographers in order to retain details from many sampling sites and, rather than generalizing, to interpret them in terms of diversity and patterning (Gaudreau 1988).

The most reliable data sources for regional-scale plant paleoecology are pollen from lakes and large bogs (Larsen and MacDonald 1993; Prentice 1985), macrofossils from multiple sample sites, and remains of medium- to large-sized herbivores. While pollen diagrams emphasize arboreal taxa at the generic level, macrofossils provide species data. Macrofossils from anywhere but archaeological sites and alluvium have the additional virtue of likely originating near where they are found. Compilations of pollen (including NAP) and macrofossil data from as many sites as possible within a region build a picture of the diversity and grain of plant distributions in the past, which can be compared and evaluated against other paleodata and modern distributions. In the display and comparison of such information at this and larger scales, GIS methods come into their own (Allen et al. 1990; Goodchild et al. 1993).

The salient determinants of vegetation environments at the regional scale are soils and topography, particularly relief and elevation. The most important climate component at this scale is effective precipitation. Herbivores and plant pathogens can be influential in cyclical changes. The palynological literature is beginning to be informative about regional-scale anthropogenic effects, typically expressed as fire records in pollen cores and the appearance of weedy species indicative of disturbance (Behre 1981, 1986; Edwards 1982; McAndrews 1988). Vegetative replacement sequences are easily seen at this scale, where they may be studied for information about climate, competition, range adjustments, and the chronology of ecosystem evolution.

The regional scale is socially relevant for human communities, well worth efforts to understand the structure and composition of its vegetation. The regional environment should have been reasonably familiar to everyone through social networking and resource procurement. Prior to development of metallurgy and urban centers, raw materials for clothing, structures, tools of all sizes, and food were likely derived from within this spatial scale. Site catchments typically fit within it. Of course, individual and unusual items on sites may represent exchange over considerable distances beyond the region. Anthropogenic effects on the vegetation environment should be visible at the regional scale when chronological control is tight. The region is significant to all biological entities; smaller scales of habitat are embedded in it and constrained by it. With greater age and the loss of fine detail in the archaeological and paleoecological record, the analytical importance of the regional scale increases.

Localities

As at the regional scale, innovative methods are necessary for successful paleovegetation reconstruction at the scale of localities. With good chronological control, all the high-resolution techniques developed for site-scale research can be applied both on-site and off at the locality scale. Archaeologists must work closely with palynologists to achieve analyses that can support interpretations of local diversity and particularity. Fine-scale work of the sort now done in site soils could be expanded to locality scales. Attention to multiple samples, large pollen counts, identification of rare specimens and particularly NAP, and complementary data on macrofossils and paleontology will support more realistic estimates of species composition and vegetation structure. Human communities subsist mainly on local plant associations, directly and indirectly.

When conditions are optimal for pollen recovery, locality-scale data can provide detailed pictures of local vegetation sequences and the effects of human activities. In an upland area in southern Wales including a Mesolithic knapping site, multiple samples in a peat blanket allowed investigators to follow vegetation sequences from the eighth millennium B.P. An early Holocene woodland was burned, damaging soil and initiating heath formation. Subsequently, small fires in the locale kept trees from invading the heath, with the effect of improving grazing for large herbivores. Impermeable soils under the heath supported the spread of blanket peat after the mid-Holocene. Small areas of woodland, reed swamp, and woody fen were recognized, demonstrating the patch structure of the ancient vegetation. The several fire episodes were of small extent and different ages, leading the investigators to conclude that the pattern is better explained by anthropogenic burning than by climate change (Smith and Cloutman 1988).

Archaeological (micro-) scales (typically less than 1 km²)

Reliable data for local vegetation reconstruction must be sought where they occur, with awareness of the range of possibilities at micro-scales. Archaeologists require small-scale data with close chronological tolerances and fine detail, especially in respect to the non-arboreal flora that provides so much human food and craft materials. For such information plant macrofossils, phytoliths, isotope ratios, and residues are already productive and promise more to come. Proxy data such as soils types and small and microscopic animals are still underutilized, despite being widely available (Avery 1982; Evans 1991). The challenge is to recover suitable materials during excavation, being alert to the range of data and the discipline required to control contexts.

The pervasiveness of human influence on pollen deposition within sites has been demonstrated by Dimbleby (1985) and many others. In a sensitive interpretation of a nineteenth-century industrial residential area, Kelso (1993) used multidisciplinary evidence and texts in conjunction with pollen data to show how human activities disrupt both vegetation and pollen deposition and influence the on-site record of pollen sedimentation. With the pollen record he was able to demonstrate differences in residential land use between mill workers and managers, showing how those also influenced micro-scale pollen deposition and preservation.

Samples may be taken both off-site and on-site. Closely spaced samples along transects give excellent resolution of local vegetative patchiness (patchy distribution), as demonstrated by studies of a small Yorkshire stream catchment (Turner et al. 1993). Sampling of interior spaces (e.g., caves, houses) requires techniques that are sensitive to the variety of special circumstances involved, such as airflow patterns, access to airborne pollen, and the potential multiplicity of pollen vectors. Coles and

Gilbertson (1994) describe a study of pollen deposition within caves that displays the difficulties and the rewards; although their situation was unusually difficult, the lessons are applicable to other cave studies and to the evaluation of pollen signatures from enclosed or semi-enclosed rooms.

Pollen cores from small ponds or depositional basins are helpful when the collection points are close to an archaeological site (Burden et al. 1986; Edwards 1991). Macrofossils and residues can be directly dated by AMS, improving chronological control. Soils micromorphology can identify relict soil conditions, including changes in such characteristics as drainage. Remains of small non-food animals can help date and specify aspects of ground cover and undergrowth in the vicinity (e.g., Evans 1984). Plant materials represented in artifacts or raw materials, because they may originate far from the site where they were recovered, are not reliable data for paleovegetation investigations. Non-cultural deposits such as packrat middens are useful when locally available (Betancourt et al. 1990).

Phytogeography at the site scale should include mapping of present vegetation on transects or quadrats for comparison with modern pollen rain (Bryant and Hall 1993). This is the best foundation for interpreting ancient pollen rain and macrofossil distributions, which are compared to modern conditions by means of difference or dissimilarity statistics. Ancient and modern plant and pollen distributions plotted onto soils maps reveal changes due to anthropogenic, edaphic, or climatic developments.

All archaeological macrofossil assemblages have environmental implications at some scale, although archaeologists more usually emphasize the economic significance of such materials. Materials utilized in paleoenvironmental interpretations from archaeological sites must be critically evaluated to determine their taphonomic status as either naturally or anthropogenically deposited. For example, scattered charcoal fragments in site soils likely have many depositional histories, making them poor choices for paleoenvironmental reconstructions of any sort (Hally 1981; Minnis 1981). Tracking the source areas of plant materials found on sites helps to define site catchment areas, and thus the spaces and habitats significant for a human community. Interpretation of the range of plant materials found can indicate the diversity of utilized environments, some of which may be located at great distances. Distributions of plant remains across a site or region, when not obviously related to environmental parameters, can indicate human manipulation of either the source or depositional environments. All such analyses require close chronological resolution to be maximally useful; the smaller the spatial scale implicated, the more exact the chronology must be to minimize interpretational distortion.

The suite of plant materials recovered from site-scale investigations represents only an assemblage of plant remains and proxies – an assemblage partly formed with cultural criteria specific to the site residents and the investigators. Claims that the materials represent a natural association of any kind would entail a rigorous demonstration based on sound ecological principles and exhaustive taphonomic analyses. This is not to deny that indications of plant associations may be recovered. The paleoenvironmental literature offers notable instances of the recognition of local patches of special vegetation (e.g., Turner and Peglar 1988) and of local vegetation burns and landscape sequences (Smith and Cloutman 1988). The best instances of such demonstrations result from combining microfaunal data with plant remains from well-dated on-site contexts (e.g., Allen and Robinson 1993). Such small-scale reconstructions benefit from interpretation within the larger context of regional-scale investigations, where the prevalent patterning of diverse vegetation associations can be evaluated.

The special virtues of site-scale data are the details they provide on vegetal environments valued, tolerated, and utilized by people – intimate glimpses of human habitats and niche behavior. The remains recovered represent choices made by inhabitants of the site, not all of whom were human. Anthropogenic influences on plant associations and distributions may be visible, if not always interpretable. Thus, site-specific data and the inferences drawn from them must not be pressed too hard into the service of larger-scale paleoenvironmental understandings.

Vegetation study at the site scale aids identification of items of diet (see below). When dietary items can be defined, it is possible to consider the effects on the landscape of human preferences for those vegetative species, whether cultivated or not.

COMMUNITIES IN PALEOECOLOGY

> Death and the passage of time transform living ecological communities into the assemblages which are exhumed by paleoecologists and archaeologists. The analysis of these remains provides the best, and often the only, indication of the composition of the original community.
>
> GEE AND GILLER 1991: 1

In significant contrast to the physical systems of the atmosphere and geosphere, systems in the biosphere are characterized by openness and thus are not predictable at medium and large scales. The inherent dynamism and responsiveness of open systems precludes confident, bounded predictions of either past or future states and conditions.

Community concept

> [T]here are aspects of contemporary ecological practice and theory that will benefit
> environmental archaeologists, and others that in their present state will not.
>
> GEE AND GILLER 1991: 10

Historically, the discipline of plant ecology developed under the guidance of an organismic concept of biological communities as coexisting groups (societies) of species which changed along predictable trajectories toward mature "climax" formations defined by climate, which was itself considered stable within observed limits. The term "community" carried connotations of organization and structured interaction among associated organisms, with structure conceived along two analytical dimensions. One dimension involved resource partitioning in space, including competitive interactions; the other involved "networks" of predation and dependency (food webs) or, alternatively, the hierarchy of **trophic levels** (feeding levels involving food producers, consumers, secondary consumers [carnivores], and decomposers). The idea of structured interactions carries the further implication that communities might be products of co-evolution and therefore recurrent entities, with stability being characteristic of climax associations. This concept of community was influential in the ecosystem models introduced by the mid-twentieth century (Golley 1993).

Recently observation, experiment, and mathematical modeling have shown that "communities" observable in the present are essentially short-term, scale-dependent associations of species, variable in time and space. Associations at local scales are the stages where competition is enacted. Observations of species at local scales reveal that competitive interactions do not always have the same outcomes, casting serious doubt on the theoretical defensibility of the concept of communities co-evolving along predictable trajectories (Gee and Giller 1991; Kikkawa and Anderson 1986; Tilman 1988). Randomness and historical factors play larger roles than were realized: the role of initial conditions (contingencies) in historical trajectories has been underestimated (Table 14.2). Among biologists the concept of community has been redefined into a heuristic research approach (Anderson and Kikkawa 1986; Hoffman 1979), a familiar label for "synecology" – the study of organisms in ecological relationships with specifiable habitats at several scales (Birks and Birks 1980: 26, 232; Moore et al. 1991: 7; Tallis 1991).

Community ecology continues as an active and healthy discipline, pursued in both field studies and experiments, featuring lively controversies about the nature of life and living creatures (Allen and Hoekstra 1992). The community concept has been notably productive in elucidating interactive processes in dynamic **biocoenoses** (living associations), particularly those processes involved in resource partitioning.

Table 14.2 Some determinants of plant associations

- Insolation (aspect, latitude, elevation)
- Temperature (latitude, elevation, aspect, wind direction and speed, season, continentality)
- Effective precipitation (rainfall, wind speed, temperature, drainage)
- Substrate (texture, chemistry, available nutrients, depth, maturity)
- Availability of parent populations (distance, physical barriers)
- Propagule dispersal mechanisms and vectors
- Age of association
- Competition
- Pathologies
- Predation (herbivory)
- Frequency of disturbances

Process models are the strength of ecological studies of biological interactions. The results of such study are essential to paleoecology for explaining the observed dynamism which, nevertheless, can be extended into past associations only analogically. Contrasts between the data sets and analytical concepts available to "neoecologists" working with living communities and to paleoecologists working with death assemblages are succinctly and clearly summarized for archaeologists by Gee and Giller (1991). Dodd and Stanton (1990) and chapters in volumes edited by Diamond and Case (1985) and Gee and Giller (1986) consider the issues for biologists.

Much of the quantitative strength of **neoecology** (the study of living communities) is inaccessible to paleoecology as presently practiced (Barber 1991). Community ecology is at its best when quantification is possible for constituents and processes such as species abundances, trophic levels, competition, reproduction rates, and replacement rates. Quantification is rarely possible in paleoenvironmental reconstructions, which deal best with qualitative aspects of past plant associations. Despite the attractiveness of some concepts of community ecology, there are benefits in avoiding the conceptual baggage of the term "community" in paleoenvironmental reconstructions, and dealing instead with species associations, biomes, and ecosystems at relevant, diverse scales. The extent that even those can be inferred from death assemblages remains a salient problem of paleoecology. Archaeologists can use neo-ecological data and methods for their special purposes only to the extent that they understand the strengths and limitations barely indicated here (Delcourt and Delcourt 1981; Tallis 1981).

Any paleolandscape is the result of partitioning of resources among all its living inhabitants. The ecological concept of niche is helpful in understanding how this partitioning takes place. Each kind of organism is potentially able to exist in a finite range of physical and biological conditions; that range is the "fundamental," or **potential niche**. The limits of the potential niche are defined by the organism's success in acquiring, in the presence of competitors, the resources essential for its well-being and procreation. The conditions under which organisms of one kind are usually successful on those terms are the **realized niche** of the species.

The niche concept applied to plants has been frequently utilized in paleoenvironmental studies as a guide to associations and to scaling the distributions of species. Once the limitations of the community concept for paleoecology were fully realized, the usefulness of the niche concept in reconstructions faded. The only method available for modeling the potential niches of plants is extrapolation from current observations. The only aspect of niche ecology that is observable is realized niches contingent on modern conditions. Plants growing today cannot be expected to display the full range of their genetic potential in the face of the limited diversity, stability, and duration of Holocene environments affected by people. It follows logically, therefore, that plant potential niches are imperfectly known, and once back in time among no-analog conditions we cannot rely on current knowledge to model the past. These constraints necessarily reflect poorly on the "indicator species" approach to the descriptive reconstruction of ancient plant associations, which suffers from the same limitations for predictions as do other analog models.

A genuine landscape paleoecology awaits the development of methods for recognizing in assemblages of dead organisms indications of relevant controls on species composition and diversity. "No organizing principles exist in nature to order the lives of plants in communities" (Colinvaux 1993: 443). Neoecology demonstrates that temperature, moisture, substrate and soils, topography, species availability, competition, predation, pathogens, fire susceptibility, and human activities, among other things, are involved (e.g., Risser 1987; Table 14.2). While considerable data on these phenomena are retrieved by paleoenvironmental research, details are nevertheless constrained by preservation and recovery conditions, sample resolutions, and chronology (Pilcher 1993).

Plant associations from fossil remains

Of course the greater the degree of spatial and temporal integration that took place as the death assemblage formed, the lesser the degree of spatial and temporal resolution in any conclusions drawn from the analysis of the assemblage.

GEE AND GILLER 1991: 3

A few analytical and interpretive concepts derived from neoecology and ecosystems theory that are commonly invoked in paleoecology merit introduction here. They

shape the kinds of reconstructions paleoecologists offer, with the result that the speculative worlds of paleoecology resemble descriptions typical of modern biocoenoses
and ecosystems. Such reconstructions, it should be clear, are analogs based implicitly
on the community concept and tend to overextend uniformitarianism.

Qualities

Ecologists describe the vegetative components of **ecosystems** in terms of structural
characteristics such as **diversity** or **density** of plant species, patchiness of distribution, and the **biomass** of the standing vegetation (a quasi-quantitative measure of the
standing crop). A more complete picture of an ecosystem includes the animals living
among the plants; that requires consideration of the trophic levels (Chapter 16). The
species diversity and density within a plant association depend on a number of variables that are particular to a time and place (Table 14.2), including the dominant or
keystone species, which may be plants but are more often herbivores.

The ecotone concept has achieved an important role in archaeological modeling
of human resource acquisition behavior because the biologically enriched zone
between areas of contrasting biomes or ecosystems is considered especially attractive
for intensive exploitation or strategic location. Ecotones are notoriously difficult to
define since even the contrastive areas are totally dependent on the scale of observation (Rhoades 1978). Applications of the concept to paleoenvironmental reconstructions are problematic unless supported by independent data on contrastive
substrates or climatic areas.

Processes

The metaphor of plant species "migration" is frequently met in the literature when
range adjustments, or distribution changes, are addressed. Range adjustments by
plant species, discussed below, involve diverse strategies for propagation, dispersal of
propagules, and competition. Distribution changes are best considered in terms of
the mechanisms by which individual species extend or contract their ranges, or the
changed conditions which initiate such responses. Generalizations about mechanisms, effective causes, or strategies can be misleading.

Competition for light, water, and space is fundamental to the maintenance of
species spacing and resource partitioning. Both within and between species, plants
compete actively by means of different requirements for light and water, different
metabolic routes and growth patterns, and by the production of phytotoxins to deter
herbivores or neighbors. Despite the importance of these processes, competitionist
theory in ecology is poorly developed for plants (Grace and Tilman 1990: 232).

The concept of **succession** was formulated by early community ecologists to
explain the sequencing of plant species within a habitat over time, even in the

absence of major climate change. Plants that first colonize bare ground ("pioneers") such as that created, e.g., by flooding, are in time replaced by other suites of species. Although prediction is unsuccessful unless major variables can be held constant, modern census data and computer models demonstrate that pioneer associations are characterized by low competitive pressure, short generation length, moderate diversity, usually low density, and low stability. Primary succession occurs on bare ground; secondary succession is triggered by disturbance in standing vegetation. Because climate and other major influences on plant associations display little constancy, succession is a normal characteristic of vegetation, and needs less explanation than was believed when equilibrium models reigned.

Subsequent to primary succession, the first plants are replaced by associations that display more competition, greater species density and biomass due to the different heights of shrubs and other plants under tree canopies, longer generation length, and greater stability. Eventually, such characteristics of "mature" vegetation associations produce a peak of diversity, followed by a decline, unless development is interrupted by perturbations such as fires, storms, severe insect infestations, or pathogens (Colinvaux 1993). Disturbance sequences must have been observed by prehistoric peoples who managed vegetation by burning to increase the diversity of shrubs and grasses valued as food for people or animals.

Pollen assemblages

Palynologists define pollen "zones" on pollen diagrams to demarcate periods of relatively stable pollen assemblages; for a number of reasons these are not equivalent to plant associations or neoecological communities (Table 14.3; Chapter 13). Permanent or long-lasting species covariance seems restricted to **symbionts** and parasites, at fairly small or intimate spatial scales. These observations lie behind the abandonment of modern plant associations as reliable analogs for past community composition and structure, or species relationships (Gee and Giller 1991). Species associations in the past can be partially inferred on the basis of contexts of recovery. Both the natural and cultural aspects of such contexts are essential to understanding the spatial referents of the associations.

The major restriction on quantification or specificity in paleoecological reconstructions is the taphonomic bias in the material remains of organisms in the fossil record. The depositional, preservational, and retrieval conditions for material remains of past ecosystems render those remains fundamentally incomparable to observable associations of living organisms (Chapter 13). Ancient system states and conditions may be characterized in terms of dissimilarity or divergence from system characteristics observable at present. For example, maps of regional vegetation assemblages in the past can be compared to maps representing the modern pollen

Table 14.3 Limitations of pollen assemblages for paleoecological interpretations

- Pollen is identified at the taxonomic level of genus or higher in most cases, while adaptation takes place at the species level.
- Pollen production and dispersal are unrelated to species numbers in particular places.
- Palynology provides poor discrimination within the NAP group, where important community constituents are represented. This is especially the case in forested environments where tree pollen dominates and masks abundances of smaller plants.
- Palynological samples include little pollen from insect-pollinated flowering plants.
- Modern plant associations used for comparisons or analogs are to unknown degrees unstable, immature, or transitory.
- Environmental tolerances and competitive relationships of species can change through time, weakening comparisons.
- Pollen may be transported from unknowable distances, redeposited from older sediments, and introduced by humans.
- Pollen ratios are affected by disturbance and preservation factors.

rain, and the differences expressed mathematically or descriptively (e.g., Birks and Gordon 1985).

Paleoecologists seeking other means to bring fossil assemblages (**thanato-coenoses**) into some semblance of life turned to "indicator species" for guidance, hoping that species with dependable environmental associations today could be clues to the past, less fraught with complications than "communities." The indicator-species approach assumes unchanging ecological tolerances and static competitive environments (Birks and Birks 1980: 233–255), assumptions that have fared no better than the community analog, as discussed above. The more data available, the less uniformity is observable; the more diversity, the less predictability. Taphonomic histories, informed by sampling theory, are the best means currently available for controlling the links between methods, data, and inferences and implicating some of the crucial initial conditions that have affected change in biological systems. Paleoecologists must respect the data and refrain from pushing the limits more aggressively than information warrants. As data bases and theory grow, surprises do not diminish; they proliferate.

Phytogeography and phytosociology

Pollen diagrams are rich intellectual food for paleoecologists who seek distribution patterns and sequences in data. The study of past vegetation configurations in environmental archaeology is derived from those. However, as death assemblages, pollen suites are not readily amenable to studies of species associations or interactions and therefore of processes of any sort. Carefully used, death assemblages are acceptable bases for describing distributions in terms of presences (never absences) of species and species assemblages.

Phytogeography is concerned with describing and interpreting distributions of plant species in space – the extent of habitats and the associations that occupy them. Isochron and isopoll maps compiled from multiple pollen diagrams are excellent tools for spatial analysis and some paleoecological applications. Taphonomic complications prevent such maps from achieving the degree of temporal and spatial resolution possible with surveys of living plant associations, regardless of the desire of many archaeologists to employ them as if they did. Scale considerations also limit their appropriateness for archaeological modeling. Within the generalizations entailed by sampling errors and age approximations, they are certainly preferable to the use of modern phytogeographical maps that were pressed into archaeological service until quite recently.

Phytosociology began as a method for describing the observed diversity in plant communities and systematizing the results into nested hierarchies, each unit related to a specific range of habitat elements and each successively higher level increasingly generalized (Table 14.4). The approach, actively under development, is widely used in descriptive ecology in Europe (Ellenberg 1988; Küster 1991; Oberdorfer 1979). The method and its assumptions have been criticized for excessive arbitrariness and rigidity, and the system has been ignored in most English-language ecological literature. A notable exception is Jones (1988). Even though phytosociological methods are applicable only to living communities of plants and are inappropriate for paleobotany, aspects of the classificatory hierarchy are referenced by historical phytogeographers in literature archaeologists use. Table 14.4 displays the structure of the terminological scheme so that archaeologists can recognize it.

Vegetation range adjustments in the Pleistocene

The vegetation story following deglaciation everywhere is one of range adjustments as plant taxa recolonized exposed sediments and later the maturing soils. Throughout the Pleistocene, especially in middle to high latitudes, range adjustments were essentially continuous; stability was not reached in any interglacial period. Typically, range expansion in one direction is complemented by range contraction elsewhere. These phenomena, the most obvious examples of instability

Table 14.4 Phytosociological hierarchy

Unit	Suffix	Example
Formation:		water plants; forest
Class	*-etea*	deciduous forests
Order	*-etalia* + modifier	mesophytic deciduous forests
Alliance	*-ion* + modifier	forest of oak and hornbeam, beech forest
Association		"generally . . . the smallest units in the phytosociological system" may be subdivided into Subassociations

Note: The several units are named with basic terms derived from Latin names of plant taxa typical of the unit, with suffixes indicative of the level in the hierarchy. Some terms take modifiers; some are hyphenated compounds. The system was developed in Central and Western Europe and is incomplete, but under development. Although terms from this system are used descriptively in the paleobotanical literature, it is not recommended for archaeobotanists (Hillman 1991; Küster 1991).

in the paleobiological record, represent changes in species distributions, abundances, and associations resulting from many complex factors.

> The main influences upon a [plant] taxon's arrival in any locality are (1) distance from refugia; (2) competitive ability; (3) prevailing climatic, ecological and edaphic conditions; (4) agencies of establishment – those that affect or alter local substrate and light condition, notably disturbance agencies; and (5) vectors of spread . . . the means of effecting dispersal over short or long distance, such as wind, water, birds . . . or mammals.
>
> CHAMBERS 1993A: 251

Range adjustments are the principal means of plant adaptation to changing conditions in Quaternary time. Throughout the Pleistocene, little evidence has been found of plant genetic adaptation to either specific environmental changes or the pace of change (Chaloner 1991). In such circumstances, plant species with short generation lengths, numerous progeny, and effective means of long-distance dispersal of seed are favored in the short run. These pioneer species dominate the early centuries of deglaciation episodes. Plant species with long generation lengths typically adapt to adverse short-term changes, even of large magnitude, by dormancy behavior; they are severely disadvantaged when adverse climatic conditions persist. Successful adaptation to a range of microhabitats, and the exploitation of mobile vectors for seed dispersal (such as birds and animals with large ranges), are the best survival mechanisms for long-generation species. Here is another aspect of the no-analog problem: some of the likely seed vectors include species now extinct, such as the passenger pigeon of

North America. Equally, the microhabitat range of species under modern conditions need not be equivalent in detail to that of the past. Domesticated plants and crop weeds exemplify notable changes in dispersal mechanisms and habitat ranges.

Pollen can travel far in wind and water but it cannot procreate directly. Seeds or spores are required to establish new plants. Therefore, it should be no surprise that macrofossils, indicative of established plants or of transported seeds, may outrace pollen during range adjustments except for grains of the far-travelling species such as pine (Gear and Huntley 1991; McWeeney 1994). In periods of rapid environmental change, neither pollen diagrams nor macrofossil finds closely reflect the dynamics of plant species range adjustments and competition.

Archaeological paleoecology critically needs better theoretical models for plant competition as well as enhanced resolution in paleoenvironmental data. Archaeologists can enrich the record by collecting vegetation samples broadly during site excavations and by resourcefully applying site-scale data to the challenges of microhabitat reconstruction. They can also help by refraining from overgeneralized applications of palynological data to site-scale reconstructions.

Climatic control of plant distributions

A long-standing controversy in ecology about whether climate is the principal factor controlling plant distributions is resolving into an issue of scale. Climatic control appears to be supported at the mega- and macro-scales in both space and time, but there are so many locational factors operating at smaller scales that the issue remains unresolved. It may be the wrong question. Chambers notes (1993a: 252) that climatic forcing of species' distributions may be relevant mainly at the edges of ranges. All the factors listed above as contributing to range expression (Table 14.2) likely modify any pure climatic effects. Vegetation ranges at scales from global to microhabitat most closely match climate during periods of relative stability, which, as discussed above, may be characteristic of neither the Pleistocene nor the Holocene.

However, the situation is less extreme as distance increases from glaciers and glacial climates. Vegetation ecology and history are underdeveloped in the southern hemisphere and the tropics, so that it is much too early to predict what kinds of insight into plant ecology might emerge from those regions that were unglaciated and therefore might have more stable plant associations in some areas, or different kinds of responses to stressors at many scales.

LANDSCAPES WITH PEOPLE

The idea that "natural" biological associations lacking human influence were the prehistoric norm has egregiously misled paleoecological thought and practice.

Wherever they exist humans affect their environments, as do all living creatures. A productive and realistic approach to human influences on phytogeography is to ask not whether people affected the distribution and composition of vegetation but *when, how, and how much.* Whether purposely or inadvertently, people are among the determinants of plant species' composition, diversity, density, biomass, and productivity at local and, recently, larger scales.

This pervasive influence for change is exerted by affecting plant populations directly or by changing their habitat conditions. Human activities change soils by clearing or burning vegetation and by trampling, draining, flooding, disturbing, enriching, polluting, and increasing erosion or leaching. Humans change microclimates by increasing albedo or exposure to sunshine, and by affecting hydrography through raising or lowering water tables or blocking and diverting streams. Humans influence plant distributions and associations both favorably and unfavorably to individual species. Positive effects on species include establishing them in new areas, increasing their ranges and densities by selecting, tending, encouraging, and cultivating them, and reducing their competitors by clearing land, weeding stands, burning underbrush, and hunting or fencing herbivores. Negative effects include reducing ranges or densities by removing or limiting growth, reducing habitat by direct competition, increasing herbivory, intensifying economic exploitation, and facilitating access by disease vectors (see essays on elm decline). Human intervention in plant community composition typically increases ecological risk for both the favored plant species and human managers: the elimination of competitors results in simplified specialized communities (monocultures) with attendant loss of resilience and increased susceptibility to diseases.

Ecological relationships work mutually. Humans affect plant assemblages; equally, changes in plant assemblages affect human behavior and lifeways by redefining the range of opportunities presented in the habitat. Elm disease, spreading through Europe near the beginning of agriculture, may have indirectly aided introduction of domesticated plants by creating clearings on rich soils. The rise of atmospheric CO_2 at the end of the glacial period likely supported a natural expansion of grasses, including the cereals that eventually were domesticated. A hemlock decline observed in mid-Holocene eastern North America may have opened the forests for an expansion of nut trees; the vegetation changes coincided with dramatically increased human population densities in the region (Mulholland 1979). Changes in plant ecology at regional scales necessarily entail new adaptations on the part of herbivores of all kinds.

Old ideas of people as passive occupiers of natural environments have influenced archaeologists' selection of theoretical models of ecological dynamics and large-scale generalizations for reconstructing past habitats. The no-analog challenge to the community concept in paleoecology has exposed the weakness in such premises (Behre and Jacomet 1991). Although there are no absolute first principles on which paleocommunities can be elaborated, sound ecological theory is an excellent source for hypotheses and models for interpreting data so long as scale congruence is maintained.

Plants in human niche space

The interpretation of paleoenvironments from remains is the first step in archaeological applications. The ultimate purpose is to interpret the human uses of and relationships with those environments. "Paleoethnobotany . . . is the analysis and interpretation of the *direct* interrelationships between humans and plants for whatever purpose as manifested in the archaeological record. Its objective is the elucidation of cultural adaptation to the plant world and the impact of plants upon a prehistoric human population, not simply the recognition of useful plants" (Ford 1979: 286). This volume is not the place to elaborate upon paleoethnobotanical methods, case studies, or contributions. Rather, the argument here is that paleoenvironmental reconstruction is not an end in itself; significant anthropological and historical study of the human past moves beyond description (Gremillion 1997).

Paleoethnobotany significantly expands knowledge of the **autecology** of humans by displaying former aspects of the human realized niche. Reconstruction of landscapes near archaeological sites and the anthropogenic changes in them, as well as the recognition of **synanthropic** plant associations that developed in and near sites, are illuminating the coadaptation of human behavior and other beings influenced by it.

Anthropogenic influences on human environments are manifested both subtly and obviously. The subtle effects are among the most significant, although they may be revealed very slowly. Among them are the reflexive effects that work through the ecosystem and loop back to influence human health and well-being within breeding populations and communities (Dincauze 1993b). Human disturbance of forests and other established plant formations redefines the densities and distributions of wild plants used for food, medicines, and raw materials as well as those of plants without obvious economic value.

Paleoecological investigations on both sides of the North Atlantic are converging to implicate human disturbance of ecosystems in the formation of extensive wetlands during the course of the Holocene. Chapters by Moore and Warner in Chambers (1993) show how human destruction of forests on two continents led to heaths, blanket bogs, and floating bogs.

The crucial constituent of human realized niches is human technology. Technology is also the defining trait for archaeology: where there is no technology, there is no material culture. Technologies based on plant materials include food gathering, fire production, crop production, food preparation and storage, medicines, and artifact manufacture using plant tissues and fibers. All these exploitations and technological modifications of plant materials fall into the domain of ethnobotany and paleoethnobotany (Hastorf and Popper 1988; Pearsall 1989). Within human niches, interactions with plants begin at the microscopic level with pollen allergies and plant extracts used in medicine, and progress through the Plant Kingdom to construction timber. The roles of plants, phytochemicals, bacteria, and fungi in human nutrition, diseases, pharmacopoeia, paints and dyes, and toxins are lightly touched upon below. All are salient aspects of human ecology and paleoecology.

Cultivars

The innovation of plant cultivation was not a unique historical moment; rather, distinct processes of discovery, experimentation, and technological development were played out in many areas of the world (Harlan 1995). The immediate motivations for these multiple events remain elusive. No single new state or condition seems to explain all, but some phenomena appear to be essential. Near the end of the last ice age, global atmospheric circulation and the latitudinal range of the jet stream changed, as did oceanic circulation and the monsoonal cycles. The Holocene rise of atmospheric carbon dioxide concentration stimulated productivity in C_3 grasses (Field et al. 1992), some of which became early domesticates in the Old World. This atmospheric factor may explain why domestication did not begin sooner in unglaciated areas at lower latitudes. Comparable changes probably happened during previous interglacial episodes as well but, this time, modern human beings were on the scene.

Human relationships with plants begin with tasting and experimenting, becoming familiar with plant properties in their natural states. The continuum of use ranges through harvesting, with its unintended effects on gene pool, to tending with intervention in growth cycles, to transplanting, to storing and dispersing (planting) seeds. Once a plant species loses the ability to propagate itself without human intervention, it is a genetically dependent human artifact. Cowan and Watson (1992: 4) make the distinction by defining a "cultigen" as a wild plant species that is tolerated or encouraged for use, while a "domesticate" is dependent upon human intervention for growth and reproduction.

Obviously, early stages of cultivation are essentially invisible in the archaeological record, and the emergence of domestication is so gradual as to be very elusive indeed

(Harris 1996). By the time seed characteristics are morphologically different from their wild ancestors, domestication is well established and changes in plant associations, distributions, and relative frequencies in landscapes are underway. Well before domestication of plants can be recognized archaeologically, intensified utilization would have affected plant ecologies, blurring the changes attendant upon cropping. Attention to on-site behavioral remains can lead to recognition of the intensified cropping, crop cleaning, and storage that should accompany the development of domestication, but the point at which a plant species becomes dependent on human intervention in its propagation will remain elusive unless DNA studies improve.

Pollen can signal the critical disturbance of native flora that accompanies farming, but careful reasoning is needed to avoid error. Even the recognition of cereal grain pollen can be complicated. Wild grasses related to barley and wheat have pollen very similar in size to that of the domesticates, which can be difficult to distinguish from the latter (Aaby 1994: 143). In the Americas, pollen data are disappointing in elucidating the process of plant domestication or the spread of cultigens, partly because pollen grains of the relevant plants do not spread far in air.

Archaeologists have other strings to their bows for investigating the development and spread of cropping, although the full set is rarely used. Pollen investigation, especially when problem-oriented and conducted at high resolution (e.g., McAndrews and Boyko-Diskonow 1989; Peglar 1993), can reveal land preparation and clearance episodes, and record the presence of exotic cultigens. As discussed below, alertness to the information in distributions of weed pollen and macrofossils can also help, as can attention paid to insect faunas that are especially relevant for identifying pasture land. On-site data such as seeds and seed stores, macrofossils (leaves, stems, and cuticle fragments), pollen, phytoliths, and plant residues can establish the presence of introduced plants that may be recognizable as domesticates (Hillman et al. 1993; Miller and Gleason 1994). Analysis of human and animal bones reveals isotopic indicators of exotic domesticates (Chapter 13).

Weeds

Weeds are plants growing where people don't want them. They are by-products of human land management. Farming communities at first influenced their landscapes only locally and minimally, little more than did hunter-gatherer managers of browse. However, since farming nearly always provides an immediate surplus of storable food, investment in storage as well as cleared land tied people to places to unprecedented degrees. Repeated meddling in natural systems induces measurable change, not simply perturbations from which systems recover. Farmers reduce the diversity of natural associations and increase the species richness of domesticated plants, crop weeds, and **ruderals** – plants that spread on disturbed ground. Some ruderals were desirable food plants; others were not. Their increase modified the numbers and distributions of other plants as well as animals dependent on plants.

As pollen or phytoliths, weeds are identifiable only to the family level. While charring may inhibit identification at the species level, uncarbonized plant remains in terrestrial archaeological matrices are likely intrusive and should not be interpreted as old (Keepax 1977; Miksicek 1987; Minnis 1981). Taphonomic questions necessarily dominate interpretations. How was the weedy material introduced to the site; how was it deposited; what were its associations; how was it carbonized (as waste, fuel, by accident, or in a conflagration)? On-site seed deposits introduced by harvesting practices may have been an integral part of the crop, or the waste of crop-processing; seeds can be introduced in thatch, flooring, bedding, or dung. In western Europe, the familiar crop weeds such as *Rumex* and *Plantago* in pollen diagrams have been used as indicators of farming, because they were assumed to accompany the Neolithic spread of cultivation and forest clearance. With the recognition that such plants are natural components of understory, increasing after any kind of disturbance, there are well-founded doubts about such direct assumptions (e.g., Bjerck 1988).

Weeds offer rich opportunities for interpretation about both paleoenvironments and human behavior, topics which are difficult to separate when crop cultivation is at issue. At the simplest level, one wants to know whether the weedy plants were crop weeds, food remains, or simply ruderals invading the disturbed ground of a site. Modern floral ecology is a poor guide to such reasoning (Hillman 1991; Küster 1991); archaeologists should rely on close interpretation of the contexts of the finds as guides to associations and taphonomy. The interpretation will vary as the finds were associated with coarse crop material, cleaned seed, fodder, flooring, roof thatch, dung, cleaning waste in trash pits, or the background pollen in site soils.

Weedy plant materials closely associated with crop remains are excellent indicators of the soil chemistry and moisture of fields in which the crops grew (Holm et al. 1997). For example, the range of non-crop seeds intermingled with crop remains at the Danebury hillfort in England showed that the fort "was receiving cereal crops from throughout its territory" (Jones 1984: 493). European weed sequences trace the progressive drying of soils in central and western Europe since the early Neolithic. Damp-ground weeds have been replaced with sunny or dry field types following forest clearing, increased evaporation from sunny surfaces, lowered water tables, and some drainage (e.g., in Holland). Trade and contact have also contributed to changing weed assemblages through millennia (Küster 1991). British grassland, a major component of modern landscapes, has developed since the Bronze Age (Greig 1991).

Plowing and harvesting techniques stress plants differentially, so that suites of crop weeds change through time. The direction of change can be interpreted in terms of land management practices (Hillman 1991). Hillman's observations in Southwest Asia show that ard-cultivated fields have a rich flora of perennial and biennial weeds that is destroyed by moldboard plows, while annual weeds are comparable under both styles of tillage (Hillman 1984). Rough crop cuttings with weeds can indicate whether sheaves were cut tall or short; short weed plants will be included only if the crop was cut near the ground. Weeds can also indicate the season of harvest, an inference otherwise difficult for crop plants in deep antiquity.

In eastern North America, field weeds are rarely identified in pollen diagrams prior to the appearance of European exotics. There is much to be learned about prehistoric field clearance and management practices in the eastern woodlands, where interpretation has typically been based on a few seventeenth-century eyewitness accounts and long-distance analogs such as subtropical "milpa" cultivation (swidden or slash-and-burn). Seed stores for *Zea mays* will probably not yield traces of weeds because of the way maize seeds form, are harvested, and stored. Nevertheless, careful search for weed traces in site soils and in nearby pollen catch-basins could enrich knowledge of field management and environments (e.g., Burden et al. 1986; Gremillion 1993). In the arid American Southwest, Suzanne Fish's attention to anthropogenic pollen suites revealed floras different from off-site pollen assemblages and unlike any observable today. She found insect-pollinated species abundant in archaeological sites, in contrast to off-site assemblages of wind-pollinated plants (Fish 1985).

PLANTS IN PEOPLE

People ingest plants and plant derivatives for food, flavorings, hallucinogens, analgesics (pain killers), and medication; the latter may also be applied topically. Poisons and allergens are usually ingested or inhaled ignorantly, accidentally, or inadvertently. Worldwide, people have learned independently, through ingenuity or hard lessons, to process toxic plants into nutritious food. Plants and plant extracts influence human health and mortality and thereby phenotypes, genotypes, and demographics. Archaeobotanists address these issues through ethnobotany and ethnoscience, as well as analyzing human remains for evidence of diet and disease. Alert archaeologists can collect crucial on-site evidence of plant use in macro- and microfossil contexts, as residues on artifacts, and as trace elements in human remains.

Diet: human foodways

Food is the fundamental ecological link between an organism and its environment. Diet, the choice and consumption of food, is a principal component of niche behavior. It is not surprising, therefore, that anthropological studies of human diet borrow theoretical concepts from ecology and investigate human food webs or diet breadth.

"We are now considerably closer to being able both to build past human food webs through direct evidence of what their components are and how they are energetically or nutritionally linked, and to explore the dynamics of those constructed webs and consider the consequences for the trajectories of past human ecosystems" (Jones 1992: 210). Food webs link human cultural behavior closely to the biomes that provide sustenance. The food-web model implicates networks of dependency in an ecosystem – each consumer depends upon the availability of its food items, down to the plant producers that depend in turn on decomposers recycling nutrients in the soil. Trophic level or food pyramid models typically culminate in carnivores. Such linear models are awkward for omnivores such as humans, who dine at several trophic levels. Acknowledging this, it should be obvious that the study of human diet or diets is seriously undertheorized for the extreme diversity of niche behavior in humans.

The unique diversity of human dietary behaviors is based on the species' capacity for omnivory. Both dentition and digestive tract are adapted to the utilization of plant and animal foods to nearly their full variety, although tradition and culture limit the actual selection in each case. Starting with the control of fire, development of food-preparation techniques has expanded the catalog of plant foods available for human nutrition, as people learned to soften, pulverize, and liquefy hard substances, to skim fat from otherwise inedible plant and animal matter, and to detoxify plant tissues that, untreated, would sicken or kill (Etkin 1994).

Plant cultivation, leading eventually to agriculture supporting towns, cities, and states, is clearly an outgrowth of herbivory. It could occur only among people already closely familiar with the growth habits and requirements of a range of useful plants, such that they could encourage them locally and finally control their productivity. This essential familiarity developed over millennia of observation and experiment; it involved knowledge not only of plant growth but also of the efficacy of plant products and tissues for nutrition and for non-food uses such as analgesics and medicines, hallucinogens, and poisons. The implications are for a staggering degree of experiment and evaluation, entailing both successes and failures.

Dietary reconstruction

Archaeological dietary reconstruction begins with a compilation of all the foods known to be available to the human group in question, at the intra-site, site, society, and culture scales. Such compilation draws from every possible source of data, beginning with organic remains found at the site and extending to data derived from landscape units of the same age (e.g., Fritz 1994; Mason et al. 1994). Macrobotanic, microbotanic, archaeozoological data and information from chemical residues are complemented by data more directly derived from humans – coprolites, chewed **quids**, and bone analyses. Artifacts used in food preparation may yield residues as tissue, phytoliths, or pollen adhering to grinding and pounding tools and to food vessels. All information about foodstuffs existing in the environment, ingested or chewed, and the nutritional elements actually incorporated into body tissues, is relevant.

Once the list of available edibles is compiled, the challenge is to determine what was actually used, how it was used, in what quantities and frequencies, in what seasons, and by whom. Every society selects from among the total of available foodstuffs. Some available edibles are ignored or rejected as dietary constituents: for example, Western peoples tend to ignore insects. The edibles selected are adopted into traditional cookery in ratios different from their representations in source populations. Within a society foodstuffs are rarely made available equally to all ages, genders, and statuses. Diets often vary seasonally, being sometimes inadequate in diversity, quality, or quantity. Such issues of variance are crucial to understanding diets; when possible, their resolution requires data solidly grounded on adequate, disciplined sampling in the field and accurate, informed analysis and interpretation. The enterprise is fundamentally interdisciplinary, demanding broad understanding of many approaches (Farb and Armelagos 1980; Sandford 1993b; Sobolik 1994; Wing and Brown 1979).

All adequate human diets include carbohydrates, proteins, fats, vitamins and minerals, and water. These essential components of nutrition are extracted from the range of foodstuffs available. Most diets are based on a few "staples" that provide the basic calories; diversity is provided by foods that are seasonal or supplementary to the bulk staples. The ratios of essential elements consumed depend on the amount and composition of food eaten over a short term, and may be less than optimal. Ratios of nutrients inadequate for metabolism and growth will be betrayed in the composition and structure of body tissues. Because diet is closely tied to health, the study of ancient diets involves paleopathology (Huss-Ashmore et al. 1982).

Archaeological data on ancient diets will always be incomplete, biased by unequal preservation and recovery, especially of minor constituents or perishables that are preserved only in rare circumstances. The list of available foods should include everything implicated by all possible data sources, supplemented by informed ideas of what constitutes a viable, adequate diet. When human remains can be analyzed, evidence of nutritional stress can indicate dietary components that were in short supply; the lack of evidence for stress implies healthy populations untroubled by episodic shortages – an uncommon situation.

Food chemistry

Cooks were the first chemists. The impetus behind detoxifying plants to make them edible and nutritious surely derives from failed experiments in dietary expansion and is closely involved with the development of poisons and medicines. The subtlety of observation, thought, and action behind traditional combinations of foods that create balanced diets (Farb and Armelagos 1980; Wing and Brown 1979) is matched by the achievements rendering edible such toxic plant products as fava beans, cassava root, bitter potatoes, and acorn meal (Johns 1990). Fermentation characterizes many traditional foodways today (e.g., Uzogara et al. 1990); it was developed repeatedly in separate parts of the world to preserve, transform, or detoxify plant foods. Also, fermentation is used to produce intoxicating beverages such as beer, wine, and chicha, which are valued for their keeping qualities as well as for their effects on the nervous system.

Nutrition

The reach from dietary reconstruction to understanding of ancient human nutrition still exceeds our grasp. Efforts to deduce diets from analyses of stable isotopes and trace elements in bone have revealed numerous unsolved problems in the relationships between bone chemistry and the foods that lie behind it (Radosevich 1993; Sillen 1989; Sobolik 1994; Chapter 16). Sobolik has noted the lack of integration among disciplines involved in archaeological research on diets and health. This lack has prevented strong inference and led to misperceptions (Sobolik 1994: 1).

Investigations of ancient diets and nutrition continue because the subject is crucial to understanding the physical and cultural histories of our species. "Human populations are both geographically and temporally diverse, and they adapt to different environments by both biological and cultural means. It would be remarkable if, given that evolution, all populations shared the same nutritional requirements" (Sutton 1994: 108). We know that humans can adapt to diets inadequate in either quality or quantity; they do so today and have done in the past. The development of agriculture did not necessarily or always improve human nutrition when it increased the quantity of food available. Diets were not merely enriched by the abundance provided by cultigens; they were impoverished by reduced diversity of wild plants consumed and of nutrients so provided (Cohen and Armelagos 1984).

Even imperfect archaeological data can expand knowledge of human diets. Archaeologists must communicate effectively with specialists on the physiological processes of metabolism and disease, who alone can translate dietary information into understanding of nutrition.

Plant products in disease and healing

In addition to providing the bulk of human foods, plants are sources of analgesics, sleep inducers, and medicines. Plant products also cause disease and psychotropic disorders, and death by toxins. The complexity of these relationships is represented in the Greek word *pharmakon* from which comes pharmacy; the original word meant both poison and drug, a tension that continues today. Human experimentation with plants early revealed the capacity of plant derivatives to ease pain; to induce sleep, relaxation, or altered mental states; to ease or terminate pregnancies; and to facilitate healing of wounds and illnesses. Since deep antiquity, people have treated the discomforts of injuries and illnesses with infusions and poultices derived from various plants.

Diseases caused by plants are among the most personal of environmental effects on humans; metaphorically, plant allergens are attacks by the habitat. Medicinal uses of plant derivatives likely developed concurrently with the recognition that contact with plants could result in diseases such as skin lesions induced by poison "oak" and ivy and stinging nettles. Although prior to the development of microscopes the role of pollen in inducing "hay fevers," or of bacteria, viruses, and algae (not strictly plants) in infections, was not realized, plant derivatives were used to counter the assaults. Many traditional medicines are demonstrably effective. Both efficacious plant medicines and plant toxins influence the human gene pool.

Archaeologists should be alert to recover evidence for non-dietary plant use and plant effects in the archaeological record. The primary source has been paleopathological data from human remains although to date most of those address nutrition. Increased attention to the full range of seeds, plant residues, and charred and desiccated plant waste products in sites should improve the situation. Since plant extracts leave few remains, attention to processing debris is most productive. DNA studies may be useful (Weising et al. 1995). Many medicinal plants are today considered weeds; overlooking their active effects on humans may be wasteful of evidence. Non-dietary plant remains should be investigated thoroughly and compared to traditional and modern lists of chemically active plants used for medicines, narcotics, and hallucinogens.

DISCUSSION

Archaeologists typically rely on specialists to identify plant remains recovered in excavations, and adapt descriptive and interpretive research off-site from many different disciplines. Moving from these basic data-gathering exercises toward understanding of human paleoenvironments involves difficult tasks of integration and interpretation. The tasks are made more daunting by poor communication between disciplines as well as by linguistic and geographical isolation within archaeology.

Paleobotanists have their own paleobotanical agendas, leading to phytogeographical maps, paleoecological scenarios, and sometimes ultimately paleoclimatic interpretations. Even when working with archaeologists, they may not advance archaeological goals especially well. This should not be surprising; phytoecology is not human paleoecology. In an insightful discussion of a volume of interdisciplinary reports, John Birks remarked, "there is surprisingly little in common between the questions about the cultural landscape being addressed by pollen analysts and the problems being studied by cultural landscape ecologists" (Birks 1988: 464). Birks saw problems of scale incongruence in time and space contributing to the miscommunications, along with inductive approaches to interpretation that left the appropriateness of theoretical assumptions unexamined. Within archaeology, vegetation studies typically focus on understanding economic uses and sources of exploited plants and plant products, and on the human behaviors associated with those specimens. Such studies are equally not human paleoecology. Valuable information is falling into the cracks.

There is still no consensus in paleoenvironmental disciplines, including archaeology, about the pervasiveness of anthropogenic effects on paleoenvironments. However, the last few years have seen significant convergence toward acceptance of the maxim that today's observable vegetation (the basis for modern ecology) is everywhere a culturally influenced landscape. On this basis, the observable world offers few if any examples of biomes uninfluenced by people, or otherwise comparable to states and conditions of the past. To understand the past we must seek it on its own terms, in paleodata from paleobotany and archaeology, interpreted as independently as possible of modern conditions.

A genuine human paleoecology must be interested in vegetative environments at human scales – those represented by standing vegetation in the neighborhood of sites, by food and drugs, by exotics imported for use or display, and by allergens and disease organisms. It must see paleoenvironments evolving (changing) as constituent species adjust to each other's presence and influence. It must see humans as integral parts of the ecological dynamism, full participants in synecology. As a species, we are what we are as the result of millennia of adaptation to unique, dynamic environments. Vegetation on the Earth is what it is because humans, as well as all other animals and plants, have defined the mix. Plant environments are dependent not only on climate, soils, and topography; they have adapted to the influences of human and other inhabitants over millennia. Human modifications of human niche space impinge on the niche space of other organisms. The effects are subtle, pervasive, recursive, and ancient, reaching far beyond human awareness.

The environmentalist ethos that inspired paleoenvironmental studies in the past quarter-century has also set agendas and defined expectations for results. Anthropogenic change imposed on environments should not be hastily judged "habitat destruction." Such changes deserve detailed analysis of their direct and recursive effects. Habitat management typically reduces diversity, deplored by ecologists but offering short-term advantages to exploiters. Even extensively reorganized habitats have continued to support large human populations; the changes suit new lifestyles. Certainly, they define new habitats for humans while constituting either habitat destruction or expansion for other species. Paleoecology must offer insights into such double-edged relationships, not ideological messages. Paleoenvironmental archaeology might yet aspire to the goal of a genuine human ecology (Butzer 1982) when it is able to consider the human role in global ecology from a long historical perspective.

THE PALEOECOLOGY OF THE ELM DECLINE

The case study in Part III summarized five different explanations for the mid-Holocene European elm decline and found all either inadequate or inconclusive. Climatic deterioration, soils depletion, human exploitation of the species, human competition for the tree's habitat, and disease were all shown to be inadequate to comprehend the evidence. The hypothesis invoking climatic deterioration to explain the widespread loss of elms from the temperate forests was poorly supported on several counts, as was the hypothesis of soils depletion. The diversity of habitats, elm species, soils, and topography across the prehistoric elm range in central and western Europe undermines the appropriateness of both these hypotheses as explanations. Looking for single causal explanations for the behavior of complex systems is fruitless (Chapter 2).

Decline in elm pollen began in southeastern Europe early in the sixth millennium B.P., even as the Holocene spread of elms reached its maximum distribution (Huntley and Birks 1983: 412). The decline was time-transgressive westward until around 5000 B.P., when it spread rapidly to its northern limits (Fig. A). The near-coincidence with evidence for the initiation of farming in northern Europe long supported speculation that the elms were killed by pastoralists and farmers establishing agricultural landscapes.

Among the dominant hypotheses, only that of disease was supported by good correlations with the rate, spatial scale, and time of the elm loss. Vegetation mapping at the continental scale indicated that the elm decline spread through the mid-Holocene forests of northern Europe at a rate of 4 km per year (Huntley and Birks 1983: 414), a rate consistent with observed pathogen spread in contemporary forests (Birks 1986: 50). The proposed mechanism is infection by a fungus, *Ceratocystis ulmi*, carried by a beetle vector (*Scolytus scolytus*) to elms, in which it is usually fatal (see

Figure A The elm decline in Europe. The lines A, B, C, and D mark the approximate northwestern limits of sites where elm pollen values declined markedly over the periods
6.5–7.0 ka ago (A), 6.0–6.5 ka ago (B), 5.5–6.0 ka ago (C), and 5.0–5.5 ka ago (D). Lines
e and f mark the southeastern limits of sites with ≥ 2% elm pollen 7.0 and 5.0 ka ago,
respectively. Line g marks the southern limit of regions where *Ulmus glabra* may have
been the only elm species 5 ka ago. Simplified from the maps in Huntley and Birks
(1983). (Reproduced from Tallis 1991: Fig. 12.11, with permission of Chapman & Hall;
original caption.)

review by Girling [1988]). Finding *S. scolytus* beetle fragments in peat of the right age in London demonstrated the presence of the vector, at least. The disease kills quickly; with time, surviving elms genetically resistant to the fungus can reestablish populations (Birks 1986: 51).

The unresolved debate about the elm decline was conducted on the basis of regional-scale data, especially in northwest Europe. Regionally, elm pollen declined from averages as high as 20–25% of all tree pollen to post-decline averages of 1–5% (Birks 1986: 49). The loss of trees is well established, but not the effects of their loss on the forests. What the pollen percentage figures mean in terms of actual forest composition is not clear. Data on prehistoric densities of elms either before or after the decline are spotty and diverse. Elm pollen densities are patchy within the continuous elm range in Europe, probably reflecting local edaphic and microclimatic factors (Huntley and Birks 1983). Elms are major components of canopy. A thinned canopy filters out less grass and cereal pollen from the pollen rain, thus increasing the percentage representation of non-arboreal pollen, including cereals and weeds, in deposits (Perry and Moore 1987). The coincidence of cereal and weed pollen increasing with the loss of elm pollen might be an artifact of pollen dispersal and percentage counts rather than a prime indicator of forest clearance for agriculture (Edwards and Hirons 1984; Groenman-van Waateringe 1983; Tauber 1967).

Can fine-resolution pollen studies at the local scale help? Garbett's (1981) study failed to support the climatic explanation; he concluded for anthropogenic factors rather than disease in northwest England. A few years later, close-interval sampling on a pollen core in annually varved sediment supported a different conclusion at Diss Mere in eastern England (Peglar 1993). Pollen percentages and influx calculation, as well as charcoal counts, for 181 samples from 252 sediment years showed periods of woodland disturbance by humans both before and after the elm decline signal. Cereal pollen appeared in two intervals prior to the decline, with evidence for soil disturbance and forest burning. Elm pollen counts did not change with the disturbances, but later moved dramatically; *Ulmus* pollen counts fell 73% within six years. This rate is comparable to observed pathogen effects on modern elms and other species.

Fine-resolution sampling and better chronological control in pollen studies have shown that, not only was the elm decline not exactly synchronous with the initiation of farming in northern Europe, it is no longer demonstrably a single chronostratigraphic marker. Close-interval sampling in small upland pollen basins in Britain revealed sequences of *Ulmus* decline events over time spans of a millennium or more (e.g., Simmons and Innes 1996; Smith and Cloutman 1988; Whittington et al. 1991).

Fundamental to understanding the intransigence of the elm decline problem is recognition of its reliance on early twentieth-century methods of paleobotany (wide sampling intervals, percentage diagrams, ignoring of non-arboreal pollen), and its peripherality to archaeological methods. Archaeologists in Europe were galvanized by Iversen's claims (1941) of evidence for initiation of farming. The loss of elms roughly coincident with the first appearance of cereal and weed pollen in northern European bogs was a revelation. Iversen's landnam model of slash-and-burn farmers in a primeval forest readily suited archaeologists accustomed to such farming practices in the anthropological literature. The analogy was adopted without cavil or test as an archaeological interpretation which, although originating in northwestern Europe, could be broadly applied.

The anthropogenic explanation has appealed as the best, perhaps even sufficient, explanation in northwest Europe (e.g., Edwards 1993). While archaeologists remained uninvolved, the debate was mainly carried on among and for paleobotanists. Thus, it is not surprising that circular reasoning is implicated in definitions of farming used in the discussions. At diverse times and places the initiation of farming has been claimed on the basis of the appearance in a given region (rarely locale) of (a) pottery, (b) cereal pollen, (c) weed pollen, and even (d) the elm decline itself. Loose definitions cannot support claims for strong correlations, let alone explanations.

Beginnings are notoriously elusive. While the elm decline can be identified and dated in terms of a quantifiable change in the frequency of elm pollen in sediment samples, the beginning of cereal farming or animal husbandry is not so easily specified. It is not equivalent to the deposition of cereal pollen in sediment that happened to be intercepted by a pollen corer. The beginning of farming may always be essentially a matter of definition (Thomas 1991). Archaeologists must define the issues and seek the evidence in archaeological contexts and in archaeological systems of meaning. Pollen analysis is a valued contributor to archaeological data sets but it is generated from non-archaeological data and styles of thought and practice and will always require archaeological contextualization and interpretation.

The hypotheses for human roles in the loss of elms resolve essentially into (1) intensive human harvesting of elm leaves for animal food, and (2) human competition for the genus' habitat as preferred locations for agricultural fields and pasturage. These ideas are components of the classic landnam model with the foddering model of Troels-Smith (1960), which dominated the elm decline debates during the seventh and eighth decades of the twentieth century. Provision of tree fodder to Neolithic herd animals was demonstrated at the Egolzwil 3 site in Switzerland (Rasmussen 1993), where elm branches and twigs were found in animal scat and mats of waterlogged elm leaves were recognized. Elm, however, did not dominate among other tree species in the scat. The large scale of forest damage required to "cause" the elm decline, in the face of the small-scale scatter of early farming communities in the archaeological record (Rowley-Conwy 1982), further reduces the relevance of these models.

Archaeological evidence currently fails to show good spatial or temporal correlation between the timing and range of the elm decline (Huntley and Birks 1983) and any particular criterion of early farming (Dennell 1992; Thomas 1991; Zvelebil 1986). Cereal pollen precedes the elm decline even into parts of northern Europe (Edwards and Hirons 1984; Göransson 1985; Groenman-van Waateringe 1983; Huntley and Birks 1983). Outside of Britain and northern Europe, *archaeological* evidence for farming communities precedes the elm decline (Zvelebil 1986). Farming and the elm decline are not synchronous.

Recently, biological opinions have converged toward a synergistic model of the elm decline. Human activities related to the initiation of agriculture may have brought pathogens or the vector beetle into forests not previously exposed to one or either, and human activities aided their effectiveness. In 1980, Oliver Rackham proposed that agriculture and disease in combination were more destructive than either alone (Rackham 1980: 266). Among others, Birks (1986), Faegri and Iversen (1989), Göransson (1984, 1986), Huntley (1988), Huntley and Birks (1983), Moore et al. (1991: 189), and Peglar (1993) accept that mid-Holocene human disruption of forests contributed to the virulence of an elm pathogen by opening clearings and harvesting elms.

On the other hand, reduction of elm populations by disease is an alternative mechanism for opening the forest canopy and increasing the frequency and size of clearings (Whittington et al. 1991). Additional sunlight on the forest floor permitted more understory and groundcover plants. The effect was to increase, without human labor, available pasturage or arable land on the best soils. People could take advantage of opportunities to intensify pasturing, gardening, and/or cereal agriculture. The elm decline might have enabled intensification of food production earlier than would have been the case without it.

The reduction of elm pollen marks a definitive change in the composition of mid-Holocene European arboreal pollen rain, and possibly in the forest canopies. It may also represent a point of intensification of human dominance of ecosystems. The crucial issue for understanding these relationships may have been ancient human forest-management practices, not aggressive forest clearing to establish a new mode of life. Forest management by tree girdling, controlled burning, and foddering of animals, with or without cropping, began before the elm declines, apparently within the Mesolithic period in the northwest. Analytically distinguishing elm loss from the initiation of food production, while recognizing their historical near-coincidence, opens a productive reexamination of ideas about mechanisms of human ecology in temperate forests. Understanding early European farming or the decline of elms may require the integration of mechanisms from both processes.

PART VII

Fauna

PLATE VII

FAUNAL PALEOENVIRONMENTS:
CONCEPTS AND METHODS

> The days when excavation directors allowed the animal bones to be thrown onto the spoil heap, by default if not by deliberate policy, are now largely past.
>
> GAMBLE AND BAILEY 1994: 81

The complex relationships between human populations and components of their environments are particularly intense within the Animal Kingdom. Humans and other animals evolved together for over 3 million years in Africa. While the span of coevolution is shorter in other parts of the world, the expansion of human populations and the growth of technology in recent millennia mean that no animal species is likely to be environmentally unaffected by the existence of *Homo sapiens sapiens*. Complementarily, as humans encounter and come to know other species, we find our lives interconnected in many subtle ways.

Paleolithic archaeology in the Old World developed from vertebrate paleontology in European caves and gravels, and thus since its nineteenth-century beginnings has employed vertebrate remains as rough guides to paleoclimates. Zooarchaeology (archaeozoology in Europe; osteoarchaeology) as it has developed recently is far from being a simple transfer of paleontological methods and assumptions to archaeological contexts. Most of the optimistic simplifying assumptions about animal remains in archaeological sites that were routinely applied in initial studies have been refuted in the past twenty years by the advance of taphonomic understanding. With their passage has come awareness of the rich complexity of information in faunal remains. No longer simply applied paleontology, faunal analysis is a specialization within archaeology whose practitioners conduct research alongside archaeologists. The methods derive from biology, paleontology, and archaeology; the theory is still

411

immature. The goals of faunal analysis in archaeology necessarily diverge from those of paleontology, being anthropocentric by definition. The faunal assemblages are samples of archaeological contexts, not of natural communities. The processes which defined the samples are identified and evaluated for their relevance to the understanding of human lives and environments. The critical evaluation of faunal data to define the supportable limits of inference has fed back into archaeological practice with demands for more precise techniques of excavation, sampling, collecting, and reporting, and for heightened awareness of context.

The dominant part of zooarchaeological literature is devoted to the interpretation of human behavior in respect to animals. Hunting and butchery patterns, management of domestic herds, utilization of animal products and such are the typical subjects of zooarchaeological study. Here, attention is directed to paleoenvironmental applications of faunal data both to animal environments as those elucidate human environments, and to the animals in human environments and within humans themselves. To keep this purpose clearly in focus, I employ the term "archaeozoology" in the text that follows.

Faunal remains in archaeological contexts support inferences about the environments of the animals themselves (climate and habitats) as well as aspects of human environments that animals affect or reflect. It is well to keep in mind which of these environments is of interest in any particular case, since proxy value and relevant scales vary with species (Fig. 15.1). An animal's sensitivity to environmental factors such as climate and habitat varies roughly in inverse proportion to its size, such that small invertebrates are typically better indicators of both than are large vertebrates. At the base of the chain, bacteria and parasitic organisms are typically host-specific, and therefore **stenotopic** indicators of narrowly defined interior environments. Insects are sensitive indicators of temperature and moisture (both critical aspects of climate), of food sources and, sometimes, the soils and herbaceous substrates on which they live. Animals resident in water bodies are often informative about water chemistry and temperatures. On the other hand, migratory fish and birds reflect climates and seasonality only at the regional scale. Many animals that reflect seasonality in their growth cycles reveal very little about other aspects of their environments beyond gross habitat characteristics. Pets and **commensals** (consumers of human foods) inform about conditions in human domestic spaces, while larger domesticates reveal something about land use such as the pastures and transhumance required by large herbivores in some environments. Interpretations of animal range locations and season of availability are important aspects of paleoenvironmental research that are widely honored in the study of archaeological animal remains; they directly implicate human behaviors in animal exploitation, particularly hunting and

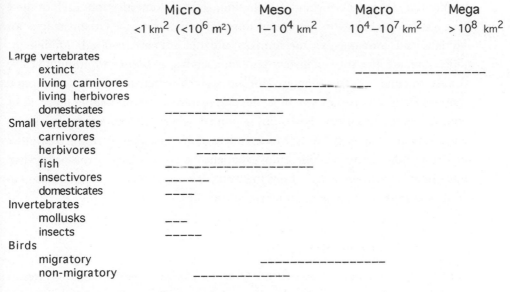

Figure 15.1   Environmental scaling with fauna. The chart displays various faunal data classes appropriate to paleoenvironmental modeling at micro-, meso-, macro-, and mega-scales. There is no chronological (vertical) dimension to the chart; time-scale is appropriately that of an individual animal's life span.

pastoralism. The importance of the latter in Eurasia and Africa explains the emphasis large-animal archaeology receives in those areas.

For paleoenvironmental research, interest in faunal remains cannot be restricted to only large vertebrates, or only bones. The full range of animal remains in archaeological contexts can be informative, particularly about the ecology of the species archaeologists care about most. Preservation conditions will control the availability of animal tissues in any place – whether archaeologists encounter bones, antler, horn, **chitin**, hair, skin or other tissues, feathers, bird eggs or mollusk shells, parasite cysts, or chemical residues. The full range should be recognized, sampled, and treated appropriately to establish conditions for successful analysis. This desirable outcome is only possible when the potential diversity of information in animal remains is anticipated in a project's research design.

Theory in faunal studies is best developed for systematics and taphonomy (from paleontology), and for human behavioral interpretations (from anthropology and archaeology). Issues around animals as environmental factors are undertheorized. Animal remains have long been analogically interpreted as climate proxies. They have been much less appreciated as factors influencing human existence as distinct from human behavior (e.g., hunting). The behavioral theory is relevant to (1) scavenging,

(2) hunting, (3) butchering and distribution, and (4) domestication. Each of these four classes of behavior implicates different environmental circumstances for humans and consequences for humans and the animals involved. Among the differences are the species involved in interactions, exposure to communicable disease, the amount of time required for success in the enterprise (both planning and execution), the relative amount of facilitation required, any mutualities involved, as with domesticated animals. For example, animals scavenged for meat experience no environmental change from the human interaction, since they were killed by other predators. The carnivore killers do experience a change in environment when humans are able to drive them from their prey. The human change is in diet and in confrontation with (and management of) carnivores.

ANIMAL KINGDOM

Far from being merely the exploitable Others in the biosphere – basic resources – animals are major environmental factors for humans. People and animals mutually use and are used, eat and are eaten, share living space and define the conditions of life for each other. Whenever humans actively exploit or use animals, or vice versa, animals are significant elements of the human environment. As the top carnivores in most of the world's food chains, humans prey on other animals, eating whales and insects and most kinds and sizes of animals between. Humans also dominate animals by domestication, controlling them as breeders, feeders, transporters, protectors, trainers, harnessers, drivers, riders, keepers of pets, and as appropriators of milk, blood, hair, and progeny. The superior muscular strength of large animals provides human domesticators with power beyond their own capabilities, as animals pull plows and vehicles, drive mills and pumps, and confer on those who ride horses, camels, and elephants speed and mobility far beyond the limits of bipedalism. From animals humans obtain diverse, unique, even indispensable raw materials such as bone, antler, shell, teeth and tusks, claws and horns, hides, furs, feathers, sinew, organs for containers, fat, bones, and dung for fuel as well as dietary meat, fat, blood, and milk.

As active agents in human environments, animals directly affect human life and living conditions. Some occasionally prey on humans, mainly under unusual conditions of threat, stress, or provocation. Parasites and decomposers, on the other hand, freely feed as opportunity allows. Animals compete with humans for basic resources such as shelter (cats, bears, canids, and some reptiles in caves) and food. From deer in the garden to rodents and insects in stored grain, herbivores compete actively with humans for food. Widespread extirpation is the price the world's major carnivores have paid for their competition for human meat supplies. Domestic animals impose on their keepers the burdens of feeding and protecting them, which dramatically modify human lifestyles and define new selective pressures on physique and temperament. Both as parasites and as vectors for transmissible diseases (e.g., fleas, lice, mosquitoes, snails, rodents, dogs, cattle, and swine) animals directly affect human morbidity and mortality and thus ultimately the species' gene pool. Long before domestication and the infection theories of disease, humans recognized animals' influence upon their own physical well-being. Regarding them with awe and envy, not scorn, they celebrated the powers of animals as aspects of divinity and manifestations of vital force. Successful dominance of large animals is a quick route to status among humans.

Animal environments

Animal remains in paleoenvironmental reconstruction provide information relative only to the areal range and life spans of *individual animals*. Extrapolation to breeding populations is a further speculative step. This is especially true and onerous in the case of animals in archaeological sites. Therefore, the scales of reconstructions must vary with the size and mobility of the animal indicators. The larger, longer-lived, or more mobile an animal, the less specific it is as proxy for environment. Applications of such reconstructions to problems on human scales require that the relevance of the animal indicators of environments to the anthropocentric problem be demonstrated through contextual or other evidence. Failing such demonstrated relevance, reconstructions of animal environments are not directly referable to problems on human scales, such as the span of site occupancy or the extent of site catchment area.

Reconstruction of animal biogeography cannot be based on proxy data. Paleovegetation and paleoclimates implicate associated animal species only in the case of requisite symbionts. To take an extreme example, which vegetation and climate would implicate the presence of humans? The niches and habitats activated in a particular paleo time and place can only be approximated on the basis of associated animal remains, with reliance on analogies drawn from modern conditions or associations. Analogies lose relevance as ancient conditions diverge from the present.

Taxonomy (systematics)

Zoological taxonomy is a formal system of naming and representing genetic relationships among animals. Naming follows formal rules mediated by international

Table 15.1 Examples of zoological taxonomy: Kingdom Animalia
(principal categories only, without intermediates)

Phylum Chordata				
Subphylum	Vertebrata			
Class	Mammalia			
Order	Artiodactyla		Carnivora	
Family	Cervidae		Canidae	
Genus	*Odocoileus*		*Canis*	
Species	*virginianus*	white tail deer	*lupus*	wolf
Class	Osteichthyes	bony fishes		
Order	Salmoniformes		Clupeiformes	
Family	Salmonidae		Clupeidae	
Genus	*Salmo*		*Clupea*	
Species	*salar*	Atlantic salmon	*harengus*	Atlantic herring
Class	Aves	birds		
Order	Anseriformes		Falconiformes	
Family	Anatidae		Falconidae	
Genus	*Anser*		*Falco*	
Species	*albifrons*	white-fronted goose	*peregrinus*	Peregrine falcon
Phylum	Mollusca	shellfish		
Class	Bivalvia		Gastropoda	
Order	Myoida		Mesogastropoda	
Family	Myidae		Littorinidae	
Genus	*Mya*		*Littorina*	
Species	*arenaria*	soft-shelled clam	*littorea*	periwinkle
Phylum	Arthropoda			
Class	Crustacea		Insecta	
Order	Decapoda		Coleoptera	
Family	Homaridae		Carabidae	
Genus	*Homarus*		*Aphodius*	
Species	*americanus*	lobster	*rufipes*	dung beetle

committees, governed by precedence and a hierarchical scale (for an historical review, see Mayr and Ashlock [1991]). The seven major levels of taxonomic categories are displayed in Table 15.1 along with examples of classification in order of increasing specificity from kingdom to species. The proper scientific name for an identified organism is the binomial combination of genus and species, italicized.

Archaeozoologists should be aware that taxonomy is undergoing fundamental revision under the direction of the International Commission on Zoological Nomenclature (ICZN). The current version of official publications and field guides should be consulted for identification and naming (e.g., *Bulletin of Zoological Nomenclature*).

Systematic reference collections are essential guides to identification. Anyone working with archaeological bone assemblages must have access to formal collections or develop one appropriate to the area from which the assemblage was derived. Archaeologists need comparative specimens that are not only whole but also fragmented, burned, and leached; they should expand comparative collections in those directions. Formal training in vertebrate and invertebrate paleontology is essential for good work; it typically involves apprenticeship. With some experience in a research area archaeologists can learn to do rough sorting, but responsible and authoritative identification and interpretation of animal bones require specialization. Specialization is essential, of course, when animal remains include not only bones but also teeth, tissues, hair, sinew, fibers, or residues. There is a large specialist literature on identification and description of animal remains, and a very large vocabulary involved. Manuals are easily exhausted, requiring recourse to journal articles and publications of limited circulation. Some volumes particularly useful to archaeologists include those by Cornwall (1964), Gilbert (1980), Gilbert et al. (1981), Hillson (1986, 1992), Lavocat (1966), Olsen (1964, 1968), Schmid (1972), Walker (1985), and Wheeler and Jones (1989).

Identification of animal remains from archaeological contexts begins with sorting the pieces and fragments so that identification can proceed efficiently. Sorting may be done several ways according to the condition of the bones or debris or the problems being addressed. A first sort can be made according to immediately visible large categories, equivalent to the taxonomic level of class, such as the "fur, fin, feather, or scale" groups of vertebrates (i.e., mammal, fish, bird, or reptile bones), and bivalve vs. gastropod for mollusks. A method used especially by investigators relying on published keys is sorting by **element**, that is, by body part (Fig. 15.2). Cranial elements (skull bones, horns, antler, teeth, etc.) are separated from postcranial elements (everything else) and the latter according to axial (e.g., rib cage, vertebral column) or appendicular (e.g., limbs, extremities, etc.) elements, then by size. Sorting by element simplifies dealing with fragments, which may be grouped as elements even when not identifiable to the generic level.

Regardless of fragmentation, identification of animal remains may be achieved to some level of taxonomic specificity. Just recognizing "animal" gets to the kingdom level, and sorting for bone/antler, shell, or chitin will achieve the phylum

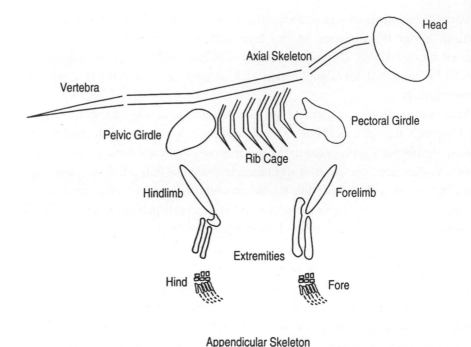

Figure 15.2 Divisions of the vertebrate skeleton, showing elements. The head, spinal
column, rib cage, and sternum comprise the axial skeleton. The girdles, limbs,
and extremities comprise the appendicular skeleton. (After Hesse and Wapnish
1985: Fig. 27.)

level (Table 15.1). Very little more experience permits identification to class level in
terms of mammal, bird, amphibian/reptile or fish, bivalve, or gastropod. Reaching
the order level of specificity requires that diagnostic elements be recognizable in the
collection, such as the rugged third metacarpal of perissodactyles, the teeth of carnivores, and so on. The family taxon distinguishes dogs from cats, deer from antelopes, humans from apes, and so on. Family-level identification may require
comparative collections because some criteria are subtle: teeth are typically critical
at this level, as are foot bones, especially in birds (toothless, of course). Getting fish
down to the family level can be very challenging. Experimental DNA studies with
preserved animal tissues imply that genetic identification to the family level might
become routine (of course, genetic and taxonomic classifications are distinct
systems). Identification to the genus level depends on the presence of diagnostic
teeth, horn or antler shapes, or articular surfaces of crucial bones. Generic
identification frequently requires comparative collections for the particular region
or locality.

When the collection and comparative material permit identification to species, the way is clear to thinking about habitats and niches. With fragmented bones, or animals now extinct, it is less likely this level of identification can be achieved. When sorting to species level is possible, and the collection is large, resorting to count elements can open the analysis to various quantification methods. Elements sorted by size, laterality (left or right), age, and sex can support estimates of the number of individual animals contributing to the collection. The estimates are always minimal because of uncontrollable variables of taphonomy and collection. While such estimates are unnecessary for paleoenvironmental considerations (Grayson 1981), they support inferences about biology and human behavior that are at the core of zooarchaeology and paleoethnozoology. Information about seasonality of death, an environmental character, requires data about age and sometimes sex of individuals (see below).

Any attempt at quantification must include the fragments, at whatever level of taxonomic specificity they are identified (Lawrence 1978). Each category is weighed as a percentage of a bulk sample or measured as a percentage of volume of a depositional unit. Fragments should be systematically collected and analyzed whenever funding permits; if not so treated, their absence from total counts should be explicitly noted.

Interpretation of archaeological samples

The description phase of zooarchaeological analysis is complete when an inventory of the assemblage lists taxa present by depositional unit within a site. Interpretive efforts build on that. To evaluate the representativeness and reliability of the assemblage in terms of intra-site variability, comparisons can be made between depositional units, with confidence limits defined or estimated on the basis of sample sizes, inter-sample variability (including differential preservation as clue to integrity), taphonomy, recovery methods (e.g. sieve mesh size), and soil pH. These qualities are essential first steps toward understanding the usefulness of a collection for paleoenvironmental or behavioral interpretations (Shipman 1981). Intensive statistical manipulation of data should not be considered unless the representativeness is controlled at least to this degree. The difficulty of achieving representative samples, even when the problem is recognized in advance, is revealed in dismaying detail by Gamble and Bailey in their discussion of problems at Klithi Cave in Greece (Gamble and Bailey 1994).

Quantification methods are a major problem in zooarchaeological studies (e.g., Grayson 1984; Ringrose 1993). Their reliability is fundamentally challenged by growing awareness of taphonomical, excavational, and preservational uncertainties. Because statistical analyses are less important in paleoenvironmental work, where presence data are the only reliable ones (Grayson 1981), no further discussion is given here. The reader curious about NISP, **MNI** (minimum number of individuals), MGUI, and other indices is referred to the cutting edge of zooarchaeological literature – the specialist journals – for developments on this moving front (*Archaeozoology, Ethnobiology, Paleobiology,* and *Zooarchaeology* among others).

Metrical and morphological variables are important to biogeographers and paleontologists. For example, size gradients in time and space within taxa may reflect significant environmental factors such as climate or habitat changes, food quantity and quality, topographic or other controls on breeding, competition, and domestication (Klein and Cruz-Uribe 1984). Archaeologists in a position to contribute such data from their assemblages should work with specialists in measuring and describing their unusual faunal specimens or taxa. A standard set of measurement techniques is available (Driesch 1976).

Collections conservation

Conservation of recovered remains is an essential aspect of responsible excavation. Archaeologists must be prepared to treat fragile faunal material appropriately as it is recovered in the field and later prepared for study in the laboratory (Leiggi and May [1995] for vertebrate bones). Review of site conditions and structure in advance of field work should indicate whether plans need be made for field treatments such as wet wraps, vacuum tanks, hardening agents, plaster wraps, and special supportive packaging materials.

In the "heroic" early years of archaeology, field directors decided what to save and what to discard by an extraordinary variety of criteria, many purely intuitive. Archaeologists learn what careful housekeepers know – anything discarded may be regretted a short time later. Modern archaeologists know the disappointment of seeking vainly in museum storehouses for the vast quantities of faunal remains casually mentioned in reports but never analyzed. Funds and facilities permitting, it is wise to take *everything* to the laboratory for close examination. The rewards range from the discovery among bone scrap of small tools, engravings, and rare specimens, to the ability to evaluate sample quality in the several units of a site.

However, a generalized retention strategy can easily devolve into mindless accumulation. There is no substitute for intelligent evaluation of analytical tasks in terms of their relevance and productivity for the goals of investigation. The real costs in cleaning, labeling, packing, and analysis must be considered against the benefits they are likely to yield in knowledge (O'Connor 1989). As part of a cost/benefit estimation, it is usually a good idea to experiment innovatively with classes of remains that do not offer immediately realizable information. A day or two of thought directed toward extracting unusual data from usually overlooked remains can yield remarkable insights; until attention has been focused on a class of remains, it is wise not to underestimate its research potential.

VERTEBRATES

The bones and teeth of **vertebrates** (animals with backbones) are the most common animal remains in archaeological collections, although not necessarily the most common in sites. Relatively rugged and easily visible in archaeological sediments, they are rich stores of information about human and animal environments and behavior. Here we briefly survey the information potentials currently recognized in them. Emphasis will continue to be upon paleoenvironmental information.

Within human communities, animals are sources of food and raw materials, and fill the roles of domesticates or competitors. Body parts or the animals themselves may be moved by humans away from their native habitats at regional or even larger scales. The locations of consumption, use, or discard may bear no determinable relationship to source areas. Depending upon conditions of preservation, vertebrate remains may include more than hard tissues; dung and coprolites, skin and muscle fibers, hair, feathers, scales, and blood residues may all be preserved under appropriate conditions.

Chemistry and structure of vertebrate hard tissues

Mammalian bone is a dynamic system composed of organic and inorganic matter. Twisted fiber bundles of collagen comprise about 90% of the organic component; rod-like crystals of hydroxyapatite (calcium phosphate: $Ca_{10}(PO_4)_6.2OH$) and other minerals comprise the inorganic component, which accounts for about 75% of the dry weight. The structure of bone is continuously remodeled throughout life, responding to environmental circumstances such as diet and health and to structural demands on various parts of the organism. The final form expresses genetic, metabolic, and mechanical influences, being species-specific with minor individual variations. Mineralization of bone (ossification) proceeds outward from centers. Thus, cranial elements fuse along their borders after growth has achieved final form, while long bones such as those of the limbs ossify separately along the shaft and at both ends. To minimize weight without sacrificing strength, bones have spongy internal structure and smooth hard outer layers. The combination is very strong, providing attachment and leverage for muscles while supporting the body weight and protecting internal organs. Antler is similar to bone in form, but is even lighter for its size. Horn cores and hooves are dense spongy bone sheathed with keratin, a fingernail-like material of modified skin tissue. (See details in Lyman [1994: 72–82] and other sources.)

In comparison to mammal bones, bird bones characteristically minimize weight by forming thinner walls and less spongy tissue in the interiors of the shafts. Reptilian and amphibian bones differ somewhat from mammal bones in fine structure and form. Fish bones vary among the major taxa, but in general have less mineral matter and more cartilage (gelatinous connective tissue, ca. 50% collagen) than those of other vertebrates (Wheeler and Jones 1989: Ch. 7).

Teeth, simpler and harder than bones, are composed of strong elastic dentine covered by hard resistant enamel of prismatic hydroxyapatite, with connective tissue called cementum below the gumline. Tusks are specialized teeth, composed of a tough version of dentine (ivory) (Hillson 1986: Ch. 2).

Avian eggshells are composed of calcite in an organic matrix, and preserve well in alkaline contexts. Leathery reptilian eggshells rarely preserve. The bony scales of fish and amphibians grow on the skin; scutes and spines are special modifications of scales. Reptilian scales of keratinous material rarely survive burial.

Taphonomy

Concern for taphonomic processes was introduced to archaeology from vertebrate paleontology. Discussed in Part VI in respect to plant remains, the subject requires further consideration. It involves the processes affecting animal bones from death of the individual to fossilization (or total decomposition) of the remains. Table 15.2 displays some of those processes and their consequences for archaeological recovery and interpretation.

Animal remains occur in diverse archaeological contexts as intentional burials, food wastes, processing wastes, abandoned storage, and simple discard as well as post-consumption wastes. Culturally defined disposal practices defy generalizations. Whether inside or outside of dwellings or other defined spaces, materials recovered together cannot be casually assumed to have been acquired, used, or deposited at the same time or from equivalent sources. There are many routes for the introduction and removal of faunal remains into and from archaeological assemblages – some purposive, some adventitious, and others subsequent to the major deposition events (Lyman 1994; Schiffer 1987: Ch. 4).

Table 15.2 Taphonomic and diagenetic processes affecting terrestrial animal remains

	A Physical loss (scattering)	B Biological loss (consumption)	C Chemical loss (dissolution)	D Sampling loss (selection)
1. Living associations				
2. Death		✓	✓	
3. Surface processes	✓	✓	✓	✓
4. Transportation	✓			✓
5. Disarticulation	✓			✓
6. Consumption and/or decomposition		✓	✓	✓
7. Dispersal of fragments	✓			✓
8. Burial	✓	✓		✓
9. Decomposition and/or fossilization	—	—	—	—
10. Excavation	✓			✓
11. Identification	✓			✓

Note: Taphonomic and diagenetic processes affecting terrestrial animal tissues from the death of the individual (numbered rows). Not all will be active in any one case. There may be mutual exclusions, as for example between fossilization and decomposition, or repetitions, as with remobilization and deposition. The loss of mass and information at each step is indicated in columns A through D.

The death of an animal initiates a natural sequence of events that ends ultimately in chemical recycling or fossilization (Table 15.2). Bones or fossils recovered paleontologically or archaeologically represent interrupted taphonomic sequences. A dead animal is normally consumed and decomposed on the ground surface, never to begin the process of fossilization (Table 15.2 row 6). Those buried in place or after transportation (row 8) may be subjected to chemical transformations leading to preservation of part of the remains (row 9). Burial within active soil horizons adds to the history pedoturbation and diagenetic processes that result in fragmentation and dissolution of bony matter (Hare 1980). Information is lost at every step in the process (Table 15.2 columns A–D).

Taphonomy has matured into an impressive specialty within zooarchaeology, mainly although not exclusively addressed to vertebrates (Lyman 1994). Field studies and experiments expand awareness of diverse processes of decay, exposure, attrition (trampling, quarrying, collecting, carnivore gnawing and scattering), transportation, burial, preservation, and diagenesis (e.g., Behrensmeyer and Hill 1980; Binford 1978; Brain 1981; Haynes 1988; Jones 1986; Payne and Munson 1985; Yalden and Morris

1990). Studies of fossilization and diagenesis have wide implications for interpretation of field collections and for subsequent analyses (e.g., Donovan 1991; Marean 1991; Radosevich 1993). Awareness of taphonomic processes permits evaluation of taphonomic contexts in archaeology and a realistic perspective on what can be learned from recovered bone (Pate and Hutton 1988).

Taphonomic contexts comprise sediments and inclusions patterned by (1) the manner of death, (2) the transport agents, (3) the destructive processes imposed from whatever source, (4) the disposal practices of human groups, and (5) the archaeological recovery methods. Interpretation of taphonomic contexts demands informed analysis of the historical situations that have shaped them, by investigators trained in appropriate disciplinary specializations. The requirements of a good taphonomic investigation are close to those for good field archaeology (e.g., Barker 1993; Lyman 1994: 22).

Preservation and diagenesis

The circumstances of death and burial or human disposal behavior limit opportunities for preservation of animal remains. Long-term preservation of buried faunal material requires special chemical conditions: anaerobic, arid, alkaline, or mineralizing. Most organic decomposers require oxygen; in its absence decomposition of organic matter is delayed or prevented. Thus, the famous preservation of soft tissue including skin, hair, and internal organs in the wet anaerobic conditions of bogs, ponds, wells, and so forth (Coles 1984). Collagen, the pliable organic component of bone, is preserved well in acid wet matrices that dissolve away the mineral component. Bone that has lost minerals will shrink, warp, and crack upon drying. Frozen sediments are the best case of wet anaerobic conditions, preserving the quick-frozen corpses of Pleistocene animals including humans (e.g., Guthrie 1990; Spindler 1993). Special non-archaeological anaerobic situations preserving animal remains of interest to paleoecologists include salt seeps and tar pits.

Decomposers also require moisture; permanently dry conditions such as desert sands, deep caves, and tombs in either situation preserve desiccated soft tissues, bones, and hair in good condition. Fast-draining sediments in regions of low rainfall, such as deep loess deposits, preserve bones well but lose soft tissues. Alkaline archaeological environments of moderate pH value such as shell middens and ash deposits preserve bone, but not soft tissue; calcareous loesses and shelly sands have equivalent effects. Sediments and hardpans rich in Fe, Mn, Si, K, and $CaCO_3$ allow organic and mineral matter to be replaced with stable minerals that retain form while changing the chemical composition of the bone – in short, fossilizing. The mineral component of burned bone is stabilized by calcination. Exchanges of minerals between bone and sediment, with recrystallization of the inorganic fractions of buried bone, are aspects of diagenesis that have serious implications for analytical studies of excavated bone (Sandford 1993a). After recovery, animal tissues should be maintained in conditions as close as possible to those which preserved them: wet kept wet and dry, dry, and both protected from microorganisms. Matrices that are alternately wet and dry or both acid and oxidized (e.g., podzols) provide no preservation.

Coprolites are special preservative matrices that contain many kinds of animal and plant fragments otherwise rarely encountered. Reinhard and Bryant (1992) list bacterial cysts, fungal hyphae and spores, parasites, feather fragments, mammal hair, small bones, eggshell and molluskan shell fragments, scales, and insects among the non-plant remains recoverable from coprolites. Researchers in Scottish coastal sites have identified cattle and sheep dung on the basis of characteristic phytolith suites (Powers-Jones 1994: 46). Well-preserved vertebrates may include intestinal contents which have the same potential for yielding animal products as do coprolites and privy contents (Greig 1985; Reinhard et al. 1986). A late Pleistocene mastodont recovered from an Ohio bog apparently had viable enteric bacteria in its gut (Lepper et al. 1991).

Trace fossils

Traces of animal behavior, technically **ichnofossils**, may be preserved in sediments and on buried surfaces of other materials. Artifacts and butchery cuts are special kinds of ichnofossils (Gautier 1993). Footprints are the most dramatic trace fossils in paleontology, providing intimate and immediate glimpses into animal behavior, as with the Pliocene footprints at Laetoli mentioned in Part IV. Bronze Age domestic herds left footprints in a muddy boundary ditch on Dartmoor in southern England, revealing the jostling amble familiar to herders everywhere and providing an unquantified inventory of herd composition (Smith et al. 1981: 269–270, Pl. 14). Worm tracks are less dramatic ichnofossils created by animal locomotion.

Animal burrows as small as worm tunnels or as large as those of badgers, rabbits, and foxes, are ichnofossils as well as important information about taphonomic processes (bioturbation). They reveal aspects of species-specific animal environments as well as behavior. Dens and nests reveal the animal occupant's former presence, implicate some behavior, and may include materials derived from the immediate environment.

Tooth and claw marks on bones and on cave walls and floors, occasionally identifiable to the generic level, are always worth noting for information on agents affecting osseous materials or sediment and rock substrates. Coprolites are behavioral products and therefore trace fossils, as are bones and fragments chemically etched in carnivore guts (Horwitz 1990). The catalog of ichnofossils humorously annotated by Gautier (1993) alerts archaeologists to many subtle indicators of animal behaviors. Bromley (1990) offers a guide to more advanced issues.

Chemical residues, isotopes, and trace elements

Residues identifiable by diverse chemical and molecular biological analyses provide information about animals in archaeological contexts even when tangible remains are absent. Residues have been extracted and analyzed from soils, potsherds, and stone tools by methods seeking traces of bone components, amino acids, lipids (fats), and blood. Such research on archaeological bone and residues on artifacts has increased greatly over the past decade. The first efforts extended established chemical analyses of soil, revealing concentrations of calcium and phosphates that implicate the former presence of animal tissues (Eidt 1985). More fugitive organic remains such as amino acids are sought in soils, with early optimism. Osseous remains of large animals of all kinds, especially people, have been chemically analyzed for paleodietary inferences. Surfaces of stone and ceramic artifacts have been analyzed to identify various organic residues identifiable to plant and animal sources. DNA extraction from ancient tissues has raised hopes of deeper knowledge of evolutionary and genetic relationships.

Early investigations based on experimental techniques and unexamined assumptions lacked critical insights into metabolic and diagenetic processes and were reported without error estimates. With hindsight, most of the widely publicized early results have proven flawed. As is typical of media-disseminated reports of scientific work, the refutations spread much more slowly beyond the laboratories than did the initial euphoric reports. It is wise for archaeologists not involved in developing new laboratory approaches to resist being dazzled into hasty acceptance. As a group archaeologists typically lack training in evaluating scientific methods (Pollard 1995). Until new methods have been presented for critical scrutiny by the scientific community, fully explained in terms of mechanisms and tested for precision and accuracy, interpretations of results are merely promissory notes and should be so understood.

In the 1990s, the most successful analyses seeking animal residues on tools have been lipid studies on potsherds (Evershed 1993). Early work identified dairy products such as milk and butter (Ryder 1983); subsequently, plant-residue identification has been more successfully specific. As analysts gained experience, they realized that there were many sources for lipid residues on sherds, involving original use of

ceramic vessels as well as contamination in the burial environment and after excavation. Organic compounds are degraded in cooking and during decay and diagenesis;
bacteria and fungi in soils can introduce organic compounds to sherds (Evershed et
al. 1992). Initially exciting claims for family- and species-level identification of
animals from blood residues on flint tools have not been successfully replicated. The
appropriateness of immunological and crystallographic techniques as well as the
mechanisms of preservation of organic residues are under challenge for archaeological materials (Cattaneo et al. 1993; Child and Pollard 1992; Downs and Lowenstein
1994; Gurfinkel and Franklin 1988). Research on amino-acid molecules in soils has
suffered similar critiques: organic molecules degrade with time and are subject
during burial to fragmentation and contamination from bacteria and fungi. While
many of the immunological techniques have been useful in forensic investigations,
their appropriateness for materials of great age remains to be demonstrated. The
potential value to archaeological and paleoenvironmental studies of successful
identifications of organic residues can hardly be overestimated. Research continues.

Animal tissues preserved in both wet and dry burial environments have been analyzed for DNA, especially since development of the polymerase chain reaction (PCR)
technique to amplify residual DNA for analysis (Eisenstein 1990). Preliminary results
were encouraging (Lawlor et al. 1991). Articles evaluating experience with ancient
DNA extraction and interpretation indicate that much remains to be learned about
techniques, preservation, sources of contamination, and interpretation of results.
Recognized complications of work on animal sequences include contamination
from several sources, not least of all from DNA derived from burial matrices; false
positives; and uncertainty about whether fragments represent RNA or DNA
(Andrews 1994; Hedges and Sykes 1992; Lambert and Grupe 1993). The recently recognized ancient phylogenetic links between animals and fungi may go some way
toward explaining why animal DNA/RNA is so easily contaminated by fungal
sequences (Wainwright et al. 1993).

Analyses of stable isotopes and trace element concentrations in bone promise to
revolutionize the study of diet, not only of humans but also of herbivores and carnivores, once the assumptions are clarified and methods refined (Price 1989). Stable
carbon isotopes provide suggestive evidence of components of the vegetation diet in
humans and herbivores, since the C_3, C_4, and CAM pathways utilized in plant metabolism (Chapter 13) carry isotopic signals into the tissues of consumers. The relationships are neither simple nor direct; bone collagen and apatite derive carbon isotopic
signals from different components of the diet, and the signals are modified in various
ways as they move up the trophic ladder (Chisholm 1989; Katzenberg 1992;
Schoeninger and Moore 1992). Stable carbon isotope studies entered the paleodietary

literature in the 1970s, with the trend recently being toward wider awareness of complications (Ambrose 1993; Ezzo 1994; Radosevich 1993). Carbon isotopes are used as indicators of animal diets and ranges, as well as of climate variation (van der Merwe 1986, 1989, 1992). Nitrogen isotopes help define the ratios of meat to plant foods; applications of oxygen isotopes are under study. Diagenetic changes in bone after burial differentially affect carbon in collagen and apatite; the latter is subject to mineral exchanges, while collagen maintains its original ratios (Fizer et al. 1994).

Sandford (1993a) sketches the wobbly career of trace-element analyses applied to animal bones. The story is much the same as for stable isotopes: initial optimism over direct relationships between dietary components and bone chemical analyses is tempered by realization of numerous complicating factors in life and after burial (Ezzo 1994; Sandford 1993a). Trace-element concentrations and ratios are expected to be informative about dietary composition, trophic level, animal ranges (including human), and other paleoenvironmental variables reflected in animal bones (Price et al. 1994). Trace-element ratios are also being applied to the analysis of residues on ceramic vessels. In the case of animal lipids, there is still much to be learned about chemical change in burial and in extraction methods (Heron and Evershed 1993).

Recovery: sampling and screening

> The customary use of quarter-inch screens has kept many archaeologists blissfully unaware of the myriad microvertebrate and plant remains that languish in their back-dirt piles.
>
> MORLAN 1987: 123

Faunal samples that will justify analyses to test inferences about both the environmental and cultural significance of the remains entail advance planning. Evaluation of sediments prior to excavation will alert excavators about the preservation conditions on a site and the complexity of site structure, so that the range of contexts and conditions of preservation of faunal material can be utilized to the fullest. A suitable research design specifies appropriate techniques for retrieval, and a sound sampling design assures the availability of special materials for field conservation. All of these parameters vary with the size, complexity, and condition of a site, so that little general advice can be given here (Hesse and Wapnish 1985: Chs. 3 and 5; Leiggi and May 1995; manuals on organic materials other than bone).

However, whether the issue is a dry site or a wet one, large or small, complex or simple, reliance on sight alone to recover organic materials is inadequate. "In the absence of rigorous recovery methods during excavation, the sample of artifacts will speak more of the behavior and decisions during excavation than about prehistory"

(Greenfield 1991: 167). Optimal methods include fine screening and/or water separation of systematic samples of matrix from all discrete contexts. Worthwhile samples are (1) adequate in size and condition to justify further study, (2) discrete enough to maintain contextual integrity, and (3) representative of the size range and proportions present in the deposits (Gamble and Bailey 1994). Archaeologists unfamiliar with the range of potential organic materials in site sediments typically underestimate it, especially being unaware of how small are microvertebrate and fish bones and the wealth of invertebrate materials amenable to recovery by appropriate methods. Control samples from comparable contexts off-site are valuable for contrasting cultural and natural assemblages (e.g., Dillehay 1989).

Decisions about the mesh of screens or sieves will vary with the nature of the enclosing sediments, the time and crew size available, and the research goals of the excavation. In general, the finest screen size amenable to the project's constraints is recommended: a mesh size of 1 mm is not extreme if the sediments support it. Small mesh can result in many welcome surprises when analytical expertise is available (Jones 1982; O'Connor 1989; Shaffer and Sanchez 1994). Control of sample volume to assure comparability is important in fine sieving and flotation. Standardized sample volumes that can be related to the volume of the source unit permit frequency and density calculations. This consideration may entail the collection of multiple samples from large units.

On-site participation of a faunal specialist is the best way to assure proper sampling of all appropriate contexts. Direct participation also helps the analyst understand the site in all its variety, assuring maintenance of contextual integrity through the analysis. The archaeologist defines sampling locations on the basis of cultural contexts, to permit controlled comparisons as well as retrieval of small items (e.g., grave fill, stomach and gut area of burials for food remains and parasites). For the analysis of environmental and ecological data, faunal collection strategies should always provide for recovery of soft tissues such as skin, hair, and sinew when preserved, invertebrate remains, and residues. Sampling for chemical or DNA analyses should avoid contamination during collection and storage. The recovery of ichnofossils requires special awareness and care in disarticulating sediments.

Dating vertebrate remains

Using vertebrate remains for chronometry requires awareness of the complications introduced by metabolism and diagenesis. Isotopic fractionation related to an organism's preferred food and position in the food chain is an obvious complication in isotopic dating of organic remains. Diagenetic processes exchange materials between deposits and buried organic matter. The chronometric techniques most applicable to vertebrate remains are liable to such problems (see Part II). New techniques and insightful and controlled applications in radiocarbon, amino-acid racemization, and electron spin resonance dating are enhancing awareness of complications and improving results (Brooks et al. 1990; Grün and Stringer 1991; Stafford et al. 1991; Taylor 1994).

Supported by taphonomic analyses, animal remains in sediments can help refine control of the time dimension in deposits. Evaluation of the transport and depositional histories of included animal remains provides information about the history of a deposit, its relative integrity, the depositional environment, and the time duration involved in transport and deposition. For example, the condition of included animal remains is helpful in estimating the relative durations of processes of transport, deposition, and burial – less or more than a year, accumulation over many years, and so forth.

Ageing and sexing vertebrate bones

A major emphasis in zooarchaeology contributing to study of human behaviors is determining the age and sex composition of faunal assemblages once those have been sorted taxonomically. The applications are many; some have been cited in this volume. In paleoecological interpretations, such information is most often used in determining seasonality of capture, and in distinguishing incipient domestication from hunting of wild animals, on the basis of the age and sex composition of archaeological assemblages.

For large vertebrates including people, the important indicators of individual age at death are the size of bones, the degree of ossification of bones, and the number and condition of teeth. Increments in the growth of teeth, and of scales, vertebrae, and otoliths of fish, are important supplemental sources of age information. Sexing depends on shape characteristics of pelves and availability of tissues that vary with secondary sex characters such as antlers, tusks, and horns. Age and sex analyses are tasks for experienced analysts. The favored approaches, and their limits, can be reviewed in texts (Davis 1987: 39–45; Hesse and Wapnish 1985; Hillson 1986; Wheeler and Jones 1989), journals, and collections of specialist publications (e.g., Wilson et al. 1982).

Paleoenvironmental indicators

With the singular exception of humans, the remains of large animals identified to species can provide information on gross regional climate, meso-scale habitats, and relative dating (especially with extinct species). Large domesticates have unique environmental implications. Seasonality indicators may be based on a number of criteria (Table 15.3). Food remains and thus indications of both habitat and niche may be directly identified in chewed wads of food (quids or boluses), stomach contents, dung and coprolites. The dietary contributions of browse vs. grasses, and of grasses grown in areas of differing temperature and precipitation regimes, may be studied through stable isotope ratios and trace elements in herbivore bones and teeth, and in shells, giving some indication of the range of habitats available to the animals whose remains were deposited in a site. Many of these methods avoid the limitations of analogy as a means of knowing. Numerous equifinalities involved in archaeological associations remain, however, as special problems with faunal collections from archaeological sites.

Small vertebrates, especially rodents and insectivores, have small ranges and relatively narrow environmental tolerances by species. However, the remains of small animals reach archaeological deposits by a variety of routes. Some were human prey for food and/or fur; others were domesticated to serve more complex human purposes, as with barn cats, dogs, and ferrets; others were kept for food and fur, as with paca and rabbits. Some invited themselves and lived among human habitations as commensals or competitors (e.g., rodents [Auffray et al. 1988]). Individual bones, teeth, or whole mummies were introduced into middens after serving as fetishes or decorative accessories. Some animals occupied an archaeological site between periods of human use, dying in their home burrows, while others were introduced in the scat of carnivores or the regurgitated pellets of birds of prey (Andrews 1990). Each case has different implications for the spatial relevance of potential environmental clues. For example, owl ranges are likely to be larger than those of their prey. Owls are also selective; they will not deposit a sample representative of any specific area (Yalden and Morris 1990). Animals living among humans, such as granary beetles, mice and rats, cats and dogs, have wide environmental ranges regardless of their natural tolerances because they live in artificially maintained habitats. Consequently, they may reflect only the specific environments of human dwellings (Buckland 1991; Rackham 1982). The environmental significance of small-animal remains thus varies with the modes of association and deposition. The better the quality of stratigraphic and contextual resolution achieved during excavation, the better will the faunal analyst be able to discriminate among the possibilities.

Analogical inferences about bird habitats or climates must be drawn carefully, without expectations for exactitude when migrators are involved. On the other hand, home ranges of permanent residents may be at micro-scales. People transport birds and bird parts over great distances. Humans use birds and birds' eggs as food,

Table 15.3 Seasonality of death indicators

Basis of methods	Introductory references
Vertebrates	
Seasonal availability/unavailability	
Migrators	Monks 1981
Aestivators/hibernators	Monks 1981
Growth and maturation	
Epiphyseal/suture fusion	Monks 1981; Wilson et al. 1982
Antler condition and shedding	Legge and Rowley-Conwy 1988; Monks 1981
Medullary bone	Rick 1975
Porotic bone	
Egg-laying or molting	Monks 1981
Antler regeneration	Monks 1981
Tooth eruption, wear, and crown height	Hillson 1986
Tooth dentine and cementum annuli	Hillson 1986; Lieberman 1994
Vertebral annuli	Monks and Johnson 1993
Fish otoliths	Carlson 1988; Monks 1981
Fish vertebrae, scales, and spines	Carlson 1988; Monks and Johnston 1993; Wheeler and Jones 1989
Reproduction cycle	
Birth timing	Monks 1981
Eggs	Monks 1981
Invertebrates	
Seasonal unavailability	
Aestivators	Davis 1987
Hibernators	Monks 1981; Davis 1987
Dormancy	Undeveloped
Growth and maturation	
Molluskan annuli	Claassen 1993, 1998; Deith 1983; Monks and Johnston 1993
Shell annuli isotopes	Bailey et al. 1983; Kennett and Voorhies 1996; Shackleton 1973
Reproduction cycle	
Pupae	Gilbert and Bass 1967

utilize their feathers, bones, skins, and eggshells in many ways, keep them as pets, preserve them as fetishes or ornaments, and train species such as cormorants and hawks for hunting. Bird bones may also be brought to sites by other predators. Seasons of availability for migratory birds (Table 15.3) cannot be extended far back into Quaternary time, since migratory distances, routes, and timing have changed many times with changing insolation, climates, and environments. The seasons, being expressions of orbital parameters, can be read from biological clocks; months, which are cultural conventions, are not equivalent to seasons.

Amphibians and reptiles (**herpetofauna**), including their eggs, are rarely more than minor food resources for human groups because of their small sizes and solitary habits. Sea turtles and iguanas are notable, localized exceptions. Reptiles may be prized for their skins and carapaces, and they are often used as fetishes, so that humans as well as other predators introduce their remains to living sites. Herpetofauna may share caves and other sites alternately with people, without direct contact. The sensitivity of cold-blooded animals to temperature and moisture makes them useful in paleoenvironmental modeling.

Fish remains survive in archaeological sediments only when quickly buried into dry or anaerobic preservation contexts. Bones, spines, and scales are fragile and may disintegrate quickly unless calcined, but the dense ear-stones (otoliths) are both durable and identifiable to the generic and sometimes specific level. Both marine and freshwater fish provide human food; skins can be used for clothing, spines for tools, vertebral centrum bones for beads. Inferences about seasonality of site use from fish remains, unless remains are abundant, suffer the bias introduced by storage of dried fish and the importation of fish products and bony parts. Reasoning from fish remains to climatic conditions is probably justifiable only when the fish support without conflict evidence from more robust data sources (Brinkhuizen and Clason 1986; Wheeler and Jones 1989).

INVERTEBRATES

One of the striking things about insects in any habitat is their utility in the general eco-logical scheme. They seem to exist for the purpose of being eaten by a wide range of animals.

ORDISH 1985: 142

If archaeological deposits were truly representative of the worlds in which they were created, they would yield overwhelming numbers of invertebrate remains. There are vastly more high-level taxa of invertebrates than appear usually in archaeological deposits, or ever in archaeological collections. The ubiquity and pervasiveness of invertebrates in biocoenoses are rapidly lost in thanatocoenoses, even before the losses incurred during excavation.

In comparison to the publication record for aspects of vertebrate archaeozoology, the record for invertebrates is impoverished. It is dominated by marine and terrestrial mollusks and recently enriched by expanding studies of insects, particularly beetles. Parasitology has begun to demonstrate its potential in paleoecology, and the study of microfauna in marine and freshwater sediment cores is beginning to make inroads into archaeology from a strong base in paleoclimatology. Microbes are being identified in special preservation contexts; DNA research is opening a new frontier (Chapter 17). The best of the literature on invertebrates in archaeology has been written by specialists for other specialists and is relatively inaccessible to and frequently ignored by archaeologists. This situation must be reversed to permit maturation of paleoenvironmental studies, because the smallest animals carry significant information about temperature, moisture, chemistry, and biology in paleoenvironments.

Mollusks

The interpretive usefulness of shelled invertebrates was recognized early in the nineteenth century as investigations demonstrated the artifactual status of shell middens, and has been expanding ever since. Molluskan roles in human environments include food, raw material (e.g., shell, pearls), disease vectors, and scavengers. The information about temperature, moisture, and substrate carried by both aquatic and terrestrial species is well recognized in paleoenvironmental studies (e.g., Klippel and Morey 1986). Among mollusks, the most appreciated groups are the bivalves (cockles and mussels, oysters, clams, etc.) and gastropods (snails, periwinkles, whelks, etc.) (Claassen 1998). The marine mollusks most important in archaeology include an array of gastropod and bivalve dwellers on rocky, sandy, muddy, or grassy substrates near shore, whence they were gathered by humans (Waselkov 1987). Sizes of mollusks range from the tropical giant clam to soil-dwelling gastropods smaller than pinheads. While gastropod ranges are generally small, and bivalves are confined to water, shells of all taxa may be transported over vast distances by predators or as sedimentary particles.

Although the most visible gastropods are introduced to archaeological sites by humans or other predators, some are synanthropic, scavenging in gardens and domestic rubbish in search of food. Because the autecology of terrestrial snails is fairly well known, particularly in the British Isles and the rest of Western Europe, analogy supports paleoenvironmental interpretations to quite fine degrees of resolution in regard to habitats (Bobrowsky 1984; Evans 1991; Thomas 1985). Terrestrial gas-

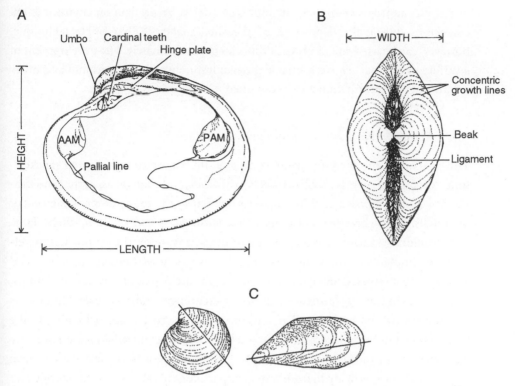

Figure 15.3 Generalized bivalve shell structure and selected terminology. "(A) inside of right valve. AAM, PAM: anterior and posterior adductor muscle scars, respectively. (B) Dorsal view of shell. (C) Axis of maximum growth in a clam (left) and a mussel (right)." (Excerpted and modified from Seed 1980: 25.)

tropods are sensitive to substrate chemistry, soil temperatures, moisture, and plant communities; they provide excellent detail on land use and plant successions at very local scales. In calcareous soils, where gastropods are numerous and well preserved and pollen grains are not, they are a valuable alternative to palynology, and a complement with strictly local relevance when pollen is available (Evans 1984).

Mollusk shells are composed of a protein matrix of conchiolin ($C_{30}H_{48}O_{11}N_9$) enclosing calcite and aragonite crystals. The shells grow outward at their edges as carbonates are secreted by the mantle tissue that encloses the soft bodies and wraps around the growing edge. Growing shells incorporate information about the chemistry and temperature of their immediate environments, as well as about their individual growth rates (Lutz and Rhoads 1980). Environmental conditions are reflected in the structure and chemistry of shell components: in the crystal size and type and growth increments (Fig. 15.3), and in isotope ratios in carbonate crystals. Analytical techniques appropriate to these attributes can derive proxy data on environmental conditions during the deposition of the shell material. "No single technique, however, can be used effectively on all species indiscriminately. The development of a variety of approaches is essential if the maximum amount of seasonal and other environmental information is to be obtained" (Deith 1983: 69).

Arthropods (crustaceans and insects; ostracods)

This numerous and diverse phylum comprises invertebrates with jointed exoskeletons – organisms such as crayfish, insects, ostracods, and water fleas. Arthropod exoskeletons are composed of chitin, material similar to the tough outer skin layers of mammals. Even when their chitinous exoskeletons are preserved in middens, large and mobile crustaceans such as crabs and lobsters provide very little information relevant to human environments, being indicative only of human collecting and exploitation strategies. Small aquatic crustaceans are proxies for water conditions, and those living among humans, such as some scavenger crabs, are useful indicators of temperature and moisture. Tiny bivalved aquatic crustaceans belonging to the taxonomic Orders Cladocera and Ostracoda, recovered from subaqueous cores, are cherished proxies in paleolimnology (Binford et al. 1983; Lowe and Walker 1984: 197–201). Ostracods living in fresh water are particularly valuable in studies of water quality and the human land-use practices that influence it (e.g., Deevey et al. 1979; Palacios-Fest 1994).

Insect exoskeletons are recoverable when buried in stable conditions maintaining either permanent wetness or permanent dryness (Buckland 1976). Elements of the exoskeletons of beetles (Coleoptera) are particularly durable (Fig. 15.4), as are the puparia (cases for the dormant stage) of common flies. While some insects provide food for humans (e.g., Madsen and Kirkman 1988; Sutton 1995), the vast majority of insect species are less welcome sharers of living space or body surfaces. Typical non-food roles of insects among human communities include disease vectors, pests, parasites (lice and fleas), decomposers of waste matter, and competitors for stored foods (Kenward 1982).

Because breeding requirements and food needs are likely to be specific, insects closely reflect habitat conditions at very small scales. In particular, many are highly sensitive to temperature. For instance, beetle assemblages from stratified Quaternary deposits show that highly mobile beetles respond much more rapidly to changes in temperature than do plant species. Thus, beetle assemblages provide sensitive indicators of past ambient temperatures that may conflict with the evidence from plant proxies (Coope 1977; Morgan et al. 1983). Analog inferences for beetle

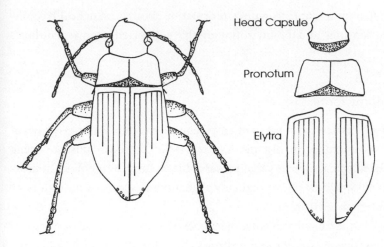

Figure 15.4   Dorsal surface of a ground beetle, showing parts typically preserved: the head capsule, pronotum (thorax cover), and elytra (wing covers). (After Elias 1994: Fig. 3.1.)

microclimates are considered well founded because the beetle species appear to be evolutionarily stable in their climatic requirements, moving to suitable places and expanding food choices rather than adapting genetically (Coope 1986; Elias 1994). That is certainly not necessarily the case for other insect taxa, whose ability to adapt genetically in response to environmental changes is notorious in the checkered history of insecticides in the past few decades.

Soft-bodied invertebrates

Worms, being soft-bodied, are rarely found preserved in archaeological materials, although they may have permeated the site sediments. earthworm casts will betray their presence and warn the excavator of the damage they have done to stratification and midden constituents (Armour-Chelu and Andrews 1994; Atkinson 1957; Stein 1983). Much of the environmental information earthworms provide is equally recoverable from chemical and particle-size analyses of the sediment itself. Larvae of insects are rarely recovered and usually difficult to identify; their usefulness as paleoenvironmental proxies is unevaluated.

Environmentally, the really informative worms are those parasitic in humans and domestic animals (nematodes and helminths); they reveal the health status of the site's inhabitants and may give clues to distant contacts as well (Fiennes 1978; Mahmoud 1989; Reinhard et al. 1986). Parasitology has begun to realize its potential in paleoecology (Reinhard 1992), providing information about human health conditions, population densities, and the environments that supported intermediate hosts and vectors.

Pathogenic microorganisms

As DNA research opens new frontiers in micropaleontology, and awareness grows of the many roles of microbes in organic life, diverse microorganisms are being identified in archaeological matrices that preserve them. Improvements in microscopy assure that they will be more regularly exploited as sensitive indicators of special, usually internal, environments.

In the study of human environments, the currently most informative microorganisms are the pathogenic bacteria and protozoa (Kingdoms Monera and Protista, respectively), which directly affect health and population size, and therefore aspects of biological evolution, in our species. Infectious pathogens may kill their hosts, and therefore have the ability to move from host to host, some across species. Pathogenic protozoans such as amoebae and *Giardia* reach humans from water or intermediate vectors, causing severe diseases including dysentery and malaria. Some bacteria live as symbionts in the intestinal tracts of all vertebrates, playing useful roles in digestion. Others are parasitic without being fatal to the host. Bacteria and their spores can be isolated from human feces and from soil and plant detritus, the problems being avoidance of contamination with recent material. Refinement of techniques for isolating and identifying microorganisms from archaeological contexts promises crucial detail on the histories of human pathologies as well as enhanced information about environmental factors that have influenced the course of evolution (Anderson and May 1982; Fiennes 1978; Roberts and Manchester 1995; Verano and Ubelaker 1993).

Invertebrate taphonomy

Invertebrates occur in archaeological sites as food remains left by a range of predators, as cohabitants, parasites, or adventitious or technological debris. Understanding their taphonomic histories requires alertness by excavators to their presence, recovery, and interpretive values. Remains of large invertebrates usually are treated as normal archaeological sedimentary particles, recorded by context units in use at the site. Small invertebrates such as terrestrial gastropods, insects, and worms burrow into sites, drawn by organically enriched soils. Burrowers of any size are taphonomic agents, capable of postdepositional sorting or homogenizing of the

sedimentary matrix. Only when their presence is correctly interpreted and their relative ages well controlled can these resident invertebrates inform on site microclimates and microenvironments. Invertebrates imported to a site by vertebrate
predators, or deposited by wind or water, reflect environments elsewhere, whose
locations need to be established if possible (e.g., Kenward 1975).

In shell middens, mollusks represent variously foods for humans or other vertebrates, industrial material (for making beads, ornaments, knives, hoes, and axes), or
merely adventitiously collected specimens associated with food species. Environmental interpretations must take account of these taphonomic possibilities; excavators should be alert to clues in context. In the heterogeneous open matrix of shell
middens, with spaces among the large particles, burrowers thrive and small particles
and shells as well as small mammal and fish bones typically lose stratigraphic integrity by falling through cracks and burrows. With integrity is lost their interpretive
usefulness as well; only small items whose position is secure within a stratigraphic
unit can be informative about the chronology, depositional environment, or cultural
activities associated with that unit.

Preservation of invertebrate remains

Concentrations of shells create a local chemistry conducive to the preservation of
shell and bone, sometimes even chitin. Diagenesis of shell involves dissolution
of the organic and mineral fractions, exchange of elements and recrystallization of
minerals. Burial conditions affect these processes differently. Discard behavior
creates the depositional environments and preservation potential. Isolated shells
are subject to rapid chemical attack in soils, and small shells are always lost before
more massive ones. The interaction of physical breakage (as in trampling and
dumping) and chemical and bacterial alteration degrades shells rapidly.
Permineralization of calcitic minerals by groundwater ions retains the form of
mollusk shells, while changing the weight and chemistry. Unlike bones, shells are
not preserved by calcination; heating in cooking or incineration speeds disintegration and therefore acid attack. Mollusks preserve well in alkaline sediments such as
calcareous crusts, loesses, and ash deposits that are inimical to pollen; therefore,
they have complementary distributions and applications (Evans 1984). In some wet
matrices shells lose mineral components and are reduced to shrunken and warped
sheets of conchiolin alone.

Preservation of soft-bodied invertebrates requires stability, either permanent
wetness or dryness; preservation in alternately wet and dry or acid and oxidized conditions is brief. Wet anaerobic conditions constraining bacterial action preserve soft

tissues, including chitin, in bogs, ponds and pools, pits and ditches, urban fills, and coastal lagoons. Recent paleoentomological research in Greenland and Iceland reminds us that chilled or frozen soils preserve insects remarkably well (Buckland et al. 1991). Permanently wet or dry sediments that preserve other organic remains may hold parasites as well as bacterial and protozoan cysts (Jones 1985; Reinhard et al. 1986). Parasitic invertebrates preserve with the desiccated soft tissues of host organisms. The eggs and cysts of parasites may survive intact in soils, floor sweepings, grave and pit fills, anaerobic tombs, and mummies.

Trace fossils

Burrows dug by invertebrates rarely survive in sediments, an important exception being tropical termite nests. Seed stores damaged by insects testify to the high costs of competition for food between humans and insect pests (Buckland 1991). Insect scats and egg cases may resemble small seeds; proper identification enriches information. Worm casts are among the most abundant terrestrial trace fossils. The activity of worms and other burrowers can sometimes be inferred from the degree of sorting, or destroyed stratification in site sediments (Allen and Robinson 1993; Crimes and Droser 1992; Gautier 1993).

Chemical residues

Identification of invertebrates in archaeological residues is not well developed. Heron and Evershed (1993: 256–257) cite a study that identified beeswax on a Greek ceramic vessel thought to have been used as a beehive. Isotope and trace-element studies have made good cases for human consumption of seafood, but the distinction between vertebrate and invertebrate fauna has not yet been made. Seafood is recognized in isotopic signatures in the marine food chain created by the carbon reservoir in the sea and the fractionation of carbon isotopes by water plants (Chisholm et al. 1982, 1983; Little and Schoeninger 1995; Schoeninger et al. 1983). With additional work on lipids and DNA, invertebrate residues might be recognized under ideal conditions of organic preservation.

Recovery

Whenever conditions might be favorable for the preservation of invertebrate remains, such as insects, special recovery techniques should be tried. Beetle remains, for instance, can be recovered from organic sediments by flotation with kerosene (paraffin), even when the remains cannot be directly observed in the sediments (Kenward et al. 1980). Dry sediments are likely to include a rich desiccated insect fauna, which can be concentrated by appropriate sampling and sieving of all sediment units on a site. The sampling might well extend beyond the site to retrieve gastropod suites and insects from nearby landforms and soils, as controls and source indicators. Local geomorphology and soils chemistry are also crucial data for evaluating native and introduced faunas, the ratios of which vary significantly across space (Evans 1991). Human burials and tombs are likely sources for remains of invertebrate parasites and decomposers (e.g., Reinhard et al. 1992).

Appropriate systematic sampling is crucial for remains such as shells in middens that are too numerous to permit collection of the entire suite, as well as for remains that are dispersed in sediments (e.g., Claassen 1998; Kent 1988: Ch. 3). Whole or rare specimens or large fragments collected during excavation complement sieved samples.

Organic materials, including shell and chitin, may require treatment to remove salt prior to storage; simple tests will help evaluate that need. Important specimens may require hardening. All should be protected from excess humidity once cleaned and dried.

Dating

Chronometry based on invertebrate remains poses special problems that should be kept well in mind. Problems with mollusk ages surfaced early in the chronicles of radiocarbon. They include the incorporation into shell calcite of old carbon from groundwater and the marine reservoir, and fractionation of carbon isotopes in nearshore marine plants and marine food chains. These complications can sometimes be corrected, but each case is local (e.g., Little 1993). The conchiolin fraction of shells, small as it is, is preferred for radiocarbon dating; AMS dating makes this feasible (Aitken 1990: 87–88). Small invertebrates such as insects are normally preserved in organic-rich matrices that offer better choices for radiocarbon dating than remains of burrowing animals. Amino-acid racemization dating of shell has been superseded by an emphasis on the method's value in paleotemperature research (Aitken 1990: 13–14). ESR dating has been successful for mollusks in geological contexts only, not for the small scale of shell middens (Aitken 1990: 199).

Interesting applications of invertebrates to dating issues include the use of insect remains to interpret the season and duration of exposure of a pit fill (Chomko and Gilbert 1991), and bivalve growth-ring sequences used to test contemporaneity of discontinuous shell deposits (Dillon and Clark 1980). The successful use of small objects or organisms for dating ultimately rests on scrupulous interpretation of the context of recovery. Small items capable of insinuation into extant deposits, or valuable items curated and transported, will frustrate efforts at dating contexts, however precise may be the determination of the object's unique age.

Paleoenvironmental indicators

Invertebrates are excellent sources of information about aspects of temperature and moisture in paleoenvironments. Not only are they sensitive to such habitat features in life, they typically incorporate into their exoskeletons habitat-specific chemical signals, such as oxygen-isotope temperature records. Soft-bodied invertebrates contribute very little to paleoenvironmental study except for the valued beetles and the information revealed by parasites and disease vectors about internal environments of vertebrates. This characteristic of parasites makes them useful proxies for their hosts: parasites in coprolites implicate the former presence of large animals otherwise unrepresented.

Marine mollusks are indicative of ranges of water temperatures and chemistry (Part III), water depth and bottom conditions, and the season of their own death (Table 15.3). They have been used to study changing human food sources and collecting patterns, marine regressions and transgressions, water temperatures and depths, tidal amplitudes, shore configurations, localized siltation rates, and currents. Freshwater mollusks (naiads) are sensitive to water temperature, chemistry, limpidity, oxygenation, and current velocity (e.g., Klippel et al. 1978). A good introductory summary of paleoenvironmental work with mollusks is in Lowe and Walker (1984).

Molluskan shell shape indicates environmental conditions such as water temperature, depth, substrate, and food availability (e.g., Kent 1988). Variations in shell increment widths inform about individual life spans and season of death (Claassen 1986; Lutz and Rhoads 1980), with a sensitivity recording not merely seasonal climates but also weather – storminess and temperature extremes. This sensitivity has been applied to the task of studying prehistoric El Niño events and other climatic variables off the coasts of northwestern South America (Rollins et al. 1986) and southwestern Africa (Cohen et al. 1992). As discussed in Chapter 8, oxygen isotopes in mollusk shells can be read in terms of atmospheric and surface water temperatures. Source waters for transported shells may be indicated by trace elements in shell chemistry (e.g., Claassen and Sigmann 1993). More research must be done before the range of variation in shell chemistry and growth patterns is well understood; archaeological analyses will be immature until these variables are better controlled. In addition, as discussed above, diagenetic changes in shell caused by leaching and recrystallization constrain results.

The abundance of insect species and their genetic plasticity make individual specimens or species a weak basis for paleoenvironmental inferences. Studies of insect
autecology are just beginning to provide analog data (e.g., Elias 1994). In this state of
affairs, Kenward (1975, 1978) urged that modern insect associations in different habitats be studied to provide reasonable analogies about climate and local habitats for
application to multi-species assemblages recovered archaeologically. Kenward's
work and that of others in archaeological contexts (e.g., Buckland et al. 1991, 1994;
Coope 1986; Kenward 1982) provide impressive examples of the specificity that can
be attained.

CODA

Archaeologists need to be sensitive to the ubiquity of faunal remains and their many
guises in archaeological matrices. Vertebrate remains are merely the most obvious,
when preserved at all. Given that faunal remains may occur as body parts dried,
waterlogged, calcined, or fossilized in a broad range of sizes, and as chemical residues, it may be that no archaeological sites are completely devoid of faunal indicators. In any condition or size, identifiable faunal remains associated with human
activities can contribute to interpretations of human behavior or human environments. A responsible sensitivity on the part of excavators to taphonomic contexts
and processes is crucial to the recovery and evaluation of such remains.

16

FAUNAL PALEOECOLOGY

Variety ... seems to be the dominant aspect of paleoecological situations.

OLSON 1980: 9–10

The truly dynamic components of the biosphere are members of the Animal Kingdom, most of whom are capable of motion and intentional behavior. Behavior (e.g., feeding, competition, migration, cooperation) immensely complicates environmental modeling by reducing predictability in system states. Here, the emphasis is on describing and interpreting the faunal components of past ecosystems, including humans, as a basis for understanding paleoecology.

Paleoenvironmental reconstruction has been important in paleontology for a very long time, beginning two centuries ago in the fossiliferous Paleolithic caves of Europe. However, interest in paleoenvironmental reconstruction from archaeological faunas did not travel intact across the Atlantic (Grayson 1981). The best American work in the genre has been done by paleontologists, whether or not working for archaeologists (e.g., Graham, Guilday, Guthrie, Klippel, Parmalee). The problem in America seems to derive from the fact that few paleontologists are interested in Holocene faunas, while neoecologists work in a timeless dimension that assumes the validity for ancient times of actualistic study in present conditions. Consequently, the development of critical theory for paleoenvironmental reconstruction from archaeological faunas in the Americas has been delayed, to the detriment of research designs and excavation strategies. Archaeozoology with an environmental emphasis is more at home in the rest of the world than in the western hemisphere, where autecological studies are in short supply and zooarchaeological emphases on human behavior dominate the archaeological literature.

Admittedly, there are stringent limitations to the applicability of archaeological data for paleoenvironmental work with fauna, as indicated below. There are also opportunities being lost worldwide as information from archaeological sites is not integrated with that from paleontological universes. While palynology dominates terrestrial paleoclimatology and paleoenvironmental reconstruction, faunal data take a lesser place because the value of microfauna as proxies for numerous environmental components is overlooked. Living animal associations result from many interacting mechanisms and random events, and therefore cannot be predicted from theoretical variables or recovered in detail from remains. With the demise of community theory in paleoecology (Chapter 14), theoretical models for ecosystem structure are imprecise; the assumption of trophic levels is about as far as they go. Trophic models are useful for fauna at the level of taxonomic order, predicting taxa adapted to a standard range of macro-niches such as herbivores, omnivores, carnivores, insectivores. However, they are non-predictors at the level of genus and species, where behavior rules species interactions and archaeologists become interested.

The concept of synecology is replacing community theory in the biosciences. Its expansion should promote the integration of human ecology with that of other organisms at all scales. Synecological insights have significantly informed recent research on anthropogenic extinctions of island faunas (e.g., Dye and Steadman 1990), as well as on the beginnings of domestication with the idea that some species, notably canids, might be self-domesticators that adapted to people even as people adapted to their close presence (Coppinger and Feinstein 1991; Morey 1994).

In archaeology, interest in faunal internal environments is growing as biological anthropologists and zooarchaeologists refine the study of diets and disease. The identification of disease vectors and conditions of hygiene in archaeological contexts has direct relevance to human biological adaptations and evolution. As such, these factors should be as important in human faunal ecology as the study of food resources and domestication.

RECONSTRUCTING FAUNAL ENVIRONMENTS

For an individual organism, the environment normally comprises three components: the non-living or abiotic world, the world of other species, and the world of conspecifics.

INGOLD 1986: 2

Faunal remains from archaeological contexts present special problems of recovery, analysis, and interpretation. Animal remains reach archaeological deposits by means of natural processes, human purposes, or combinations of both. The analytical discrimination of animal roles in such deposits, as elements of environment or human resources, is desirable but not always possible. Therefore, within the subdiscipline of archaeozoology/zooarchaeology the tasks of environmental reconstruction and the understanding of human behavior involving animals are not cleanly separable. Studies tend to cleave along the line between vertebrates and invertebrates, or large vertebrates and all other remains, with behavioral emphasis typically given to the former and paleoenvironmental emphasis to the latter. Such cleavages of convenience lead to neglect of some bodies of data, and to overextension of others. Synthesis remains the ideal (Lyman 1982).

The extraction of environmental information from animal remains suffers methodological and theoretical constraints, some peculiar to archaeological deposits, most shared with paleontology. The pervasive, inescapable problem of representativeness reminds us that we do not, and cannot, know what is the relationship of archaeological samples of animal remains to the living communities from which they were derived (Lyman 1994). It is best to consider an archaeological collection of faunal remains recovered from a single depositional unit as an "assemblage," a partially artificial conglomeration of remains from an unknown number and diversity of sources. Assemblages, therefore, are in no essential way equivalent to the associations of species that may be observed within living communities.

Methodological problems exacerbate the sampling constraints by introducing biases in terms of the portions of a site excavated, the discrimination of appropriate stratigraphic units, and the retrieval of subsets of the site population by decisions made about screen size, bulk sampling, and so forth. The only mitigation for these biases is exquisite excavation and recording techniques; not even those can completely overcome taphonomic and preservation biases, which must be addressed analytically. This set of methodological problems applies equally to archaeological site faunas and assemblages retrieved by paleontologists from natural traps.

Additionally, there is the problem of reliance on analogy to apply autecological knowledge of living species to the interpretation of death assemblages from times past. Analytical and interpretive approaches that mitigate the constraints of analogy in paleoenvironmental reconstruction are emphasized in this chapter. However, analogy necessarily plays a major role in modeling faunal paleoenvironments.

A major limitation on the applicability of analogies is the assumption that the range of variance observable today adequately represents the range of adaptation at all times and places. Rhoads and Lutz (1980: 3), speaking of marine adaptations, nevertheless express well the situation for all animals: "A species is able to grow and reproduce as long as its functional range (biospace) [here, habitat] is not exceeded by the ambient environment. Not all parts of the realized biospace promote equal growth or fecundity. Different combinations of niche parameters will be expressed as changed rates of growth, survivorship, or reproductive success."

Faunal assemblages: site data

As presented above (Chapter 15, pp. 441–443), the remains of animals arrive in archaeological deposits by a variety of routes. The analyst must keep this potential complication firmly in mind in addressing an assemblage from any site.

The first step in paleoenvironmental modeling with archaeological fauna is an enumerated list of specimens recovered – the composition of the assemblage – from each depositional context or site (a set of contexts). The list comprises entities identified by taxon. Ideally, the finds are evaluated by taphonomic criteria for assemblage integrity, taking into account the elements represented for each taxon. Integrity and synchroneity are essential characteristics of faunal assemblages that are to be used in reconstructing paleoenvironments. The stratigraphy of depositional units, with chronometric analyses, should establish whether the several contexts are synchronic, diachronic, or heterochronic (all more or less the same age, a series of ages, or a mixed-age group). If there are doubts, a series of radiocarbon ages should settle the matter, as well as defining the size of the time envelope within which the assemblage belongs. A collection involving more than one identifiable period of time or belonging to more than one depositional episode should be subdivided prior to the derivation of any inferences about paleoenvironments. If the time span is undefinable, the assemblage is of questionable value for paleoenvironmental work.

Habitats

Successful paleoenvironmental reconstruction using archaeological faunas entails sophisticated biological knowledge. Both environmental requirements and tolerance breadths of modern species must be understood in detail, and the organisms at issue must not be far removed in space or generational time from the population used as analog. Interdisciplinary data sets and isotope studies are relaxing the reliance on analogies for both vertebrate and invertebrate remains. Stable carbon isotopes have demonstrated value for interpreting herbivore diets, as well as the range of vegetation habitats utilized by a species.

External (off-site) data on habitat states and conditions enrich interpretations of archaeological faunal assemblages. Many data sources are useful for testing interpretive results in terms of congruence among multiple data sets, and they enrich the details available for delineating habitats and animal roles in ancient landscapes. Even at fairly general levels of precision, habitat reconstruction helps explain presences and absences of faunal taxa in assemblages. Its greatest value for archaeologists, of course, is providing context for sites and for human populations and their subsistence strategies.

Climate

Climatic reconstruction at mega- and macro-scales is no longer reliant in any significant degree on data from vertebrate faunas (Chapter 8). In the age of General Circulation Models, a maturing discipline of paleoclimatology provides faunal paleoecology with external data on climates at global to regional scales. Habitat reconstructions based on non-faunal data are best for evaluating the congruence of faunal data; otherwise, circular reasoning intrudes.

Climate data drawn from sources external to a faunal assemblage are the foundation for climate modeling at meso- and micro-scales. Within such contexts, local and microclimatic conditions important at site scales can be interpreted from local faunal assemblages. At this point stenotopic small vertebrates, with relatively narrow tolerances for temperature and moisture, and key invertebrate faunas achieve maximal usefulness in paleoecology. Analogies drawn from modern species ranges may be applied once their relevance can be argued or demonstrated, providing small-scale, precise temperature estimates (e.g., Morgan 1987). Oxygen-isotope values in mollusk shells and vertebrate teeth permit estimates of average ambient temperatures experienced by the individual sampled.

Landforms and soils

Faunal assemblages contribute significantly to the reconstruction of landforms and soils (Parts IV and V), while the latter enrich models of animal distributions and behaviors based on vegetation. Interpretations of small vertebrate remains benefit from landform details such as the proximity of cliffs for raptor roosts explaining concentrations of microfaunal remains, and loose rock screes explaining a high frequency of bones and nests of small rodents. Interpretation of large vertebrate remains may depend on external information about landforms and elevations, as is shown in the Star Carr case study below, where a model of cervid seasonal movements was corrected for local conditions.

The diversity of landforms and soils in a study area is likely to have a direct relationship to the patchy distribution of vegetation. The patchiness of substrates defines the size and distribution of vegetation **patches**, which in turn affect access and use by animals. The developmental stage of soils, their drainage qualities, moisture content, organic content, and particle size constrain the types and richness of vegetation supported, and thus the herbivore composition and numbers. The vegetation and moisture quality of substrates are crucial habitat conditions for invertebrate herbivores and scavengers such as insects and gastropods. This close relationship makes insects and mollusks useful supplements and even proxies for paleosol investigations, fairly reliable substitutes for direct data on soils (e.g., Evans 1991).

Marine mollusks can implicate shore conditions, supplementing geoarchaeological data on marine regressions and transgressions, water depths, shore configurations, and localized siltation rates. Geoarchaeological data on coastal configurations and sediment types may indicate source areas for food items transported to sites, and clarify the role of choice in archaeological faunal assemblages (e.g., Shackleton 1988).

Vegetation

Vegetation formations in paleoecology are typically modeled from palynological data supplemented by climate and soils (Part VI). In modeling the vegetation component of faunal habitats, off-site evidence should be kept separate from on-site data prior to final integration, to avoid circularity and refine controls. Faunal evidence providing data on microhabitats should be congruent with the external data. Faunal remains incongruent with the bulk of other evidence for vegetation should be evaluated for the likelihood of exotic origins.

Herbivores ranging in size from elephants to insects evolve specialized organs for obtaining and digesting plant food. Many such specializations contribute to taxonomic distinctions at the levels of order and family, so that herbivores are classified separately from, e.g., insectivores, and specialized grazers of grass are distinguished from leaf-eaters. Of course, grazers optionally browse on leafy vegetation when necessary or desirable, the difference indicating mainly seasonal or climatic conditions. It is unwise to overemphasize modern specializations in projecting adaptive styles into paleoenvironments. The teeth of grass-eaters typically show adaptations to abrasive diets, which could otherwise destroy teeth prematurely, such as high molar crowns or teeth that grow continuously through life. Reflecting adaptation, the body size of herbivores is roughly indicative of the requisite area of suitable habitat (Fig. 16.1).

With good preservation conditions, animal food remains indicative of both habitat and niche may be directly identified in materials adhering to teeth or in calculus, chewed wads of food, stomach contents, dung and coprolites (e.g., Markgraf 1985). The dietary contributions of browse or grasses, and of grasses originating in areas of differing temperature, precipitation regimes, or chemical substrates, may be studied through stable isotopes and trace elements in herbivore bones and in shells, giving some indication of the range of habitats available to the animals whose

FAUNA

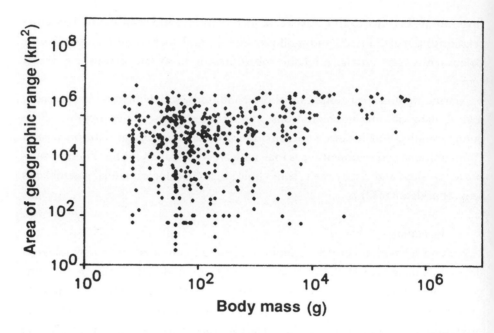

Figure 16.1   Relation between area of geographic range and body mass (plotted on logarith-
                mic axes) for the species of North American land mammals. Species of large body size
                tend to have large geographic ranges. (Reproduced with permission from Brown and
                Maurer 1989: Fig. 2, © 1989 American Association for the Advancement of Science;
                original caption.)

remains were deposited in a site. The broad, climatically controlled distribution of
C_4 plants on the North American continent may come as a surprise to archaeologists
habituated to think of maize as a unique example in temperate climates (Fig. 16.2).
Carbon-isotope values in herbivore bones, and their traces up the food chain to
people, may derive from some of these grasses.

Interactions between herbivores and their vegetative environments define the
characteristics of both in various feedback loops (Guthrie 1984). Overgrazing on
restricted tracts revises the composition of the vegetation, favoring plants unpalatable or toxic to grazers, whose numbers in turn are reduced. Herbivore cropping can
promote plant species whose reproductive organs are least at risk, favoring those
with underground reproductive organs over those that produce pollen and seeds.
Herbivore trampling favors some plant species over others and may damage substrates, initiating erosion. Elephants and other large "keystone herbivores," very
destructive to trees and other vegetation, can open and close niches for smaller
animals (Owen-Smith 1987). Selective browsing at ecotones may maintain or

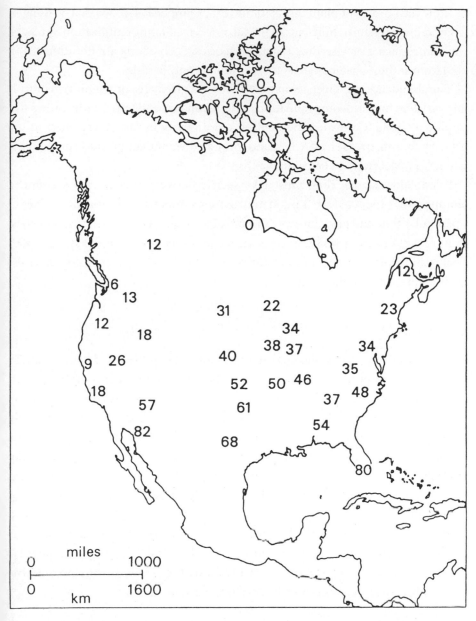

Figure 16.2 Proportion of C$_4$ species in the grass flora of various parts of North America. (Reproduced from Cox and Moore 1985: Fig. 2.5, with permission of Blackwell Science, Ltd; original caption.) Note the latitudinal cline in fitness of C$_4$ vegetation.

redefine the borders of plant associations (e.g., Campbell et al. 1994). The dung of large herbivores returns nutrients to the substrate, facilitating reutilization by plants, while introducing or reseeding palatable species. Such effects are not different in kind from anthropogenic changes that are unique only in scale.

The abundance and diversity of herbivores in a given area or region are controlling variables for carnivore populations – the secondary and tertiary consumers in a trophic pyramid. Carnivore abundances and diversity in turn affect those of the primary consumers, the herbivores, and through them the composition of the vegetation (e.g., McLaren and Peterson 1994).

Paleoecological modeling must take such reflexive processes into account: a **biotope** is the product of accommodation among **sympatric** (co-resident) species in a particular time and place, not an example of an ideal type. Extinctions, removals, or introductions from whatever cause influence other species in the system, both closing and opening niches in a habitat. Reconstructions based on analogies necessarily ignore such complications.

Scales

In recent years research has shown that understanding of process and mechanisms in living systems is improved with reduction in the scale of targeted investigation. Each successive reduction of scale closes some analytical approaches and opens others (Table 14.1; Hillman et al. 1993). At the largest scales, with the largest fauna, only grand generalizations can be made about ecology, associations, and habitats. As scales diminish, ever finer distinctions reveal differences in space and time. At the level of molecular and chemical analyses, very intimate details about individuals and internal environments are glimpsed. Scalar categories are complementary, not redundant.

Human interactions in the biosphere vary in quality from scale to scale, as humans interact with and respond to individual animals, single-species populations, biotopes and biomes. Increasingly precise methods must be employed downscale to observe the relevant variables and support interpretation.

Mega- and macro-scales
Only subdivisions of the global biosphere have relevance for human activities; the big picture is pure background. The continental scale is relevant as context; there are significant differences between, for instance, North America and Australia. At the subcontinental macro-scale of physiographic province, the composition of faunal populations and the structure of ecosystems are perceptible, if not tangible, to

human residents. Reconstruction of faunal associations at these scales is the business of paleontologists, who may utilize archaeological data.

Meso-scales

At the meso-scales of region (10^2–10^4 km^2) and locality (1–10^2 km^2) faunal associations are discussed as biomes and biotopes, respectively. Here, too, we deal with paleontological (off-site) context. Archaeological site assemblages are normally samples of these encompassing biomes and biotopes of the site region and locale. Archaeologists are partly dependent on paleontological data at these scales, but archaeological assemblages gain prominence and importance in modeling. More to the point, fauna at these scales represent significant components of the ecosystems of human societies, and the effective pool of available animal resources.

Faunal assemblages recovered away from archaeological sites are not burdened with the biases inherent in human choices. Where dating can provide good correlations, natural off-site deposits of faunal remains can be very informative about the region or neighborhood of archaeological sites. The essential chronological precision is sometimes elusive, as in the case of natural deposits such as tar pits or river gravels where the period of accumulation for the assemblage cannot be closely determined. Because of the severe constraints on chronological resolution characterizing most natural deposits, archaeologists must employ such data sources with due awareness of their limitations. Paleontologists, however, rarely agonize over half a millennium, more or less.

Micro-scales

Modeling paleobiotopes at the micro-scales of locale and site (<1 km^2) requires assemblages equally local in relevance. Whether these are strictly on-site recoveries, or are derived from very local but distinct preservation contexts (as nearby bogs with insect remains), varies with specific situations. The presence or absence of a cultural filter must be carefully determined in every case, as must be the issue of contemporaneity. On-site assemblages are fraught with behavioral implications that focus the attention of archaeologists, frequently to the exclusion of their paleoecological potential.

On-site assemblages of faunal remains are samples from distinct human habitats. They are least compromised in modeling human paleoecology at the site scale; extensions to the locale and beyond must be tempered by attention to taphonomic biases. Site-scale faunas on the whole are assembled purposefully by humans, who bring in food items, domesticates, and interesting exotics. Site-scale faunas also include animals resident in human dwellings for their own purposes, such as commensals and pests which feed locally, and parasites. Co-residents may include very large animals, such as cave bears occupying spaces alternately used by humans, but small ones are more usual. The analytical significance of small animal remains in sites thus varies with the modes of association and deposition. The better the quality of stratigraphic and contextual resolution achieved during excavation, the better will the faunal analyst be able to discriminate among the possibilities.

FROM ASSEMBLAGES TO ASSOCIATIONS

Archaeological faunal assemblages are samples of archaeological, not natural, deposits. Consequently, no direct relationship can be assumed to living animal associations at any scale. When analogical argument requires some presumption of equivalence between an assemblage as recovered and an observed neoecological association, that must be tested before it is used to advance an interpretation.

Like climatology, biology is a discipline currently developing rapidly. The rejection of classical community theory in paleoecology was discussed in Part VI. This volume is not the place to scrutinize developments in biochemistry and mathematical modeling of ecosystems and species interactions; the fields are moving too quickly. Consumers of biological and ecological data and theories must be alert to rapidly changing consensus positions. I offer here some ideas on paleoecological modeling for faunal associations as I understand them, ideas built on the shifting sands of disciplines not my own. Some of the foundation stones may be crumbling as I write.

Relaxing analogical limitations

As a means for understanding the unobservable past from its fragments, analogical reasoning is limited because it entails projecting into the past present-day individual experience or disciplinary consensus. Proxy data – tested and refined analogies – are less useful for reconstructing biotic environments than for physical environments. For avoiding the assumptions required by analogical arguments about habitats and niches of animals represented in death assemblages, especially those older than ca. 5000 years, paleoecologists have recourse to (1) evidence internal to the remains themselves, (2) the sedimentary and environmental contexts from which they were recovered, and (3) external evidence for synchronic habitat conditions.

Internal evidence
Some information about niche behavior, and therefore aspects of habitats, is integral to well-preserved animal remains. Skeletal morphology, including teeth, body size,

and health status, is suitable for interpretation in terms of the animal's health, method of locomotion and of feeding, age and condition at death. When many individuals of the same chronometric age are available within a limited area, such information can be further interpreted in terms of nutritive levels and stresses, population structure, reproductive strategies, and patterns of mortality.

Modeling a world beyond compare. A controversy over modeling the ecosystem of Beringia, the Pleistocene land bridge between eastern Siberia and Alaska and the Yukon territory, provides promising approaches based on functional interpretation of physiological attributes of fauna, supplemented by synecological principles for habitat sharing among species. Subfossil mammalian remains in Beringia feature a diverse suite of apparently numerous and widespread herbivores, some very large, implying rich grazing in high Arctic areas that supported no such biotas in the Holocene. Palynological studies in the area were interpreted as indicating a cold desert with low pollen influx, which could not support the "mammoth steppe" model of the paleontologists. This "productivity paradox" of Beringia was addressed by an interdisciplinary symposium that examined diverse interpretations and attempted mediation (Hopkins et al. 1982).

The case for the mammoth steppe model was made most fully by vertebrate paleontologist R. Dale Guthrie (1982, 1990), arguing for a seasonally variable steppic environment unlike any observed today. He based his case on evidence from the faunal suite characteristic of Beringia during the full glacial period and times immediately preceding and following. Innumerable finds in the west of woolly mammoth, bison, horse, elk, musk ox, woolly rhino, and less numerous ass, saiga antelope, and sheep imply a cool steppe habitat extending from northern Eurasia across into eastern Beringia. Many of these species display body size and secondary sex characteristics (antlers and horns) significantly larger than those of their modern relatives, which Guthrie interprets as indicating excellent nutrient status and strongly seasonal ruts. He notes that the most characteristic species have feet adapted to firm ground, unlike those of the tundra-adapted caribou, with body proportions and musculature adapted to either swift or long-distance running. Most of the resident species were poorly adapted for coping with deep snow, again unlike the modern denizens of the north, caribou/reindeer. The teeth of the largest and most common species – mammoth, horse, bison, and musk ox – were specialized for utilizing coarse grasses. Stomach contents of frozen carcasses support the inference of diets based heavily on grasses.

From the skeletal evidence of diet, and growth patterns indicative of good nourishment, Guthrie argues that the resident fauna were able to store fat reserves sufficient to allow overwintering where thin snow cover permitted subsistence feeding. Noting the widespread loess mantle of glacial Beringia, he argues that steady winter winds would have kept large areas free of deep snow. On the basis of paleontological principles, Guthrie models from the faunal remains themselves a broad grassland with a firm substrate, long, cloud-free summers permitting lush growth of grasses and herbs, and cold windy winters with little snow cover. Because the well-drained loessic substrate did not support permafrost, there was no extensive tundra or muskeg vegetation like that characterizing the modern landscape. Glacial Beringia was not a pale shadow of modern Arctic lowlands; it was distinct in almost every way.

The paradox of incompatible evidence from palynology and paleontology was not resolved as of 1998. The bibliography generated by it is extensive and growing. Whether the "mammoth steppe" model will triumph, or a compromise concept such as a "steppe–tundra" vegetation mosaic will force reconsideration, should be settled within a few years. What Guthrie has given us, in any case, is a masterful example of how informative about ancient habitats faunal remains can be. Animal remains approached with sophisticated ecological understanding and disciplined scholarship can provide evidence for climates, landforms, hydrology, vegetation, and resource partitioning within biotopes.

Contextual evidence

The enclosing matrix and sedimentary associations of archaeological faunal remains contribute to interpretation in two major ways: indicating depositional environments and defining the degree of association of plant and animal remains. Taphonomic evaluation is essential to establish whether the sedimentary units retain integrity or have been disturbed. If an undisturbed deposit accumulated from locally derived elements, the fossil contents (a thanatocoenosis) may provisionally be considered a sample of a living association (a biocoenosis). Flood deposits, for example, do not qualify. If cultural selection or mixing within the deposit is indicated, this working assumption is falsified. When a depositional environment can be inferred, it may be used to evaluate the congruence of the assumed association.

When depositional integrity supports the assumption that materials in a deposit have sampled a biocoenosis, the next step is to establish the scale – a habitat group or something larger. If biological principles support the grouping, the indicated habitats can be evaluated on the basis of landform and vegetation reconstructions. If the details are mutually supportive, one is likely dealing with local biotopes. If, however, the diversity of elements in the archaeological sample exceeds that of the apparent local landscape of the time, the thanatocoenosis probably sampled more extensive

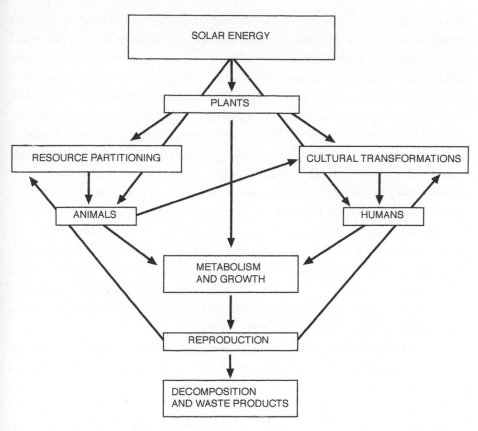

Figure 16.3   Energy flow model. A simplified model of the flow of solar energy through the biosphere. The human role is separated from the rest of animals to introduce the concept of cultural transformations, here complemented by resource partitioning. Energy is lost at each transfer – line and arrow.

biomes. Such scalar information ultimately supports evaluation of site catchments – the areas habitually exploited for food and raw materials from a site.

Synecology: trophic levels

The Beringian reconstruction summarized above employed concepts from synecology to model the lifetime interactions of a paleontological suite of species, some of which are extinct. Energy flow is the basis of synecological relationships, tracing the passage of decreasing amounts of available energy from the radiant Sun to the last decomposing bacterium (Fig. 16.3).

Trophic levels are the fundamental categories in resource partitioning. Solar energy passes up the "food pyramid" of trophic levels (Chapter 14) from plants through herbivores and carnivores, with smaller total biomass in each successive level. Ideally, such a predictable model should be simple; in fact, a representative energy-flow, food-web, or trophic-level model has so many complications that it must be highly abstracted to be comprehensible at all. A complication rarely modeled is the flexibility of eating strategies among real species in real environments: e.g., carnivores eat some plants, omnivores feed opportunistically at several trophic levels.

What is reliable about trophic-level models is that (1) animals depend on plants to make food from sunlight, (2) energy decreases along the chain, successively constraining biomass, (3) animal bodies concentrate energy, (4) carnivores feed mainly upon herbivores, (5) decomposers recycle nutrients from once-living matter back into the soil where they become available to plants, and (6, the kicker) the species census for any trophic level is not predictable. Furthermore, the cline of diminishing biomass defined by energy loss does not apply to individuals or species, only to the total biomass at each level. Herbivores can be huge, like elephants, or small, like aphids. Top carnivores can kill and eat animals many times their weight; size ratios between carnivores and prey are not determined.

The result for paleoenvironmental modeling is that species identified in assemblages and reasonably assignable to the same habitat group can be sorted into trophic levels in a general way, on the basis of mobility adaptations and teeth. Top carnivores among the animals can usually be identified in a suite. However, humans break all these rules. Not spectacularly equipped in either mobility or dentition, *Homo sapiens sapiens*, omnivore, is nevertheless the keystone species and top carnivore worldwide.

Synecology: associations

Modeling the structural characteristics of paleofaunas remains the weakest part of reconstructing ecosystems, ancient or modern. Some analytical concepts from neo-ecology suggest that aspects of structure can be modeled hypothetically, but the details are elusive, especially for vertebrates (Dodd and Stanton 1990: 333–337). For example, while diversity–density relationships among species in plant formations can be hypothesized from palynological data (Chapter 14), there is no reliable basis for quantifying diversity or species abundances in archaeological paleofaunas (Bobrowsky and Ball 1989). Lacking those basic quantities, reconstructions of biomass, predator–prey relationships, food webs, reproductive strategies, and population cycles are beyond reach except through analogies.

Qualitative characteristics are potentially definable. Species distributions can be mapped and compared to known environmental controls on distribution and density. For example, the distributions of (1) surface water in a locale or region, (2) particular classes of plant foods, or (3) geographical barriers, may be mappable. However, except in very unusual circumstances, few of these factors can be reconstructed with reasonable accuracy from archaeological-scale data at particular points in time. Climatic variables limiting animal species are elusive at scales relevant for archaeology, although adequately known for Holocene plant formations.

The patch structure of ecosystems, so central to neoecology and especially human ecology, is elusive in paleoecology. The recognition, not to say mapping, of ecotones is rarely achievable except through inference from physical attributes such as contrastive soils and landforms, at the risk of creating a past on the model of the present. Because ecotones are the most dynamic and biologically rich areas of landscape, attractors for human settlement and exploitation, this limitation is a major constraint on paleoecology in archaeology.

An exception to these disappointments is shore environments, where variation may be closely approximated in the biological inventories of shell middens with their special preservational properties. When chronology is controlled, biotic variation along a shore might be read from a sequence of middens.

Habitat groups and scales

Biologists label species sharing a single habitat or closely adjacent habitats sympatric species; species separated into discrete habitats differing in some salient characteristics are **allopatric**. For a long time, paleoecologists and archaeologists projected modern sympatries into past environments, as they did when assuming that intact biomes shifted latitudinally during the Pleistocene. The evidence for Pleistocene environments without modern representatives shattered that idea, leaving paleoenvironmental modelers adrift. Theoretical principles for grouping species in thanatocoenoses into habitat associations are not yet well defined. Paleontologists and paleoecologists provide guidance for larger-scale groupings, subject to revision (e.g., Kurtén and Anderson 1980; Shelford 1963; Stuart 1982). At the biotope scale one is heavily reliant upon zoogeography for analogies with modern related species. With increasing distance from the present, ever more historical and adaptive change stands between animal species of today and distributions and interactions of the past (e.g., see chapters in Martin and Barnosky 1993).

Bones and teeth of large mammals tend to persevere in deposits preserving any bone at all. However, for environmental studies they are arguably the most problematic of all remains. Large animals move about the landscape at micro- to mesoscales, not closely bound to narrowly defined habitats. Moreover, human interaction with large animals is likely to be highly purposeful.

Small vertebrates, smaller than foxes, typically have small individual ranges (micro-scale to locality) and often environmental tolerances narrower than those of larger species. Consequently, they may be sensitive indicators of climate and habitats at micro-scales, provided the full range of constraints on their adaptations is identified and utilized. Their fundamental niche behavior is indicated by their teeth, as carnivores, herbivores, or insectivores. Analog arguments are soundest when identification is possible at the species level and the time difference between the fossil and living groups is not great (e.g., Avery 1982; Morlan 1989).

Bird bones, thin-walled and hollow, preserve less well than those of mammals. Both bird remains and avian ecology are also less well known than those of other vertebrates (Morales Muiz 1993). The environmental sensitivity of birds varies greatly; some migrate over large distances, others remain year-round in small territories, while others, like Canada geese, may do either. Condors in Pleistocene deposits in New York state are a continent's width away from their historically known habitats in California, and equally far from observable analogies (Steadman and Miller 1987). Holocene ranges of migratory birds are recent phenomena, subject to annual adjustments according to weather and other factors such as hunting pressure.

Along with other small animals, herpetofauna fall prey to carnivores or raptors that deposit their remains beyond the home range. With their small ranges, strong seasonal control on breeding, and seasonal dormancy in temperate latitudes, herpetofauna are good indicators of habitat characteristics. Their cold-blooded metabolism makes them very sensitive to temperature; amphibians, particularly, have special moisture needs. The environmental tolerances of herpetofauna are likely always to have been less variable than those of warm-blooded animals (exceptions cited in Graham and Grimm 1990: 290).

Fish are sensitive to variable conditions in their watery habitats; their remains can inform by analogy about water temperatures, salinity, trophic states, and bottom conditions when the source waters can be identified. Different species are characteristic of ponds, lakes, small and large rivers, estuaries, and seacoasts (e.g., Wheeler 1985). Ranges may be very local, as for pond species, macro-scale for anadromous fish such as salmon, and intermediate for riverine and coastal species. Fish remains may be transported over large distances as artifacts or dried food; rationales for assuming that fish remains in archaeological sites bear any specifiable relationship to aquatic communities near their findspots must be explicated. Because normal archaeological sampling constraints are exacerbated by the fragility of fish remains, there is rarely any justification for applying quantitative techniques to refine qualitative environmental inferences from fishes.

Terrestrial gastropods are valuable members of animal assemblages, indicating qualities of substrates and vegetation. Being reliably local, they can supplement or replace pollen in paleoecological reconstruction (Evans 1984, 1991; Lowe and Walker 1984: 191–192; Robinson 1988). Marine mollusks incorporate habitat signatures in the geometry and chemistry of their shells, providing direct evidence that supplements more general ecological analogies (Rhoads and Lutz 1980). Transport and artifactual use of marine shells complicate their environmental relevance except where they are numerous at coastal sites.

Other microfauna, ranging down in size from mice and voles through invertebrates, constitute some of the best evidence for local environments if they are autochthonous in the deposits. Microorganisms in groundwater and in surface water, although rarely preserved, belong to the trophic pyramid and should be incorporated theoretically into models and interpretations. Insects, as elements of human habitats and indicators of host species, may be evaluated for congruence with inferred habitat groups. Insect mobility and ubiquity, as well as seasonal dormancy, makes this group of invertebrates able to respond successfully and rapidly to habitat opportunities (Buckland 1976; Kenward 1975). They are significant elements in the environments of all organisms.

Food webs and carrying capacities

Within the past two decades, neoecologists have redefined the classic ecological concept of carrying capacity, incidentally depriving archaeologists of a cherished notion for explaining biological population fluctuations in the past. Carrying capacity as traditionally defined depended on the concept that finite resources fixed an upper limit to the biomass of a species supportable in a particular habitat (Watt 1973: 24). In an absolute sense, that cannot be contested; the biomass of producer organisms must always exceed that of consumers. Thus, the trophic pyramid, narrowing toward the top.

However, studies in fluctuating animal populations, particularly in boreal and arctic environments and in aquatic ecosystems, have shown that the matter is (of course) much more complicated. Decades of attention to food webs, rather than trophic-level scales, have revealed relationships between species interactions and species diversity and density (e.g., Paine 1966). Ecologists have demonstrated that populations are controlled not only from the "bottom up," by availability of nutrients, but from the "top down," by competition, predation, and density-dependent disease. Top-down models alone have successfully simulated dynamic terrestrial ecosystems (Colinvaux 1993: 469–470). Animal populations are balanced by food supply, predation, and density stresses; such interactions tend to keep populations from exhausting their food supplies. "Carrying capacity," therefore, is an abstract idea, not a mechanism for population control.

People, as omnivores capable of technological innovation, are even less constrained by the mechanisms of carrying capacity than are other organisms. We are capable of expanding resources by technological innovations that permit exploitation of lower levels of the pyramid. People can expand their niches and create new ones. The idea that population pressure is the effective motive for technological innovation has long dominated in the anthropological literature (e.g., Boserup 1965). It is yielding to mature consideration of the impressively large database of technological history. Significant technological innovations appear to precede population expansion worldwide (Dickson 1988). Once an innovation in food production, energy transformation, or disease control has been accepted, it provides a temporary surplus of resources previously devoted to subsistence. The surplus in turn can support, or may require for perpetuation, an increase in population (Dincauze 1993a). The application or acceptance of an innovation may even be delayed by population limitations.

Among humans, density stresses have diverse causes: politics and ideologies as well as technologies delimit access to resources by populations or segments of populations. Food as such is not ultimately limiting for humans in the absence of cultural constraints. Currently obvious destruction of ecosystems by human exploitation cannot serve as a ruling assumption for paleoenvironmental interpretations. Human destructiveness, obvious in hindsight, has not been a goal of technological innovation in the past – only its ultimate product. People can destroy their standard of living, but their terrible adaptability has not yet led to a fatal degree of habitat destruction; it may yet do so. Population growth is not the motor of the engine, only its fuel.

Future prospects

Neoecologists are currently experimenting aggressively with biocoenoses, with the goal of establishing theoretical principles of ecosystem organization. Some experienced theoretical ecologists doubt that ecosystems ever develop sufficient stability to organize into predictable, repetitive patterns (e.g., Potts 1996). Certainly, they have not done so in the span of the Holocene, and the competitionist model based on the assumption that they did is poorly supported by field data (e.g., Wiens 1984). A second avenue of inquiry is mathematical, exploring species relationships and, at higher levels of abstraction, models of spontaneous self-organization in complex dynamic systems. J. H. Brown combines several such approaches to explore large-scale patterns of "macroecology," finding applications at scales from biomes to species (Brown 1995). A lot is at stake here, going to the very heart of our understanding of neoecology. Paleoecologists should follow these developments; if the modelers succeed, paleohabitat reconstructions will be revolutionized.

RESPONSES TO HABITAT CHANGE: BEHAVIOR AND PHYSIOLOGY

Ecological and ethological studies of extinct taxa are, of course, impossible.

LYMAN 1994: 38

Old, enduring ideas about the balance of nature are falsified by demonstrations that the Pleistocene epoch was characterized not by biological equilibrium but by dynamism at varying rates and scales (Strong et al. 1984). Both the physical and biological constituents of Earth's environments respond to change by changing in turn, enforcing other changes. The potential for rapid biological and behavioral changes among animal populations is likely to be high, but to date is not well understood.

Perturbations

The factors forcing instability in open biological systems may be external (e.g., climate change or extreme weather, tectonism, and chance events such as fires) or internal (e.g., competitive pressures, immigrants, parasitic infestations, predators, and behavioral changes). The dynamism is multicausal, and to an extent random (stochastic) (Behrensmeyer et al. 1992; Gee and Giller 1986; Potts 1996).

The climatic transition between Late Glacial and Early Holocene times was a large-scale natural experiment that has revealed responses to changing climates and landforms among plant and animal taxa worldwide. Species redistributed themselves on the landscape, some primarily responding to physical change, others accommodating to the changed biological compositions. Competitive relationships were strengthened, weakened, or redefined. Associations were sorted out in new ways: some species that were sympatric in the glacial-age temperate zones are now allopatric, and vice versa (FAUNMAP 1996). Modern biogeography continues to adjust to climatic and anthropogenic change, as pollen data imply for some tree distributions.

Biota along ecotones, where some species are near their tolerance limits for diverse habitat factors, are particularly sensitive to environmental change, while associations centrally located within biomes may change little. A strong example of such ecotonal adjustment is disclosed in research on the Late Holocene withdrawal

of Atlantic salmon (*Salmo salar*) from the southern reaches of its historical distribution in southern New England rivers. The disappearance of the anadromous salmon
began late in the eighteenth century, synchronous with early hydropower development on those rivers. On the basis of this coincidence, the dams were interpreted as
the sole cause of the loss of the salmon. A more detailed knowledge of salmon
ecology and prehistoric distribution reveals that climatic warming since the Little Ice
Age is a stronger predictor of salmon range along the western side of the Atlantic
than is the frequency, or even size, of dams (Carlson 1995). The shift of the salmon
away from their southern limit is expectable, even unavoidable, in a warming period.
The persistence in the same streams of the anadromous shad (*Alosa sapidissima*) is
then understandable; shad distribution extends much farther south. No doubt the
dams, with other industrial changes, contributed to the salmon shift. Stressors tend
to work synergistically.

Adapting to climate change

Climatic control of the distributions, compositions, densities, health status, and
breeding schedules of animal populations is most obvious in terms of the large-scale
fluctuations of Pleistocene glacials and interglacials, with global changes of mean
temperatures and varying intensity of seasonal differences in insolation and temperature ranges (Chapter 7). Mid-latitude ice-age climates were characterized by cooler
mean temperatures with seasonal contrasts more equable than today's. During the
transition to the Holocene, rapidly heightened seasonal contrasts (Fig. 7.3) were
major stressors of biota at scales from species to biomes. Sympatric associations,
some having endured for thousands of glacial years with reduced seasonality, were
fragmented.

Physiological and behavioral adjustments

Genetic adaptations to long-lasting climate regimes and habitat characteristics are
the basis of biotic evolutionary diversity. Sensitivity to climatic controls on viability
varies among species with size and mobility. Climate change at meso-scales and
above affects animals of all sizes. At micro-scales of space and time, smaller animals
are affected most directly. Evolutionary adaptations to rapid habitat changes forced
by climate are possible only for organisms with short generation length and large
reproductive cohorts, typically insects. Short-term, intensive climatic variability
stresses individuals, whose behavioral response repertory is either adequate or fatally
inadequate. Both rate (wavelength) and scale (amplitude) of change are critical
factors.

In Late Quaternary time, the dominant mode of successful adaptation to environmental change has been range adjustment (FAUNMAP 1996). Relocations begun at the end of the latest ice age are still reverberating as species jostle each other to establish viable ranges and relationships. Habitat relocation often entails some redefinition of niche behaviors; any change in niche involves new competitive pressures. The history of life in the Holocene teaches strongly that animal adaptation to rapidly varying habitats is not primarily evolutionary but behavioral.

Because mobility is so important a strategy for adapting to change, its efficacy may vary according to external constraints on distances. For example, the predominant north–south structure of the North American continent contrasts with the predominant east–west structure of Eurasia. In times of severe latitudinal climatic adjustment, the range options available to North American species may have shrunk to inadequacy, with climate zones constrained laterally by elevation and shrinking latitudinally. In Eurasia, species had lateral space in which to sort themselves out (e.g., Soffer 1993). Different extinction patterns in the several continents may partly reflect such landform characteristics.

Technology

Human cultural adaptations to climate change are briefly summarized in Chapter 4, with references. Behavioral responses dominate overwhelmingly in humans, scaling upward from an efficient minimum of adjustments of energetic cost through a grudging escalation to whatever level of innovation and effort is essential. The pace varies with the situation. In ecological terms, technological innovation is a change in niche behavior, freighted with all the attendant consequences, and never fully reversible.

Seasonal adaptations

Seasonal climates respond to orbital parameters (Chapter 3) that control the period and intensity of solar energy striking the surface of the Earth at different latitudes. Insolation directly delimits day length and, with other variables, climate – temperature range and precipitation. Biological functions under insolation control vary in periodicity with latitude, e.g., deer-antler drop, bird molt, breeding, growth period, and migration. These are reliable seasonal indicators only in terms of the solar, not calendar, year. Contingencies such as storms and volcanic dust may trigger variation in the seasonal responses of animals; precision cannot be expected in retrodicting seasons in the past (Kent 1988; Monks 1981).

Animals meet severe seasonal variation in climate and food availability by either special feeding adaptations (e.g., food storage, deer yarding in winter, migration) or dormancy (hibernation, aestivation, resting stages of insect life cycles). Both kinds of behavioral adjustments entail physiological capacities which are ultimately genetic adaptations to habitat variability. If the demands of variation exceed the adaptations, the species goes to extinction. Human responses exclude dormancy but along with storage include feeding adaptations such as food selection among different trophic levels, exchange and transport, and habitat expansions by conquest and colonization (Huss-Ashmore et al. 1989). Note that food storage, a strategy shared with animals, is more complex among people (e.g., Binford 1993). A common human long-term strategy for mitigation of periodic shortages is elimination of carnivore competitors.

Migration and dormancy responses imply, of course, that the composition of animal communities varies seasonally. The seasonality of prey species determines the seasonally varying location and energy expenditure of the predator. Coyotes and eagles, humans, and all others who kill for food experience this constraint; they adapt to it by selecting from a range of strategies and tactics for capture of various prey. Seasonally contrastive prey availability may be observed in the archaeological record directly, as remains, or indirectly, as tactics and strategies. The particular weaponry utilized by human groups may be reliable seasonal indicators, depending on the distinctiveness of the prey behavior being exploited. Seasonal behavior at individual sites is reflected in the styles and sizes of houses, storage and food preparation facilities, and soils chemistry indicative of food processing.

Table 15.3 displays several methods for determining the seasonality of death in animal remains. However, the deposition of animal remains into a site context is another matter entirely, sometimes resolvable by taphonomic methods; it cannot be equated with the time of death without careful evaluation (e.g., Star Carr case study; Soffer 1987).

Seasonality inferences in archaeology are still underdeveloped. Animal indicators are generally the best available. However, no methods yet proposed reliably discriminate year-round residence at a site from a sequence of short-term uses throughout the year. For studies of site seasonality, the full range of seasonal indicators should be considered, not merely the mode. Incongruence within a suite of seasonal indicators may represent diversity of site use, not merely ambiguity in the indicators. Furthermore, criteria needed to evaluate differences in seasonal site behaviors by food producers and by non-food producers are undefined.

Recent insightful work indicates the rewards and the difficulties of seasonal inference. For example, rigorous evaluation of animal remains in early and late Mesolithic sites in Denmark has shown that, although sites of both cultural periods were located on lake shores in situations apparently equivalent, and additionally contained similar suites of animals, in fact the seasonal use of the sites, and thus their role in the annual subsistence round, contrasted significantly (Rowley-Conwy 1993).

CODA

The potential of faunal paleoecology has yet to be fully realized in archaeology, perhaps because of complications attendant on the human presence and involvement with animals. Innovative approaches are being developed and tested. However, for innovation to be successful, there is need for informed recognition of the inadequacies of conventional approaches to the description and interpretation of ancient faunal associations, and for thoughtful application of a wide range of paleoenvironmental indicators to complement animal remains.

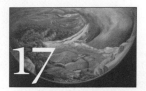

HUMANS AMONG ANIMALS

[Biological anthropologists] know, better than any other scientists know, that the human condition is an aspect of the animal condition; that people are animals and the descendants and cousins of animals, and that the seemingly unbridgeable gulf that separates us from other animals is an illusion due to the accidents of history.

CARTMILL 1994: 5

[By permission of Wiley-Liss, Inc., a subsidiary of John Wiley & Sons, Inc.]

Human ecology is a discipline fragmented among academic departments of geography, biology, anthropology, history, and economics. How central is it to archaeology, both prehistoric and historical? How central is it to understanding the human condition? The answer to the second question is the same as the answer to the first, and I choose an emphatic "Very."

Relationships between humans and other animals are the special focus of this chapter. Much of importance to individual organisms and species in the Animal Kingdom is inseparable from human concerns. As animals among animals, we share bits of DNA and somatic organization with many organisms to whom we feel no kin. Western industrial cultures share little of the awe, respect, and even fellow-feeling that people in cultures closer to the earth readily bestow on non-human animals. Nevertheless, the fates of industrialized people are equally involved with the fates of all organisms that comprise our environments (Part I). Invisible pathogens can determine the fates of individual humans and social groups. The tree that falls in the forest, the animal that dies in the trap, are significant elements in our world. Some organisms now going to extinction are unacknowledged keystone species, whose loss has consequences for untold others.

HUMAN EFFECTS IN ANIMAL ECOSYSTEMS

All living organisms have a reflexive relationship with their environment, and humans are neither unique in this respect, nor excluded from it.

O'CONNOR 1991: 3

The dominance of large animal remains over those of smaller animals and plants in archaeological sites is only partly a matter of relative preservation. More significantly, it is the result of differential visibility and inadequate recovery strategies. Years of attention to large vertebrate assemblages have produced a rich record of interpreted human cultural behaviors involving large animals, living and dead. This record is anthropocentrically skewed; the biases, now identified, are being corrected.

Interpretations of paleoecological relationships among humans and other animals require awareness of the constraints imposed by the incongruent scales of paleontological reconstructions, typically regional or larger, and observations of human behavior at local scales. Incongruency can only be overcome by integrating data from many aspects of environments. The literature on human paleoecology typically displays descriptive reconstructions of Pleistocene biotopes and biomes based on pollen spectra supplemented only by animal species lists. The level of speculative generalization involved is not explicitly discussed. These poorly supported models are vulnerable to refutation as soon as the least of the grounding assumptions is questioned.

New directions in archaeozoological research seek ecological insights into the human condition within biomes – human relationships with other organisms. This section introduces a few issues to foster awareness of research that considers sometimes unfamiliar aspects of past lives.

Predation

Human omnivores have the technological capacity to tap the flow of energy through biotic communities at several points in the trophic pyramid – as herbivores, herbivore managers, and carnivores. There are advantages to intercepting the flow at low levels where there is more energy in the system, and different advantages to tapping it at high levels, where the concentrated energy is very efficient for those with access. Paleoecologists ask where humans tap into the flow, examine the differences between societies on this dimension, and explore how humans, as members of biotopes, contribute to or deflect the flow.

Archaeological sites with large animal bones are typically valued more highly and considered more significant than those without such remains. For example, Gamble found in a survey of archaeologists that western North American Paleoindian sites with megafauna and few artifacts were considered to be more important than the larger, culturally richer, and more numerous eastern Paleoindian sites lacking organic preservation (Gamble 1993: 316). Thus archaeologists privilege carnivory and subsistence hunting over all other strategies, leading to interpretive circularity in paleoenvironmental studies. This particular perceptual bias toward animal food is also expressed widely among human societies, despite its being contrary to the realities of subsistence strategies and nutrition (Kent 1989). A balanced, theoretically informed evaluation of the roles of hunting in human societies might show that, outside particular low-diversity environments (Foley 1982), hunting large animals is primarily a mechanism for achieving and validating male status rather than a means for acquiring essential nutrients. Kent's review of agricultural societies (1989) led her to conclude that ideology rather than social competition was the explanation. Behavioral emphases in zooarchaeology support the bias toward hunting; ecological emphases may support alternative conclusions about human behaviors and human roles in animal communities. None of this is dismissive of the importance of protein and fat in human diets, nor of the widespread and dominant influence of humans within animal environments. Here, we consider the effects of human predation on animal populations and ecosystems without implying that hunting is only about food or even raw materials.

All effective carnivores stress prey populations and constrain abundance and diversity, breeding success, and range and territory of prey species. At the ecosystem level, predators influence the composition of biotopes and thus the partitioning of resources among resident species. Predator size and behavior select for genetic and behavioral characteristics of prey species related to escape and avoidance, as well as breeding success.

Preying upon sessile animals differs in its demands on the predator and its effects on the prey. Collecting marine and freshwater mollusks exemplifies the issues. Freshwater mollusks (naiads) live in a variety of substrates and water conditions that are variously accessible to humans. Marine mollusks include "epifauna" living on rocky beaches cyclically above tide, others underwater on sand in the eel grass, and "infauna" burrowing into soft substrates. These several habitats can be identified from the shells, to implicate human collecting strategies (Claassen 1986; Deith 1986). It is a matter of debate whether human collecting can eliminate shellfish from any habitat, but ecology shows that community compositions and abundances are subject to strong fluctuations from competition, predation, storms, and changes in marine currents.

Scavenging other carnivore kills, a kind of sessile prey, seems to have been the primate route toward predatory carnivory (Bunn and Ezzo 1993). Scavenging has little effect on prey populations because, as secondary predation, it does not increase predation pressure. The emergence late in the Pleistocene of effective human hunters with weapons arsenals and cooperative strategies changed animal environments wherever the hunters appeared. "The increasing focus on prime adult prey suggests a growing separation between the hominid predatory niche and the niches of sympatric carnivores, and it has a number of ecological implications for understanding humans' changing place in Upper Pleistocene animal communities" (Stiner 1991: 181). Stiner argues that human targeting of healthy adult animals instead of the vulnerable young or aged individuals in prey populations was a new predator behavior with evolutionary consequences for prey.

Optimal foraging models, borrowed into archaeology from evolutionary ecology, are useful abstractions for modeling the efficiency of various hunting strategies in relationship to prey characteristics (e.g., Keene 1983; Winterhalder and Smith 1981, reviewed by Cashdan [1982]). The models depend on a number of simplifying assumptions that are inappropriate to human behavior and may prove, with testing, to oversimplify animal behavior as well. Such models are useful first approximations to human behavior; they are incomplete but not invalid as far as they go. When compared to actual zooarchaeological data in archaeological sites, they can help highlight culturally defined strategies that diverge from the predictions of the deterministic model.

Extinctions

That *Homo sapiens* armed with guns and chain saws can cause faunal extinctions is amply proven by the Late Holocene record of species loss. Recent tragic loss of biodiversity is not, however, proof that Late Pleistocene megafauna were "overkilled" by humans. After years of search and research "the zoo-archaeological record, however tantalizing, does not directly verify either decimation or extinction as a result of prehistorical hunting" (Butzer 1982: 203); the statement stands. Many unicausal mechanisms of megafaunal extinction have been posited; any one in isolation has proven inadequate. To reveal the subtleties in extinction sequences, we need contingent, ecologically informed models. Paleontologists suggest that Late Pleistocene American megafauna, stressed by environmental change, were more vulnerable to human hunting than they would otherwise have been; their reduced populations were unable to recover from the ecological bottleneck imposed by rapid climate change and its habitat consequences (Graham 1990; Haynes 1989; Lundelius 1989). Both the rapidity of the Late Glacial changes and the presence of modern humans make the American case unique, even within the Pleistocene. Considerations of human impacts on animal ecology overwhelmingly address the megafaunal extinctions, typically ignoring the fates of smaller taxa confronted with ecosystem disturbance and habitat reduction in changing climates (Grayson 1989). The Holocene extinctions unequivocally referable to human action are of medium-sized animals in mesic and tropical environments; many are island faunas significantly including flightless birds (Steadman 1989). Archaeozoology, interpreting small units of time and space, can offer detail and richer theory on extinction mechanisms, particularly regarding avifauna and small vertebrates.

Competitive interactions

[M]an operates fundamentally as a mediator of the terms of competition between species, whether they be native or introduced, domesticated or wild, cultivated or naturalized.

WACE 1978: 229

Early in the Holocene humans emerged as keystone species in many areas of the world, setting the terms of competition for other species, arrogating ever more of the planet's resources. In defining the terms of competition, humans redefine their own environments as well, keeping the Red Queen running. Throughout the biosphere, competition provides vital dynamism. Humans compete with both plants and animals for territory and habitat. We introduce domesticated animals which in turn compete with native species. We actively reduce or eliminate carnivore populations that we perceive as direct competitors. The effect is often to relax breeding controls on prey species, allowing them unprecedented proliferation, to the jeopardy of vegetation. Human removal of predators or competitors permits range expansions of some species.

Inter-species competition can be effective whether direct or indirect; appropriating the living space available to a species can be as deadly as direct killing. Expansion, elimination, or reduction of populations all initiate new kinds of competitive interactions, changing the state and condition of entire ecosystems (Diamond and Case 1985). We have seen that plants evolve defenses against herbivores (e.g., thorns, toxins, and vegetative reproduction). Animals can learn defenses against humans, although most such are relatively ineffectual against weapons and other strategies that do not require proximity for success.

The terms of competition between humans and animals are rarely confrontational; resource partitioning is the usual issue. Small organisms pose more serious threats to people than do large ones. The most effective competitors are small and furtive. Crop pests have vastly increased their numbers and even species by stealthily occupying new niches created by humans, as do insects in stored grain (Buckland 1991). Field pests, both invertebrate and vertebrate, have diversified with monoculture. Mice and rats have increased their numbers and ranges notoriously by adapting to synanthropic niches. These relatively recent adaptations have created entirely new dimensions of competition in human ecology.

Of course, human history dramatically demonstrates that intra-species competition has devastating effects as well: both subtle and overtly aggressive competitive behaviors are pervasive even in daily interactions. Our species is not unique in that, but our effectiveness is such that we endanger ourselves critically. If we are not to compete ourselves into extinction, we urgently need to replace competition with an ethos of active cooperation extended to other organisms as well (McCay and Acheson 1987). Our relationships with domestic animals and house pets have cooperative components, but they are too controlling to be widely applicable models.

Introductions

A special place in the history of animal competition is reserved for human actions introducing animals to new habitats and the inadvertent, often regrettable, consequences that follow (Crosby 1986). Some consequences have been beneficial to people; some have been deleterious. They were rarely benign for animals residing in the areas of introduction. Paleoenvironmental reconstruction in archaeozoology contributes unique insights to the history of the world's biotas by focusing on the contexts and consequences of introductions, which are understandable from the perspectives of ecological theory (Kirch 1983; Steadman 1989).

Purposeful introductions are an ongoing process of ecosystem modification; even modern customs barriers are ineffectual filters. The spread of domesticated animals around the world is the obvious example, with obvious consequences for native herbivores. Experimentation in biological controls and breeding has moved animals such as rabbits and "killer" bees to new continents. Traders and entrepreneurs have been agents since antiquity, moving and selling exotic animals as curiosities (lions, giraffes) or exploitable resources (elephants, silkworms). Escaped or abandoned pets may compete successfully and breed feral populations without natural enemies. A misguided romantic introduced birds mentioned by Shakespeare into North America, thereby disadvantaging unique native species and imposing urban avifauna.

Inadvertent introductions are equally detrimental. They occur typically whenever people move about in large numbers and transport bulk commodities, as do warriors, explorers, traders, and colonizers. Evidence for seasonal and larger-scale movement of people has been reported by parasitologists in the Americas and Europe (Reinhard 1992), demonstrating the introduction of organisms that cannot survive in some habitats without human hosts. Animal **vectors** (organisms that carry pathogens from one host to another) of infectious diseases travel with armies; the Romans introduced rats into insular Britain, setting the stage for a series of medieval plagues. Roman conquests and colonization introduced pests in stored grain throughout Europe (Buckland 1991). The Norse brought lice and fleas to Iceland, along with dung beetles, parasites living on their domestic animals, and insects in stored hay (Buckland 1988).

Habitat modifications

Destruction, creation, and manipulation of habitats and biotopes are equally aspects of human competition with other organisms. The increase in burning observed in Holocene pollen cores (see Elm Decline essay, Part VI) is frequently interpreted as anthropogenic habitat modification for the creation of agricultural fields and pasture, or to rejuvenate forage for wild herbivores. Not all cases of burning can be so interpreted. There are claims for human agency in ancient Pleistocene burnings, especially in Australia, but the matter remains controversial there and elsewhere (Horton 1982). Forest clearance for cropping or for fuel may be irreversible under some regimes of climate and soils, resulting in soil degradation, local climate change, and the formation of heath lands, blanket bogs, or grasslands (Chambers 1993a; Roberts 1989). Domestic herd animals can modify vegetation as effectively as fire does, suppressing some species and establishing others.

Sedentary human populations added entirely new habitats – houses, barns, storage facilities, gardens, middens, and sewers – that were colonized by animals that diminished human health and comfort. Intentional landscape modification for crops and herds was carried further with the modification of surficial water bodies by the digging of irrigation canals and the draining of wetlands. Edge environments, attractive to many animals, were created by changes in waterways, by construction of roads and hedgerows, plowed fields or gardens. Small-animal populations expanded as a consequence, changing species ratios and increasing hunting opportunities for humans (Emslie 1981; Linares 1976; Szuter 1994). New wet environments provided habitats near humans for disease vectors such as snails and mosquitoes, and also infectious amoebae.

The result of human intervention in ecosystem composition is an ecosystem that no longer maintains itself. Intervention imposes upon humans the responsibility, even necessity, for active management to retain desirable features. Human ecosystem managers must adapt culturally and genetically to the special demands of the habitats and biotopes they defined. We are prisoners of our own competitive success.

Synanthropy and domestication

> Regardless of individual cases or acquired tastes, as a *species* we seem to share the high tolerance for filth characteristic of our housemates, the roaches and rats. This tolerance appears to confer major competitive and adaptive advantages at the species level.
>
> DINCAUZE 1993A: 49

Worldwide, purely natural landscapes unmodified by humans are very rare, if they exist at all. The landscapes around us are cultural to a greater or lesser degree, and the species inhabiting them reflect various degrees of adaptation to the human presence. Some have learned effective avoidance strategies; others dine in gardens or skulk about scavenging food from human waste and stores. Still others have established themselves uninvited in human shelters and in human bodies. Animals living near humans affect site depositional processes that may or may not be evident to archaeologists. Many synanthropic situations are mentioned above. Some, like body lice, are older than our species; others are as recent as the adaptational successes of raccoons (*Procyon lotor*) and coyotes (*Canis latrans*) on the close fringes of American suburbia, the former eating garbage, the latter preying on house pets. Recent and rapid adaptations such as these should remind us that animal behavior and feeding preferences are very flexible and contingent.

Vermin (rats, mice, cockroaches, houseflies, etc.) are the weeds of the Animal Kingdom – organisms that, from human perspectives, are in the wrong places. They compete directly with us, in our faces. "The number of animals that accompany people without their leave is enormous, especially if we include the clouds of microorganisms that infest their land, food, clothes, shelter, domestic animals and their own bodies" (Goudie 1993: 88). Some of these synanthropes are self-domesticated, in that they require human habitats for continuing life. Some may be on the verge of speciation.

In an essay on the distinguishing characteristics of domestication, Pierre Ducos noted that "all those features which distinguish the *domestic* animal from the wild one (whether biological or behavioral) stem not from the evolutionary dynamics of the animal but from those of the human society." Building on that insight, he offered the following definition:

> domestication can be said to exist when living animals are integrated as objects into the socioeconomic organization of the human group, in the sense that, while living,

those animals are objects for ownership, inheritance, exchange, trade, etc., as are the other objects (or persons) with which human groups have something to do. Living conditions are among the consequences of domestication, not the mark of it.

1978: 54

This definition is particularly useful because it applies as well to humans.

Among "the consequences of domestication" for humans as well are artificial environments (living conditions, habitats). Their features include food provisioning, clothing and shelter, and entire ecosystems. Domestic, artificial environments are now more or less essential for human health and safety, and are crucial for synanthropes. Domesticated animals live in artificial environments created by people-in-culture. We are a domesticated species; for better or worse, we have domesticated ourselves.

Artificial environments entail behavioral and biological changes – adjustments – in the organisms living within them. For animals, the changes result directly from human intervention in their care, management, and breeding. For humans, the entailed genetic changes are thought to have involved rather less selection, but that proposition has not been rigorously tested. Certainly, self-domestication among humans has required behavioral adaptation to intense social interactions. The domestication of other animals and their adoption into human societies has required of people additional measures of forethought and of routine labor in order to meet the responsibilities of care. Habitual association among species in domestic space imposes costs in space requirements and biological risks in terms of disease. It may impose stresses that select for biological adaptations related to cooperativeness and equable temperaments.

Efforts to identify early steps in the domestication of animals have focused on physiological changes in the target species related to dentition, and body form and dimensions (Davis 1987; Klein and Cruz-Uribe 1984; Olsen 1979). Size reduction in comparison to wild relatives is widely noted, but not yet understood; critical factors may include impoverished diets, restricted movement, crowding, disease, and selection by humans for docile individuals or other special traits. Size reduction in humans is observed among some village farming societies, but it is not universal. An animal showing physiological traits indicative of domestication has a long history of genetic change behind it. Beginnings are elusive in the archaeological record because the process of domestication can take many forms and is reversible in its early stages.

Dogs, apparently the first domesticated species after humans, appeared early in the Holocene in several parts of the world. Research in canid ethology is implying that canids, adapted to cooperative hunting and pack life, may have attached themselves to humans in symbiotic relationships (Morey 1994). The biological consequences, long before human selection created many new variants on "dog," include the retention of juvenile traits such as shortened snouts, which account for tooth crowding, and barking, which among wild canids is characteristic only of pups (Coppinger and Feinstein 1991).

A second approach to archaeological recognition of incipient domestication is the study of herd structure and culling (Davis 1987; Klein and Cruz-Uribe 1984; Olsen 1979). This requires demonstration of herd management techniques that result in characteristic slaughter patterns by age and sex of animals – typically an emphasis on culling young males, retaining females for breeding stock. Such slaughter profiles imply a degree of control of a small population, but provide no details. A pattern of stock handling that did not result in such a profile might mislead the analyst. Ritual offerings of animals showing consistent age and sex selection have also been interpreted as indications of domestication. At present, the archaeological search for the beginnings of animal domestication has been pushed to the limits of available method without resolution. The presence of domesticated animals at archaeological sites can be established on the basis of many other criteria (Davis 1987), typically the appearance of exotic species. Insect faunas associated with animal husbandry, land-use changes indicative of pasturage, and food residues in dung are indicators independent of osteological remains.

ANIMALS AS HUMAN FOODS

The animals [humans] relish range in size from termites to whales.

FARB AND ARMELAGOS 1980: 165

Worldwide, and probably throughout the time span of the species, human diets are predominantly vegetal (Harris 1992). Despite the fact that primate nutrition for all taxa is based on carbohydrates, food remains in archaeological sites are predominantly faunal (protein and fats). Thus, archaeological interpretations have inadvertently misrepresented human diets in antiquity and given hunting of animals a place in culture out of all proportion to its importance in sustenance. That misrepresentation is being corrected by paleoanthropology, ethnoarchaeology, and deeper understanding of human nutrition and metabolism. Animal foods dominate human diets only in environments where edible plants are seasonally or absolutely scarce or low in diversity, such as tundras, grassy plains, and steppes. Having considered vegetal foods earlier (Chapter 14), we here focus on animal foods.

Available foods

Paleoenvironmental modeling, not the contents of archaeological sites, is the best place to begin consideration of prehistoric human diets (Chapter 14; Lyman 1982). When something is known about the environment, we can approach answers to the question "What was out there?" The opportunities and constraints for potential human diets can be specified. The plant and animal foods available in a habitat, their seasonal variation, and the relative ease of access to dietary essentials define the parameters of human diets – the sources and quality of essential nutrients such as carbohydrates, proteins and fats, vitamins, and trace elements such as Fe, Ca, Na, K, Zn, I, and Sr (Table 12.2).

Unprocessed natural foods are not all benign; some plants are unpalatable or toxic, some animal tissues are toxic (e.g., hypervitaminosis A, see below) or infested with parasites. Humans learned about edibility by alert observation of other animals' feeding behavior or by bitter experience. The store of such knowledge is necessarily specific to a particular habitat or set of habitats. People who buy their food in markets are likely to be unaware of the diversity of such crucial information. To people who gather or produce most of their own food, it is central to health and longevity.

Food choices

Food consumption is not determined by environmental availability. Material archaeological remains provide little detail about "What went in?" – what people actually consumed at a particular site or in a region. Custom, technology, ideology, and social relations determine what foods are selected, how they are prepared, and to whom they are offered. Information about actual diets must be sought on-site and in human tissues and wastes. The quality and adequacy of diets (nutrition) is a separate matter that can be investigated only from human tissue itself.

Preservation and collection differences between sites, especially differences in screen sizes, sampling fractions, and flotation practice, mean that animal remains from archaeological sites may not closely represent site contents and thus be poorly comparable between sites (Sutton 1994). Small animals, especially, are conventionally underrepresented in collections, making their dietary contributions difficult to evaluate and too easily dismissed (Stahl 1982).

Animals are efficient sources of protein, already converted from plant tissue and easily digested by humans. Food values in terms of calories, protein, vitamins, and trace elements vary among taxa; introductory discussions are presented by Wing and Brown (1979) but details must be sought in technical publications usually produced by government offices. The nutrient values of animal flesh and organs vary seasonally and with other kinds of stress including drought, breeding, and long-distance migration. The variable quality of meats is less important in human diets, mainly composed of plant foods, than is the seasonally variable amount of available fat (Speth 1987). In paleodietary reconstructions, these variables must be considered but can rarely be specified in any useful way except through dietary stress indicators in human bones and teeth (e.g., Bunn and Ezzo 1993).

Dietary studies based on bone chemistry and isotope ratios in humans have raised expectations for detailed specification of dietary constituents and sources. The attractive catch phrase "you are what you eat" was a banner for early paleodietary studies, with the promise that, beginning with what a person "was" (i.e., bones), the analyst could interpret what was consumed to create the remains. As studies proliferated and the literature grew, it became clear that mechanisms were more complicated. The ratios of chemical signals in the bones of prey or the tissues of plant foods do not translate into ratios in the bones of consumers in any simple reflection of trophic levels (e.g., Schoeninger 1989). Differential fractionation between tissues in food organisms as well as in consumers results in different values for hard tissues, muscle flesh, and organ meats. There are diagenetic complications as well (Radosevich 1993; Wright and Schwarcz 1996). The early promises are still unmet (Ambrose 1993; Sandford 1993a). Successful paleodietary studies require deeper understanding of food webs, metabolism, and isotope fractionation. The methods applied by Little and Schoeninger (1995) in a study of coastal diets should be further developed; isotope and trace-element values of food items were directly measured and transformed by weighted values and linear mixing equations into estimates of corresponding values in human bones. Even in this sophisticated study, comparative values had to be adopted from modern analogs. In their turn, archaeologists must be diligent and rigorous in examining the context of bones to be used in such studies, so that diagenetic effects can be measured.

Nutrient *needs* vary among individuals, groups, and societies, according to physiological factors such as age and growth rates, health status and pregnancy, climatic extremes, and physical work performed (e.g., Katzenberg et al. 1993). Recent studies of health status in prehistoric societies show that access to food is rarely determined by such needs. Sociocultural values determine disparate access to dietary items; different groups within societies have different diets. Trace-element research reveals diversity and inequality in food intake within and between societies. Meat, especially, may be distributed preferentially to individuals of high status and male sex (e.g., Schoeninger 1979). Infants often suffer health deficits from poor diets, especially when, among subsistence farmers, they are weaned onto a diet of gruel that fails to provide essential nutrients (Cohen and Armelagos 1984; Martorell 1989).

Trace-element and isotope-ratio analyses are revealing that dietary reconstructions for humans require consideration of choice as well as opportunity. The importance of marine foods to the diet of Danish Mesolithic societies was revealed by carbon-isotope ratios, implicating major food collecting along coasts now submerged and therefore unrepresented in the mapped site distributions (Tauber 1981). Late Prehistoric populations on Nantucket Island, in southern New England, USA, were once assumed to be heavy consumers of maize; analysis of human bone demonstrated that seafood was more important than either maize or terrestrial animals (Little and Schoeninger 1995). Isotope and trace-element signatures in human bone have been used to indicate individuals who migrated during their lifetime. Immigrants have been identified in burial populations in southern Africa (Sealy et al. 1991) and in southeastern North America (Ezzo et al. 1997).

Everything edible has been eaten by humans at some time or place. Taboos, proscribing an available food, are also characteristic of the species' dietary habits. Animal foods are more likely than plant foods to be proscribed. Taboos that are validated by mythology and ideology are nevertheless often based on medicinal observations or economics, that is, on the long-term or short-term costs to individuals or societies of consuming such foods. Although recognizing dietary biases resulting from social proscriptions is particularly challenging in archaeology, taboos may be justified in interpretive models.

Food preparation and remains

People, eating from what is available, expand the edible portion of their environments by modifying foodstuffs not originally suited to their dentition and digestive organs. Animal flesh is typically processed by roasting or boiling; cooking softens tough portions, aids digestion, and kills parasites and **pathogens** (organisms that cause disease). Pulverizing is another approach to rendering animal food chewable. Small animals, especially insectivores and rodents in North America, were roasted and eaten whole (Stahl 1982) or pulverized prior to drying or boiling; the high ratio of meat to total weight of these animals makes them nutritious, and their abundance makes them available.

The study of paleodiets must be approached without ethnocentric preconceptions; the taboos of one's own society should not intrude. Analysis of coprolites recovered in dry areas of the Americas have shown that pulverized bone, animal hair, and insect parts passed through the human digestive tract, presumably after digestible meat was selectively incorporated into human bodies. Insects are readily eaten when abundant, requiring only simple if any preparation (Madsen and Kirkman 1988; Sutton 1995). Efficiency of food has long been a consideration in human diets. "Milk production is a very efficient way of converting vegetable protein to animal protein, the efficiency being 27% compared to 6% meat" (Ryder 1983: 239).

The remains of animal foods in archaeological sites are more various than the obvious megafaunal bones. Waste from preparation of animal foods should be typical components of middens, house floors and yards, hearths, and garbage pits. Therefore, sediments should always be searched by fine screening or flotation, as appropriate, to recover such remains. As discussed in Chapter 16, site soils and potsherds yield identifiable residues in ideal conditions, and coprolites show some of what was ingested and in what condition.

Diet and health

Organisms eat to live. Once the essential caloric requirements are met, assuring energy for the business of getting more food, diversification of diet provides the quality that underpins health. Life does not guarantee health; certainly poor health diminishes life. An individual's diet and health are intertwined in synergistic relationships that make a poorly fed individual prone to illness, and an ill individual likely to be poorly nourished (Huss-Ashmore et al. 1982; Martorell 1980).

Food collectors through prehistory have enjoyed widely diverse foods and therefore a generally nourishing diet. Most have also experienced periodic food insufficiency, and therefore periods of nutritional stress. The shift to food production significantly increased the amount of food available to farming communities with increased storage capacity, but also reduced the diversity of food sources and therefore the quality of nutrition (Cohen and Armelagos 1984). Compromised diets, whatever the restriction, result in growth interruptions in children that are indicated in bones and teeth by linear structures such as Harris lines and dental hypoplasias (growth interruptions) (Martin et al. 1985). Hypoplasias have even been identified on Neanderthal teeth (Ogilvie et al. 1989). The specific events or conditions that created the stresses so recorded can be identified only inferentially, when other data are available about the quality and quantity of diets and the prevalence of disease (Larsen 1997).

Technologies of food production lie at the foundation of the exponential growth in numbers of human beings over the past several thousands of years. Reproductive success is the measure of biological fitness; on those terms humans are phenomenally successful. Only archaeology can provide the data and analyses to demonstrate and quantify the costs for individual fitness of the subsistence mode that has triumphed globally (Goodman 1994).

Much of the adjustment to suboptimal diets resulting from reliance on cereal crops comes in the form of phenotypic changes – variation in gene expression developed during the life of individuals. Such qualities as body height and weight, and head shape, are partly defined by dietary adequacy and general health. Populations that changed from food gathering to reliance on cereal crops, if the new diets were inadequate in protein and trace nutrients, show reduced height, weight, and musculature (Goodman et al. 1984; Larsen 1997; Styles 1994). With improved living conditions and a more adequate diet, such traits can disappear within a generation. It is not clear yet whether genotypes are changed by dietary stress, but populations so stressed would be selected for plasticity in adjusting to it.

PALEOPATHOLOGY

Like other animals, man will have lived his life in balance with his pathogens, which only have serious effects at times of ecological imbalance.

FIENNES 1978: 13

Diseases and injuries effectively determine life span for most individual animals. Today, as in the past, the balance between illness and health is fundamentally an environmental issue. Infection and toxins intrude into an individual from outside, before and after birth, and are likely to be environment-specific (Potts 1996). Environmental conditions can protect individuals from disease, expose them to it, and mediate their response to it. These influences are equally relevant for injuries.

Environmental elements that affect the health of animal individuals and populations are both "natural" and social, in all possible combinations. Climatic factors – temperature and moisture – influence the distribution, abundance, and nature of pathogens and the robustness of individual response to pathogenic attack. It is not damp, chilly weather that "causes" the common cold, but rather the enhanced susceptibility of chilly people to ubiquitous rhinoviruses, the infectious organisms that irritate the membranes in air passages. The variable duration and intensity of daily activity patterns determine an individual's exposure to a wider or narrower range of pathogens and influence the body's energy status, which in turn affects the robustness of immune response. Activity patterns also influence an individual's exposure to injury. The nutritional adequacy of one's diet is central to good health and an effective immune system. As briefly discussed above, quality, quantity, and variety of foods are all crucial to good health and the avoidance of serious illness. Population structure, density, and mobility also influence exposure to pathogenic attack; a large number of organisms of the same kind clustered in one place are more vulnerable to pathogenic attack than are the same number scattered in small groups, because the pathogens must "find" them. Mobility is both a defense against pathogenic attack and a danger of exposure to new pathogens, as in the case of Crusaders bringing old urban diseases westward into medieval Europe. The relative hygiene of an individual's domicile can be differentially supportive of pathogens – dirty surroundings are unhealthy for large animals, as is now known but was not understood during most of our species' existence. Vermin, insects and other small invertebrates, and bacteria, of course, thrive in our dirt. Most immediately significant for humans, animals are reservoirs of diseases that afflict people directly or, more typically, indirectly through intermediate animal vectors.

Pathologies that affect the bony skeleton and teeth are central to paleopathology, which rarely has softer tissues to work with. Thus, analyses of growth abnormalities, bone lesions, and dentition dominate this specialist literature (e.g., Boddington et al. 1987; Larsen 1997; Ortner and Aufderheide 1991; Rothschild and Martin 1992; Waldron 1994). Evidence for diseases that affect only soft tissues, and direct evidence of internal parasites, is recovered only in unusual preservation conditions (arid or saturated). Expansion of analytical techniques is increasing our ability to utilize those special cases. Trace-element analysis may identify toxins in soft tissues, as with arsenic and lead in hair. Amplified DNA promises to refine the identification of even submicroscopic pathogens (Eisenstein 1990). However, efforts to extract and amplify old DNA too often reveal only fungal sequences (Chapter 13). Until more is known about the diagenesis and extraction of DNA from archaeological materials, such research must be considered experimental. Recent success in isolating DNA characteristic of *Mycobacterium tuberculosis*, the tuberculosis pathogen, from human remains is promising (Baron et al. 1996; Taylor et al. 1996).

Other sources of paleopathological evidence occur in archaeological sites, according to the type of sediments. Chitinous exoskeletons of insect and arthropod disease vectors and parasites, and the egg cases of some parasitic worms may be found in floor sweepings and pit fills, in coprolites and dung. Sometimes their type and sometimes their context can reveal their source as either animal or human. In either case, their presence in archaeological sediments should be noted and reported.

Kinds of pathologies

Disease is part of the ecology of an individual. It represents the impact of the environment and part of the body's reaction to it.

HILLSON 1986: 283

Ill health in animals takes many forms. Pathogenic organisms include a variety of invertebrates, microbes, and fungi ranging in size from tapeworms to viruses.

Non-infectious illnesses may be nutritional, genetic, developmental, toxic, or traumatic.

Parasites and pathogens

Parasites are basically of two forms: ectoparasites, those feeding on the surface of the host's body, and endoparasites, invasive organisms that live inside their hosts. Ectoparasites such as fleas and lice do not necessarily cause disease, but they permit disease organisms to penetrate the body's external defenses. They typically have a spectrum of potential hosts and little concern with whose hide they feed in; they may therefore be efficient disease vectors. Endoparasites vary from helminths (flatworms) and nematodes (roundworms) through protozoans, bacteria, and viruses. Both invasive and infectious, they enter host bodies by a variety of routes. Many may pass between species under facilitative conditions, especially the **zoonoses** that infect humans from animal hosts in uncooked meat or milk, through the medium of vectors, or by other means. Immunological adaptations to such infections may be effective enough to kill the parasite, but more typically simply keep the numbers in check, leaving "the enemy within" to eat unbidden and unwanted in a host that is maintained in a suboptimal nutritional state. Hosts lacking effective immunological defenses against virulent pathogens may die from the assault.

Direct recovery of parasites permits a richer interpretation of disease ecology. Although endoparasites are soft-bodied, some have identifiable reproductive structures that carry spores outside to other hosts; these may be recovered from feces. A large literature is accumulating on archaeological helminth infestations (Reinhard 1992). Suites of helminths are characteristic of most vertebrate taxa; with good preservation in dung, they may help identify the animals involved in the absence of other remains. Ectoparasites include arthropods whose identifiable exoskeletons may be preserved in archaeological contexts.

Non-infectious pathologies

Some illness is ingested, as mineral, plant, fungal, and animal toxins. Dietary deficiencies and imbalances play pervasive roles in illness; they may be direct causes, or may play a synergistic role to exacerbate the expression of other threats. Poorly fed animals are likely to suffer a range of unrelated illnesses. Genetic or metabolic diseases, although non-infectious, are costly to victims and societies and are potentially fatal. Some illness results from injury to the body, usually complicated by infections at the wound site. The expression as illness of these several kinds of stressors may be similar or indistinguishable in their effects on bones, so that paleopathological diagnosis depends on external evidence or very large samples of individuals (Roberts and Manchester 1995).

Pathology in non-human animals

Pathological conditions of animal bones, interesting in themselves, indicate environmental circumstances affecting prey species and domesticates important to humans (Baker and Brothwell 1980). Animal pathologies implicate environmental, nutritional, and social stresses (hunting and fighting, human management) affecting or imposed by people. The distribution, age, and virulence of zoonoses are important for the history of human health and sickness, and therefore merit more attention from archaeologists than they typically receive. Fiennes (1978) presents a fascinating catalog, albeit in an anthropologically naive narrative. The expression of zoonoses may vary in humans and other animals, as does the immune response.

Nutritional deficiencies may explain the observed size reduction in early domesticated animals; this explanation can be tested by paleopathological analytical methods applied to animal bones from archaeological sites. Animals under restraint, as with bridles and bits for horses, or harnessed for traction, develop wear or stress responses in bones and teeth that are available for interpretation of the intensity of human exploitation.

An instructive example of research in animal environments and disease is the investigation of microfauna in byres (animal barns) where domestic stock was sheltered through long, intense winters in medieval Norse Greenland (McGovern et al. 1983). The byres were apparently dark and stuffy with floors deep under food waste and dung, ideal breeding grounds for disease vectors threatening the health of animals and their human keepers. The culturally created microenvironment, required to shelter exotic animals from the extreme climate and maintain their existence, itself tipped the balance against health.

Human paleopathology

Pathogens are the principal predators of humans. Consequently, infectious disease is a characteristic of human habitats of paramount importance to the evolutionary history of our species (McKeown 1988). Genotypes change as humans adapt to parasite loads and endemic diseases such as malaria, and to stresses of crowding, dietary changes, and unique new domestic environments. The adaptational consequences of novel diets and changed activity patterns introduced with food production are with us all today (Fig. 17.1)

For humans, the most important aspects of environment in relation to health are cultural. Before the acceptance of the "germ" theory of disease (infectious organisms), humans defined disease as a punishment from others – animals, enemies, God or gods, witches or devils. The elaboration of human ideological behavior probably

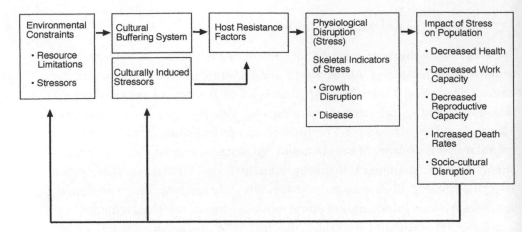

Figure 17.1 Environmental, cultural, and biological factors in the generation and expression of stress in archaeological human populations. Stressors include disease, climate, work, and other factors discussed in the text. Limiting resources include food, water, and shelter. (After Goodman and Armelagos 1989: Fig. 1.)

began as responses to such threats from undeterminable environmental sources. The externalization of disease sources was an appropriate concept, although incomplete. Only recently have pathogenic mechanisms been identified. We now confront them internally, with medicines or surgery. To our loss, conventional modern medical practice ignores or dismisses the contributions of organic and social-environmental factors, which are never trivial.

Much of the disease experience of modern human populations derives ultimately from domestication – the self-domestication of our species into locally dense numbers and crowded living conditions, the self-domestication of small mammals and invertebrates which become disease vectors in human domiciliary environments, and our purposeful domestication of fauna, flora, and landscapes. The density-dependent diseases of monoculture, zoonoses associated with animal husbandry and organic pollutants, and the density-dependent contagious diseases of humans are self-inflicted results of human experiments in domestication and sedentism.

Infectious diseases

Humans adapt to infectious disease by developing immune responses following exposure, or by ingesting antibodies in mother's milk (Gillen et al. 1983). The mode of adaptation is necessarily particular to specific environments and diseases. Different populations and subsets of populations and social groups are differentially exposed and are differentially vulnerable to infections. Vulnerabilities vary with location and mobility, age, physical condition, and social status and gender.

The history and distribution of human diseases cannot be discussed here; there is a large literature (Kiple 1993). For archaeologists, however, it is useful to touch on some topics and cases of direct interest. Only some few infectious diseases are recognizable in bones, so that disease is likely underrepresented in archaeological populations. The distribution and variety of infectious diseases have been expanded by domestication, landscape modifications, and the worldwide multiplication of our species. Construction of canals and reservoirs increased stagnant-water environments supportive of invertebrate parasites and vectors, and brought them close to human habitats. Parasites moved from the tropics to the Arctic by sheltering in human bodies and clothes. Population concentrations supported by food production permit the explosions of density-dependent contagious diseases that have periodically decimated populations since at least medieval times in Eurasia. Disease prevalence, being environmentally specific and culturally defined, is well worth the attention of archaeologists.

Parasitic infections by roundworms and flatworms, normal to human populations, adversely affect the health status and energy level of the host organisms. Most such parasites cycle between hosts according to the stages of their reproductive cycle; for some, the specificity of intermediate hosts can be a strong environmental signal. Eggs, cysts, and body parts of parasites can be identified, when preservation permits, in the gut contents and feces of humans and other animals (Faulkner 1991; Reinhard et al. 1986). Human feces may be distinguished from other scats by the specific parasite contents (Greig 1985; Jones 1985).

The inference of pathologies from human remains, however, is a task for specialists alone (Waldron 1994). Bacterial infections in bones form visible lesions on the periosteum or in the cortical bone. If the individual survives the disease, the bone will be remodeled before death. Many of the modifications of bones observed as pathologies are not specific to a single disease. Changes in bone mass and density described as *cribra orbitalia* and porotic hyperostosis indicate the body's response to inadequate numbers of red blood cells – anemias. The condition that stimulated those responses could be nutritional deficiencies or any number of infectious diseases (Reinhard 1992). Among diseases that may form characteristic changes in bone morphology are bacterial infections such as leprosy, tuberculosis, and treponemas (syphilis, yaws), the viral disease poliomyelitis (e.g., Chamberlain 1994: 29–31), and some parasitic infestations.

Non-infectious diseases and traumas

Human health can be compromised by a variety of factors distinct from pathogens. Dietary deficiencies resulting in such diseases as rickets, scurvy, caries, and iron-deficiency anemia are expressed in abnormalities of bones and teeth, which have been observed in human populations from Neanderthal age to contemporary.

Metabolic and genetic diseases resulting in dwarfism, cancers, arthritis, and osteoporosis may show in bones; gallstones and kidney stones may be recoverable from graves. Asthma and autoimmune diseases such as allergies typically leave no evidence for archaeologists, although there are exceptions. Toxins such as those in shellfish derived from algal blooms cannot yet be identified, but improvements in chemical analyses may change this. Metal poisoning such as from lead and arsenic is traceable in body tissues. A report of possible vitamin A poisoning in *Homo erectus* is notable for its antiquity (Walker et al. 1982); hypervitaminosis contracted from carnivore livers is a threat even today in the Arctic. Broken bones show patterns that may implicate situations that led to the damage: forearm parry-wounds from fending blows are characteristic of interpersonal violence, and falls have their own signature breaks (Chamberlain 1994: 28–29; Ubelaker 1978: 79).

Disease in populations

In contrast to the population-based quantitative data on which modern studies of disease and demography are based, paleopathological information from archaeological sites is best for individuals, equivalent to anecdotal evidence. Not even the study of entire cemetery populations can produce data equivalent to censuses and epidemiology. Extending well beyond the typical sampling limitations of taphonomy and representativeness, the sample requirements of the quantitative methods that support modern epidemiology are not met in archaeological populations (Waldron 1994). Paleodemographers and epidemiologists grapple as well as they can with these deficiencies (Buikstra and Mielke 1985; Kiple 1993). What can be learned (and sometimes claims that go well beyond that) is on review in volumes such as those by Larsen (1997), Verano and Ubelaker (1993), and Webb (1994). The enterprise is well worth the efforts being made: population studies are fundamentally important to understanding human evolution and adaptations – past, present, and future.

CODA

Animal lives are embedded in the contingencies of their larger environments – physical, biological, and social. While humans are animals among animals, our species brings unique destabilizing qualities to the environments of which we are parts (Part I). Archaeologists have unparalleled opportunities to expand knowledge of all three aspects of environments. Sensitivity to the opportunities for knowledge that occur in the contents and matrices of archaeological sites can contribute significantly to understanding human health, longevity, and the quality of lives in the past and present, for the future.

HOW DO WE READ THESE BONES? SEASONS
OF USE AT STAR CARR

The Star Carr site represents a turning point in prehistoric archaeology, especially in the paleoenvironmental archaeology of wet sites. Grahame Clark's monograph of 1954 established new standards for excavation, recovery, and interpretation. It has since inspired several reinterpretations. The site was reopened for additional field work in the 1980s and 1990s (Cloutman and Smith 1988; Mellars and Dark 1998). Such ongoing interest is a tribute to the quality of the original work and to the continuing importance of its role in archaeology.

Star Carr, a wetland site near the north edge of the Vale of Pickering in eastern Yorkshire, England, comprises a deposit of early Mesolithic artifacts of stone, bone, antler, bark, and wood, preserved with other organic remains in peat. It is culturally affiliated with the Danish Maglemosian, Mesolithic woodland hunter-gatherers who lived partly on terrain now inundated by the North Sea, during the early Holocene Preboreal period about 9600 radiocarbon years ago (see Day and Mellars 1994). Artifacts and organic debris were deposited on the shore and shallow margin of a lake occupying the Vale of Pickering.

The outstanding feature of the site was a "platform" of birch trunks and branches exposed by careful excavation of the overlying peat and mud. The platform lay on and in a reed swamp bordering the lake, between dry ground and open water where the latter was closest to land. A wide range of artifacts lay on and in the platform, raising questions about the purpose and use of the platform feature and activities undertaken at the site.

The stratigraphy of the platform area and enclosing reed swamp appeared to indicate at least one interruption in the occupation; the research team could not refine the depositional sequence more precisely than that. Human activities at the site appeared not to have hindered the growth of reeds (Clark 1954: 38), supporting the inference that people were not present during the spring and early summer growing season.

The animal bones preserved on the platform, the wettest part of the site, were studied by Fraser and King of the British Museum of Natural History, London (Fraser and King 1954). Their work revealed unexpected potential for interpretation of archaeological bone; subsequent development of zooarchaeology/archaeozoology built on their foundation. Prior to the establishment of modern conventions for describing and quantifying zooarchaeological remains, Fraser and King counted all identifiable whole and fragmentary bone and antler specimens, summed and described them by species, and tried to determine the number, size, and age of individual animals represented, their seasons of death, and the habitats their presence implied.

Interpretation of the site's role in a human society requires determination of the season(s) of use; for that the animal bones appeared to offer the best evidence. This essay features the arguments advanced and the evidence used to interpret season of site use *from the bones*; despite their inherent fascination, none of the other issues about Star Carr is considered in any detail here.

Fraser and King assigned the largest number of osteological specimens to red deer (*Cervus elaphus*), represented by whole and fragmentary antlers as well as by bones. The analysts counted individuals represented in terms of the largest number of bones of single elements unduplicated by side, anticipating the MNI method developed later. Antlers were included with postcranial elements to derive the totals of individuals for the cervid species (red deer, roe deer, and elk), although some antlers had been naturally shed and thus were brought in by people separately from carcasses. "The figures indicate *minimum* numbers, being based on the numbers of individuals of each species distinguished with certainty" (Fraser and King 1954: 91). Since antlers contributed to the total of individual animals counted, it was a short step to consider the condition of the antlers as clues to the season of death. The preponderance of red deer antler in mature winter condition became a major criterion for inferring use of the site in winter.

> In general the evidence supplied by the cervid specimens points to occupation during the winter months to about April. Perhaps the most interesting implication is that the occupants of the site were apparently absent from it during the period from April till September when the red deer antlers would have been of least use for working into spearheads and for other purposes.
>
> FRASER AND KING 1954: 93

Efforts at seasonal interpretation of the deaths of the roe deer, elk, aurochs, wild pig, and a small group of fur-bearers at the site were inconclusive. One individual each of nine bird species contributed nothing to the argument at first. No fish bones were found; Clark argued that their absence supported the inference of winter season use (Clark 1954: 16). Recovery methods may be a factor in their absence.

In 1972, Clark offered a thoughtful extended essay placing the site into regional context. Arguing from ecological studies of Scottish highland red deer that the species wintered in lowlands and summered in the hills to escape swarming insects, Clark proposed a two-season hunting strategy involving shifting human settlement – winter at Star Carr near yarded deer and summer on the heights of the North Yorkshire Moors (Clark 1972). This conclusion was shortly strengthened by evidence of partially healed weapon-inflicted wounds in deer and elk shoulders (Noe-Nygaard 1975). The argument was that only winter hunting at yarding areas would likely permit encounters with the same animals twice in a short time.

Three articles in 1978 opened a debate about the criteria for seasonality, two calling into question the use of antlers as seasonality indicators when they could have been, and in this case likely were, collected and brought to the site as raw materials or artifacts (Caulfield 1978; Jacobi 1978). Caulfield was dubious about the migration model. Jacobi supported it but also noted the presence of fawns and roe deer with antlers; finding these to be "clear indications that some at least of the occupations at Star Carr were continued into early summer," he wondered about the absence of fish in the circumstance (Jacobi 1978: 319). A timely ecological explanation was offered by Wheeler (1978), who argued that freshwater game fish such as pike may not have been established in British inland waters so early in postglacial time.

An innovative interpretation of site function and seasonality was proposed by Pitts, who argued that the site was an industrial area for making antler tools and tanning hides in summer (Pitts 1979). The organic richness of the plant debris in the water on the birch platform would have been conducive to hide tanning, while antler soaking in the water would be softened for easier working. Enthusiastically, he suggested that the Star Carr shore was "probably one of the oldest cases of vegetable preparation and tannage of hides documented" (Pitts 1979: 37). Of course, it is not documented, only postulated. Pitts dismissed antlers from the calculation of individual animals represented, partly on the excellent grounds that they were incongruent with the sex ratios of the postcranial elements. This criterion takes antlers out of consideration as seasonality indicators for this assemblage. Pitts' reworked data implied to him that "there was activity at the site throughout the year. However, this is not to say that the same group of people were always present" (1979: 40). Grigson also cautioned against including antlers in counts of prey individuals or in seasonality estimates, calling attention to the presence at the site of the remains of summer birds (Grigson 1981).

Graduate students in a seminar at the University of Arizona, USA, applied emergent archaeological models to the task of reinterpreting Star Carr. Their assumptions, not always clear, were adopted variously from the original report, revisions, current interpretive modes, and taphonomic principles. Rejecting Pitts' industrial argument, they postulated that the site was used for game drives into the lake, with hunters awaiting their prey on the reed swamp at the tip of a peninsula. They claimed that "both plant and animal remains definitely imply use of the site during the summer and autumn" and found "little reason to believe use in one season predominates" (Andresen et al. 1981: 33).

Price, reviewing the accumulating revisionist literature, argued that Star Carr was a base camp. More strongly convinced by the arguments of Pitts than those of Andresen et al., he concluded that use in all seasons was "clearly evident," and that a "distinct seasonal occupation cannot be demonstrated at Star Carr" (Price 1982 [1989 reprint: 110]).

Up to this point, Noe-Nygaard was the only participant in the seasonality debates who had directly examined specimens from Star Carr. As many revisionists had advised, it was time to confront the data directly. Legge and Rowley-Conwy took up the challenge, expecting that new archaeozoological methods would clarify the seasonality of the site (Rowley-Conwy 1987: 74). They visited museums where the Star Carr animal bones were curated to restudy the entire extant set of the large herbivore and pig bones, examined systematic collections of deer bones, and undertook field studies of carcasses (Legge and Rowley-Conwy 1988: 51). Their restudy was based on their own broad experience, the best methods current in archaeozoology, and much information about Pleistocene fauna unavailable to the original analysts. They revised the identification of some specimens, changed the counts of three species, and added bear. They introduced analysis of tooth wear and crown heights to compile age cohorts for the deer taken, and thus identified the season of death for roe deer juveniles killed in late spring or summer. While adult individuals could have been killed in other seasons, and the site could have been occupied at any or all seasons, their data weakened arguments for winter occupation. Because the migratory upland herd analogy favored by Clark was not the best choice in the moderate elevations of wooded early Holocene Yorkshire, they concluded that strong seasonality of hunting opportunities was unlikely. On the basis of their revised age charts for roe and red deer, the authors concluded that Star Carr was a temporary summer camp, occupied most intensively between May and September. This estimate of seasonality is necessarily based on a minority of the individuals represented in the assemblage, with the assumption that all the animals were killed and brought to the site by resident humans. No evidence for non-human predators is reported. This reinterpretation goes far beyond the issue of seasonality, having implications for a thoroughly new understanding of the site and its role in the regional subsistence/ settlement system (Legge and Rowley-Conwy 1988; Schadla-Hall 1990).

Within ten years, other studies of Star Carr deer teeth led to different conclusions about the seasonal kills of juvenile roe and red deer (Carter 1997, 1998). Using radiographs to score the developmental stage at death of juvenile teeth, Carter produced revised individual counts and age profiles of the deer collection. He also concluded that 47% of the red deer rami were from subadults, further distancing the antler counts from any relevance. On the basis of the small sample suitable for his research, he concluded that the "killing of these [juvenile] animals is evenly spread over the cooler months of the year" (Carter 1998: 855). Thus, since the first report, interpretations proposed for Star Carr faunal seasonality moved from a "winter" site to a year-round one, to one used from late spring into summer, to use for at least some purposes in fall and winter – with corresponding reevaluations of site function.

Interpreting newly gathered vegetation histories and isotope analyses from the site, Day (1996: 786) confirmed "two separate phases of human activity" at the site, "each lasting several decades and resulting in significant changes to the local vegetation." The conclusions of her detailed close-interval sampling and interpretation of pollen and charcoal are further developed in the monograph report on the restudy of the site (Mellars and Dark 1998).

Full understanding of this productive site requires integration of data from bones and insects, animal behavior (e.g., Coles and Orme [1983] suggest that the birch trees of the platform were felled by beaver), macrobotanical and microbotanical remains, detailed consideration of the use and distribution of stone tools (e.g., Dumont 1990), geochemistry, and isotope physics. The restudy monograph may well ignite further productive discussion of this compelling case.

PART VIII

Integration

ANTHROPOCENTRIC

PALEOECOLOGY

In all scientific endeavour, the relationships and communications between allied disciplines are of paramount importance; if we define archaeology quite broadly as the application of all man's current knowledge and techniques to the study of all man's past knowledge and techniques, then archaeologists are compelled more than any profession to communicate with their disciplinary neighbours.

BODDINGTON ET AL. 1987: 3

In the first sentence of Chapter 1, we quoted Hardesty (1977: 290) defining ecology as "that branch of science concerned with [the study of] the relationships between organisms and their environment." In Part VI, we introduced "neoecology" as a special aspect of ecology devoted to the study of living species in their environments or in laboratory situations, and "paleoecology" as the application of principles from neoecology along with disciplined inference to the study of organisms in environments no longer directly observable. On the basis of these definitions, paleoecology is the best that archaeologists can do in researching societies of the past. Furthermore, because archaeologists are particularly devoted to the ecology of human beings, our study is necessarily anthropocentric. This volume is an extended argument for the centrality to archaeology of an anthropocentric paleoecology; the concept imposes on research and interpretation broader contexts and goals than are typically included in the currently controversial term "environmental archaeology."

The argument that human beings can exist and act independently of their environments is a fallacy deeply rooted in Western culture (Glacken 1967). The false dichotomization of nature and culture is supported by religious and technological ideologies, and embraced by development economics. The environmental crises of today are direct results of such dismissal of interactive mutualities between organisms and their physical and social environments. The argument here is that humans and human societies exist embedded in synecological relationships. No social science can thrive by focusing on culture or human behavior to the exclusion of historical contingencies, the initial conditions that constrain the spectrum of possible behaviors.

Successful description of human paleoecologies entails not only integration of all available information from both organic and inorganic components, but its interpretation, which must be informed by a sophisticated awareness of both the potential and the limitations of recovered data samples. Data from all five spheres of the climate system are essential for knowledge of past conditions of interest to the investigator of ancient human environments. Utilization of many disparate data sources provides investigators with both (1) scientific modes of control over the accuracy of descriptions and (2) access to powerful interpretive synergisms. The case studies presented in this volume illustrate the power of multidisciplinary integration to advance understanding of the unobservable past. The opportunity to test and evaluate competing interpretations, which is the strength of multidisciplinary research, must be a normal component of archaeological investigations.

Anthropocentric paleoecology (i.e., fully contextualized environmental archaeology) offers opportunities to redress long-standing imbalances in the ecological literature. It should be clear, from consideration of cases cited throughout this book, that humans are a highly interactive element (catalyst) in all environments and ecosystems, and have been for a very long time.

Archaeologists need environmental scientists to help them understand the contexts of human evolution and human behavior. The better those contexts are understood and integrated, the clearer will be our evaluations of the roles of human society and culture in history and prehistory. Equally, environmental scientists need archaeologists to help them understand the role of human communities in the evolution of landforms, climates, and biotas through the millions of years of coexistence and interaction. The human (cultural) dimension cannot be banished from the study of past environments, even if its role in forming and modifying those may have been more elusive in the past than it is today.

Archaeologists are in uniquely privileged positions to look for anthropogenic signals in environmental records. Those signals will appear in unexpected, unusual observations. Analysts satisfied with the broad brush will miss them. Interpreters who extend and extrapolate data across space and time will erase them. The unimaginative will never see them. The use of diverse data sets as complements brings out the details in all paleoenvironmental reconstructions. Only the details at fine resolutions can help us see ancient circumstances clearly.

As past environments are more assiduously studied, because of the growing environmental crises today, surprises are to be expected. Data from the Greenland glacier demonstrate that even atmospheric pollution began over 2000 years ago. Analyses of particulate matter in Greenland ice cores reveal that "Greek and Roman lead and silver mining and smelting activities polluted the middle troposphere on a hemispheric scale two millennia ago" (Hong et al. 1994: 1841). During the centuries of Classical-period industrial metallurgy, toxic metallic aerosols, notably copper and lead, circulated the northern hemisphere and precipitated as far north as the Arctic. Reduced during the Dark Ages, metallurgical atmospheric pollution rose again during the Middle Ages and increased until improved production techniques and recent emission-control devices reversed the direction of change. Roman copper metallurgy produced copper aerosol precipitation in Greenland heavier than that from any time between the early Industrial Revolution and the twentieth century (Hong et al. 1996). Bronze Age metallurgy did not produce a measurable rise in copper aerosols in Greenland ice. These quantifiable results imply that carbon dioxide release from ancient smelters' charcoal fires was also considerable. The deforestation that fed the ovens contributed heavily to degrading soils and landforms.

Human influence on physical and biological aspects of Earth's environments is even more ancient. Domestication, the imposition of social and cultural values on environmental variables, began with the evolution of the genus *Homo*. It subsequently expanded into the biosphere, the hydrosphere, the geosphere, and the atmosphere. All classes of proxy data for past climates are susceptible to influence by human activity. Anthropogenic effects on environments and proxies may be initially small but, even then, by increasing variation they reduce determinacy in the systems and may exaggerate perturbations. How confident can we be that our observations of past environmental states or processes are untainted by our particular subject of study, the planet's most meddlesome species? Excellent recent discussions of human influences on a wide range of environmental variables focus on diverse spans of human history, beginning with very ancient foragers (e.g., Bell and Walker 1992; Goudie 1993; Jamieson et al. 1993; Roberts 1989).

Traditional ecological emphases in archaeology, in which the environment is considered the independent factor in environment–human relationships, are clearly inadequate theoretical formulations. They have led to some quite sterile research results, properly decried within the last decade. The time has come for researchers to acknowledge that environmental changes are not infrequently or insignificantly influenced by human actions, inadvertence notwithstanding. The study of human impacts on environments is a more productive research orientation at local scales and for archaeological techniques than is the study of environmental impacts on human communities. The results should be awareness of mutual influences and interdependencies and of interactive trajectories of change, and avoidance of the impasse of causal indeterminacy or the fallacy of overdetermination.

Archaeology's interest in human behavior is enriched by attention paid to human actions as they influence and respond to changes in environmental variables. Human behaviors are value-driven, not automatic responses to simple stimuli. Consequently, their predictability is very low. Awareness of ancient environments in their complexity will stimulate archaeological interpretations of the past to situate human actions in their cultural and cognitive contexts, and to contextualize the record of human existence within that of an evolving and mutable world.

The physical, biological, and climatic contexts of human lives – human habitats – cannot be declared irrelevant to a humanistic study such as archaeology. The term "contextual archaeology" emerged in the decade of the 1970s in reference to expanded ecological study of environments in archaeology (Butzer 1978). Almost immediately the term was also claimed by partisans of a reflexive, cognitive archaeology. This confusion of terms has led archaeologists into polar positions about what kind of context is worth considering. What is needed is expansion of archaeological study and interpretation to embrace all contexts as having relevance for some problems, and development of precise analytical and synthetic concepts and terminology that will allow us to get on with it.

Human volition and planning are constrained and sometimes frustrated by unpredictable natural forces. Strains of fatalism in all philosophies derive from experiences of storms, floods, earthquakes, volcanism, and pestilence among other untimely deaths. Random natural events have swung the fates of empires, as did the storms that blasted the Spanish Armada. On the other hand, human ingenuity has built great economies and civilizations on predictable natural events such as the Nile floods, and has moved public opinion by politically motivated predictions of astronomical events such as eclipses and heliacal risings. As we learn more about the mechanisms of environmental change, even at the scale of weather, archaeology is enabled to incorporate both cyclic and unpredictable natural events into culture history. The study of the ENSO weather pattern of the equatorial Pacific is emerging as a powerful tool for evaluating cultural change in many parts of the globe, because it influences weather in both hemispheres (Diaz and Markgraf 1993). Collection and integration of data by archaeologists aware of the El Niño signature in coastal landforms, shellfish, fluvial and aeolian deposits, and sudden changes in sociocultural conditions will support interpretations of change that are richer and pervade many different environmental and social systems in many parts of the world. Well-dated ice-core studies of weather and volcanism are already supporting vastly enriched evaluations of sudden events in the archaeological record. New data classes are enabling archaeologists to expand the variables considered in special cases (e.g., Grattan and Gilbertson 1994). No realized or foreseeable accuracy in social theory can substitute for the ability to identify unpredictable natural events in the archaeological record.

The price of ignoring the complexities of environments beyond the social is descriptions of the past that are vacuous, misrepresenting the contexts and exaggerating the independence of human actions. The challenge of including in archaeological interpretations a significant range of environmental variables is also daunting. The preceding chapters are intended to ease access to the range of variables currently considered by specialists in paleoclimatology and paleoecology. The range is expanding even as I write; my hope is that increased familiarity with the theory, methods, and research designs of specialists in the geosciences and biosciences, and with sound archaeology that includes significant environmental variables, will empower archaeologists to include more of those variables than they have been willing or able to do.

Throughout this volume, "complexity" runs as a refrain, sometimes an intimidating one, whether in reference to the climate system, life, or methods and theory for investigating those. Awareness of complexity should not lead through disillusionment with analytical techniques to despair about the limits of knowledge; rather, awareness should lead to enlightenment. Students must understand the usefulness, even the centrality, of uncertainty (Pollard 1995). Familiarity with the theory underpinning a body of knowledge makes that knowledge accessible, reducing apparent complexity and providing guiding concepts. While apparent complexity overwhelms and may alienate the perceiver, apparent simplicity encourages misuse. Archaeologists determined to simplify cannot effectively confront the complexities of their research universes.

Researchers dealing with physical systems can use theory to predict data, to the extent that theory and data remain congruent. Physical systems in paleoenvironmental studies, for which theory can be so used, include those of climate, geomorphology, hydrology, and soils exclusive of the organic components. In open biological systems, on the other hand, theory cannot predict data, because of the multiplicity of contingent variables and initial conditions. As indicated in preceding chapters, approaches to the biosphere in paleoecology are at present undertheorized. We should eagerly anticipate research in ecology that will have theoretical implications for paleoecology. Theory, whether descriptive, analytical, or predictive (very rare in biology), is a powerful tool for researchers, helping to define questions, isolate significant variables, and indicate appropriate and productive techniques for collection and analysis of variables.

THE MANY VARIABLES OF ENVIRONMENTAL STUDIES

> [A]rchaeology is by nature a multi-disciplinary subject and its study a highly eclectic affair.
>
> POWERS 1988: 459

One refrain repeated in critiques of the literature and practice of environmental archaeology is the idea that the study is technique-driven, that it follows a model of positivist, mechanistic science that ignores the influence of human thought and action. Such polarization of science vs. social science is fallacious. Science is not synonymous with method and technique; it is a mode of disciplined inquiry that utilizes technical methods to expand observation to scales larger or smaller than those for which humans are biologically suited. Observation is fundamentally driven by concepts (theories and hypotheses) that direct inquiry toward variables and processes thought to be productive for solving particular problems. The skillful application of a precise technique to an inappropriate problem is a futile gesture. Formal theories and methods carry investigators beyond quotidian taken-for-granteds into potentially larger conceptual spaces.

Archaeologists often evince a consumer attitude about science. They want quick, brief, non-controversial answers to their disembedded, particularistic questions. "What is this rock?" "Where was it collected?" "Where did this copper come from?" "How old is this artifact found near this charcoal fragment?" "How important was meat to the diet of the society which this specimen individual represents?" Such expectations betray inadequate understanding of the roles of technique and of data in the achievement of understanding. Archaeologists who would be participants in scientific learning must pay attention to the fundamental theories, methods, and interpretive styles of the disciplines from which they seek answers to their cross-disciplinary questions (Pollard 1995).

The data of any discipline are defined and explained by theoretical concepts (paradigms) specific to a particular time, place, data set, and investigator. Borrowed data come with theoretical baggage attached, which must be explicitly acknowledged and understood by the borrower. When data cross disciplinary boundaries, their theoretical context is changed, and must be translated and evaluated by informed investigators. The significance of data, then, is always contingent, and cannot be considered immutable or permanently reliable. Even if one cherishes the positivist notion of data as reality, data *meanings* cannot be considered unchangeable or unchallengeable.

When data cannot be accommodated in a theoretical model, the model must change. Of course, data can often be accommodated in unsuitable or incomplete models.

Successful interdisciplinary research, therefore, demands of each member of the team a healthy degree of respect for and understanding of each discipline's guiding theory and current assumptions. This is rarely taken seriously enough, especially by archaeologists whose training in "hard" science may be casual and whose respect for scientific discipline may be exaggerated posturing. Cross-disciplinary communication is neither easy nor natural. All investigators are deeply invested in their own disciplinary paradigms (modes of doing and taken-for-granteds). The deep questioning of each other's assumptions that is essential to understanding and critical awareness can be challenging, even confrontational. Some way must be found to encourage productive exchange of ideas and interpretive models without personal alienation. Understanding how questions are asked and answers found in disciplines not one's own makes cross-disciplinary communication possible.

Scaling paleoenvironmental variables

Data for investigating paleoenvironments are derived from contexts not easily partitioned into discrete units that themselves make "sense" (that is, satisfy our intuitive expectations). As argued throughout this volume, there are relationships and interactions at all levels. Matters can be rationalized by grouping problems and variables into sets defined by the several levels of temporal and spatial scales and by the five spheres of the climate system.

When borrowing data or interpretations, the investigator should aim for consistency of scale. Within scalar levels of observation and analysis the choice of data and methods for solving problems or for interpreting data sets can be rationalized and controlled. When analytical scales and relevant variables are specifiable, the appropriate range of human choices and constraints in given situations can be approximated and environmental determinism avoided. Relationships dominated by chance or randomness can be more easily identified when scaled. In archaeology, both temporal and spatial scales are significant aspects of problems. Spatial congruence is usually more easily expressed and realized than is temporal congruence. This is so not least because of the many different ways in which archaeologists measure time (Part II), each of which has its characteristic uncertainties and inherent errors. Calibration of chronometric techniques is a constant challenge, demanding discipline to evade serious errors of interpretation and comparison.

The five spheres model of environmental variables offers important advantages for ordering data and interpretations within scalar units. Environmental states and conditions in any particular sphere can be described or inferred using data from all or most of the five, as argued and exemplified in Parts III through VII above.

The early years of environmental archaeology were characterized by emphasis on specification of past climatic states. As far as it goes, such emphasis is not a problem; climate cannot be ignored as context, and paleoclimatology is maturing impressively. However, environments are more than climate, even if all are ultimately shaped by it. Climate is not fate for human societies or individuals, even though catastrophic weather may well be so in particular circumstances. Different kinds of climate exert physiological stresses on organisms through water or temperature stresses. Such stresses on humans may be met by either cultural (short-term) or physical (long-term) adaptations. Adaptations to changed circumstances by plants or animals in human space modify species distributions and frequencies, entailing further changes. Even disease vectors are influenced by climate change, becoming more or less virulent or pervasive. The description or specification of changed climatic variables is only the beginning of consideration of environmental change. This is especially so when climate-change models are derived from data gathered off-site and at regional or larger scales of analysis. Few studies achieve or even aspire to climatic reconstruction at the site scale, where the effects are most relevant for humans.

The five spheres in paleoenvironments

This text is organized into sections by environmental categories familiar to archaeologists, with the five spheres of the climate system (atmosphere, geosphere, hydrosphere, cryosphere, biosphere) discussed within each. The five spheres are not only elements of the climate system; they also represent classes of resources critical for humans and other organisms. Here, we utilize the spheres themselves to integrate arguments, rearrange contexts, and avoid repetition.

Atmosphere carries climates at all scales of space and time. New and powerful data sources and integrative models are available for describing ancient atmospheric states and conditions (Chapter 3 and Part III). Deep cores from marine sediments and glacial ice are the most recent new sources of data; they reveal direct evidence for atmospheric aerosols, and proxy data for temperatures in isotope ratios. In combination, these data help indicate the directions from which air masses came and, by further inference, the atmospheric conditions that moved them. Bubbles in ice hold tiny samples of ancient atmospheres. General Circulation Models (GCMs) provide powerful models of atmospheric mechanisms carrying weather patterns worldwide, albeit at fairly large scales of analysis. Climatic data from other spheres can also be indicative of atmospheric conditions, sometimes down to the local scale in space. It is possible to answer queries about temperature and precipitation regimes with isotope proxies.

The mineral matter of the planet, in the forms of tectonic plates, rocks, and minerals or sediments, comprises the geosphere. Past geospheric states and conditions are observed in landforms, sediments and soils, and, more intimately, in archaeological matrices. One cardinal principle in the study of past geospheric states is that, over time, essentially every unit may have moved in space. Spatial congruence is as challenging as temporal congruence in defining and selecting variables for description of past geological entities. In terms of human paleoecology, the farther back one goes in time, the less solid is the ground beneath one's feet, and the more salient is the need to evaluate sediments, soils, landforms, and continental configurations. Mineral matter is important for human tool-making, plant-growing, architecture, and residence siting. The states and conditions of such resources are significant both vitally and culturally.

The hydrosphere is crucial in paleoenvironmental study for two major lines of inquiry: (1) the conditions and states of the hydrosphere control the availability and quality of water on which all organic life depends, and (2) water is a controlling factor in climates. Hydrospheric conditions are investigated through proxy data derived mainly from sediments and landforms (fluvial, lacustrine, and marine shores and basins, as well as cultural constructions such as canals, wells, and reservoirs). Secondarily, they are studied in elements of the biosphere (especially tree rings). Atmospheric states as described in GCMs also imply information about the hydrosphere. Humans do not differ from other organisms in their need for water; in fact, we need more per unit of body mass than others. The locations, timing, and durations of civilizations have been water-dependent throughout history and prehistory. Increasing skill in water management has permitted the expansion of human populations in both numbers and geographic distribution (e.g., the case of Classic Maya urban reservoirs [Scarborough and Gallopin 1991]). Nevertheless, no one has found a way to increase the finite quantity of water on the planet, and drastic rearrangement of it is not a route to release of the constraint. Human paleoecological studies must always take account of the hydrosphere as an essential resource that is a limiting condition, subject to some degree of management.

Although highly variable in amount and distribution, the cryosphere is an influential component of planetary environments and of environmental studies. It exchanges water with the hydrosphere, modifies the geosphere, influences the conditions and states of the atmosphere, and restricts the extent of the biosphere. It is studied through proxy data in landforms, marine and terrestrial sediments, and biotas, and directly in ice cores. The fact that glaciers were prominent hemispheric-scale elements in paleoenvironments throughout the three or more million years of the evolution of our species is likely to have been a defining condition of our physical and mental development (Vrba et al. 1995). The transporting and transforming of ice is gaining economic salience; ice and ice-making are becoming important resources and commodities.

Life, of course, is the biosphere, a relatively thin layer on and in the surface of the Earth, and in the near-surface zones of the atmosphere and hydrosphere. Paleoecology is the study of past states and conditions in the biosphere, and human paleoecology is merely one small aspect of that. Vegetation, the kingdom of auto-trophic organisms that make food from gases, trace elements, and light, is the primary source of information about past conditions and states of the biosphere. Palynology is the most developed set of analytical techniques for its study. At archae-ological scales, botanical macrofossils are additional significant sources of data. Study of ancient vegetation is facilitated by the fact that direct evidence is widely available, and reliance on proxies is minimized. Vegetation offers widely utilized, but variably reliable, proxy data for understanding past climates and animal associa-tions. Human dominance over and domestication of vegetation is the major route through which our species modifies the world we inhabit. Beyond their centrality to habitat, plants are crucial resources for humans, for food, fuel, and raw materials including structural timbers. As members of the animal part of the biosphere, humans consume food produced by other organisms. Animal environments are the seas humans swim in; we are poorly prepared to recognize our own roles in those contexts. Animals provide an array of resources including food, raw materials, work energy, and companionship. Ideologies define the terms in which we evaluate our roles in the biosphere: dominance or membership. The study of paleoenvironments and of environmental change has been unduly complicated and long delayed by ideological barriers to observation and interpretation.

Acknowledging complexity: ideologies and analogies

Successful projects in environmental archaeology often are restricted to investiga-tion of a small area, a few events, and (ideally) a short time span. Such work is essen-tial to the social sciences and humanities for multiplying instances of human behavior and response beyond the written record, allowing richer appreciation of human lives and the human condition in the past. The larger purpose of environ-mental research within archaeology is gathering data to test generalizing notions about the human condition with evidence revealing contingent circumstances not observable today.

By increasing the fund of cases, environmental archaeology is the best available antidote to the tyranny of actualistic studies untested against a fully contextualized past. Analogies and normalizing arguments fail to do justice to the differences between present and past, and may be supposed typically to mislead. Analogies are Trojan horses, freighted with hidden dangers in the forms of unexamined implications and postulates. They are powerful aids for defining research strategies, but are not themselves reliable guides to unbiased and original research outcomes.

An example of a subtle assumption that leads to pervasive misunderstanding of past human and general environmental conditions is the modern, unprecedented population density of our species. Our familiarity with its effects biases analog models for both culture and environment. Our sense of a filled world is not compatible with the situation even in the nineteenth century, and is orders of magnitude different from times prior to that. Our density and technological dominance give us advantages never before enjoyed by another species. For example: "Human beings currently use 20 to 40% of the solar energy that is captured in organic material by land plants . . . Never before in the history of the Earth has a single species been so widely distributed and monopolized such a large fraction of the energetic resources" (Brown and Maurer 1989: 1149). How can we justify using current circumstances anywhere on Earth as examples for situations in the past, particularly when any quantification is involved?

Given past excesses of predation, competition, and reduction in variety in many aspects of earthly environments, there is no longer even any "wilderness" against which we humans can evaluate our influence. Humans are mediators of competition, and therefore in large part define the terms of biological fitness, throughout the biosphere. Our presence affects even species of whose existence we are unaware. Essentially every living creature, with the possible exceptions of organisms living in deep caves and oceanic thermal vents, must adjust to the human presence. The adjustments may not yet be clearly visible, but they are real. An example is a 1995 report from the site of the 1986 Chernobyl nuclear meltdown (N. Williams quoted in *Science* 269: 304). A fence excludes people from an area within 10 km of the plant. The enclosure is now occupied by populations of wild boar, birds, deer, rodents, and wolves. Despite the elevated levels of radioactivity within the fence, the animals are apparently thriving and increasing in numbers. Genetic damage is expressed in high mutation rates, but the absence of humans outweighs for the animals the negatives of radioactivity. This example shows how strongly the human presence stresses animal populations, and illustrates the subtlety of damage inflicted, some of which is not obvious although genetic damage is already measurable. No matter how long these populations survive, they will never return to a state unaffected by humans. Even without the complications of radiation, who can say that any tract of woodland or steppe, no matter how apparently natural, has a past unmodified by human intervention?

The disciplines of paleoenvironmental studies are uniquely situated to evaluate the relative integrity of habitats of today and their representativeness for those of the past. Archaeology can contribute to identification and understanding of ecoprocesses leading to the modern state of humanity and to the history of stresses that have been effective in the evolution of human culture and the human genome. "It is significant that the archaeological evidence for stratified societies appears in tropical Polynesia after indigenous land animals have been depleted and the natural environment has been transformed into a cultural landscape" (Dye and Steadman 1990, *American Scientist* 78: 215). Humanity's position at the top of the food chain, the keystone species worldwide, is simultaneously a triumph and a tragedy. Ideological clashes in the public domain, opposing the values of dominance to those acknowledging interdependence of living things, display this conflict. The welter of conflicting interests obscures the wide range of possible analogies from which we choose a few.

This situation provides archaeologists with opportunities to do research with relevance for administrative policies. Government planning offices need the kinds of information that well-defined archaeological research projects can provide. A report prepared for the US National Research Council posed explicit examples of significant research questions applicable to policy planning. Some are directly suitable for archaeological paleoenvironmental research: "What forces drive the human activities that are major contributors to environmental degradation and how do these forces operate? . . . Which interventions are most effective for changing environmentally destructive activities?" (Stern et al. 1992, referenced in Stern 1993: 1897).

Traditional paleoecological questions and research approaches must be reconsidered for their dependence on contemporary analogies and ideologies if inquiry is to lead toward understanding rather than misuse of the fragmentary archaeological record, and if results are to avoid tautology. Among the important questions that only excellent anthropocentric paleoecology can address is the large one: "How have people lived with the world and shaped it?" Good answers to this question may be archaeology's crucial contribution to society. Richly contextualized answers can address ideologies, politics, historical views of intentionality and the roles of individuals, and also philosophy (the issue of free will).

IMPLICATIONS FOR RESEARCH PRACTICE

> Scientists might think of disciplined reflexivity as a necessary calibration of the instrument by means of which anything (including Nature) will ever be (humanly) known.
>
> LEDERMAN 1996: 398

Awareness of the numerous aspects of environment brings significant implications for research practice in both archaeology and geology: (1) the necessity for diligence, rigor, and imagination; (2) the awareness that data complexity and interrelated variables invalidate models of linear causative chains. Throughout this volume, there has been an effort to avoid discussing causes and effects as direct relationships.

The classic linear model of causation implies a direct, undeviating, determinative relationship between an active agent and the result of action. Take, for example, the expectable result of applying an open flame to the edge of a piece of paper. Is the result invariably an expansion of fire? If we assume that, other things being equal, that result will always occur, we overlook how many other things must be held equal and, moreover, we rarely try to specify them. Consider: if the paper is thoroughly wet, the flame may not spread to it. If the paper has been treated with a fire-retardant chemical, the flame may not spread. If a strong breeze is blowing across the paper toward the flame, the flame may not reach the paper. If the experiment is tried in a drenching rainstorm, the result may be that the flame is extinguished. Undoubtedly many other variables could be invoked or observed to render inaccurate the confident prediction of "effect." On what basis, then, may we assume what variables are irrelevant in any particular historical context?

The assumption of "other things being equal" (*ceteris paribus* in formal logic) is an intolerable burden for dealing with open, complex, dynamic systems. Every link in a linear causal chain actually brings with it (entails) a unique set of initial conditions, depending on the link's state at the moment of its inclusion in the chain. The relationship of any link to the next in a chain will vary with the initial conditions in play at the time of its inclusion. The following link in the chain is difficult to predict accurately without detailed knowledge of the initial conditions entailed by each preceding link. Even though the span of time between two links, or phenomena, or actions, in a causal chain may be minute, its reality opens the possibility for some deviance in initial conditions. For example, between the statement that a piece of paper will incinerate when contacted by a flaming match, and the actual contact, water may saturate the site of the event and void the prediction. Moreover, there may be reflexive loops in a chain, that is, it may not be linear if initial conditions require or permit more complex relationships.

For either historical research or future prediction involving open complex systems, all things cannot be held equal for the convenience of the investigator without artificially constraining part of the historical or future context under investigation. Once this fundamental property of complex, dynamic open systems is understood, it is clear that explanation in historical sciences requires that the range of *possible* variables and states be accommodated in models and hypotheses employed for reasoning. Because of the centrality of contingency, of the historical particular, one must work with multiple hypotheses, and explain away as many of those as the evidence permits. Variables not identified in an explanation may nevertheless have been operant in the event; their omission, or relegation to the status of residuals, will bias any explanation thus impoverished.

The "instrument" whose calibration is advocated by Lederman (epigraph above) is, of course, the brain. The "disciplined reflexivity" for calibrating it begins with explicit awareness of one's own basic premises, and proceeds to a mature willingness to test those premises against whatever evidence and arguments are encountered during the task of learning. Calibration requires a quasi-formal process of research practice, running from problem formulation through the definition of research design, coordination with specialist collaborators, designing excavation practice, recovering critical data, specifying appropriate analyses, integrating the products of the several analyses, evaluating the research goals, and interpreting the results for several audiences.

Research practice in archaeology

Approaches to problem formulation have been addressed throughout this volume, and cannot be elaborated here. Instead, the implications for archaeological practice in the field, laboratory, and publication are briefly reviewed for optimizing results contributing to the goal of an anthropocentric paleoecology. The burden of data collection and the success of integration and interpretation in such projects falls on the archaeologist, who should take all possible measures to assure successful outcomes.

Planning for field work requires as first priority a responsibility to data collection that recognizes the importance of sampling. Sampling for interdisciplinary analyses must seek samples that (1) are representative of the diversity existing in the contexts explored; (2) are adequate in size, content, and diversity for addressing the research problems; (3) are congruent in scale; and (4) preserve data about original associations (Chapter 2). An essential part of any sampling strategy is taking control samples from contrastive matrices and contexts, in order to provide a basis for evaluating the uniqueness of central samples, and to support multiple-hypothesis testing. Off-site sediment samples are the most obvious kind of control samples, but by no means the only kind. Intra-site samples of feature fill, for example, must be supported by samples of sediments taken by the same means outside the limits of the feature but nearby.

Excavation with paleoenvironmental information

Application during excavation of informed knowledge of the world is an important methodological requirement. Excavators should be aware of the richness of data sets in the contexts and matrices in which they are working. Always there is the requirement for alertness to the unexpected. Alert and curious excavators are positioned to benefit from the unexpected, and are prepared to sample it usefully. Conclusions drawn from a narrowly predetermined set of data or focused in support of one hypothesis can be utterly convincing and, at the same time, entirely wrong.

Prior to excavation, but after initial mapping of a site, whether surficially or by remote sensing, it is advisable to dig a strategically scattered set of test pits or cores to collect samples of the observable sedimentary units. Each distinct sedimentary unit should be scrutinized through physical and chemical analyses in order to disclose the range of contexts or environments in the site and the range of materials likely to be encountered or preserved in each (e.g., Fig. 12.5). Such an inventory of site contents and structural relationships permits advance planning for recovery and sampling of contexts, whether depositional, cultural, pedological, or disturbed. Knowledge of the range of included materials supports planning for retrieving, sampling, conserving, storing, and analyzing those materials that will contribute most to the investigations, as well as arranging for specialist consultations or collaboration. Such knowledge is also essential for training field crews to recognize and name the phenomena they will encounter and try to record at the site.

Excavators informed about the range of materials available at a site are much more productively aware of changes in matrices, and less likely to overlook or discard significant information of whatever size. The discussions above of microbiological and macrobiological materials and ichnofossils (Parts VI and VII), climate proxies (Part III), and sedimentary materials and pedological processes (Part V) highlight classes of information too often ignored during excavations. Observations and interpretations of such materials are essential elements of sound paleoenvironmental research.

Because chronology is the foundation of all archaeological interpretation, whether for sequences or processes, stratigraphic observation and recording should be at the finest resolution consistent with research goals. When administrative or financial constraints require trimming of ideal strategies for an excavation, stratigraphic control must be protected at all costs; only crew safety is more important. Field record forms that support the Harris matrix analysis are excellent for revealing ambiguities in the field while they can still be resolved (e.g., Barker 1993). Designers of research strategies as well as excavators must be alert to collect all available chronological evidence in stratigraphic relationships and to collect natural and cultural materials appropriate for chronometry in their full diversity (Part II). Contexts of all finds and samples should always reference a depositional unit, whatever other grid controls may be used. Arbitrary levels and Cartesian coordinates, by their very nature, abstract finds from depositional contexts, always with the loss of some relational information. Reliance on grids alone can lead to the kind of absurdity I once encountered in field records, wherein depths of finds were referenced to elevation "above sea level" – a variable abstraction, as explained in Chapter 10, no substitute for site datum.

Taphonomic relationships are keys to the history of deposition and disturbance in sediments and thus to the chronology and associational integrity of materials in contexts; they must be given high priority during excavation. Excavators should be alert to recognize and interpret signs of disturbance, changes of context and matrix (facies), and differences in preservation conditions (Schiffer 1987), all the while being sensitive to equifinality (Parts VI and VII). Multiple hypotheses intensively discussed in the field are the most valuable interpretive aids; all versions should be entered into the record, with explanations of the criteria that permit disproof of any. Field observations relevant to understanding the rates and effects of pedogenesis and diagenesis in the sediments should be valued (Part V).

Collaboration

Projects that involve several disciplinary data sets and specialist analyses challenge the cooperative commitment, sense of humor, and patience of everyone involved. Success in integrating multiple results requires knowledge, judgment, and (above all) honesty to assure that the necessary evaluation, interpretation, and reconciliation are achieved. There are no shortcuts to reliable conclusions. There is the need to evaluate others' work by the same rigorous standards we bring to our own, questioning and clarifying until congruence and mutual comprehension are achieved.

Cross-disciplinary collaboration is expected to benefit all parties; nevertheless, it is complicated and sometimes frustrated by scale differences in field data among archaeologists, biologists, and geoscientists, deriving from distinct research orientations. Collaborators aware of the problems can usually resolve them and realize mutual benefits. Differences of terminology and basic concepts of the world are more elusive difficulties. The archaeologist, as principal coordinator with responsibility for the entire project, must be alert to such problems of communication and be able to address them from familiarity with the terminology and theory of several disciplines. Dillehay (1993) provides an insightful discussion of issues in the practice of interdisciplinary investigations.

The company of collaborators, as much as the range of materials recovered, will designate the kinds of technical analyses imposed on the materials. These are limited only by available knowledge, skills, equipment, and funds, and so must be specified in terms of the research goals and the administrative constraints. As analytical possibilities are expanding rapidly, no attempt is made here to recommend any basic set. Analyses should be selected to permit evaluation of evidence from several complementary directions on a range of materials. This is only possible with samples that are defensibly representative, congruent, and appropriate.

Environmental information generated by collaborators should not be relegated to appendices. Appendices are properly for descriptive data, not interpretation. To realize its richest contribution to archaeology, cross-disciplinary information must be fully integrated into interpretations.

Integration of data and problems

Description precedes interpretation. We only observe what we can name in some fashion. The chapters above have introduced technical terms from a number of disciplines outside archaeology. This was not done lightly: unfamiliar specialist terms can be daunting, and the response may be negative. The purpose of special terminology is not only to improve communication among disparate disciplines; these terms and the concepts they label increase archaeologists' analytical vocabulary and interpretive acuity.

Integration follows description and interpretation of basic data. Most of the interpretation of field and analytical data is likely to be done by specialists – archaeologists and all their consultants. Integration requires that one brain (or very few), likely those of archaeologists, literally incorporate the information and work through it all to achieve congruence and insight. Integration is expensive and difficult; it is labor-intensive work, demanding rigor, scholarship, ingenuity, and open minds. Complete integration of paleoecological projects is rarely achieved; the larger and more complex the data set, the more ambiguities and incongruities find room. Uncertainties do not represent failures; they should not be suppressed in final reports.

Because we are trying to understand a dynamic and utterly complex world, in many manifestations and states, paleoenvironmental research cannot be automated. In such a multivariate world, success in research is most likely to reward the best juggler – that is, someone capable of (1) keeping a lot of balls in the air (multiple variables interacting), (2) taking risks (expanding a repertoire of skills and knowledge), and (3) enjoying the undertaking.

Interpretation

The processes of data integration and final interpretation are not strictly sequential; they flow reflexively. Synthesis in multidisciplinary archaeological investigations is the responsibility of the archaeologist, who must attempt to make human sense of the data presented in several different disciplinary dialects. Interpretive hypotheses will raise questions not anticipated during initial integrations, and integrations may have organized data sets in such a way as to refute a favored hypothesis or foil testing of others. Assumptions must be stated clearly, despite the difficulty of identifying them for oneself. The archaeologist must be willing to report unresolved differences, warts and all, to make clear the residue of ambiguities.

Assumptions, ambiguities, errors of recording or of analysis recognized in hindsight – these are the things that go bump in the night as one attempts to understand. Recognizing them acknowledges our humanity more than our fallibility. The case studies in this volume display the process of reevaluation and rethinking, exemplifying the benefits of reconsideration and the participation of many investigators. "The archaeological scientist approaches the evidence on the premise that close examination of it in the light of current theory might serve to modify working interpretations concerning past events and conditions. Absolute certainty is not on offer" (O'Connor 1991: 1).

A genuinely holistic appreciation of human beings can be approached from the perspective of synecology, a theoretical position that respects growth and behavior in particular physical, biological, and social contexts. Life on this singular planet is based on conditions given by its situation – particular forms of astronomical cycles, of materials and energetics, and the contingencies defined by them. Synecology accepts humans as integral parts of the biosphere, responsive to phenomena in all spheres. It demonstrates, moreover, that within the biosphere human lives are uniquely complex.

Because of these inevitable parameters of life on Earth, the study of the human condition is not separable from the ecology of the home planet. Environments ordain nothing but change; they are not deterministic, but they do impose both opportunities and constraints. Life is responsive to situations resulting from contingencies; life entails strategizing. Humans are the best strategists the world has produced – flexible, clever, and manipulative. Nevertheless, this is not a world in which long-term agendas are fully realized. Archaeological research that is sensitive to the implications of place, time, and the presence of other beings will more fully realize its potential than studies that ignore context and interactions.

Archaeological interpretation of research results is itself contextualized in the needs of the sociopolitical worlds in which it appears. Results that are addressed only to other archaeologists risk marginalization, even irrelevance. The language of archaeology, and of environmental archaeology in particular, tends toward the esoteric; it is often either inaccessible to non-archaeologists or dismissed by them for a variety of communicative failings. The task of interpretation, therefore, does not end with a report to one's archaeological peers.

The canons of academic science tend to devalue popularization of research, probably because efforts to reach a larger audience so often result in excessive simplification and serious distortion of meanings. Means must be found by which the results of archaeological and anthropocentric paleoecological research can be communicated effectively to a larger public where they may contribute to the debates that inform public policies and enrich cultural values in non-exclusionary terms.

EXAMPLE OF SUCCESSFUL INTEGRATION AND INTERPRETATION

> Interdisciplinary research . . . refers to the incorporation of other scientists into all phases of research, from the initial stages of problem formulation and research design to the intermediary stages of data extraction and analysis to the final interpretative stage.
>
> DILLEHAY 1993: 411–412

Integration of several lines of paleoenvironmental inquiry has to date been most successful at small spatial and temporal scales. Mingies Ditch, an Iron Age site on a tributary of the River Thames in England, provides an example of what can be accomplished with clear research goals and a well-preserved site. The site, quarried away in 1980, was a small farmstead occupied for a century or less by a few people tending livestock on the valley floor of the Windrush River, from about 2200 radiocarbon years ago. The data recovered support a reconstructive drawing of the site, with houses, outbuildings, boundary ditches and hedges, and pasture and animal pens (Fig. 18.1). The summary following is derived from the site report, where more details and the cultural description are presented (Allen and Robinson 1993); commentary is by the present author.

The site was located on an island of alluvium within anastomosing channels of the Windrush and its small tributaries. At the time of occupation, no trees grew there. Bronze Age deforestation apparently had removed large vegetation, resulting in rough pasturage for the Iron Age occupants. During the occupation, the water table was low enough to prevent flooding and to permit earthworm activity in the soil, but the boundary ditches held water most of the time. Subsequent to abandonment, the water table rose; the site was buried under alluvium early in the Saxon period. The higher water table assured preservation of organic materials in the buried ditches.

Figure 18.1   Reconstruction drawing of the Mingies Ditch Iron Age farmstead, showing ditch pattern, indicated vegetation, and inferred land use and structural associations. (Reproduced from Allen and Robinson 1993, with permission of the Oxford Archaeological Unit and Danion Rey.)

Excavations inside the central ditches revealed indications of five houses, some occupied sequentially, with outbuildings and pits. Construction and resituating of outbuildings, ditches, roads, and pits was a feature of the site, which was apparently abandoned on one or two occasions for a period of months. The house floors were swept clean, as was the immediate vicinity of external storage structures; midden trash accumulated elsewhere in the compound and in pits. The area between the compound boundary ditch and the concentric ditch beyond it was apparently used for animal pens. The ditch boundaries must have been enhanced by less permanent gates and fencing. No evidence of Iron Age plowing was encountered.

Bronze Age deforestation had reduced the biological diversity of both plants and animals. The only wild animal remains recovered were beaver, duck, and plover. The Iron Age settlement added medium-sized and large herbivores, whose activities at pasture led to increased diversity and density of ruderals, which were distinct from the crop weeds that came into the site with cereal grains. No remains of fish or edible mollusks were recovered, either because they were not utilized or because they were simply not preserved.

Regional-scale archaeological studies conducted from Oxford prior to this investigation had established that Iron Age agricultural settlements were located on the gravel terraces flanking the Windrush valley. The nearest were 1 to 2 km distant from Mingies Ditch. The settlement on the valley floor specialized in keeping cattle, horses, and sheep, while importing its cereal foods in the form of wheat and barley grains, likely from the farms on the terraces. Domestic animals were butchered at the site; either live animals or animal products or both could have been traded for cereals. Structural timbers were also necessarily imported to the treeless site.

Investigation and data collection

Investigation of this productive site was conducted under less than ideal conditions, having been undertaken with volunteer labor under threat of site destruction in 1977 through 1978. It benefited from the long-term regional studies conducted by some of the same personnel (e.g., Lambrick and Robinson 1979; Robinson and Lambrick 1984). The interdisciplinary analysis and integration was carried to completion in 1985. The decision to publish in 1993 was taken despite some continuing rethinking of arguments and conclusions. Absence of closure of the interpretive process is expectable in any challenging project. Perfect knowledge is never fully achieved, nor could we be confident of recognizing it if it were. As argued in Chapter 2, science is learning, not knowing.

The site was observed in aerial photographs prior to investigation; the photos guided the placement of exposures. A gridded open plan with stratigraphic controls and collection of a wide range of environmental data classes guided the excavations. Saturated organic materials in old river channels and Iron Age ditches provided pollen, botanical macrofossils, and Coleoptera. Charred plant materials, soil mollusks, soil profiles and sedimentary textures, and animal bones were the main categories of environmental data exploited on site. Autecological analogs indicated the presence during the Iron Age settlement of several local, contrastive habitat groups of plants and beetles, including among others: standing water, wet vegetation, wet and dry grassland and disturbed open ground, large herbivores, and scrub/hedge associations. "The different lines of evidence could often be used to complement each other. For instance, pollen and insect evidence were useful for assessing the general character of the vegetation around the site, whereas the seeds were valuable in determining the particular species which comprised the plant communities inferred from the more general landscape information" (Allen and Robinson 1993: 165). Remains from intra-site wet deposits indicated aspects of local environments, while those in alluvium and channel deposits were related to more extensive riverine environments.

Uncertainties and ambiguities

The authors are laudably forthcoming about the degrees of uncertainty and inconclusiveness they recognize in the project. A technical appendix offers unusual detail on the processes of decision-making that informed the interpretations offered. The discussions are refreshingly reflexive, and helpfully evaluative.

We have already noted above the considerable reliance on modern analogs for community studies of vegetation and Coleoptera; such analogs bring with them uncertainties in respect to degree of stability in the associations of organisms through time. In reporting their analysis of the domestic animal bones, Wilson and Bramwell specify the decision criteria they employed, and specifically evaluate the reliability of their samples and of the inferences drawn from them. Unlike most of the specialist reports, the bones analysis focused on inferences about human behavior because the sample was overwhelmingly of domesticated herbivores introduced and controlled by the human occupants of the site. Nevertheless, interpretation of the site economy was inconclusive: the archaeologists could not definitively decide whether the site occupants were tending animals in their own interests or for members of the larger local Iron Age community. The presence of numerous horses, contrasting with the otherwise straitened appearance of the material culture at the site, supports the second alternative. Although some kitchen gardening seems likely, the staple cereal foods were processed, but not produced, at the site. "The overall impression is of almost entirely local trade . . . The utilitarian character and very local style of the pottery, the evidence for limited metalworking and weaving all suggest that the settlement aimed at a high degree of self-sufficiency" (Allen and Robinson 1993: 147).

A very high level of competent observation of sedimentary surfaces and sequences during excavation enhances this report, providing details on construction sequences, the trampling and relative cleanliness of yards and floors, and the fills of ditches and pits. A single sequence of house occupancy was not achieved, but it seems likely that house rebuilding and even reorganization of the site plan followed at least one period of abandonment. Changes in social relationships are implicated by such activity, but the evidence is inconclusive. Other unfinished interpretations are frankly and fairly presented in the report.

Chronology, at least, was not a serious problem at this site; it emerges as such only in discussions about behavior related to building and ditch sequences. What was exposed was essentially a short-term, single-component site with some internal changes, expectable for a span of occupancy not exceeding a century. The excellent controls on archaeological contexts permit the assumption of essential contemporaneity in the paleoecological data from the ditches and pits. The regional data from fluvial deposits have no such direct relationship, of course.

In this instance, disciplined and resourceful investigators, working within a constrained budget, were able to achieve an unusual degree of verisimilitude in the reconstructive description of the farmstead. The report presents significant socioeconomic details and interpretations. "It is suggested that the Mingies Ditch enclosure was a pioneer pastoral settlement, bringing what had been underexploited land marginal to the gravel terrace settlements into more intensive use" (Allen and Robinson 1993: 143). If the site functioned as common grazing for the larger community, the stock-keepers may have retained only food animals over the winter. If the farm was producing for trade, the commodities were likely dairy products, cattle, and horses. Noting the plainness of the material culture inventory and the small sizes of the houses, the authors conclude: "It is most unlikely that the site would have been entirely autonomous; its inhabitants probably had links with and obligations of service or kind to a higher social organization such as was responsible for the massive enterprise of hillfort construction" (Allen and Robinson 1993: 149). In such a case, the inhabitants of the Windrush valley floor may have been able to call on work parties to help build the ditches at the establishment of the site.

A FUTURE FOR PALEOENVIRONMENTAL STUDIES

[A]rchaeological reconstructions are continually presented – not just to keep pace
with newly devised means of increasing the accuracy of our understanding of the past
– but to keep pace with the changing concerns of our own society.

LEONE AND PALKOVICH 1985: 428

Budgets as well as methodological and tactical constraints appear to favor studies of
small sites. Examples throughout the literature and featured in this volume show
that moving observations down-scale offers real advantages in meeting costs and
providing insight into environmental mechanisms. Meticulous dissection of limited
archaeological contexts may give the best detailed results. Intensive, technical,
instrumental, and laboratory analyses are more easily affordable when sample populations are moderate.

However, there are dangers in constraints. Tight budgets inevitably and quickly
lead to sample populations too small to be representative. Compromised sample
quality will limit interpretations. Large-scale interpretive models cannot be built on
the sum of small, discrete projects. Nor can interpretations developed on large-scale
modern analogs be tested on the ground in small archaeological sites. The geosciences have learned that mechanisms observed locally are not always representative of
large-scale processes; archaeologists must keep this caveat in mind, while struggling
with inadequate resources to define research projects that will generate new insights
and knowledge of the human past. Reliable paleoenvironmental research must
include a significant regional component, and yet be fine-scaled enough to permit
evaluation of diversity and exceptions.

Integration of results from large research projects at complex sites or those involving regional sequences has proven much more elusive than in the project at Mingies
Ditch. Many of the large and already extensively published multidisciplinary projects undertaken since World War II remain unintegrated. Chronological resolution
is typically a major hindrance to integration, as is the burden of vast, diverse detail on
the principal investigator and team. Complex sites investigated by multidisciplinary
teams nonetheless have greatly enriched the methodological literature and, more
importantly, have offered significant insights into human ecology in the past, as with
the excavations of Viking and Roman York, medieval Iceland, Abu Hureyra in Syria,
Franchthi Cave in Greece, and workers' housing in industrial Lowell, Massachusetts,
among others.

A major barrier to broadly applicable results in environmental archaeology and
human paleoecology is the parochialism of the literature. Despite my expectations

pon undertaking the reviews that support this volume, I found that only the paleo-vegetation literature is characterized by a semblance of international and multilingual integration. Good archaeological and paleoenvironmental work is being done, and published, in other languages, but it is difficult and expensive for an English-speaker, even one who can read some of the languages, to access those literatures. The reverse is also often true. I suspect that a large amount of inefficient reinvention is one result of this fragmentation into linguistic communities. I know that this is true between the French-speaking and English-speaking archaeological communities in northeastern North America and, more disturbingly, I know it to be true between English-speakers on separate continents. American and British researchers in paleo-environments, to a far greater degree than social theoreticians, live in separate tight little citation circles and independently invent research approaches. International conferences are improving the situation, and electronic communication may presently erase the intellectual isolation along with its inefficient burden of duplicative research.

With more sophisticated awareness of what can be done in archaeological data recovery and analysis must come requirements for better training in science for archaeologists, making the language and concepts of other disciplines less exotic. It will necessarily follow that the interpretive literature will become something less of a literary exercise and instead move toward the exposition of testable statements and propositions about diversity in time and space.

Funding for archaeology will improve only as archaeologists demonstrate that they produce not only entertainment (tempered by severe physical labor) but also socially useful information that can inform policies for contemporary societies. The ability to measure the extent and timing of human influence in ecosystems could be the foundation for enlightened environmental policies. For instance, misinformed efforts to "restore wilderness" in various parts of the world could be redirected into social planning that will accommodate the biological and material diversity that is the essential basis for the continuity of life.

Awareness of humans as elements in planetary ecosystems requires new thinking about dominance and destiny. Human ecology is the story of self-domestication, of decisions made, risks taken, and limits defined or defied. It is also the untold story of the consequences of strategies. Decisions and risks are defined ideologically as they are lived, and their outcomes are enshrined ideologically in today's politics. The results of paleoecological research are distorted for purposes of public policy because of the thick cultural screen between scientifically informed publications and the ideologically freighted language of public discourse. The continuing debate about human responsibility for global warming, for example, is consuming resources and time better spent on planning for reducing those threats we can control and for adapting realistically to those we cannot. Management policies directed to human society rather than to human habitats can improve the quality of our self-domestication by offering space and resources to other forms of life. Anthropocentric paleoecology may help us learn to manage ourselves for continuing existence.

REFERENCES

Aaby, B. 1988 The cultural landscape as reflected in percentage and influx pollen diagrams from two Danish ombrotrophic mires. In *The cultural landscape – past, present and future*, edited by H. H. Birks, H. J. B. Birks, P. E. Kaland, and D. Moe, pp. 209–288. Cambridge University Press.

— 1994 Review of *Climate change and human impact on the landscape: studies in paleoecology and environmental archaeology*, edited by F. M. Chambers, 1993. *Journal of Archaeological Science* 21: 143.

Aaby, B., and G. Digerfeldt 1986 Sampling techniques for lakes and bogs. In *Handbook of Holocene palaeoecology and palaeohydrology*, edited by B. E. Berglund, pp. 181–194. Chichester: John Wiley and Sons.

Ager, D. V. 1993 *The nature of the stratigraphical record*. 3rd edition. Chichester: John Wiley and Sons.

Ager, T. A. 1982 Vegetational history of western Alaska during the Wisconsin glacial interval and the Holocene. In *Paleoecology of Beringia*, edited by D. M. Hopkins, J. V. Matthews, Jr., C. E. Schweger, and S. B. Young, pp. 75–93. New York: Academic.

Aitken, M. J. 1985 *Thermoluminescence dating.* Orlando: Academic.

— 1990 *Science-based dating in archaeology.* London: Longman.

Aitken, M. J., H. N. Michael, P. P. Betancourt, and P. M. Warren 1988 The Thera eruption: continuing discussion of the dating. *Archaeometry* 30: 165–182.

Aitken, M. J., C. B. Stringer, and P. A. Mellars (editors) 1993 *The origin of modern humans and the impact of chronometric dating.* Princeton University Press.

Akersten, W. A., T. M. Foppe, and G. T. Jefferson 1988 New source of dietary data for extinct herbivores. *Quaternary Research* 30: 92–97.

Akin, W. E. 1991 *Global patterns: climate, vegetation, and soils.* Norman: University of Oklahoma Press.

Allchin, B., A. Goudie, and K. Hegde 1978 *The prehistory and palaeogeography of the Great Indian Desert.* London: Academic.

Allen, K. M. S., S. W. Green, and E. B. W. Zubrow

(editors) 1990 *Interpreting space: GIS and archaeology*. London: Taylor and Francis.

Allen, T. F. H., and T. W. Hoekstra 1992 *Towards a unified ecology*. New York: Columbia University Press.

Allen, T. G., and M. A. Robinson 1993 *The prehistoric landscape and Iron Age enclosed settlement at Mingies Ditch, Hardwick-with-Yelford, Oxon*. Thames Valley Landscapes: The Windrush Valley, vol. 2. Oxford University Committee for Archaeology.

Alley, R. B., D. A. Meese, C. A. Shuman, A. J. Gow, K. C. Taylor, P. M. Grootes, J. W. C. White, M. Ram, E. D. Waddington, P. A. Mayewski, and G. A. Zielinski 1993 Abrupt increase in Greenland snow accumulation at the end of the Younger Dryas event. *Nature* 362: 527–529.

Allison, T. D., R. E. Moeller, and M. B. Davis 1986 Pollen in laminated sediments provides evidence for a mid-Holocene forest pathogen outbreak. *Ecology* 67: 1101–1105.

Ambrose, S. H. 1993 Isotopic analysis of paleodiets: methodological and interpretive considerations. In *Investigations of ancient human tissue: chemical analyses in anthropology*, edited by M. K. Sandford, pp. 59–130. Langhorne, Penn.: Gordon and Breach.

Ambrose, S. H., and M. J. DeNiro 1989 Climate and habitat reconstruction using stable carbon and nitrogen isotope ratios of collagen in prehistoric herbivore teeth from Kenya. *Quaternary Research* 31: 407–422.

Ambrose, S. H., and N. E. Sikes 1991 Soil carbon isotope evidence for Holocene habitat change in the Kenya Rift Valley. *Science* 253: 1402–1405.

Andersen, S. T. 1986 Palaeoecological studies of terrestrial soils. In *Handbook of Holocene palaeoecology and palaeohydrology*, edited by B. E. Berglund, pp. 165–177. Chichester: John Wiley and Sons.

Anderson, D. J., and J. Kikkawa 1986 Development of concepts. In *Community ecology: pattern and process*, edited by J. Kikkawa and D. F. Anderson, pp. 3–16. Oxford: Blackwell Scientific.

Anderson, R. M., and R. M. May (editors) 1982 *Population biology of infectious diseases*. New York: Springer-Verlag.

Andresen, J. M., B. F. Byrd, M. D. Elson, R. H. McGuire, R. G. Mendoza, E. Staskie, and J. P. White 1981 The deer hunters: Star Carr reconsidered. *World Archaeology* 13: 31–46.

Andrews, D. L. 1994 Molecular approaches to the isolation and analysis of ancient nucleic acids. In *Method and theory for investigating the peopling of the Americas*, edited by R. Bonnichsen and D. G. Steele, pp. 165–175. Corvallis, Oreg.: Oregon State University.

Andrews, P. J. 1990 *Owls, caves, and fossils*. University of Chicago Press.

Anthes, R. A., J. J. Cahir, A. B. Fraser, and H. A. Panofsky 1981 *The atmosphere*. 3rd edition. Columbus: Charles E. Merrill.

Armour-Chelu, M., and P. Andrews 1994 Some effects of bioturbation by earthworms (Oligochaeta) on archaeological sites. *Journal of Archaeological Science* 21: 433–443.

Artzy, M., and D. Hillel 1988 A defense of the theory of progressive soil salinization in ancient Southern Mesopotamia. *Geoarchaeology* 3: 235–238.

Ashton, N. M., J. Cook, S. G. Lewis, and J. Rose (editors) 1992 *High Lodge: excavation by G. de G. Sieveking 1962–1968 and J. Cook 1988*. London: British Museum.

Atkinson, R. J. C. 1957 Worms and weathering. *Antiquity* 31: 219–233.

Auffray, J. C., E. Tchernov, and E. Nevo 1988 Origine du commensalisme de la souris domestique (*Mus musculus domesticus*) vis-à-vis l'homme. Paris: *Comptes rendues de l'Académie des sciences* 307(3): 517–522.

Avery, B. W. 1980 *Soil classification for England and Wales (higher categories)*. Soil Survey Technical Monographs no. 14, Harpenden: Soil Survey of England and Wales.

Avery, D. M. 1982 Micromammals as palaeoenvironmental indicators and an interpretation of the Late Quaternary in the southern Cape Province, South Africa. *Annals of the South African Museum* 85: 183–374.

Bailey, G. N. 1983 Concepts of time in Quaternary prehistory. *Annual Review of Anthropology* 12: 165–192.

Bailey, G., J. Chappell, and R. Cribb 1994 The origin of *Anadara* shell mounds at Weipa, North Queensland, Australia. *Archaeology of Oceania* 29: 69–80.

Bailey, G. N., M. R. Deith, and N. J. Shackleton 1983 Oxygen isotope analysis and seasonality determinations: limits and potential of a new technique. *American Antiquity* 48: 390–398.

Bailey, G., G. King, and D. Sturdy 1993 Active tectonics and land-use strategies: a Palaeolithic example from northwest Greece. *Antiquity* 67: 292–312.

Bailey, G., and J. Parkington (editors) 1988 *The archaeology of prehistoric coastlines*. Cambridge University Press.

Baillie, M. G. L. 1990 Checking back on an assemblage of published radiocarbon dates. *Radiocarbon* 32(3): 361–366.
 1995 *A slice through time: dendrochronology and precision dating*. London: Batsford.

Baillie, M. G. L., and D. M. Brown 1988 An overview of oak chronologies. In *Science and archaeology, Glasgow 1987*, edited by E. O. Slater and J. O. Tate, pp. 543–548. Oxford: BAR British Series 196(ii).

Baillie, M. G. L., and M. A. R. Munro 1988 Irish tree rings, Santorini and volcanic dust veils. *Nature* 332: 344–346.

Baker, J. R., and D. R. Brothwell 1980 *Animal diseases in archaeology*. London: Academic.

Barba P. L. A., L. Manzanilla, R. Chavez, L. Flores, and A. J. Arzate 1990 Caves and tunnels at Teotihuacan, Mexico: a geological phenomenon of archaeological interest. In *Archaeological geology of North America*, edited by N. P. Lasca and J. Donahue, pp. 431–438. Centennial Special Volume 4. Boulder: Geological Society of America.

Barber, K. E. 1991 On the relationship between palaeoecology and neoecology. In *Modelling ecological change*, edited by D. R. Harris and K. D. Thomas, pp. 13–16. London: Institute of Archaeology.

Bard, E. 1997 Nuclide production by cosmic rays during the last ice age. *Science* 277: 532–533.

Bard, E., B. Hamelin, R. G. Fairbanks, and A. Zindler 1990 Calibration of the ^{14}C timescale over the past 30,000 years using mass spectrometric U–Th ages from Barbados corals. *Nature* 345: 405–410.

Barker, P. 1982 *Techniques of archaeological excavation*. 2nd edition. London: Batsford.
 1993 *Techniques of archaeological excavation*. 3rd edition. London: Batsford.

Barney, G. O. 1980 *The global 2000 report to the President of the US: entering the 21st century*. Vol. 1: *The Summary Report*. New York: Pergamon.

Baron, H., S. Hummel, and B. Herrmann 1996 *Mycobacterium tuberculosis* complex DNA in ancient human bones. *Journal of Archaeological Science* 23: 667–671.

Bartlein, P. J., M. E. Edwards, S. L. Shafer, and E. D. Barker, Jr. 1995 Calibration of radiocarbon ages and the interpretation of paleoenvironmental records. *Quaternary Research* 44: 417–424.

Barton, C. M., and G. A. Clark 1993 Cultural and natural formation processes in Late Quaternary cave and rockshelter sites of western Europe and the Near East. In *Formation processes in archaeological context*, edited by P. Goldberg, D. T. Nash, and M. D. Petraglia, pp. 33–52. Madison, Wis.: Prehistory.

Bar-Yosef, O. 1993 Site formation processes from a Levantine viewpoint. In *Formation processes in archaeological context*, edited by P. Goldberg, D. T. Nash, and M. D. Petraglia, pp. 13–32. Madison, Wis.: Prehistory.

Batt, C. M. 1997 The British archaeomagnetic calibration curve: an objective treatment. *Archaeometry* 39: 153–168.

Baumgartner, T. R., J. Michaelsen, L. G. Thompson, G. T. Shen, A. Soutar, and R. E. Casey 1989 The recording of interannual climatic change by high-resolution natural systems: tree-rings, coral bands, glacial ice layers and marine varves. In *Climatic change in the eastern Pacific and western Americas*, edited by D. Peterson, pp. 1–14. Washington, D.C.: Geophysical Monograph Series 55, AGU.

Beck, C. (editor) 1994 *Dating in exposed and surface contexts*. Albuquerque: University of New Mexico Press.

Becker, B. 1993 An 11,000-year German oak and pine dendrochronology for radio-carbon calibration. *Radiocarbon: Calibration 1993* 35: 201–215.

Behre, K.-E. 1981 The interpretation of anthropogenic indicators in pollen diagrams. *Pollen et spores* 23: 225–246.

——— (editor) 1986 *Anthropogenic indicators in pollen diagrams*. Rotterdam: Balkema.

Behre, K.-E., and S. Jacomet 1991 The ecological interpretation of archaeobotanical data. In *Progress in Old World palaeoethnobotany*, edited by W. van Zeist, K. Wasylikowa, and K.-E. Behre, pp. 81–108. Rotterdam: Balkema.

Behrensmeyer, A. D., and A. P. Hill (editors) 1980 *Fossils in the making*. University of Chicago Press.

Behrensmeyer, A. K., J. D. Damuth, W. A. DiMichele, R. Potts, H. D. Suess, and S. L. Wing (editors) 1992 *Terrestrial ecosystems through time*. University of Chicago Press.

Belknap, D. R., and J. C. Kraft 1981 Preservation potential of transgressive coastal lithosomes on the U.S. Atlantic shelf. *Marine Geology* 42: 429–442.

Bell, M. 1982 The effects of land-use and climate on valley sedimentation. In *Climatic change in later prehistory*, edited by A. F. Harding, pp. 127–142. Edinburgh University Press.

——— 1992a The prehistory of soil erosion. In *Past and present soil erosion: archaeological and geographical perspectives*, edited by M. Bell and J. Boardman, pp. 21–35. Oxbow Monograph 22. Oxford: Oxbow Books.

——— 1992b Archaeology under alluvium: human agency and environmental process. Some concluding thoughts. In *Alluvial archaeology in Britain*, edited by S. Needham and M. G. Macklin, pp. 271–276. Oxbow Monograph 27. Oxford: Oxbow Books.

Bell, M., and J. Boardman (editors) 1992 *Past and present soil erosion: archaeological and geographical perspectives.* Oxbow Monograph 22. Oxford: Oxbow Books.

Bell, M., and M. Walker 1992 *Late Quaternary environmental change: physical and human perspectives.* London: Longman.

Bellomo, R. V. 1993 A methodological approach for identifying archaeological evidence of fire resulting from human activities. *Journal of Archaeological Science* 20: 525–553.

Berger, A., J. Imbrie, J. Hays, G. Kukla, and B. Saltzmann (editors) 1983 *Milankovitch and climate* (vols. 1 and 2). Dordrecht: D. Reidel.

Berglund, B. E. (editor) 1986 *Handbook of Holocene palaeoecology and palaeohydrology.* Chichester: John Wiley and Sons.

Berglund, B. E., and M. Ralska-Jasiewiczowa 1986 Pollen analysis and pollen diagrams. In *Handbook of Holocene palaeoecology and palaeohydrology*, edited by B. E. Berglund, pp. 455–484. Chichester: John Wiley and Sons.

Bernabo, J. C., and T. Webb, III 1977 Changing patterns in the Holocene pollen record of northeastern North America: a mapped summary. *Quaternary Research* 8: 64–96.

Berner, R. A. 1990 Atmospheric carbon dioxide levels over Phanerozoic time. *Science* 249: 1382–1386.

Betancourt, J. L., T. R. Van Devender, and P. S. Martin (editors) 1990 *Packrat middens: the last 40,000 years of biotic change.* Tucson: University of Arizona Press.

Betancourt, P. P. 1987 Dating the Aegean Late Bronze Age with radiocarbon. *Archaeometry* 29: 45–49.

Betancourt, P. P., and H. N. Michael 1987 Dating the Aegean Late Bronze Age with radiocarbon: addendum. *Archaeometry* 29: 212–213.

Bettis, E. A., III (editor) 1995 *Archaeological geology of the Archaic period in North America.* Boulder: Geological Society of America Special Paper 297.

Biers, W. R., and P. E. McGovern 1990 *Organic contents of ancient vessels: materials analysis and archaeologic investigation.* Research Papers in Science and Archaeology No. 7, Museum of Applied Science Center for Archaeology [MASCA]. Philadelphia: University of Pennsylvania.

Binford, L. R. 1965 Archaeological systematics and the study of cultural process. *American Antiquity* 31: 203–210.

1978 *Nunamiut ethnoarchaeology.* New York: Academic.

1981 *Bones: ancient men and modern myths.* New York: Academic.

1993 Bones for stones: considerations of analogues for features found on the central Russian plain. In *From Kostenki to Clovis: Upper Paleolithic–Paleo-Indian adaptations*, edited by O. Soffer and N. D. Praslov, pp. 101–124. New York: Plenum.

Binford, M. W., M. Brenner, T. J. Whitmore, A. Higuera-Gundy, E. S. Deevey, and B. Leyden 1987 Ecosystems, paleoecology and human disturbance in subtropical and tropical America. *Quaternary Science Reviews* 6: 115–128.

Binford, M. W., E. S. Deevey, and T. L. Crisman 1983 Paleolimnology: an historical perspective on lacustrine ecosystems. *Annual Review of Ecology and Systematics* 14: 255–286.

Bintliff, J. L. 1977 *Natural environment and human settlement in prehistoric Greece.* Oxford: BAR Supplementary Series 28 (i, ii).

1992 Erosion in the Mediterranean lands: a reconsideration of pattern, process and methodology. In *Past and present soil erosion: archaeological and geographical perspectives*, edited by M. Bell and J. Boardman, pp. 125–131. Oxbow Monograph 22. Oxford: Oxbow Books

Birkeland, P. W. 1984 *Soils and geomorphology*. New York: Oxford University Press.

Birks, H. H., H. J. B. Birks, P. E. Kaland, and D. Moe (editors) 1988 *The cultural landscape – past, present and future.* Cambridge University Press.

Birks, H. J. B. 1986 Late-Quaternary biotic changes in terrestrial and lacustrine environments, with particular reference to north-west Europe. In *Handbook of Holocene palaeoecology and palaeohydrology*, edited by B. E. Berglund, pp. 3–65. Chichester: John Wiley and Sons.

1988 Conclusions. In *The cultural landscape – past, present and future*, edited by H. H. Birks, H. J. B. Birks, P. E. Kaland, and D. Moe, pp. 464–467. Cambridge University Press.

Birks, H. J. B., and H. H. Birks 1980 *Quaternary paleoecology*. London: Edward Arnold.

Birks, H. J. B., and A. D. Gordon 1985 *Numerical methods in Quaternary pollen analysis*. London: Academic.

Bjerck, L. G. B. 1988 Remodelling the Neolithic in southern Norway: another attack on a traditional problem. *Norwegian Archaeological Review* 21: 21–52, with comments.

Blackford, J. 1993 Peat bogs as sources of proxy climatic data: past approaches and future research. In *Climate change and human impact on the landscape: studies in paleoecology and environmental archaeology*, edited by F. M. Chambers, pp. 47–56. London/New York: Chapman and Hall.

Blinn, D. W., R. H. Hevly, and O. K. Davis 1994 Continuous Holocene record of diatom stratigraphy, paleohydrology, and anthropogenic activity in a spring-mound in southwestern United States. *Quaternary Research* 42: 197–205.

Bloom, A. L. 1983 Sea level and coastal changes. In *Late-Quaternary environments of the United States*. Vol. 2: *The Holocene*, edited by H. E. Wright, Jr., pp 42–51. Minneapolis: University of Minnesota Press.

Boardman, J., and M. Bell 1992 Past and present soil erosion: linking archaeology and geomorphology. In *Past and present soil erosion: archaeological and geographical perspectives*, edited by M. Bell and J. Boardman, pp. 1–8. Oxbow Monograph 22. Oxford: Oxbow Books.

Bobrowsky, P. T. 1984 The history and science of gastropods in archaeology. *American Antiquity* 49: 77–93.

Bobrowsky, P. T., and B. F. Ball 1989 The theory and mechanics of ecological diversity in archaeology. In *Quantifying diversity in archaeology*, edited by R. D. Leonard and G. T. Jones, pp. 4–12. Cambridge University Press.

Boddington, A., A. N. Garland, and R. C. Janaway 1987 Flesh, bones, dust and society. In *Death, decay and reconstruction: approaches to archaeology and forensic science*, edited by A. Boddington, A. N. Garland, and R. C. Janaway, pp. 3–9. Manchester University Press.

Bohrer, V. L. 1986 Guideposts in ethnobotany. *Journal of Ethnobiology* 6: 27–43.

Bond, G., W. Showers, M. Cheseby, R. Lotti, P. Almasi, P. deMenocal, P. Priore, H. Cullen, I. Hajdas, and G. Bonani 1997 A pervasive millennial-scale cycle in North

Atlantic Holocene and glacial climates. *Science* 278: 1257–1266.

Boserup, E. 1965 *The conditions of agricultural growth.* Chicago: Aldine.

Bowen, D. Q. 1991 *Quaternary geology.* New York: Pergamon.

Bowman, S. 1990 *Radiocarbon dating.* Interpreting the Past series. Berkeley: University of California Press.

Boyle, E. A. 1990 Quaternary deepwater paleoceanography. *Science* 249: 863–870.

Bradley, R. S. 1985 *Quaternary paleoclimatology.* Boston: Allen and Unwin.

1999 *Paleoclimatology: Reconstructing climates of the Quaternary.* San Diego: Academic.

(editor) 1991 *Global changes of the past.* UCAR/Office for Interdisciplinary Earth Studies, Boulder.

Brady, N. C. 1990 *The nature and properties of soils.* 10th edition. New York: Macmillan.

Brain, C. K. 1981 *The hunters or the hunted? An introduction to African cave taphonomy.* University of Chicago Press.

Brandt, R. W., W. Groenman-van Waateringe, and S. van der Leeuw (editors) 1987 *Assendelver Polder Papers 1.* Amsterdam.

Brasier, M. D. 1980 *Microfossils.* London: Allen and Unwin.

Braziunas, T. F. 1994 Review of *Global climates since the Late Glacial maximum,* edited by H. E. Wright, Jr., J. E. Kutzbach, T. Webb, III, W. F. Ruddiman, F. A. Street-Perrott, and P. J. Bartlein, 1993, University of Minnesota Press. *Quaternary Research* 42: 363.

Brenton, B. P. 1994 Paleonutrition: implications for contemporary Native Americans. In *Paleonutrition: the diet and health of prehistoric Americans,* edited by K. D. Sobolik, pp. 294–305. Occasional

Paper No. 22. Carbondale: Center for Archaeological Investigations, Southern Illinois University.

Brinkhuizen, D. C., and A. T. Clason (editors) 1986 *Fish and archaeology.* Oxford: BAR International Series 294.

Broecker, W. S. 1994 Massive iceberg discharges as triggers for global climate change. *Nature* 372: 421–424.

Broecker, W. S., and G. H. Denton 1990 What drives glacial cycles? *Scientific American* (Jan. 1990): 49–56.

Broecker, W. S., J. P. Kennett, B. P. Flower, J. T. Teller, S. Trumbore, G. Bonani, and W. Wölfli 1989 The routing of meltwater from the Laurentide Ice Sheet during the Younger Dryas cold episode. *Nature* 341: 318–321.

Bromley, R. G. 1990 *Trace fossils: biology and taphonomy.* London: Unwin Hyman.

Brooks, A. S., P. E. Hare, J. E. Kokis, G. H. Miller, R. D. Ernst, and F. Wendorf 1990 Dating Pleistocene archeological sites by protein diagenesis in ostrich eggshells. *Science* 248: 60–64.

Browman, D. L. 1981 Isotopic discrimination and correction factors in radiocarbon dating. In *Advances in Archaeological Method and Theory* 4: 241–295.

Brown, A. G. 1997 *Alluvial geoarchaeology.* Cambridge University Press.

Brown, J. E. 1973 Depositional histories of sand grains from surface textures. *Nature* 242: 396–398.

Brown, J. H. 1995 *Macroecology.* University of Chicago Press.

Brown, J. H., and B. A. Maurer 1989 Macroecology: the division of food and space among species on continents. *Science* 243: 1145–1150.

Bryant, V. M., Jr., and S. A. Hall 1993 Archaeological palynology in the United

States: a critique. *American Antiquity* 58: 277–286.

Bryant, V. M., Jr., R. G. Holloway, J. G. Jones, and D. L. Carlson 1994 Pollen preservation in alkaline soils of the American Southwest. In *Sedimentation of organic particles*, edited by A. Traverse, pp. 47–58. Cambridge University Press.

Bryson, R. A. 1985 On climatic analogs in paleoclimatic reconstruction. *Quaternary Research* 23: 275–286.

1989 Late Quaternary volcanic modulation of Milankovitch climate forcing. *Theoretical and Applied Climatology* 39: 115–125.

Buck, C. E., C. D. Litton, and E. M. Scott 1994 Making the most of radiocarbon dating: some statistical considerations. *Antiquity* 68: 252–263.

Buckland, P. C. 1976 The use of insect remains in the interpretation of archaeological environments. In *Geoarchaeology*, edited by D. A. Davidson and M. L. Shackley, pp. 369–396. Boulder: Westview.

1988 North Atlantic faunal connections – introduction or endemics? *Entomologica scandinavica supplement 1988*: 7–29.

1991 Granaries stores and insects: the archaeology of insect synanthropy. In *La Préparation alimentaire des céréales*, edited by F. Sigaut and D. Fournier, pp. 69–81. Strasbourg: Council of Europe.

Buckland, P. C., A. J. Dugmore, and K. J. Edwards 1997 Bronze Age myths? Volcanic activity and human response in the Mediterranean and North Atlantic regions. *Antiquity* 71: 581–593.

Buckland, P. C., A. J. Dugmore, D. W. Perry, D. Savory, and G. Sveinbjarnardóttir 1991 Holt in Eyjafjallasveit, Iceland: a paleoecological study of the impact of landnám. *Acta Archaeologica* 61: 252–271.

Buckland, P. C., R. A. Housley, and F. Brian Pyatt 1994 Paint, date, bog stratigraphy and murder: some comments on Lindow Man. In *Whither environmental archaeology?*, edited by R. Luff and P. A. Rowley-Conwy, pp. 7–12. Oxbow Monograph 38. Oxford: Oxbow Books.

Buikstra, J. E., and J. H. Mielke 1985 Demography, diet, and health. In *The analysis of prehistoric diets*, edited by R. L. Gilbert, Jr., and J. H. Mielke, pp. 359–422. Orlando: Academic.

Bull, W. B. 1991 *Geomorphic responses to climatic change*. Oxford University Press.

Bullock, P., N. Fédoroff, A. Jongerius, G. Stoops, and T. Tursina 1985 *Handbook for soil thin section description*. Wolverhampton: Waine Research Publications.

Bumsted, M. P. 1985 Past human behavior from bone chemical analysis – respects and prospects. *Journal of Human Evolution* 14: 539–551.

Bunn, H. T. 1981 Archaeological evidence for meat-eating by Plio-Pleistocene hominids from Koobi Fora and Olduvai Gorge. *Nature* 291: 574–577.

Bunn, H. T., and J. A. Ezzo 1993 Hunting and scavenging by Plio-Pleistocene hominids: nutritional constraints, archaeological patterns, and behavioural implications. *Journal of Archaeological Science* 20: 365–398.

Burden, E. T., J. H. McAndrews, and G. Norris 1986 Palynology of Indian and European forest clearance and farming in lake sediment cores from Awenda Provincial Park, Ontario. *Canadian Journal of Earth Sciences* 23: 43–54.

Butler, S. 1992 X-radiography of archaeological soil and sediment profiles. *Journal of Archaeological Science* 19: 151–161.

Butzer, K. W. 1969 Changes in the land. Review

of *The Mediterranean valleys*, by C. Vita-Finzi. *Science* 165: 52–53.

1971 *Environment and archaeology: an ecological approach to prehistory.* 2nd edition. Chicago: Aldine-Atherton.

1976 *Geomorphology from the Earth.* New York: Harper and Row.

1978 Toward an integrated, contextual approach in archaeology: a personal view. *Journal of Archaeological Science* 5: 191–193.

1980 Holocene alluvial sequences: problems of dating and correlation. In *Timescales in geomorphology*, edited by R. A. Cullingford, D. A. Davidson, and J. Lewin, pp. 131–142. Chichester: John Wiley and Sons.

1981a Rise and fall of Axum, Ethiopia: a geoarchaeological interpretation. *American Antiquity* 46: 471–495.

1981b Cave sediments, Upper Pleistocene stratigraphy and Mousterian facies in Cantabrian Spain. *Journal of Archaeological Science* 8: 133–183.

1982 *Archaeology as human ecology.* Cambridge University Press.

Cadogan, G. 1978 Dating the Aegean Bronze Age without radiocarbon. *Archaeometry* 20: 209–214.

Campbell, C., I. D. Campbell, C. B. Blyth, and J. H. McAndrews 1994 Bison extirpation may have caused aspen expansion in western Canada. *Ecography* 17: 360–362.

Canada Soil Survey Committee 1978 *The Canadian system of soil classification.* Canadian Department of Agriculture Publication 1646. Ottawa: Supply and Services Canada.

Carlson, C. 1988 An evaluation of fish growth annuli for seasonality determination. In *Recent developments in environmental analysis in Old and New World archaeol-*

ogy, edited by E. Webb, pp. 67–87. Oxford: BAR International Series 416.

1995 The (in)significance of Atlantic salmon in New England. In *New England's creatures: 1400–1900*, edited by P. Benes, pp. 13–23. Boston University.

Carter, R. J. 1997 Age estimation of the roe deer (*Capreolus capreolus*) mandibles from the Mesolithic site of Star Carr, Yorkshire, based on radiographs of mandibular tooth development. *Journal of Zoology* 241: 495–502.

1998 Reassessment of seasonality at the early Mesolithic site of Star Carr, Yorkshire based on radiographs of mandibular tooth development in red deer (*Cervus elaphus*). *Journal of Archaeological Science* 25: 851–856.

Carter, R. W. G. 1988 *Coastal environments: an introduction to the physical, ecological and cultural systems of coastlines.* New York: Academic.

Cartmill, M. 1994 Reinventing anthropology. *Yearbook of Physical Anthropology* 37: 1–9.

Cashdan, E. 1982 The ecology of human subsistence. *Science* 216: 1308–1309.

Catt, J. A. 1986 *Soils and Quaternary geology: a handbook for field scientists.* Oxford: Clarendon.

1988 *Quaternary geology for scientists and engineers.* New York: Halsted.

Catt, J. A., and A. H. Weir 1976 The study of archaeologically important sediments by petrographic techniques. In *Geoarchaeology*, edited by D. A. Davidson and M. L. Shackley, pp. 65–90. Boulder: Westview.

Cattaneo, C., K. Gelsthorpe, P. Phillips, and R. J. Sokol 1993 Blood residues on stone tools: indoor and outdoor experiments. *World Archaeology* 25: 29–43.

Caulfield, S. 1978 Star Carr – an alternative

view. *Irish Archaeological Research Forum* 5: 15–22.

Chaloner, W. G. 1991 Global change and the biosphere. *Annals of Botany* 67, Supplement 1: 1–3.

Chamberlain, A. 1994 *Human remains.* Berkeley: University of California Press.

Chambers, F. M. 1993a Late-Quaternary climatic change and human impact: commentary and conclusions. In *Climate change and human impact on the landscape*, edited by F. M. Chambers, pp. 247–259. New York: Chapman and Hall.

(editor) 1993b *Climate change and human impact on the landscape: studies in paleoecology and environmental archaeology.* New York: Chapman and Hall.

Chapman, J., and J. M. Adovasio 1977 Textile and basketry impressions from Icehouse Bottom, Tennessee. *American Antiquity* 42: 620–625.

Charters, S., R. P. Evershed, L. J. Goad, A. Leyden, P. W. Blinkhorn, and V. Denham 1993 Quantification and distribution of lipids in archaeological ceramics: implications for sampling potsherds for organic residue analysis and the classification of vessel use. *Archaeometry* 35: 211–223.

Child, A. M., and A. M. Pollard 1992 A review of the applications of immunochemistry to archaeological bone. *Journal of Archaeological Science* 19: 39–47.

Chisholm, B. S. 1989 Variation in diet reconstruction based on stable carbon isotope evidence. In *The chemistry of prehistoric human bone*, edited by D. Price, pp. 10–37. Cambridge University Press.

Chisholm, B. S., D. E. Nelson, K. A. Hobson, H. P. Schwarcz, and M. Knyf 1983 Carbon isotope measurement techniques for bone collagen: notes for the archaeol-

ogist. *Journal of Archaeological Science* 10: 355–360.

Chisholm, B. S., D. E. Nelson, and H. P. Schwarcz 1982 Stable-carbon isotope ratios as a measure of marine versus terrestrial protein in ancient diets. *Science* 216: 1131–1132.

Chomko, S. A., and B. M. Gilbert 1991 Bone refuse and insect remains: their potential for temporal resolution of the archaeological record. *American Antiquity* 56: 680–686.

Chorley, R. J., S. A. Schumm, and D. E. Sugden 1984 *Geomorphology.* London: Methuen.

Claassen, C. P. 1993 Problems and choices in shell seasonality studies and their impact on results. *Archaeozoologia* 5(2): 55–76.

1998 *Shells.* Cambridge University Press.

Claassen, C. P., and S. Sigmann 1993 Sourcing *Busycon* artifacts of the eastern United States. *American Antiquity* 58: 333–347.

Clark, A. 1990 *Seeing beneath the soil.* London: Batsford.

Clark, J. G. D. 1954 *Excavation at Star Carr: an early Mesolithic site at Seamer near Scarborough, Yorkshire.* Cambridge University Press.

1972 *Star Carr: a case study in bioarchaeology.* Reading, Mass.: Addison-Wesley Monograph in Archaeology 10.

Clark, M. J. (editor) 1988 *Advances in periglacial geomorphology.* New York: John Wiley and Sons.

Clark, P. U., and W. W. Fitzhugh 1992 Postglacial relative sea level history of the Labrador coast and interpretation of the archaeological record. In *Paleoshorelines and prehistory: an investigation of method*, edited by L. L. Johnson and M. Stright, pp. 189–213. Boca Raton: CRC.

Clarke, D. L. 1968 *Analytical archaeology.* London: Methuen.

1973 Archaeology: the loss of innocence. *Antiquity* 47: 6–18.

CLIMAP group 1976 The surface of the ice-age Earth. *Science* 191: 1131–1144.

Cloud, P. 1988 *Oasis in space: Earth history from the beginning.* New York: Norton.

Cloutman, E. W., and A. G. Smith 1988 Palaeoenvironments in the Vale of Pickering Part 3: environmental history at Star Carr. *Proceeding of the Prehistoric Society* 54: 37–58.

Clymo, R. S. 1984 Sphagnum-dominated peat bog: a naturally acid ecosystem. *Philosophical Transactions of the Royal Society of London* B305: 487–499.

Cohen, A. L., J. E. Parkington, G. B. Brundrit, and N. J. van der Merwe 1992 A Holocene marine climate record in mollusc shells from the southwest African coast. *Quaternary Research* 38: 379–385.

Cohen, M. N., and G. J. Armelagos (editors) 1984 *Paleopathology at the origins of agriculture.* Orlando: Academic.

COHMAP members 1988 Climatic changes of the last 18,000 years: observations and model simulations. *Science* 241: 1043–1052.

Coles, B. J. (editor) 1992 *The wetland revolution in prehistory: proceedings of a conference held by the Prehistoric Society and WARP at the University of Exeter April 1991.* WARP Occasional Paper 6. Exeter: Prehistoric Society and the Wetland Archaeology Research Project.

Coles, G. M., and D. D. Gilbertson 1994 The airfall-pollen budget of archaeologically important caves: Creswell Crags, England. *Journal of Archaeological Science* 21: 735–755.

Coles, J. M. 1984 *The archaeology of wetlands.* Edinburgh University Press.

Coles, J. M., and B. J. Coles 1994 Japanese wetland archaeology, March 1994. *News WARP* 15: 3–8. Wetland Archaeology Research Project newsletter.

Coles, J. M., and B. J. Orme 1983 *Homo sapiens* or *Castor fiber*? *Antiquity* 57: 95–102.

Colinvaux, P. A. 1978 On the use of the word "absolute" in pollen statistics. *Quaternary Research* 9: 132–133.

1981 Photosynthetic pathways in paleoecology: a paleothermometer of promise. *Quarterly Review of Archaeology* 2(2): 5.

1993 *Ecology 2.* New York: John Wiley and Sons.

Conyers, L. B., and D. Goodman 1997 *Ground-penetrating radar: an introduction for archaeologists.* Walnut Creek, Calif.: Sage Publications.

Coope, G. R. 1977 Quaternary Coleoptera as aids in the interpretation of environmental history. In *British Quaternary studies: recent advances,* edited by F. W. Shotton, pp. 55–68. Oxford: Clarendon.

1986 Coleoptera analysis. In *Handbook of Holocene palaeoecology and palaeohydrology,* edited by B. E. Berglund, pp. 703–714. Chichester: John Wiley and Sons.

Coope, G. R., A. Morgan, and P. J. Osborne 1971 Fossil Coleoptera as indicators of climatic fluctuations during the last glaciation in Britain. *Palaeogeography, Palaeoclimatology and Palaeoecology* 10: 87–101.

Coppinger, R., and M. Feinstein 1991 "Hark! Hark! The dogs do bark . . ." and bark and bark. *Smithsonian* 21(10): 119–129.

Cordell, L. S. 1984 *Prehistory of the Southwest.* Orlando: Academic.

Cordell, L., and F. Plog 1979 Escaping the confines of normative thought: a reevaluation of Puebloan prehistory. *American Antiquity* 44: 405–429.

Cornwall, I. W.   1958   *Soils for the archaeologist.* London: Phoenix House.

—   1964   *Bones for the archaeologist.* 3rd printing. London: Phoenix House.

Courty, M.-A., P. Goldberg, and R. Macphail   1989   *Soils and micromorphology in archaeology.* Cambridge University Press.

Cowan, C. W., and P. J. Watson (editors)   1992   *The origins of agriculture: an international perspective.* Washington, D.C.: Smithsonian Institution Press.

Cowgill, G. L.   1970   Some sampling and reliability problems in archaeology. In *Archéologie et calculateurs*, edited by J. C. Gardin, pp. 161–175. Paris: Centre national de la recherche scientifique.

—   1986   Archaeological applications of mathematical and formal methods. In *American archaeology past and future*, edited by D. J. Meltzer, D. D. Fowler, and J. A. Sabloff, pp. 369–393. Washington, D.C.: Smithsonian Institution.

—   1989   Formal approaches in archaeology. In *Archaeological thought in America*, edited by C. C. Lamberg-Karlovsky, pp. 74–88. Cambridge University Press.

Cox, C. B., and P. D. Moore   1985   *Biogeography: an ecological and evolutionary approach.* 4th edition. Oxford: Blackwell Scientific.

Cremeens, D. L., and J. P. Hart   1995   On chronostratigraphy, pedostratigraphy, and archaeological context. In *Pedological perspectives in archaeological research*, edited by M. E. Collins, B. J. Carter, B. G. Gladfelter, and R. J. Southard, pp. 15–33. SSSA Special Publication No. 44. Madison, Wis.: Soil Science Society of America.

Crimes, P., and M. L. Droser   1992   Trace fossils and bioturbation: the other fossil record. *Annual Review of Ecology and Systematics* 23: 339–360.

Cronyn, J. M.   1992   *The elements of archaeological conservation.* London: Routledge.

Crosby, A. W.   1986   *Ecological imperialism: the biological expansion of Europe, 900–1900.* Cambridge University Press.

Crowley, T. J., and G. R. North   1991   *Paleoclimatology.* Oxford Monographs on Geology and Geophysics No. 16. Oxford University Press.

Cullingford, R. A., D. A. Davidson, and J. Lewin (editors)   1980   *Timescales in geomorphology.* Chichester: John Wiley and Sons.

Daniels, R. B., and R. D. Hammer   1992   *Soil geomorphology.* Somerset, N.J.: John Wiley and Sons.

Dansgaard, W., H. B. Clausen, N. S. Gundestrup, C. U. Hammer, S. J. Johnsen, P. M. Kristinsdottir, and N. Reeh   1982   A new Greenland deep ice core. *Science* 218: 1273–1277.

Dansgaard, W., S. J. Johnsen, H. B. Clausen, and C. C. Langway, Jr.   1971   Climatic record revealed by the Camp Century ice core. In *The Late Cenozoic ice ages*, edited by K. K. Turekian, pp. 37–56. New Haven: Yale University Press.

Dansgaard, W., S. J. Johnsen, J. Møller, and C. C. Langway, Jr.   1969   One thousand centuries of climatic record from Camp Century on the Greenland Ice Sheet. *Science* 166: 377–381.

Davidson, D. A.   1980   Erosion in Greece during the first and second millennia B.C. In *Timescales in geomorphology*, edited by R. A. Cullingford, D. A. Davidson, and J. Lewin, pp. 143–158. New York: John Wiley and Sons.

Davis, M. B.   1981   Outbreaks of forest pathogens in Quaternary history. *Proceedings of the IV International Palynological Conference at Lucknow* vol. 3: 216–227.

1986 Foreword. *Vegetatio* 67: 63.

Davis, O. K. 1984 Multiple thermal maxima during the Holocene. *Science* 225: 617–619.

Davis, O. K., and J. A. Overs (editors) 1995 *Aspects of archaeological palynology: methodology and applications.* Dallas: American Association of Stratigraphic Palynologists, Contribution Series 29.

Davis, O. K., J. Sheppard, and S. Robertson 1986 Contrasting climatic histories for the Snake River Plain, Idaho, resulting from multiple thermal maxima. *Quaternary Research* 26: 321–339.

Davis, S. J. M. 1987 *The archaeology of animals.* New Haven: Yale University Press.

Davis, S. J. M., and F. R. Valla 1978 Evidence for domestication of the dog 12,000 years ago in the Natufian of Israel. *Nature* 276: 608–610.

Dawson, A. G. 1992 *Ice age Earth: Late Quaternary geology and climate.* New York: Routledge.

Day, P. 1996 Dogs, deer and diet at Star Carr: a reconsideration of C-isotope evidence from early Mesolithic dog remains from the Vale of Pickering, Yorkshire, England. *Journal of Archaeological Science* 23: 783–787.

Day, S. P., and P. A. Mellars 1994 "Absolute" dating of Mesolithic human activity at Star Carr, Yorkshire: new palaeoecological studies and the identification of the 9600 BP radiocarbon "plateau." *Proceedings of the Prehistoric Society* 60: 417–422.

Deagan, K. A. 1996 Environmental archaeology and historical archaeology. In *Case studies in environmental archaeology,* edited by E. J. Reitz, L. A. Newsom, and

S. J. Scudder, pp. 359–376. New York: Plenum.

Dean, J. S. 1978 Independent dating in archaeological analysis. *Advances in Archaeological Method and Theory* 1: 223–255.

1993 Geoarchaeological perspectives on the past: chronological considerations. In *Effects of scale on archaeological and geoscientific perspectives,* edited by J. K. Stein and A. R. Linse, pp. 59–65. Boulder: Geological Society of America Special Paper 283.

Dean, J. S., D. M. Meko, and T. E. Swetnam (editors) 1996 *Tree rings, environment and humanity: Proceedings of the International Conference. Radiocarbon* 38.

Deevey, E. S., D. S. Rice, P. M. Rice, H. H. Vaughan, M. Brenner, and M. S. Flannery 1979 Maya urbanism: impact on a tropical karst environment. *Science* 206: 298–306.

Deith, M. R. 1983 Seasonality of shell collecting, determined by oxygen isotope analysis of marine shells from Asturian sites in Cantabria. In *Animals and archaeology: 2. Shell middens, fishes and birds,* edited by Caroline Grigson and Juliet Clutton-Brock, pp. 67–76. Oxford: BAR International Series 183.

1986 Subsistence strategies at a Mesolithic camp site: evidence from stable isotope analyses of shells. *Journal of Archaeological Science* 13: 61–78.

Delcourt, P. A., and H. R. Delcourt 1981 Vegetation maps for eastern North America: 40,000 yr B.P. to the present. In *Geobotany II,* edited by R. C. Romans, pp. 123–165. New York: Plenum.

Delcourt, H. R., P. A. Delcourt, and T. Webb, III 1983 Dynamic plant ecology: the spectrum of vegetational change in space and time. *Quaternary Science Reviews* 1: 153–175.

Denevan, W. M., K. Mathewson, and G. Knapp (editors) 1987 *Pre-Hispanic agricultural terraces in the Andean region*. Oxford: BAR International Series 359 (1).

Dennell, R. W. 1985 Neolithic advances. Review of *The Neolithic transition and the genetics of populations in Europe* by A. J. Ammerman and L. L. Cavalli-Sforza. Princeton University Press. *Science* 227: 1331.

— 1992 The origins of crop agriculture in Europe. In *The origins of agriculture: an international perspective*, edited by C. W. Cowan and P. J. Watson, pp. 71–100. Washington, D.C.: Smithsonian Institution.

Denton, G., and T. Hughes (editors) 1980 *The last great ice sheets*. New York: John Wiley and Sons.

DeVries, J. 1981 Measuring the impact of climate on history: the search for appropriate methodologies. In *Climate and history: studies in interdisciplinary history*, edited by R. I. Rotberg and T. K. Rabb, pp. 19–50. Princeton University Press.

Diamond, J., and T. J. Case (editors) 1985 *Community ecology*. New York: Harper and Row.

Diaz, H. F., and V. Markgraf (editors) 1993 *El Niño: historical and paleoclimatic aspects of the Southern Oscillation*. Cambridge University Press.

Dickinson, W. R., D. V. Burley, and R. Shutler, Jr. 1994 Impact of hydro-isostatic Holocene sea-level change on the geological context of island archaeological sites, northern Ha'apai group, Kingdom of Tonga. *Geoarchaeology* 9(2): 85–111.

Dickson, D. B. 1988 Circumscription by anthropogenic environmental destruc-tion: an expansion of Carneiro's (1970) theory of the origin of the state. *American Antiquity* 52: 709–716.

Dillehay, T. D. 1989 *Monte Verde: a Late Pleistocene settlement in Chile*. Vol. 1: *Palaeoenvironment and site context*. Washington, D.C.: Smithsonian Institution.

— 1993 Interdisciplinary research on culture and environment at Monte Verde, Chile: problems and prospects. In *Culture and environment: a fragile coexistence*, edited by R. W. Jamieson, S. Abonyi, and N. A. Mirau, pp. 411–419. Archaeological Association, University of Calgary.

— 1997 *Monte Verde: a Late Pleistocene settlement in Chile*. Vol. 2: *The archaeological context and interpretation*. Washington, D.C.: Smithsonian Institution.

Dillon, J. F., and G. R. Clark, II 1980 Growth-line analysis as a test for contemporaneity in populations. In *Skeletal growth of aquatic organisms*, edited by D. C. Rhoads and R. A. Lutz, pp. 395–415. New York: Plenum.

Dimbleby, G. W. 1985 *The palynology of archaeological sites*. London: Academic.

Dincauze, D. F. 1976 *The Neville site: 8000 years at Amoskeag, Manchester, New Hampshire*. Peabody Museum Monographs 4. Cambridge, Mass.: Peabody Museum of Archaeology and Ethnology.

— 1984 An archaeo-logical evaluation of the case for Pre-Clovis occupations. *Advances in World Archaeology* 3: 275–323.

— 1993a The gardeners of Eden. In *Ela' Qua: essays in honor of Richard B. Woodbury*, edited by D. S. Krass and R. B. Thomas, pp. 41–59. Amherst: Department of Anthropology, University of Massachusetts.

1993b The Oops Factor: unintended conse-
quences in biocultural evolution. In
*Culture and environment: a fragile coexis-
tence,* edited by R. W. Jamieson, S.
Abonyi, and N. A. Mirau, pp. 3–10.
Archaeological Association, University of
Calgary.

Dodd, J. R., and R. J. Stanton, Jr. (editors) 1990
Paleoecology: concepts and applications.
2nd edition. New York: Wiley.

Donovan, S. K. 1991 *The processes of fossilization.* New York: Columbia University
Press.

Dorale, J. A., L. A. González, M. K. Reagan, D. A.
Pickett, M. T. Murrell, and R. G. Baker
1992 A high-resolution record of
Holocene climate change in speleothem
calcite from Cold Water Cave, northeast
Iowa. *Science* 258: 1626–1630.

Doran, G. H., and D. N. Dickel 1988 Multidisciplinary investigations at the
Windover site. In *Wet site archaeology,*
edited by B. A. Purdy, pp. 263–289.
Caldwell, N.J.: Telford.

Downey, W. S., and D. H. Tarling 1984
Archaeomagnetic dating of Santorini
volcanic eruptions and fired destruction
levels of Late Minoan civilization. *Nature*
309: 519–523.

Downs, E. F., and J. M. Lowenstein 1994
Identification of archaeological blood
proteins: a cautionary note. *Journal of
Archaeological Science* 22: 11–16.

Driesch, A. von den 1976 *The measurement of
animal bones from archaeological sites.*
Peabody Museum Bulletin 1. Cambridge,
Mass.: Peabody Museum of Archaeology
and Ethnology.

Ducos, P. 1978 "Domestication" defined and
methodological approaches to its recognition in faunal assemblages. In
Approaches to faunal analysis in the

Middle East, edited by R. H. Meadow and
M. A. Zeder, pp 53–56. Peabody Museum
Bulletin 2. Cambridge, Mass.: Peabody
Museum of Archaeology and Ethnology.

Dugmore, A. J., and A. J. Newton 1992 Thin
tephra layers in peat revealed by X-
radiography. *Journal of Archaeological
Science* 19: 163–170.

Dumont, J. V. 1990 Star Carr: the results of a
micro-wear study. In *The Mesolithic in
Europe: papers presented at the Third
International Symposium, Edinburgh,
1985,* edited by C. Bonsall, pp. 231–240.
Edinburgh: John Donald.

Dunbar, J. S., S. D. Webb, and M. K. Faught 1992
Inundated prehistoric sites in Apalachee
Bay, Florida, and the search for the Clovis
shoreline. In *Paleoshorelines and prehis-
tory,* edited by L. L. Johnson and M.
Stright, pp. 117–146. Boca Raton: CRC
Press.

Dye, T., and D. W. Steadman 1990 Polynesian
ancestors and their animal world.
American Scientist 78: 207–215.

Eddison, J., and M. Gardiner (editors) 1995
Romney Marsh: the debatable ground.
Oxford University Committee for
Archaeology, Monograph 41.

Edwards, K. J. 1982 Man, space, and the woodland edge: speculations on the detection
and interpretation of human impact on
pollen diagrams. In *Archaeological
aspects of woodland ecology,* edited by M.
Bell and S. Limbrey, pp. 5–22. Oxford:
BAR International Series 146.

1991 Using space in cultural palynology: the
value of the off-site pollen record. In
Modelling ecological change, edited by
D. R. Harris and K. D. Thomas, pp. 61–73.
London: Institute of Archaeology.

1993 Models of mid-Holocene forest
farming for north-west Europe. In

Climate change and human impact on the landscape, edited by F. M. Chambers, pp. 133–145. London: Chapman and Hall.

Edwards, K. J., and K. R. Hirons 1984 Cereal pollen grains in pre-elm decline deposits: implications for the earliest agriculture in Britain and Ireland. *Journal of Archaeological Science* 11: 71–80.

Edwards, R. L., J. W. Beck, G. S. Burr, D. J. Donahue, J. M. A. Chappell, A. L. Bloom, E. R. M. Druffel, and F. W. Taylor 1993 A large drop in atmospheric $^{14}C/^{12}C$ and reduced melting in the Younger Dryas, documented with ^{230}Th ages of corals. *Science* 260: 962–968.

Eidt, R. C. 1985 Theoretical and practical considerations in the analysis of anthrosols. In *Archaeological geology*, edited by G. Rapp, Jr., and J. A. Gifford, pp. 135–190. New Haven: Yale University Press.

Eighmy, J. L., and D. R. Mitchell 1994 Archaeomagnetic dating at Pueblo Grande. *Journal of Archaeological Science* 21: 445–453.

Eisenstein, B. I. 1990 The polymerase chain reaction. *New England Journal of Medicine* 322: 178–181.

Elias, S. 1994 *Quaternary insects and their environments*. Washington, D.C.: Smithsonian Institution.

Ellenberg, H. 1988 *Vegetation ecology of central Europe*. Translated by G. K. Strutt. 4th edition. Cambridge University Press.

Emslie, S. D. 1981 Prehistoric agricultural ecosystems: avifauna from Pottery Mound, New Mexico. *American Antiquity* 46: 853–861.

Erlandson, J. M. 1984 A case study in faunalturbation: delineating the effects of the burrowing pocket gopher on the distribution of archaeological materials. *American Antiquity* 49: 785–790.

Esau, K. 1977 *Anatomy of seed plants*. 2nd edition. New York: John Wiley and Sons.

Etkin, N. L. (editor) 1994 *Eating on the wild side: the pharmacologic, ecologic, and social implications of using noncultigens*. Tucson: University of Arizona Press.

Evans, C., and I. Hodder 1987 Between the two worlds: archaeological investigations in the Haddenham level. In *European wetlands in prehistory*, edited by J. M. Coles and A. J. Lawson, pp. 180–191. Oxford University Press.

Evans, J. G. 1976 *Land snails in archaeology, with special reference to the British Isles*. London: Seminar.

——— 1984 Land snail analysis. In *Danebury: an Iron Age hillfort in Hampshire*. Vol. 2. *The excavations 1969–1978: the finds*, B. Cunliffe and others, pp. 474–481. London: Council for British Archaeology Research Report No. 52.

——— 1991 An approach to the interpretation of dry-ground and wet-ground molluscan taxocenes from central-southern England. In *Modelling ecological change*, edited by D. R. Harris and K. D. Thomas, pp. 75–89. London: Institute of Archaeology.

Evershed, R. P. 1993 Biomolecular archaeology and lipids. *World Archaeology* 25: 74–93.

Evershed, R. P., C. Heron, S. Charters, and L. J. Goad 1992 The survival of food residues: new methods of analysis, interpretation and application. In *New developments in archaeological science*, edited by A. M. Pollard, pp. 187–208. Proceedings of the British Academy 77. Oxford University Press.

Ezzo, J. A. 1994 Putting the "chemistry" back into archaeological bone chemistry analysis: modeling potential paleodietary indicators. *Journal of Anthropological Archaeology* 13: 1–34.

Ezzo, J. A., C. M. Johnson, and T. D. Price 1997
Analytical perspectives on prehistoric
migration: a case study from east-central
Arizona. *Journal of Archaeological
Sciences* 24: 447–466.

Faegri, K. 1950 On the value of palaeoclimato-
logical evidence. *Centenary proceedings of
the Royal Meteorological Society* 1950, pp.
188–195. New York.

Faegri, K., and J. Iversen 1989 *Textbook of
pollen analysis.* 4th edition by K. Faegri,
P. E. Kaland, and K. Krzywinski. New
York: Wiley.

Fahn, A. 1990 *Plant anatomy.* 4th edition.
Oxford: Pergamon.

Fankhauser, B. 1994 Protein and lipid analysis
of food residues. In *Tropical archaeobotany,* edited by J. G. Hather, pp. 227–250.
London: Routledge.

Fanning, D. S., and M. C. B. Fanning 1989 *Soil
morphology, genesis, and classification.*
New York: John Wiley and Sons.

Farb, P., and G. Armelagos 1980 *Consuming
passions: the anthropology of eating.*
Boston: Houghton Mifflin.

Farrand, W. R. 1984 Stratigraphic
classification: living within the law.
Quarterly Review of Archaeology 5 (1):
1, 4, 5.

Faulkner, C. T. 1991 Prehistoric diet and parasitic infection in Tennessee: evidence
from the analysis of desiccated human
paleofeces. *American Antiquity* 56:
687–700.

FAUNMAP Working Group 1996 Spatial
response of mammals to Late
Quaternary environmental fluctuations.
Science 272: 1601–1606.

Faure, G. 1986 *Principles of isotope geology.* 2nd
edition. New York: John Wiley and Sons.

Ferring, C. R. 1992 Alluvial pedology and geoarchaeological research. In *Soils and
archaeology: landscape evolution and
human occupation,* edited by V. T.
Holliday, pp. 1–39. Washington, D.C.:
Smithsonian Institution.

Field, C. B., F. S. Chapin, III, P. A. Matson, and
H. A. Mooney 1992 Responses of terrestrial ecosystems to the changing atmosphere: a resource-based approach.
Annual Review of Ecology and Systematics
23: 201–235.

Fiennes, R. N. T.-W. 1978 *Zoonoses and the
origins and ecology of human disease.*
London: Academic.

Fish, S. 1985 Prehistoric disturbance floras of
the lower Sonoran Desert and their
implications. *American Association of
Stratigraphic Palynologists Contribution
Series* 16: 77–88.

Fisher, W. F., and G. K. Kelso 1987 The use of
opal phytolith analysis in a comprehensive environmental study: an example
from 19th-century Lowell,
Massachusetts. *Northeast Historical
Archaeology* 16: 30–48.

Fishman, B., H. Forbes, and B. Lawn 1977
University of Pennsylvania radiocarbon
dates XIX. *Radiocarbon* 19: 188–228.

Fitzhugh, W. W., and H. F. Lamb 1985
Vegetation history and culture change in
Labrador prehistory. *Arctic and Alpine
Research* 17: 357–370.

Fitzpatrick, E. A. 1980 *Soils.* London:
Longman.
  1993 *Soil microscopy and micromorphology.*
New York: John Wiley and Sons.

Fizer, M., A. Mariotti, H. Bocherens, B. Lange-
Badré, B. Vandermeersch, J. P. Borel,
and G. Bellon 1994 Effect of diet,
physiology and climate on carbon and
nitrogen stable isotopes of collagen in a
Late Pleistocene anthropic palaeoeco-
system: Marillac, Charente, France.

Journal of Archaeological Science 22: 67–80.

Flannery, K. V. 1968 Archaeological systems theory and early Mesoamerica. In *Anthropological archaeology in the Americas*, edited by B. J. Meggers, pp. 67–87. Anthropological Society of Washington.

——— 1972 The cultural evolution of civilizations. *Annual Review of Ecology and Systematics* 3: 399–426.

Flint, R. F., and B. J. Skinner 1974 *Physical geology*. New York: John Wiley and Sons.

Foley, R. 1982 A reconsideration of the role of predation on large mammals in tropical hunter-gatherer adaptation. *Man* n.s. 17: 393–402.

——— 1984 Putting people into perspective: an introduction to community evolution and ecology. In *Hominid evolution and community ecology*, edited by R. Foley, pp. 1–24. Orlando: Academic.

Foody, G., and P. Curran (editors) 1994 *Environmental remote sensing from regional to global scales*. New York: Wiley Interscience.

Ford, R. I. 1979 Paleoethnobotany in American archaeology. *Advances in Archaeological Method and Theory* 2: 286–336.

Forman, R. T. T., and M. Godron 1986 *Landscape ecology*. New York: John Wiley and Sons.

Fraser, F. C., and J. E. King 1954 Faunal remains. In *Excavations at Star Carr: an early Mesolithic site at Seamer near Scarborough, Yorkshire*, by J. G. D. Clark, pp. 70–95. Cambridge University Press.

Friedman, I., F. W. Trembour, and R. E. Hughes 1997 Obsidian hydration dating. In *Chronometric dating in archaeology*, edited by R. E. Taylor and M. Aitken, pp. 297–321. New York: Plenum.

Friedrich, W. L., P. Wagner, and H. Tauber 1990 Radiocarbon dated plant remains from the Akrotiri excavation on Santorini, Greece. In *Thera and the Aegean world III*. Vol. 3: *Chronology*, edited by D. A. Hardy, with A. C. Renfrew, pp. 188–196. Proceedings of the Third International Congress. London: Thera Foundation.

Fritts, H. C. 1991 *Reconstructing large-scale climatic patterns from tree-ring data: a diagnostic analysis*. Tucson: University of Arizona Press.

Fritz, G. J. 1994 The value of archaeological plant remains for paleodietary reconstruction. In *Paleonutrition: the diet and health of prehistoric Americans*, edited by K. D. Sobolik, pp. 21–33. Occasional Paper No. 22, Center for Archaeological Investigations. Carbondale: Southern Illinois.

Fritz, W. J., and J. N. Moore 1988 *Basics of physical stratigraphy and sedimentology*. New York: John Wiley and Sons.

Fry, G. F. 1985 Analysis of fecal material. In *The analysis of prehistoric diets*, edited by R. I. Gilbert, Jr., and J. H. Mielke, pp. 127–154. Orlando: Academic.

Gale, S. J., and P. G. Hoare 1991 *Quaternary sediments: petrographic methods for the study of unlithified rocks*. New York: John Wiley and Sons.

Gallup, C. D., R. L. Edwards, and R. G. Johnson 1994 The timing of high sea levels over the past 200,000 years. *Science* 263: 796–800.

Gamble, C. 1993 The center at the edge. In *From Kostenki to Clovis: Upper Paleolithic–Paleo-Indian adaptations*, edited by O. Soffer and N. D. Praslov, pp. 314–321. New York: Plenum.

Gamble, C., and G. Bailey 1994 The faunal specialist as excavator: the impact of recovery techniques on faunal interpretation at Klithi. In *Whither environmental archaeology?*, edited by R. Luff and P. Rowley-Conwy, pp. 81–89. Oxbow Monograph 38. Oxford: Oxbow Books.

Ganopolski, A., C. Kubarzki, M. Claussen, V. Brovkin, and V. Petoukhov 1998 The influence of vegetation–atmosphere–ocean interaction on climate during the mid-Holocene. *Science* 280: 1916–1919.

Garbett, G. G. 1981 The elm decline: the depletion of a resource. *New Phytologist* 88: 573–585.

Gardner, M. 1960 *The annotated Alice: Alice's adventures in Wonderland and Through the looking glass by Lewis Carroll.* New York: Clarkson N. Potter.

Gasche, H., and Ö. Tunca 1983 Guide to archaeostratigraphic classification and terminology: definitions and principles. *Journal of Field Archaeology* 10: 325–335.

Gates, W. L. 1976 Modeling the ice-age climate. *Science* 191: 1138–1144.

Gaudreau, D. G. 1988 The distribution of Late Quaternary forest regions in the northeast: pollen data, physiography, and the prehistoric record. In *Holocene human ecology in northeastern North America*, edited by G. P. Nicholas, pp. 215–256. New York: Plenum.

Gaudreau, D. G., and T. Webb, III 1985 Late-Quaternary pollen stratigraphy and isochrone maps in the northeastern United States. In *Pollen records of Late-Quaternary North American sediments*, edited by V. M. Bryant, Jr., and R. G. Holloway, pp. 247–280. Dallas: American Association of Stratigraphic Palynologists Foundation.

Gautier, A. 1993 Trace fossils in archaeozoology. *Journal of Archaeological Science* 20: 511–523.

Gear, A. J., and B. Huntley 1991 Rapid changes in the range limits of Scots pine 4000 years ago. *Science* 251: 544–547.

Gee, J. H. R., and P. S. Giller 1991 Contemporary community ecology and environmental archaeology. In *Modelling ecological change*, edited by D. R. Harris and K. D. Thomas, pp. 1–12. London: Institute of Archaeology.

(editors) 1986 *Organization of communities, past and present.* Oxford: Blackwell Scientific.

Gerrard, J. 1992 *Soil geomorphology: an integration of pedology and geomorphology.* London: Chapman and Hall.

Ghose, B., A. Kar, and Z. Hussain 1979 The lost courses of the Saraswati river in the Great Indian Desert: new evidence from Landsat imagery. *Geographical Journal* 145: 446–451.

Giddings, J. L., Jr., and D. D. Anderson 1986 *Beachridge archeology of Cape Krusenstern. Eskimo and pre-Eskimo settlements around Kotzebue Sound, Alaska.* Washington, D.C.: US Department of the Interior, National Park Service Publications in Archaeology No. 20.

Gifford, D. P. 1981 Taphonomy and paleoecology: a critical review of archaeology's sister disciplines. *Advances in Archaeological Method and Theory* 4: 365–438.

Gifford, J. A., G. Rapp, Jr., and V. Vitali 1992 Palaeogeography of Carthage (Tunisia): coastal change during the first millennium BC. *Journal of Archaeological Science* 19: 575–596.

Gilbert, B. M. 1980 *Mammalian osteology.* Laramie, Wyo.: B. Gilbert.

Gilbert, B. M., and W. M. Bass 1967 Seasonal dating of burials from the presence of fly pupae. *American Antiquity* 32: 534–535.

Gilbert, B. M., L. D. Martin, and H. G. Savage
1981 *Avian osteology*. Laramie, Wyo.: B. Gilbert.

Gillen, F. D., D. S. Reiner, and C.-S. Wang 1983 Human milk kills parasitic intestinal protozoa. *Science* 221: 1290–1292.

Girling, M. A. 1988 The bark beetle *Scolytus scolytus* (Fabricius) and the possible role of elm disease in the early Neolithic. In *Archaeology and the flora of the British Isles*, edited by M. Jones, pp. 34–38. Oxford University Committee for Archaeology Monograph 14.

Girling, M. A., and J. Greig 1985 A first fossil record for *Scolytus scolytus* (F.) (elm bark beetle): its occurrence in elm decline deposits from London and the implications for Neolithic elm disease. *Journal of Archaeological Science* 12: 347–352.

Glacken, C. J. 1967 *Traces on the Rhodian shore: nature and culture in Western thought from ancient times to the end of the eighteenth century*. Berkeley: University of California Press.

Glass, L., and M. C. Mackey 1988 *From clocks to chaos, the rhythms of life*. Princeton University Press.

Gleick, J. 1987 *Chaos: making a new science*. New York: Penguin.

Goldberg, P. 1992 Micromorphology, soils, and archaeological sites. In *Soils in archaeology: landscape evolution and human occupation*, edited by V. R. Holliday, pp. 145–167. Washington, D.C.: Smithsonian Institution.

Golley, F. B. 1993 *A history of the ecosystem concept in ecology: more than the sum of the parts*. New Haven: Yale University Press Press.

Goodchild, M. F., B. O. Parks, and L. T. Steyaert (editors) 1993 *Environmental modeling with GIS*. Oxford University Press.

Goodman, A. H. 1994 Cartesian reductionism and vulgar adaptationism: issues in the interpretation of nutritional status in prehistory. In *Paleonutrition: the diet and health of prehistoric Americans*, edited by K. D. Sobolik, pp. 163–177. Occasional Paper No. 22, Center for Archaeological Investigations. Carbondale: Southern Illinois University.

Goodman, A. H., and G. J. Armelagos 1989 Infant and childhood morbidity and mortality risks in archaeological populations. *World Archaeology* 21: 225–243.

Goodman, A. H., D. Martin, G. J. Armelagos, and G. Clark 1984 Indications of stress from bones and teeth. In *Paleopathology at the origins of agriculture*, edited by M. N. Cohen and G. J. Armelagos, pp. 13–49. Orlando: Academic.

Göransson, H. 1984 Pollen analytical investigations in the Sligo area. In *The archaeology of Carrowmore. Environmental archaeology and the Megalithic Tradition at Carrowmore, County Sligo, Ireland*, edited by G. Burenhult, pp. 154–193. Stockholm: Theses and Papers in North-European Archaeology 14. .

1985 On arguing in a circle, on common sense, on the smashing of paradigms, on thistles among flowers, and on other things. *Norwegian Archaeological Review* 18: 43–45.

1986 Man and the forests of nemoral broadleafed trees during the Stone Age. *Striae* 24: 143–152.

Goudie, A. (editor) 1981 *Geomorphological techniques*. London: George Allen and Unwin.

1983 *Environmental change*. 2nd edition. Oxford: Clarendon.

1984 *The nature of the environment*. Oxford: Blackwell.

1993 *The human impact on the natural environment.* 3rd edition. Oxford: Blackwell.

Gould, S. J. 1965 Is uniformitarianism necessary? *American Journal of Science* 263: 223–228.

1986 Evolution and the triumph of homology, or why history matters. *American Scientist* 74: 60–69.

1989 *Wonderful life: the Burgess shale and the nature of history.* New York: W. W. Norton.

1993 *Eight little piggies: reflections in natural history.* New York: W. W. Norton.

Gove, H. E. 1992 The history of AMS, its advantages over decay counting, applications and prospects. In *Radiocarbon after four decades. An interdisciplinary perspective,* edited by R. E. Taylor, A. Long, and R. S. Kra, pp. 214–229. New York: Springer.

Grace, J. B., and D. Tilman (editors) 1990 *Perspectives on plant competition.* San Diego: Academic.

Graham, R. W. 1986 Plant–animal interactions and Pleistocene extinctions. In *Dynamics of extinction,* edited by D. K. Elliott, pp. 131–154. New York: John Wiley and Sons.

1990 Evolution of new ecosystems at the end of the Pleistocene. In *Megafauna and man: discovery of America's heartland,* edited by L. D. Agenbroad, J. I. Mead, and L. W. Nelson, pp. 54–60. The Mammoth Site of Hot Springs, South Dakota, Inc., Scientific Papers 1.

Graham, R. W., and E. C. Grimm 1990 Effects of global climate change on the patterns of terrestrial biological communities. *Trends in Ecology and Evolution* 5: 289–292.

Grattan, J. P., and D. D. Gilbertson 1994 Acid-loading from Icelandic tephra falling on acidified ecosystems as a key to understanding archaeological and environmental stress in northern and western Britain. *Journal of Archaeological Science* 21: 851–859.

Grayson, D. K. 1981 A critical view of the use of archaeological vertebrates in paleoenvironmental reconstruction. *Journal of Ethnobiology* 1: 28–38.

1984 *Quantitative zooarchaeology: topics in the analysis of archaeological fauna.* Orlando: Academic.

1989 The chronology of North American Late Pleistocene extinctions. *Journal of Archaeological Science* 16: 153–165.

Greenfield, H. J. 1991 Fauna from the Late Neolithic of the central Balkans: issues in subsistence and land use. *Journal of Field Archaeology* 18: 161–186.

Greig, J. R. A. 1982 The interpretation of pollen spectra from urban archaeological deposits. In *Environmental archaeology in the urban context,* edited by A. R. Hall and H. K. Kenward, pp. 47–65. London: Council for British Archaeology, Research Report 43.

1985 Garderobes, sewers, cesspits and latrines. *Current Archaeology* 85: 49–52.

1991 The British Isles. In *Progress in Old World palaeoethnobotany,* edited by W. van Zeist, K. Wasylikowa, and K.-E. Behre, pp. 299–334. Rotterdam: Balkema.

Gremillion, K. J. 1993 Crop and weed in prehistoric eastern North America: the *Chenopodium* example. *American Antiquity* 58: 496–509.

(editor) 1997 *People, plants, and landscapes: studies in paleoethnobotany.* Tuscaloosa: University of Alabama Press.

Grigson, C. 1981 The Mesolithic: fauna. In *The Mesolithic in British prehistory,* edited by I. G. Simmons and M. J. Tooley, pp. 110–124. Ithaca, N.Y.: Cornell University Press.

Grimm, E. C. 1988 Data analysis and display. In *Vegetation history*, edited by B. Huntley and T. Webb, III, pp. 43–76. Dordrecht: Kluwer Academic.

Grimm, E. C., G. L. Jacobson, Jr., W. A. Watts, B. C. S. Hanson, and K. A. Maasch 1993 A 50,000-year record of climate oscillations from Florida and its temporal correlation with the Heinrich Events. *Science* 261: 198–200.

Grissino-Mayer, H. D. 1995 An updated list of species used in tree-ring research. *Tree-Ring Bulletin* 53: 17–43.

Groenman-van Waateringe, W. 1983 The early agricultural utilization of the Irish landscape: the last word on the elm decline? In *Landscape archaeology in Ireland*, edited by T. Reeves-Smith and F. Hammond, pp. 217–234. Oxford: BAR British Series 116.

Groenman-van Waateringe, W., and M. Robinson (editors) 1988 *Man-made soils*. Oxford: BAR International Series 410.

Grove, J. 1988 *The Little Ice Age*. London: Methuen.

Grün, R. 1997 Electron spin resonance dating. In *Chronometric dating in archaeology*, edited by R. E. Taylor and M. J. Aitkin, pp. 217–260. New York: Plenum.

Grün, R., and C. Stringer 1991 Electron-spin resonance dating and the evolution of modern humans. *Archaeometry* 33: 153–199.

Gu, Daifang, and S. G. H. Philander 1997 Interdecadal climate fluctuations that depend on exchanges between the tropics and extratropics. *Science* 275: 805–807.

Gumerman, G. J. (editor) 1988 *The Anasazi in a changing environment*. SAR Advanced Seminar Series. Cambridge University Press.

Gurfinkel, D. M., and U. M. Franklin 1988 A study in the feasibility of detecting blood residue on artefacts. *Journal of Archaeological Science* 15: 83–97.

Guthrie, R. D. 1982 Mammals of the mammoth steppe as paleoenvironmental indicators. In *Paleoecology of Beringia*, edited by D. M. Hopkins et al., pp. 307–326. New York: Academic.

1984 Mosaics, allelochemics, and nutrients: an ecological theory of Late Pleistocene megafaunal extinctions. In *Quaternary extinctions: a prehistoric revolution*, edited by P. S. Martin and R. G. Klein, pp. 259–298. Tucson: University of Arizona Press.

1990 *Frozen fauna of the mammoth steppe: the story of Blue Babe*. University of Chicago Press.

Guthrie, R. L., and J. E. Witty 1982 New designations for soil horizons and layers and the new Soil Survey Manual. *Soil Science Society of America Journal* 46: 443–444.

Haigh, J. D. 1996 The impact of solar variability on climate. *Science* 272: 981–984.

Haines-Young, R. H., and J. R. Petch 1983 Multiple working hypotheses: equifinality and the study of landforms. *Transactions, Institute of British Geographers*, n.s. 8: 458–466.

Hall, G. D., S. M. Tarkam, Jr., W. J. Hurst, D. Stuart, and R. E. W. Adams 1990 Cacao residues in ancient Maya vessels from Rio Azul, Guatemala. *American Antiquity* 55: 138–143.

Hall, S. A. 1981 Deteriorated pollen grains and the interpretation of Quaternary pollen diagrams. *Review of Palaeobotany and Palynology* 32: 193–206.

Hallam, A. 1981 *Facies interpretation and the*

stratigraphic record. Oxford: W. H. Freeman.

Hallberg, G. A. 1985 The U.S. system of soil taxonomy: from the outside looking in. In *Soil taxonomy: achievements and challenges*, edited by R. B. Grossman, H. Eswaran, and R. H. Rust, pp. 45–59. Madison, Wis.: Soil Science Society of America.

Hally, D. J. 1981 Plant preservation and the content of paleobotanical samples: a case study. *American Antiquity* 46: 723–742.

Hambrey, M. J., and J. Alean 1992 *Glaciers.* Cambridge University Press.

Hammer, C. U. 1989 Dating by physical and chemical seasonal variation and reference horizons. In *The environmental record in glaciers and ice sheets*, edited by H. Oeschger and C. C. Langway, Jr., pp. 99–121. New York: Wiley-Interscience.

Hammer, C. U., H. B. Clausen, W. L. Friedrich, and H. Tauber 1987 The Minoan eruption of Santorini in Greece dated to 1645 BC? *Nature* 328: 517–519.

Hardesty, D. L. 1977 *Ecological anthropology.* New York: John Wiley and Sons.

1980 The use of general ecological principles in archaeology. *Advances in Archaeological Method and Theory* 3: 157–187.

Hardy, D. A., with J. Keller, V. P. Galanopoulos, N. C. Flemming, and T. H. Druitt (editors) 1990 *Thera and the Aegean world III.* Vol. 2: *Earth sciences.* Proceedings of the Third International Congress. London: Thera Foundation.

Hardy, D. A., with A. C. Renfrew 1990 *Thera and the Aegean world III.* Vol. 3: *Chronology.* Proceedings of the Third International Congress. London: Thera Foundation.

Hare, P. E. 1980 Organic geochemistry of bone and its relation to the survival of bone in the natural environment. In *Fossils in the making*, edited by A. K. Behrensmeyer and A. P. Hill, pp. 208–219. University of Chicago Press.

Hare, P. E., T. C. Hoering and K. King, Jr. (editors) 1980 *Biogeochemistry of amino acids.* New York: John Wiley and Sons.

Hare, P. E., D. W. Von Endt, and J. E. Kokis 1997 Protein and amino acid diagenesis dating. In *Chronometric dating in archaeology*, edited by R. E. Taylor and M. J. Aitken, pp. 261–296. New York: Plenum.

Harlan, J. 1995 *The living fields.* Cambridge University Press.

Harris, D. R. 1992 Human diet and subsistence. In *The Cambridge encyclopedia of human evolution*, edited by S. Jones, R. Martin, and D. Pilbeam, pp. 69–74. Cambridge University Press.

(editor) 1996 *The origins and spread of agriculture and pastoralism in Eurasia.* London: University College.

Harris, D. R., and G. C. Hillman (editors) 1989 *Foraging and farming: the evolution of plant exploitation.* London: Unwin Hyman.

Harris, E. C. 1989 *Principles of archaeological stratigraphy.* 2nd edition. London: Academic.

Harrison, K. G., W. S. Broecker, and G. Bonani 1993 The effect of changing land use on soil radiocarbon. *Science* 262: 725–726.

Hastorf, C. A., and V. S. Popper (editors) 1988 *Current paleoethnobotany.* University of Chicago Press.

Hather, J. G. (editor) 1994 *Tropical archaeobotany: applications and new developments.* London: Routledge.

Havinga, A. J. 1984 A 20-year investigation into differential corrosion susceptibility of pollen and spores in various soil types. *Pollen et spores* 26: 541–558.

Hay, John 1981 *The undiscovered country.* New York: W. W. Norton.

Hay, R. L. 1981 Paleoenvironment of the Laetolil Beds, northern Tanzania. In *Hominid sites: their geologic settings,* edited by G. Rapp, Jr., and C. F. Vondra, pp. 7–24. Boulder: Westview.

Haynes, G. 1988 Mass deaths and serial predation: comparative taphonomic studies of modern large mammal death sites. *Journal of Archaeological Science* 15: 219–236.

1989 Late Pleistocene mammoth utilization in northern Eurasia and North America. *ArchaeoZoologia* 3: 81–108.

1991 *Mammoths, mastodonts, and elephants: biology, behavior, and the fossil record.* Cambridge University Press.

Hedges, R. E. M. 1993 Review of *Radiocarbon: Calibration 1993,* edited by M. Stuiver. *Journal of Archaeological Science* 20: 715–716.

Hedges, R. E. M., and B. C. Sykes 1992 Biomolecular archaeology: past, present and future. In *New developments in archaeological science,* edited by A. M. Pollard, pp. 267–283. Proceedings of the British Academy 77. Oxford University Press.

Helskog, K. 1974 Two tests of the prehistoric cultural chronology of Varanger, north Norway. *Norwegian Archaeological Review* 7: 97–103.

Heron, C., and R. P. Evershed 1993 The analysis of organic residues and the study of pottery use. *Archaeological Method and Theory* 5: 247–284. Tucson: University of Arizona Press.

Herz, N., and E. G. Garrison 1998 *Geological methods for archaeology.* Oxford University Press.

Hesse, B., and P. Wapnish 1985 *Animal bone archeology: from objectives to analysis.* Manuals on Archeology 5. Washington, D.C.: Taraxacum.

Hester, T. R., H. J. Shafer, and K. L. Feder 1997 *Field methods in archaeology.* 7th edition. Mountain View, Calif.: Mayfield.

Hillman, G. 1984 Interpretation of archaeological plant remains: the application of ethnographic models from Turkey. In *Plants and ancient man: studies in palaeoethnobotany,* edited by W. van Zeist and W. A. Casparie, pp. 11–41. Rotterdam: Balkema.

1991 Phytosociology and ancient weed floras: taking account of taphonomy and changes in cultivation methods. In *Modelling ecological change,* edited by D. R. Harris and K. D. Thomas, pp. 27–40. London: Institute of Archaeology.

Hillman, G., S. Wales, F. McLaren, J. Evans, and A. Butler 1993 Identifying problematic remains of ancient plant foods: a comparison of the role of chemical, histological and morphological criteria. *World Archaeology* 25: 94–124.

Hillson, S. 1986 *Teeth.* Cambridge University Press.

1992 *Mammal bones and teeth: an introductory guide to methods of identification.* London: Institute of Archaeology, University College.

Hodder, I. 1986 *Reading the past.* Cambridge University Press.

(editor) 1987 *The archaeology of contextual meanings.* Cambridge University Press.

Hoffman, A. 1979 Community paleoecology as an epiphenomenal science. *Paleobiology* 5(4): 357–379.

Hofmann-Wellenhof, B., H. Lichtenegger, and J. Collins 1993 *Global positioning system: theory and practice.* New York: Springer.

Holliday, V. T. 1990 Pedology in archaeology. In *The archaeological geology of North*

America, edited by N. P. Lasca and J. Donahue, pp. 525–540. Boulder: Geological Society of America.

(editor) 1992 *Soils in archaeology: landscape evolution and human occupation.* Washington, D.C.: Smithsonian Institution.

Holliday, V. T., C. R. Ferring, and P. Goldberg 1993 The scale of soil investigations in archaeology. In *Effects of scale on archaeological and geoscientific perspectives,* edited by J. K. Stein and A. R. Linse, pp. 29–37. Special Paper 283. Boulder: Geological Society of America.

Holliday, V. T., and J. K. Stein 1989 Variability of laboratory procedures and results in geoarchaeology. *Geoarchaeology* 4: 347–358.

Holm, L., J. Doll, E. Holm, J. Pancho, and J. Herberger 1997 *World weeds: natural histories and distribution.* New York: Wiley.

Hong, S., J.-P. Candelone, C. C. Patterson, and C. F. Boutron 1994 Greenland ice evidence of hemispheric lead pollution two millennia ago by Greek and Roman civilizations. *Science* 265: 1841–1843.

1996 History of ancient copper smelting pollution during Roman and medieval times recorded in Greenland ice. *Science* 272: 246–249.

Hopkins, D. M., J. V. Matthews, Jr., C. E. Schweger, and S. B. Young (editors) 1982 *Paleoecology of Beringia.* New York: Academic.

Horton, D. R. 1982 The burning question: Aborigines, fire and Australian ecosystems. *Mankind* 13: 237–251.

Horwitz, L. K. 1990 The origin of partially digested bone recovered from archaeological contexts in Israel. *Paléorient* 16: 97–106.

Housely, R. A., R. E. M. Hedges, I. A. Law, and C. R. Bronk 1990 Radiocarbon dating by AMS of the destruction of Akrotiri. In *Thera and the Aegean world III.* Vol. 3: *Chronology,* edited by D. A. Hardy, with A. C. Renfrew, pp. 207–215. Proceedings of the Third International Congress. London: Thera Foundation.

Hubberten, H.-W., M. Bruns, M. Calamiotou, C. Apostolakis, S. Filippakis, and A. Grimani 1990 Radiocarbon dates from the Akrotiri excavations. In *Thera and the Aegean world III.* Vol. 3: *Chronology,* edited by D. A. Hardy, with A. C. Renfrew, pp. 179–186. Proceedings of the Third International Congress. London: Thera Foundation.

Hughen, K. A., J. T. Overpeck, S. J. Lehman, M. Kashgarian, J. R. Southon, and Larry C. Peterson 1998 New ^{14}C calibration data set for the last glaciation based on marine varves. *Radiocarbon* 40: 483–494.

Hughes, M. K., P. M. Kelly, J. R. Pilcher, and V. C. LaMarche, Jr. (editors) 1982 *Climate from tree rings.* Cambridge University Press.

Hunt, C. B. 1974 *Natural regions of the United States and Canada.* San Francisco: Freeman.

Huntley, B. 1988 Europe. In *Vegetation history,* edited by B. Huntley and T. Webb, III, pp. 341–383. Dordrecht: Kluwer Academic.

1990 European vegetation history: palaeovegetation maps from pollen data – 13,000 yr BP to present. *Journal of Quaternary Science* 5: 103–122.

Huntley, B., and J. B. Birks 1983 *An atlas of past and present pollen maps for Europe: 0–13000 years ago.* Cambridge University Press.

Huss-Ashmore, R., J. J. Curry, and R. K. Hitchcock (editors) 1989 *Coping with seasonal constraints.* MASCA Research Papers in Science and Archaeology 5. Philadelphia: University Museum, University of Pennsylvania.

Huss-Ashmore, R., A. H. Goodman, and G. J. Armelagos 1982 Nutritional inferences from paleopathology. *Advances in Archaeological Method and Theory* 5: 395–474.

Hutson, W. H. 1977 Transfer functions under no-analog conditions: experiments with Indian Ocean planktonic foraminifera. *Quaternary Research* 8: 355–367.

Imbrie, J., and K. P. Imbrie 1979 *Ice ages: solving the mystery.* London: Macmillan.

Ingold, T. 1986 *The appropriation of nature: essays on human ecology and social relations.* Manchester University Press.

Ingram, M. J., G. Farmer, and T. M. L. Wigley 1981 Past climates and their impact on man: a review. In *Climate and history,* edited by T. M. L. Wigley, M. J. Ingram, and G. Farmer, pp. 3–50. Cambridge University Press.

Isaac, G. Ll., and D. C. Crader 1981 To what extent were early hominids carnivorous? An archaeological perspective. In *Omnivorous primates,* edited by R. S. O. Harding and G. P. Teleki, pp. 37–103. New York: Columbia University Press.

Ivanovitch, M., and R. S. Harmon (editors) 1992 *Uranium-series disequilibrium.* 2nd edition. Oxford University Press.

Iverson, J. 1941 Landnam i Danmarks stenalder (Land occupation in Denmark's Stone Age). *Danmarks Geologiske Undersøgelse,* series 11 (66): 1–68.

Jacobi, R. M. 1978 Northern England in the eighth millennium bc: an essay. In *Early postglacial settlement of northern Europe,* edited by P. Mellars, pp. 295–332. London: Duckworth.

Jacobs, J. A. 1994 *Reversals of the Earth's magnetic field.* 2nd edition. Cambridge University Press.

Jacobs, J. S. 1995 Archaeological pedology in the Maya Lowlands. In *Pedological perspectives in archaeological research,* edited by M. E. Collins, B. J. Carter, B. G. Gladfelter, and R. J. Southard, pp. 51–80. Madison, Wis.: Soil Science Society of America.

Jacobson, G. L., Jr. 1988 Ancient permanent plots: sampling in paleovegetational studies. In *Vegetation history,* edited by B. Huntley and T. Webb, III, pp. 3–16. Dordrecht: Kluwer Academic.

Jacobson, G. L., Jr., T. Webb, III, and E. C. Grimm 1987 Patterns and rates of vegetation change during the deglaciation of eastern North America. In *North America and adjacent oceans during the last deglaciation,* edited by W. F. Ruddiman and H. Wright, Jr., pp. 277–288 + end maps. The Geology of North America, vol. K-3. Boulder: Geological Society of America.

Jacoby, G. C., R. D. D'Arrigo, and T. Davaajamts 1996 Mongolian tree rings and 20th-century warming. *Science* 273: 771–773.

Jamieson, R. W., S. Abonyi, and N. Mirau (editors) 1993 *Culture and environment: a fragile coexistence.* Proceedings of the twenty-fourth annual conference. Archaeological Association of the University of Calgary.

Jashemski, W. M. F. 1979 *The gardens of Pompeii, Herculaneum and the villas destroyed by Vesuvius.* New Rochelle, N.Y.: Caratzas Bros.

Jenny, H. 1941 *Factors of soil formation.* New York: McGraw-Hill.

Johns, T. 1990 *With bitter herbs they shall eat it:*

chemical ecology and the origins of human diet and medicine. Tucson: University of Arizona Press.

Johnson, D. L., E. A. Keller, and T. K. Rockwell 1990 Dynamic pedogenesis: new views on some key soil concepts, and a model for interpreting Quaternary soils. *Quaternary Research* 33: 306–319.

Johnson, D. L., and D. Watson-Stegner 1990 The soil-evolution model as a framework for evaluating pedoturbation in archaeological site formation. In *Archaeological geology of North America*, edited by N. Lasca and J. Donahue, pp. 541–560. Centennial special vol. 4. Boulder: Geological Society of America.

Johnson, L. L., with M. Stright 1992 *Paleoshorelines and prehistory: an investigation of method.* Boca Raton: CRC.

Jones, A. K. G. 1982 Bulk-sieving and the recovery of fish remains from urban archaeological sites. In *Environmental archaeology in the urban context*, edited by A. R. Hall and H. K. Kenward, pp. 79–85. London: Council for British Archaeology, Research Report 43.

1985 Trichurid ova in archaeological deposits: their value as indicators of ancient faeces. In *Palaeobiological investigations: research design, methods and data analysis*, edited by N. R. J. Fieller, D. D. Gilbertson, and N. G. A. Ralph, pp. 105–114. Oxford: BAR International Series 266.

1986 Fish bone survival in the digestive systems of the pig, dog and man: some experiments. In *Fish and archaeology*, edited by D. C. Brinkhuizen and A. T. Clason, pp. 53–61. Oxford: BAR International Series 294.

Jones, G. E. M. 1991 Numerical analysis in archaeobotany. In *Progress in Old World palaeoethnobotany*, edited by W. van Zeist, K. Wasylikowa, and K.-E. Behre, pp. 63–80. Rotterdam: Balkema.

Jones, M. K. 1984 The plant remains. In *Danebury: an Iron Age hillfort in Hampshire.* Vol. 2: *The excavations 1969–1978: the finds*, B. Cunliffe and others, pp. 483–495. London: Council for British Archaeology, Research Report 52.

1988 The phytosociology of early arable weed communities with special reference to southern England. In *Der prähistorische Mensch und seine Umwelt*, edited by H.-J. Küster, pp. 43–51. Forschungen und Berichte zur Vor- und Frühgeschichte in Baden-Württemberg 31. Stuttgart: Theiss.

1991 Sampling in palaeoethnobotany. In *Progress in Old World palaeoethnobotany*, edited by W. van Zeist, K. Wasylikowa, and K.-E. Behre, pp. 53–62. Rotterdam: Balkema.

1992 Food remains, food webs and ecosystems. In *New developments in archaeological science*, edited by A. M. Pollard, pp. 209–219. Proceedings of the British Academy 77. Oxford University Press.

Jones, M., L. P. Zhou, E. Marseglia, and P. Mellars 1994 New analysis of ESR spectra of fossil tooth enamel. *Cambridge Archaeological Journal* 4: 139–146.

Judson, S. 1963 Erosion and deposition of Italian stream valleys during historic time. *Science* 40: 898–899.

Kaiser, J. 1996 Acid rain's dirty business: stealing minerals from soil. *Science* 272: 198.

Kaplan, L., M. B. Smith, and L. A. Sneddon 1992 Cereal grain phytoliths of southwest Asia and Europe. In *Phytolith systematics*, edited by G. Rapp, Jr., and S. C. Mulholland, pp. 149–174. New York: Plenum.

Katzenberg, M. A. 1992 Advances in stable isotope analysis of prehistoric bones. In *The skeletal biology of past peoples: research methods*, edited by S. R. Saunders and M. A. Katzenberg, pp. 105–120. New York: John Wiley and Sons.

Katzenberg, M. A., S. R. Saunders, and W. R. Fitzgerald 1993 Age differences in stable carbon and nitrogen isotope ratios in a population of prehistoric maize horticulturists. *American Journal of Physical Anthropology* 90: 267–281.

Kauffman, S. 1995 *At home in the universe: the search for the laws of self-organization and complexity*. Oxford UniversityPress.

Keene, A. S. 1983 Biology, behavior, and borrowing: a critical examination of optimal foraging theory in archaeology. In *Archaeological hammers and theories*, edited by A. S. Keene and J. A. Moore, pp. 137–155. New York: Academic.

Keepax, C. 1977 Contamination of archaeological deposits by seeds of modern origin. *Journal of Archaeological Science* 4: 221–229.

Keith, M. L., G. M. Anderson, and R. Eichler 1964 Carbon and oxygen isotopic composition of mollusk shells from marine and fresh-water environments. *Geochimica et Cosmochimica Acta* 28: 1757–1786.

Kelley, J. H., and M. P. Hanen 1988 *Archaeology and the methodology of science*. Albuquerque: University of New Mexico Press.

Kellogg, D. C. 1988 Problems in the use of sea-level data for archaeological reconstructions. In *Holocene human ecology in northeastern North America*, edited by G. P. Nicholas, pp. 81–104. New York: Plenum.

Kelso, G. K. 1993 Pollen-record formation processes, interdisciplinary archaeology and land use by mill workers and managers: the Boott Mills Corporation, Lowell, Massachusetts, 1836–1942. *Historical Archaeology* 27: 70–94.

——— 1994 Pollen percolation rates in Euroamerican-era cultural deposits in the northeastern United States. *Journal of Archaeological Science* 21: 481–488.

Kennett, D. J., B. L. Ingram, J. M. Erlandson, and P. Walker 1997 Evidence for temporal fluctuations in marine radiocarbon reservoir ages in the Santa Barbara Channel, southern California. *Journal of Archaeological Science* 24(11): 1051–1059.

Kennett, D. J., and B. Voorhies 1996 Oxygen isotopic analysis of archaeological shells to detect seasonal use of wetlands on the southern Pacific coast of Mexico. *Journal of Archaeological Science* 23: 689–704.

Kent, B. 1988 *Making dead oysters talk: techniques for analyzing oysters from archaeological sites*. St. Mary's City: Maryland Historical Trust.

Kent, S. 1989 Cross-cultural perceptions of farmers as hunters and the value of meat. In *Farmers as hunters: the implications of sedentism*, edited by S. Kent, pp. 1–17. Cambridge University Press.

Kenward, H. K. 1975 Pitfalls in the environmental interpretation of insect death assemblages. *Journal of Archaeological Science* 2: 85–94.

——— 1978 *The analysis of archaeological insect assemblages: a new approach*. The Archaeology of York 19/1. London: Council for British Archaeology.

——— 1982 Insect communities and death assemblages, past and present. In *Environmental archaeology in the urban context*, edited by A. R. Hall and H. K. Kenward, pp. 71–78. London: Council for British Archaeology, Research Report 43.

Kenward, H. K., A. R. Hall, and A. K. G. Jones 1980 A tested set of techniques for the extraction of plant and animal macrofossils from waterlogged archaeological deposits. *Science and Archaeology* 22: 3–15.

Kerr, R. A. 1996 A new dawn for Sun–climate links? *Science* 271: 1360–1361.

Kershaw, A. P. 1978 Record of last interglacial–glacial cycle from northeastern Queensland. *Nature* 272: 159–161.

Kikkawa, J., and D. J. Anderson (editors) 1986 *Community ecology: pattern and process.* Oxford: Blackwell.

King, J. E. 1985 Palynological applications to archaeology: an overview. In *Archaeological geology*, edited by G. Rapp, Jr., and J. A. Gifford, pp. 135–154. New Haven: Yale University Press.

Kiple, K. F. (editor) 1993 *The Cambridge world history of human disease.* Cambridge University Press.

Kirch, P. 1983 Man's role in modifying tropical and subtropical Polynesian ecosystems. *Archaeology in Oceania* 18: 26–31.

Kirch, P. V., and T. L. Hunt (editors) 1993 *The To'aga site. Three millennia of Polynesian occupation in the Manu'a Island, American Samoa.* Berkeley: Contributions of the University of California, Archaeological Research Facility 51.

Kitagawa, H., and J. van der Plicht 1998 Atmospheric radiocarbon calibration to 45,000 yr B.P.: Late Glacial fluctuations and cosmogenic isotope production. *Science* 279: 1187–1190.

Klein, R. C., and K. Cruz-Uribe 1984 *The analysis of animal bones from archeological sites.* University of Chicago Press.

Klippel, W. E., G. Celmer, and J. R. Purdue 1978 The Holocene naiad record at Rodgers Shelter in the western Ozark highlands of Missouri. *Plains Anthropologist* 23(1): 257–271.

Klippel, W. E., and D. F. Morey 1986 Contextual and nutritional analysis of freshwater gastropods from Middle Archaic deposits at the Hays site, middle Tennessee. *American Antiquity* 51: 799–813.

Knuepfer, P. L. K., and L. D. McFadden (editors) 1990 *Soils and landscape evolution.* Amsterdam: Elsevier.

Kolb, M. F., N. P. Lasca, and L. G. Goldstein 1990 A soil-geomorphic analysis of the midden deposits at the Aztalan site, Wisconsin. In *Archaeological geology of North America*, edited by N. P. Lasca and J. Donahue, pp. 199–218. Centennial special vol. 4. Boulder: Geological Society of America.

Körber-Grohne, U. 1991 Identification methods. In *Progress in Old World palaeoethnobotany*, edited by W. van Zeist, K. Wasylikowa, and K.-E. Behre, pp. 3–24. Rotterdam: Balkema.

Kra, R. 1986 Standardizing procedures for collecting, submitting, recording, and reporting radiocarbon samples. *Radiocarbon* 28, No. 2A: 765–775.
1995 From the Editor. *Radiocarbon* 37(1): iii–iv.

Kraft, J. C., I. Kayan, and O. Erol 1980 Geomorphic reconstructions in the environs of ancient Troy. *Science* 209: 776–782.

Krinsley, D., and J. C. Doornkamp 1973 *Atlas of quartz sand surface textures.* Cambridge University Press.

Kukla, G., and Z. An 1989 Loess stratigraphy in central China. *Palaeogeography,*

Palaeoclimatology, Palaeoecology 72: 203–225.

Kuniholm, P. I., B. Kromer, S. W. Manning, M. Newton, C. E. Latini, and M. J. Bruce 1996 Anatolian tree rings and the absolute chronology of the eastern Mediterranean, 2220–718 BC. *Nature* 381: 780–783.

Kurtén, B., and E. Anderson 1980 *Pleistocene mammals of North America.* New York: Columbia University Press.

Küster, H. 1991 Phytosociology and archaeobotany. In *Modelling ecological change,* edited by D. R. Harris and K. D. Thomas, pp. 17–26. London: Institute of Archaeology.

Kutzbach, J. E. 1976 The nature of climate and climatic variations. *Quaternary Research* 6: 471–480.

——— 1987 Model simulations of the climatic patterns during the deglaciation of North America. In *North America and adjacent oceans during the last deglaciation,* edited by W. F. Ruddiman and H. E. Wright, Jr., pp. 425–446. The Geology of North America, vol. K-3. Boulder: Geological Society of America.

Kutzbach, J. E., and F. A. Street-Perrott 1985 Milankovitch forcing of fluctuations in the level of tropical lakes from 18 to 0 kyr BP. *Nature* 317: 130–134.

Lakoff, G., and M. Johnson 1980 *Metaphors we live by.* University of Chicago Press.

LaMarche, V. C., Jr., and K. K. Hirschboeck 1984 Frost rings in trees as records of major volcanic eruptions. *Nature* 307: 121–126.

Lamb, H. H. 1972 *Climate, present, past and future,* vol. 1. London: Methuen.

Lambert, J. B., and G. Grupe (editors) 1993 *Prehistoric human bone: archaeology at the molecular level.* Berlin: Springer.

Lambert, J. B., S. V. Simpson, J. E. Buikstra, and D. K. Charles 1984 Analysis of soil associated with Woodland burials. In *Archaeological chemistry III,* edited by J. B. Lambert, pp. 97–113. Washington, D.C.: American Chemical Society.

Lambrick, G., and M. Robinson 1979 *Iron Age and Roman riverside settlement at Farmoor, Oxfordshire.* London: Council for British Archaeology Research Report 32.

Larick, R., and R. L. Ciochon 1996 The African emergence and early Asian dispersals of the genus *Homo. American Scientist* 84: 538–551.

Larsen, C. P. S., and G. M. MacDonald 1993 Lake morphometry, sediment mixing and the selection of sites for fine resolution palaeoecological studies. *Quaternary Science Reviews* 12: 781–792.

Larsen, C. S. 1997 *Bioarchaeology: interpreting behavior from the human skeleton.* Cambridge University Press.

Laville, H. 1976 Deposits in calcareous rock shelters: analytical methods and climatic interpretation. In *Geoarchaeology,* edited by D. A. Davidson and M. L. Shackley, pp. 137–155. Boulder: Westview.

Lavocat, R. (editor) 1966 *Faunes et flores préhistoriques de l'Europe occidentale.* Paris: Boubée.

Lawlor, D. A., C. D. Dickel, W. W. Mausworth, and P. Patham 1991 Ancient HLA genes from 7000 year old archaeological remains. *Nature* 349: 785–788.

Lawrence, B. 1978 Analysis of unidentifiable bone from Çayönü: an early village farming community. In *Approaches to faunal analysis in the Middle East,* edited by R. H. Meadow and M. A. Zeder, pp. 11–13. Peabody Museum Bulletin 2. Cambridge, Mass.: Peabody Museum of Archaeology and Ethnology.

Lawrence, D. R. 1988 Oysters as geoarchaeological objects. *Geoarchaeology* 3: 267–274.

Leakey, M. D., and R. L. Hay 1979 Pliocene footprints in the Laetolil Beds at Laetoli, northern Tanzania. *Nature* 278: 317–323.

Leakey, M. D., R. L. Hay, G. H. Curtis, R. E. Drake, M. K. Jackes, and T. D. White 1976 Fossil hominids from the Laetolil Beds. *Nature* 262: 460–466.

Lederman, R. 1996 Anti anti "anti-science." Book review essay on concepts of objectivity. *American Anthropologist* 98: 396–398.

Legge, A. J., and P. A. Rowley-Conwy 1987 Gazelle killing in Stone Age Syria. *Scientific American* 255(8): 88–95.

——— 1988 *Star Carr revisited*. Centre for Extra-Mural Studies, University of London.

Leick, Alfred 1995 *GPS satellite surveying*. New York: Wiley.

Leiggi, P., and P. May (editors) 1995 *Vertebrate paleontological techniques*, vol. 1. Cambridge University Press.

Leone, M. P., and A. M. Palkovich 1985 Ethnographic inference and analogy in analyzing prehistoric diets. In *The analysis of prehistoric diets*, edited by R. L. Gilbert, Jr., and J. H. Mielke, pp. 423–431. Orlando: Academic.

Leopold, L. B. 1994 *A view of the river*. Cambridge, Mass.: Harvard University Press.

Lepper, B. T., T. A. Frolking, D. C. Fisher, G. Goldstein, D. A. Wymer, J. E. Sanger, J. Gordon Ogden, III, and P. E. Hooge 1991 Intestinal contents of a Late Pleistocene mastodont from midcontinental North America. *Quaternary Research* 36: 120–125.

Lieberman, D. E. 1994 The biological basis for seasonal increments in dental cementum and their application to archaeological research. *Journal of Archaeological Science* 21: 525–539.

Limbrey, Susan 1975 *Soil science and archaeology*. London: Academic.

——— 1992 Micromorphological studies of buried soils and alluvial deposits in a Wiltshire river valley. In *Alluvial archaeology in Britain*, edited by S. Needham and M. G. Macklin, pp. 53–64. Oxbow Monograph 27. Oxford: Oxbow Books.

Linares, O. 1976 "Garden Hunting" in the American tropics. *Human Ecology* 4: 331–349.

Lincoln, R. J., G. A. Boxshall, and P. F. Clark 1982 *A dictionary of ecology, evolution and systematics*. Cambridge University Press.

Liritzis, Y. 1985 Archaeomagnetism, Santorini volcanic eruptions and fired destruction levels on Crete. *Nature* 313: 76.

Little, E. A. 1993 Radiocarbon age calibration at archaeological sites of coastal Massachusetts and vicinity. *Journal of Archaeological Science* 20: 457–471.

Little, E. A., and M. J. Schoeninger 1995 The Late Woodland diet on Nantucket Island and the problem of maize in coastal New England. *American Antiquity* 60: 351–368.

Lockwood, J. G. 1985 *World climatic systems*. London: Edward Arnold.

Long, A., and R. M. Kalin 1992 High-sensitivity radiocarbon dating in the 50,000 to 70,000 B P range without isotopic enrichment. *Radiocarbon* 34: 351–359.

Lowe, J. J. 1993 Isolating the climatic factors in early- and mid-Holocene palaeobotanical records from Scotland. In *Climate change and human impact on the landscape: studies in paleoecology and environmental archaeology*, edited by F. M. Chambers, pp. 67–82. London: Chapman and Hall.

Lowe, J. J., and M. J. C. Walker 1984
    Reconstructing Quaternary environments.
    London: Longman.
Lundelius, E. L., Jr. 1989 The implications of
    disharmonious assemblages for
    Pleistocene extinctions. *Journal of
    Archaeological Science* 16: 407–417.
Lutz, R. A., and D. C. Rhoads 1980 Growth pat-
    terns within the molluskan shell. In
    Skeletal growth of aquatic organisms,
    edited by D. C. Rhoads and R. A. Lutz,
    pp. 203–254. New York: Plenum.
Lyman, R. L. 1982 Archaeofaunas and subsis-
    tence studies. *Advances in Archaeological
    Method and Theory* 5: 331–393.
    1994 *Vertebrate taphonomy.* Cambridge
    University Press.
McAndrews, J. H. 1988 Human disturbance of
    North American forests and grasslands:
    the fossil pollen record. In *Vegetation
    history,* edited by B. Huntley and T.
    Webb, III, pp. 673–695. Dordrecht:
    Kluwer Academic.
McAndrews, J. H., and M. Boyko-Diskonow
    1989 Pollen analysis of varved sediment
    at Crawford Lake, Ontario: evidence of
    Indian and European farming. In
    *Quaternary geology of Canada and
    Greenland,* vol. 1, edited by R. J. Fulton,
    pp. 528–530. Ottawa: Geological Survey
    of Canada.
McBride, M. B. 1994 *Environmental chemistry
    of soils.* Oxford University Press.
McBurney, C. B. M. 1960 *The Stone Age of
    northern Africa.* Harmondsworth:
    Penguin.
McCay, B. J. and J. M. Acheson (editors) 1987
    *The question of the commons: the culture
    and ecology of communal resources.*
    Tucson: University of Arizona Press.
McCoy, W. D. 1987 The precision of amino
    acid geochronology and paleothermo-

metry. *Quaternary Science Reviews* 4:
    43–54.
McDowell, P. F., T. Webb, III, and P. J. Bartlein
    1990 Long-term environmental change.
    In *The Earth as transformed by human
    action: global and regional changes in the
    biosphere over the past 300 years,* edited by
    B. L. Turner, II, W. C. Clark, R. W. Kates,
    J. F. Richards, J. T. Mathews, and W.
    Meyer, pp. 143–162. Cambridge
    University Press.
McGovern, T. H. 1981 The economics of
    extinction in Norse Greenland. In
    *Climate and history: studies in past cli-
    mates and their impact on man,* edited by
    T. M. Wigley, M. J. Ingram, and G.
    Farmer, pp. 404–433. Cambridge
    University Press.
McGovern, T. H., P. C. Buckland, D. Savory, G.
    Sveinbjarnardottir, C. Andreasen, and P.
    Skidmore 1983 A study of the faunal
    and floral remains from two Norse farms
    in the Western Settlement, Greenland.
    Arctic Anthropology 20: 93–120.
McKeown, T. 1988 *The origins of human
    disease.* New York: Blackwell.
Macklin, M. G., and S. Needham 1992 Studies
    in British alluvial archaeology: potential
    and prospect. In *Alluvial archaeology in
    Britain,* edited by S. Needham and M. G.
    Macklin, pp. 9–23. Oxbow Monograph
    27. Oxford: Oxbow Books.
McLaren, B. E., and R. O. Peterson 1994
    Wolves, moose, and tree rings on Isle
    Royale. *Science* 266: 1555–1558.
Macphail, R. I. 1981 Soil and botanical studies
    on the 'Dark Earth'. In *The environment
    of man: the Iron Age to the Anglo-Saxon
    period,* edited by M. Jones and G.
    Dimbleby. Oxford: BAR British Series 87:
    309–331.
    1987 A review of soil science in archaeology

in England. In *Environmental archaeology: a regional review*, vol. 11, edited by H. C. M. Keeley, pp. 332–379. Occasional Papers 11. London: Historic Buildings and Monuments Commission.

1994 The reworking of urban stratigraphy by human and natural processes. In *Urban–rural connexions: perspectives from environmental archaeology*, edited by A. R. Hall and H. K. Kenward, pp. 13–43. Symposium of the Association for Environmental Archaeology 12. Oxford Books.

Macphail, R. I., M.-A. Courty, and A. Gebhardt 1990 Soils and early agriculture. *World Archaeology* 22: 53–69.

McWeeney, L. J. 1994 Archaeological settlement patterns and vegetation dynamics in southern New England in the Late Quaternary. Ph.D. dissertation, Yale University, New Haven.

Madrey, S. L. H. 1990 The realities of hardware. In *Interpreting space: GIS and archaeology*, edited by K. M. S. Allen, S. W. Green, and E. B. W. Zubrow, pp. 173–183. London: Taylor and Francis.

Madsen, D. B., and J. E. Kirkman 1988 Hunting hoppers. *American Antiquity* 53: 593–604.

Magny, M. 1982 Atlantic and Sub-Boreal: dampness and dryness? In *Climatic change in later prehistory*, edited by A. F. Harding, pp. 33–43. Edinburgh University Press.

Mahmoud, A. A. F. 1989 Parasitic protozoa and helminths: biological and immunological challenges. *Science* 246: 1015–1022.

Mangerud, J., E. Larsen, H. Furnes, I. L. Kristiansen, and L. Lomo 1984 A Younger Dryas ash bed in western Norway, and its possible correlations with tephra in cores from the Norwegian Sea and the North Atlantic. *Quaternary Research* 21: 85–104.

Manning, S. W. 1988 The Bronze Age eruption of Thera: absolute dating, Aegean chronology and Mediterranean cultural relations. *Journal of Mediterranean Archaeology* 1: 17–82.

1990 The Thera eruption: the Third Congress and the problem of the date. *Archaeometry* 32: 91–100.

Marean, C. W. 1991 Measuring the post-depositional destruction of bone in archeological assemblages. *Journal of Archaeological Science* 18: 677–694.

Margulis, L., and K. V. Schwartz 1982 *Five kingdoms: an illustrated guide to the phyla of life on Earth.* San Francisco: Freeman.

Marinatos, S. 1939 The volcanic destruction of Minoan Crete. *Antiquity* 13: 425–439.

Markgraf, V. 1985 Late Pleistocene faunal extinctions in southern Patagonia. *Science* 228: 1110–1112.

Marsh, G. P. 1965 [1864] *Man and nature: or, physical geography as modified by human action.* Edited by D. Lowenthal. Cambridge, Mass.: Belknap.

Martin, D. L., A. H. Goodman, and G. J. Armelagos 1985 Skeletal pathologies as indicators of quality and quantity of diet. In *The analysis of prehistoric diets*, edited by R. L. Gilbert, Jr., and J. H. Mielke, pp. 227–279. Orlando: Academic.

Martin, R. A., and A. D. Barnosky (editors) 1993 *Morphological change in Quaternary mammals of North America.* Cambridge University Press.

Martorell, R. 1980 Interrelationships between diet, infectious disease, and nutritional status. In *Social and biological predictors of nutritional status, physical growth and neurological development*, edited by

L. Greene and F. Johnston, pp. 81–106. Orlando: Academic.

1989 Body size, adaptation and function. *Human Organization* 48: 15–20.

Maschner, H. D. G. (editor) 1996 *New methods, old problems: Geographic Information Systems in modern archaeological research.* Occasional Paper 23, Center for Archaeological Investigations Visiting Scholar Program. Carbondale: Southern Illinois University.

Mason, O. K. 1992 A geoarchaeological methodology for studying prograding coastal sequences: beach-ridge geo-morphology in Kotzebue Sound, Alaska. In *Paleoshorelines and prehistory: an investigation of method,* edited by L. L. Johnson and M. Stright, pp. 55–81. Boca Raton: CRC.

Mason, S. L. R., J. G. Hather, and G. Hillman 1994 Preliminary investigation of the plant macro-remains from Dolní Vestonice II, and its implications for the role of plant foods in Palaeolithic and Mesolithic Europe. *Antiquity* 68: 48–57.

Matthews, J. A. 1993 Radiocarbon dating of arctic–alpine palaeosols and the recon-struction of Holocene palaeoenviron-mental change. In *Climate change and human impact on the landscape,* edited by F. M. Chambers, pp. 83–96. London: Chapman and Hall.

Matthews, W., and J. N. Postgate, with S. Payne, M. P. Charles, and K. Dobney 1994 The imprint of living in an early Mesopotamian city: questions and answers. In *Whither environmental archaeology?,* edited by R. Luff and P. Rowley-Conwy, pp. 171–212. Oxbow Monograph 38. Oxford: Oxbow Books.

May, R. M., and J. Seger 1986 Ideas in ecology. *American Scientist* 74: 256–267.

Mayewski, P. A., L. D. Meeker, S. Whitlow, M. S. Twickler, M. C. Morrison, R. B. Alley, P. Bloomfield, and K. Taylor 1993 The atmosphere during the Younger Dryas. *Science* 261: 125–197.

Mayewski, P. A., L. D. Meeker, S. Whitlow, M. S. Twickler, M. C. Morrison, P. Bloomfield, G. C. Bond, R. B. Alley, A. J. Gow, P. M. Grootes, D. A. Meese, M. Ram, K. C. Taylor, and W. Wumkes 1994 Changes in atmospheric circulation and ocean ice cover over the North Atlantic during the last 41,000 years. *Science* 263: 1747–1751.

Mayr, E., and P. D. Ashlock 1991 *Principles of systematic zoology.* 2nd edition. New York: McGraw-Hill.

Mazer, J. J., C. M. Stevenson, W. L. Ebert, and J. K. Bates 1991 The experimental hydration of obsidian as a function of relative humidity and temperature. *American Antiquity* 56: 504–513.

Meese, D. A., A. J. Gow, P. Grootes, P. A. Mayewski, M. Ram, M. Stuiver, K. C. Taylor, E. D. Waddington, and G. A. Zielinski 1994 The accumulation record from the GISP2 core as an indicator of climate change throughout the Holocene. *Science* 266: 1680–1682.

Mellars, P., and P. Dark 1998 *Star Carr in context: new archaeological and palaeo-ecological investigations at the early Mesolithic site of Star Carr, North Yorkshire.* Cambridge: McDonald Institute Monographs.

Mellars, P., and D. Gibson 1996 *Modelling the early human mind.* Cambridge: McDonald Institute.

Merrill, R. T., and P. L. McFadden 1990 Paleomagnetism and the nature of the geodynamo. *Science* 248: 345–350.

Meyer, F. G. 1980 Carbonized food plants of Pompeii, Herculaneum, and the villa at

Torre Annunziata. *Economic Botany* 34: 401–437.

Michael, H. N., and E. K. Ralph (editors) 1971 *Dating techniques for the archaeologist.* Cambridge, Mass.: Massachusetts Institute of Technology Press.

Middleton, W. D., and I. Rovner 1994 Extraction of opal phytoliths from herbivore dental calculus. *Journal of Archaeological Science* 21: 469–473.

Miksicek, C. H. 1987 Formation processes of the archaeobotanical record. *Advances in Archaeological Method and Theory* 10: 211–247.

Miller, N. F., and K. L. Gleason 1994 *The archaeology of garden and field.* Philadelphia: University of Pennsylvania Press.

Minnis, P. E. 1981 Seeds in archaeological sites: sources and some interpretive problems. *American Antiquity* 46: 143–152.

Misra, V. N., and S. N. Rajaguru 1989 Palaeoenvironment and prehistory of the Thar Desert, Rajasthan, India. In *South Asian Archaeology 1985*, edited by K. Frifelt and P. Sørensen, pp. 296–320. Scandinavian Institute of Asian Studies, Occasional Papers 4. London: Curzon.

Moffat, A. S. 1993 Clearcutting's soil effects. *Science* 261: 1116.

Monks, G. G. 1981 Seasonality studies. *Advances in Archaeological Method and Theory* 4: 117–240.

Monks, G. G., and R. Johnston 1993 Estimating season of death from growth increment data: a critical review. *ArchaeoZoologia* 2: 17–40.

Monmonier, M. 1993 *Mapping it out: expository cartography for the humanities and social sciences.* University of Chicago Press.

Mook, W. G. 1986 Recommendations/resolutions adopted by the Twelfth International Radiocarbon Conference. *Radiocarbon* 28, No. 2A: 799.

Moore, P. D., J. A. Webb, and M. E. Collinson 1991 *Pollen analysis.* 2nd edition. Oxford: Blackwell Scientific.

Morales Muiz, A. (editor) 1993 *Archaeornithology: birds and the archaeological record. Archaeofauna* 2.

Moran, E. F. 1982 *Human adaptability: an introduction to ecological anthropology.* Boulder: Westview.

Morey, D. F. 1994 The early evolution of the domestic dog. *American Scientist* 82: 336–347.

Morgan, A. V. 1987 Late Wisconsin and Early Holocene paleoenvironments of east-central North America based on assemblages of fossil Coleoptera. In *North America and adjacent oceans during the last deglaciation*, edited by W. F. Ruddiman and H. E. Wright, Jr., pp. 353–370. The Geology of North America, vol. K-3. Boulder: Geological Society of America.

Morgan, A. V., A. Morgan, A. C. Ashworth, and J. V. Matthews, Jr. 1983 Late Wisconsin fossil beetles in North America. In *Late-Quaternary environments of the United States. Vol. 1: The Late Pleistocene*, edited by S. C. Porter, pp. 354–363. Minneapolis: University of Minnesota Press.

Morlan, R. E. 1987 Archaeology as palaeobiology. *Transactions of the Royal Society of Canada*, series V, vol. 11: 117–124. Ottawa: The Royal Society of Canada.

1989 Paleoecological implications of Late Pleistocene and Holocene microtine rodents from the Bluefish Caves, northern Yukon Territory. *Canadian Journal of Earth Science* 26: 149–156.

Morowitz, H. 1983 Two views of life. *Science '83*: 21, 24–25.

Moseley, M. E. 1987 Punctuated equilibrium: searching the ancient record for El Niño. *Quarterly Review of Archaeology* 8(3): 7–10.

Moseley, M. E., D. Wagner, and J. B. Richardson, III 1992 Space shuttle imagery of recent catastrophic change along the arid Andean coast. In *Paleoshorelines and prehistory: an investigation of method*, edited by L. L. Johnson and M. Stright, pp. 189–235. Boca Raton: CRC.

Muckelroy, K. (editor) 1980 *Archaeology under water: an atlas of the world's submerged sites*. New York: McGraw-Hill.

Mulholland, M. T. 1979 Forest succession and population change in a temperate forest environment. In *Ecological anthropology of the middle Connecticut Valley*, edited by R. Paynter, pp. 45–56. Research Reports 18. Amherst: Department of Anthropology, University of Massachusetts.

Nelson, D. E., J. S. Vogel, and J. R. Southon 1990 Another suite of confusing radiocarbon dates for the destruction of Akrotiri. In *Thera and the Aegean world III*. Vol. 3: *Chronology*, edited by D. A. Hardy, with A. C. Renfrew, pp. 197–206. Proceedings of the Third International Congress. London: Thera Foundation.

Netting, R. McC. 1977 *Cultural ecology*. Menlo Park: Cummings.

Newell, R. R. 1984 The archaeological, human biological, and comparative contexts of a catastrophically-terminated *Kataligaag* house at Utqiagvik, Alaska (BAR-2). *Arctic Anthropology* 21: 5–51.

Nitecki, M. H., and D. V. Nitecki (editors) 1987 *The evolution of hunting*. New York: Plenum.

NOAA 1994 *Pollen database manual*. Boulder: National Geophysical Data Center.

Noe-Nygaard, N. 1975 Two shoulder blades with healed lesions from Star Carr. *Proceedings of the Prehistoric Society* 41: 10–16.

North American Commission on Stratigraphic Nomenclature 1983 North American stratigraphic code. *American Association of Petroleum Geologists Bulletin* 67: 841–875.

Oberdorfer, E. 1979 *Pflanzensoziologische Exkursionsflora*. 4th edition Stuttgart.

O'Connor, T. P. 1989 Deciding priorities with urban bones: York as a case study. In *Diet and crafts in towns: the evidence of animal remains from the Roman to the post-medieval periods*, edited by D. Serjeantson and T. Waldron, pp. 189–200. Oxford: BAR British Series 199.

1991 Science, evidential archaeology and the new scholasticism. *Scottish Archaeological Review* 8: 1–7.

Oeschger, H., and C. C. Langway, Jr. (editors) 1989 *The environmental record in glaciers and ice sheets*. New York: Wiley-Interscience.

Ogilvie, M. N., B. K. Curran, and E. Trinkhaus 1989 Incidence and patterning of dental enamel hypoplasia among Neanderthals. *American Journal of Physical Anthropology* 79: 25–41.

O'Hara, S. L., F. A. Street-Perrott, and T. P. Burt 1993 Accelerated soil erosion around a Mexican highland lake caused by prehistoric agriculture. *Nature* 362: 48–51.

Oldfield, F. 1993 Forward to the past: changing approaches to Quaternary palaeoecology. In *Climate change and human impact on the landscape: studies in palaeoecology and environmental archaeology*, edited by F. M. Chambers, pp. 13–21. London: Chapman and Hall.

O'Leary, M. H. 1988 Carbon isotopes in photosynthesis. *BioScience* 38: 228–335.

Oliver, J. E., and J. J. Hidore 1984 *Climatology, an introduction*. Columbus: Charles E. Merrill.

Olsen, S. J. 1964 *Mammal remains from archaeological sites, Part I: Southeastern and southwestern United States*. Papers of the Peabody Museum of Archaeology and Ethnology, No. 56, Pt. 1. Cambridge, Mass.: Peabody Museum.

—— 1968 *Fish, amphibian and reptile remains from archaeological sites, Part I: Southeastern and southwestern United States*. Papers of the Peabody Museum of Archaeology and Ethnology, No. 56, Pt. 2. Cambridge, Mass.: Peabody Museum.

—— 1979 Archaeologically, what constitutes an early domestic animal? *Advances in Archaeological Method and Theory* 2: 175–197.

Olson, E. C. 1980 Taphonomy: its history and role in community evolution. In *Fossils in the making: vertebrate taphonomy and paleoecology*, edited by A. K. Behrensmeyer and A. P. Hill, pp. 5–19. University of Chicago Press.

Ordish, G. 1985 *The living garden: the 400-year history of an English garden*. Boston: Houghton-Mifflin.

Orme, B. (editor) 1982 *Problems and case studies in archaeological dating*. Exeter Studies in History 4; Exeter Studies in Archaeology 1. University of Exeter.

Ortloff, C. R., and A. L. Kolata 1993 Climate and collapse: agro-ecological perspectives on the decline of the Tiwanaku state. *Journal of Archaeological Science* 20: 195–221.

Ortner, D., and A. C. Aufderheide (editors) 1991 *Human paleopathology: current syntheses and future options*. Washington, D.C.: Smithsonian Institution.

Overpeck, J. T. 1991 Century- to millennium-scale climatic variability during the Late Quaternary. In *Global changes of the past*, edited by R. S. Bradley, pp. 139–173. Boulder: UCAR/Office for Interdisciplinary Earth Studies.

Owen-Smith, N. 1987 Pleistocene extinctions: the pivotal role of megaherbivores. *Paleobiology* 13: 351–362.

Pace, N. R. 1997 A molecular view of microbial diversity and the biosphere. *Science* 276: 734–740.

Paine, R. T. 1966 Food web complexity and species diversity. *American Naturalist* 100: 65–75.

Painter, T. J. 1994 Preservation in peat. *News WARP* 15: 30–36. Wetland Archaeology Research Project newsletter.

Palacios-Fest, M. R. 1994 Nonmarine ostracode [*sic*] shell chemistry from ancient Hohokam irrigation canals in central Arizona: a paleohydrochemical tool for the interpretation of prehistoric human occupation in the North American Southwest. *Geoarchaeology* 9: 1–29.

Parker, M. L., L. A. Jozsa, S. G. Johnson, and P. A. Bramhall 1984 Tree-ring dating in Canada and the northwestern U.S. In *Quaternary dating methods*, edited by W. C. Mahaney, pp. 211–225. Amsterdam: Elsevier.

Parmalee, P. W. 1993 An archaeological avian assemblage from northwestern Alabama. *ArchaeoZoologia* v(2): 77–92.

Pate, F. D., and J. T. Hutton 1988 The use of soil chemistry data to address post-mortem diagenesis in bone mineral. *Journal of Archaeological Science* 15: 729–739.

Patton, P. C., and S. A. Schumm 1981 Ephemeral stream processes: implications for studies of Quaternary valley fills. *Quaternary Research* 15: 24–43.

Payne, S., and P. J. Munson 1985 Ruby and how

many squirrels? The destruction of bones by dogs. In *Palaeobiological investigations: research design, methods and data analysis*, edited by N. R. J. Fieller, D. D. Gilbertson, and N. G. A. Ralph, pp. 31–48. Oxford: BAR International Series 226.

Pearcy, R. W., J. Ehleringer, H. A. Mooney, and P. W. Rundel (editors) 1989 *Plant physiological ecology: field methods and instrumentation*. London: Chapman and Hall. Reprinted 1991.

Pearsall, D. M. 1989 *Paleoethnobotany*. San Diego: Academic.

Pecker, J.-C., and S. K. Runcorn (editors) 1990 *The Earth's climate and variability of the Sun over recent millennia: geophysical, astronomical and archaeological aspects*. London: Royal Society.

Peglar, S. M. 1993 The mid-Holocene *Ulmus* decline at Diss Mere, Norfolk, UK: a year-by-year stratigraphy from annual laminations. *The Holocene* 3: 1–13.

Perry, I., and P. D. Moore 1987 Dutch elm disease as an analogue of Neolithic elm decline. *Nature* 326: 72–73.

Peteet, D. M. 1995 Global Younger Dryas. *Quaternary International* 28: 93–104.

Pilcher, J. R. 1993 Radiocarbon dating and the palynologist: a realistic approach to precision and accuracy. In *Climate change and human impact on the landscape: studies in palaeoecology and environmental archaeology*, edited by F. M. Chambers, pp. 23–32. London: Chapman and Hall.

Piperno, D. R. 1987 *Phytolith analysis*. San Diego: Academic.

1989 The occurrence of phytoliths in the reproductive structures of selected tropical angiosperms and their significance in tropical paleoecology, paleoethnobotany

and systematics. *Review of Palaeobotany and Palynology* 61: 147–173.

Pirazzoli, P. A. 1991 *World atlas of Holocene sea-level changes*. New York: Elsevier.

Pitts, M. 1979 Hide and antlers: a new look at the gatherer-hunter site at Star Carr, North Yorkshire, England. *World Archaeology* 11: 32–42.

Plog, S., and J. L. Hantman 1990 Chronology construction and the study of prehistoric culture change. *Journal of Field Archaeology* 17(4): 439–456.

Plummer, M. A., F. M. Phillips, J. Fabryka-Martin, H. J. Turin, P. E. Wigand, and P. Sharma 1997 Chlorine-36 in fossil rat urine: an archive of cosmogenic nuclide deposition during the past 40,000 years. *Science* 277: 538–540.

Pollard, A. M. 1995 Why teach Heisenberg to archaeologists? *Antiquity* 69(263): 242–247.

Ponnamperuma, C., and E. Friebele 1982 The antiquity of carbon. In *Nuclear and chemical dating techniques*, edited by L. A. Currie, pp. 391–409. Washington, D.C.: American Chemical Society.

Pope, K. O., and T. van Andel 1984 Late Quaternary alluviation and soil formation in the southern Argolid: its history, causes, and archaeological implications. *Journal of Archaeological Science* 11: 281–306.

Porter, S. C. 1986 Pattern and forcing of northern hemisphere glacier variations during the last millennium. *Quaternary Research* 26: 27–48.

Potts, R. 1984 Hominid hunters? Problems of identifying the earliest hunter/gatherers. In *Hominid evolution and community ecology*, edited by R. Foley, pp. 129–166. Orlando: Academic.

1996 *Humanity's descent: the consequences*

of ecological instability. New York: Morrow.

Powers, A. 1988 Phytoliths: animal, vegetable and mineral? In *Science and archaeology, Glasgow 1987,* edited by E. A. Slater and J. O. Tate, pp. 459–472. Oxford: BAR British Series 196 (ii).

Powers-Jones, A. H. 1994 The use of phytolith analysis in the interpretation of archaeological deposits: an Outer Hebridean example. In *Whither environmental archaeology?,* edited by R. Luff and P. Rowley-Conwy, pp. 41–49. Oxbow Monograph 38. Oxford: Oxbow Books.

Prentice, I. C. 1985 Pollen representation, source area, and basin size: toward a unified theory of pollen analysis. *Quaternary Research* 23: 76–86.

1988 Records of vegetation in time and space: the principles of pollen analysis. In *Vegetation history,* edited by B. Huntley and T. Webb, III, pp. 17–42. Dordrecht: Kluwer Academic.

Price, T. D. 1982 Willow tales and dog smoke. *Quarterly Review of Archaeology* 3(1): 4–7.

1989 Multi-element studies of diagenesis in prehistoric bone. In *The chemistry of prehistoric human bone,* edited by T. D. Price, pp. 126–154. Cambridge University Press.

Price, T. D., C. M. Johnson, J. A. Ezzo, J. Ericson, and J. H. Burton 1994 Residential mobility in the prehistoric southwest United States: a preliminary study using strontium isotope analysis. *Journal of Archaeological Science* 21: 315–330.

Pryor, F. 1991 *Flag Fen.* London: Batsford.

1995 A wall for each season – the new Preservation Hall at Flag Fen, Peterborough, England. *NewsWARP* 18: 21–23.

Purdy, B. A. (editor) 1988 *Wet site archaeology.* Caldwell, N.J.: Telford.

Pye, K. 1987 *Aeolian dust and dust deposits.* London: Academic.

Pye, K., and H. Tsoar 1990 *Aeolian sand and sand dunes.* London: Unwin Hyman.

Pyle, D. M. 1990 The application of tree-ring and ice-core studies to the dating of the Minoan eruption. In *Thera and the Aegean world III.* Vol. 3: *Chronology,* edited by D. A. Hardy, with A. C. Renfrew, pp. 167–173. Proceedings of the Third International Congress. London: Thera Foundation.

Rackham, D. J. 1982 The smaller mammals in the urban environment: their recovery and interpretation from archaeological deposits. In *Environmental archaeology in the urban context,* edited by A. R. Hall and H. K. Kenward, pp. 86–93. London: Council for British Archaeology, Research Reports 43.

Rackham, O. 1980 *Ancient woodland: its history, vegetation and uses in England.* London: Edward Arnold.

Radosevich, S. C. 1993 The six deadly sins of trace element analysis: a case of wishful thinking in science. In *Investigations of ancient human tissue: chemical analyses in anthropology,* edited by M. K. Sandford, pp. 269–332. Langhorne, Penn.: Gordon and Breach.

Rambler, M. B., L. Margulis, and R. Foster 1989 *Global ecology: towards a science of the biosphere.* San Diego: Academic.

Rapp, G., Jr. 1975 The archaeological field staff: the geologist. *Journal of Field Archaeology* 2: 229–237.

Rapp, G., Jr., and C. L. Hill 1998 *Geoarchaeology.* New Haven: Yale University Press.

Rapp, G., Jr., and S. C. Mulholland (editors) 1992 *Phytolith systematics: emerging issues.* New York: Plenum.

Rasmussen, P. 1993 Analysis of goat/sheep faeces from Egolzwil 3, Switzerland: evidence for branch and twig foddering of livestock in the Neolithic. *Journal of Archaeological Science* 20: 479–502.

Reineck, H. E., and I. B. Singh 1980. *Depositional sedimentary environments.* New York: Springer.

Reinhard, K. J. 1992 Parasitology as an interpretive tool in archaeology. *American Antiquity* 57: 231–245.

Reinhard, K. J., and V. M. Bryant, Jr. 1992 Coprolite analysis: a biological perspective on archaeology. *Advances in Archaeological Method and Theory* 4: 245–288.

Reinhard, K. J., P. R. Greib, M. M. Callahan and R. H. Hevly 1992 Discovery of colon contents in a skeletonized burial: soil sampling for dietary remains. *Journal of Archaeological Science* 19: 697–705.

Reinhard, K. J., S. A. Mrozowski, and K. A. Orloski 1986 Privies, pollen, parasites and seeds: a biological nexus in historic archaeology. *MASCA Journal* 4: 31–36.

Renfrew, A. C. 1973 *Before civilization: the radiocarbon revolution and prehistoric Europe.* New York: Knopf.

1979 Systems collapse as a social transformation: catastrophe and anastrophe in early state societies. In *Transformations: mathematical approaches to culture change,* edited by A. C. Renfrew and K. Cooke, pp. 481–506. New York: Academic.

Renfrew, J. M. 1973 *Palaeoethnobotany: the prehistoric food plants of the Near East and Europe.* London: Methuen.

Retallack, G. J. 1984 Completeness of the rock and fossil record: some estimates using fossil soils. *Paleobiology* 10: 59–78.

1990 *Soils of the past: an introduction to palaeopedology.* London: HarperCollins.

Rhoades, R. E. 1978 Archaeological use and abuse of ecological concepts and studies: the ecotone example. *American Antiquity* 43: 608–614.

Rhoads, D. C., and R. A. Lutz 1980a Introduction: skeletal records of environmental change, in *Skeletal growth of aquatic organisms: biological records of environmental change,* edited by D. C. Rhoads and R. A. Lutz, pp. 1–19. New York: Plenum.

(editors) 1980b *Skeletal growth of aquatic organisms: biological records of environmental change.* New York: Plenum.

Rick, A. M. 1975 Bird medullary bone: a seasonal dating technique for faunal analysts. *Bulletin of the Canadian Archaeological Association* 7: 183–190.

Rick, J. W. 1976 Downslope movement and archaeological intra-site spatial analysis. *American Antiquity* 41: 133–144.

Ridings, R. 1996 Where in the world does obsidian hydration work? *American Antiquity* 61: 136–148.

Ringrose, T. J. 1993 Bone counts and statistics: a critique. *Journal of Archaeological Science* 20: 121–157.

Rink, W. J., H. P. Schwarcz, H. K. Lee, V. Cabrera Valdés, F. Bernaldo de Quirós, and M. Hoyos 1996 ESR dating of tooth enamel: comparison with AMS ^{14}C at El Castillo Cave, Spain. *Journal of Archaeological Science* 23: 945–951.

Risser, P. G. 1987 Landscape ecology: state of the art. In *Landscape heterogeneity and disturbance,* edited by M. G. Turner, pp. 3–14. New York: Springer.

Ritchie, J. C. 1986 Climate change and vegetation response. *Vegetatio* 67: 65–74.

Ritchie, J. C., and L. C. Cwynar 1982 The Late Quaternary vegetation of the north Yukon. In *Paleoecology of Beringia,* edited by D. M. Hopkins, J. V. Matthews, Jr., C. E. Schweger, and S. B. Young, pp. 113–126. New York: Academic.

Ritchie, J. C., L. C. Cwynar, and R. W. Spear 1983 Evidence from north-west Canada for an Early Holocene Milankovitch thermal maximum. *Nature* 305: 126–127.

Roberts, B. K. 1987 Landscape archaeology. In *Landscape and culture*, edited by J. M. Wagstaff, pp. 77–95. Oxford: Basil Blackwell.

Roberts, C., and K. Manchester (editors) 1995 *The archaeology of disease*. 2nd edition. Ithaca, N.Y.: Cornell University Press.

Roberts, N. 1989 *The Holocene: an environmental history*. Oxford: Basil Blackwell.

Robinson, M. A. 1988 Molluscan evidence for pasture and meadowland on the floodplain of the upper Thames basin. In *The exploitation of wetlands*, edited by P. Murphy and C. French, pp. 101–110. Oxford: BAR British Series 186.

Robinson, M. A., and G. H. Lambrick 1984 Holocene alluviation and hydrology in the upper Thames basin. *Nature* 308: 809–814.

Rollins, H. B., J. B. Richardson, III, and D. H. Sandweiss 1986 The birth of El Niño: geoarchaeological evidence and implications. *Geoarchaeology* 1: 1–15.

Rolph, T. C., J. Shaw, E. Derbyshire, and Z. An 1994 Determining paleosol topography using seismic refraction. *Quaternary Research* 42: 350–353.

Rothschild, B. M., and L. Martin 1992 *Paleopathology: disease in the fossil record*. Boca Raton: CRC.

Rovner, I. 1983 Plant opal phytolith analysis: major advances in archaeobotanical research. *Advances in Archaeological Method and Theory* 6: 225–266.

1988 Macro- and micro-ecological recon-

struction using plant opal phytolith data from archeological sediments. *Geoarchaeology* 3: 155–163.

Rovner, I., and J. C. Russ 1992 Darwin and design in phytolith systematics: morphometric methods for mitigating redundancy. In *Phytolith systematics: emerging issues*, edited by G. Rapp, Jr., and S. C. Mulholland, pp. 253–276. New York: Plenum.

Rowley-Conwy, P. A. 1982 Forest grazing and clearance in temperate Europe with special reference to Denmark: an archaeological view. In *Archaeological aspects of woodland ecology*, edited by M. Bell and S. Limbrey, pp. 85–96. Oxford: BAR International Series s146.

1987 Animal bones in Mesolithic studies: recent progress and hopes for the future. In *Mesolithic Northwest Europe: recent trends*, edited by P. A. Rowley-Conwy, M. Zvelebil, and H. P. Blankholm, pp. 74–81. Sheffield: Department of Archaeology and Prehistory.

1993 Season and reason: the case for a regional interpretation of Mesolithic settlement patterns. In *Hunting and animal exploitation in the later Palaeolithic and Mesolithic of Eurasia*, edited by G. Peterkin, H. M. Bricker, and P. Mellars, pp. 179–188. Archaeological Papers of the American Anthropological Association 4. Washington, D.C.: American Anthropological Association.

Ruddiman, W. F. 1987 Synthesis: the ocean/ice sheet record. In *North America and adjacent oceans during the last deglaciation*, edited by W. F. Ruddiman and H. E. Wright, Jr., pp. 463–478. The Geology of North America, vol. K-3. Boulder: Geological Society of America.

Ruddiman, W. F., and A. McIntyre 1981

Oceanic mechanisms for amplification of 23,000 year ice-volume cycle. *Science* 212: 617–627.

Rundgren, M. 1995 Biostratigraphic evidence of the Allerød–Younger Dryas–Preboreal oscillation in northern Iceland. *Quaternary Research* 44: 405–416.

Rutter, N. W., R. J. Crawford, and R. D. Hamilton 1985 Dating methods of Pleistocene deposits and their problems: IV. Amino acid racemization dating. In *Dating methods of Pleistocene deposits and their problems*, edited by N. W. Rutter. Toronto: Geological Association of Canada, Reprint Series 2: 23–30.

Ryder, M. L. 1983 Milk products. In *Integrating the subsistence economy*, edited by M. Jones, pp. 239–250. Oxford: BAR International Series 181.

Rymer, L. 1978 The use of uniformitarianism and analogy in palaeoecology, particularly pollen analysis. In *Biology and Quaternary environments*, edited by D. Walker and J. C. Guppy, pp. 245–257. Canberra: Australian Academy of Science.

Saarnisto, M. 1986 Annually laminated lake sediments. In *Handbook of Holocene palaeoecology and palaeohydrology*, edited by B. E. Berglund, pp. 343–370. Chichester: J. Wiley and Sons.

Sahlins, M. 1972 *Stone Age economics.* Chicago: Aldine.

Sandford, M. K. 1993a Understanding the biogenic–diagenetic continuum: interpreting elemental concentrations of archaeological bone. In *Investigations of ancient human tissue: chemical analyses in anthropology*, edited by M. K. Sandford, pp. 3–57. Langhorne, Penn.: Gordon and Breach.

——— (editor) 1993b *Investigations of ancient human tissue: chemical analyses in anthropology.* Langhorne, Penn.: Gordon and Breach.

Sandor, J. A. 1992 Long-term effects of prehistoric agriculture on soils: examples from New Mexico and Peru. In *Soils in archaeology: landscape evolution and human occupation*, edited by V. T. Holliday, pp. 217–245. Washington, D.C.: Smithsonian Institution.

Sandweiss, D. H., J. B. Richardson, III, E. J. Reitz, H. B. Rollins, and K. A. Maasch 1996 Geoarchaeological evidence from Peru for a 5000 years B.P. onset of El Niño. *Science* 273: 1531–1533.

Savelle, J. M. 1984 Cultural and natural formation processes of a historic Inuit snow dwelling site, Somerset Island, Arctic Canada. *American Antiquity* 49: 508–524.

Scarborough, V. L., and G. G. Gallopin 1991 A water storage adaptation in the Maya lowlands. *Science* 251: 658–662.

Schadla-Hall, R. T. 1990 The Vale of Pickering in the early Mesolithic in context. In *The Mesolithic in Europe: papers presented at the Third International Symposium, Edinburgh, 1985*, edited by C. Bonsall, pp. 218–224. Edinburgh: John Donald.

Scharpenseel, H. W., and P. Becker-Heidmann 1992 Twenty-five years of radiocarbon dating soils: paradigm of erring and learning. *Radiocarbon* 34: 541–549.

Schiffer, M. B. 1987 *Formation processes of the archaeological record.* Albuquerque: University of New Mexico Press.

Schmid, E. 1972 *Atlas of animal bones for prehistorians, archaeologists and Quaternary geologists.* Amsterdam: Elsevier.

Schoch, W. 1986 Wood and charcoal analysis. In *Handbook of Holocene palaeoecology and palaeohydrology*, edited by B. E. Berglund, pp. 9–626. Chichester: John Wiley and Sons.

Schoeninger, M. J. 1979 *Dietary reconstruction at Chalcatzingo, a Formative period site in Morelos, Mexico.* Museum of Anthropology, Technical Reports 9. Ann Arbor: University of Michigan.

1989 Reconstructing prehistoric human diet. In *The chemistry of prehistoric human bone*, edited by T. D. Price, pp. 38–67. Cambridge University Press.

Schoeninger, M. J., M. J. DeNiro, and H. Tauber 1983 Stable nitrogen isotope ratios of bone collagen reflect marine and terrestrial components of prehistoric human diet. *Science* 220: 1381–1383.

Schoeninger, M. J., and K. Moore 1992 Bone stable isotope studies in archaeology. *Journal of World Prehistory* 6: 247–296.

Schumm, S. A. 1977 *The fluvial system.* New York: Wiley-Interscience.

1991 *To interpret the Earth: ten ways to be wrong.* Cambridge University Press.

Schuster, H. G. 1988 *Deterministic chaos, an introduction.* 2nd edition. Weinheim: VCH Verlagesellschaft.

Schweger, C. 1985 Geoarchaeology of northern regions: lessons from cryoturbation at Onion Portage, Alaska. In *Archaeological sediments in context*, edited by J. K. Stein and W. R. Farrand, pp. 127–141. Orono, Maine: Center for the Study of Early Man.

Scollar, I. 1990 *Archaeological prospecting and remote sensing.* Cambridge University Press.

Scott, E. M., D. D. Harkness, and G. T. Cook 1998 Interlaboratory comparisons: lessons learned. *Radiocarbon* 40: 331–342.

Scuderi, L. A. 1990 Tree-ring evidence for climatically effective volcanic eruptions. *Quaternary Research* 34: 67–85.

1993 A 2000-year tree ring record of annual temperatures in the Sierra Nevada mountains. *Science* 259: 1433–1436.

Sealy, J. C., N. van der Merwe, A. Sillen, F. Kruger, and H. Krueger 1991 $^{87}Sr/^{86}Sr$ as a dietary indicator in modern and archaeological bone. *Journal of Archaeological Science* 18: 399–416.

Sease, C. 1987 *A conservation manual for the field archaeologist.* Archaeological Research Tools, vol. 4, Institute of Archaeology. Los Angeles: University of California Press.

Seed, R. 1980 Shell growth and form in the Bivalvia. In *Skeletal growth of aquatic organisms*, edited by D. C. Rhoads and R. A. Lutz, pp. 23–67. New York: Plenum.

Seidler, H., W. Bernhard, M. Teschler-Nicola, W. Platzer, D. zur Nedden, R. Henn, A. Oberhauser, and T. Sjøvold 1992 Some anthropological aspects of the prehistoric Tyrolean Ice Man. *Science* 258: 455–457.

Sellers, P. J., R. E. Dickinson, D. A. Randall, A. K. Betts, F. G. Hall, J. A. Berry, G. J. Collatz, A. S. Denning, H. A. Mooney, C. A. Nobre, N. Sato, C. B. Firle, and A. Henderson-Sellers 1997 Modeling the exchanges of energy, water, and carbon between continents and the atmosphere. *Science* 275: 502–509.

Seltzer, G. O., and C. A. Hastorf 1990 Climatic change and its effect on prehispanic agriculture in the central Peruvian Andes. *Journal of Field Archaeology* 17: 397–414.

Serpell, J. (editor) 1995 *The domestic dog, its evolution, behaviour and interactions with people.* Cambridge University Press.

Shackleton, J. C. 1988 Reconstructing past shorelines as an approach to determining factors affecting shellfish collecting in the prehistoric past. In *The archaeology of prehistoric coastlines*, edited by G. Bailey and J. Parkington, pp. 11–21. Cambridge University Press.

Shackleton, N. J. 1973 Oxygen isotope analysis as a means of determining season of occupation of prehistoric midden sites. *Archaeometry* 15: 133–141.

1977 Oxygen-isotope stratigraphy of the Middle Pleistocene. In *British Quaternary studies: recent advances*, edited by R. W. Shotton, pp. 1–16. Oxford: Clarendon.

Shackleton, N. J., J.-C. Duplessy, M. Arnold, P. Maurice, M. A. Hall, and J. Cartlidge 1988 Radiocarbon age of last glacial Pacific deep water. *Nature* 335: 708–711.

Shackleton, N. J., and N. D. Opdyke 1973 Oxygen-isotope and paleomagnetic stratigraphy of equatorial Pacific core V28-238: oxygen isotope temperatures and ice volumes on a 10^5 year and 10^6 year scale. *Quaternary Research* 3: 39–55.

Shaffer, B. S., and J. L. J. Sanchez 1994 Comparison of 1/8″- and 1/4″-mesh recovery of controlled samples of small-to-medium-sized mammals. *American Antiquity* 59: 525–530.

Sheets, P. D. 1992 *The Ceren site: a prehistoric village buried by volcanic ash in Central America*. Fort Worth: Harcourt Brace.

Sheets, P. D., and D. K. Grayson (editors) 1979 *Volcanic activity and human ecology*. New York: Academic.

Sheets, P. D., and B. R. McKee (editors) 1994 *Archaeology, volcanism, and remote sensing in the Arenal region, Costa Rica*. Austin: University of Texas Press.

Shelford, V. E. 1963 *The ecology of North America*. Urbana: University of Illinois Press. (6th printing 1972.)

Shennan, I. 1988 *Quantifying archaeology*. Edinburgh University Press.

Shimada, I., C. B. Schaaf, L. G. Thompson, and E. Mosley-Thompson 1991 Cultural impacts of severe droughts in the prehis-toric Andes: application of a 1,500-year ice core precipitation record. *World Archaeology* 22: 247–270.

Shipman, P. 1981 *Life history of a fossil: introduction to taphonomy and paleoecology*. Cambridge, Mass.: Harvard University Press.

Shlemon, R. J., and F. E. Budinger, Jr. 1990 The archaeological geology of the Calico sites, Mojave Desert, California. In *Archaeological geology of North America*, edited by N. P. Lasca and J. Donahue, pp. 301–314. Centennial special volume 4. Boulder: Geological Society of America.

Short, N. M., and R. W. Blair, Jr. (editors) 1986 *Geomorphology from space: a global overview of regional landforms*. Washington, D.C.: National Aeronautics and Space Administration.

Shukla, J. 1998 Predictability in the midst of chaos: a scientific basis for climate forecasting. *Science* 282: 728–731.

Sibrava, V., D. Q. Bowen, and G. M. Richmond (editors) 1986 *Quaternary glaciations in the northern hemisphere*. Report of the International Geological Correlation Programme, Project 24. *Quaternary Science Reviews* 5. New York: Pergamon.

Sillen, A. 1989 Chemistry and palaeodietary research: no more easy answers. *American Antiquity* 54: 504–512.

Simmons, I. G., and J. B. Innes 1996 Prehistoric charcoal in peat profiles at North Gill, North Yorkshire Moors, England. *Journal of Archaeological Science* 23: 193–197.

Simpson, I. A. 1997 Relict properties of anthropogenic deep top soils as indicators of infield management in Marwick, West Mainland, Orkney. *Journal of Archaeological Science* 24: 365–380.

Skinner, B. J., and S. C. Porter 1995 *The

dynamic Earth: an introduction to physical geology. 3rd edition. New York: John Wiley and Sons.

Smart, T. L., and E. S. Hoffman 1988 Environmental interpretation of archaeological charcoal. In *Current paleoethnobotany,* edited by C. A. Hastorf and V. S. Popper, pp. 167–205. University of Chicago Press.

Smith, A. G., and E. W. Cloutman 1988 Reconstruction of Holocene vegetation history in three dimensions at Waun Fignen Felen, an upland site in South Wales. *Philosophical Transactions of the Royal Society* [B], 322: 159–219.

Smith, K., J. Coppen, G. J. Wainwright, and S. Beckett 1981 The Shaugh Moor project: third report – settlement and environmental investigations. *Proceedings of the Prehistoric Society* 47: 205–274.

Sobolik, K. D. (editor) 1994 *Paleonutrition: the diet and health of prehistoric Americans.* Occasional Paper 22, Center for Archaeological Investigations. Carbondale: Southern Illinois University Press.

Soffer, O. 1987 Radiocarbon accelerator dates for Upper Paleolithic sites in European USSR. In *Archaeological results from accelerator dating,* edited by J. A. J. Gowlett and R. E. M. Hedges, pp. 109–115. Oxford University Committee for Archaeology, Monograph 11.

1993 Upper Paleolithic adaptation in central and eastern Europe and man–mammoth interactions. In *From Kostenki to Clovis: Upper Paleolithic–Paleo-Indian adaptations,* edited by O. Soffer and N. D. Praslov, pp. 31–49. New York: Plenum.

Soil Survey Staff 1975 *Soil taxonomy – a basic system of soil classification for making and interpreting soil surveys.* Washington,

D.C.: USDA, SCS, Agriculture Handbook 436.

Solomon, A. M., and T. Webb, III 1985 Computer-aided reconstruction of Late-Quaternary landscape dynamics. *Annual Review of Ecology and Systematics* 16: 63–84.

Sparks, R. S. J. 1985 Archaeomagnetism, Santorini volcanic eruptions and fired destruction levels on Crete. *Nature* 313: 74–75.

Speth, J. D. 1987 Early hominid subsistence strategies in seasonal habitats. *Journal of Archaeological Science* 14: 13–29.

Spindler, K. 1993 *Der Mann im Eis.* Munich: Bertelsmann.

Stace, H. C. T., G. D. Hubble, R. Brewer, K. H. Northcote, J. R. Sleeman, M. J. Mulcahy, and E. G. Hallsworth 1968 *A handbook of Australian soils.* Adelaide: Rellim Technical.

Stafford, T. W., Jr., P. E. Hare, L. Currie, A. J. T. Jull, and D. Donahue 1991 Accelerator radiocarbon dating at the molecular level. *Journal of Archaeological Science* 18: 35–72.

Stahl, P. W. 1982 On small mammal remains in archaeological context. *American Antiquity* 47: 822–829.

Stahle, D. W., and D. Wolfman 1985 The potential for archaeological tree-ring dating in eastern North America. *Advances in Archaeological Method and Theory* 8: 279–302.

Stanley, D. J., and H. Sheng 1986 Volcanic shards from Santorini (Upper Minoan ash) in the Nile Delta, Egypt. *Nature* 320: 733–735.

Stanley, D. J., and A. G. Warne 1994 Worldwide initiation of Holocene marine deltas by deceleration of sea-level rise. *Science* 265: 228–231.

Starkel, L. (editor) 1987 Anthropogenic sedimentological changes during the Holocene. *Striae* 26: 1–64.

Steadman, D. W. 1989 Extinction of birds in eastern Polynesia: a review of the record, and comparisons with other Pacific island groups. *Journal of Archaeological Science* 16: 177–205.

Steadman, D. W., and N. G. Miller 1987 California condor associated with spruce-jack pine woodland in the Late Pleistocene of New York. *Quaternary Research* 28: 415–426.

Stein, J. K. 1983 Earthworm activity: a source of potential disturbance of archaeological sediments. *American Antiquity* 48: 277–289.

 1985 Interpreting sediments in cultural settings. In *Archaeological sediments in context*, edited by J. K. Stein and W. R. Farrand, pp. 5–19. Orono, Maine: Center for the Study of Early Man.

 1987 Deposits for archaeologists. *Advances in Archaeological Method and Theory* 11: 337–395.

 1990 Archaeological stratigraphy. In *Archaeological geology of North America*, edited by N. P. Lasca and J. Donahue, pp. 513–523. Centennial Special Volume 4. Boulder: Geological Society of America.

 1992 Organic matter in archaeological contexts. In *Soils in archaeology*, edited by V. T. Holliday, pp. 193–216. Washington, D.C.: Smithsonian Institution.

 1993 Scale in archaeology, geosciences, and geoarchaeology. In *Effects of scale on archaeological and geoscientific perspectives*, edited by J. K. Stein and A. R. Linse, pp. 1–10. GSA Special Paper 283. Boulder: Geological Society of America.

Stein, J. K., and A. R. Linse (editors) 1993 *Effects of scale on archaeological and geoscientific perspectives*. GSA Special Paper 283. Boulder: Geological Society of America.

Stern, P. C. 1993 A second environmental science: human–environment interactions. *Science* 260: 1897–1899.

Stern, P. C., O. R. Young, and D. Druckman (editors) 1992 *Global environmental change: understanding the human dimensions*. National Research Council, Washington, D.C.: National Academy.

Sternberg, R. S. 1990 The geophysical basis of archaeomagnetic dating. In *Archaeomagnetic dating*, edited by J. L. Eighmy and R. S. Sternberg, pp. 5–28. Tucson: University of Arizona Press.

Stevenson, C. M., P. J. Sheppard, D. G. Sutton, and W. Ambrose 1996 Advances in the hydration dating of New Zealand obsidian. *Journal of Archaeological Science* 23: 233–242.

Stickel, E. G., and E. G. Garrison 1988 New applications of remote sensing: geophysical prospection for underwater archaeological sites in Switzerland. In *Wet site archaeology*, edited by B. A. Purdy, pp. 69–88. Caldwell, N.J.: Telford.

Stiner, M. C. 1991 An interspecific perspective on the emergence of the modern human predatory niche. In *Human predators and prey mortality*, edited by M. C. Stiner, pp. 149–184. Boulder: Westview.

Straus, L. G. 1990 Underground archaeology: perspectives on caves and rockshelters. *Archaeological Method and Theory* 2: 255–304.

Street-Perrott, F. A. 1991 General circulation (GCM) modelling of palaeoclimates: a critique. *The Holocene* 1: 74–80.

Street-Perrott, F. A., Y. Huang, R. A. Perrott, G. Eglinton, P. Barker, L. Ben Khelifa, D. D. Harkness, and D. O. Olago 1997 Impact of lower atmospheric carbon dioxide on tropical mountain ecosystems. *Science* 278: 1422–1426.

Stright, M. J. 1986a Evaluation of archaeological site potential on the Gulf of Mexico continental shelf using high-resolution seismic data. *Geophysics* 51: 605–622.

1986b Human occupation of the continental shelf during the Late Pleistocene/Early Holocene: methods for site location. *Geoarchaeology* 1: 347–364.

Strong, D. R., Jr., D. Simberloff, L. G. Abele, and A. B. Thistle (editors) 1984 *Ecological communities. Conceptual issues and the evidence.* Princeton University Press.

Stuart, A. J. 1982 *Pleistocene vertebrates in the British Isles.* London: Longman.

Stuiver, M. (editor) 1993 *Radiocarbon: calibration 1993* 35(1). Tucson: University of Arizona Press.

Stuiver, M., and B. Becker 1993 High-precision decadal calibration of the radiocarbon time scales, AD 1950–6000 BC. *Radiocarbon* 35: 35–65.

Stuiver, M., T. F. Braziunas, B. Becker, and B. Kromer 1991 Climatic, solar, oceanic, and geomagnetic influences on Late-Glacial and Holocene $^{14}C/^{12}C$ change. *Quaternary Research* 35: 1–24.

Stuiver, M., B. Kromer, B. Becker, and C. W. Ferguson 1986 Radiocarbon age calibration back to 13,300 years B.P. *Radiocarbon* 28B: 969–979.

Stuiver, M., and G. W. Pearson 1993 High-precision bidecadal calibration of the radiocarbon time scale, AD 1950–500 BC and 2500–6000 BC. *Radiocarbon* 35: 1–23.

Stute, M., P. Schlosser, J. G. Clark, and W. S. Broecker 1992 Paleotemperatures in the southwestern United States derived from noble gases in ground water. *Science* 256: 1000–1003.

Styles, B. W. 1994 The value of archaeological faunal remains for paleodietary reconstructions: a case study for the Midwestern United States. In *Paleonutrition: the diet and health of prehistoric Americans,* edited by K. D. Sobolik, pp. 34–54. Occasional Paper 22, Center for Archaeological Investigations. Carbondale: Southern Illinois University Press.

Sullivan, D. G. 1988 The discovery of Santorini Minoan tephra in western Turkey. *Nature* 333: 552–554.

Sullivan, M., and S. O'Connor 1993 Middens and cheniers: implications of Australian research. *Antiquity* 67: 776–788.

Summerfield, M. A. 1991 *Global geomorphology: an introduction to the study of landforms.* Harlow, Essex: Longman Scientific & Technical.

Sutton, M. Q. 1994 Indirect evidence in paleonutrition studies. In *Paleonutrition: the diet and health of prehistoric Americans,* edited by K. D. Sobolik, pp. 98–111. Occasional Paper 22, Center for Archaeological Investigations, Southern Illinois University, Carbondale.

1995 Archaeological aspects of insect use. *Journal of Archeological Method and Theory* 2: 253–298.

Swetnam, T. W., and J. L. Betancourt 1990 Fire–Southern Oscillation relations in the southwestern United States. *Science* 249: 1017–1020.

Szuter, C. R. 1994 Nutrition, small mammals, and agriculture. In *Paleonutrition: the diet and health of prehistoric Americans,* edited by K. D. Sobolik, pp. 55–65. Occasional Paper 22, Center for Archaeological Investigations, Southern Illinois University, Carbondale.

Tallis, J. H. 1991 *Plant community history.* London: Chapman and Hall.

Tankard, A. J., and F. R. Schweitzer 1976 Textural analysis of cave sediments: Die Kelders, Cape Province, South Africa. In *Geoarchaeology*, edited by D. A. Davidson and M. L. Shackley, pp. 289–316. Boulder: Westview.

Tarling, D. H. 1978 Magnetic studies of the Santorini tephra deposits. In *Thera and the Aegean world*. Vol. 11: *Papers presented at the 2nd international scientific congress*, edited by C. Doumas, pp. 195–201. London: Thera and the Aegean World, 1978–1980.

Tattersal, I. 1998 *Becoming human: evolution and human uniqueness*. New York: Harcourt Brace.

Tauber, H. 1967 Investigations of aerial pollen transport in a forested area. *Dansk Botanisk Arkiv* 32: 1–121.

1981 $\delta^{13}C$ evidence for dietary habits of prehistoric man in Denmark. *Nature* 292: 332–333.

Taylor, K. C., P. A. Mayewski, R. B. Alley, E. J. Brook, A. J. Gow, P. M. Grootes, D. A. Meese, E. S. Saltzman, J. P. Severinghaus, M. S. Twickler, J. W. C. White, S. Whitlow, and G. A. Zielinski 1997 The Holocene–Younger Dryas transition recorded at Summit, Greenland. *Science* 278: 825–827.

Taylor, L. R. 1987 Objective and experiment in long-term research. In *Long-term studies in ecology: approaches and alternatives*, edited by G. E. Likens, pp. 20–70. New York: Springer.

Taylor, R. E. 1987 *Radiocarbon dating: an archaeological perspective*. Orlando: Academic.

1994 Radiocarbon dating of bone using accelerator mass spectrometry: current discussions and future directions. In *Method and theory for investigating the peopling of the Americas*, edited by R. Bonnichsen and D. G. Steele, pp. 27–44. Corvallis: Oregon State University Press.

Taylor, R. E., M. Stuiver, and P. J. Reimer 1996 Development and extension of the calibration of the radiocarbon time scale: archaeological applications. *Quaternary Science Reviews* 15: 665–668.

Tenner, E. 1996 *Why things bite back: technology and the revenge of unintended consequences*. New York: Knopf.

Thomas, J. 1991 *Rethinking the Neolithic*. Cambridge University Press.

Thomas, K. D. 1985 Land snail analysis in archaeology in theory and practice. In *Palaeobiological investigations: research design, methods and data analysis*, edited by N. J. R. Fieller, D. D. Gilbertson, and N. G. A. Ralph, pp. 131–156. Oxford: BAR International Series 266.

Thompson, L. G. 1991 Ice-core records with emphasis on the global record of the last 2000 years. In *Global changes of the past*, edited by R. S. Bradley, pp. 201–224. Boulder: UCAR/Office for Interdisciplinary Earth Studies.

Thompson, L. G., M. E. Davis, E. Mosley-Thompson, T. A. Sowers, K. A. Henderson, V. S. Zagorodnov, P.-N. Lin, V. N. Mikhalenko, R. K. Campen, J. F. Bolzan, J. Cole-Dai, and B. Francou 1998 A 25,000-year tropical climate history from Bolivian ice cores. *Science* 282: 1858–1864.

Thompson, L. G., E. Mosley-Thompson, M. E. Davis, J. Bolzan, J. Dai, N. Gundestrup, T. Yao, X. Wu, L. Klein, and Z. Zichu 1990 Glacial stage ice core records from the subtropical Dunde ice cap, China. *Annals of Glaciology* 14: 288–297.

Thompson, L. G., E. Mosley-Thompson, M. E. Davis, P.-N. Lin, K. A. Henderson,

J. Cole-Dai, J. F. Bolzan, and K.-b. Liu 1995 Late Glacial stage and Holocene tropical ice core records from Huascarán, Peru. *Science* 269: 46–50.

Thompson, L. G., E. Mosley-Thompson, and P. Thompson 1992 Reconstructing inter-annual climate variability from tropical and subtropical ice-core records. In *El Niño: historical and paleoclimatic aspects of the Southern Oscillation*, edited by H. F. Diaz and V. Markgraf, pp. 296–322. Cambridge University Press.

Thorn, C. E. 1988 *Introduction to theoretical geomorphology*. Boston: Allen and Unwin.

Thornes, J. B. 1983 Geomorphology, archaeology and recursive ignorance. *The Geographical Journal* 149: 326–333.

Thorson, R. M. 1990a Geologic contexts of archaeological sites in Beringia. In *Archaeological geology of North America*, edited by N. P. Lasca and J. Donahue, pp. 399–420. Centennial Special Volume 4. Boulder: Geological Society of America.
    1990b Archaeological geology. *Geotimes* Feb. 1990: 32–33.

Tieszen, L. L., M. M. Senyimba, S. K. Imbamba, and J. H. Troughton 1979 The distribution of C_3 and C_4 grasses and carbon isotope discrimination along an altitudinal and moisture gradient in Kenya. *Oecologia* 37: 337–350.

Tilman, D. 1988 *Plant strategies and the dynamics and structure of plant communities*. Princeton University Press.

Toll, M. S. 1988 Flotation sampling: problems and some solutions, with examples from the American Southwest. In *Current paleoethnobotany: analytical methods and cultural interpretations of archaeological plant remains*, edited by C. A. Hastorf and V. S. Popper, pp. 36–52. University of Chicago Press.

Tolonen, K. 1986 Charred particle analysis. In *Handbook of Holocene palaeoecology and palaeohydrology*, edited by B. E. Berglund, pp. 485–496. Chichester: John Wiley and Sons.

Tooley, M. J. 1981 Methods of reconstruction. In *The environment in British prehistory*, edited by I. Simmons and M. J. Tooley, pp. 1–48. London: Duckworth.

Tooley, M. J., and I. Shennan (editors) 1987 *Sea-level changes*. Institute of British Geographers Special Publications Series, vol. 20. New York: Basil Blackwell.

Törnqvist, T. E., T. R. Kidder, W. J. Autin, K. van der Borg, A. F. M. de Jong, C. J. W. Klerks, E. M. A. Snijders, J. E. A. Storms, R. L. van Dam, and M. D. Wiemann 1996 A revised chronology for Mississippi River subdeltas. *Science* 273: 1693–1696.

Tricart, J., and A. Cailleux 1972 *Introduction to climatic geomorphology*. Translated by C. J. Kiewiet de Jonge. London: Longman.

Troels-Smith, J. 1954 Ertebøllekultur–Bondekultur. Resultater af de sidste 10 aars undersøogelse i Aamosen, Vestsjaelland (Ertebølle culture–farmer culture. Results of the past ten years' excavation in Aamosen Bog, West Zealand). *Aarbøger for Nordisk Oldkyndighed og Historie* 1953: 5–62.
    1960 Ivy, mistletoe and elm. Climate indicators/fodder plants. *Danmarks Geologiske Undersøgelse*, IV 4: 1–32.

Trumbore, S. E., O. A. Chadwick, and R. Amundson 1996 Rapid exchange between soil carbon and atmospheric carbon dioxide driven by temperature change. *Science* 272: 393–396.

Tuniz, C., J. R. Bird, D. Fink, and G. F. Herzog 1998 *Accelerator Mass Spectrometry: ultrasensitive analysis for global science*. Boca Raton: CRC.

Turner, A. 1984 Hominids and fellow-travellers: human migration into high latitudes as part of a large mammal community. In *Hominid evolution and community ecology*, edited by R. Foley, pp. 193–217. Orlando: Academic.

Turner, J., J. B. Innes, and I. G. Simmons 1993 Spatial diversity in the mid-Flandrian vegetation history of North Gill, North Yorkshire. *New Phytologist* 123: 599–647.

Turner, J., and S. M. Peglar 1988 Temporally-precise studies of vegetation history. In *Vegetation history*, edited by B. Huntley and T. Webb, III, pp. 753–777. Dordrecht: Kluwer Academic.

Ubelaker, D. H. 1978 *Human skeletal remains: excavation, analysis, interpretation*. Chicago: Aldine.

Ugent, D. 1994 Chemosystematics in archaeology: a preliminary study of the use of chromatography and spectrophotometry in the identification of four prehistoric root crop species from the desert coast Peru. In *Tropical archaeobotany*, edited by J. G. Hather, pp. 215–226. London: Routledge.

Uzogara, S. G., L. N. Agu, and E. O Uzogara 1990 A review of traditional fermented foods, condiments and beverages in Nigeria: their benefits and possible problems. *Ecology of Food and Nutrition* 24: 267–288.

van Andel, T. H. 1985 *New views on an old planet: continental drift and the history of Earth*. Cambridge University Press.

van Andel, T. H., and N. Lianos 1984 High-resolution seismic reflection profiles for the reconstruction of postglacial transgressive shorelines: an example from Greece. *Quaternary Research* 22: 31–45.

van Andel, T. H., C. N. Runnels, and K. O. Pope 1986 Five thousand years of land use and abuse in the southern Argolid, Greece. *Hesperia* 55: 103–128.

van der Leeuw, S. E., and R. W. Brandt 1988 Research design and wet site archaeology in the Netherlands: an example. In *Wet site archaeology*, edited by B. A. Purdy, pp. 153–175. Caldwell, N.J.: Telford.

van der Merwe, N. J. 1986 Carbon isotope ecology of herbivores and carnivores. *Palaeoecology of Africa* 17: 123–131.

1989 Natural variation in ^{13}C concentration and its effect on environmental reconstruction using ^{13}C/^{14}C ratios in animal bones. In *The chemistry of prehistoric human bone*, edited by T. D. Price, pp. 105–125. Cambridge University Press.

1992 Light stable isotopes and the reconstruction of prehistoric diets. In *New developments in archaeological science*, edited by A. M. Pollard, pp. 247–264. Proceedings of the British Academy 77. Oxford University Press.

van Valen, L. 1973 A new evolutionary law. *Evolutionary Theory* 1: 1–30.

Verano, J. W., and D. Ubelaker (editors) 1993 *Disease and demography in the Americas*. Washington, D.C.: Smithsonian Institution.

Verosub, K. L. 1988 Geomagnetic secular variation and the dating of Quaternary sediments. In *Dating Quaternary sediments*, edited by D. J. Easterbrook, pp. 123–139. Special Paper 227. Boulder: Geophysical Society of America.

Verosub, K. L., and P. J. Mehringer, Jr. 1984 Congruent paleomagnetic and archeomagnetic records from the western United States: A.D. 750 to 1450. *Science* 224: 387–389.

Villa, P. 1982 Conjoinable pieces and site formation processes. *American Antiquity* 47: 276–290.

Villa, P., and J. Courtin 1983 The interpretation of stratified sites: a view from underground. *Journal of Archaeological Science* 10: 267–281.

Vita-Finzi, C. 1969 *The Mediterranean valleys: geological change in historical time.* Cambridge University Press.

Vrba, E. S., G. H. Denton, T. C. Partridge, and Ll. H. Burckle (editors) 1995 *Paleoclimate and evolution, with emphasis on human origins.* New Haven: Yale University Press.

Wace, H. H. 1978 Human modification of the natural ranges of plants and animals. In *Biology and Quaternary environments,* edited by D. Walker and J. C. Guppy, pp. 225–244. Canberra: Australian Academy of Science.

Wagner, G. A., M. J. Aitken, and V. Mejdahl 1983 *Thermoluminescence dating.* Handbooks for Archaeologists, No. 1. Strasbourg: European Science Foundation.

Wagner, G., and P. van den Haute 1992 *Fission-track dating.* Norwell, Mass.: Enke, Stuttgart, and Kluwer.

Wagner, G. E. 1988 Comparability among recovery techniques. In *Current paleoethnobotany: analytical methods and cultural interpretations of archaeological plant remains,* edited by C. A. Hastorf and V. S. Popper, pp. 17–35. University of Chicago.

Wagstaff, J. M. 1981 Buried assumptions: some problems in the interpretation of the "Younger Fill" raised by recent data from Greece. *Journal of Archaeological Science* 8: 247–264.

(editor) 1987 *Landscape and culture.* Oxford: Basil Blackwell.

Wainwright, P. O., G. Hinkle, M. L. Sogin, and S. K. Stickel 1993 Monophyletic origins of the metazoa: an evolutionary link with fungi. *Science* 260: 340–342.

Waldron, T. (H. A.) 1994 *Counting the dead: the epidemiology of skeletal populations.* Chichester: J. Wiley and Sons.

Waldrop, M. M. 1992 *Complexity: the emerging science at the edge of order and chaos.* New York: Simon and Schuster.

Walker, A., M. R. Zimmerman, and R. E. F. Leakey 1982 A possible case of hypervitaminosis A in *Homo erectus. Nature* 296: 248–250.

Walker, R. 1985 *A guide to post-cranial bones of East African animals.* Norwich: Hylochoerus.

Warren, P. 1984 Absolute dating of the Bronze Age eruption of Thera (Santorini). *Nature* 308: 492–493.

1988 The Thera eruption III: further arguments against an early date. *Archaeometry* 30: 176–179.

Waselkov, G. A. 1987 Shellfish gathering and shell midden archaeology. *Advances in Archaeological Method and Theory* 10: 93–210.

Washburn, A. L. 1980 *Geocryology.* New York: John Wiley and Sons.

Wasylikowa, K. 1986 Analysis of fossil fruits and seeds. In *Handbook of Holocene palaeoecology and palaeohydrology,* edited by B. E. Berglund, pp. 571–590. Chichester: John Wiley and Sons.

Waters, M. R. 1992 *Principles of geoarchaeology.* Tucson: University of Arizona Press.

Watkins, N. D., R. S. J. Sparks, H. Sigurdsson, T. C. Huang, S. Federman, S. N. Carey, and D. Ninkovich 1978 Volume and extent of the Minoan tephra from Santorini: new evidence from deep-sea sediment cores. *Nature* 271: 122–126.

Watson, P. J., and M. C. Kennedy 1991 The development of horticulture in the eastern woodlands of North America:

women's role. In *Engendering archaeology: women and prehistory*, edited by J. M. Gero and M. W. Conkey, pp. 255–275. Oxford: Basil Blackwell.

Watson, P. J., S. A. LeBlanc, and C. L. Redman 1984 *Archeological explanation: the scientific method in archeology*. New York: Columbia University Press.

Watt, K. E. F. 1973 *Principles of environmental science*. New York: McGraw-Hill.

Wattez, J., and M.-A. Courty 1987 Morphology of ash of some plant remains. In *Micromorphologie des sols – soil micromorphology*, edited by N. Fédoroff, L. M. Bresson, and M.-A. Courty, pp. 677–683. Plaisir: Association française pour l'étude du sol.

Webb, S. 1994 *Paleopathology of aboriginal Australians*. Cambridge University Press.

Webb, T., III, and P. J. Bartlein 1992 Global changes during the last three million years: climatic controls and biotic responses. *Annual Review of Ecology and Systematics* 23: 141–173.

Webb, T., III, and D. R. Clark 1977 Calibrating micropaleontological data in climatic terms: a critical review. In *Amerinds and their paleoenvironments in northeastern North America*, edited by W. S. Newman and B. Salwen. New York Academy of Sciences, *Annals* 288: 93–118.

Wehmiller, J. F. 1984 Relative and absolute dating of Quaternary mollusks with amino acid racemization: evaluation, applications and questions. In *Quaternary dating methods*, edited by W. C. Mahaney, pp. 171–193. Amsterdam: Elsevier.

Weiner, J. S. 1955 *The Piltdown forgery*. Oxford University Press.

Weinstein, G. A., and H. N. Michael 1978 Radiocarbon dates from Akrotiri, Thera. *Archaeometry* 20: 203–209.

Weising, K., H. Nybom, K. Wolff, and W. Meyer 1995 *DNA fingerprinting in plants and fungi*. Boca Raton: CRC.

Weiss, H., M.-A. Courty, W. Wetterstrom, F. Guichard, L. Senior, R. Meadow, and A. Curnow 1993 The genesis and collapse of third millennium North Mesopotamian civilization. *Science* 261: 995–1004.

Wendorf, F., R. Schild, A. E. Close and associates 1993 *Egypt during the last interglacial: the Middle Paleolithic of Bir Tarfawi and Bir Sahara East*. New York: Plenum.

Wheeler, A. 1978 Why were there no fish remains at Star Carr? *Journal of Archaeological Science* 5: 85–90.

  1985 *The world encyclopedia of fishes*. London: Macdonald.

Wheeler, A., and A. K. G. Jones 1989 *Fishes*. Cambridge University Press.

White, E. M., and L. A. Hannus 1983 Chemical weathering of bone in archaeological soils. *American Antiquity* 48: 316–322.

White, R., and I. Page (editors) 1992 *Organic residues in archaeology: their identification and analysis*. London: UKIC Archaeology Section.

White, W. B. 1988 *Geomorphology and hydrology of karst terrains*. Oxford University Press.

Whittington, G., K. J. Edwards, and P. R. Cundill 1991 Palaeoecological investigations of multiple elm declines at a site in north Fife, Scotland. *Journal of Biogeography* 18: 71–87.

Wiens, J. A. 1984 On understanding a non-equilibrium world: myth and reality in community patterns and processes. In *Ecological communities, conceptual issues and the evidence*, edited by D. R. Strong, Jr., D. Simberloff, L. G. Abele, and A. F. Thistle, pp. 439–457. Princeton University Press.

Wigley, T. M. L., M. J. Ingram, and G. Farmer
(editors) 1981 *Climate and history:
studies in past climates and their impact
on man.* Cambridge University Press.

Wild, A. 1993 *Soils and the environment: an
introduction.* Cambridge University
Press.

Wilding, L. P. 1967 Radiocarbon dating of bio-
genetic opal. *Science* 156: 66–67.

Wilding, L. P., N. E. Smeck, and G. F. Hall
(editors) 1983 *Pedology and soil taxonomy.* New York: Elsevier.

Wilkinson, T. J., and P. Murphy 1986
Archaeological survey of an intertidal
zone: the submerged landscape of the
Essex coast, England. *Journal of Field
Archaeology* 13: 177–194.

(editors) 1995 Archaeology of the Essex
coast. Vol. 1: *The Hullbridge Survey.* East
Anglian Archaeology 71.

Williams, M. A. J., D. L. Dunkerley, P.
DeDeckker, A. P. Kershaw, and T. Stokes
1993 *Quaternary environments.* London:
Edward Arnold.

Wilson, B., C. Grigson, and S. Payne (editors)
1982 *Ageing and sexing animal bones
from archaeological sites.* Oxford: BAR
British Series 109.

Wing, E. S., and A. B. Brown 1979
Paleonutrition. New York: Academic.

Winterhalder, B., and E. A. Smith (editors) 1981
*Hunter-gatherer foraging strategies: eth-
nographic and archeological analyses.*
University of Chicago Press.

Wintle, A. G. 1993 Luminescence dating of
sands: an overview. In *The dynamics and
environmental context of aeolian sedimentary systems,* edited by K. Pye, pp. 49–58.
London: Geological Society Special
Publication 72.

1996 Archaeologically-relevant dating techniques for the next century. Small, hot

and identified by acronyms. *Journal of
Archaeological Science* 23: 123–138.

Wintle, A. G., and D. J. Huntley 1982
Thermoluminescence dating of sediments. *Quaternary Science Review* 1:
31–53.

Wintle, A. G., N. Lancaster, and S. R. Edwards
1994 Infrared stimulated luminescence
(IRSL) dating of Late-Holocene aeolian
sands in the Mohave Desert, California,
U.S.A. *The Holocene* 4: 74–78.

Woillard, G. M. 1978 Grand Pile peat bog: a
continuous pollen record for the past
140,000 years. *Quaternary Research* 9:
1–21.

Wolfman, D. 1984 Geomagnetic dating
methods in archaeology. In *Advances in
Archaeological Method and Theory* 7:
363–458.

1990a Mesoamerican chronology and
archaeomagnetic dating, A.D. 1–1200. In
Archaeomagnetic dating, edited by J. L.
Eighmy and R. S. Sternberg, pp. 261–308.
Tucson: University of Arizona Press.

1990b Retrospect and prospect. In
Archaeomagnetic dating, edited by J. L.
Eighmy and R. S. Sternberg, pp. 313–364.
Tucson: University of Arizona Press.

Wood, W. R., and D. L. Johnson 1978 A survey
of disturbance processes in archaeological site formation. *Advances in
Archaeological Method and Theory* 1:
315–381.

Wright, L. E., and H. P. Schwarcz 1996
Infrared and isotopic evidence for
diagenesis of bone apatite at Dos Pilas,
Guatemala: palaeodietary implications.
Journal of Archaeological Science 23:
933–944.

Wylie, A. 1985 The reaction against analogy.
*Advances in Archaeological Method and
Theory* 8: 63–111.

Yalden, D. W., and P. A. Morris 1990 *The analysis of owl pellets.* Occasional Publication 13. London: The Mammal Society.

Zahn, R. 1994 Fast flickers in the tropics. *Nature* 372: 621–622.

Zangger, E. 1992 Neolithic to present soil erosion in Greece. In *Past and present soil erosion: archaeological and geographical perspectives*, edited by M. Bell and J. Boardman, pp. 133–147. Oxbow Monograph 22. Oxford: Oxbow Books.

Zeuner, F. E. 1946 *Dating the past: an introduction to geochronology.* London: Methuen.

Zielinski, G. A., and M. S. Germani 1998a New ice-core evidence challenges the 1620s BC age for the Santorini (Minoan) eruption. *Journal of Archaeological Science* 25: 279–289.

1998b Reply to: Correction. New GISP2 ice-core evidence supports 17th century BC date for the Santorini (Minoan) eruption: response to Zielinski & Germani (1998). *Journal of Archaeological Science* 25: 1043–1045.

Zvelebil, M. (editor) 1986 *Hunters in transition: Mesolithic societies of temperate Eurasia and their transition to farming.* Cambridge University Press.

Index